THE *unofficial* GUIDE®
ᵀᴼCruises

10TH EDITION

THE *unofficial* GUIDE®

TO Cruises

10TH EDITION

KAY SHOWKER *with* BOB SEHLINGER

WILEY

Please note that prices fluctuate in the course of time, and travel information changes under the impact of many factors that influence the travel industry. We therefore suggest that you write or call ahead for confirmation when making your travel plans. Every effort has been made to ensure the accuracy of information throughout this book, and the contents of this publication are believed correct at the time of printing. Nevertheless, the publishers cannot accept responsibility for errors or omissions or for changes in details given in this guide or for the consequences of any reliance on the information provided by the same. Assessments of attractions and so forth are based upon the author's own experience, and therefore, descriptions given in this guide necessarily contain an element of subjective opinion, which may not reflect the publisher's opinion or dictate a reader's own experience on another occasion. Readers are invited to write the publisher with ideas, comments, and suggestions for future editions.

Published by:
John Wiley & Sons, Inc.
111 River Street
Hoboken, NJ 07030

Produced by Menasha Ridge Press

Cover design by Michael J. Freeland

Interior design by Michele Laseau

For information on our other products and services or to obtain technical support, please contact our Customer Care Department within the United States at (800) 762-2974, outside the United States at (317) 572-3993, or fax at (317) 572-4002.

John Wiley & Sons, Inc. also publishes its books in a variety of electronic formats. Some content that appears in print may not be available in electronic formats.

ISBN 978-0-470-08791-6

Manufactured in the United States of America

5 4 3 2 1

CONTENTS

LIST *of* MAPS

LAURELS
for the
LABORERS

THIS EDITION MARKS the 11th year and 10th edition for the *Unofficial Guide to Cruises.* It goes almost without saying that a book of this scope—covering more than 100 cruise lines with upward of 400 ships sailing to destinations from the North Pole to the South Pole and around the world—is the work of many people. Over the decade it has required extensive research, interviews with passengers, seemingly endless discussions with specialized travel agents and other knowledgeable people about cruises, not to mention the incredible amount of follow-up due to the constantly changing nature of the cruise industry.

So many people have been tireless in their effort to help that it would take another book to name them all, but we would be remiss not to mention some.

Alan Wilson, editor/publisher of *Cruise News Daily,* an online newsletter; Mike Driscoll's online newsletter, *Cruise Week*; George Devol's monthly publication, *Ocean Cruise News,* and its online version by Bill Miller; *Cruisemates;* and *Travel Agent* and *Travel Weekly* magazines' online editions have been steady sources of information helping us keep abreast of the constantly changing cruise industry.

Lloyd Cole of Valerie Wilson Travel, Dr. Bradley Feuer of Pace Travel, and Lisa Haber of Cruise Professionals have given us plentiful insights and never seemed to tire of our endless questions.

We are grateful to all our public-relations friends at the cruise lines who helped us check the nitty-gritty details and who have been our hosts over the years without any obligation.

TEXT CONTRIBUTIONS

TIME CONSTRAINTS IN WRITING A BOOK such as this make it impossible for two people to visit and revisit every ship prior to our deadlines, as we would want to do. Throughout the years, we have called on colleagues for help, particularly writers who specialize in cruising and are as qualified as we to write this book.

Some of these folks contributed material written specifically for the book, others shared their knowledge from recent cruises or allowed us to use material from recently published research, while still others reviewed or helped with the updating of information we had already written. Specifically for Part Two, sections were written by Dave Houser (Cruise West); Ted Scull (American Safari Cruises; Saga Cruises) and Susan Young (Oceania Cruises); for Part Three, Ted Scull (Norwegian Coastal Cruises and European Cruise Ferries); Dave Houser (Freighter Cruises); Ted Scull and P. J. Mooney (Hapag-Lloyd Cruises), and Ann Kalosh, Marcia Levin, and Susan Milne, who not only wrote parts of this book but also generously contributed their insights and information to many of the cruise lines and ships profiled in Part Two. For Part Three, sections were written by Shann Davies (Yangtze River Cruises in China) and Carla Hunt (Cruceros Australis). Mary Brennan prepared the itineraries. Many other writing colleagues shared their firsthand experience with us, too. We particularly want to thank Arlene and Sam Bleecker, Anne Campbell, George Devol, Michael Driscoll, Marilyn Green, Mary Ann Hemphill, Michael Iachetta, and Molly Staub.

Many, many friends, friends of friends, travel agents, and cruise passengers along the way willingly gave us their time for interviews, helped with ship ratings, and phoned and sent us letters about their latest cruise, and to them we express our heartfelt thanks.

Last but not least, we thank the staff of Menasha Ridge Press, who worked tirelessly on the manuscript every step of the way.

Kay Showker
Bob Sehlinger

THE *unofficial* GUIDE®
ᵀᴼCruises

10TH EDITION

INTRODUCTION

About **THIS GUIDE**

HOW COME "UNOFFICIAL"?

THE MATERIAL IN THIS GUIDE has not been edited or directed by the cruise lines profiled. In this "unofficial" guide we represent and serve you, the consumer. If a ship serves mediocre food, has cramped cabins, or offers poor shore excursions, we will say so. Through our independence, we hope we can make selecting a cruise efficient and economical and your cruise experience on-target and fun.

MAKING IT EASY

IN THE NEARLY TWO YEARS it took to write the first edition of this book, Kay had pinned on a wall in front of her a note that read: "This book has one purpose: To help readers select the right cruise— i.e., the cruise that's right for them." She kept it there to make sure we never lost sight of that goal.

Most guides to cruising approach their subject on a ship-by-ship basis, giving only the briefest attention to the cruise line and emphasizing ships—the hardware. But people don't buy ships, they buy cruises, and those cruises—the software—have been designed according to cruise lines' business plans, which define the types of cruises they offer. The cruise lines are challenged daily by their competitors and all the other leisure products vying for your attention—from the latest car and computer to a Disney vacation—to make their cruises irresistible. Yet they freely admit that although there's a cruise for everyone, not every cruise is for everyone. What it boils down to is that you can listen to Beethoven's Ninth Symphony played by the Boston Symphony Orchestra, or you can hear it played by the New York Philharmonic. It's the same music, but it's going to come out differently.

This book is designed to help you recognize the differences. By understanding the cruise lines and the experiences they offer, you will be able to recognize the different types of cruises available and identify the ones likely to appeal to you. Each line offers cruises with features that distinguish them from the others. It is these features—or "style" as we call it—that are the essence of the cruise experience.

A Carnival cruise is a Carnival cruise, for example. Each Carnival ship offers a "Fun Ship" vacation, and, except for the cruise's length and destinations, the experience varies little among their ships. Carnival has designed it that way.

The same is true of Costa, Holland America, Seabourn, and every other line that has built ships of a class or style from the same mold. However, a Carnival cruise is as different from a Princess, Holland America, Crystal, or Seabourn cruise as night is from day.

As cruise lines continue to standardize their operations to keep costs down and distinguish themselves from their competition, it becomes more important for you (or your travel agent), as you select a cruise, to understand the line and the type of cruises it offers. With that goal in mind, this guidebook is organized in three parts:

Part One, Planning Your Cruise Vacation, covers basic information on what cruises contain, tips on finding the best values, and preparing for your cruise.

Part Two, Cruise Lines and Their Ships, profiles all major "mainstream" cruise lines that sell primarily to U.S. and Canadian travelers. At the end of Part Two are cruise lines—some small, some also in the mainstream—but not necessarily on this side of the Atlantic. Most, but not all, are based in Europe, cruise less-traveled routes, and cater mainly to Europeans.

Part Three, Cruising Alternatives, describes other options, such as river cruises, adventure and expedition cruises, plus freighters, coastal ships, cruise ferries, and sailing ships.

LETTERS, COMMENTS, AND QUESTIONS FROM READERS

MANY WHO USE THE *Unofficial Guides* write to us with questions, comments, or their own strategies for planning and enjoying travel. We appreciate all such input, both positive and critical. Readers' comments are frequently incorporated into revised editions of the *Unofficial Guides* and have contributed immeasurably to their improvement. Please write to:

Kay and Bob
The Unofficial Guide to Cruises
P.O. Box 43673
Birmingham, AL 35243

Please put your return address on both your letter and envelope; the two sometimes become separated. Also, include your phone number if you are available for a possible interview. And remember, our work often requires that we be out of the office for long periods, so forgive us if our response is slow. If you'd like a faster response, you can also try e-mailing us at unofficialguides@menasharidge.com.

A Reader Survey is included at the end of the book. We urge you to copy or clip it out, add your impressions, and send it in.

CRUISING: *A Look Back, A Look Ahead*

IN 2006, MODERN CRUISING MARKED its 40th anniversary. December 19, 1966, is recognized as a landmark because on that date a series of cruises was launched that, for the first time, had been created and packaged as a mass-market product and sold on a year-round basis. The ship, the *Sunward* of the Norwegian Caribbean Line (later renamed the Norwegian Cruise Line), sailed from Miami to Nassau with 540 passengers on the first three- and four-day cruises to be offered year-round between Miami and the Bahamas. No one, including the creators, imagined where that small step would lead. Indeed, many in the steamship business dismissed the idea as crazy, declaring there was not enough of a market to support such cruises.

Cruising, of course, did not actually start in 1966; it evolved over a span of 150 years. But it's true that until the 1960s the closest most people got to a big ship was on the big screen, either in movies about glamorous people living romantic lives, or in newsreels of the Duke and Duchess of Windsor arriving on the *Queen Mary*, or F. Scott and Zelda, the Astors, the Vanderbilts, and other celebrities sailing stylishly to Europe aboard an elegant ocean liner.

From the start of the first regular transatlantic steamship service by Samuel Cunard in 1840, a voyage on a great liner became the ultimate dream shared by people worldwide. In the early days, a sea voyage was more of an expedition, requiring passengers to endure hardships with few amenities on board ship or at ports. Passenger comfort, even in first class, was not a priority. But as competition developed and steamship travel gained popularity, each generation of ships brought enhanced comfort.

Then, too, throughout the late 19th century and up to World War I, ships carrying passengers had other purposes. Among them was transporting thousands of immigrants to the New World and a new life. To meet the demand—and reap large profits—many steamship companies were born and ships built, and, except for the war years when the vessels transported troops, ocean liners paraded across the Atlantic and Pacific in an endless stream, with the world's elite in their top decks and the huddled masses below.

Then in 1921, passage of the Immigration Act, intended to slow the torrent of new arrivals, forced steamship companies to change course.

To make up for lost revenue from steerage, companies created cabin or tourist class in the several decks below first class and unwittingly took the next step toward modern cruising. Although a voyage remained a means of getting from one continent to another, it was no longer a pastime only for the privileged. Cabin class did not have the elegance and panache of first class, but it wasn't bad. It found a ready market in the GIs who had fought in Europe and wanted to return with their families, immigrants who had made good and wanted to visit relatives in their homelands, and America's growing middle class, who wanted to emulate the celebrities and aristocrats in first class.

THE GOLDEN AGE

THE ROARING TWENTIES was a golden age for steamship travel. It was a time of new prosperity, blithe spirits—and Prohibition in America. With alcoholic beverages legal at sea, ship companies offered a new type of short cruise—the party, or booze cruise—that made getting there half the fun.

In the dining room, passengers sat at long tables on chairs bolted to the floor (ships did not have stabilizers). In 1910, Ritz restaurants, replicating the setting of their shoreside operations, introduced round tables and carpeted floors in first class on ships of Hapag-Lloyd of Germany. The style soon became the standard for other ships. Private bathrooms were available in first class on the grandest liners, but in cabin class, passengers shared bath facilities until the 1950s. Air-conditioning was introduced by P&O Lines in the 1930s but did not become common until the 1950s.

The first indoor swimming pool appeared in 1910 on the *Olympic* of White Star Line. (It was the first of the line's three superliners; the others were the *Titanic* and the *Gigantic,* later renamed *Britannic.*) Known as a plunge bath, it had a balcony where others could watch the bathers. The first permanent outdoor pool was introduced in 1926 on the *Roma* of Italian Lines. Until the late 1950s, the top deck was fitted with machinery and was off-limits to passengers. Today, it's usually a sports deck.

A NEW ERA

AFTER WEATHERING THE GREAT DEPRESSION and another war, ocean liners resumed their traditional role, and by the 1950s were conveying hordes of students to Europe and masses of refugees to U.S. shores. The glamour returned with the comings and goings of a young Liz Taylor and the sailing of Grace Kelly to her fairyland prince. After World War II, the addition of radar and improved navigational equipment made passenger ships safer and more accurate in regard to arrival times, enabling operators to plan reliable itineraries. By the mid-1950s, most ocean liners had stabilizers. Radios were added in staterooms. The tradition to separate first class and tourist class on transatlantic service continued, but in 1958, Holland America launched the *Rotterdam,* which could be converted to one class. However, by decade's end, most elite passengers had taken flight—literally.

The final blow came in 1958, when the first commercial jets streaked across the Atlantic, cutting travel time from five days to just over five hours. Instead of dying out, however, the ships changed course and became part of the revolution that took place on the sea as well as in the sky.

THE CRUISE REVOLUTION

THE TURNAROUND OF THE 1960S brought radical changes. New cruise lines, untethered to the past, exchanged formality for fun and brought a new atmosphere to shipboard life. The barriers of separate classes were removed, and the space was used for sports, recreation, and entertainment, turning the ships into floating resorts. Getting there was no longer half the fun—it *was* the fun. Passengers no longer bundled under blankets in deck chairs. Instead, they bounced in aerobics classes, swung at golf and tennis balls, plunged into the sea with masks and fins, soaked in hot tubs, and luxuriated in shipboard spas. Bingo survived, but it now competed with jazzy casinos, Broadway shows and discos, wine and piano bars, comics and cabarets. New and younger passengers were attracted by the activity and informality. Families with children, too, were finding cruises to be ideal vacations.

But change came wrapped in skepticism. For example, the hot news in 1968 was the new, mod look of the SS *Independence.* With a red, orange, and yellow sunburst splashed across the length of its sides and a riot of interior color, it was quickly dubbed the psychedelic ship. A magazine called the shakedown cruise a "floating water pad for the turned on generation" and suggested that "dancing until the wee hours . . . the informal atmosphere of the one-class ship, and ever-changing program of top-talent entertainment may prove a real drawing card."

The 1970s began with Royal Caribbean Cruise Lines making its debut with a fleet of ships built specifically for Caribbean cruising. It was followed two years later by Carnival Cruise Lines, which developed the "Fun Ship" concept to scuttle the elitist traditions of ocean liners and appeal to a mass market of younger, first-time passengers from all walks of life.

As the revolution's final irony, the spectacular growth in cruise vacations really took off in the 1970s, when cruise lines joined forces with airlines, which had almost put the steamship companies out of business. The union created air/sea programs that combined air transportation and ground transfers with a cruise in one package at one price. The programs enhanced the value of cruise vacations, simplified their purchase, and eliminated hassles for travelers. With the packages, cruise lines virtually brought their ships to people's doorsteps, regardless of where they lived. The marriage enabled cruise lines to base their ships in warm-weather ports from where they could cruise year-round and to fly passengers from faraway places to begin their cruises.

A relaxed, informal holiday in the sun—and available year-round—became the essence of modern cruising. Flying passengers to their ships saved time and enabled cruise lines to offer shorter, less expensive cruises that fit into the national trend toward shorter vacations. People who might never have considered taking a cruise booked them. It also allowed cruise lines to open new parts of the world to cruising; itineraries multiplied. No matter how many cruises a person took, new ones remained. Or so it seemed, until the oil crisis of the early 1970s, when dark clouds again threatened the future of vacations at sea.

Then, in 1978, despite skyrocketing fuel prices and predictions that cruising was doomed, Carnival Cruise Lines ordered a large, technologically advanced passenger ship. It became the forerunner of the 1980s superliners. Two years later, Norwegian Cruise Line shocked the cruise world by buying the fabulous *France* and transforming her into the *Norway*. The floating resort set cruise trends for the decade, introducing innovations, including a variety of entertainment lounges, a theater for Broadway-scale productions, a shopping plaza, and a "sidewalk" cafe. Holland America followed with *Nieuw Amsterdam* and *Noordam,* twin ships with square sterns that allowed over 20 percent more deck space for recreation, including two swimming pools. The ships also introduced computer keys to open cabin doors and other innovations.

Princess Cruises' stylish *Royal Princess,* which debuted in 1984, set new standards of comfort with all outside cabins fitted with minibars, television, and baths with tubs in every category. About the same time, the *QE2* introduced the first Golden Door spa at sea, the first computer learning center, and the first satellite-delivered newspaper.

Among the most interesting entries in the 1980s was the *Windstar,* a cruise ship with computerized sails. *Windstar* married the romance of sailing under canvas with the comforts of a cruise ship and the electronic age. At the same time, Carnival's superliners, *Holiday, Jubilee,* and *Celebration,* were introduced. Their madcap design totally changed the look of ship interiors and the use of public space.

Yet nothing since the *Norway* caused as much excitement as the 1988 debut of Royal Caribbean Cruise Line's *Sovereign of the Seas.* The world's largest cruise ship at the time, she became the pacesetter for the 1990s. Among her features was the first shipboard atrium, rising through five decks and creating a new environment. The ship offered such numerous and varied entertainment and recreation options that passengers needed several cruises to experience them all. As the decade closed, some old lines disappeared in mergers, and new lines popped up. Health and fitness facilities were integrated into cruising. Healthful foods were readily available. Well-equipped gyms, elaborate spas, VCRs, cable television, and worldwide direct-dial telephones were rapidly becoming standard amenities. Small boutique ships, including those of the Seabourn and Silversea lines, brought new levels of luxury to cruising. Special-interest lines were finding their niche. Increased interest in adventure and nature cruises caused some traditional cruise lines to add them.

Environmental concerns had a major impact on cruise ship technology. The late 1960s and early 1970s saw the conversion of ocean liners to cruise ships and the first ships built specifically for cruising, but the 1980s and 1990s became the decades of innovation, particularly aboard ships designed to sail in warm climates.

IN THE NEW MILLENNIUM

NOW INTO ITS FIFTH DECADE, the cruise boom shows no signs of slowing down. In that time, the number of passengers has swelled from under 500,000 annually to almost 13 million in 2006. Ten of the nineteen members of the Cruise Lines International Association, the major cruise trade association, did not exist 20 years ago.

The 1990s were a blockbuster decade, with more than three dozen new ships costing an estimated $12 billion in the water; and followed by another $15 billion in the new century, resulting in at least five dozen more ships by 2005. There's apparently no letup. In 2007, 38 ships were on order, with about a dozen ships to be delivered each year for the next three years. Most of the ships are bigger, with more dazzle, and travel specialists are asking, "Where's the sky?"

The ships over 80,000 tons—and particularly those over 100,000 tons—represented a new generation of megaliners. Most had new design features and facilities—such as the highly publicized 18-hole miniature golf course on *Legend of the Seas,* the virtual-reality theater on Princess Cruises' *Grand Princess,* and the interactive computers on Celebrity's *Century* and *Galaxy.*

But the capper was *Voyager of the Seas,* the first of the three 142,000-ton ships built by Royal Caribbean, which debuted in November 1999 with cruising's first rock-climbing wall and ice rink. The climbing wall proved to be so popular that RCL has installed them fleetwide.

Meanwhile, Cunard's *Queen Mary 2,* which debuted in December 2003, assumed the title as the biggest, widest, longest, and most expensive ship ever built, and at 150,000 tons she dwarfed all predecessors. The much-anticipated *QM2* came with the first and only spa at sea operated by the world-famous Canyon Ranch health resorts; the world's first and only planetarium at sea; the largest ballroom at sea; the largest library at sea; the largest wine cellar at sea; ten dining venues, including the first and only shipboard restaurant by popular American chef Todd English; and a learning center with guest lecturers from Oxford University.

However, the *QM2* lost her "biggest" status in 2006, when RCCL launched its first ultra-megaliner, as the 162,000-ton *Freedom of the Seas* was being called. But that will not be the end to the contest. RCCL is already outdoing itself with Project Genesis, its largest ship yet, at 220,000 tons and capable of carrying 5,400 passengers. The ships are being built by Aker Yards of Finland for a 2009 delivery, at an estimated cost of $1.5 billion per ship. Carnival Cruises, Cunard's owners, is said to be planning an even larger one.

Innovations keep coming. In 2006, Norwegian Cruise Line debuted the first bowling alley at sea on its new *Norwegian Pearl*, Costa Cruises introduced a Grand Prix (Formula One) race car simulator on the new *Costa Concordia*, and Royal Caribbean launched the first boxing ring at sea on the *Freedom of the Seas*. Along with innovations, the new ships have enhanced the cruise experience. Standard cabins on most new ships are larger and there are many more verandas across the price spectrum. More dining options are becoming standard, with Norwegian Cruise Lines setting the pace with 11 dining venues. There are also more entertainment choices, more sports opportunities, greatly expanded children's facilities, larger, more elaborate spas, Internet cafes, in-cabin Internet access, wireless facilities, and cell phones that work at sea.

Other ways the cruise experience is being enhanced are through innovative enrichment programs, such as Crystal Cruises' Creative Learning Center, offering courses in cooking, art, business, technology, and health, and on the line's new *Crystal Serenity*, even learning to play the piano in an arrangement with Yamaha that provides instructors. Passengers can also take classes in fine art, drawing, sculpture, painting, floral design, and interior design by faculty from the Parsons School of Design in New York.

Another such program is Princess Cruises' Scholarship Sea (which Princess calls "edutainment"), introduced on the *Coral Princess* with topics ranging from cooking taught in a demonstration kitchen like those seen on television, to pottery classes with the first shipboard kiln; and Holland America's Culinary Arts Institute, which is part of the line's ambitious $225 million Signature of Excellence, a multi-faceted program that has seen the upgrading and expansion of all its shipboard facilities and amenities to appeal to maturing baby boomers, the growing family and multigeneration vacationer market.

There has also been a vast improvement in the variety and number of shore excursions (although not an improvement in price), particularly in the Caribbean, for active passengers to enjoy hiking, biking, kayaking, golf, swimming with dolphins, and much more. Now, too, many cruise lines enable passengers to book shore excursions online. Cruise lines faced with intense competition—again, particularly in the Caribbean—have looked for new and more varied itineraries, but the biggest shift, particularly after September 11, 2001, has come with a new emphasis on "homeland" cruising. That has resulted in more ships based in new U.S. ports and many more itineraries along the East and West coasts of the United States, Mexico, and Central America. In addition to attracting travelers who do not want to stray far from home, this has stimulated a market of drivers who do not want to fly out of fear or who prefer not to deal with the security hassles and delays at airports.

Although innovation and product refinement is common throughout the cruise industry, Princess Cruises and Norwegian Cruise Lines have led the way. Most of the innovations address longstanding complaints of cruise passengers (they really do read all those survey forms). For cruisers who disliked being relegated to a specific seating for dinner, or for that matter, eating in the same restaurant each night, many vessels, particularly the newest ones, now offer multiple dining venues that operate like shoreside restaurants. Make a reservation or just show up at the restaurant of your choice.

Specialties at these stand-alone eateries cover a wide variety of cuisines, from Japanese to Mexican and Italian to Chinese. Princess and Holland America, for example, have installed steakhouses on their fleets. The Princess Personal Choice Dining program also includes an Italian trattoria, a Southwestern restaurant, and a 24-hour buffet and bistro. Norwegian Cruise Line's Freestyle Cruising offers as many as 11 restaurants on a single ship, each with its own identity and area of specialization. On the Disney Cruise Line, passengers rotate to a different restaurant each night. The line also features a reservations- and adults-only Italian restaurant on each ship.

Carnival introduced "Total Choice" dining, enabling passengers to choose from four seating times in the main dining room instead of the usual two. The four seatings stagger the arrival of diners, preventing the galley from being inundated and allowing the waitstaff to concentrate on a smaller number of passengers at any given time. Carnival has also added a supper club with gourmet cuisine on all its new ships, which has proven enormously popular.

Although more choice in dining sounds like a definite perk, there's a downside, particularly on large ships. A great number of singles and couples depend on meeting new friends at their assigned table in the main dining room. For many, their assigned dinner companions become their social circle for the duration of the cruise. Each night, they meet over dinner and discuss the day's activities. Some coordinate shore tours or enjoy each other's company outside the dining room, and it is a common occurrence for tablemates to become close friends and to keep in touch once they return home. Needless to say, it's much harder to get acquainted and form friendships when your assigned dinner companions are off trying the alternative dining venues each night.

Among other notable initiatives is the Princess Flight-Choice program that confirms air itineraries purchased through Princess 60 days prior to the cruise date, allowing passengers ample time to make changes if desired. In a related program, Princess has also established an express check-in, where passengers can avoid the hassle of dockside check-in by completing boarding documents online or mailing them to Princess in advance.

Norwegian Cruise Line has taken a much-welcomed and long-overdue crack at easing the discomfort of disembarkation. On most large vessels, you are run off the ship by 8 a.m. to make way for passengers going on the next cruise. Norwegian's program allows passengers to occupy their stateroom until midmorning and enjoy a leisurely breakfast before disembarking. Along similar lines, the Disney Cruise Line allows passengers to disembark whenever they please as soon as the ship has been cleared by customs. If ever there were initiatives we'd like to see emulated industry-wide, it's these.

More and more cruise lines enable passengers to "stay connected" by providing Internet access, including wireless connection. A few offer it free, but most charge a high fee per usage. Some have plans for unlimited Internet access during a cruise for a single rate, which is a better deal for frequent users. Crystal Cruises enables passengers to have their own shipboard e-mail address. Crystal, as well as several other lines, has computer schools at sea. In 2006, staying connected also meant using your cell phone as more and more cruise lines installed the equipment to enable passengers to use them at sea.

Another bow to the electronic age: When you sail with Princess Cruises or Norwegian Cruise Line, you will receive your tickets and other documentation via email unless you or your travel agent tell the cruise line otherwise. Expect other cruise lines to follow suit soon.

For those who believe it is better to receive than send, there has been a proliferation of live, real-time television available on your stateroom. In addition to CNN, the Discovery Channel, ESPN, TNT, and CNBC are now available on many cruise liners, depending on their location.

THE BIG THREE

ALTHOUGH NOT MANY CRUISERS know it, three companies control the lion's share of the American cruise market. These companies set the pace and establish norms for the mass-market cruise industry. Then, too, when there's a depressed travel market, as there was after 9/11, their discounts impact even the luxury end of the market.

First of the three is Carnival Corporation, which owns Carnival, Holland America, Cunard, Seabourn, Costa Cruises, P&O (which includes P&O Australia), and Princess Cruises (which in turn included P&O Australia, Swan Hellenic Cruise Lines, and several small lines created to serve specific markets, such as Germany).

Next is Royal Caribbean International (RCI), which operates Royal Caribbean Cruise Line and Celebrity Cruises/Celebrity Expedition Cruises, and recently purchased Pullamtur, a major Spanish tour and cruise operator. RCI made a bid to buy Princess Cruises, but lost out to Carnival Cruises.

Number three, Star Cruises, is Asia's largest cruise line and owns Norwegian Cruise Line/NCL America and Orient Line; together, they have almost as many ships as Carnival Cruises or RCI. The deep pockets of Star Cruises have enabled NCL to grow with new ships that are among the most innovative and put NCL once again in its role as the trendsetter of the cruise industry.

Cruise lines big and small got off to a rough start in 2001. First, there was the soaring price of fuel, followed by a serious dip in the economy. These hit at a time when the big three, as well as several other lines, were awash with new ships with thousands of extra berths to fill. By the time the first quarter of calendar year 2001 ended, ships were sailing with empty cabins, and the fight for available passengers was running at full tilt.

Then came the events of September 11, 2001, as cruising, along with travel in general, came to a screeching halt. By the 2001 Christmas season, cruising had begun its slow comeback, and the winter season, particularly in the Caribbean, was better than anticipated. Nonetheless, three cruise lines went out of business, and a fourth declared bankruptcy.

Among the casualties were American Classic Voyages, parent company of American Hawaii and Delta Queen Steamboat Company, and Renaissance. Just the year before, two other smaller cruise lines, Premier and Commodore, went belly-up, while several others struggled and remained vulnerable. By 2003, two more—Regal Cruises and World Explorer Cruises—had departed. The loss of these lines was especially sad because they were small, moderately priced operators serving areas that the big lines had ignored or could not serve with their huge ships.

On the bright side, two new cruise lines were launched in summer 2003: Oceania Cruise Lines, using two of Renaissance Cruises' former vessels and modeling itself, more or less, after that now-defunct line, and Discovery World Cruises, sailing on less-traveled routes. Despite the soft travel market, Oceania did well, added a third ship, and now is building two new ships. Other former Renaissance ships have found their way to exploration and cultural cruise lines, and as a result, set a new deluxe standard for these types of cruises.

The big three have staying power. They don't like compromising yields, but they'll do it to fill cabins and build their customer base. As we have already seen, the cruise lines that really felt the pinch were the smaller and medium-sized ones—lines that don't have the advertising dollars or market clout to compete head-to-head with the big guys and that cannot afford to offer comparable discounts.

The loss of each small or medium cruise line is important because it diminishes competition and concentrates more power in the larger lines, especially in the American market. Interestingly, some of the ships of these defunct cruise lines have found their way to small European cruise lines, particularly British-based lines, such as Fred Olsen Cruise Lines and Saga Cruises, to name a few. And they have stepped up their promotional efforts to attract U.S. and Canadian passengers who prefer small ships.

THE FUTURE

THE TWO OVERRIDING FACTORS that will influence all travel and particularly cruises for years to come, will be the Internet and the maturing of the baby boomer generation. With someone in the United States turning 50 every seven seconds, it's easy to see who the cruise lines passengers will be and why so many trends already in place or developing are a result, directly or indirectly, of these elements.

With regard to new ships, the trend toward larger ships will continue with capacity approaching 5,000 passengers before the end of the decade. These ships will have features designed to attract and satisfy the growing market of family and multigeneration vacationers and will further develop the concept of the ship as the destination with more and more elaborate spas, climbing walls, demonstration kitchens, and children's facilities. Most cabins on new ships will have balconies.

Look also for ships more than eight years old to undergo major modifications and conversions that go beyond the required refurbishing to cater to the changing tastes of consumers and the maturing baby boomers. Examples include Holland America's $225 million investment in its "Signature of Excellence" program, Seabourn Cruises' doubling the size of its gyms, and Costa Cruises' adding balconies to one of its newest ships, which did not have them.

Even as ships continue to get larger, we are likely to see the entry of more small ships, tailored to specific markets. It's already happened in Europe—German ships for German speakers, British ships for Brits and Anglophiles—and those designed for specific segments of the market, such as easyCruise, the new no-frills cruise line, similar in concept to low-cost, no-frills airlines. Small and midsize ships are likely to gain in popularity as a segment of travelers, particularly among experienced cruisers, will look for greater privacy, ships with fewer people, and fellow passengers with more common interests.

The average price of cruises will remain low for cruise lines to remain competitive and continue broadening the market. However, they will be under the constant pressure of rising operating costs for food, labor, shipbuilding, fuel, amenities, and entertainment. Thus, they must look for ways, particularly through onboard revenue, to offset these increased costs, since there is a limit to reducing operating costs without weakening the product and little elasticity in prices.

Already labor cutbacks can be seen on the large, mass-market ships. In the past, cabin attendants might have been assigned 12 cabins, but now they care for 20. In the dining rooms, headwaiters and waitstaff might have had a dozen tables to serve, but now they have 20 and the wine steward is gone. There have been cutbacks in food quantity (and in some cases quality) as reflected in fewer courses at breakfast and lunch and/or fewer selections for each course.

New cruisers may not be aware of these changes and experienced ones may not care if it helps keep down prices. Then, too, there has always been too much food and too many choices served on most ships. What's more, people's interests and lifestyles have changed. As a result, cruise lines are switching their emphasis to activities and amenities, rather than food, as in the past. Food is still important but changing.

Look for a wider range of amenities and dining options with more venues, more types of food, and specialty restaurants onboard. We've seen the beginning of a trend—restaurants run by well-known chefs or shoreside restaurants. Todd English on the QM2 is an example. The downside: passengers will be charged for their use, not only in the food outlets but perhaps for such items as movies and entertainment. Already it has been shown that passengers are willing to pay for some enhancements.

Another trend to watch: ships staying overnight in port, giving passengers the opportunity to explore ports in more depth. This could be particularly appropriate for destination-oriented cruise lines and be a result of a maturing cruise market. It also reflects a shift from the old formula of more ports being seen as value to experienced cruisers understanding the value of overnight port stays.

Now that ResidenSea has shown the way, look for new lines to try a variety of new ideas, such as cruise ships with apartments for sale as time-shares, or cabins booked for one to four months at a time or even a year.

Another trend that has picked up steam in recent years is cruise lines investing in port development in the United States—Royal Caribbean in Philadelphia and Bayonne, New Jersey; Carnival in Mobile, Alabama, and Jacksonville, Florida—as well as in Mexico (Costa Maya), the Caribbean (Grand Turk), and the Mediterranean, often giving the line exclusive rights as well as new or vastly improved ports. Carnival's latest involvement is building a new port in Roatan, Honduras.

The availability of Internet access on cruise ships has grown by leaps and bounds in the last two years, and now the availability of wireless connection and cell phone use is being added almost as rapidly. At the same time, the acceptance of personal computers as part of our lives and the ease of using them to book travel will have more and more people booking cruises on the Internet and the number of mom-and-pop travel agencies shrinking. Already those agencies had dropped from 33,000 in 2001 to about 17,000 in 2004, and some predict there will be fewer than 5,000 by the end of the decade. Meanwhile, the number of home-based travel agents has skyrocketed and now account for one-third of all cruise sales. They are expected to reach a half-million agents before the decade ends. And the Internet may even force cruise lines to simplify their pricing, including, we hope, brochure prices that today have no relation to reality.

Despite the setbacks and uncertainties, cruising as a vacation choice continues to attract new travelers by the thousands and has devotees returning year after year. That's because the fundamental attraction of cruising—value for money—has not and is not likely to change.

PART ONE

PLANNING *Your* CRUISE

UNDERSTANDING CRUISES

THE INCLUSIVE CRUISE VACATION

MOST CRUISES ARE INCLUSIVE—that is, their basic components are typically purchased together rather than à la carte. In general, a cruise—or what a travel agency or cruise line might describe as a "cruise-only" product—includes:

1. Shipboard accommodations.
2. Three full-service dining room meals daily (breakfast, lunch, and dinner), plus alternative breakfast, lunch, evening buffets, and late-night snacks. On most ships, room service meals do not cost extra. Many ships also offer options, such as early-bird breakfast, morning bouillon, and afternoon events, including tea, pizza snacks, ice-cream parties, and poolside cookouts.
3. Most shipboard entertainment, including music, dancing, and shows in the lounges, discos, live bands, Las Vegas–style productions, nightclubs, karaoke, and movies.
4. Most shipboard sports and recreational facilities, including swimming pools, health club or exercise room, promenade or jogging track, whirlpool, sauna, library, game room, and child-care facilities. (Spa and beauty treatments, some specialized exercise classes such as Pilates, and sports equipment normally cost extra.)
5. Most shipboard activities, including casino entry, onboard games and contests, lectures, demonstrations, and most children's programs (where applicable, babysitting services are extra).
6. Stops at ports of call on the itinerary.

The features listed above are almost universally a part of any cruise vacation, and an inclusive cruise vacation is often a very good value, particularly when compared with the cost of similar pieces booked on a resort vacation. That said, other inclusions or lack of inclusion are line specific. Some cruise lines do include transfers—basically a bus or van ride from the airport to ship and ship to airport. Other lines charge for those transfers, unless you buy your air tickets through the line in what travel agents call an air/sea package.

Port charges (usually noted in the bottom fine print of any cruise advertising or brochure) are usually included in the cruise price. Still, it pays to check carefully or ask your travel agent, as port charges can range from $120 to $200 or even more on a seven-day Caribbean cruise, depending on the itinerary.

Taxes, optional shore excursions, alcoholic beverages and soft drinks, casino play, onboard shopping, some computer classes, use of Internet connection, and tips are not included in most cases. On a few very upscale lines, gratuities and wine and alcoholic beverages are included in the cruise price. On some, tips are pooled (you are asked to contribute a suggested amount per day to be divided among all staff except officers and senior staff) and now, more and more cruise lines are adding a service charge to your shipboard account in lieu of tipping. With most lines you have the option of paying it or having it removed and handling the tipping yourself. We include a section on tipping in Part Two.

CRUISING'S UNFORTUNATE STEREOTYPES

YOU HAVE PROBABLY HEARD that "cruising is not for everyone." But that's like saying travel is not for everyone. If you like to travel, you will almost certainly enjoy cruising. It's that simple. Cruising, however, has accumulated unfortunate stereotypes, which continue to recycle.

MYTH NO. 1: I'LL BE BORED Many people, particularly men and younger, active folks, believe cruising is dull and sedentary. They picture bulk loaders crowding buffets while active folks sit bored and unstimulated. Sorry, not so.

Today, most cruises offer around-the-clock activities. Ships have workout rooms with high-quality equipment, jogging tracks, pools, and daily exercise classes. Some larger ships have volleyball courts, basketball courts, and even climbing walls, golf simulators, and ice rinks. At ports of call, a variety of sports—from golf to cycling, snorkeling to kayaking—are offered. There are far more opportunities for sports and athletics than most of us have at home. Some lines now even offer extreme adventures like off-road vehicle trips or mountain biking. If you go on a cruise and sit on your butt, that's your decision.

For the active but less athletic, most ships offer swimming, shuffleboard, table tennis, walking areas, and spa amenities, including hot tubs and saunas. Many ships offer yoga or stretching classes. At night, for the energetic, there's dancing in many forms, from ballroom to reggae to line dancing to salsa.

A range of organized activities targets gregarious and fun-loving people. Versions of television game shows are popular, as are more traditional events, such as bridge tournaments, arts and crafts classes, and dancing lessons. Most cruise ships have casinos, and almost all have bingo.

If learning is your goal, dozens of cruises specialize in providing educational experiences and exploration of a region accompanied by experts. Like floating graduate schools, these cruises may focus on political and natural history, or may even offer lectures on topics unrelated to the ship's destinations.

Finally, there is no place better than a cruise ship to relax. The favorite cruise activity for many people is curling up in a comfortable deck chaise with a good book. Even a big ship with constant activity offers quiet spots for meditation, reading, or just enjoying the beauty of the sea.

MYTH NO. 2: CRUISING IS FOR RICH PEOPLE; I CAN'T AFFORD A CRUISE
If you take a vacation of three or more days during which you stay in hotels and eat in restaurants, you can afford a cruise. In fact, a cruise may be cheaper than a deluxe resort vacation.

Let's compare cruising with a modest vacation: Vic and Edna's one-week trip to Gatlinburg, Tennessee, and the Smoky Mountains. Driving from their home near Cleveland, Ohio, Vic and Edna spent about $400 on gas for the Chevy. They averaged $75 a night plus tax for motels, or $577 for the week. For breakfast and lunch, it was Shoney's- or Denny's-type restaurants. They'd go more upscale for dinner, and they liked beer or wine with their meal. Total for seven days' food: $588. In the mountains, they mostly hiked and drove around. One day, however, they played golf; on another they visited a museum and a theme park. On the Friday before heading home, they rented horses for half a day. Golf, admissions, and horses came to approximately $260. Recapping:

VIC AND EDNA'S SPLENDID VACATION	
Lodging	$577
Gas	$400
Meals	$588
Admissions	$260
Total	$1,825

During the same period, a good middle-of-the-market cruise line (not super-budget or super-luxury) offered a seven-night Caribbean cruise for $899 per person, including round-trip airfare. The cruise visited San Juan, St. Thomas, Martinique, Tortola, the British Virgin Islands, Antigua, and St. Maarten. Even better values could have been had with promotional fares, which were as low as $579.

These were promotional rates, not the "rack" rates listed in the brochures. The point is, on the seven-night cruise, Vic and Edna could have enjoyed the amenities of a full resort, dined in grand style, danced to live music, visited six beautiful tropical islands, and soaked in a whirlpool under the Caribbean moon for about the same amount they spent on their road trip. We are not suggesting Vic and Edna should swap the Smokies for the Caribbean, only that they could afford to do so if they are inclined.

MYTH NO. 3: CRUISES ARE STUFFY, ELITIST, AND FORMAL Most cruises are none of the above, though the description might fit some passengers. Cruises cover a broad range of dress and social protocols. You can choose a cruise at whatever level of formality or casualness feels right for you. Overall, cruises have become very casual and informal. Even on "formal" nights—such as the captain's welcome-aboard party and/or farewell party—only half of the men wear business suits, and women don cocktail or party dresses. Newer ships offering alternative (to the main dining room) dining options make it possible to avoid formal events entirely. Yet, on the most informal ships, like Carnival, people dress to the nines—and it's often the men more so than the women. And they love it.

MYTH NO. 4: CRUISES ARE TOO REGIMENTED FOR ME Granted, it takes organization to get everyone on board a cruise ship. It takes similar regimentation to get everyone off at the end of the cruise. At ports, you need only get back on board before the ship sails.

Some folks lump cruises into the same category as whirlwind bus tours—eight countries in five days and that sort of thing. A cruise might visit eight countries in five days, but you will have to check in and unpack only once. That's the beauty of cruising—you can hang out on the ship and just enjoy the ride, or you can get off at each port and pursue your own agenda.

Also, the trend toward more relaxed dining hours and alternative (to the main dining room) dining venues has resulted in notably less regimentation aboard ship.

MYTH NO. 5: I'M AFRAID I'LL GET SEASICK Well, you might, but the vast majority of people don't, particularly on a Caribbean cruise. Even those who get queasy in a car can usually handle a cruise. Over-the-counter antinausea medications like **Bonine** (doesn't make you drowsy) or **Dramamine** get most folks over the acclimatization period of the first few hours at sea. Bring some: you may never need it, but having it is comforting. Usually, Dramamine or Bonine is available from the purser's desk or the ship's medical unit.

Some guests swear by **Sea Bands**—a pair of elasticized wristbands (similar to tennis bands), each with a small plastic disk that applies pressure to the inside wrist, according to acupressure principles. They are particularly useful for people who have difficulty taking medication. Sea Bands are sold in drug, toiletry, and health-care stores (sometimes on board ships as well) and can be ordered from **On the Go Travel Accessories** (5603 NW 159th Street, Miami, FL

33014; ☎ 888-303-3039; **www.onthegoaccessories.com**). If you take precautions and become seasick anyway, the ship's doctor can administer more powerful medication.

In regard to seasickness, remember: don't dwell on your fear, and if you become queasy, take medicine immediately. When you deal with symptoms quickly, relief is quick.

Minimize the probability of getting seasick by choosing an itinerary in calmer waters: Alaska's Inside Passage, the Caribbean, the Mediterranean, and the Gulf of Mexico. Less smooth are voyages on the Atlantic, Pacific, or Indian oceans or the South China Sea. And remember the time of year may also matter. The Caribbean can be less smooth during hurricane season. You are unlikely to be in the storm's way, but water conditions can kick up far from the trouble zone.

MYTH NO. 6: I'M APPREHENSIVE ABOUT WALKING ON A MOVING SHIP If you are not agile or fit on land, you might envision tortuous trips down narrow gangways or climbing ladders through tiny hatches while the ship rolls and pitches. But those images are really in the past. Generally, if you can handle a hotel, you can handle a cruise ship. Large vessels have wide, carpeted halls with hand railings, and slip-resistant outside decks. Elevators serve all passenger decks, so using the stairs may not even be necessary. Passengers use no tricky ladders or tiny hatches.

Modern cruise ships have state-of-the-art stabilizers, and even in bad weather and heavy seas they are amazingly stable. Small ships, depending on their draft and build, may be more subject to the motion of the ocean and are a little more challenging to get around. Being smaller, however, there's less territory to cover. Most ships launched in the last ten years were built with consideration for passengers with ambulatory disabilities. Most new ships offer wheelchair-accessible cabins and ramps.

A TYPICAL DAY ON A CRUISE

LET'S SAY YOU'RE CRUISING the Caribbean. You can start your morning with an early-bird breakfast or a walk or jog around deck, or you can have breakfast from the menu in the dining room. Late sleepers can order breakfast from room service or catch the breakfast buffet, which stays open later than the dining room. It may be served on the "lido" deck—a casual indoor/outdoor dining facility on the same deck as the swimming pool or sports facilities. The lido buffet has longer and more flexible hours, enabling you to come and go at will.

Days at sea are the most relaxing of the cruise itinerary. The casino, shopping arcade, spa, exercise room, and shore-excursion desk are open. Programs and activities are virtually nonstop on large ships; many folks, however, hang out by the pool or on deck to enjoy the beauty of the sea and the relaxing movement of being underway. The captain may update passengers over the public-address system on the ship's progress toward the next port. The captain or cruise director may also point out interesting sights.

Lunch works much like breakfast: you can eat in the dining room and order from the menu, or you can stay in your swimsuit and eat burgers or pizza by the pool, where there is likely to be a music combo playing upbeat rhythms. You can join the pool games—always a good way to meet people—or just watch or ignore them. You then might work out, read, nap, play bridge, learn the latest dance steps, or attend orientation lectures about the next port. Recently released movies are shown in the ship's movie theater or on cabin television in the afternoon. On some ships, afternoon tea is a big deal—white gloves and all. At cocktail hour, there is usually live music by the pool, often with special drinks or appetizers, or happy hour in one of the bars.

As dinner approaches, it's time to dress for the evening. The dress code generally is specified on the daily agenda slipped under your door every evening. It is also spelled out in the cruise line's brochure, so you can pack accordingly. (More information on dress codes is available under "Preparing for Your Cruise.")

Some passengers stroll the deck before dinner, particularly at sunset, a beautiful time at sea. Others have a drink in one of the lounges. Dinner in the dining room is a social culmination of the day's activity. Spirits are always high.

After lingering over several well-prepared courses, it's off to the showroom, where live entertainment, ranging from Las Vegas–style variety shows to Broadway musicals, is offered nightly. After the show, early risers and those who had a long day of touring retire to their cabins. The more active or party-minded guests head for the casino, disco, or a lounge with entertainment. Midnight buffets are about gone these days. On select nights there may be a special late-night buffet or light snack fare. Now, too, on many ships, you have another option—a 24- (or almost 24-) hour alternative restaurant, often dressed up for the evening with table service and music. Before turning in, stretch out in a chaise lounge on deck with a glass of wine. Breathe in the balmy salt-sea air and be caressed by the warm breeze. Lose yourself among the million stars of the Caribbean night.

Usually, cruise ships sail through the night and arrive at the next port early in the morning. If you have risen in time to enjoy the early morning—another gorgeous time at sea—you can watch your ship dock. It's interesting and fun. After breakfast, the captain announces that the ship has been cleared by local officials and that passengers may disembark. Those signed up for shore excursions are given last-minute instructions about when and where to meet and are normally first to go ashore.

Although port calls range from two hours to two days (with an overnight at dock), most are four to ten hours—enough time to get a taste of an island or city. As you disembark, crew members remind you of the sailing time and make sure you are carrying your cruise identification, which you must present to reboard. Once ashore, some people explore on foot on their own, take walking tours, shop, and perhaps try a shoreside restaurant. Others hire a cab for a driving tour, and most take shore excursions purchased aboard ship.

Shore excursions take many forms. Some are passive (bus tour), but others are active (snorkeling, sailing, hiking, biking, or fishing). Surprisingly, many folks, particularly repeat cruisers, stay aboard ship. It's quiet—almost empty of passengers—but it's in full operation, except for casinos and shops. Lunch is served on schedule in the dining room.

About an hour before sailing, you reboard the ship. Don't be late. The ship will not wait for you! Just before castoff, go topside to watch the crew prepare for departure. Leaving port is always interesting, and a ship's higher decks offer a great viewing platform. Once at sea, the ship settles into its normal nighttime routine, and so do you.

SO MANY CRUISES TO CHOOSE FROM

TO THE FIRST-TIME CRUISER and even many veterans, the number of cruise lines, ships, and itineraries is staggering. Travel agencies that sell only cruises ease their customers into the array of choices by comparing cruise lines with well-known hotel chains, and such comparisons are useful. They might see Carnival, for example, as the Holiday Inn of cruises. Holland America and Celebrity Cruise Line are up a notch, perhaps at the Hyatt level.

Ritz-Carlton–type cruises might appeal to the most discriminating cruisers and are at the upper end of price, service, and amenities. Large and medium ships in this class include those of Crystal Cruises and Regent Seven Seas Cruises (which also has a small ship in Tahiti). Boutique cruises overlap the luxury category and include the smaller, all-suite ships of Silversea and Seabourn, as well as the cruise/sail ships of Windstar.

Be aware that none of the hotel chains mentioned (except Radisson and Hyatt) have anything to do with cruising, and these are only a handful of the lines available. Although the foregoing comparison may help you see where you fit into the general scheme, you must dig much deeper to find your perfect cruise.

GETTING YOUR ACT TOGETHER

CRUISES VARY WIDELY. To pinpoint your requirements and preferences in a cruise, you need to ask yourself dozens of questions. Once you settle on what you want, it's easier to match your demands and budget with the appropriate line and ship.

1. What Is My Vacation Budget?

Unless price is no object, one place to start planning is your general budget. How much can you afford, and what are you willing to spend

unofficial **TIP**
Have flexibility and an
open mind.

for your cruise? Consider what you must or may add to the cruise price: port charges and taxes, shore excursions, shopping, drinks and dinner wine (on most ships), gambling in the casino, spa services, laundry, and tips for crew members. Once you figure a range within your uppermost limit for all costs, you can begin to explore what kind of cruise you can buy. A good travel agent may tell you about a special promotion that provides value or added perks on a cruise you may think is beyond your price range. In the end, it may cost less, and if it does cost more, you may decide it is the best choice due to "extras" you receive. In other words, use your budget as a starting point.

Although we will revisit this issue in "How to Get the Best Deal on a Cruise," let's say three-day cruises start at about $295 a person, assuming two people to a cabin. Seven-day cruises begin at about $650, and ten-day cruises are about $920 and up. These prices are deeply discounted and represent the least you would expect to pay, usually for a cabin without windows.

2. How Many Days Do I Want to Cruise?

Your available vacation time and budget are among the factors in your ultimate cruise selection. Generally, the larger your budget, the more cruise days you can buy. That is, the longer the cruise, the more it will cost. If your budget isn't up to the number of days you have your heart set on, you still have options. First, trade luxury for cruise days; consider a cruise on a less-luxurious ship. The fee for a week on an upscale

unofficial **TIP**
Don't veer too far from
your lifestyle or interests,
or you will be disap-
pointed with your cruise.

ship will easily buy two weeks on a midrange vessel. Second, cruise during the off-season, when prices are lowest. Third, consider the least expensive cabin. Once aboard, all passengers have the same privileges, eat the same meals, and enjoy the same entertainment. Unless you plan to spend an extraordinary amount of time in your cabin, you might select less-expensive accommodations. We're not talking about special suites, just the difference between the highest deck outside cabin (with a window or veranda) and the lowest deck inside cabin (no window). For example, on a seven-day Celebrity Cruise Line itinerary to Bermuda, the upper-deck outside cabin costs more than twice as much as the lower-deck inside cabin.

In the Caribbean and Mexico, a seven-day cruise is about right for your first trip, but a three- or four-night cruise will give you a good enough overview of ship life that you can determine whether cruising is something you'll enjoy again in the future.

3. Where Do I Want to Go?

You can cruise just about anywhere there is enough water to float a ship. This includes all of the world's oceans and seas and many rivers.

Where you want to cruise depends primarily on your own "wild goose." It also hinges on your preferred style of cruising and whether you enjoy the destinations or the ship more.

Some destinations, including Alaska and Europe, are seasonal. Others, like the Caribbean and Mexico, are year-round. Almost all cruises worldwide are tailored to the market and the weather. Many to the Caribbean and Mexico, for example, are festive and high-spirited, emphasizing activity and fun. Mild temperatures allow time outdoors, and passengers tend to be younger. By contrast, Alaskan, Canadian, North Atlantic, Scandinavian, and Baltic Sea cruises are more passive, focusing on the beauty of the forests, islands, fjords, and glaciers. Still, Alaska cruises can have very active shore trips. For these northerly venues, longer cruises and colder temperatures contribute to a more sedate experience and attract families or older passengers. Mediterranean itineraries generally revolve around antiquities and port cities of southern Europe, northern Africa, and the Middle East. Most ships visit a port each day, and sightseeing is the backbone of the vacation. On ships where English is spoken and the majority aboard are Americans, the passengers are likely to be 50 years of age or older, and affluent. On cruise ships where Europeans predominate, passengers are often younger, and sun and fun are emphasized, like in the Caribbean.

Hawaiian cruises occupy the middle, emphasizing both festivity and scenery, though passengers are, at times, older on average than those in the Caribbean. For other North Pacific, South Pacific, Indian Ocean, and South China Sea settings, the distance of the cruise areas and home ports from the United States ensures an older, wealthier market. As with Mediterranean cruises, sightseeing and cultural attractions are the focus.

Though a great way to see exotic places without shuffling among hotels, cruises allow only a cursory glimpse of the countries visited. Ten hours in Venice on a cruise is no substitute for visiting Italy. Even in the Caribbean, short stopovers on small islands leave much undiscovered. Yet, many guests will enjoy seeing something new, and probably would never travel to all these destinations on their own.

unofficial **TIP**
Some travelers use cruising to sample cities and countries to determine whether they might want to return later for a more prolonged visit.

If you are interested in further exploring a destination, consider the add-ons most lines offer at the beginning and end of cruises. Two- or three-night packages include a hotel and some sightseeing. They are usually well priced and can be booked at the time you buy your cruise. Also consider picking an itinerary that offers "overnights" in certain high-profile ports such as St. Petersburg, Russia, or Venice, Italy. These cruises offer more intense destination time ashore.

DEFINING THE CARIBBEAN On a map with the arm of the compass pointing north, the islands closest to the United States are the Greater

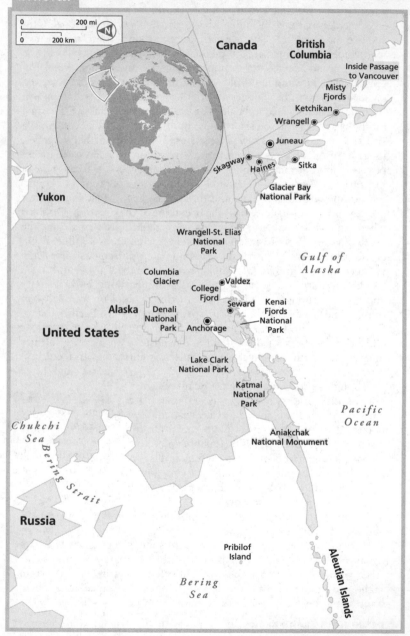

alaska

0   200 mi
0   200 km

Canada

British
Columbia

Inside Passage
to Vancouver

Misty
Fjords

Ketchikan

Wrangell

Juneau

Skagway

Haines

Sitka

Glacier Bay
National Park

Yukon

Wrangell-St. Elias
National
Park

Gulf of
Alaska

Columbia
Glacier

College
Fjord

Valdez

Seward

Kenai
Fjords
National
Park

Alaska

Denali
National
Park

Anchorage

United States

Lake Clark
National Park

Katmai
National
Park

Chukchi
Sea

Bering Strait

Aniakchak
National Monument

Pacific
Ocean

Russia

Pribilof
Island

Aleutian Islands

Bering
Sea

Antilles; they include Cuba, the Caymans, Jamaica, Haiti, the Dominican Republic, and Puerto Rico. All but Cuba are visited by ships from
U.S. ports and have daily, direct air service from major U.S. cities.

The Bahamas and the British colony of the Turks and Caicos lie
north of the Greater Antilles and southeast of Florida. They are
entirely in the Atlantic Ocean, but because their tropical environment is similar to that of the Caribbean, they are viewed as part of
the region. The Bahamas, and occasionally the Turks and Caicos, are
cruise stops; both have air service from the United States mainland.

In the eastern Caribbean are the Lesser Antilles, starting with the
Virgin Islands in the north and curving south to Grenada. The north-
ern of these many small islands are called the Leewards and comprise
the U.S. and British Virgin Islands, Anguilla, St. Maarten, St. Barts,
Saba, St. Eustatius, St. Kitts, Nevis, Antigua, Barbuda, Montserrat,
and Guadeloupe. The south islands, called the Windwards, include
Dominica, Martinique, St. Lucia, Barbados, St. Vincent and the
Grenadines, and Grenada.

The Virgin Islands, St. Maarten, Antigua, Guadeloupe, Martinique, St. Kitts, St. Lucia, and Barbados are frequent cruise stops
and have direct air service from the United States mainland or via
Puerto Rico. The others are reached through local airlines, and most
are stops for small ships, particularly during winter cruise season. In
the south are Aruba, Bonaire, Curaçao, and Trinidad and Tobago,
which lie off Venezuela. Aruba and Curaçao are major ports on
southern Caribbean and Panama Canal cruises. In the western
Caribbean are Jamaica and the Cayman Islands, and off the Yucatán
Peninsula are the Mexican islands of Cancún and Cozumel. All are
major cruise destinations.

Along the 2,000-mile Caribbean chain, nature has been extravagant with its color, variety, and beauty. Verdant mountains rise from
sun-bleached shores. Between towering peaks and the sea, rivers and
streams cascade over rocks and hillsides and disappear into mangrove
swamps and deserts. Fields of flowers, trees with brilliant blossoms,
and a multitude of birds and butterflies fill the landscape. The air,
refreshed by tropical showers, is scented with spices and fruit.

Yet what makes the Caribbean islands unique is their combination
of exotic scenery and the kaleidoscope of diverse cultures. The cultures have evolved from traditions, music, dance, art, architecture,
and religions from around the world.

To be fair, we should warn you that the exponential growth of
cruising in the Caribbean has had a tremendous, and many would say
negative, impact on some islands. Cruise ships disgorging thousands
of passengers a day on a tiny island disrupt the normal rhythms,
changing a quaint, sleepy, laid-back port into a frenetic, artificial
tourist attraction. Sprawling malls have sprung up like ragweed
around the docks, and whole local populations have abandoned their

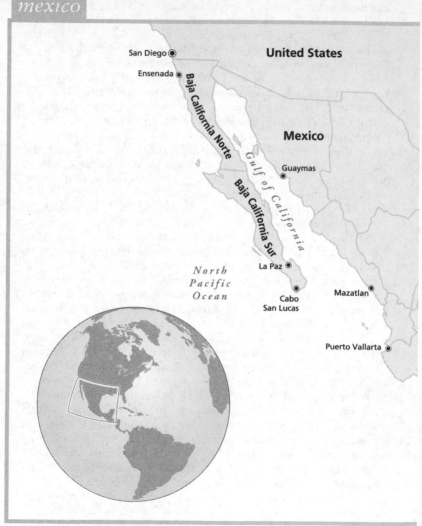

mexico

San Diego

Ensenada

United States

Baja California Norte

Mexico

Gulf of California

Guaymas

Baja California Sur

North
Pacific
Ocean

La Paz

Cabo
San Lucas

Mazatlan

Puerto Vallarta

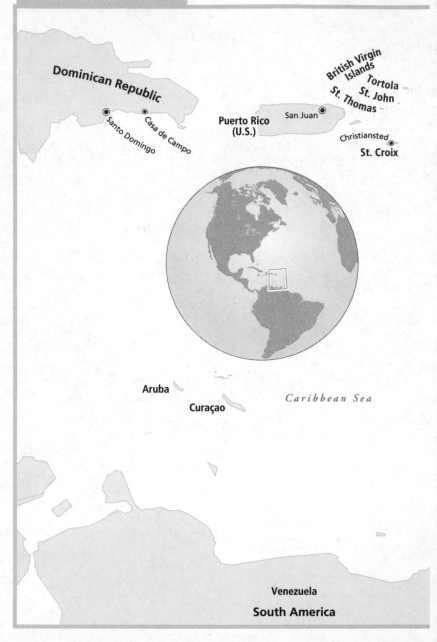

eastern caribbean

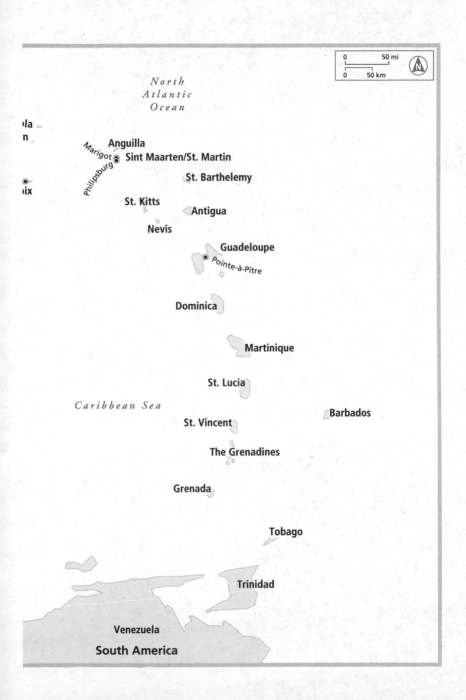

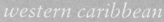

western caribbean

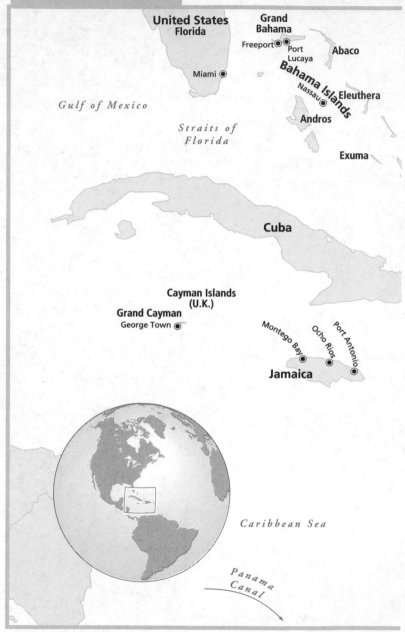

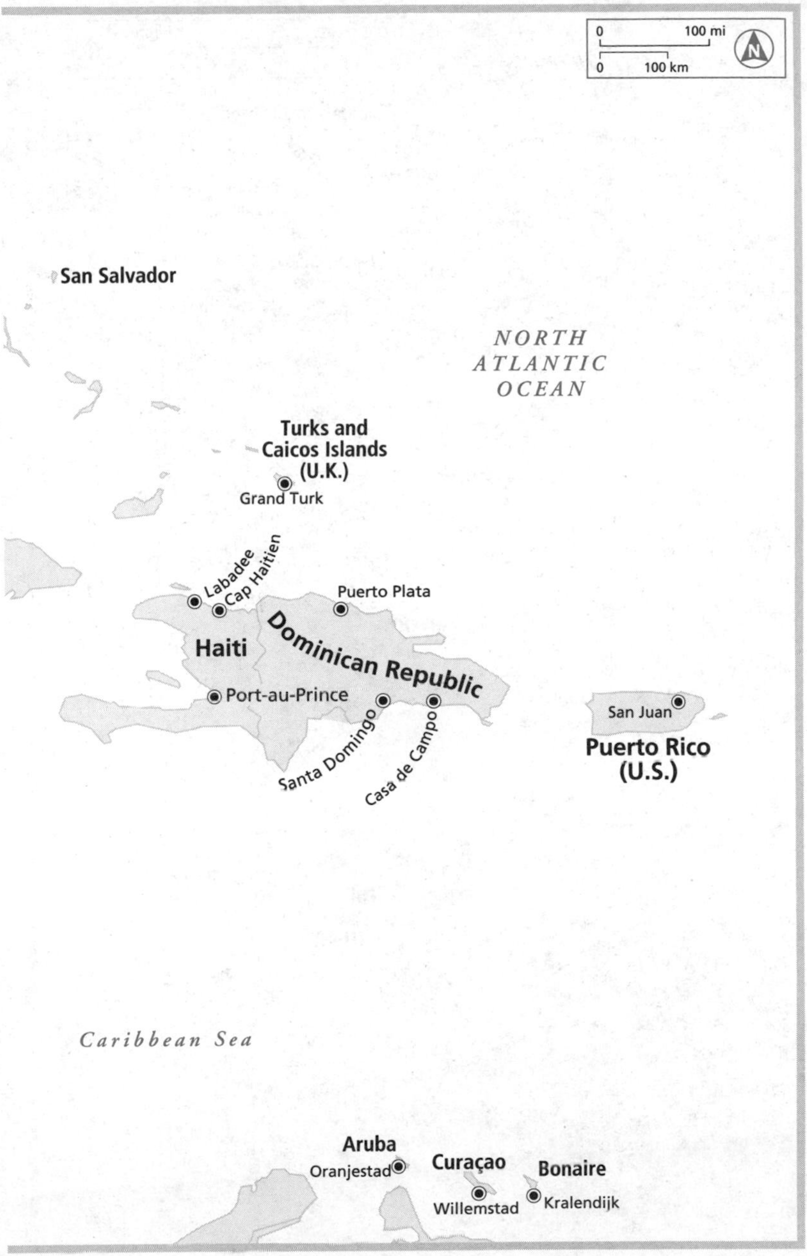

San Salvador

0   100 mi
0   100 km

NORTH
ATLANTIC
OCEAN

Turks and
Caicos Islands
(U.K.)
Grand Turk

Labadee
Cap Haïtien

Puerto Plata

Haiti

Dominican Republic

Port-au-Prince

Santa Domingo

Casa de Campo

San Juan

Puerto Rico
(U.S.)

Caribbean Sea

Aruba
Oranjestad

Curaçao

Bonaire
Kralendijk

Willemstad

south america

australia

0   500 mi
0   500 km

Arafura Sea
Gulf of Carpentaria
Coral Sea
Great Barrier Reef
Bathurst Island
Darwin
Cooktown
Cairns
Hayman Island
Northern Territory
Queensland
Indian Ocean
Western Australia
South Australia
Brisbane
New South Wales
Perth
Fremantle
Great Australian Bight
Adelaide
Victoria
Sydney
Melbourne
Tasmania
Tasman Sea
Hobart

new zealand

0   200 mi
0   200 km

Three Kings Islands
Bay of Islands
Great Barrier Island
Auckland
North Island
Bay of Plenty
Auckland
Tasman Sea
Taranaki
Cook Strait
Hawke's Bay
Wellington
Nelson
Marlborough
Westland
Canterbury
Christchurch
South Pacific Ocean
Milford Sound
South Island
Otago
Southland
Dunedin
Stewart Island
Foveaux Strait

the orient

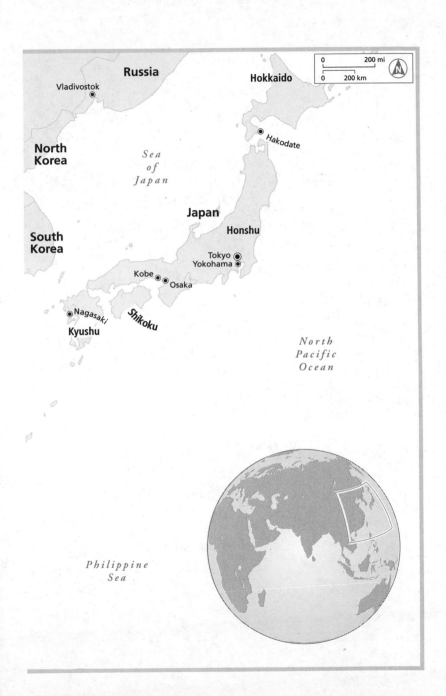

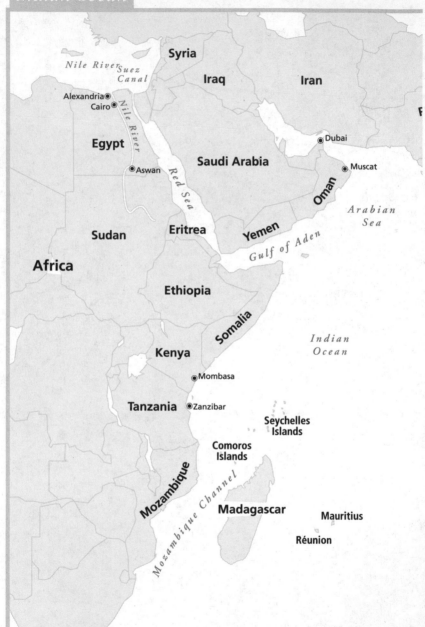

indian ocean

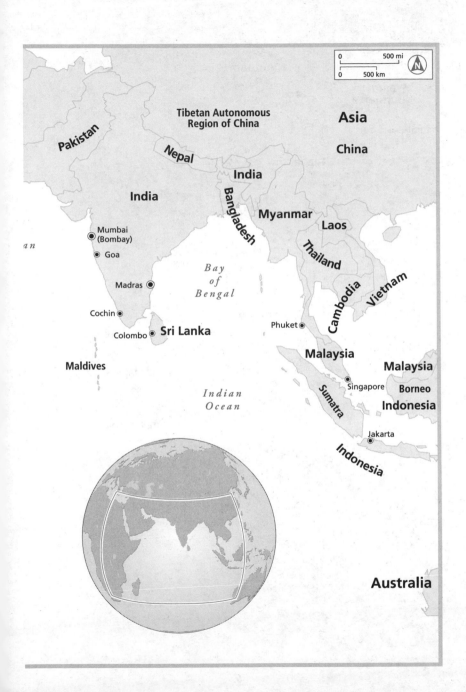

0   500 mi

0   500 km

Tibetan Autonomous
Region of China

Asia

Pakistan

China

Nepal

India

India

Bangladesh

Myanmar

Laos

Mumbai
(Bombay)

Thailand

Goa

Cambodia

Vietnam

Madras

Bay
of
Bengal

Cochin

Phuket

Colombo   Sri Lanka

Malaysia

Maldives

Malaysia

Singapore   Borneo

Sumatra

Indonesia

Indian
Ocean

Jakarta

Indonesia

Australia

southeast asia

China

Hong Kong

Vietnam

Hanoi

Myanmar
(Burma)

Laos

(Rangoon)
Yangon

Thailand

Laos

Da Nang

South China Sea

Bangkok

Kampuchea
(Cambodia)

Vietnam

Mai

*Andaman
Sea*

Phnom Penh

*South
China
Sea*

Ho Chi Minh City
(Saigon)

Phuket

Gulf of Thailand

South China Sea

Strait of Malacca

Kota Kinabula

Penang
Malaysia

Brunei

Nias

Kuala Lumpur

Malacca

Malaysia
Borneo

Singapore

Indonesia

Indonesia

Sumatra

In

*Java
Sea*

Jakarta

Semarang

Java

Surabaya

Bali

Kom

*Indian
Ocean*

western mediterranean

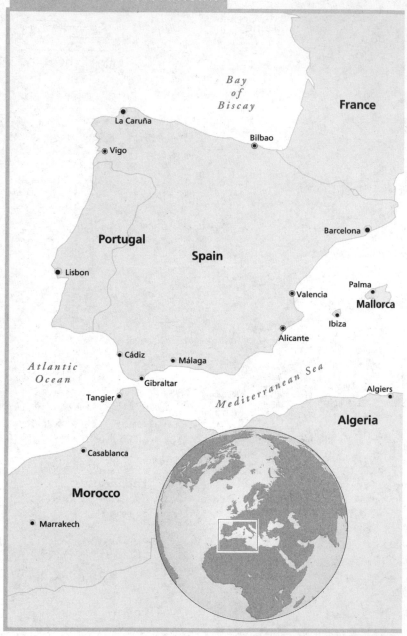

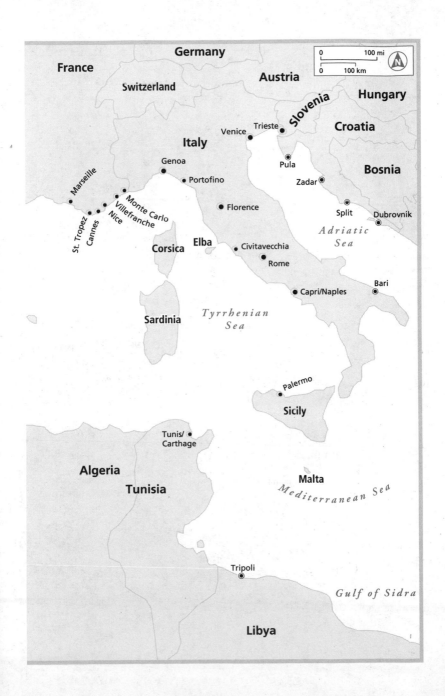

scandanavia and northern europe

Iceland
Reykjavik

Faroe Islands

Spitsbergen

North Cape
Hammerfest
Kirkenes

Russia

Tromso
Harstad

Lofoten Islands

Narvik

Bodo

Norwegian Sea

Sweden

Finland

Trondheim
Kristiansund
Molde

Geiranger Fjord

Sogne Fjord

Gulf of Bothnia

Norway

Flam
Bergen

Oslo

Stavanger

Helsinki

Turku

St. Petersburg

Stockholm

Gulf of Finland

Tallinn

Estonia

Russia

Kristiansand

Göteborg

Riga

Latvia

North Sea

Denmark

Baltic Sea

Lithuania

Esbjerg

Copenhagen

Belarus

Netherlands

Gdansk

Hamburg

Amsterdam

Berlin

Poland

Germany

Belgium

Czech

lifelong vocations to cater to tourists. Some Caribbean islands have become the equivalent of private islands owned by several cruise lines: plastic, idealized versions more familiar to fans of *Gilligan's Island* than to veteran Caribbean travelers.

4. When Do I Want to Go?

Cruises follow the sun, visiting destinations during their best weather. Hence, for some exotic destinations and such seasonal cruise areas as Alaska, the British Isles, Canada, and Antarctica, you have only a two- to five-month window of opportunity. For the Caribbean, Mexico, Hawaii, and Asia, among others, cruises are available all year.

Below is a sampling of popular destinations and cruising seasons.

Africa	Year-round, but mostly May–October for north Africa; November–April for eastern and southern Africa
Alaska	May–September
Asia and the Orient	Mainly October–March
Baltic	May–October
Bermuda	May–October
Black Sea	April–October
Canada	May–October
Caribbean	Year-round
Hawaii	Year-round
India and Southeast Asia	Year-round, but mostly November–April
Mediterranean	Year-round, but mostly March–November
Mexico	Year-round
New England	May–October
Panama Canal	Year-round, but mostly September–May
South America	North coast, year-round; other areas, September–April
South Pacific	Year-round, but mainly November–April

For every area, periods of peak demand are called high season; moderate demand, shoulder season; and low demand, low season or value season. Usually high season occurs when good weather in the cruise area coincides with times when people want to take vacations. In the Caribbean, that's between Christmas and the middle of April, and from June 15 to August 15. But in the Caribbean, for example, immediately after the Christmas–New Year holiday, demand drops and the first two weeks in January offer value-season rates. If you can be flexible, shifting cruise dates a week or two may offer big savings. Ask your travel agent to compare pricing

unofficial **TIP**
Within high season, there are often valleys when prices are likely to be their lowest for the year, offering you an opportunity to save a bundle.

on a week-to-week basis before you book. Always check the period immediately before or after your selected dates to find out your options.

The January to April market targets seniors and Northerners seeking a respite from the winter. Although weather in summer is not generally as good as between January and April, families create high demand during midsummer. When demand tapers off, shoulder season follows, giving way to low season as cruise demand continues to decline.

During high season, ships generally are full and cruises are more expensive (because demand is high). If your plans are flexible, it is usually possible to identify several times in the year when your destination's weather is predictably good but cruise demand is moderate or low. Cruising during these periods provides lower prices, less-crowded ships, and good weather. Caribbean cruises in November and early December, before Christmas, are good examples. Hurricane season is over, prices are lower, and ships are significantly less crowded. Early May for Alaska is another excellent time.

If your travel schedule is not flexible, shoulder seasons (early June or late August) may be your best bet.

5. What Sort of Lifestyle or Activity Level Am I Seeking?

As baby boomers enter middle age and relative affluence, and as younger couples and families discover the economy of cruise vacations, cruising's demographics are changing. On most midmarket cruises of two weeks or less, passengers are amazingly diverse. Responding to a widening range of energy and interests among these passengers, lines have developed activities that offer something for almost everyone.

Even so, lines continue to fine-tune their product for their primary markets. Thus, although Celebrity Cruises might develop programs and activities for younger clients, these cruisers continue to be a secondary market. The line's real focus is the 45-to-65 age group. That means a younger person will have a good time on Celebrity, but an over-40 person will probably have a better time because the cruise is built around the latter's preferences.

How cruise lines serve their primary, secondary, and even tertiary markets makes relevant the question, "What sort of lifestyle or activity level am I seeking?"

In each of our cruise-line and ship profiles, we pinpoint the style, tenor, and activity level of the cruises offered. Look for an activity and social mix that seems right for you, but don't get bogged down in demographics. Many older people are active, athletic, and like to party, and many young people appreciate a sedate cruise and may spend their days doing nothing more than reading in a lounge chair.

The choice to participate in activities or party all night is entirely yours. Do, however, pay attention to the ship's size. A small ship carrying 250 or fewer passengers may have only one or two lounges and limited deck space. If you don't care for a full day or evening of shipboard activity, you'll enjoy its low-key ambience. Large ships have the resources to offer considerable variety. Carnival Cruise Lines, for example, pretty much wrote the book on party cruising, but even on a Carnival ship it is possible to relax. Ships carrying 1,000 or more passengers have plenty of places to escape the festivities.

Most ships offer a variety of dance music. Many even have separate nightclubs offering different types of music, dancing, and entertainment. Some even offer teen night spots.

Cruise lines design their promotional brochures to appeal to their target markets. If you identify with the people and activities depicted in the brochure, you probably will feel at home on one of that line's ships. Lines that do not cater to families, for instance, do not feature them in their literature. Study the brochures from your travel agent. Are the passengers pictured your age or of varied ages? Is the emphasis on shipboard activities or ports and scenery? Does shipboard life look like a 24-hour party, or do photos show a more laid-back experience? Onboard facilities need no interpretation. They're spelled out.

6. What Level of Formality Do I Prefer?

Most cruises give passengers an opportunity to play dress-up. On certain evenings in the main dining room, men may be requested to wear jackets, tuxedos, or dark suits, and women to wear cocktail dresses or gowns. Most ships have a dress protocol that passengers are expected to observe, and it varies widely by line. (See "Dress Codes" under "Preparing for Your Cruise.")

unofficial **TIP**
Even an informal ship might ask passengers not to wear shorts and tank tops in the dining room and be strict about it.

Formality (or lack thereof) is a way cruise lines set themselves apart. A luxury line targeting highly affluent passengers may be more formal than a midmarket line. Family and budget lines can be less formal, but even the "fun ships" of Carnival have some formal nights, and adventure cruises are usually the most informal.

The bottom line is how much formality you want. The great majority of cruises vary attire from night to night and won't punish someone who breaks the dress code. If, for example, a man wears a dark suit instead of a tuxedo for the captain's party, it's likely no one will notice. Check the ship's dress code before you book.

7. What Standards Do I Require for Dining and Food Quality?

Food—its quality and the overall dining experience—is cited by most passengers as a critical element of their cruise. The fare on cruise ships is generally very good—impressive considering that shipboard meals represent the ultimate extension of catered banquet dining.

Feeding 300 to 1,600 persons at a sitting is challenging under any circumstances. Doing it at sea with attention to detail, quality ingredients and preparation, multiple courses, and beautiful presentation is one of cruising's miracles. Ships have made an art of serving palatable food to crowds of diners. Hotel food and beverage managers could learn a lot from cruise ship chefs.

However, you can't expect the same excellence from a galley serving hundreds of dinners as you can from an upscale restaurant cooking to order for a small number of guests. A few small ships have cuisine rivaling better land-based restaurants, and small alternative or specialty restaurants on newer large ships can hold their own with the best of them.

The quality of meals and sophistication of the dining experience vary considerably among ships. Although luxury ships serving fewer passengers in single seatings have the greatest potential for serving memorable meals, midmarket lines like Celebrity, Holland America, and Princess have shown they can approach similar standards of excellence serving larger numbers.

If you have a refined palate and eat exclusively in the finest restaurants, you may meet your dining requirements only in the high-end group of cruise ships. If, however, you dine regularly in restaurants of varying quality, are acquainted with the world's major cuisines, and understand the limitations of cruise food service, you will find numerous ships capable of meeting or exceeding your expectations.

For those not hung up on gourmet food, there are many suitable, and even better, affordable, cruises. You can use your cruise dining experience to broaden your culinary horizons, or you can save bucks aboard a ship specializing in good but less-expensive American fare.

Many people pay for food much fancier than their taste requires. Meat-and-potatoes people get a better deal putting their dollars into a cabin upgrade on a midmarket line rather than paying for fancy food on a luxury line.

Cruise lines have tended to offer good dining-room meals or good buffets, but seldom both. Almost all lines have eliminated the midnight buffet, except for one special late-night extravaganza on some ships when chefs go all out to show off their culinary skills.

Under Norwegian Cruise Line's "Freestyle Cruising" program, you can eat in one of two main dining rooms, at whatever time you choose during normal hours of operation, or you can make reservations at any of six alternative restaurants. On the *Norwegian Sun,* for example, Le Bistro serves French cuisine; East Meets West offers Pacific Rim and Asian fusion fare; Las Ramblas offers tapas bar fare; Il Adagio offers Italian cuisine; Pacific Heights specializes in healthy, light California cuisine; and Ginza offers sushi, sashimi, and teppanyaki dining. If none of that works for you, the Garden Café operates a buffet around the clock, or alternatively there's 24-hour room service. The reservations-only alternative restaurants impose a surcharge of $10 to $30 per person, but it's worth it. The restaurants are elegant, quiet, and intimate, and the food rivals that of good onshore restaurants—or perhaps more relevant, the fare served on ships in the luxury market. Boomers love the flexibility these multiple restaurants provide. Aside from the surcharge, the main downside is that you don't have the opportunity to meet people and form friendships as you would in a conventional dining arrangement, where you eat in the same place, at the same assigned table, and with the same people, every night—a feature important to more "traditional cruisers."

Among other cruise-dining innovators, Princess's Personal Choice Dining program offers multiple restaurants and no assigned seating; or alternatively, passengers can opt for the traditional dining arrangement. The Disney Cruise Line also features several dining venues, but on the Disney ships, passengers rotate among three different themed restaurants according to a prearranged schedule. And, in a concession to those passengers who develop a fondness for their waitstaff, their waiter and assistant rotate right along with them. Carnival, with yet another approach, offers "total choice" dining, where passengers can choose from four seating times in the main dining room, instead of the usual two; some other lines are also doing this. The four seatings stagger the arrival of diners, preventing the galley from being inundated, and allowing both chefs and waitstaff to concentrate on a smaller number of diners at a given time.

Weather and lifestyle have clearly affected cruise dining. Because most ships spend all or part of the year in the Caribbean and Mexico, where passengers remain in their bathing suits most of the day, the lines found that it makes sense and saves money to expand the lido breakfast and lunch. Lido dining also gives passengers relief from the regimentation of dining-room hours.

A recent trend in onboard dining is the availability of stand-alone specialty restaurants in addition to the main dining room and buffet. Found mostly on ships carrying 1,000 or more passengers, and operating like a restaurant on shore, these specialized eateries offer an intimacy and ambience impossible to match in the ship's grand dining room. Like most upscale restaurants, the seagoing versions accept reservations; alternatively, you can just show up during operating hours and hope to get a table. Cuisines and specialties available run the gamut from steak to sushi, Cantonese to California nouvelle cuisine. Almost all charge a fee ranging from $10 to $30, and most are worth every penny. Especially notable are QM2's Todd English, Princess's Sabatini, and Carnival's ship-top steak and seafood restaurants.

8. How Gregarious Am I (Are We)?

Generally, it's easier to meet folks on a small ship if that is one of your prime goals on board. There are fewer passengers, and you see the same people more often. Conversely, on a large ship, the only folks you see regularly may be your dinner-table companions (hope you like them!). On larger ships, if you meet somebody you would like to see again, get their name and cabin number. We once met a nice woman checking in on the 2,300-passenger *Monarch of the Seas*. In a week aboard, we never again saw her. Then again, many people who are frazzled in their daily work life come aboard for escapism and personal pampering. Some don't need or want this socializing.

Large ships offer many social settings. It's possible to meet people in bars, lounges, and nightclubs; on shore excursions; in the health club; around the pool; and in the casino. But the easiest time to meet them is at planned activities. Whether it's aerobics and line dancing or bridge and wine tasting, such activities help people with similar interests come together.

The style of a cruise is important. If you are gregarious, you might prefer a ship that promotes a party atmosphere. If you are more solitary or are taking a romantic cruise with your significant other, you may prefer a less-frenetic social agenda.

Most cruisers solve the problem of companionship by taking significant others, friends, relatives, or all of the above with them. As on Noah's ark, the majority of passengers arrive already paired up. This is attributable in part to the double-occupancy norm for cabins. On most ships, solo passengers pay a hefty "singles supplement" for the privilege of having a cabin to themselves. Ships schedule gatherings where singles can meet, and some try to seat singles at the same dining tables, but singles generally have to scout around to find other people who are sailing solo.

9. The Other Passengers: What Kind of People Am I Most Comfortable With?

The less expensive the cruise, the more varied the passengers. Aboard a recent, affordable, four-day cruise were retired seniors, middle-aged professionals, 20-something newlyweds, a bowling team from Pennsylvania, families with young children, a group of pipe fitters, and college students on spring break.

On upscale cruises of two weeks or longer, the cost ensures that passengers are somewhat more affluent and perhaps less diverse. On a seven-day Caribbean or Mexico cruise with midmarket lines, such as Princess, Celebrity, and Holland America, you will find more seniors, more professionals, fewer tradespeople, fewer families with children (except during summer), and fewer people younger than age 25. Passengers are even less varied on the same lines' seven-day or longer cruises to the more expensive destinations of Alaska and the Mediterranean.

On the most upscale lines, including Seabourn, Regent Seven Seas, and Silversea, the average passenger is older than age 50 and affluent. Passengers younger than age 20 are likely traveling with parents or grandparents. Some lines don't take children or discourage their presence because they do not have the facilities or atmosphere for them. Couples account for 80% of those on board. Singles are likely to be widows, widowers, or mature travelers able to afford the lifestyle. Many lines get a fair number of mother-daughter pairings.

For our profiles of cruise lines and ships, we carefully scrutinized their passengers so you'll know what to expect. We believe the inclusion of this information is one element that makes this book different from other guidebooks on cruises. If you have strong feelings about whom your fellow passengers will be, pay close attention to these descriptions.

WARNING: CHILDREN ABOARD One person's darling can be another person's pain in the neck. We have received a surprising number of complaints from readers about children on their cruises. However, most referred to cruises during holidays, spring break, and summer, when there can be 400 or more children aboard a ship. On Disney Cruise Line, the number could be much greater. In such cases, even people who adore children might find their patience wearing thin if the children are rowdy and ill-behaved, or if the cruise lines fail to supervise them adequately. As cruise popularity and family travel increase, the two converge with greater frequency.

unofficial **TIP**
The simple fact is that cruising can be a wonderful family vacation.

If you do not want to cruise with children, avoid holiday periods, particularly on mass-market lines that promote family travel and cruise to the most popular Caribbean, Mexican, and Alaskan destinations. If, however, these are the only times you can travel (if you are a teacher, for example), search for ships that sail off the beaten track or focus on enrichment rather than entertainment. Finally, an experienced travel agent should be able to help you find the right ship—or the ones to avoid.

10. What Kind of Itinerary Do I Prefer?

Among itineraries, there's a world to choose from. You can have mostly days at sea, mostly days in port, or a balance of the two. Your cruise can be educational or just fun. There are theme cruises where entertainment or education is the focus, such as a jazz festival, and cruises where specific activities are emphasized, such as scuba diving, golf, sailing, or viewing wildlife.

Start by deciding how much time at sea versus time in port you prefer. If you are more interested in visiting ports, seek an itinerary with many of them. (Be aware that when a ship visits more than five ports on a seven-day cruise, some stops will be half-day.) Port-intensive itineraries are most plentiful on Mediterranean, Baltic, and eastern Caribbean cruises. Compare itineraries for different lines listing the same ports. When figuring your time in each port, remember that your ship must clear customs on arrival before passengers are allowed to disembark. A ship making port at 8 a.m. may not put passengers ashore before 9 or 9:30 a.m. Most ships require passengers to be aboard 30 minutes or more before leaving port. Thus your time in port could be trimmed by an hour or more coming and going.

Another important consideration, if you want to maximize your time in port, is whether your ship ties up at the dock or anchors offshore. Having to use a tender (a small commuting boat) to reach shore can take a big bite out of your port time. The larger the ship, the more likely the need to use a tender. The published itinerary or your travel agent will provide information on tendering.

Many passengers, particularly older, experienced cruisers who have "been there, done that" relish the serenity of being at sea. In recent years, they have been very vocal in opposing cruise lines' cramming ports into their itineraries to attract first-time cruisers who commonly perceive value in the number of ports visited. Increasingly though, as boomers and even younger travelers—both renowned as "collectors" of destinations—come on board in greater numbers, the port or land focus has become more important to cruise lines. As a result, it's more difficult to find itineraries featuring days spent at sea than to uncover itineraries with daily port calls. Some itineraries actually tout "overnights" in highly desirable ports like St. Petersburg, Russia, or Venice. Most three-, four-, and seven-day cruises spend more daylight hours in port than at sea. Longer cruises typically feature more time at sea. Itineraries list days spent under way as "cruising" or "at sea."

A map highlighting ports of call in the world's cruise areas shows the hundreds of ports ships can add to their itineraries. With the possible exception of the Atlantic coast of Africa, most ports are close enough to one another to allow a port visit every day. Fortunately, most itineraries of seven or more days strike a balance. A typical seven-day itinerary includes two days at sea. Three or four days of cruising is typical of ten-day itineraries; four to five days on 12- to 14-day itineraries.

unofficial **TIP**
Repositioning cruises are the best buys for those who crave more days at sea. They are also the best bargains.

Repositioning cruises occur at the end of the season in a cruise area when lines reposition their ship(s) by dispatching them to other areas where new seasons are beginning. Thus, Princess, Holland America, and many other lines reposition some of their Caribbean fleet in late April (the end of Caribbean high season) to the Pacific Northwest for summer cruises to Alaska. At the same time, Costa, Celebrity, Holland America, MSC Cruises, Princess, and others might dispatch ships from the Caribbean to Europe or the Mediterranean. Repositioning cruises stop at some ports, but there usually is a high ratio of sea days to days in port. Because such voyages occur only twice a year, they are difficult for lines to promote, and passage usually is discounted significantly.

11. Specialized Itineraries and Specialized Ships

Passengers aboard most large ships determine for themselves how they will use their time. Specialty cruises, by contrast, focus on a specific activity or pursuit. Some may specialize in whale-watching, others in exploring ancient ruins. Sometimes the vessel sets the focus. Smaller (20- to 150-passenger) ships can dock in small ports and anchor in secluded coves. This facilitates fishing, swimming, snorkeling, scuba diving, and water skiing (participants sometimes carry their own sports equipment) and makes a difference in the way passengers use their time.

Traditional ships sometimes offer theme cruises. For example, professional football players may be aboard and reruns of famous games are shown. Passengers should inquire about themes and book the cruise only if they're interested. A cruise ship can be the medium for countless activities and themes. For additional information on specialty cruises, see Part Three, "Cruising Alternatives."

Big Ships versus Small Ships

Hardly a week passes that some cruise line doesn't announce plans for another ship—bigger and, of course, better than the last. But bigger isn't necessarily better for a cruise.

New words have crept into the cruise lexicon. Not everyone agrees on their definitions, but for the purpose of comparison, these are the parameters we will use:

ULTRALINER A cruise ship over 140,000 tons and with a basic capacity (that is, 2 people per cabin) of over 2,500 passengers.

MEGALINER A cruise ship with a basic capacity of more than 2,000 passengers.

SUPERLINER A cruise ship with a basic capacity of about 1,000 to 2,000 passengers.

MIDSIZE A cruise ship with a basic capacity of 400 to 900 passengers.

SMALL SHIP A cruise ship with a basic capacity of under 400 passengers.

BOUTIQUE SHIP A luxury cruise or expedition ship with a basic capacity of under 300 passengers.

OCEAN LINER Generally, any oceangoing passenger vessel, but tends to be used for ships that provided transatlantic and worldwide service and have since been converted into cruise ships. Although the new QM2 could be called an ocean liner, she's also an ultraliner since she holds 2,800 passengers and offers transatlantic service on a regular basis.

Until you sail on small ships, you may not realize their special pleasures. Small ships are fewer but more diverse in style than larger ones. They range from traditional sailing ships, such as Star Clipper's tall ships, to computer-driven ones like Windstar Cruises' ships, and in the degree of comfort and service from the modest vessels of

American Canadian Caribbean Lines to Silversea's ultraluxurious fleet. Prices likewise vary from the moderate Windjammer Barefoot Cruises to *très cher* Seabourn Cruises.

unofficial **TIP**

Small ships are people-sized. It's easy to learn the layout on the first day. Life aboard is casual, even on the most luxurious ships. Informality and friendliness go hand in hand. Passengers are fewer, and making friends is easy—an advantage for singles.

It's difficult to generalize, but all small ships are cozy, imparting warmth never felt on a superliner. The smallest ones, such as American Safari's 12- to 21-passenger ships, are like private yachts—yet surprisingly affordable. The congenial atmosphere also enhances inter-action between passengers and crew, who are likely to call you by name from the first day. If you covet privacy and personal space, though, this type of cruise may not be your best bet.

Small ships with their shallow drafts, turn-on-a-dime maneuverability, and fewer passengers can gain access and acceptability in places where large ships simply cannot go. Their size makes them welcome at private islands and exclusive resorts and allows them to nudge into shallow bays and hidden coves. Their ports tend to be offbeat and uncommercialized.

Some small cruisers have bow or stern ramps, enabling them to disembark passengers directly onto beaches or into remote villages. Others carry Zodiacs and/or sea kayaks to transport passengers into wilderness. Some have retractable marinas, enabling passengers to water ski or swim from the ship.

A small ship offers exclusivity, even if it is unintended. Seating is unassigned at single seatings for meals. (On luxury ships, dining may be at the time of your choosing.) There are no crowds, no long lines, almost no regimentation. Best of all, on shore, you don't feel like part of a herd, unless you book a bus tour.

Today's superliners, megaliners, and ultraliners are self-contained floating resorts with facilities that operate almost around the clock. The bigger the vessel, the more the ship becomes the focus, although itineraries and ports are still important.

For small ships, destinations are key, and sightseeing is the main activity. These ships offer more varied and unusual itineraries than larger ships can, and often carry experts to discuss destinations and accompany passengers on shore excursions.

Small ships draw experienced, discriminating, and independent travelers who enjoy low-key ambience and often appreciate what is *not* available as much as what is. Many neither want nor need non-stop activities. Still, check with your travel agent, as some small ships, like *Celebrity Expedition,* are also great for active pursuits like diving, hiking, or hefty nature activities. A few small vessels have tiny casinos and small-scale entertainment, but most substitute conversation and companionship, or lectures by various experts, for chorus lines and cabarets.

The smaller size attracts all age groups. Sailing ships, particularly schooners, draw the young and adventuresome, attracted by the lower price and the opportunity to work alongside the crew. Deluxe ships and those with longer itineraries attract older travelers, many of whom are young in spirit and intellectually curious. They appreciate an island's culture and are eager to interact with the locals.

Sound appealing? Then consider one of the three basic types of small ships: Ultraluxurious liners offer privacy and pampering, exclusivity and elegance, tastefully opulent suites, gourmet dining, and often formal evenings. In sharp contrast are adventure-oriented ships, whose destinations are chosen for their natural beauty, wildlife, or cultural interest. Activities include hiking, kayaking, and birding. Cabins usually are modest, service minimal, and cooking down-home. They appeal to many people who spurn luxurious pampering but are keenly interested in participatory travel. A third type strikes a middle ground, offering comfortable (but not lavish) accommodations, good food, and attentive service. There is some adventure, some history and wildlife, and some time for sports. Evening entertainment includes games, movies, local talent, and guest speakers.

Even with these choices, small-ship cruising is not for everyone. Some would find it boring or confining. But if you abhor lines or regimentation, can operate on your own juices, yearn for a more intimate environment, or want to try trimming the sails or floating in luxury, small ships might be right for you.

Old Ships versus New Ships

Poets praise the beauty of sailing ships. But observers of classic cruise ships like the *QE2* have been equally captivated by noble grace that is both massive and subtle. Unfortunately, *Norway* is gone—out of the U.S. fleet and possibly headed for the scrap yard. Alas, such ships will never be built again.

Are old or new vessels better? The debate rages. Classic ships still in service, as opposed to those merely old, offer ambience that no newer ship can duplicate. But the newest cruise vessels have advantages only dreamed of in 1960. Because there are well-maintained and up-to-date older ships in service, you have a choice between the old and the new afloat. Find your preference by surveying what each type of ship has to offer.

Notice first the appearance of any vessel, old or new. The newest ships are designed from the inside out to provide more and better public rooms and the most amount of usable deck space. These vessels spend most of their days in calm seas. None but *Queen Mary 2* will cut through the North Atlantic at full speed to maintain a schedule, so the fine lines and razor-sharp bow of the *QE2* aren't needed. Instead, new ships have squared sterns and chunky superstructures that provide many benefits internally but none externally.

As with some prima donnas, most new ships have one or two good angles. Publicity materials show profile shots and aerials of raked stems and funnels and broad decks for recreation.

Once inside your cabin, however, you may forget your ship's outward appearance. The space available to modern designers has generally made possible standard, usually larger, cabins for everyone. Some older ships offer comfortable space in every cabin, but they can't match the improved bathrooms and lighting of newer ships.

Luxury versus Midprice and Economy Cruises

Some of the most extraordinary spas, gyms, pools, lounges, and showrooms are found on the megaships of affordable midmarket lines such as Carnival and Princess. Likewise, dropping big bucks will not ensure that your ship is newer, nicer, or more competently and courteously staffed. (Check the ratio of passengers to crew. The lower the ratio, the more service you should get.) Booking a luxury cruise may get you a larger cabin (suites aboard Silversea or Seabourn Cruise Line) and almost certainly buys a roomier bath with tub and shower.

unofficial **TIP**
Spending more on a cruise does not necessarily get you more or better facilities.

Regarding food, luxury lines have the edge. Usually they feed fewer passengers at a single seating spanning a couple of hours. Passengers arrive at the dining room a few at a time, like at a restaurant ashore. The staggered arrivals allow the galley the flexibility to provide more choice and cook dishes to order.

Most midmarket and economy cruises have two seatings for each meal. When their seating is called, passengers stampede into the dining room like marines hitting the beach. Surprisingly, however, the quality of meals on some luxury ships is only marginally better than that of better midmarket lines. A number of midmarket cruise lines such as Princess, Norwegian, and Disney offer exclusive, stand-alone specialty restaurants in addition to their main dining rooms. These restaurants require reservations and passengers must pay a surcharge (usually between $10 and $30), but some serve fare that rivals the cuisine served in dining rooms aboard luxury vessels.

SPECIAL PEOPLE WITH SPECIAL NEEDS

SOME PASSENGERS REQUIRE SPECIAL SERVICES or accommodations. If you are a honeymooner, single, disabled, require a special diet, or plan to travel with young children or teens, read on.

Singles

Safety and security, comfort, convenience, companionship, fun, and freedom—all are reasons that cruises are among the fastest-growing options available to travelers who want to go it alone.

A cruise ship is about the safest, most secure environment you can find. A woman might hesitate to talk with someone in a hotel bar, dine alone in a fancy restaurant, or walk alone into a nightclub, but such barriers don't exist on a ship. As always, though, for female travelers, common sense remains a good attribute.

Furthermore, the fun is at your fingertips. The nightclub, disco, casino, and theater are walking distance from your cabin. Relieved of the need for an escort and with ready-made companions for dinner or activities, single people—men and women—vacation on their own terms.

Cruise prices are based on two people sharing a cabin. For one person to occupy a cabin alone, cruise lines impose an extra charge over the per-person double-occupancy rate. This "single supplement" varies from 10% to 100% (expressed as 110–200%), depending on the line, ship, itinerary, season, and cabin category. The most frequent charge is 150% except for suites, which usually go for 200%. Brochures always publish the rate. Your choices are to pay it, bring a friend, or take one of these options:

GUARANTEED SINGLE RATE You pay a set price published in the brochure, which is comparable to the low end of a per-person double-occupancy rate. The line assigns your cabin at embarkation. You don't have a choice, but you do have a guarantee of price and privacy.

You are likely to be assigned an inside cabin. If you select low season (October in the Caribbean), the start of a new season (May in Alaska), or a repositioning cruise when the ship is unlikely to be full, you might get a nice outside cabin. Currently, however, ships are sailing at full occupancy, making even these upgrades less likely than in past years. Royal Caribbean International and Norwegian Cruise Line offer a guaranteed single fare. Some lines do not show a guaranteed single rate in their brochure but will accept a reservation when bookings are light. Be sure to ask.

LOW SINGLE SUPPLEMENT Some lines have single supplements of 115% or less. Seabourn offers 110% on some cruises; Silversea has a few at 110%, though most are at 150%. In all cases, you pay slightly more than the per-person double rate, but you get privacy, and in the case of Seabourn and Silversea, all accommodations are deluxe suites.

FLAT RATE Star Clipper and some other lines charge a flat rate for single occupancy. You pay more but are ensured privacy and choice.

GUARANTEED SHARE The line plays travel matchmaker. You pay the per-person double-occupancy price, and the line matches you with a cabin mate (same gender and smoking preference). If the line does not find a suitable mate, you get the cabin to yourself at no extra charge. The savings—and drawbacks—are obvious. It's a bit of Russian roulette. You stand a better chance of having a cabin to yourself during low season or on a repositioning cruise. Some lines don't publicize a guaranteed share program but will accept a reservation. Be sure to ask.

SINGLE CABIN Some older ships have single cabins. The price is set but not necessarily comparable to a per-person double rate. More likely, a surcharge has been built into the price.

Also, some lines charge singles minimal or no surcharge for less desirable cabins, such as inside rooms, particularly when bookings are slow.

Helpful Hands

Golden Age Travellers (Pier 27, The Embarcadero, San Francisco, CA 94111; ☎ 800-258-8880 or 415-296-0151; **www.gatclub.com**), offers about 300 cruises a year and provides a cabin-mate matching service and lower supplements based on bargaining clout. Limited to those age 50 and up. Annual fee is $10 per person; $15 per couple.

Travel Companion Exchange (P.O. Box 833, Amityville, NY 11701; ☎ 800-392-1256 or 631-454-0880; **www.travelcompanions.com**), offers membership, a matching service, and bimonthly issues of a 20-page newsletter for $159 (first-time enrollment; regular annual rate is $298).

Finally, watch for specials and find a knowledgeable travel agent to help you. A smart, experienced agent knows which, when, and how cruise lines make special deals for singles, and she can often unearth ways to apply purchase and special promotional fares, even though based on double occupancy, to single travelers.

OTHER TIPS FOR SAILING SOLO The cruise industry has a long way to go in handling the singles market. The probability of finding love at sea varies according to age group. Twenty-somethings should look to the Caribbean on cruise lines that target a younger market, though the average passenger age remains above age 35.

Singles wanting to meet people should participate in activities, shore excursions, and sports. On a small ship, the chances of meeting many singles are slim. Big ships are considered better for meeting a wide range of people and also often have a get-acquainted session or other event for singles. Among small ships, adventure and educational cruises are singles' best choices; camaraderie quickly develops among passengers. Also, the number of unattached men is likely to be higher than on traditional cruises.

If you're 40-something or an older single woman who loves to dance, book a ship that employs gentlemen hosts—single males, age 50 or older, who dine and dance with all unattached women—no favoritism or hanky-panky allowed. Crystal, Cunard, Delta Queen, and Holland America have them.

On singles cruises offered several times annually, Windjammer Barefoot Cruises all but guarantees a 50-50 ratio of males and females. Ages vary widely. You get no break on price—the single supplement is 150%—unless you are willing to share.

CRUISING FOR SINGLES

S = Single cabins available
GSP = Guaranteed share program available
Single Supplement = Percentage of fare based on per-person double-occupancy rate

CRUISE LINE	S	GSP	SINGLE SUPPLEMENT
American Canadian Caribbean	Yes	Yes	175%
American West Steamboat	No	Yes	150–200%
Carnival Cruise Lines	Yes	Yes	150–200%
Celebrity Cruises	Yes	No	200%
Clipper Cruise Line	No	Yes	Varied
Costa Cruise Lines	Yes	No	180–200%
Cruise West	Yes	Yes	150%
Crystal Cruises	No	No	125–150%
Cunard Line	Yes	No	175–200%
Delta Queen	Yes	Yes	150–200%
Disney Cruise Line	No	No	175–200%
Glacier Bay Cruiseline	No	No	175%
Holland America Line	Yes	Yes	150–190%
MSC Cruises	No	No	150–200%
Norwegian Cruise Line	No	No	150–200%
Oceania Cruises	No	No	125–200%
Orient Lines	No	Yes	105–200%
Princess Cruises	No	No	150–200%
Regent Seven Seas Cruises	No	No	30–100%
Royal Caribbean International	No	No	200%
Seabourn Cruise Line	Yes	No	125–175%
Silversea Cruises	No	No	110–200%
Star Clippers	No	No	150%
Windstar Cruises	No	No	175%

A common complaint we hear from singles concerns table assignment for dining. Some singles are unhappy because they're seated with married folks. Others are annoyed because they're seated with other singles and resent the cruise line playing matchmaker. Response varies, but your best bet is to submit a written request in advance outlining your preference in dining companionship. Aboard, if you are disenchanted with your table mates, ask the maître d'hôtel to move you; you may, in fact, even talk with the maître d' before the first night at a table, to state your preferences.

Honeymooners

If there is a better honeymoon option than a cruise, we can't think of it. There is nothing more romantic than balmy nights and sunny days under a Caribbean or Mediterranean sky. Your cabin is your honeymoon suite; room service usually is complimentary, so you never have to leave unless you want to. Forget the car, unpack only once, and still visit exotic places. Many lines (with advance notice) will provide a cozy table for two in the dining room. Regardless, tell the cruise line you are newlyweds. You will probably get preferential treatment, a bottle of Champagne, flowers in the room, a souvenir photo, or even a cabin upgrade.

If you are contemplating a cruise honeymoon, consider: if you marry on Saturday, then Sunday or Monday departures are most convenient. Check on the availability of bathtubs versus showers if that is important to you. Ask whether room service is available at all three meals and whether you can choose from the regular menu (room service menus are often limited).

Nonambulatory Disabled Passengers

Many people who use a wheelchair or other mobility aids have discovered the pleasures of cruising firsthand. However, you need to be very direct and specific when exploring your options. Dining rooms, showrooms, or public restrooms are not wheelchair accessible on many older or smaller ships. A few small ships have no elevators; on others, particularly older ships, elevators do not serve every deck. Most ships require that you bring your own wheelchair, often one that is collapsible or narrow-gauge. Do not count on a lot of wheelchair-accessible facilities or cabins. On the most wheelchair-accessible ships, no more than two dozen cabins will have wheelchair-accessible bathrooms, and there usually is no way to get a wheelchair into a regular cabin's bathroom. If you need an accessible cabin, book well in advance. We list the number of wheelchair-accessible cabins available under each line's Standard Features and each ship's Cabin Specifications. Look for a ship with a lot of elevators relative to its complement of passengers. Divide the number of passengers by the number of elevators. Generally, the lower the calculated number, the less time you will spend waiting for elevators.

It is important that you book your cruise through an agency specializing or experienced in travel for physically challenged guests.

If you power your own wheelchair, unaided by a companion, bring something to extend your reach. A rubber-tipped teacher's pointer is good, a collapsible one is ideal. You need the pointer to reach elevator buttons, some light switches, and the closet rod and higher storage space in your cabin, even in some wheelchair-accessible rooms.

Make sure that dining rooms, restrooms, showrooms, lounges, promenade decks, and the pool areas are wheelchair accessible. Determine whether gangways are accessible at ports. If tenders are used, will you be able to board in a wheelchair? In the dining room, will your table accommodate your wheelchair, or must you shift to a regular chair? If you cannot shift yourself, will you need a companion to help or are crew members allowed to assist? Can crew members help in your cabin and elsewhere aboard ship? Must you sign a medical waiver or produce documentation from your physician to obtain a wheelchair-accessible cabin? No matter how dependable your travel agent is, call the cruise line and double-check all important arrangements yourself.

Partially Ambulatory Disabled

If you use a wheelchair sometimes but can walk a little, you will do fine on most ships large enough to have elevators. You will be able to get around your cabin and into the bathroom on foot. A collapsible wheelchair will enable you to cover longer distances. Crutches are iffy on ships, walkers better, but the safest way for the partially ambulatory to get around is in a wheelchair.

Larger ships have wide passageways, spacious public areas, and, most likely, an adequate number of elevators. Smaller ships may have tight passageways, steep stairs, and no elevators. Older vessels may have bulkhead doors with raised thresholds, blocked passageways with steps to the next level, and no elevator access to some decks.

Choose a cabin near the elevators. Book one with a shower (with metal chair or stool); many ships' bathtubs are higher and/or deeper than yours at home. Ask whether the cabin's bath has sturdy handgrips.

Consider booking an itinerary on calmer water, such as Alaska's Inside Passage or the Mississippi River. If you cruise on the open sea, choose a cabin on a lower deck in the vessel's center; this area is least susceptible to motion.

Passengers with Sight and/or Hearing Impairments

Many people with sight or hearing impairments travel with a nondisabled companion. Regardless, be sure to inform your cabin steward of your disability. In the event of an emergency, he should know to check your cabin immediately to make sure your companion is with you and to assist you if not. If you are hearing-impaired, your steward should be given permission to enter your cabin in an emergency if there is no response to a knock.

Passengers with Diet Restrictions

Diet restrictions usually pose no problem on cruise ships. The galley will prepare meals to your specification and serve them at regular seatings in the dining room. Orthodox religious practitioners who must verify that a meal is prepared in a certain way should ask whether such verification will be possible. All lines request advance notice—either at the time of booking for some lines, or no less than 30 days prior to departure for others—for specific needs. We provide this information under cruise lines' Standard Features. Also, cruise line brochures detail procedures for diet requests.

Families with Younger Children

Although some lines are equipped to handle younger children, we do not recommend cruising for kids younger than age 5 on most lines, and ages 3 and up on lines like Royal Caribbean that have a special program for toddlers and their families. Lines that really want family business advertise that fact. If you have young children and want them to enjoy the cruise, but do not necessarily want to tend to them 24 hours a day yourself, book with a line specializing in family cruises. Its ships will have play areas, supervised activities, and some-times a separate swimming pool for children. Best of all, the chaperoned children's program provides a respite from constant par-enting. If, however, your rich Aunt Hattie wants to treat you and your little nippers to a luxury cruise, don't decline because the ship's brochure doesn't picture kids. Little ones on essentially adult cruises fare reasonably well. Although planned activities may be few or none, globally astute kids who relish history, culture, new sights, and meeting new people will get along fine. Kids who need constant entertainment and attention should not be brought along.

Usually, the children's center will be a sort of seagoing day-care facility. Group babysitting in the children's center is available on most ships in the evening. A few ships offer in-cabin babysitting. If the lat-ter and all-meal room service are available, you've got it made. Sign up for second seating in the dining room, or go late if there is only one. Let the kids enjoy room service in the cabin, or take them to the buffet or informal dining area. Then turn the fed-and-scrubbed munchkins over to the sitter and head for the dining room. Of course, you can take your children to the dining room, but if they are age 6 or younger, once may be enough. If you prefer to dine with your children in the dining room, you should sign up for the early seating.

If your ship has a supervised children's program, your kids will be on the go all the time. However, we've seen children who scarcely countenance their parents at home refuse to leave them and go to the children's center aboard ship. To avoid this issue, before you leave home, explain how things work and negotiate what time you will spend together and apart. If your children are too young to negotiate such deals, save the family cruise for another year or put the kids into the children's center and deal with any fallout.

Consider accommodations: Cabins are much more confining than children's homes or bedrooms. Your kids will size up your cabin in about ten seconds and figure there is not much to do there. From that point, they will be obsessed with running loose around the ship. Anticipate this response. Set limits in advance about bedtime, naps, meals, and parental private time, and plan for each day. Television, when available, is usually limited to a news channel, movies, and information about the ship and shore excursions. While family-focused lines may offer a cartoon channel or Nickelodeon, it's still good to bring games, books, and toys to keep the children reasonably content in the cabin.

If you can afford it, putting the children in an adjoining cabin is best, if the line's policy permits. If you buy kids their own cabin, the cruise line will sometimes include airfare in the deal. If you bunk the young ones in your cabin, you have to buy their airfare as an add-on. A few cruise lines offer a discount on a connecting cabin, where available, especially during low seasons.

Families with Teens

Teens do pretty well on cruises. They are old enough not to need constant supervision, will definitely eat their money's worth of food, and collect new experiences they can talk about back home. Teens are allowed to enjoy everything aboard except the casino and some lounges. On some ships, teens accompanied by parents are allowed in the disco and other adult areas. Family and midmarket ships often have clubs where teens can dance, and arcades with Ping-Pong, pool, or electronic games.

A cruise is a totally new environment for children—some embrace it with gusto, eager to learn, to find every nook and cranny, but others are intimidated and need help. For the right kids, it's a fabulous, fun, learning experience. With teens, as with younger kids, negotiate and set your limits before you leave home. Because teens can be messy and monopolize the bathroom, we stress our recommendation that you get them an adjoining cabin, again, if the line's policy permits. Finally, though we believe teens on their own are safe aboard ship, we suggest you keep them under tight rein ashore. If this is your first cruise and you have qualms about taking children, go without them and size up the situation. All of you might enjoy it more if you know the territory.

Additional Information

In both the cruise lines' Standard Features and the cruise ship profiles, we include a section on children's facilities. These references are a start. Also consult **Family Travel Times** (40 Fifth Avenue, New York, NY 10011; ☎ 212-477-5524; **www.familytraveltimes.com**), an online publication of TWYCH (Travel With Your Children) that frequently reports on family cruises, down to the last playpen and high chair. Annual subscriptions are $39, which buys you access to six online issues.

Cruising for Children

This chart includes only those cruise lines with facilities for children; for details, see the line's profile in Part Two. Many lines not included on this chart accept children and offer cruises appropriate for them, but have no special facilities for children. Also, note that age limits vary from "no age restriction" to "no children younger than age 18 permitted." Always check with the cruise line before making plans.

CARNIVAL CRUISE LINES		CELEBRITY CRUISES		COSTA CRUISES	
REDUCED CRUISE RATE (with 2 full-fare adults)[1]	A	REDUCED CRUISE RATE (with 2 full-fare adults)[1]	A	REDUCED CRUISE RATE (with 2 full-fare adults)[1]	S
AIR/SEA RATE (same as or less than full-fare passengers)	A	AIR/SEA RATE (same as or less than full-fare passengers)	–	AIR/SEA RATE (same as or less than full-fare passengers)	A
BABYSITTING AVAILABLE[2]	A	BABYSITTING AVAILABLE[2]	AH	BABYSITTING AVAILABLE[2]	A
CRIBS AVAILABLE[3]	A	CRIBS AVAILABLE[3]	A	CRIBS AVAILABLE[3]	A
QUAD/FAMILY CABINS AVAILABLE	A	QUAD/FAMILY CABINS	A	QUAD/FAMILY CABINS AVAILABLE	A
ESCORTED SHORE TOURS	S	ESCORTED SHORE TOURS	–	ESCORTED SHORE TOURS	–
MENUS	A	MENUS	A	MENUS	A
MOVIES	A	MOVIES	A	MOVIES	A
PARTIES	A	PARTIES	A	PARTIES	A
POOL (just for kids)	A	POOL (just for kids)	S	POOL (just for kids)	S
TEEN CENTER OR DISCO	A	TEEN CENTER OR DISCO	A	TEEN CENTER OR DISCO	S
TEEN COUNSELOR	A	TEEN COUNSELOR	A	TEEN COUNSELOR	S
VIDEO GAMES	A	VIDEO GAMES	A	VIDEO GAMES	A
YOUTH CENTER/PLAYROOM	A	YOUTH CENTER/PLAYROOM	A	YOUTH CENTER/PLAYROOM	A
YOUTH COUNSELOR	A	YOUTH COUNSELOR	A	YOUTH COUNSELOR	A

HOLLAND AMERICA LINE		MSC CRUISES		NORWEGIAN CRUISE LINE	
REDUCED CRUISE RATE (with 2 full-fare adults)[1]	A	REDUCED CRUISE RATE (with 2 full-fare adults)[1]	A	REDUCED CRUISE RATE (with 2 full-fare adults)[1]	–
AIR/SEA RATE (same as or less than full-fare passengers)	A	AIR/SEA RATE (same as or less than full-fare passengers)	A	AIR/SEA RATE (same as or less than full-fare passengers)	A
BABYSITTING AVAILABLE[2]	A	BABYSITTING AVAILABLE[2]	A	BABYSITTING AVAILABLE[2]	A
CRIBS AVAILABLE[3]	A	CRIBS AVAILABLE[3]	S	CRIBS AVAILABLE[3]	A
QUAD/FAMILY CABINS AVAILABLE	A	QUAD/FAMILY CABINS AVAILABLE	ST	QUAD/FAMILY CABINS AVAILABLE	A
ESCORTED SHORE TOURS	S	ESCORTED SHORE TOURS	A	ESCORTED SHORE TOURS	S
MENUS	A	MENUS	A	MENUS	A
MOVIES	A	MOVIES	A	MOVIES	S
PARTIES	A	PARTIES	A	PARTIES	A
POOL (just for kids)	S	POOL (just for kids)	S	POOL (just for kids)	S
TEEN CENTER OR DISCO	A	TEEN CENTER OR DISCO	S	TEEN CENTER OR DISCO	SH
TEEN COUNSELOR	A	TEEN COUNSELOR	S	TEEN COUNSELOR	AH
VIDEO GAMES	A	VIDEO GAMES	S	VIDEO GAMES	A
YOUTH CENTER/PLAYROOM	A	YOUTH CENTER/PLAYROOM	S	YOUTH CENTER/PLAYROOM	S
YOUTH COUNSELOR	A	YOUTH COUNSELOR	S	YOUTH COUNSELOR	AH

REGENT SEVEN SEAS CRUISES		ROYAL CARIBBEAN INTERNATIONAL		SEABOURN CRUISES	
REDUCED CRUISE RATE (with 2 full-fare adults)[1]	–	REDUCED CRUISE RATE (with 2 full-fare adults)[1]	–	REDUCED CRUISE RATE (with 2 full-fare adults)[1]	–
AIR/SEA RATE (same as or less than full-fare passengers)	–	AIR/SEA RATE (same as or less than full-fare passengers)	–	AIR/SEA RATE (same as or less than full-fare passengers)	–
BABYSITTING AVAILABLE[2]	–	BABYSITTING AVAILABLE[2]	H	BABYSITTING AVAILABLE[2]	S
CRIBS AVAILABLE[3]	–	CRIBS AVAILABLE[3]	A	CRIBS AVAILABLE[3]	–
QUAD/FAMILY CABINS AVAILABLE	–	QUAD/FAMILY CABINS AVAILABLE	A	QUAD/FAMILY CABINS AVAILABLE	–
ESCORTED SHORE TOURS	–	ESCORTED SHORE TOURS	A	ESCORTED SHORE TOURS	–
MENUS	–	MENUS	A	MENUS	–
MOVIES	–	MOVIES	A	MOVIES	–
PARTIES	S	PARTIES	A	PARTIES	–
POOL (just for kids)	–	POOL (just for kids)	S	POOL (just for kids)	–
TEEN CENTER OR DISCO	–	TEEN CENTER OR DISCO	S	TEEN CENTER OR DISCO	–
TEEN COUNSELOR	–	TEEN COUNSELOR	A	TEEN COUNSELOR	–
VIDEO GAMES	–	VIDEO GAMES	S	VIDEO GAMES	S
YOUTH CENTER/PLAYROOM	–	YOUTH CENTER/PLAYROOM	A	YOUTH CENTER/PLAYROOM	–
YOUTH COUNSELOR	S	YOUTH COUNSELOR	A	YOUTH COUNSELOR	H

KEY

A = All ships

S = Some ships and/or destinations

T = No 4-berth cabins available, but some triples

H = Only seasonal, usually Christmas, Easter, or summer holiday periods. Whenever children are aboard, most ships strive to accommodate them and their needs; the more children are aboard, the greater the variety of special activities.

CRYSTAL CRUISES

REDUCED CRUISE RATE (with 2 full-fare adults)[1]	A
AIR/SEA RATE (same as or less than full-fare passengers)	A
BABYSITTING AVAILABLE[2]	A
CRIBS AVAILABLE[3]	A
QUAD/FAMILY CABINS AVAILABLE	T
ESCORTED SHORE TOURS	AH
MENUS	AH
MOVIES	A
PARTIES	AH
POOL (just for kids)	AH
TEEN CENTER OR DISCO	S
TEEN COUNSELOR	AH
VIDEO GAMES	AH
YOUTH CENTER/PLAYROOM	A
YOUTH COUNSELOR	AH

CUNARD LINES

REDUCED CRUISE RATE (with 2 full-fare adults)[1]	A
AIR/SEA RATE (same as or less than full-fare passengers)	A
BABYSITTING AVAILABLE[2]	S
CRIBS AVAILABLE[3]	A
QUAD/FAMILY CABINS AVAILABLE	A
ESCORTED SHORE TOURS	A
MENUS	A
MOVIES	A
PARTIES	S
POOL (just for kids)	–
TEEN CENTER OR DISCO	S
TEEN COUNSELOR	H
VIDEO GAMES	S
YOUTH CENTER/PLAYROOM	S
YOUTH COUNSELOR	H

DISNEY CRUISE LINE

REDUCED CRUISE RATE (with 2 full-fare adults)[1]	A
AIR/SEA RATE (same as or less than full-fare passengers)	A
BABYSITTING AVAILABLE[2]	A
CRIBS AVAILABLE[3]	A
QUAD/FAMILY CABINS AVAILABLE	A
ESCORTED SHORE TOURS	A
MENUS	A
MOVIES	A
PARTIES	A
POOL (just for kids)	A
TEEN CENTER OR DISCO	A
TEEN COUNSELOR	A
VIDEO GAMES	A
YOUTH CENTER/PLAYROOM	A
YOUTH COUNSELOR	A

OCEANIA CRUISES

REDUCED CRUISE RATE (with 2 full-fare adults)[1]	–
AIR/SEA RATE (same as or less than full-fare passengers)	–
BABYSITTING AVAILABLE[2]	–
CRIBS AVAILABLE[3]	–
QUAD/FAMILY CABINS AVAILABLE	A
ESCORTED SHORE TOURS	–
MENUS	–
MOVIES	–
PARTIES	–
POOL (just for kids)	–
TEEN CENTER OR DISCO	–
TEEN COUNSELOR	–
VIDEO GAMES	–
YOUTH CENTER/PLAYROOM	–
YOUTH COUNSELOR	–

ORIENT LINES

REDUCED CRUISE RATE (with 2 full-fare adults)[1]	A
AIR/SEA RATE (same as or less than full-fare passengers)	A
BABYSITTING AVAILABLE[2]	–
CRIBS AVAILABLE[3]	–
QUAD/FAMILY CABINS AVAILABLE	A
ESCORTED SHORE TOURS	–
MENUS	–
MOVIES	–
PARTIES	H
POOL (just for kids)	–
TEEN CENTER OR DISCO	–
TEEN COUNSELOR	H
VIDEO GAMES	–
YOUTH CENTER/PLAYROOM	–
YOUTH COUNSELOR	H

PRINCESS CRUISES

REDUCED CRUISE RATE (with 2 full-fare adults)[1]	–
AIR/SEA RATE (same as or less than full-fare passengers)	–
BABYSITTING AVAILABLE[2]	S
CRIBS AVAILABLE[3]	S
QUAD/FAMILY CABINS AVAILABLE	S
ESCORTED SHORE TOURS	S
MENUS	A
MOVIES	A
PARTIES	A
POOL (just for kids)	S
TEEN CENTER OR DISCO	S
TEEN COUNSELOR	A
VIDEO GAMES	A
YOUTH CENTER/PLAYROOM	S
YOUTH COUNSELOR	A

SILVERSEA CRUISES

REDUCED CRUISE RATE (with 2 full-fare adults)[1]	–
AIR/SEA RATE (same as or less than full-fare passengers)	A
BABYSITTING AVAILABLE[2]	–
CRIBS AVAILABLE[3]	–
QUAD/FAMILY CABINS AVAILABLE	T
ESCORTED SHORE TOURS	–
MENUS	–
MOVIES	–
PARTIES	–
POOL (just for kids)	–
TEEN CENTER OR DISCO	–
TEEN COUNSELOR	–
VIDEO GAMES	–
YOUTH CENTER/PLAYROOM	–
YOUTH COUNSELOR	–

NOTES

1. On most cruises, infants travel free. Where applicable, maximum age is 1 to 3 years.

2. Where available, babysitting is arranged on board and not guaranteed.

3. Where available, cribs arranged for at time of booking.

4. Children under age of 12 not encouraged.

Source: Cruise Line International Association (CLIA)

SHOPPING *for and* BOOKING *Your* CRUISE

GATHERING INFORMATION

NOW THAT YOU HAVE OUTLINED your requirements and preferences, compare them against the profiles of the cruise lines and ships described in this book. After you, or you and your travel agent, identify several lines that seem to meet your needs, obtain promotional brochures either through the agent or by contacting the lines directly, using phone numbers and addresses in the profiles.

A travel agent specializing in cruises or selling them routinely can be a tremendous source of information. Many agents who have sailed repeatedly can provide firsthand information about ships and lines. Also, many will put you in touch with clients willing to share thoughts and opinions. However, always understand from a self-interest perspective that cruise lines pay the agent a commission on every cruise the agent sells.

In addition to obtaining promotional materials, buy several Sunday newspapers: (1) one in a primary geographic market for the cruise industry, including New York, Chicago, Dallas, or Los Angeles; and (2) the paper of the largest city within 200 miles of your home. The travel sections in these papers indicate where the itineraries and deals are. If you live in a medium-sized city like Charleston, South Carolina, for example, you may uncover cruise deals in the Atlanta paper that beat anything in your local paper.

Finally, here are some helpful magazines, periodicals, and Internet sites: **www.cruisecritic.com, www.cruisemates.com, cruises.about.com, www.shipsandcruises.com, www.southerncruising.com,** and **www.cruisediva.com** are written by veteran cruise writers. Their candid ship reviews are based on firsthand experience. They also have cruise line information, news updates, information on promotions, and best deals.

Another Web site, **www.cruiseopinion.com,** offers lots of detailed ship evaluations written by passengers who submit monthly reviews. AnotherWeb site worth checking out is found at **www.i-cruise.com,** which has a "beat your best price" feature. The sites listed sell cruises in addition to providing comparative information. Also check **www.cruise.com.** All provide reviews, deck plans, tips for singles, and, of course, hot deals.

For those with an interest in the cruise industry as well as cruises, we recommend **www.cruisenewsdaily.com,** which publishes a daily newsletter that costs $47.95 for a semiannual subscription for new subscribers.

Cruise Travel magazine (P.O. Box 342, Mount Morris, IL 61054; ☎800-877-5893; **www.cruisetravelmag.com**) is unabashedly rah-rah cruising and contains no critical content, but it's a good source of information. Its six issues a year contain ads from dozens of cruise discounters, consolidators, and cruise-specialty travel agents. Subscriptions run about $20 a year in the United States, $40 in Canada.

Cruise Week (Lehman Publishing, 502 Seafarer Drive, Carolina Beach, NC 28428; ☎ 800-593-8252; fax 775-402-7614; **cruiseweek@ aol.com; www.cruise-week.com**), a two-page weekly industry newsletter available by fax or e-mail, is produced by an editor who has reported on the industry for many years. It's directed to the travel industry, but consumers interested in tracking news about cruising will find it a timely resource. Subscriptions are $125 annually.

Ocean & Cruise News (P.O. Box 4850, Stamford, CT 06907; ☎ 203-329-2787; **www.oceancruise.com**) reports on the industry and reviews a different ship in each issue. A much-publicized annual evaluation of lines and ships in the February issue is based on subscribers' votes, which tend to reflect seasoned cruisers' preferences for established lines. Subscriptions are $35 annually for 12 issues for U.S. readers ($40 elsewhere).

Porthole (P.O. Box 469066, Escondido, CA 92046-9066; ☎ 800-776-port; **www.porthole.com**) is by far the most attractive and lively magazine on cruises. It offers a range of interesting articles by knowledgeable writers, although criticism is rare. Subscriptions are $19.95, one year (six issues), U.S.A.; US $24.95, Canada; all other countries: first-class mail US $39.95, airmail US $79.95. **TravLtips** magazine (P.O. Box 580188, Flushing, NY 11358-0218; ☎ 800-872-8584; info@travltips.com; **www.travltips.com**) is a good bet if you are interested in freighter cruising, expedition cruising, or bargain around-the-world cruising on conventional cruise ships; it's published bimonthly. Subscriptions are $20 for introductory U.S. membership for one year, $35 for two years and include a special edition of *TravLtips: Roam the World by Freighter & Small Ship*. Canadian membership, $30 for one year, and $45 for two years. Call for overseas membership rates.

HOW TO READ A CRUISE LINE BROCHURE

CRUISE BROCHURES ARE VERY ELABORATE. Because they contain so much information, we offer a systematic approach to evaluating and understanding their contents.

Look at the Pictures

All photos in the brochures have been carefully chosen to excite the people for whom the cruise line tailors its product. If you identify with the activities depicted, this may be a good cruise line for you. Pay attention to ages of the people shown. Do you see yourself in the activities?

Sizing up the Ships

Look at the ships. Are they too big, too small, about right, or you don't care as long as they float? Talk to a travel agent about your vacation style. A good agent can help you make the right fit with a line and ship. Most brochures also contain a deck-by-deck schematic of the ship. Concentrate first on the ship's layout, looking for features important to you. If you work out, look at the relative size of the exercise room and try to find a photo of it so you can check the equipment. Ask about exercise classes, the spa, and such features as a jogging track or lap pool. If you have mobility problems, look for elevators. Because upper decks offer the best views at sea, note inside and outdoor public areas, particularly on the top two and promenade decks.

Itineraries

Read the itineraries, making preliminary selections on where and how long you want to cruise. On what days and at what times does the cruise begin and end? Do these work for you? Focus on a couple of cruises. Read the itineraries, observing how much time the ship spends at sea and in port, how much cruising is during waking hours, and whether the number of ports and the time allowed to see them suits you.

For practice, let's look at a ten-day itinerary from Copenhagen to London/Tilbury.

The cruise sails at 6 p.m. Sunday, allowing several options. Because most flights from the United States to Europe depart in the late afternoon and evening, a person living in the eastern United States could work most or all of Friday and catch an evening flight to Copenhagen, arriving Saturday morning. He would have until about 3:30 p.m. Sunday to rest and see Copenhagen. Alternately, he could fly out Saturday evening and arrive in Copenhagen on Sunday morning with four or five hours at his disposal before boarding, although we do not recommend this. Remember, flights do cancel or have serious delays at times. Come in the day before. Why take a chance of missing your ship? A third possibility, of course, would be to arrive before Saturday and enjoy a

DAY	DATE	PORT	ARRIVE	DEPART
Sunday	June 4	Copenhagen		6 p.m.
Monday	June 5	Cruising		
Tuesday	June 6	Helsinki	8 a.m.	6 p.m.
Wednesday	June 7	St. Petersburg	8 a.m.	
Thursday	June 8	St. Petersburg		6 p.m.
Friday	June 9	Stockholm	4 p.m.	
Saturday	June 10	Stockholm		3 p.m.
Sunday	June 11	Cruising		
Monday	June 12	Oslo	8 a.m.	5 p.m.
Tuesday	June 13	Cruising		
Wednesday	June 14	London/Tilbury	7 a.m.	

leisurely weekend. The first day (Monday) at sea is a wonderful start, providing a chance to catch up on jet lag and explore the ship.

This cruise calls on four ports, not counting ports of origination and termination. This is fewer than average for a ten-day cruise, but all are major cities. The itinerary gives lots of time in each port. In St. Petersburg and Stockholm, the ship anchors overnight. If you're interested in St. Petersburg and Stockholm and a lot of sightseeing, this works well. If not, it's a long time in port. Full days (8 a.m. to 5 or 6 p.m.) are planned in Helsinki and Oslo. In total, the cruise is 229 hours, of which 153 hours (67%) are at sea and 76 hours (33%) are in port. However, only 71 hours of the 153 hours at sea are during waking hours (7 a.m. to 10 p.m.).

Rates

Flip to the rate charts to determine whether the cruises you like fall roughly within your budget. We do mean roughly: you should anticipate paying 10% to 50% less depending on the line, ship, itinerary, season, and market condition. We describe available discounts in "How to Get the Best Deal on a Cruise."

unofficial **TIP**
Almost no one pays the brochure rates. Brochure rates are helpful only in providing a base for calculating discounts.

Most lines present their fares in a chart like the one on page 71 for Princess Cruise Line's *Grand Princess* on a seven-day western Caribbean itinerary in November. The fares are per-person at the brochure rate, based on two persons sharing a cabin (double occupancy). If the per-person fare for a cabin on the Lido Deck, category BA, with private balcony and two lower beds is $1,569; you and your traveling companion would pay $3,138 ($1,569 x 2) for the cabin. For singles supplement, see "Singles" in this chapter for a rate explanation.

As many as four persons may share a cabin, depending on its configuration. Rates for the third, fourth, and fifth persons are deeply discounted, sometimes as much as 66% off the double-occupancy fare. Let's say Tom, Ed, John, and Earl are willing to share a Dolphin Deck, Category AC cabin that goes for $1,749 per person double occupancy. The line charges the double-occupancy price ($1,749) for two of the four men, and the third/fourth person rate of $399 for the remaining two. Thus, the tab for all four:

PERSON 1	$1,749	Cruise Only
PERSON 2	$1,749	Cruise Only
PERSON 3	$399	Cruise Only
PERSON 4	$399	Cruise Only
TOTAL	$4,296	

Usually, for cruise lines that bundle airfare to the port into the total price of the cruise (as part of an air/sea package), the airfare is normally included only for the two persons paying the double-occupancy rate. The cruise line will arrange airfare, often at a discounted rate, for the third and fourth persons.

If Tom, Ed, John, and Earl want to split the cost of their Princess cruise equally, here's the way the finances average out:

Cruise fare for all four guys	$4,296
Final cost per person	$1,074

Because standard cabins on almost all cruise ships are small with tiny bathrooms and little storage, we do not recommend cruising with more than two persons in a cabin unless, for budgetary reasons, there's no other choice. If you do elect to cruise with extra people in your cabin, select your roommates with care. Make sure everyone is compatible regarding smoking, snoring, and sleeping hours. Most of all, be tolerant and bring your sense of humor. Start with a cruise in a warm clime, when you can spend more time on deck than in your cabin. In the Caribbean, you might find yourself doing little more than sleeping and changing clothes there.

Most newer cruise ships are distinguished by the number of cabins with private balconies. These cabins become more affordable year by year and are highly recommended for those who want a quiet, private space to relax.

Sailing Dates

Check the sailing dates of cruises that interest you, looking for those compatible with your schedule. Check dates around these to see if a slight shift puts you into a lower-priced season.

Cabin Category and Ship Deck Plans

Now look at the types of cabins available. Many brochures include floor plans for several types of cabins showing their size, configuration, and placement of furniture and fixtures. Some brochures include color photographs of cabins.

Although some upscale lines offer only suites, most ships provide a choice of cabins. The top of the line—usually on the top decks— are the palatial owner's suite or royal suite, comparable to the presidential suite in a good hotel. Next are a small number of one- or two-bedroom suites, followed by a larger number of minisuites. After these deluxe accommodations come standard cabins, which account for about 85% of accommodations on most ships. Now, on more of the new, large ships, many standard cabins have verandas. In fact, on some ships 60% to 80% of all accommodations feature these balconies, which are becoming a must-have amenity for many guests. Outside standard cabins with a window are generally preferred to inside standard cabins without windows, but they are more expensive. Usually, the higher the deck, the higher the cabin's price. For outside standard cabins with windows, many cruise lines offer different categories and rates for windows with an unencumbered view,

Grand Princess Rate Chart

Single-occupancy fares for categories GS–AD, BA–BD, and CC is 200% of the double-occupancy fare. For categories C–G and K: 150% of the double-occupancy fare.

	STATEROOM CATEGORIES	LIST PRICE PER PERSON	EARLY BOOKING PRICES STARTING FROM
BALCONY STATEROOMS/SUITES			
Lido Deck	GS	$2,949	$2,949
Baja Deck	OS	$2,449	$2,449
Caribe Deck	PH	$2,149	$2,149
Baja & Caribe Decks	PS	$2,099	$2,099
Dolphin & Emerald Decks	VS	$2,049	$2,049
Dolphin Deck	XS	$1,999	$1,999
Dolphin Deck	AA	$1,949	$1.349
Dolphin Deck	AB	$1,849	$1,249
Dolphin Deck	AC	$1,749	$1,149
Emerald Deck	AD	$1,649	$1,049
Lido & Caribe Decks	BA	$3,599	$1,749
Aloha, Caribe & Dolphin	BB	$1,569	$969
Aloha & Baja Decks	BC	$1529	$929
Baja Deck	BD	$1,449	$849
OCEANVIEW STATEROOMS (no balcony)			
Lido Deck	CC	$1,429	$829
Aloha Deck	C	$1,419	$819
Emerald Deck	DD	$1,399	$799
Plaza Deck	D	$1,370	$799
Plaza Deck	EE	$1,359	$759
OCEANVIEW STATEROOMS (partially obstructed view)			
Emerald Deck	E	$1,339	$739
Emerald Deck	FF	$1,319	$719
Emerald Deck	F	$1,309	$709
Emerald Deck	GG	$1,299	$699
INTERIOR STATEROOMS			
Lido & Aloha Decks	II	$1,139	$639
Aloha & Baja Decks	I	$1,129	$629
Baja & Caribe Decks	JJ	$1,119	$619
Caribe, Emerald, Dolphin	J	$1,109	$609
Plaza Deck	K	$1,099	$599

Grand Princess Rate Chart (continued)

STATEROOM CATEGORIES	LIST PRICE PER PERSON	EARLY BOOKING PRICES STARTING FROM
3RD/4TH GUESTS		
Suite/Minisuite	$499	$499
Balcony	$399	$399
Oceanview	$299	$299
Interior	$199	$199

Rates include port charges. Air transportation and certain taxes and fees are additional. All rates quoted in U.S. dollars, per person, double occupancy.

versus windows that are mostly or partially blocked, by a lifeboat for example.

Standard cabins on ships built since 1988 generally are the same throughout the ship. Windows may decrease in size as you descend from deck to deck. If the window view is obstructed, this information should be indicated on the rate charts. If not, ask.

Cabins toward the middle of the ship are considered more desirable than cabins on either end, because center cabins are closer to stairs and elevators and are less affected by the ship's back-and-forward motion (pitching). The side-to-side motion (rolling) is more pronounced the higher you go and is felt least on lower decks. But the fact is, on large cruise ships, you will feel very little motion of the sea, except perhaps on the highest decks.

unofficial **TIP**
The most stable cabins are at the waterline near the center of the lower passenger decks—the best cabins for travelers prone to motion sickness.

Before selecting a cabin category, study the ship's deck plan. Normally, the schematic is near scale and is color-coded for cabin category. Checking the Princess Cruise Line rate chart with the ship schematic for the *Grand Princess,* the most expensive accommodations are on the Lido, Baja, and Caribe Decks, the first, third, and fourth highest decks respectively with passenger accommodations. All three decks are removed from noise of the galley, engines, lounges, pool area, and showroom.

Check the drawing for decks where passengers walk or jog. Avoid cabins beneath jogging tracks or promenades. Similarly, avoid cabins where the window overlooks a track or walkway. Pinpoint lounges, showrooms, the casino, discos, and other potentially noisy, late-night areas. Avoid cabins directly above or below them. Engine noise may be audible in lower-deck cabins toward the stern.

Although private verandas, or balconies, have become increasingly popular and affordable, not all balconies are created equal. When shopping, always ask about balcony size and configuration. Some are

PRINCESS CRUISES ⁂.

MINISUITE WITH
PRIVATE BALCONY

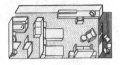

(Categories AA, AB, AC,
AD, and AE)

Large bedroom with twin beds, which make up into a queen bed. Sitting area with sofa bed and desk. 2 TVs, walk-in closet, refrigerator. Bath with tub and shower.

OUTSIDE DOUBLE WITH
PRIVATE BALCONY

(Categories BA, BB, BC,
BD, BE, and BF)

Two lower beds, which make up into a queen bed. TV, closet, refrigerator. Bath with shower.

OUTSIDE OR
INSIDE DOUBLE

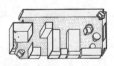

(Categories C, DD, D, EE, E, FF, F,
GG, G, HH, II, I, JJ, J, K, L, and M)

Outside staterooms have a picture window. (Categories E–HH obstructed.) Two lower beds, which make up into a queen bed. Many staterooms with two upper berths. Television, closet, refrigerator. Bath with shower.

PRINCESS CRUISES

GRAND PRINCESS

Plaza   Fiesta   Promenade   Emerald   Dolphin

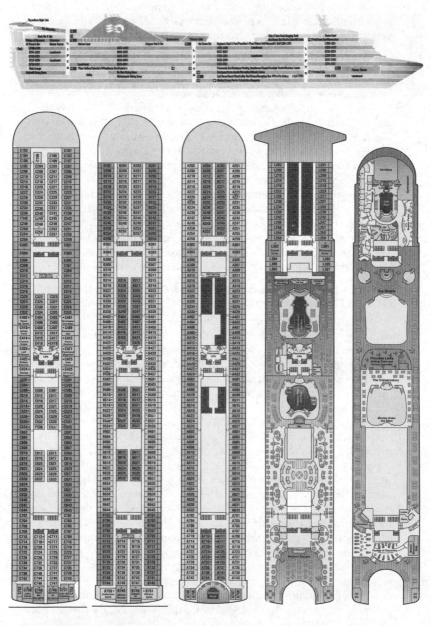

Caribe   Baja   Aloha   Lido   Sun

barely large enough for a chair, while others can accommodate a chaise lounge, a couple of chairs, and a table. Some balconies are covered, providing both shade and privacy, but others are open to the weather, perfect for sun bathing, but also subject to the nosy gaze of passengers on higher decks. Balconies on the bow face forward and are often subject to a great deal of wind when the ship is under way. Stern balconies, on the other hand, offer more protection and additionally provide sweeping views to either side of the ship.

Even veteran cruisers have difficulty gleaning this information from a deck plan, but a knowledgeable travel agent knows how to check out these details when you ask. Analyze what you get for a few dollars more or less. In the chart above, for example, a balcony cabin on Baja Deck is only $20 more than an oceanview (no balcony) cabin on the higher Lido Deck.

Be aware that the newer megaships are very long indeed. The *Grand Princess* is 951 feet long, more than the length of three football fields. If you have a cabin toward the stern, it's quite a trek to the ship's main theater near the bow. One round-trip would be roughly a half mile. With the way the public areas are distributed throughout the ship, it's easy to log upward of four miles of walking on an average day.

A PRELIMINARY LOOK AT DISCOUNTS AND INCENTIVES

YOU SHOULD NOW KNOW whether you are interested in a cruise offered in the brochure you are reading. If you are, the next step is to check the line's price incentives and discounts.

After two decades of steady growth, with dozens of new ships coming online, the supply of cabins outstripped demand (the number of people to fill them). Competition put pressure on cruise lines to cut deals to keep their ships filled, and a buyer's market prevailed. But that began to change in 2004, and for 2005, when a seller's market with high occupancy and fewer discounts prevailed. In 2006, something happened that took the cruise industry by surprise. For the first time, excepting the downturn in all travel following 9/11, demand dropped significantly for Caribbean cruises. Reasons hypothesized for the decline include the growing sophistication of cruisers, the increased demand for cruises in Europe, the negative impact of large-ship cruising on the culture of the Caribbean, and in the year following Katrina, fear of hurricanes. If the Caribbean market remains soft, look for above-average discounts in 2007 and possibly 2008.

Another destination where deep discounts on cruises seem likely is Hawaii. In this case, the number of ships and berths exceeds demand. Competition for passengers in this market has posed major problems, especially for Norwegian Cruise Lines. NCL's Hawaii fleet includes a number of American-flagged vessels that are more expensive to operate than ships flying a foreign flag (owing to U.S. minimum-wage requirements, taxes, and safety regulations). Consequently, NCL can't drop its prices to meet the competition without incurring a vastly reduced operating profit or a loss.

In the next couple of years there will be fewer new ships coming online than in the preceding three years, bringing supply more in line with demand. However, because the new ships entering service are so large (most carry more than 2,000 passengers), we're unlikely to see anything approaching a real seller's market. So there will still be bargains, but primarily in specific markets such as Hawaii, the Caribbean, and Alaska.

Incentives and discounts offered in the lines' brochures are varied. First, the line sets prices according to times of greatest demand. High season is most expensive, followed by shoulder season, then low season. Savings may not be spectacular, judging from the brochure prices.

Remember: fares in the brochure are base prices to which discounts are applied. Also, ships are less crowded and cabin upgrades somewhat more available during low and shoulder seasons.

After studying seasonal discounts, check early-booking discounts. Lines offer substantial discounts to travelers willing to book six months to a year ahead. The line has use of your money in advance and gets critical information on whether a particular cruise is filling. Early-booking discounts commonly are 15% to 50% off the seasonal rate, or may be expressed as a two-for-one deal. Either way, early-booking incentives are generally the largest discounts given directly by the lines, and once they're gone, they're gone. You get other benefits, too: your choice of cabin, often the most direct air routing, and your dining-room seating preference (if the line bases seating on first come, first served). That's the kind of information available in fine print or from an experienced travel agent.

Cruise lines also may offer cabin upgrades, credit for shipboard purchases, receptions with the captain, or a couple of nights at a hotel at the originating or terminating port. In addition to an early-booking discount, almost all lines offer other discounts (often up to 50%) to repeat passengers. Some discounts from cruise lines, travel agents, wholesalers, and consolidators never appear in the cruise lines' basic brochures. For help in finding them, read the section "How to Get the Best Deal on a Cruise."

ROUND-TRIP AIRFARE

UNLESS YOU LIVE WITHIN DRIVING DISTANCE of your cruise's originating port, you will require transportation to it. Until a few years ago, most lines included air transportation in the cruise cost and promoted it as "free air." But times have changed.

What Happened to "Free Air"?

First, check the cruise brochure to determine whether prices include air transportation. When lines include air transportation in their packages (for a higher cruise cost, of course), they agree to fly you round-trip from specific "gateway" cities. These gateway cities vary among cruise lines, but usually include all major U.S. and Canadian cities and many smaller cities. If air transportation is part of the cruise package but your gateway city is especially far from the port, an air supplement—an extra charge—may be levied.

Until the late 1990s, air/sea packages were touted as all-inclusive, with "free" airfare. Nothing, of course, was ever free. Cruise lines built air transportation into the cruise cost and called it free. By buying in advance and in large volume, lines could negotiate big discounts on airfares. These discounts enabled the cruise lines to offer complete vacation packages—the cruise with airfare—for a good price. Since 1997, however, cruise lines have increasingly published their rates as "cruise-only" fares and sell the air transportation as an add-on. The reason for the change is that as demand for air travel increased, airlines radically reduced the availability and size of discounts for cruise lines. Even in a post-9/11 world, airlines can fill their planes without offering reduced fares to major ports, particularly for weekend flights when cruise lines need them most. Today, cruise lines can obtain the discounts required for a good air/sea package only by buying airlines' least desirable flights, including late-night flights, circuitous routes, and multiple stops. Luxury cruise lines are the exceptions, as they continue to offer air-inclusive packages to ensure that their customers get the most direct and convenient flights.

At the same time, many passengers often discover they can get better airfares and routing on their own or by using their frequent-flier points. Plus, they receive their tickets well in advance. Often with air/sea packages, airlines issue tickets only at the last minute (to distribute passengers equally among available flights). The practice panics cruise passengers near departure who wonder where their tickets are. As it happens, cruise lines accumulate reservations for several months before contacting the airlines and nailing down flight itineraries and seats. Standard practice is to advise you of your air itinerary 30 to 45 days prior to sailing (Princess has a program called Flight Choice, in which flight notification is made 60 days in advance). Understand, however, that we're only talking about flight *information*. Actual ticketing does not begin until about 30 days from your sailing date, and your tickets might not arrive until a week or two before you walk out of the door. The process affords the cruise line maximum flexibility but vastly increases the probability of your receiving an inconvenient itinerary with multiple connecting flights, and with little time left to make changes. As a kicker, you may be surprised to discover that making your reservations well in advance doesn't mean that you'll get one of the better flight itineraries. A few lines give priority to early bookers, with flight itineraries based on the "seniority" of cruise reservations that are paid in full. With many other lines, it matters not whether you booked eight months or eight weeks ahead—you'll get what's available at the time the cruise line finally books the air travel.

If the air itinerary provided by the cruise line is not acceptable, you can request a change or a particular routing through your travel agent. Many cruise lines maintain "Air Deviation" desks to handle requests from passengers who want to change their assigned routing. Changes can cost $35 to $100 (as if you changed a ticket directly with an airline), and an additional air supplement may be charged if no seats are available in your designated airfare category. So, you ask, how bad can flight itineraries arranged by the cruise line be? A California couple was ushered off their ship and shuttled to the San Juan, Puerto Rico, airport at 9:30 a.m. for a flight home that departed at 6 p.m. Following a cruise, a family of six was split up with four of the party scheduled for an early flight and the other two reserved for a flight that arrived eight hours later.

If you purchase an air-inclusive cruise vacation but elect to arrange (and pay for) your own air transportation, the cruise fare will be decreased because you are not using the air-travel part of the package. The amount to be lopped off your package price is shown at the bottom of the rate sheet as "Cruise-Only Travel Allowance." The allowance, for example, is about $250 on one-week Caribbean air/sea packages.

unofficial **TIP**
Flights arranged by the cruise lines are often not eligible for frequent-flier mileage. Plan to call the airline directly after the ticket has been issued to try to get proper credit.

Price and itineraries, however, are not the only considerations in buying air from the cruise line. When you buy the line's air add-on or an air-inclusive cruise, transfers are almost always included. The cruise line will meet you at the airport and transfer you to the ship. Likewise, at the end of the cruise, the line will return you to the airport.

When you purchase your air transportation independently or if you use frequent-flier awards, you can usually buy airport transfers from the cruise lines. Carnival, for example, offers one-way and round-trip transfers, which must be booked 14 days in advance; price varies with location. Without such an arrangement, you must set up your own transfers. This seems complicated, but travel agents can handle such details for you—and we advise you to let them. Be aware that at cruise's end only, some lines provide this transportation service regardless of whether you bought your air through them.

When arriving at the embarkation airport, you will claim your baggage. Those on an air/sea package or with transfers will board a bus and their luggage will be transported with them to the pier. There, luggage will be taken by porters, and you will see it several hours later, after it is delivered directly to your cabin. If the airline booked by the cruise line loses your luggage, the cruise line will do its best to get it to you (once it's recovered), even if the ship has sailed.

During busier times, cruise lines may fly you to the port city a day in advance and provide hotel accommodations. If you live in the western United States and are sailing from an eastern port, the cruise line may fly you to the port city on a late-night flight with arrival between midnight and 9 a.m. More considerate lines arrange hotel day rooms where you can rest before boarding your ship later in the day. Similar arrangements are sometimes made for East Coast passengers embarking on the West Coast, and passengers on European or Asian cruises.

The line, when it puts you in a hotel, assumes responsibility for transporting you to the pier. If you are to be accommodated in a hotel before embarkation, pack an overnight bag; you may not have access to your luggage until you're aboard ship.

Most air transportation purchased through cruise lines is coach class. Your travel agent can arrange seat assignments, boarding passes, and upgrades (when available).

If you are cruising during autumn (excluding holiday periods) or when airfares are discounted in your city, or if you can reach the port on a discount airline (like Southwest), you may want to book your own air travel to save money. If you can book your flights at or near the cruise line's air allowance, you will be able to choose your airline, ensure a good flight itinerary, accrue frequent-flier miles, and receive your tickets well before your departure date.

If you choose the air-inclusive package or buy air transportation as an add-on, take these precautions:

1. **DO YOUR HOMEWORK.** Ask the cruise line if preferred air itineraries are allocated according to reservations seniority (that is, those who book earliest get the best itineraries). Also ask when your booked flight itinerary will be available. If the cruise line does not give priority to those who book early or does not provide flight information far enough in advance to make changes, book your own air.

2. **CALL EARLY TO RESERVE.** Remember that cruise lines contract for a specific number of seats for every cruise—when they're filled, the line has to scramble for additional ones. That's when you're likely to get a circuitous routing. But, to put this in perspective: the airline crunch comes at holiday times—Labor Day, Thanksgiving, Christmas, spring break through Easter—and can be exacerbated by bad weather. So, if you plan a cruise during a holiday period, arrange it early and save yourself a pile of headaches. As a veteran travel agent advised, "Passengers should seriously consider taking the air/sea package from the cruise line during the winter months, especially if they are flying from a cold-weather gateway. If there are weather- or equipment-related delays, the cruise line will help air/sea passengers get to the ship. If passengers have booked their own air, they are on their own if they miss the ship. Passengers who do their own air would also be well advised to purchase

third-party travel insurance that covers trip interruption, delay, or cancellation due to weather- or equipment-related problems."

The travel agent's advice is valid, but only up to a point. The cruise line sees itself as merely an airline ticketing agent. As a matter of customer relations, many cruise lines will step in and assist a passenger who is delayed or misses the boat because of problems with flights that the cruise line booked. The salient point, however, is that the cruise line is under no obligation to help. If you read the terms and conditions of your passage contract, you'll almost immediately bump into language like the following: "Under no circumstances does [X Cruise Line's] responsibility extend beyond the ship. All arrangements made for the guests with independent contractors [such as airlines] are made solely for the convenience of the guest and are at the guest's risk." We'll explore the ramifications of this and related issues later under "When Things Go Wrong." For now, let us add that we recommend third-party travel insurance whether you book air through the cruise line or not.

3. **ASK YOUR TRAVEL AGENT WHEN YOU CAN EXPECT YOUR TICKETS.** Most cruise brochures tell this in the fine print. If not, your travel agent will know from experience or can ask the cruise line. Normally, they arrive two to three weeks before departure. Smaller cruise lines generally deliver earlier than the big lines do.

4. **PLAN YOUR ROUTE.** If you have a specific route you want to fly to your departure port, tell your travel agent when you book or as soon as possible, so that your plane tickets can be issued properly. If you receive tickets requiring layovers and a change of planes, have your agent contact the cruise line's Air Deviation desk.

HOW TO GET THE BEST DEAL ON A CRUISE

TO GET A GOOD DEAL on a cruise, know the players and how the game is played. In the case of cruising, game rules pivot on the unalterable reality that a cruise is a time-sensitive product. If a cabin is not sold by sailing time, it loses all of its value. This makes selling cruises like playing *Beat the Clock*. From the time a cruise is announced, the line is on a countdown to sell all the cabins. The immense expense of operating a cruise ship makes the selling a high-pressure, big-stakes endeavor. Yet, for 2007 and beyond, lines are running well ahead of the norm in advance bookings, and this is tightening up the availability of discounts.

For consumers, the time sensitivity is a major plus. Any time a dealer must make a sale or write off the inventory (empty cabins, in this case), wheeling and dealing are likely, and this almost always benefits the buyer. However, we emphasize that there's more to buying a cruise than its price. If you allow yourself to be influenced only by "getting the best deal," you are likely to end up on the wrong cruise. Talk to your agent and evaluate all factors.

Note that in American ports, it is no longer possible to show up at the dock, suitcase in hand, and negotiate a last-minute fare with the purser. For security reasons, cruise ships must submit passenger manifests to the FBI about a week prior to departure.

The Players: Cruise Lines

Lines have sales offices and, more and more, Web sites that can sell cruises directly to consumers. But as many as 95% of all cruises are sold through travel agents or other players, and you usually get a better price by buying from them. To their credit, cruise lines are loyal to those who sell their product and usually won't undercut the prices available to them. Practically, the lines don't want the bother, and until the Internet came along, it wasn't cost-effective. It costs cruise lines far more to maintain sales offices to serve the general public than it does to maintain a sales network through travel agencies and Internet sellers (which are expected to increase to 25% over the next few years). Note, however, that sales directly to consumers on the Internet are not necessarily at a discount.

But now many lines have "equalized" pricing and will penalize and even ban agencies from selling their products if they advertise a lower price. Carnival Cruise Lines, saying that it "would rather have thirty-five thousand people selling Carnival than ten," closed ranks with the little guys by offering the same prices to all of its accounts. Royal Caribbean has gone even farther: whether small agencies or giants, it announced recently it would no longer deal with any agency that is found undercutting prices by rebating commissions. In addition, Celebrity, Oceania Cruises, and Norwegian Cruise Lines now have similar antirebating practices. Other major lines say, off the record, to be prepared for others to follow suit. For now, some lines continue to offer large operators preferential pricing, but that practice is dwindling. To gain an even greater advantage, the big sellers also use their extensive resources to gobble up blocks of cabins at group rates and then resell the cabins one at a time to individual travelers. That too may eventually become passé as major lines are beginning to forbid this practice as well. They hope to stabilize prices and avoid abuse of their policies.

The smaller agencies are also smacked by the way the cruise lines handle "distressed inventory," for example, cabins yet unsold as the sailing date for a cruise approaches. Once again, not unexpectedly, these bargain-basement goodies are sometimes handed over to the line's big-volume brick-and-mortar and Internet accounts to move. Although most of us like to root for the underdog, it's tough to walk away from the great prices offered by larger sellers. It's worth remembering, however, that the big guys usually can't compete with a good hometown travel agent when it comes to service, accessibility, and peace of mind.

With the cruise industry expanding exponentially, be alert for foreign cruise lines and new cruise lines trying to break into the American market. Sometimes these lines offer incredible deals to lure customers from the United States. In 2005, for example, the then-new Italian Line, MSC Cruises, offered seven-night Caribbean cruises for as little as $545 for an inside cabin and $945 for a balcony stateroom. Your travel agent may not be familiar with new players in the market, so you'll probably have to ask or do some research on your own, and you may want to use a cruise-only agent who knows a host of cruise products.

The Players: Wholesalers and Megasellers

Wal-Mart founder Sam Walton taught Americans that the more of something you buy, the lower the price should be. Businesspeople call it buying in quantity or volume discounting. In cruising, travel wholesalers and megasellers are volume buyers. Booking well in advance, they buy large numbers of cabins on specific cruises with the intention of reselling the cabins at a profit. Advance purchasing and volume discounts, coupled with the fact that the cruise lines do not have to pay commissions, allow them to buy at prices substantially below what an individual could obtain. Some cabins that go unsold can be returned to the cruise company by a certain date; others are bought on a nonreturnable basis. In the latter case, the wholesaler or megaseller absorbs the costs of any cabins that aren't sold. The biggest cruise discounts available to any player go to those who buy cabins in bulk on a nonreturnable basis. Wholesalers sell to travel agents and, often, like megasellers, directly to consumers. If the wholesaler sells a cruise through a travel agency, then the wholesaler pays the agent a commission.

Note that these players generally deal with lines having large ships, or they offer the best deals on a limited number of ships and lines. If they spread themselves too thinly over the spectrum of cruises, they diminish their clout with specific lines. Remember: it's in the wholesaler's or megaseller's interest to steer you to ships where they get the best deal. That may or may not be in your best interest.

The Players: Travel Agents

Travel agents act as sales representatives of the cruise lines. Unlike wholesalers and consolidators, they don't buy cabins. Instead, they sell from the line's inventory, on commission. Like cruise lines and wholesalers, however, agents earn the most when they sell in volume.

Some full-service travel agencies specialize in cruises, whereas others are cruise-only agencies, selling nothing but cruises and cruise-related travel. The latter sell so many cabins for certain lines that they earn "override commissions"—a higher percentage level of commission over the norm. There is usually a volume threshold where the override kicks in. Some general travel agencies and independent agencies cash in on override commissions by joining a consortium—a group of agencies that pool their sales to receive the overrides.

To make the most in commissions and overrides, some agents push selected cruise lines, known in the industry as preferred suppliers. If the line that interests you is among your agent's preferred suppliers, great. If not, your agent may try to interest you in a line with which the agency has such an arrangement. However, a good agent who wants to stay in business will never put a customer on an inappropriate cruise just to earn one commission check. Remember, agents rely heavily on good word of mouth for their business. Their goal is to satisfy you, so you will come back. Most will sell you any cruise if you specifically ask for it.

Because most cruises are sold by travel agents, it is critically important for cruise lines to develop extensive systems of loyal travel agents. Competition among cruise lines to influence agents is so heated that consumers sometimes become pawns in a marketing chess game.

Over the years, for example, Holland America has awarded its agencies bonus points redeemable for chocolate, picnic lunches, dinners in local restaurants, or any number of other choice perks. Such incentives may influence agents' recommendations and narrow consumers' choices. All cruise lines are not necessarily a good fit for all of an agent's customers. Good agents place their clients' needs and preferences first, but some agents go for the largest commissions and the most goodies.

As we noted earlier, in the past, many agents sacrificed part of their commission or override to make a cruise more affordable to a good customer and to compete with large-volume discount agencies. Some agencies selling cruises in volume still take lower commissions to underprice other agencies. But again, recent cruise-line policy changes have cut these practices but have not eliminated them. In many locations, competition among agencies for cruise business is as keen as it is among cruise lines, particularly with the proliferation of cruise-only agencies and large Internet sellers. And now, with airlines having decreased agents' commissions, the competition for cruise business has grown even hotter.

In the final analysis, buyer beware. Protect yourself best by developing a long-term relationship with a knowledgeable travel agent who works to put you on the cruise that's right for you.

HELPING YOUR TRAVEL AGENT HELP YOU When you call a travel agent, ask whether he or she has cruised, how many times, and on what lines. Firsthand knowledge is invaluable. If the answer is no, find another agent or be prepared to give your agent copious direction. Ask who your agent's preferred vendors are. Just asking that question will tell the agent you are a savvy buyer. Compare the agent's recommendations with information in this guide. Request permission to contact other clients who have been on the cruise line recommended, and ask your friends. Someone you know may have sailed on the line. Also check the independent cruise Web sites listed earlier under "Gathering Information." These sites feature cruise reviews from both travel writers and the general public.

To help your travel agent obtain the best possible deal, do the following things:

1. Determine from brochures, friends' recommendations, the Internet, and this book a general idea (a framework, if you will) of where and when you want to cruise, which lines offer the kind of cruise that most appeals to you, and how much you can spend. Remember that your cruise tickets are only a part of your costs. Budget also for air travel and for shore excursions, alcoholic beverages, tips, and shopping. Many a cruise passenger has rung up an onboard credit account that rivals the cost of the cruise itself.

2. Check cruise ads in the Sunday travel section of your local newspaper and compare them to ads in the newspapers of a key cruising market (New York, Philadelphia, Los Angeles, Phoenix, Dallas, Chicago, Boston, Washington, or Atlanta) near you. Look for deals that fit your plans and that include a line you like. Also, read ads in specialty magazines, such as *Cruise Travel* and *Frommer's Budget Travel,* and check out Internet sites selling discounted cruises.

3. Call consolidators or retailers (including Internet sites) whose ads you have collected. Ask about their offers, but do not book your trip with them directly.

4. Tell your agent about cruises you find, and ask if he or she can match or beat the price or provide any "added value." Some producers may offer a bottle of wine, a fluffy robe, or another perk. Be aware that promotional ads are often bait to get your attention. The "lead" price probably applies to a limited number of cabins on a specific sailing. This element is probably the trickiest part of obtaining the best deal. Every ship has 6 to 20 categories of cabins. Often, unless you can pinpoint the date, itinerary, and cabin category being advertised, it may be hard to know whether you are getting a good deal. Nobody said this was easy.

5. Choose among options uncovered by you and your travel agent. Whatever option you elect, have your agent book it. It may be commissionable (at no additional cost to you) and will provide the agent some return on the time invested on your behalf. Also, your agent should be able to help you verify the quality and integrity of the deal, and be there to assist if any glitches arise.

HOW THE GAME IS PLAYED: THE SALES COUNTDOWN

CRUISE LINES WORK WELL IN ADVANCE to schedule cruises and

develop promotional brochures. It is essential to roll out marketing campaigns quickly to avoid "fire sales" as sailing dates near.

Most itineraries and dates are announced 10 to 18 months in advance. Particularly attractive dates on popular ships and itineraries sell out quickly. Likewise, cruises to seasonal destinations like Alaska fill fast. The highest- and lowest-priced cabins sell out first. Usually the last cruises to fill are low- and shoulder-season cruises to year-round areas. Many consumers used to wait for last-minute discounts available when cruise lines hit the panic button. The lines finally wised up, reasoning that early-booking discounts could generate cash flow and indicate sales prospects for each cruise. Although some distress selling continues, cruise lines are learning to control the inventory more efficiently.

Breakthrough Pricing

Pioneered by Brian Rice, Royal Caribbean's chief financial officer, breakthrough pricing seeks through the analysis of many variables (season, weather, price- sensitivity data, competitive pressures, and the like) to determine a minimum floor price for each type of cabin on a particular sailing month before the sailing date. The floor price is theoretically the lowest price to be offered for a particular cruise and is predicated to stimulate early demand and cash flow in the form of deposits. If the ship fills according to expectations, demand for the sailing will increase as the number of available cabins decreases as they're sold. This puts the cruise line in a position to raise fares for passengers who book later rather than earlier. As it's communicated to the public, the cruise line is essentially saying that you'll get a better deal by buying now than if you wait. Therefore, a consumer who books a November cruise in the preceding April would pay less than a passenger who books in June. That passenger, in turn, would pay less than someone booking in August, and so on.

This strategy allows the line and the travel agent to tell the customer that "this cruise will not be cheaper than today." The line can maintain the discounted rate if the ship is filling slowly, or raise it incrementally as the cruise approaches being sold out.

Identifying the pricing model is useful, because then it's easier to understand what the cruise line does to nudge the ship to capacity.

In practice, cruise lines operate two pricing systems. Primary is breakthrough pricing. If the cruise sells to near capacity, only that model will be employed. If sales lag behind expectations, however, the line goes to its separate and collateral model: the special-situations system.

Special-Situations System

Special-situations initiatives—usually time-limited and tightly targeted efforts for boosting sales—run concurrently with, and independently of, the escalating base-rate system. Examples of such initiatives include a deeply discounted senior citizen's rate, a direct mailing to previous customers offering a big discount, a regional campaign, advertising last-minute bargains on the Internet, or a heavily discounted group-sales overture to a large company for their executives or employees.

Each special-situation initiative targets a carefully selected market segment. Initiatives may run sequentially or concurrently but usually are short-lived and end when the cruise sells out. What is really important about special-situation initiatives is that the price offered might be less than the breakthrough pricing minimum floor. If you can locate such an initiative, you may have found the lowest possible fare. If the special is advertised in Atlanta and you live in Buffalo, the package's air component will be useless to you. However, if you can buy the cruise-only part of the special and arrange affordable airfare from Atlanta, you've got a deal.

A common special-situations approach is for the cruise line to join forces with specific travel agents or Internet sellers. Like travel agents who have preferred suppliers, cruise lines have preferred retailers. When a cruise is not selling to expectations, some lines have policies permitting them to enlist favorite big-volume agencies to help move the remaining cabins; other lines' policies may prohibit this, in an effort to give all retailers equal opportunities for sales. When this tactic is used, it develops promotions with these agents featuring extra-deep discounts and special incentives, such as cabin upgrades or discounted air add-ons. Many preferred agencies and Web sites sell cruises only and field hundreds of calls daily. If they have an especially juicy deal to offer, they can sell lots of cabins fast. Big-volume, cruise-only agencies advertise in magazines, including *Cruise Travel, Travel & Leisure, Frommer's Budget Travel,* and *Condé Nast Traveler,* and in large-market newspapers.

The Dump Zone

In the cruise marketplace, anything can happen. Sometimes, lines expert in special-situations initiatives don't fill their cruises. The upshot is that a goodly number of empty cabins may be sold at distress prices during the final eight weeks before sailing, especially in the off-season.

When time is short, agents and cruise lines know it is much easier and less complicated to sell a cruise to someone who doesn't require air transportation to the port. Florida is a huge market for late-breaking deals because of its large population of retirees and its proximity to ports. Major ports on the Pacific Coast and Northeast likewise enjoy distress sales. If you live within easy driving distance of a major cruise-ship port, you live in a dump zone. You are well situated to benefit from last-minute discounts, but you probably will have no choice in cabin selection or dining-room seatings.

Discount Alphabet Soup

Before you shop for discounts, pick the cruise type that appeals to you. Once you start looking, don't get sidetracked by price alone. Instead, stay doggedly on the trail of the cruise that meets your needs and will satisfy and exceed your vacation expectations. Never equate cheapest with best, but don't equate it with worst, either.

More than a dozen types of cruise discounts are commonly offered, other than seasonal discounts. As you encounter them, be aware that catchy marketing come-ons, like "two-for-one" or "sail three days free," aren't always what they seem. For example, a promotion advertising 50% off the second person in the cabin (a frequent gimmick) is nothing more than 25% off for both (you probably could have done better with an early-booking discount). The best method for comparing rates, with or without discounts, is to calculate the per diem (cost per day) of your cruise vacation. Add the cruise cost and the airfare cost if it isn't included, plus taxes, port charges, and other applicable fees (transfers, etc.). Divide the total by the number of nights you will stay on the ship or in hotels included in the package.

Always compare apples to apples. Some cruising areas are more expensive. For example, Caribbean cruises should be compared with Caribbean cruises, not with Alaskan or Mediterranean cruises. Remember also that cruise lines are not created equal. Comparing a seven-day Carnival (Holiday Inn–type) cruise with a seven-day Silversea (Ritz-Carlton–type) cruise is meaningless. The cruise line profiles in Part Two will describe the differences.

Early-Booking Discounts

The more common of two kinds of early-booking discounts, the breakthrough pricing model, was described earlier. Minimum floor rates are capacity-controlled and can be withdrawn or escalated without notice. Most of the major lines employ capacity-control pricing. A similar type of early-booking discount is the flat cutoff date. If you book before the specified date, you get the discount. This, too, is common practice on selected itineraries. Passengers who pay in full by a specified date (as much as six to nine months before the cruise) receive a 10–20% discount. This discount is popular with Crystal, Silversea, and others in the luxury market.

Free Days

Passengers are offered 7 days' cruising for the price of 6, or 12 for the price of 10. Variations include complimentary days (with hotel) in the port city before and/or after the cruise, or "book a seven-day cruise and receive a free two- or three-day land package." Divide the double occupancy price by the number of days in the package to get a per-diem cost for comparative purposes.

Two-for-One and Second Passenger Cruises Free

The deal is that two passengers cruise for the price of one, but some tricky math is involved. Pick your cruise and cabin category and find the double-occupancy price per person, air included, on the brochure's rate chart. The two-for-one price is this rate less the cruise line's air cost for one person from your gateway city.

Let's say the brochure's air-inclusive double-occupancy rate is $2,000. If the brochure does not give it, ask your travel agent to call the cruise line to learn the round-trip airfare cost from your gateway city. This amount is subtracted from $2,000, and the remainder is your cruise-only cost for two persons. You must then make your own air arrangements or buy airfare from the cruise line as an add-on. Celebrity, Oceania, Princess, Costa, and Holland America are among the lines frequently offering two-for-one promotional fares. These fares work well if you can travel to and from the port on frequent-flier miles or by car. If you have to pay for air, however, comparative math might demonstrate that a discounted air/sea package is a better deal.

unofficial **TIP**
Normally, two-for-one fares are offered far in advance, with a cutoff date to secure early bookings.

Two-for-one offers come and go with supply and demand. It's difficult to keep up with them. They also might pop up on short notice. Such fire-sale fares aim to boost short-term sales and can be withdrawn at any time.

Flat Rates

This is an early-booking program in which every cabin in the ship, except probably the luxury accommodations, is sold for the same flat rates (one for inside cabins and one for outside cabins) on a first-come, first-served basis. The earlier you book, the nicer your cabin. Flat rates are usually cruise only, but airfare may be purchased as an add-on. Flat rates are frequently offered by Princess, Crystal, and Norwegian Cruise Lines.

X Percent Off Second Passenger in a Cabin

In this very common discount offered by many cruise lines: The first passenger pays the double-occupancy brochure rate and the second passenger gets 40% to 70% off. Some simple averaging demonstrates that this works out to a discount of 20% to 35% per passenger.

Reduced Rate Air Add-ons

If you purchase airfare from the cruise line separately (as opposed to included in the cruise price), that is an air add-on. Sometimes cruise lines will couple a discounted cruise-only rate (no airfare) with a very attractive air add-on. This usually occurs when the cruise line is able to negotiate an exceptionally good bulk airfare purchase with an airline from a specific gateway city. In essence, the cruise line is passing some of their savings along to the consumer. Typically, this kind of deal applies only to specific cities and is offered only for a short time. It often results from an airline's slow sales and its need to stimulate air travel from a particular area, as opposed to being a cruise-line initiative.

Senior Citizen Discounts

Because seniors have traditionally been the backbone of the cruise market, they are often one of the first groups targeted for a discount program if a line is having difficulty filling a cruise. Usually the discount requires that one person sharing the cabin must be at least 55 years old. The discount size varies, as does the inclusion of airfare. Also, Carnival and some other cruise lines have year-round discounts for members of AARP, the American Association of Retired Persons.

Kids or Third/Fourth Passengers Go Free or at Reduced Rate

This discount is fairly common for lines like Carnival, Disney, and Celebrity that target families and younger cruisers. Third and fourth persons or children sharing a cabin cruise free or at a substantial discount. Airfare for the third/fourth person or children is usually not included. Third-fourth-person rates are generally part of a cruise line's basic rate structure (rather than promotional fares). They normally appear in the cruise line's brochure and are applicable year-round. Their promotional use might come into play seasonally by being reduced or waived altogether, perhaps in summer to stimulate family travel or in the shoulder season to stimulate first-timers to buy a cruise when three or four friends can share the cost.

Back-to-Back or Contiguous Segments Discounts

The seven-day cruise is the most popular product offered by any cruise line, as it suits the vast majority of people in terms of time and cost. However, there are people who have both the time and means for longer cruises. To satisfy both groups, the cruise lines have several choices. They may break longer cruises into seven-day segments, enabling a passenger to board in one port and depart from another. Or, they may offer two 7-day segments with different itineraries as one 14-day cruise, offering the second week at a greatly reduced price. For example, a ship departing from Miami sails one week to the eastern Caribbean and the next week to the western Caribbean. In combining the two, the only port repeated in 14 days is Miami, the departure port. Throughout our cruise line profiles, we highlight ships whose itineraries lend themselves to this sort of coupling and offer attractive discounts for the second segment.

unofficial **TIP**
When a cruise line moves a ship from one cruise area to another, this is called a repositioning cruise—and it represents one of the year's biggest bargains.

Repositioning Cruises

Rather than dispatch a ship empty, lines sell their repositioning cruises; to attract as many passengers as possible, they offer them at cut-rate prices. The majority of repositioning cruises are in spring and fall when the great "migration" of ships occurs—mostly when ships that have spent the winter on Caribbean, Panama Canal, and Mexico cruises are dispatched to Alaska or to New England/Canada and/or Europe for the summer; and again in autumn, when these ships return.

Repositioning cruises with interesting and unusual itineraries, such as from the Caribbean to New England via the Eastern Seaboard, are unlikely to have as much of a discount as those with few ports of call, such as transatlantic crossings. Those with more days at sea, however, appeal to folks who really love to cruise and cherish having uninterrupted days or weeks at sea. However, *Queen Mary 2,* for example, has a wealth of onboard activities designed for every type of traveler.

Group Discounts

Persons traveling together can almost always negotiate a group rate. The larger the group, the better the rate. For a big group, at least one free berth or cabin is customarily provided for the organizer. What constitutes a group varies among cruise lines, but eight or more persons traveling together and occupying at least four cabins generally can obtain a discount, extra amenities, or a cabin upgrade.

Standby Rates

Lines may offer deeply discounted standby rates for specific itineraries and sailing dates. Normally, you rank your ship, departure, and cabin preferences and submit them to the line with a deposit. If your preferred date is available, the line notifies your travel agent at least 30 days in advance. If you are offered your first choice, the deposit is nonrefundable. Airfare is additional.

Cabin Upgrades

Four basic ways to get a cabin upgrade are:

1. ADVERTISED OR UNADVERTISED SPECIALS Usually publicized primarily (some are in press releases to media) to travel agents, upgrade programs give them a powerful selling tool. Upgrades apply to specific sailings and can be guaranteed by the agent and line at time of booking. Such specials allow consumers to buy the cheapest fare and be upgraded from one to five cabin levels.

2. SOFT SAILING UPGRADES A soft sailing refers to a cruise that is likely to depart at substantially less than full capacity. Booking the least expensive cabin category on a low- or shoulder-season cruise offers the best opportunity for receiving an upgrade. Early booking an inside cabin on a ship with few inside cabins (study the ship's deck plans) might result in upgrading to an outside cabin. But with today's high occupancy rates, you might be stuck with the inside cabin. Just be prepared to accept it if you are not upgraded.

3. GUARANTEES If a cruise is sold out of the cabin category you request when booking, the line will offer a guarantee, promising a cabin in your preferred category or better. You pay the same rate as for the cabin you requested, including early-booking or other applicable discounts. Because guarantees are offered only when a cruise is sold out or oversold in a requested category, chances of getting the upgrade are good. Cabin location is up to the cruise line.

4. PAID UPGRADES A number of lines, particularly on soft sailings, sell upgrades. Sometimes the upgrades are as little as $15 per person per cabin category.

Confusion among passengers regarding cabin-upgrade availability often leads to frustration and disappointment. A travel agent wrote us:

> *PLEASE, PLEASE tell your readers that cabin upgrades are a privilege and not a right. . . . With most ships sailing at [near] 100% capacity, most people have a slim-to-none chance of getting upgraded—and almost certainly not from an inside cabin to an outside cabin. Many cabin upgrades are given at the time of booking, but "guaranteed cabin categories" do not mean guaranteed upgrades—these are based solely on availability. The only thing that is guaranteed is that they will get a cabin in at least the category they are booked in! Former passengers and people who book the earliest are the most likely to get upgrades, if they become available. If a certain cabin category is that important to someone, they should book it and pay for it, and not hope to be upgraded to it. . . . Plus, any travel agent that tells [clients] to take a "guaranteed" or "run of ship" rate to increase their chances of being upgraded is setting up their clients for disaster. The agent may say one thing, but the client hears the word "upgrade" and thinks this is a given. Then when it doesn't happen, the client gets angry with the travel agent and the cruise line.*

Free Stuff

Cruise lines might offer cameras, binoculars, and other goods as booking incentives. Or, freebies may be tied to a theme cruise; for example, a photography cruise sponsored by a camera manufacturer. Big-volume producers and savvy smaller agencies may offer a bottle of wine or a photo album.

Organizational Discounts

Cruise lines commonly develop relationships with organizations like the American Automobile Association or AARP. Check for discounts available through organizations to which you belong.

Credit Card Programs

Some cruise lines have credit card programs. Whenever you use the credit card, you accrue points or "cruise dollars." These can be applied toward a cruise or taken as a credit to spend aboard. Cardholders receive mailings promoting discounts, and charging a cruise on the card may result in cabin upgrades. Similarly, miles accrued on the American Express program offering one mile for every dollar charged are redeemable for cruises.

Travel Agents' Discounts

We have found that agents selling the same discount program for a cruise may quote different prices. Usually the difference is small, 2% to 5%. What's going on is that a few retailers are sacrificing part of their override commissions to lowball the competition. Big-volume, cruise-only agencies routinely do this, but local agents frequently will knock a few dollars off their commission to retain a good customer. Ads that claim, "We will beat or match your best offer," usually mean an agent is rebating some commission to his or her clients. But beware of this practice. Commissions represent an agent's costs and profit. As any businessperson knows, if you give away your profit, you will end up with red ink. In addition, cruise lines including Carnival, Oceania, Norwegian Cruise Line, Royal Caribbean, and Celebrity have cracked down on agencies that rebate in any advertised price. So the number of agencies rebating at all is greatly reduced.

Cruise Loan Programs

Pioneered by Princess, cruise loan programs are seen by the lines and travel agents as "a tool for taking away one of the clients' biggest stumbling blocks: paying in full for a cruise before sailing." Loans may also help sellers trade the customer up. Basically, you borrow your cruise's cost on a revolving line of credit (like most credit cards) and pay off the loan in 24, 36, or 48 installments, like a mortgage or car loan. The main difference between a mortgage or car loan and a cruise loan is that the former are secured by pledging your home or car as collateral. Because there is nothing to pledge as collateral on a cruise loan, interest rates are much higher. In 2006, the lowest annual percentage rate for a cruise loan was 9%; the highest, 31%. Loans are administered by participating banks that are unaffiliated with the cruise lines. If you obtain the lowest interest rate for cruise loans on a 36-installment loan, the monthly payment for a seven-day cruise costing $5,000 per couple is $161 per month. Multiply the $161 by 36 months to see you'll actually be paying $5,796 for your cruise. Most people would do better taking out a loan on their own.

Lost in the Information Haze

Deals come and go so rapidly that a travel agency has to be knowledgeable, well staffed, and computerized to keep on top of the action. Although big cruise-only agencies are the best equipped to handle the information flood, even they occasionally lag.

The National Association of Cruise-Only Agencies (NACOA) can provide a list of member agencies in your area. Check out **www.cruising.org** for a list of member agencies of Cruise Lines International Association (CLIA). Discount agencies usually advertise widely. Always check the reliability of any agency with whom you do business.

CRUISING THE INTERNET FOR CRUISES

CRUISE INFORMATION ON THE INTERNET has increased more than 1,000% in the past five years. There are thousands of Web sites to investigate. The majority are travel agencies, large and small. Even if you're a whiz at searches, you'll still need a great deal of time and infinite patience to find the facts you need. Despite Google and Yahoo and other useful search engines, cyberspace remains chaotic. We can't organize it for you, but here are facts that can help you navigate the ocean of information on your own.

Essentially, cruise-related information on the Internet is precisely that—information. You can ask questions and order brochures, and recently, a few cruise lines have taken the next step, enabling you to buy a cruise directly from them on the Internet (the numbers are expected to increase substantially over the next decade). The best way to find out if a particular cruise line is selling online is to check out its Web site. The Web addresses for all cruise lines with Web sites are included in this book.

The Internet has become a particularly handy tool for advertising last-minute specials. There are a number of sites that, after you sign up, will automatically send you an e-mail advertising deeply discounted cruises. Many sites specialize in cruises, while others offer air, hotels, rental cars, and a range of other travel products. Many sites will provide a form for you to complete listing the kind of deals (cruises, air, hotels, etc.) that you're interested in. When they send out their weekly e-mail, they limit the message to those products. Some of the best deals we've seen are on these Web sites, but buyer beware. Some Web sites have sold cruises without advising the customer of required passport and visa requirements or other pertinent information.

One of the most useful Web sites, **www.CruiseCompete.com,** calls itself "the world's exclusive competitive cruise vacation pricing Web site." Recently, it added an advanced search tool to help travelers find their ideal cruise at the best available price, enabling travelers to find multiple cruise itineraries based on a preferred port of call or country. Cruisers also can narrow their search by departure port, date range, cruise length, and cruise line at the same time. After selecting a cruise based on destination, you can then click on a sail date to request competing quotes from nearly 100 member travel agencies across the country, potentially helping consumers save substantially on their cruise vacations. If, for example, you want to take a cruise to St. Kitts in the Caribbean, you type "St. Kitts" in the search tool, and in a few seconds, CruiseCompete.com finds all of the cruises that go there. Next, set up an account for quotes (no charge). Another click and you'll get the best prices. We are not aware of any other site on the Internet offering this type of function and ease of use. Information is also available from these sources:

- **Cruise associations** Trade organizations, including Cruise Lines International Association, that have their own Web sites (**www.cruising.org**).

- **Travel agencies** Hundreds of agencies have Web sites, and others participate through their trade organizations. Most take bookings online or via e-mail.

- **Travel publications** Major travel magazines, such as *Travel & Leisure* and *Travel Weekly*, and book publishers, including John Wiley & Sons (which publishes this book), have Web sites.

- **Individuals** Recognized travel experts and some people who consider themselves cruise experts or are interested in cruises have created their own sites.

- **Subscriber services** Many, such as AOL and cruises@about.com, have specialized programs on cruises and most feature special deals.

The typical cruise-line Web site offers about the same information available in a cruise brochure. However, fares are likely to be sample prices only. Cabin sizes or configurations aren't specific. You usually can request a brochure by e-mail or on the Web (you may be required to give a phone number or e-mail address), but such sites are most useful when you know where and when you plan to cruise. Information, of course, covers the host cruise line only.

Some sites are well done, fun, clever, and even amusing, and they are getting better. Others are basic and slow to load—you would learn more by reading the line's brochure. The best sites have special features, such as itineraries with links to maps and port information, or the facility to search by ZIP code for travel agencies near you. Often, the site is linked to other cruise-related information.

The range of information is as broad as it is voluminous—Princess Cruises' Web site is huge! But it is also one of the best. Among other things, it enables you to book shore excursions in advance—a service that is becoming available from more and more cruise lines. There is no uniformity in presentation, style, or amount of detail between cruise lines. On Windstar Cruises' Web site, you can go through a typical day on board, see a sample dinner menu, review itineraries with sailing dates, and read about special fares and onboard credits for Internet users. Carnival Cruise Lines, with one of the most extensive sites, offers pictures and descriptions of each cabin category, including drawings and pictures of cabin layouts—a rare feature. Some of the smallest cruise lines have the best Web sites; of course, with fewer or smaller ships, it easier to provide information and easier for consumers to navigate the site.

For news, guidance, and evaluations, **www.cruisecritic.com** is maintained by a team of cruise specialists and knowledgeable persons. Included are candid, continuously updated ship reviews and evaluations on more than 100 ships, with descriptions on facilities, activities, amenities, itineraries, and fellow passengers; news on industry developments; and features ranging from seasickness to bargains. The Cruise Critic library contains trip reports and travel tips.

Similar information is available from **www.cruisemates.com, cruises.about.com, www.shipsandcruises.com,** and **www.southerncruising.com,** sites by established writers who specialize in cruises. In addition to constantly updated information on special deals, Cruisemates promotes several specially priced cruises throughout the year. The site has message boards where people can ask questions or post their opinions on cruises, ports, and related matters. Its ship reviews are timely and in-depth.

Cruise Opinion (**www.cruiseopinion.com**) claims to have the largest database of cruise ship reviews on the Web. All are recently written and based on personal experiences. Each reviewer evaluates the ship in 42 categories using a rating of 0 to 100 and describes the cruise experience. Most reviews were provided within the last year. A recent check showed over 4,500 reviews on file, with more added daily.

CruiseReviews (**www.cruisereviews.com**) is limited but more current than Cruise Opinion. The site lists about 20 major cruise lines and another 20 smaller lines and all their ships. About a third had been reviewed recently. Those we checked were short but pointed.

Other sites you might want to check out include:

- **www.expedia.com, www.orbitz.com,** and **www.travelocity.com.** The three big players in Internet travel sales. Besides offering copious content, each post weekly discounts on a broad range of travel products.
- **www.lastminutetravel.com** offers a full range of travel products, including cruises and air.
- **www.lowestfare.com** sells all travel products but limits its e-mails to a small number or particularly hot deals.
- **www.cheaptickets.com** posts a weekly newsletter advertising mostly air and hotel deals.
- **www.bestfares.com** is a good all-purpose travel discount site.
- **www.bestpricedcruisedeals.com** has what its name implies.

Additional Web sites specializing in cruise information and discounts include **www.seasaver.com** or **www.cruiseonly.com, www. cruise.com, www.i-cruise.com, www.cruiseplanners.com, www. cruiseholidays.com, www.cruisebrothers.com,** and **www.cruise411.com.**

Many of these Web sites offer deck plans; ship descriptions and reviews; tips on insurance; advice for couples, singles, seniors, and the disabled; and of course, hot deals. Last-minute specials and bargain rates can be found on all the sites.

Buying on the Internet

If you want to purchase a cruise from an Internet company, first try to run the transaction through your travel agent. If possible, make the booking through the site's phone number as opposed to purchasing electronically. Even if you handle the entire transaction electronically, verify by calling the seller's phone number that competent help in the form of a live person is available if you need it. Because many online sites specialize in last-minute deals, you probably won't have much time to resolve a problem should one occur. Before you book, ask the seller when your reservation will be recorded as fully paid in the cruise line's system. Repeat the process with the airline if you buy air from the cruise line. On the date provided by the seller, call the cruise line and airline directly to confirm that everything is order. If time is short when you make your reservations, you should request overnight delivery; it's worth the cost for the peace of mind. Regarding air travel purchased through the cruise line, you are likely to get electronic ticketing. At least it saves you from having to worry about paper tickets being delivered on time.

unofficial **TIP**
If the deal is available only through the Internet direct to the consumer, make sure before you buy that the site provides a phone number so that you can get a real person on the line if something goes amiss.

Online Auctions

A twist in discounting is auctioning cruises online at such sites as **www.ubid.com** and **www.allcruiseauction.com**. If ever there were a need for "buyer beware," it is here. We know that some people have scored true bargains, but we also hear of people bidding more for a cruise than they would have paid through their travel agent. The bottom line: If you want information, cruising the Internet can be useful and fun. It can also be frustrating and time-consuming. You will learn quickly which sites are worthwhile.

unofficial **TIP**
Be cautious about comments on message boards, forums, and chat rooms from unidentified sources whose reliability you can't check.

We believe that this book—we say in all modesty—together with cruise lines' compendiums and a knowledgeable travel agent, remains the most efficient and effective way to help you select the right cruise—that is, the cruise right for you.

Price Protection

The airlines and cruise lines encourage you to book early to obtain the lowest fares. But what if you plunk down $1,200 for a cruise and discover a few months later that the same class of cabin on the same cruise is selling for $800? Getting a refund for the difference or being able to cancel and rebook at the lower rate is known as price protection. The cruise lines claim to be flexible and cooperative in this regard, but when it comes to giving back money already in their pocket, things usually get sticky. Sometimes customers must "qualify" for deals offered at lower prices. These qualifications sometimes make sense, as when a deal is offered to persons over 65 years of age, or to a promotional fare offered on a strictly regional basis, for example to residents of Dade County, Florida. Often, however, the qualifications for obtaining the lower rate are specious in the extreme. A common practice among cruise lines is to reject requests to rebook after the passenger has made his final payment. If you have been a good little passenger and paid on time, you're rewarded for your punctuality by being prohibited from taking advantage of lower fares available to most everyone else. Another way cruise lines accomplish the same thing is to limit the lower fare to "new bookings only." In other words, if the right fist doesn't get you, the left will.

Almost all cruise lines assess penalties for canceling within a certain number of days from the sailing date. If you cancel before the applicable penalty date, you're free to rebook at the lower promotional fare. Problem is, cruise lines time the announcement of cut-rate deals to fall well inside the penalty period.

The most straightforward and consumer-friendly policy we were able to uncover is offered by Royal Caribbean and Celebrity. These lines will allow a passenger to rebook at any lower rate for which they qualify until the "sailing closes" (usually one or two days prior to departure). If you're age 50 and try to take advantage of a senior deal, you won't qualify, but for deals offered to the broader market, you'll be allowed to rebook without penalty.

Finally, the best price protector you'll ever have is a good travel agent. A good agent can often use her influence and clout to beat some of the silly arbitrariness out of the cruise lines. If the agent can't arrange an actual rebate, she frequently can get you compensated through other concessions such as cabin upgrades, shipboard credit, and the like. Remember that your agent will probably have dozens, if not hundreds, of clients booked on various cruises at any one time. Thus, it's unrealistic to expect her to monitor discount deals circulated by the cruise lines. It's your job to check for lower prices periodically, and if you find something, bring it to her attention. But again, increasingly, lines are cracking down on retailers who advertise low-ball pricing, and there will be less of this battle mentality in pricing for different agencies.

PULLING IT ALL TOGETHER

YOU KNOW THE PLAYERS and how the game is played. Now it's time to put your knowledge into action.

Step 1. To Agent or Not to Agent

Your first big decision is whether to use a travel agent. This guide, cruise lines' brochures, Sunday newspaper travel sections, cruise specialty magazines, and the Internet will enable you to narrow your choices. Even so, a reliable travel

unofficial **TIP**
Try to select a travel agent near your age or one who shares your interests and lifestyle.

agent can contribute immeasurably in offering advice and facilitating the process. If you have a travel agent who has served you well, particularly if you're a volume customer, you should use her. If you don't have a regular agent, ask your friends for recommendations. Make sure the agency has a good reputation and that the agent with whom you are dealing is experienced in selling cruises. Using a travel agent will not cost you more, since the cruise line pays any commissions.

Step 2. Narrow Down

Using this book and the other material, make a priority list of four lines, ships, and cruises. Be flexible. Also be alert to the possibility of travel agents' pushing their preferred suppliers, who may not be on your list. If so, ask why the agent feels the supplier might meet your needs. You might be surprised at the response. Sometimes consumers are not the best judge of the right cruise fit for themselves.

Step 3. Scout the Discounts

Using information collected from newspaper travel sections, Internet, and other sources, ask your agent if she can meet or top any special deals you have found or provide extra "value" in some way. Call a few high-volume, cruise-only agencies on your own. Ask about cruises on your priority list, then ask what's the best deal the agency is selling. Always ask for the bottom-line cost in dollars rather than the percentage discount. Repeat the quote to the agent and verify what is included (airfare, accommodations, transfers, and so on). Take notes.

unofficial **TIP**
Never fall into the trap of buying a cruise simply because it sounds like a great deal—especially if you are buying your first cruise.

Your top priority is to determine which cruise is right for you. Only then is it time to scout deals. The best way to ruin your cruise vacation is to book the wrong ship or the wrong cabin in an effort to save a few dollars.

Step 4. Buy Early or Buy Late

As we said, the biggest discounts are usually given for buying early (four to eight months before sailing) or late (during the last six weeks). First-time cruisers have greater choice and peace of mind taking the early-bird route. Experienced cruisers are in a better position to play the best-deal game. But any time you hold out for a deal, you decrease your options for getting the cabin, dining room seating, and airline routing you prefer. In the long run, these factors are much more important to the quality of your cruise than saving $50 or $100.

Step 5. Give the Seller a Price to Beat

When you've narrowed the field to one or two cruises and you're ready to buy, call the three or so agents who quoted the best prices in your first round of inquiries. Say, "I've been quoted a price of X dollars for this particular cruise; can you beat it?" Give your travel agent a chance to match it. If he can't, he may be able to verify the deal's integrity or uncover hidden problems. If the deal is commissionable, have your agent book it, or if the agent has invested a lot of time on your behalf, offer a $50 or $100 consultation fee.

Step 6. Check It Out

If you decide to buy from an agency outside your city or state, try to determine whether it's bonded and a member of its local Better Business Bureau and/or Chamber of Commerce. Also check whether it's a member of the American Society of Travel Agents (ASTA), the Association of Retail Travel Agents (ARTA), the National Association of Cruise-Only Agencies (NACOA), or Cruise Line International Association (CLIA). Membership isn't a guarantee of ethical business practices, but the organizations have a vested interest in maintaining the good reputation of cruising and try to attract only upstanding members.

American Society of Travel Agents ☎ 703-739-2782 **www.astanet.com**

Association of Retail Travel Agents ☎ 800-969-6069 **www.artonline.com**

Cruise Line International Association ☎ 212-921-0066 **www.cruising.org**

National Association of Cruise-Only Agencies ☎ 305-663-5626
www.nacoaonline.com

To find out how consolidators and wholesalers respond to questions about their affiliations and accreditations, we called all of the cruise discounters advertising in *Cruise Travel* and *Condé Nast Traveler* magazines. Some agencies were gracious and seemed to understand that customers have a right to check their credentials. An amazing number, however, were surly and uninformative. "Who are you?" and "What do you need to know that for?" were typical responses. Representatives from four agencies said they didn't know the answers to our questions but would call us back. Of course, we never heard from them. When you call to check an agency, accept nothing less than complete courtesy, openness, and cooperation. Life's too short, and your cruise is too important, to deal with rude salespeople. Remember to show the same respect. Good travel agents will work hard for you, but they can spot someone on a fishing expedition. Just be prepared. Some agents will not put quotes in writing if they feel you are only "shopping around" and will buy on price alone and not on price *and* service.

Step 7. Protect Yourself

When you pay for your cruise, use a credit card and insist that the charge be run through the cruise line's account, not the agency's account. This precaution is important. Financially shaky agencies sometimes use their customers' payments to settle agency debts instead of to secure the customer's booking. If these agencies fold, the customer is often left with no cruise and no refund. Paying with a credit card allows you to cancel payment if the cruise is not provided as promised. Reputable travel agents and other sellers are more than happy to run the charge through the cruise line's account and will absolutely not be offended by your request. Financially sound sellers make a practice of running credit card charges through the cruise line's account anyway. This is done so that the cruise line will have to pay the credit-card merchant fees. If you purchase your cruise from any seller other than your usual travel agent, ask the seller when the paid reservation will be posted in the cruise line's system. On the date provided, call the cruise line directly to confirm the reservation.

Protect your cruise investment with travel insurance. Most comes with lots of bells and whistles, but three things should concern you: (1) loss of your paid fare if you must cancel or if your cruise is interrupted, (2) the potentially huge costs of emergency medical evacuation, and (3) major medical expenses while traveling that your primary health insurance doesn't cover.

Although overpriced at about $5 to $8 per every $100 of coverage, travel insurance nevertheless is a prudent expenditure. You never know when you might become ill, have a death in the family, or miss your sailing because of a flight cancellation or delay.

Although travel insurance coverages can be purchased separately, they are usually "bundled." We recommend you purchase good coverage for trip cancellation/interruption and emergency medical evacuation. Trip cancellation/interruption insurance covers the insured traveler and traveling companion(s) against losses caused by illness, injury, or death. Most policies cover losses resulting from the interruption of your trip by the death, serious injury, or serious illness of a close family member back home. **Access America** (**www.accessamerica.com**) and **Travel Guard** (**www.travel-guard.com**) also offer coverage for the illness, injury, or death of a business partner.

If you must cancel your cruise before departure, most cancellation/interruption insurance plans will reimburse you for the cruise's full cost, less any refund you receive from the cruise line. Although cancellation and refund policies vary, most lines provide a full refund if you cancel 61 or more days before your departure date. Remember that these policies generally cover only

unofficial **TIP**
If you buy a cruise at the double-occupancy rate and your companion must cancel, your policy should cover the single supplement if you want to continue alone.

the extent of your investment. If you are buying a $1,500 cruise, you don't need $10,000 in insurance.

Ideally, insurance will allow you to cancel your trip for any reason. Most policies, however, stipulate situations that qualify for coverage. At a minimum, insist on being covered for death, injury, illness, jury duty, court appearances, accidents en route to the airport or pier, and disasters at home, including fire or flood. The same coverage applies to your traveling companion(s).

Policies usually cover airline or ship worker strikes, but not earthquakes or other disasters at scheduled ports of call. Cruise lines reserve the right to alter the itinerary once under way to avoid bad weather or other problems. Also, please keep in mind that some insurance companies may only allow you to cancel *for any reason* up to 24 or 48 hours *prior* to scheduled departure.

The fine print in many policies can be tricky, and seemingly innocuous loopholes limit the carrier's obligation. One essential question regarding cancellation/interruption insurance is whether it covers preexisting conditions: any for which you were treated by a physician in the 60 days (90 days in Maryland) before the policy was purchased. In better policies, if the preexisting condition is controlled by medication, it is covered. In insurance company language, however, "controlled" is very different from "treated." If you have high blood pressure and medication maintains it at normal, safe levels, your condition is controlled. If you have a tumor and are receiving radiation, carriers would say you are being treated, but that your condition is not controlled. If your tumor caused you to cancel your cruise, the policy would not reimburse you. The same stipulations regarding preexisting conditions apply to your family back home. If, for example, your mother dies while you're traveling, your trip interruption coverage would be void if her death was related to a preexisting condition. We recommend that you question the insurance carrier directly about any health problems, obtaining written confirmation of coverage if necessary. One reputable travel agency advised us that you stand a better chance of having preexisting conditions covered with private insurance than with many cruise-line insurance plans.

Pregnancy is covered by most policies if you cruise during your first two trimesters. If a complication arises, the policy will pay. Amazingly, if you deliver your baby normally while on a cruise, you are not covered. Many cruise lines won't accept a pregnant passenger in her third trimester.

Another potential land mine in cancellation/interruption insurance is operator failure. What if your travel agent, airline, or cruise line goes belly-up? Although brochures and most policies say they will pay in the event of operator failure or default, fine print sometimes defines *failure* and *default* as bankruptcy. Because many businesses fail without declaring bankruptcy, this is an important distinction. Note that most policies exclude the failure of the company that sold the cruise (usually a travel agent) or the company that sold the insurance. If you buy insurance from a travel agency, you're covered if the cruise line or airline fails, but not if the agency fails. This is yet another reason you should pay for your cruise with a credit card and insist that the charge be run directly through the cruise line's account, not the travel agent's. It's also a good reason to buy travel insurance directly from the insurance company, something easily done on the Internet. If all of this sounds far-fetched, think again. Four established cruise lines—Commodore, Premier, Renaissance, and American Hawaii—went under within the past few years.

Trip interruption coverage, sold with trip cancellation policies, supplements what you recover from the cruise line if something goes wrong during your trip. If a family member dies, for example, and you must fly home from a port midcruise, the interruption coverage will pay for your plane ticket home plus reimburse you for the unused portion of your cruise (less any refund you receive from the cruise line). The policy also would pay the single supplement of your cabin companion if he or she remains on the cruise. Some insurance companies also place a certain dollar limit on their trip interruption coverage and normally list the amount in their policy. Try to find a company with the highest percentage—say 150% of the trip cost rather than just 100%. Remember, when plans change, you may incur additional air or hotel charges.

Trip interruption insurance covers fire, flood, vandalism, burglary, and natural disaster as it affects your home, but does not cover similar catastrophic events if they occur at your place of business. In our estimation this is a huge gap in travel insurance coverage. As it turns out, it's also a gap in standard business-casualty insurance. If your office building burns down while you're cruising in Alaska, chances are about 99 to 1 that your business insurance will decline to reimburse you for the cost of returning home or for the unused portion of your cruise.

Something much less likely than a fire at your office, however, is now covered. As a consequence of the September 11, 2001, terrorist attacks, most travel insurance policies offer coverage for cancellation or interruption occasioned by an act of terrorism. Coverage varies from policy to policy.

A common but very important coverage exclusion relates to "travel arrangements canceled or changed by an airline, cruise line, or tour operator, unless the cancellation is the result of bad weather or financial default." What this means is that your trip cancellation/interruption insurance doesn't cover you if, say, your flight is cancelled for reasons other than weather, and you miss the boat. Logically, one would think, this is exactly the sort of circumstance for which you need travel insurance. When we asked the insurance companies why such events are excluded, their response, to quote one company representative, was, "Oh, we couldn't cover that. It happens too often." Isn't that reassuring?

Bundled with trip cancellation/interruption is emergency medical evacuation insurance. This pays to transport you to a place where you can obtain high-quality medical care. In some areas of the Caribbean and even more remote cruise areas in Africa, Asia, or Latin America, you might prefer not to entrust your care to local doctors. The insurer in conjunction with a qualified physician usually must verify your condition and authorize the evacuation. Once authorized, the insurer usually selects the means of transportation.

As a rule, evacuation insurance does not cover hospital stays, doctors, diagnostic procedures, treatments, or medications, though medical coverage sometimes is bundled with a comprehensive policy covering trip cancellation/interruption. Ask your primary health insurer, Medicare, or HMO whether you are covered for medical attention required when traveling abroad. If you are not covered, buy supplemental insurance.

If you book an upscale cruise and pack Rolex watches, gems, and other valuables, check your homeowner's policy to determine what's covered when you travel. If you aren't covered, take out a rider. When you travel, carry your valuables on your person, not in checked luggage. Even better, leave them at home.

Cruise lines and travel agencies, as a rule, do not self-insure. In other words, the policy they sell is an off-the-shelf or customized product of an independent travel insurance company. This is true even when the policy has the cruise line's name in the title, for example, "Happy Sea Cruise Line Total Protection." As mentioned earlier, any third party selling a policy is automatically excluded from "supplier default" coverage. Thus, if you buy that Happy Sea travel insurance and Happy Sea Cruise Line goes belly- up, you could get caught holding the bag. Because of many cruise lines, wholesalers, and travel agencies defaulting (going out of business) in the wake of 9/11, most travel insurance companies now maintain a list of travel suppliers, including cruise lines and cruise retailers, that they will *not* cover. Most of the failed cruise lines were on those lists prior to their ultimate collapse.

Finally, most travel insurance companies post their policies, as well as their list of excluded travel suppliers, on the Internet. Read the policies before you buy, and call the company's customer service representative if you have any questions. Here are several major insurers and their phone numbers and Internet sites:

Access America Service Corporation ☎ 866-807-3982
   www.accessamerica.com
CSA Travel Protection ☎ 800-873-9855 **www.travelsecure.com**

Travelex ☎ 888-457-4602 **www.travelex-insurance.com**

Travel Guard ☎ 800-826-4919 **www.travelguard.com**

Travel Insured ☎ 800-243-3174 **www.travelinsured.com**

There are also other smaller firms that may have good plans as well; ask your agent. When shopping for travel insurance, remember that language in the brochure is marketing language. The language in the policy legally defines the carrier's obligations.

If your cruise line underwrites its own policy, compare it with one or more of the policies listed above. If the cruise policy is comparable and the line's in good shape financially, consider it. The line has a greater interest in your satisfaction than an insurance company does and may be more helpful in a crisis. Be aware, however, that there is some risk involved with buying your insurance from the cruise line. If the line goes out of business, as Commodore, Renaissance, American Hawaii, and Premier did, your claim will be thrown in with claims of all the cruise line's creditors waiting to be reimbursed, and you may get back only pennies on the dollar, if anything.

When you buy travel insurance, make sure the policy covers you *from the date of purchase until the day you arrive home from your vacation.* This is extremely important: you can't imagine the problems some folks have had with policies that did not take effect until departure time or that didn't cover the travelers' whole time away from home. In one example, a couple from Texas bought travel insurance from a cruise company. On their own, they scheduled a two-night hotel stay at their originating port and another two-night stay at their port of disembarkation. When the husband became ill on the second day after the cruise, they tried to invoke the medical coverage on their travel insurance. Much to their chagrin, they were told that their policy covered only the days of the cruise, not the extra precruise and postcruise days the couple had arranged themselves. This is yet another example of why it's usually preferable to purchase your policy directly from the travel insurance company.

Finally, be aware before you leave home that if you need to make a claim, the travel insurance companies will hold you to an exacting standard of documentation. From the time you book your cruise, hang onto every correspondence, invoice, statement, canceled check, and receipt. For trip cancellation/interruption, travel delay, and/or medical claims, you will need some or all of the following:

1. Proof of complete trip payment.
2. Proof of insurance payment.
3. Invoice from your travel agent or tour operator showing complete trip costs and cancellation penalties.
4. If your situation involves illness, accident, or death, you'll need to produce doctor's medical records, hospital records, and/or a death certificate.

5. Paid receipts for all expenses incurred.
6. Original travel documents.

A *final note:* If you have made the decision to forgo travel insurance, consider a few important points before declining. Understand the serious financial and personal difficulties you could find yourself in should an unexpected illness or family emergency develop. First, most travelers decline because they say, "Oh, I have insurance with my company or Medicare." Understand that these plans generally only cover you while you are within the United States, not overseas. If a serious illness develops, you will be taken off the ship and deposited in a foreign land. Travel insurance almost always comes with resources, such as a 24-hour help line to provide support while you are dealing with medical problems in a foreign land. Yes, travel insurance may not immediately pay the bills on site at a foreign hospital, but it will reimburse you later for those fees so you don't forfeit your kids' college fund or your own retirement nest egg unnecessarily. Understand as well that treatment while on board a ship is not free and not necessarily inexpensive. For example, one travel agent reports she had a 29-year-old customer who was in excellent health prior to his cruise. He took no travel insurance, then suffered a massive heart attack; his bill for one day in the ship's medical center until he could be evacuated was $6,000. That didn't count the charges from the land-based hospital. Travel insurance is not really a nicety, but a necessity.

WHEN THINGS GO WRONG

AS YOU'VE ASCERTAINED from the discussion of travel insurance above, there are a number of things that can go wrong between the time you book your cruise and the day you arrive back home. Long-range planning minimizes surprises and generally allows sufficient time to work out any snags. Last-minute deals can sometimes save a ton of money, but cramming all of your planning and arrangements into a few short weeks or days before departure increases the probability of a problem arising with little or no time to resolve it.

Eliminating problems should be an integral part of your long-term planning. Begin by analyzing your risks. Take a look at your health and the health of your family and business associates. There may be foreseeable risks that suggest it's not really the best time to take a cruise. Before you book your cruise, get a handle on the financial stability of your intended cruise line. Make sure you pay with a credit card and have the charge run through the cruise line's account as opposed to the travel agent's or other third-party sellers. Buy travel insurance that takes effect on the date of purchase and provides coverage until you get home. Buy it directly from the insurance company. If you are traveling to a part of the world where you'd prefer not to be treated by the local health-care industry, make sure emergency medical-evacuation coverage is included in your policy. Go over all preexisting medical conditions with the insurance carrier before you buy. Make sure you have already acquired trip cancellation/interruption coverage. If you have special concerns, such as the possible death of an aging parent or business partner, make sure those situations are covered by the policy. Realize that there are a number of cir-

unofficial **TIP**
If you bought your cruise through the Internet or from a nonlocal seller, call the cruise line first to make sure your reservation is in their system and that full payment has been received.

cumstances besides death that may require your unexpected return home. We have readers whose cruises were interrupted by a fire at their place of business, a tree falling on their home, a burglary, and an unexpected lawsuit, to name a few. In short, the broader and more inclusive your trip cancellation/interruption coverage, the better.

Problem 1: Missing Flight Information

If you purchased your air from the cruise line, or if air was included in the price of your cruise, you should receive your flight *itinerary* 30 to 45 days prior to departure. If fewer than 30 days remain prior to departure and you haven't received your information, call your travel agent and have her find out what's going on. If everything checks out, phone the seller. Work your way from reservationist to supervisor to manager to owner as required until you get a satisfactory explanation. Take the same approach with the seller if the cruise line has no record of your reservation.

Problem 2: Missing Cruise Documents or Airline Tickets

Your date of departure is looming, but you haven't received your airline tickets and/or cruise documents. If you have a good travel agent, you are virtually assured that everything will get sorted out in plenty of time. If you purchased on your own through a print ad, the Internet, or from a seller with whom you do not ordinarily do business, the situation is much iffier. In that case, start by calling the cruise line directly and making sure that your reservation is in order and *that full payment has been received*. If you purchased air with your cruise, and you know your flight itinerary, go through the same process with the airline. If everything is properly recorded, next call the seller. You'll probably be told that late delivery of documents, especially airline tickets, is standard practice (unfortunately true) and not to worry. Most of the time this will be valid advice, but if something is actually screwed up (documents lost in mail, misplaced, etc.), you won't have much time, once the seller acknowledges a problem, to resolve it. The one thing you can count on is that the cruise line and airline are going to refer you back to the seller for resolution.

The only exception to this is when your cruise reservation is paid in full and the cruise line knows that the seller has gone belly-up. In this case, the cruise line will usually arrange for you to pick up your cruise documents at the pier. Regarding the airline, if your reservation is in the system and fully paid, and if you have an electronic ticket, you're home free. Just go to the airport and produce your photo ID and confirmation. If paper tickets are lost, you're back to dealing with the seller. If it's a weekend or holiday and you can't contact the seller, call the airline and ask for a customer-service representative. All airlines have different policies, but the representative will usually try to help if the reservation is in the airline's system and fully paid.

If your reservations, either air or cruise, are not in the cruise line's or airline's system, you've got a big problem. It could be a simple as a transmission error between the seller and the cruise line, or it could mean that the seller lost your reservations, failed to record your payments, erroneously cancelled your reservations, or is about to, or has, gone out of business. Assuming the seller is still in business, call the seller, explain your situation, and then start working your way up the chain of command until you get someone on the phone with the knowledge and authority to address your problem.

Most of these situations can be avoided, of course, by doing business with a brick-and-mortar travel agent in your hometown, by a reputable Internet seller affiliated with a reliable travel consortium, and by arranging your air itinerary through the travel agent (or on your own) rather than through the cruise line. Buying your own air, unfortunately, puts you at some risk for a couple of other unpleasant eventualities having to do with missing the ship and losing your luggage, but we'll deal with those problems later. Finally, on the topic of arranging your own flight itinerary, we don't want to overstate the case. While working on this section of the guide, we received a direct-mail promo from an excellent European cruise line offering outside cabins at half price with air to Europe included. Would we hesitate to buy because the cruise line is providing air? Not for a second.

Problem 3: Bad Weather or Air-Traffic Delays on Departure Day

When you book your air, either on your own or through the cruise line, give some thought to what weather and air-traffic conditions are likely to be on your day of departure. If you're traveling the same day as your cruise departure, over a holiday period, or at a time of year when bad weather is likely, you might want to take some precautions. Begin analyzing your airport choices. In the New York area, for example, be aware that Newark and Kennedy have longer runways, more de-icing equipment, and electronic traffic-control systems that often allow them to function when La Guardia is shut down. New Yorkers can also take a Washington-bound train directly to the

Baltimore–Washington Airport (BWI) from Penn Station in under three hours. (Washingtonians can do the same on a northbound train.) BWI has a better track record than any of the three New York airports for on-time departures.

unofficial **TIP**
Always book the earliest flight of the day on an airline that offers a number of flights throughout the day to your destination.

During holiday periods or bad weather, the chance of a serious snafu increases exponentially with every flight connection you have to make. If, with a little inconvenience, you can eliminate a connection, it's usually worthwhile to do so. Let's say you live in Louisville, Kentucky; Columbus, Ohio; or Charleston, West Virginia, and you're flying to Fort Lauderdale, Florida, for a cruise out of Port Everglades. If there's no direct flight, you might be better off driving to the Cincinnati airport (located in northern Kentucky) and taking a direct flight from there to Fort Lauderdale, thereby eliminating the connecting flight.

Early morning flights have a much better on-time record than do flights later in the day. Plus, if there's an equipment problem or a cancellation, the airline can put you on a later flight. *For maximum peace of mind, travel to the port of departure one or two days prior to your sailing date. If things go awry on your travel day, you've still got sufficient time to make alternative arrangements.* Why risk jeopardizing a cherished vacation? Arrive a day early at minimum.

You've probably heard the ongoing debate regarding electronic versus paper airline tickets. Generally speaking, we prefer electronic tickets with the proviso that you double-check with the airline to insure that your correct itinerary is in their system and that your reservations are shown as fully paid. The one situation where paper tickets are preferable is when your flight is cancelled and your airline cannot book you on another flight. In this case, you'll want to make arrangements with an alternative carrier. Most carriers will honor the tickets of another airline in the event of cancellations or labor actions, but they will require paper tickets or some form of documentation as proof of purchase.

Problem 4: Missing the Boat

This is the nightmare scenario that haunts all cruisers. If you're savvy in your travel planning, and especially if you plan to arrive at your departure port a day or so ahead of time, you'll almost eliminate the likelihood of missing the boat. We all know, however, that travel, like life, can get mixed up in ways that we never anticipate.

If you purchase your air from the cruise line, the cruise line will do its utmost to get you on the ship. There are many, many documented cases of ship departures being delayed while awaiting the arrival of a delinquent flight full of cruise passengers. Likewise, cruise lines have flown passengers who actually missed the boat to rendezvous with the ship at the first port of call. The more passengers that are affected by late flights, the more likely the cruise line is to hold the ship. The most important thing to understand, however, is that the cruise line is absolutely not under any legal obligation to hold the ship or to assist in any other manner. If you read the terms and conditions of your passage contract, you'll almost immediately encounter language like the following: "Under no circumstances does [X Cruise Line's] responsibility extend beyond the ship. All arrangements made for the guests with independent contractors [such as airlines] are made solely for the convenience of the guest and are at the guest's risk." What you *can* count on, exclusively as a matter of customer relations, is for the cruise line to do what is practicable. Do 30 late-arriving guests on a weather-delayed flight from Cleveland justify delaying the departure of a 3,000-passenger cruise ship? Perhaps, but don't count on it. We know of at least one situation when the ship sailed while two busloads of flight-delayed passengers waited at the airport to be driven to the port, 20 minutes away.

Sometimes, when air is arranged through the cruise line, and passengers miss the boat owing to flight delays, the airline will help out. Assistance usually comes in the form of a meal and perhaps a hotel room. If the airline flies to your first port of call, it will try to book you on a flight so that you can meet the ship. Because the airline is not responsible for weather or air-traffic delays, it has no legal obligation to help. Like the cruise line, any assistance rendered is primarily a matter of customer relations.

If you book your own travel arrangements to the departure port, you're on your own. As far as the cruise line is concerned, you're totally responsible for getting to the ship. If you miss the ship through no fault of your own, however, as in the case of a delayed flight, you will have that travel insurance we recommended to fall back on. Travel insurance is also your safety net if you miss the boat because of sickness, or because of bankruptcy of the cruise line. Missing the boat because of an airline strike is also usually covered by travel insurance, though the conditions for coverage vary from policy to policy. If you or your cruise line book you on an airline involved in a labor dispute, discuss the situation with your insurance carrier to determine under what circumstances you're covered. When it comes to travel insurance, don't, as the saying goes, leave home without it. Also, ask a ton of questions and compare plans carefully.

Problem 5: Lost Luggage

If you book air through the cruise line, the cruise line will make every effort to get your luggage to you (once it's recovered), including flying it to meet you at a port of call. Once again, this assistance is purely voluntary as opposed to obligatory. If you handle your own air, you must depend on the airline (generally without any assistance from the cruise line) to get your recovered luggage to you. In such situations, the probability of your luggage catching up with you while on your cruise is slim. Minimize the chances of your luggage being lost by arriving in port a day early and/or eliminating connecting flights where possible. Buy travel insurance, and make sure it pays if your bags are delayed more than 24 hours. The possibility of lost luggage is a good reason to pack essentials for an overnight in your carry-on luggage.

Problem 6: You Get Sick during Your Cruise

Although most cruise ships carry a physician and usually one registered nurse, only the new large ships are equipped to handle serious problems; and some, such as Princess's ships, maintain satellite contact with stateside hospitals when serious diagnosis is needed. Nonetheless, the majority of cruise ships fly under foreign flags, and hence their physicians are not required to be licensed to practice in the United States. From the cruise physician's perspective, shore-based facilities are better equipped to handle serious illness and emergencies. In practical terms, this means the cruise physician will want to transfer you to a hospital on shore at the first opportunity if he anticipates your illness taxing the limitations of his clinic. Also, you should know that according to the fine print in your passage contract, the cruise line is not responsible for medical care you receive while on board. As with the problems discussed earlier, travel insurance is a must. When you purchase your policy, make sure any preexisting condition is covered and understand the policy's medical-evacuation coverage.

In the last several years a media circus has swirled around the periodic occurrence of gastrointestinal viruses aboard cruise ships. Referred to in the media as "outbreaks" and "epidemics," these cases of viruses have been so sensationalized that they have become known as the "cruise ship disease." The facts, however, tell a different story. The viruses, known as Norwalk virus, Norwalk-like virus, and norovirus (collectively known as NLV) occur everywhere (on land as well as at sea), ranking second only to the common cold in the number of cases reported. Because of the extraordinary sanitation practices aboard cruise ships (operated and monitored in partnership with the U.S. Centers for Disease Control and Prevention[CDC]), these NLV occur far less frequently on cruise ships than among the general population. Expressed differently, NLV is a very common ailment and incidents occur far more often in the home, office, and at school than on cruise ships. Most cruise ship outbreaks are not caused by a "sick ship" but by sick people who bring it on board.

Symptoms can include vomiting, diarrhea, abdominal cramps, and a low-grade fever. NLV is not an upper respiratory virus such as the flu, and is usually not life-threatening, unless someone has other, more serious, medical problems.

NLV is transmitted from person to person through direct contact, and indirectly from surfaces that are then touched by another person.

NLV can also be transmitted through a food or water source; the CDC has concluded that person-to-person transmission has been the means of transmission on almost all cases reported on cruise ships.

"We continue to work very closely with the cruise lines," said David Forney, chief of Vessel Sanitation Program of the CDC. "These ships are maintaining the highest standard of sanitation in the world."

If cases of a gastrointestinal virus are reported, cruise lines take extensive precautions to contain the spread through aggressive sanitation measures and open communication with their guests prior to boarding and while on board the ship. Some of the measures employed when responding to reported cases may include:

- Passengers with obvious symptoms may not be allowed to board.

- To avoid the risk of spreading the virus, passengers who experience typical gastrointestinal symptoms are usually told to remain in their cabins until they are noncontagious but could be asked to disembark at the next available port. The CDC endorses this procedure.

- Crew with symptoms may be similarly quarantined until they are noncontagious but may also disembark the ship at the next available port.

- An aggressive onboard communications effort to encourage guests to frequently wash their hands. Washing one's hands regularly (each hour or two) is a very good way to reduce the spread of contact viruses.

- Aboard ship, staterooms and public areas are cleaned and disinfected daily, including, but not limited to, counters, bathroom surfaces, door handles, railings and grab bars, exercise equipment, and TV remote controls. Some lines also offer hand sanitizers at the entrance to the gangway or at a buffet line.

- On turn-around days, extra crew are brought on board to disinfect the ship with the CDC-recommended chlorine-based solution from top to bottom before additional passengers board.

- Onboard medical facilities and staff are always available to prescribe medication for symptomatic treatment of gastrointestinal symptoms.

Be aware that the cruise lines are so sensitive to bad press surrounding NLV and the need to assure that as many guests as possible remain well that some have enacted rather draconian policies, endorsed by the CDC. A man from Maryland on a Caribbean cruise sought care for gastrointestinal symptoms and was notified that he would be involuntarily disembarked at the next port of call. Although there were any number of alternative explanations for the symptoms, and no diagnostic testing was done, the man and his wife were ordered ashore the next day. Quarantined until time of disembarkation, his symptoms completely resolved after about ten hours. Onboard medical staff, realizing then that the symptoms could not be attributed to NLV, apologized but informed the couple that the decision was made by the line's home office and could not be reversed. After the man's return home, laboratory tests ordered by his doctor showed no evidence of a viral infection. The cruise line was so intent on getting the man off the ship that it evidently failed to clear the couple's entry into the port. Later, when they went to the airport for their flight home, they were detained by immigration for supposedly entering the country illegally. In case you're wondering, the cruise line did pay the couple's travel expenses home. Granted, this is a worst-case scenario, but it always helps to know what could happen.

Problem 7: Onboard Complaints

If your stateroom toilet backs up, the air conditioner conks out, or the showroom performers quit, don't expect a refund. If it's not resolved on board when it happens, the best you are likely to get is a discount on a subsequent cruise. Once again, it's that pesky passage contract that purports to absolve the cruise line from all responsibility, anytime, anywhere. In point of law, however (as any attorney who specializes in travel will tell you), some of the language is nothing but smoke, totally unenforceable and made part of the contract as a bluff to inhibit you from taking legal action. Understand, however, if you decide to sue, that cruise lines operate under maritime law, and you might have to file the lawsuit in the country where the ship is registered. It's not an accident that so many cruise ships fly under the so-called flags of convenience, particularly those of Liberia and Panama.

Legalities aside, it's always preferable to settle problems on the spot. Usually, you will direct your complaint to the chief purser or to the hotel manager, and usually they will be quite responsive. Be polite and friendly, and keep your anger under control. As a last resort, if your complaint is not addressed, fax the president of the cruise line. Resend each day until your problem is resolved. Keep copies of your faxes in case the complaint goes unremedied for the entire cruise. As of this writing, Carnival is the only cruise line that will allow you to cancel your cruise and disembark at the first port of call once under way if things are not satisfactory. You can get a refund for the *unused* portion of your cruise fare.

If you are really unlucky, like when your cabin is for some reason uninhabitable and the ship is completely full, your only option is to negotiate the best deal you can or leave the ship on your own initiative at a port of call. If you jump ship, regardless of the reason, you're on your own. Consequently, we recommending contacting your travel-insurance carrier for advice about how to best proceed before taking action.

Problem 8: Credit Hold

It has become common practice for cruise lines to ask passengers to complete a form prior to leaving home authorizing the cruise line to hold X dollars in credit per day for each day of the cruise. On a Holland American cruise, for example, the line held $60 per day. The same credit card covered both husband and wife, so the credit hold amounted to a not insignificant $2,160. In practicality, if the card had a $3,000 credit limit, the credit hold would leave only $840 of available credit on that card for the couple to use for onshore shopping, restaurants, etc.

Cruise lines use credit holds to make sure a passenger's onboard charges are covered. On land, each transaction on your card is approved and processed individually. On a cruise it doesn't make sense for the line to pay $10 or so in satellite telecommunications to process that $4 beer you enjoyed on the Lido Deck. Consequently, charges are recorded but not processed until the end of the cruise. At that time they are totaled and the ship runs through a single transaction. To make sure you have the credit available to pay your onboard charges, the line puts a credit hold on what it estimates you'll charge. Among other things, the practice largely eliminates messy credit problems at the time of disembarkation.

Although using credit holds addresses a legitimate problem (passengers without sufficient funds or credit to pay their onboard tabs), there are a couple of problems. First, the cruise lines do not communicate what they are doing very well, and some of the credit-hold preauthorization forms are confusing. Because many passengers don't realize what's going on, they are surprised and embarrassed when their credit card is subsequently rejected when they attempt to purchase something ashore.

The second problem is that the cruise line may hold much more per day that you'll actually charge onboard. The solution to these problems is to carefully review any form the cruise line sends, particularly one that requires your signature. If the credit amount the cruise line holds is out of line with your normal onboard spending habits, negotiate with the purser a lower per-day amount when you board the ship. Remember, however, those spa treatments and shore excursions are expensive. Your onboard spending may very likely exceed your bar bill and a couple of T-shirts for the grandchildren.

Be aware that cruise lines that do not send preauthorization forms for credit holds will probably put a similarly calculated credit hold on your card when you present it during embarkation. The salient point in the latter case is to ask the amount of the credit hold. Finally, remember that a credit hold is not a charge on your credit card. The credit hold is an amount reserved, and nothing is actually charged to your card until your total onboard bill is processed at the end of the cruise.

Problem 9: Itinerary Changes/Cancelled Ports of Call

You will discover that the cruise line has complete discretion in regard to changing the itinerary or canceling a scheduled port stop.

This discretion is necessary to ensure the safety of the passengers, ship, and crew. It is this flexibility that permits a ship to circumvent storms or offload a passenger at a nonscheduled port for medical reasons or other emergencies.

Problem 10: Shore Excursion Problems

Because shore excursions are conducted off the ship and produced by local tour companies, the cruise line will decline responsibility for any problem you have, however serious. Sometimes, however, as a matter of customer relations, a cruise ship might offer you a refund or assist you in obtaining satisfaction from the tour operator. Nevertheless, you should always register your complaint with the cruise line immediately after the tour. Although of little comfort to you, so doing may result in the cruise line forcing an errant tour operator to clean up its act.

WHAT'S THE REAL COST OF A CRUISE?

SOME READERS REPORT BEING SURPRISED by all the extras that are not covered by their cruise fare: items like beverages on board, spa services, photos taken by the ship's photographer, shore excursions, wine tastings, specialized cooking, exercise or computer classes, and even designer ice-cream treats. Although all these things add up to a hefty sum, we don't consider them to be "hidden" charges. Except for port charges (if the cruise line doesn't include them in the fare), such purchases are optional. Any travel provider will try to sell you stuff; it's like the popcorn or beer vendors at the ballpark. You know they'll be there and that what they sell will be expensive. Buy or not as you see fit, but don't be surprised by their presence. The cruise lines find these services to be very lucrative profit centers, which help them keep basic cruise prices down. Also, these multiple options increase guest choices onboard, which attracts different types of customers to cruise ships. Because most folks don't like to scrimp on their vacation, however, it's wise to anticipate these expenditures. Even the little stuff like beverages and photos can tack on $200 to $400 to a weeklong cruise. So be forewarned.

Concerning port charges, after some lawsuits in Florida seeking to redress the less-than-forthright ways that certain cruise lines represented port charges, almost all cruises from Florida to the Caribbean now include port charges in the cost of the cruise rather than tack them on as a separate charge. Still, watch out for port charges, particularly for Europe and Asia.

PREPARING *for Your* CRUISE

A CRUISE MAY BE ABOUT THE EASIEST vacation you can take when it comes to making preparations, because so much is done for you, particularly when you buy an air/sea package. During the cruise, entry formalities are handled by the ship for its passengers in most cases, sparing you the need to fill out immigration forms or clear customs in each port of call.

In most ports you can simply walk off your ship after it has been cleared by local authorities, spend the day sightseeing, shopping, enjoying a sport or other pleasant pursuits, and return to your ship without having to do anything more than pass through metal detectors and put your purchases through an X-ray machine for security reasons, and show your boarding pass.

The destination of your cruise will make some difference—the more exotic the location, the more you may have need for planning, perhaps for inoculations, visas, and the like. And of course, the weather during your cruise will determine the wardrobe you select.

Such advice may seem obvious to those who have traveled, and if it does, let this information serve simply as a reminder or checklist. Even the most seasoned travelers have been known to pack their cruise tickets and passports in their checked luggage or leave their traveler's checks at home.

CRUISE LINE BROCHURES

THE EASIEST PLACE TO START YOUR PREPARATION is by reading the brochures from the cruise line you selected for your cruise. These have a wealth of useful information. To be sure, much of it is glossy pictures and promotional puff to entice you to take a cruise, but almost all materials contain several pages, usually toward the back, aimed at answering the questions people ask most often.

These include the specifics about dining hours, smoking/nonsmoking provisions, paying for incidentals on board, embarkation and sailing times, and similar tips. In this book, too, each of the major cruise line profiles in Part Two includes a chart entitled Standard Features, which will answer similar questions pertaining to a specific cruise line and its ships.

CRUISE LINE VIDEOS/DVDS

MOST CRUISE LINES HAVE VIDEOTAPES or DVDs of the cruise you are taking that they would be happy to send you—for a fee. Most cost about $15 to $20. Essentially, it is a promotional video, but it will give you an idea of what to expect, particularly if your cruise is to an area of the world in which you have not traveled previously. You will probably receive a flyer from the cruise line to order the tape directly from a distributor. Some cruise line Web sites allow for purchasing the video online; some sites feature virtual ship tours and shore excursions.

TRAVEL DOCUMENTS

IN 2005, THE U.S. STATE DEPARTMENT began phasing in a new border-control program that will ultimately require a valid passport to both enter and leave the country. The Western Hemisphere Travel Initiative (WHTI) brings an end to decades of travel to Mexico, Canada, and the majority of Caribbean nations with only a birth certificate as proof of citizenship. Implementation dates for WHTI have been postponed several times and several exemptions are currently under consideration.

- As of **January 23, 2007** ALL persons, except as described below, including U.S. citizens, traveling by air between the United States and Canada, Mexico, Central and South America, the Caribbean, and Bermuda will be required to present a valid passport, Air NEXUS card, or U.S. Coast Guard Merchant Mariner Document, or an Alien Registration Card, Form I-551, if applicable.

- As early as **January 1, 2008,** but not later than **June 2009** ALL persons, except as described below, including U.S. citizens, traveling between the U.S. and Canada, Mexico, Central and South America, the Caribbean, and Bermuda by land or sea (including ferries), may be required to present a valid passport or other documents as determined by the Department of Homeland Security. While recent legislative changes permit a later deadline, the Departments of State and Homeland Security are working to meet all requirements as soon as possible. Ample advance notice will be provided to enable the public to obtain passports or passport cards for land/sea entries.

Exceptions

- **U.S. Territories** The passport requirement does NOT apply to U.S. citizens traveling to or returning directly from a U.S. territory. U.S. citizens returning directly from a U.S. territory are not considered to have left the United States and do not need to present a passport. U.S. territories include the following: Guam, Puerto Rico, the U.S. Virgin Islands, American Samoa, Swains Island, and the Commonwealth of the Northern Mariana Islands.

- **Youth Travel** Under a Department of Homeland Security proposed rule, U.S. and Canadian children ages 15 and younger, with parental consent, would be permitted to enter the United States with a certified copy of their birth certificates. The same would be true for U.S and Canadian citizens ages 16 through 18 traveling with public or private school groups, religious groups, social or cultural organizations, or youth athletic teams. The proposed rule notwithstanding, some cruise lines may require that passengers under 18 years of age have a passport in order to board.

Aliens residing in the United States need to have valid alien registration cards and passports. All non-U.S. citizens must have valid passports and necessary visas when boarding any cruise ship departing from and returning to U.S. ports.

Passengers on some cruises visiting Europe, former Soviet bloc countries, Asia, Africa, and South America may also be required to have a visa. *A valid passport usually means one that will not expire for at least six months.* If yours has less than six months left, it may be rejected by either the cruise line or ports of call.

Often, on cruises to these destinations, ship authorities will ask you to surrender your passport when you check in and will keep it until the end of your cruise. This enables them to clear the ship more quickly in foreign ports. In such cases, you do not need to worry about giving over your passport to the ship. The passports are locked away securely and are taken out only if local authorities ask to see them. Finally, never pack your passport in your suitcase; carry it with you at all times.

TRAVEL REQUIREMENTS

SPECIFIC REQUIREMENTS FOR PASSPORTS, visas, and vaccinations will be provided by your cruise line or travel agent. However, obtaining the necessary visas and any other documentation required for embarkation, debarkation, and reentry into the United States is your responsibility; if you do not have the proper documents, you will be denied boarding. If you buy your cruise on the Internet or from a seller not located in your city, the seller may neglect to inform you of required travel documents and other pertinent information. Even when you purchase from your local travel agent, however, it's a good idea to independently confirm document, visa, and vaccination requirements for the countries you'll be visiting. Nobody likes a last-minute surprise.

Documents that will be accepted as proof of identification vary with each cruise line. You will need to inquire in advance if the information is not provided in the cruise line's brochure, which it usually is—in the fine print.

Children traveling with anyone other than their parents or legal guardian must have permission in writing for the child to travel. Failure to comply with this requirement can also result in denial of boarding.

DRESS CODES AND PACKING

WHAT TO PACK WILL BE DETERMINED by your ship, its destinations, and, to some extent, the itinerary. An adventure cruise might be three weeks long, but not a single night will be formal or even very dressy. The dress code is usually explained in the cruise line's brochure; we also note it in the Standard Features in each cruise line's profile in Part Two.

There are no limits on the amount of luggage you can bring on board, but most cabins do not have much closet and storage space.

More importantly, because you are likely to be flying to your departure port, you need to be guided by airline regulations regarding excess baggage. All airlines have weight restrictions. Buy too many souvenirs and you will pay. So pack light on the outbound journey with that in mind.

As a consequence of the 9/11 terrorist attacks, all checked and carry-on luggage is carefully screened before being allowed on board. Even if you pack something in your checked baggage as seemingly innocuous as a corkscrew, knitting needles, or a pair of small scissors, these items might possibly be confiscated and not returned until you disembark. Moreover, none of your checked luggage will be delivered in the normal fashion to your cabin. After an hour or two of panic, thinking your baggage is lost, you'll be summoned to ship security. There, you will be asked to identify the offending luggage and objects and to sign forms acknowledging that you brought such items aboard, and that they have been impounded for the duration of the cruise. While on your cruise, be aware also that purses, bags, and packs that you carried ashore will be searched before you're allowed back on board. Ditto for anything you purchased while ashore.

Despite the image you may have about fancy parties and clothes, the reality is that shipboard life is very casual. You will spend your days in slacks, shorts, T-shirts, and bathing suits. Lightweight mix-and-match ensembles with skirts, shirts, blouses, shorts, and slacks are practical. For women, colorful scarves are another way to change the look of an outfit. Cocktail dresses or dressy pantsuits are appropriate for evening wear.

Men usually are asked to wear a jacket at dinner in the dining room. A dark suit and white shirt work fine in place of a tuxedo if the evening is black tie. Add a selection of slacks and sport shirts, and one or two sports jackets. If you are heading for a warm-weather cruise (Caribbean, Mexico, Hawaii, Tahiti), pack as you would for any resort destination. Lightweight, loose-fitting clothing is ideal, and cotton or cotton blends are more comfortable than synthetic fabrics for the tropics. Include two bathing suits if you are likely to be spending much time in the sun and at the beach. Don't forget a cover-up and flip-flops for the short jaunt between your cabin and the pool or other outside decks, as cruise ships ask passengers not to wear bathing suits or go barefoot in the public rooms.

Bring cosmetics and suntan lotion, but don't worry if you forget something. It will most likely be available on board or in portside duty-free shops. Sunglasses and a hat or sun visor for protection against the sun are essential. A tote bag comes in handy for carrying odds and ends, as do plastic bags for wet towels and bathing suits on returning from a visit to an island beach. You might also want to keep

unofficial **TIP**
For a one-week or shorter cruise, you should be able to fit everything you need into one suitcase.

camera equipment in plastic bags as protection against the salt air, water, and sand.

The first and last nights of your cruise are usually casual, and the nights your ship is in port almost always call for informal dress. At least one night will be the captain's gala party, where tuxedos for men and long dresses for women are the norm, but a jacket and tie for men and a cocktail dress for women are also just fine.

Bring your most comfortable walking shoes for shore excursions. Tennis, deck, or other low-heeled rubber or nonskid shoes are recommended for walking about the ship, up and down gangways, getting in and out of the ship's tenders, and for sightseeing. And you will need a sweater for breezy nights at sea or for the air-conditioning in the dining room or shore-excursion bus. A small flashlight, a fold-up umbrella, and a light jacket are often handy.

Pack lightly. But most of all, be comfortable. You do not need to rush out and buy an expensive wardrobe. Obviously, if your cruise is in a cool or cold climate, you will need to plan accordingly. A Baltic or Scandinavian cruise in summer is likely to encounter colder temperatures than you might think—similar to a New England fall—but then can quickly turn to a hot summer day. Plan for layers when the weather is uncertain.

As we mention elsewhere, it's a sound practice to have a small carry-on bag for your medications and cosmetics and to include a change of clothing for your first afternoon aboard your ship, in the event of a delay in the delivery of your luggage. Also, bring a fold-away bag to carry all those souvenirs, gifts, and duty-free bargains that probably won't fit in your suitcase.

Every evening, an agenda for the following day is delivered to your room; it states the dress code for the following evening. It may be:

CASUAL Comfortable day wear, such as slacks, shorts, or jeans, but some cruise lines will state specifically that T-shirts, tank tops, or shorts are not allowed in the dining room for dinner.

INFORMAL Dresses and pantsuits are suggested for the ladies; jackets for the men, but ties are optional.

FORMAL Cocktail dresses or gowns for the ladies, and tuxedo, dinner jacket, or dark business suit for men; jacket and tie are required.

It varies greatly by line, but as a general rule, the lineup might be like this:

3- to 4-night cruises One formal, one informal, and one or two casual.

7- to 8-night cruises Two formal, two informal, two or three casual.

10- to 14-night cruises Three or four formal; four or six informal; four or five casual.

You are asked to comply with the ship's stated dress code, if for no other reason than out of respect for your fellow passengers. Generally, the suggested attire is respected throughout the evening or at least until after the shows in the main showroom and the late-night buffet, when it is a gala event. Often, those who want to stay up late for the disco or casino change to more comfortable dress, if they prefer.

COSTUMES

A FEW SHIPS STILL HAVE ONE NIGHT as a masquerade party, and others have theme nights for which some people bring an outfit—a 1950s and 1960s night or a country-and-western night, for example. It's entirely up to you whether or not to participate. The cruise line's brochure usually tells you about theme nights, or you can ask your travel agent for theme nights featured on your cruise, if you want to join in. If you don't have space for a costume, the cruise staff can help you make one.

SPORTS EQUIPMENT

IF YOU PLAN TO PLAY GOLF or tennis frequently, you might want to bring your own equipment, and of course, you'll need the appropriate clothes and shoes. Ships that have golf practice facilities and shoreside golf programs sometimes supply the equipment for a nominal fee. Inquire.

Fins and a snorkeling mask (particularly if you have one fitted with your eyeglass prescription) are bulky, but might save you a $10 to $20 fee each time you go snorkeling on your own. If you buy the ship's shore excursions, the snorkeling equipment is included. Scuba gear is usually included in dive packages, too, and except for your regulator, is impractical to bring on a cruise.

Hiking boots, jogging shoes, riding attire, and other sporting gear will depend entirely on you and the nature of your cruise. For adventure or expedition cruises, such as to Antarctica, your cruise line will give you ample information about dress and the equipment you need; some supply guests with winter parkas and boots.

MONEY MATTERS

DOLLARS ARE READILY ACCEPTED throughout the Caribbean and in some other regions, as are traveler's checks and major credit cards. In Europe or Asia, the ship's purser or front office usually offers foreign currency exchange facilities, or the ship brings someone aboard to provide the facility in each port of call.

If you do exchange money (it's a great opportunity to teach kids about other currencies—euros in Martinique, Dutch guilders in Curaçao, pesos in Mexico), exchange only small amounts for your immediate use. Seldom will you have time to exchange the money back before returning to your ship, and you lose money every time you make the exchange. An exception is a European cruise. If you are visiting multiple European countries, say France, Italy, Spain and Greece, simply exchange a lot of dollars in advance for euros, which can be used in many countries.

Even with U.S. dollars, always carry small denominations—ones, fives, tens. Chances are, if you are owed change, it will be returned in the local currency. Incidentally, U.S. coins are seldom accepted in foreign countries and are impossible to exchange except in quantity at foreign-exchange banks. Likewise with foreign coins when you want to exchange them back into U.S. currency. Most become souvenirs.

Some travelers report problems cashing traveler's checks in foreign cruise ports, especially on the weekend. Major credit cards have become the currency of travelers worldwide and are accepted in most places. On a cruise, you will often find them the most convenient method of payment for settling your account aboard ship, for shopping at duty-free shops, and for payment of local restaurant or hotel bills. However, do not expect to use them in select off-the-beaten-track locations. The Cuna Indians of the San Blas Islands—an exotic stop on Panama Canal cruises—want your greenbacks. After you return home and receive your credit card bills, review them carefully. The theft of credit card numbers is a worldwide problem and cruise passengers, who are normally in for only a day, are easy prey.

PRESCRIPTION MEDICINE AND OTHER MEDICAL REQUIREMENTS

AS WITH ANY TRIP, whether on land or sea, you should have all your required medicine with you and carry it in original bottles and in your hand luggage, not packed in your suitcase. As a further precaution, bring copies of your medicine prescriptions—and for your eyeglasses, too.

If you have dietary requirements, you or your travel agent should communicate them to your cruise line at the time you book your cruise. Most ships can accommodate normal requirements of low salt and low fat, but more complex ones that require special stores be carried aboard require planning. Do not take anything for granted. Inquire. For example, many ships do not normally stock skim milk. In each of the cruise line profiles in Part Two under Standard Features, the amount of advance notice a cruise line requires to handle special diets is indicated.

Cruise ships that travel beyond coastal waters are required to have a doctor on board; most large ships have nurses and adequate medical facilities for normal circumstances. The doctor and nursing staff have limited daily office hours, which are printed in the ship's daily agenda, and they are always on call for emergencies. There are charges for most medical services.

who's who on the cruise ship

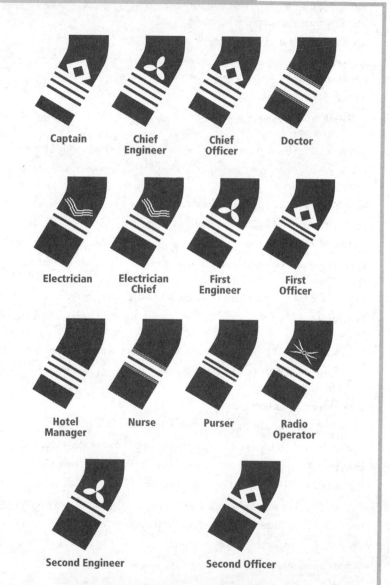

Uniform designations of Seabourn Cruise Line; other cruise lines may vary.
Courtesy of Seabourn Cruise Line.

Cruise Lingo

Add-on A supplementary charge added to the cruise fare, usually applied to correlated airfare and/or postcruise land tours.

Aft Near, toward, or in the rear (stern) of the ship.

Air/sea A package consisting of the two forms of travel, that is, air to and from the port of embarkation, transfers to and from the port, as well as the cruise itself.

Astern Beyond the ship's stern.

Batten down To secure all open hatches or equipment for seaworthiness while the ship is under way.

Beam Width of the ship (amidships) between its two sides at its widest point.

Berth Dock, pier, or quay (pronounced "key"); also, the bed in the passenger cabins.

Bow Front or forward portion of the ship.

Bridge Navigational and command control center of the ship.

Bulkhead Upright partition (wall) dividing the ship into cabins or compartments.

Category The price level of a cabin, based on location on the ship, dimensions, and amenities.

Colors A national flag or ensign flown from the mast or stern post.

Course Direction in which the ship is headed, usually expressed in compass degrees.

Crow's nest Partially enclosed platform at the top of the mast, used as a lookout.

Deck plan An overhead deck-by-deck diagram illustrating cabin and public room locations in relation to each other.

Disembark Depart from the ship.

Dock Berth, pier, or quay (pronounced "key").

Draft Measurement in feet from waterline to lowest point of ship's keel.

Even keel The ship in a true vertical position with respect to its vertical axis.

Fathom Measurement of distance equal to six feet.

First seating The earlier of several meal times in the ship's main dining rooms.

Fore The forward mast or the front (bow) of the ship.

Forward Toward the fore or bow of the ship.

Funnel The smokestack or "chimney" of the ship.

Galley The ship's kitchen.

Gangway The opening through the ship's bulwarks (or through the ship's side) and the ramp by which passengers embark and disembark.

Gross registered ton A measurement of 100 cubic feet of enclosed revenue-earning space within a ship (see "Space ratio").

Hatch The covering over an opening in a ship's deck, leading to a hold.

Helm Commonly the ship's steering wheel, but more correctly the entire steering apparatus consisting of the wheel, the rudder, and their connecting cables or hydraulic systems.

Hold Interior space(s) below the main deck for storage of cargo.

House flag The flag denoting the company to which the ship belongs.

Hull The frame and body (shell) of the ship exclusive of masts, superstructure, or rigging.

Knot A unit of speed equal to 1 nautical mile per hour (6,080.2 feet), as compared with a land mile of 5,280 feet.

League A measure of distance approximating 3.45 nautical miles.

Leeward In the direction of that side of the ship opposite from which the wind blows.

Manifest A list or invoice of a ship's passengers, crew, and cargo.

Midship In or toward the middle of the ship; the longitudinal center portion of the ship.

Nautical mile 6,080.2 feet, as compared with a land mile of 5,280 feet.

Open seating Seating in the main dining room(s) is not assigned. You eat where and with whom you wish.

Paddlewheel A wheel with boards around its circumference, and, commonly, the source of propulsion for traditional American riverboats.

Pitch The rocking back and forth (bow to stern) motion of a ship that may be felt in heavy seas when the ship is under way.

Port The left side of the ship when facing toward the bow.

Port charge Port taxes, collected by the line and paid to a local government authority; it may include other miscellaneous charges, such as gasoline surcharge and fees, as well as fees to dock in a particular port.

Port tax A charge levied by the local government authority to be paid by the passenger.

Prow The bow or the stem (the front) of the ship.

Cruise Lingo (continued)

Purser A senior management position on board ship. In most cases, the purser is like the general manager of a hotel, but in some cases, he or she is more the financial or administration officer.

Quay (pronounced "key") A dock, berth, or pier.

Registry The country under whose flag the ship is registered and with whose laws the ship and its owners must comply, in addition to compliance with the laws of the countries at which the ship calls and/or embarks/disembarks passengers/cargo.

Rigging The ropes, chains, and cables that support a sailing ship's masts, spars, kingposts, cranes, and the like.

Roll The alternate sway of a ship from side to side.

Running lights Three lights (green on the starboard side, red on the port side, and white at the top of the mast) required by international law to be lighted when the ship is in motion between the times of sunset and sunrise.

Second, third, or fourth seating The later meal times in the ship's dining room(s).

Space ratio A measurement of cubic space per passenger. Gross registered ton divided by the number of passengers (basis two) equals space ratio.

Stabilizer A gyroscopically operated finlike device extending from both sides of the ship below the waterline to steady the ship and reduce its roll.

Stack The funnel or chimney from which the ship's gases of combustion are released into the atmosphere.

SUNBURNS

YOU WILL NEED TO TAKE PRECAUTIONS against the sun when you are on a Caribbean, Mexican, Antarctic, southern European, or southeast Asian cruise. The sun in these regions is much, much stronger than the sun to which most people are accustomed. Always use a sunscreen with an SPF of 15 or higher, preferably 30 and above, and do not stay in the direct sun for long stretches at a time. Nothing can spoil a vacation faster than a sunburn.

LEARNING THE LINGO

CRUISE SHIPS HAVE A LANGUAGE all their own. Although it is not necessary to enroll in a Berlitz course to learn it, becoming familiar with a few terms will be worthwhile so you won't feel lost at sea, if you will forgive the pun.

Passengers don't reserve rooms on a ship, they book **cabins,** which cruise lines sometimes call by a fancier name, **staterooms.** The price level of a cabin is known as its **category.**

Starboard The right side of the ship when facing toward the bow.

Stateroom Cabin or suite.

Steward Personnel on board ship.

Stem The extreme bow or prow of the ship.

Stern The extreme rear of the ship.

Suite Upscale accommodations with more space, more in-room amenities, a bigger balcony and, at times, more rooms than standard or balcony cabins.

Superstructure The structure of the ship above the main deck or waterline.

Tender A small vessel, sometimes the ship's lifeboat, used to move passengers to and from the shore when the ship is at anchor.

Transfers A bus or van ride between the ship and other locations, such as airports, hotels, or departure points for shore excursions.

Upper berth A single-size bed higher from the floor than usual (similar to a bunk bed), usually folded or recessed into the wall or ceiling by day.

Wake The track of agitated water behind a ship in motion.

Waterline The line at the side of the ship's hull that corresponds to the surface of the water.

Weigh To raise; for example, to weigh the anchor.

Windward Toward the wind, to the direction from which the wind blows.

When you reach your ship, you will **board** or **embark;** when it's time to leave the ship, passengers **disembark.** If the ship arrives at a port where it cannot pull into the dock, the ship will anchor and passengers are taken ashore in a **tender,** one of the small ancillary vessels or lifeboats that travel on board the ship.

Several terms will assist you in finding your way around the ship. The **bow** is the front of the ship, the **aft** is the rear, and the center portion is **midship.**

Heading forward, toward the **bow,** the right side of the ship is known as the **starboard side;** the left side of the ship is called the **port side.** Ships have **decks,** never floors. Decks are named after such things as precious stones (Emerald Deck), activities (Sports Deck), places (Monte Carlo Deck), and planets (Venus Deck).

If you've built up an appetite from all this exploring, you can go to the **main seating** (or sitting) and eat early, or the **second seating** and dine late. Both times are assigned by the line. Some lines also offer two early and two late seatings. Some ships have **single seating,** which means that all passengers eat at the same time for all three meals. Some ships also have **open seating,** in which case you may sit anywhere—at any unoccupied table or join others. By invitation, you may even find yourself at the **captain's table.**

On board, there are people to help you decode ship lingo. The **purser's office** is the information center, similar to a check-in desk at a hotel. The **hotel manager** is in charge of all passenger-related shipboard services, such as dining, housekeeping, and so on. The **chief steward** is responsible for cabin services, and **cabin stewards** or **stewardesses** take care of cabins; the **dining steward** is your waiter. The **cruise director** functions as the emcee, and the **cruise staff,** who are his assistants, run all activities and entertainment and make sure you are having a good time. Finally, there's the **captain,** who is in charge of everything. Cruise lingo is part of the fun, so don't take it too seriously.

TIME *to* GO

If YOU PURCHASE AN AIR/SEA PACKAGE, your cruise begins from the moment you arrive at the airport. Here's how.

unofficial **TIP**
Be sure to carry all documents and essential literature you receive from your cruise line or travel agent with you. Do not pack them in your luggage.

CRUISE DOCUMENTS

NORMALLY, YOU RECEIVE your travel documents—including tickets, transfer vouchers, boarding forms, and luggage tags—about two weeks before departure. Some cruise lines, particularly deluxe and smaller ones going to offbeat destinations, begin sending material a month or more in advance, and often include information on ports of call and on shore excursions sold on board ship. A "Welcome Aboard" brochure is intended to familiarize you with your ship. Read it.

The final documents will include your airline and cruise tickets. Your agent should have checked them before sending them to you. Check them yourself. If you buy your cruise late, documents may come directly to you from the cruise line. Check them, too. Remember that you must show your cruise ticket when you check in at the dock.

In 2007, Princess Cruises and Norwegian Cruise Lines began sending cruise tickets and other documentation to passengers via email, unless you or your travel agent request otherwise. You can expect other cruise lines to follow suit in the near future. Actually, it's better for you as you will receive the tickets earlier and you will have a chance to examine them sooner to correct any errors that might have occurred.

Luggage tags show the cruise line's name and logo. They have spaces for your name and address and the name of your ship, cruise and cabin numbers, and departure date and port. Complete the luggage tags using information contained in your cruise ticket. Attach at least one tag to every piece of your luggage, including your handbags. (An amazing number of people, in their excitement, leave hand luggage behind on an airplane, in the airport, or on a motorcoach. If it's tagged, airline or port personnel will know immediately what to do with it.)

When you arrive at the airport, you will claim luggage and it will ride on the transfer bus with you for the drive to the pier. There, it will be taken by baggage handlers and will show up in your cabin in a few hours. If not, do not panic. Cruise ships, especially large ones, have thousands of bags to load and sort as passengers arrive. In our experience, luggage is moved from the airport to your cabin with amazing speed.

AIRPORT ARRIVAL AND TRANSFERS

AS YOU LEAVE YOUR AIRPLANE in Miami, Fort Lauderdale, San Juan, Vancouver, or any major departure city, you will be met by uniformed cruise line representatives, usually holding a placard showing your ship's name. The representatives gather their charges and escort or direct them to a waiting motorcoach. Keep your transfer voucher handy; you must show it to board the bus.

If you do not spot your cruise line representative, ask airline personnel or other cruise lines' reps for help. Or go to an airport "red" phone and ask that your line's representative be paged. Or proceed to where motorcoaches pick up passengers for transfer to the pier.

ADVANCE ARRIVALS OR DELAYED RETURNS

ALMOST ALL LINES HAVE HOTEL and sightseeing packages for people who choose to arrive at their port of departure in advance of their cruise or linger there afterward. Packages are described in your cruise brochure. If your cruise begins after a long flight, lines normally schedule the first day for cruising to give passengers time to overcome jet lag. If the itinerary calls for immediate ports of call, you might consider arriving a day before departure.

Give the most serious consideration to a day-in-advance arrival when you buy the cruise by itself, are arranging your own transportation to the departure port, or your travel falls during busy travel periods when weather in the northern United States often turns bad and flights are delayed (such as Thanksgiving, Christmas, New Year's, and Presidents' Day weekend).

If you're on an air/sea program, your line has a greater incentive—although not necessarily a legal one—to get you to the ship when you've been delayed, either by postponing the sailing or by arranging a hotel room and transporting you to the first port of call. In such instances, you're likely to be one of many stranded passengers.

Your name is on a passenger list, and the cruise line representative at the airport expects you. He or she is in touch with the airline and your ship and probably is setting strategy before you arrive. If you're traveling on your own and are delayed, your cruise ship has no record of your flight and no obligation to help, although most will try. If you arrive at least a day early, you can avoid this hassle.

This is highly recommended whenever possible. Why risk missing the ship due to a flight snafu? Some people advise arriving early to avoid standing in line for check-in. We view this as the least valid reason unless you want to be on as early as physically possible to enjoy onboard amenities. Queues at the airport and dockside departure gates are a fact of life in mass-market travel. If you're so impatient that you cannot stand in a check-in line—even if it takes an hour— without having your blood pressure skyrocket, then you're probably on the wrong cruise. Megaships have megapassengers, and they must be individually processed. (It would speed the process if everyone arrived with all their documents completed properly.)

AT THE PIER

IF YOU'RE LUCKY, you will be among the first to arrive from the airport and the first in line for check-in. More likely, you'll be among several hundred others, and, depending on the cruise line, day of the week, size of the ship, and other contingencies, you will stand in line ten minutes to two hours. Pull out a magazine or travel book and start reading.

Large ships have a check-in system, asking you to line up behind your letter in the alphabet. Despite occasional glitches, this works well. You often have until 60 minutes before departure to board the ship. Some lines let you board until 15 to 30 minutes before departure, but we don't suggest cutting it that close.

Normally, lines begin processing passengers at noon or 1 p.m. for a 4 or 5 p.m. departure. But they seldom allow passengers to embark sooner than two or three hours before departure, because time is needed for previous passengers to disembark and the crew to clean the ship and prepare your cabin. Some luxury or premium lines will let you come aboard sooner sometimes for a fee, but you must remain in public areas.

VISITORS

FOR SECURITY REASONS, lines do not allow visitors. If your friends or family want to send you off in style, they can contact your travel agent to arrange a party for you in your cabin, complete with flowers, wine, and Champagne, or a birthday cake or anniversary surprise in the dining room when the ship is at sea.

SETTLING IN

BOARDING YOUR SHIP

SOME SHIPS, PARTICULARLY the most luxurious ones, have uni-formed cabin stewards and stewardesses at the gangway to take you to your cabin and carry your hand luggage. Your escort may offer a quick orientation or ask you to wait for your regular steward, whose name is probably on a small tent card on your dresser. Also in your cabin is ship's literature, including an agenda for the day's events, a deck plan, and possibly stationery.

CHECKING OUT YOUR CABIN

TAKE A QUICK LOOK AROUND THE CABIN to be sure everything is working—it usually is on new ships, not necessarily on old ones. Check how to operate air- conditioning, lights, and the hot-water faucets—some fancy new ones are tricky, and the water can scald you. Check the location of life preservers, blankets, and pillows—do you have enough? If anything is missing or not as you requested—twin beds instead of a double—report it now. If you cannot locate your steward, go to the purser or front desk. If you do not get satis-faction, work your way up to the hotel manager.

HAIR DRYERS/ELECTRIC SHAVERS

ALMOST ALL CABINS ON MODERN SHIPS have standard 110-volt AC electrical outlets: your small hair dryer and electric razor won't need an adapter. A few older ships need them. Most new ships have hair dryers. We list this information in the ships' profiles in Part Two, in Standard Features, under Cabin Amenities.

LAUNDRY AND DRY CLEANING

ALMOST ALL SHIPS HAVE LAUNDRY SERVICE. Far fewer have dry-cleaning facilities. Generally, laundry service is good and reasonable but ship laundries tend to use lots of bleach. Price lists and laundry bags are in your cabin. Give your articles to be cleaned or pressed to your steward. They usually are returned in a day, and same-day ser-vice is available for an extra fee. For safety reasons, ships ask that passengers not use irons in their cabin, but many have public laun-derettes with an iron and ironing board, as well as coin-operated washers and dryers. The Standard Features section in our cruise line's profile details the availability of launderettes.

TELEPHONES AND OTHER COMMUNICATIONS

ALL BUT A FEW SHIPS HAVE TELEPHONES in cabins with instruc-tions for using them. Most phones have direct-dial to the United States 24 hours a day, but be aware of the price. Usually, you are charged $6 to $10 per minute for a ship-to-shore call. Receiving a call or a fax may cost $5 to $7 or more per minute. Policies vary. Some allow you to call collect or charge your call to your shipboard account. Shore to Ship has technology enabling passengers to dial toll-free numbers in the United States directly from their cabins. The price is $6.95 per minute, maximum ten minutes per call. Crystal Cruises was among the first to enable passengers to send and receive e-mail with relative ease. Now, most cruise ships, including even small adventure ships, have e-mail facilities and more and more are adding wireless access.

If someone wants to reach you at sea, they can telephone the ship by calling ☎ 800-SEA-CALL, asking for the ship by name, and giving its approximate location. The specific phone number for your ship is often included in the documents you receive from the cruise line in advance of your cruise. Charges for this call will appear on the caller's long-distance telephone bill. Ship-to-shore telephone and fax services are normally available only at sea. When the ship is in port, onshore communications must be used.

Until recently, cell phones worked locally in ports and up to about two miles at sea, depending on the phone and the location. But now, cruise ships, especially new ones, are installing technology that enables passengers to use their own cell phones at sea with the cost being charged to the passengers' cell phone account. Be warned: it's expensive. With e-mail becoming so readily available on cruise ships, it is the best, least costly means to stay in touch with family and friends, or to tend to business during a cruise.

Almost all new ships have an Internet cafe with a dozen or more computer terminals, and older ships and many small ones have installed at least one or two terminals for passengers' use. Many older ships have also been retrofitted with these cafes. Charges range from 25 cents to 75 cents per minute, including dial-up time, which can often take five minutes or more at sea. On weeklong or longer cruises, many ships offer weekly rates. Wi-Fi access is rapidly becoming the norm on large ships; cards usually cost $10 per day. Internet cafes in ports of call are now available around the world and are usually very inexpensive to use to send and retrieve mail—certainly much less costly than shipboard facilities.

CHECKING OUT YOUR SHIP

AFTER YOU CHECK OUT YOUR CABIN, you might want to tour the ship or, alternatively, relax in a lounge or visit the spa. The ship will be your home for a while, and it's nice to feel at home as quickly as possible.

CHECKING ON YOUR DINING RESERVATIONS

WHEN YOU BOOK YOUR CRUISE, your travel agent should state your dining preference and request reservations. On ships with assigned seating times, you may request first or second seating, or on ships with four seating times, any of those. Tables for two, four, six, or eight are available; and guests can ask for smoking or nonsmoking areas, although most ships departing from U.S. ports now have smokeless dining

unofficial TIP
If assigned arrangements are not what you requested, make a beeline for the maître d'hôtel.

rooms. Most lines say they honor requests on a first-come, first-served basis, yet few confirm them in advance. Generally, dining reservations are confirmed only by the maître d'hôtel on board.

Royal Caribbean International is among the few lines that print passengers' dining reservations on their cruise tickets. Why, in this computer age, all can't do the same is a mystery—unless it's to allow the maître d'hôtel to control last-minute shuffling and to ensure he gets his tips.

You may receive confirmation of your dining arrangements on check-in, or it may be in your cabin. If not, check on it. Even lines that give you a dining reservation in advance may ask you to confirm it with the maître d'hôtel. If you have a problem with your dining arrangements, know that most cruise lines will accommodate your change request, though not necessarily on the first night. Rest assured, you won't be the only one. No other item causes more consternation than dining-room reservations.

If you let the cruise line or maître d'hôtel place you randomly at a table and you are unhappy with your companions, do not hesitate to ask the maître d'hôtel to move you. Nothing is worse than spending a week dining with people with whom you have nothing in common and no basis for conversation. And you don't need to.

DINING HOURS

CONSUMERS OFTEN ASK ABOUT dining hours before they cruise. They vary so much that it is difficult, if not impossible, to give an accurate generic overview. Keep in mind that each line, each itinerary, and sometimes each ship may have varied hours. You will get a complete list of hours on board, and some general information before boarding about dining times and seatings. Ask your travel agent or cruise line.

But before booking, it is more important to assess how you will dine and to pick a line that meets your needs. Do your homework up front. What type of dining do you prefer? Are you more structured or flexible in dining times? Do you like to socialize with other passengers every night or do your own thing? Check brochures, Web sites, consumer cruise bulletin boards, and ask questions of your agent or friends. Find out exactly what the dining policies and dining style are on every ship you are thinking of sailing on (see our descriptions in Part II).

For those seeking the most flexibility, some luxury lines offer open seating and anytime dining programs. On the mass-market side,

Norwegian Cruise Line offers the highly flexible Freestyle Dining—guests eat where, when, and with whom they want; and guests can also access a host of onboard alternative restaurant choices in addition to the main dining room. Some are free, some come with a charge. Expedition and small ship lines may have open seating but set very specific times for their dining service.

Princess, in another twist, offers both a flexible dining experience and a more traditional fixed one; guests choose which so they can have the best of both worlds. Some lines also have open seating for breakfast and lunch, yet more structured, assigned seating times and tables for dinner. That means you are assigned a table with other guests and you dine at that same table, at that same time, every evening; of course you don't have to dine there every night. Guests often take a break and have room service one night, or visit an alternative restaurant or the buffet restaurant on another. But if you do dine in the dining room on any evening you will eat at that table and with those people each night.

Generally, there are two fixed dinner seatings between 5:30 and 7:30 p.m. and between 8 and 10 p.m. But even those times can vary. Carnival and Holland America have both adopted four seatings within the same period to offer more flexibility for guests. So if you have strong preferences, tell your travel agent, who can explain what the dining hours and choices are on individual lines.

Whichever line you pick, you won't go hungry. In addition to the regular meals, most lines offer a host of other options. These might include room service, ice cream on deck, pizza parlors (some 24 hours), a late-night snack or buffet, afternoon tea, barbecues on deck, early-bird coffee and continental breakfast in a lounge, cocktail canapés, and a host of alternative dining options.

ESTABLISHING SHIPBOARD CREDIT

MOST LINES USE A CASHLESS SYSTEM aboard ship. At check-in, you receive a card—like a credit card—which will be your identification card and probably your cabin door key. If you want to establish credit for purchases on board, drinks at the bar, wine in the dining room, and so forth, you must present a major credit card at check-in or the purser's office (you will be told at check-in) to have an imprint made and signed.

On the last night of the cruise, you receive a printout of your charges for review. You can pay the amount with cash or traveler's checks or have it billed to your credit card. In profiles in Standard Features in Part Two, we list credit cards each cruise line accepts. Also see our discussion of credit holds on pages 113–114.

PREPARING *for* TIME ASHORE

PORT TALKS AND SHOPPING GUIDELINES

ALL SHIPS OFFER "PORT TALKS"—briefings on the country or island and port where the ship will dock. The quality of these talks varies enormously among lines and ships, depending largely on the cruise director's knowledge and the importance the line puts on such programs.

Most mainstream lines with large ships do a lousy job with port talks. On the other hand, adventure and expedition cruises offer superb talks. Small ships generally have a better track record than large ones.

Avoid being misled. If, during a port talk, the cruise director or anyone else recommends one store over another, shop around before buying. The store recommended may be the best place to buy—or it may not.

Also, be cautious of advice that fabulous buys are available in duty-free shops on board and in ports. Most often, you can do as well or better at discount stores and factory outlets at home. If you are considering sizable purchases of jewelry, cameras, china, or crystal, bring a list of prices from home and comparison shop. Be sure you are comparing similar products. Prices in shipboard shops are a good gauge; they usually are competitive with those in ports.

In the Caribbean, expect to save up to 20% on such well-known brands as Gucci, Fendi, and Vuitton, and on French perfumes, which must be sold at prices set by the makers. Any store caught undercutting the price will be dropped from distribution. The biggest savings are on cigarettes and liquor, not because the price is so much less, but because you save the hefty U.S. taxes imposed on them.

When preparing for your day ashore, be aware also that purses, bags, and packs that you carry along will be searched before you're allowed back on board. Purchases you make while shopping will likewise be inspected.

SHORE EXCURSIONS:
SOME PITFALLS AND COSTS

ALTHOUGH THERE HAS BEEN much improvement recently, "shore excursions"—the tours passengers buy from the cruise line to take at ports—are often the weakest element of the cruise vacation. Cruise lines are finally recognizing the needs of younger, more active passengers by providing more adventurous excursions featuring horseback riding, hiking, mountain biking, scuba diving, snorkeling, sailing, and even a MiG flight over Moscow. But the core product— large to medium group sightseeing tours—needs more work, given the shore excursion's importance to the cruise experience.

All the latest cruise lines' research indicates that what attracts customers to buy a particular cruise are the specific ports of call on the itinerary. Travelers often view their shore trips as one of the more important aspects of the cruise. In response, major cruise lines have beefed up their shore excursion departments to offer more compelling tours, which often include exploring a destination on foot as well as by bus, van, or boat.

Shore excursions are available at every stop on a ship's itinerary, almost always at additional cost. The exceptions are adventure and expedition cruises, where shore visits are an integral part of the experience (and one reason these cruises appear to be more costly than mainstream ones). Also, cruises in China usually include the cost of shore excursions, not because cruise lines are altruistic, but because the Chinese want it that way.

Shore excursions have traditionally been sold aboard ship either by a shore excursion office or, rarely, from the purser or cruise director. It has been assumed that people prefer to buy excursions on board because their interests and plans change once the cruise begins. However, that assumption may have no foundation in fact. After you have been subjected to the way shore excursions are sold aboard many ships, you might say as we do: there must be a better way.

unofficial **TIP**
More and more, cruise lines are enabling passengers to purchase shore excursions in advance on the line's Web site, and some even by phone or mail.

Often you must choose your excursions on the first night of the cruise, especially for the first port of call. Unless you have done your homework in advance of your cruise, you will be buying blind. The shore excursion office usually has limited hours. For the first few days of a cruise, particularly on large ships, ticket lines are long. Therefore, it really pays to read your cruise literature plus books and magazine articles about your destinations in advance.

If possible, take advantage of the opportunity to book shore excursions in advance. In addition to significantly increasing your chances of getting the excursion you want, you also avoid the hassle of booking on board. Usually, a pamphlet on shore excursions is included in the literature sent prior to your cruise. Not all brochures list prices, but they are listed on those cruise lines' Web sites that provide a booking facility. Absent that convenience, you can request prices through your travel agent, if you need them for budgeting purposes. We are happy to report that more lines are including prices in their literature. Also, more often pamphlets are specific to cruise itineraries, making it easier to select tours of interest.

Shore excursions normally are operated by local tour companies. Motorcoaches seating 30 to 50 passengers are the most common form of transportation, particularly on general sightseeing tours offered by large ships. Minibuses and vans are common for smaller groups; location and terrain are also factors in the choice of conveyance. Most tours assume that passengers are on their first visit to the locale—one reason shore excursions are a weak link.

Standard shore excursions vary little among cruise lines and are, for the most part, passive and unimaginative city and/or countryside tours to the best-known sights. There are exceptions, like the excursions on Greek Isles cruises, where escorts are university graduates who must pass stiff examinations to qualify as guides, and customized tours offered by smaller ships and luxury liners. Happily, many cruise lines have added a variety of sports activities and tours that emphasis nature and culture in an effort to appeal to younger travelers and in response to passengers' requests.

After years of being bad to awful, shore excursions available on Caribbean cruises have recently shown a great improvement, as cruise lines have worked with local operators to be more creative, provide greater variety of tour offerings, and enhance the tour experience with more substance and better-trained guides.

As a rule of thumb, most standard half-day tours cost $25 to $35 in the Caribbean, but they can cost twice that in Alaska and Europe. Adventure excursions run $50 and up, mainly because the groups are small and hence cost more per person to operate. Full-day tours can run as much as $70 to $150, and some, like helicopter tours, might cost $200 or more. Often the most expensive are the first to sell out. That's usually because the number of participants is limited, or they are perceived as a great value or a once-in-a-lifetime experience, or it's an excursion that would be difficult to arrange on one's own. Variables that affect price include the locale, the number of participants, local costs, and mode of transport.

As you study excursions offered by your line, look for options that keep things simple. Excursions that involve multiple activities, sights, and stops could drive some people nuts. It's on the bus, off the bus, back on the bus, head counts. "Wait, Thelma's in the restroom!" "Where are Harry and Louise?" "I left my credit card in the stuffed parrot shop! I'll be right back." With few exceptions, you'll spend more time driving among sites and loading and unloading the bus than you will touring or doing something interesting.

When you read descriptions of available excursions, check how long the primary activity or event is. If the written material doesn't say, ask the cruise director. You'll sometimes discover that the half-day "riverboat excursion" spends only an hour on the water. The remainder of the time is spent commuting and waiting for fellow passengers to shop.

In ports where most attractions you want to see are clustered in a small area, you may save time by taking a cab or walking. Rental cars are another option. By forgoing a $48-per-person half-day shore excursion, two people can apply the $96 toward cab fares, rental cars, and admissions to attractions. In most ports, you can see and do a lot for $96.

Ask probing questions about each port. Is it a good and safe place to explore on foot? What are the local people like? At some ports, tourists are subjected to swarms of in-your-face hucksters and peddlers. In such places, escorted tours, though regimented and inefficient, can be a less stressful way to visit.

When the ship arrives in port, people who have purchased shore excursions are allowed to disembark first and are usually asked to follow a departure schedule to avert a traffic jam at the gangway. This is seldom a problem when the ship docks and passengers can disembark quickly. It can be a problem when the ship must tender, because it cuts an hour or more (depending on ship size) from the time you have in port if you plan to tour on your own.

At the END of YOUR CRUISE

TIPPING

THERE ARE NO DEFINITIVE RULES about tipping, but because it causes so much consternation for passengers, cruise lines offer guidelines, distributing them aboard ship. Some even publish them in their cruise brochures, which is helpful if you want to budget for tipping in advance. In Part Two, the cruise ship profiles' Standard Features includes Suggested Tipping. The guidelines are similar: Tip slightly less on budget cruises, slightly more on luxury cruises. Lines will also tell you if gratuities are included or if they are automatically added to your bill. Follow guidelines or your inclinations. Ship officers and senior management are never tipped. For all service personnel, tips are their main source of compensation. Only a few deluxe ships include tipping in the cruise cost (noted in the cruise line profiles).

In a session at voyage's end, the cruise director will discuss disembarkation procedures and outline tipping guidelines. There no longer is anything subtle about tipping. Either the line will automatically add the tips or it won't; if not, on the final cruise day, your cabin steward will leave a supply of envelopes for distributing your tips, possibly with guidelines. Lately, the envelopes are crassly stamped with titles—Cabin Steward, Dining Steward, Waiter—in case you did not know whom to tip!

On ships without "automatic" tipping, tips are usually given to individuals—your cabin stewards and dining room waiters. On ships with Greek crews and on many small vessels, tips are pooled for distribution to include those behind the scenes, such as kitchen staff.

The advent of alternative dining venues has confused tipping customs in recent years. Passengers sometimes were deducting from the amount given to their dining room waitstaff to compensate for gratuities rendered at the alternative restaurants. To create a more uniform approach, a number of cruise lines add gratuities directly to your shipboard bill. Most of these offer the option of decreasing or increasing the amount on your bill depending on how you felt about the service. Whatever the tipping protocol on your cruise, you can be sure it will be explained to you in detail, probably several times.

If tips are not added to your shipboard bill, custom dictates that you distribute tips the last night of the cruise. Some lines, particularly deluxe ones, will arrange prepayment of tips. Check the Standard Features section in our cruise line profiles for each line's "Suggested Tipping" information.

DEPARTING

TO SMOOTH DISEMBARKATION, your captain and cruise director will ask you to follow procedures outlined in the cruise director's final talk and repeated on closed-circuit television in your cabin and in the daily agenda. On the last day, your cabin steward will give you luggage tags to be completed and attached to your bags. You are asked to place your bags (except hand luggage) outside your cabin door before you retire. Times vary; some lines want them out by 8 or 10 p.m.—an unreasonable hour for passengers dining at the late seating. Such requests are for the ship's convenience, because no luggage can be unloaded until the ship docks. Do what's convenient for you and tell your cabin steward what to expect.

The last night of a cruise is almost always casual; plan your packing accordingly. And don't pack everything. Remember you still need to dress the next day. It's not unheard of for people to pack shoes, underwear, and even needed travel documents in their exuberance to put their bags out.

Luggage tags use a color-coded, alphabetic system that enables the ship to disembark passengers by cabin locations and airline departure times for those on air/sea packages. (Passengers on the earliest flights disembark first.) Tags also identify your airline so that your bags will go to the correct place at the airport.

Ships normally dock about 7 or 8 a.m. the last day and require about an hour to unload luggage, meaning no passengers will disembark before 9 a.m. The ship is very eager to unload passengers as quickly as possible. Some people find disembarkation so abrupt that it's unpleasant. Try to remember that the next group of passengers will arrive soon, and staff and crew have only about four hours to prepare the ship and be all smiles for them.

Breakfast is served either at normal hours with the full menu or at abbreviated hours with a short menu. Room service usually isn't available. You will be called to depart by the color of your luggage tags. After leaving the ship, you encounter chaos that varies depending on the port. Usually, you proceed first to immigration and then to the baggage holding area, where your luggage has been placed according to the color of your tags. You are responsible for finding it and taking it to customs. In Miami, for example, baggage handlers help you, and the customs official stands by the exit to take the declaration form you completed aboard ship. He or she may check your passport, so have it handy.

After clearing customs, your luggage will go with you to the airport on the transfer bus. Find the motorcoach going to your airline's departure area, show your transfer voucher, give the driver your luggage, and climb aboard. If you aren't on an air/sea package, you may be allowed aboard the motorcoach unless you have lots of luggage. Otherwise, taxis are nearby.

PART TWO

CRUISE LINES *and* THEIR SHIPS

 The **HEART** *of the* **MATTER**

PART TWO CONSISTS OF IN-DEPTH cruise line and ship profiles—the heart of this guide—serving the U.S. and Canadian markets. Listed alphabetically by cruise line, each line has three parts: a company profile, its ships' standard features, and ship descriptions. Cruise lines profiled in this section are listed in the Table of Contents. For listings of specific ships, itineraries, destinations, or for a general subject index, refer to the respective indexes at the end of this book.

CRUISE LINE PROFILES

THE FIRST THREE TO FOUR PAGES focus on the cruise line and the type of cruises it offers. At-a-glance summaries— **Type of Ships, Type of Cruises, Cruise Line's Strengths, Cruise Line's Shortcomings, Fellow Passengers, Recommended for, Not Recommended for**—help you select cruise lines of potential interest.

Summaries are followed by background on the line, its fleet, and cruise areas to reveal the company behind the cruise. The **Style** section defines the experience you can expect on any ship of that cruise line. **Distinctive Features** highlights amenities or facilities that are innovative or unusual.

Rates

The **Rates** section explains discounts, special fares, and packages and provides a range of per-person daily (per diem) costs. These figures were derived by averaging cruise-only (no airfare) brochure rates for each cabin class on every ship in the line. Calculations exclude Owner's Suites, Presidential Suites, and other extraordinary accommodations. The rate table aims to indicate the most and the least you would pay per day for a cruise if you paid brochure rates. Savvy shoppers almost certainly will be able to chip away 10% to 50% or more of the listed per diem by taking advantage of common discounts. (Our average rate is not calculated by adding the highest and lowest rates in the brochure table and dividing by two. Rather, the average per diem takes into account the number of each type of accommodation available in the line's cabin inventory. The per diem box averages rates for all ships of the line.)

Past Passengers tells what repeat customers can expect, and **The Last Word** is our summary of the line—the big picture.

Standard Features

Information on elements common to all ships of a line—including officers, staff, dining facilities, dress code, cabin amenities, and electricity—is listed in one chart for handy reference.

Cruise Ship Profiles

The cruise line's fleet, starting with its flagship (or the most representative) vessel, is covered in depth. Sister ships with identical design are clustered. Other ships that vary only in degree receive shorter treatment. We recommend that readers review the entire section for a given cruise line to have a complete picture of the cruise experience offered.

QUALITY RATINGS To differentiate ships by overall quality of the cruise experience and to allow comparison of ships from different lines, we give ships a rating of 1 to 10, with 10 being the best. The numerical rating is based on the quality and diversity of the ship's features and service, taking into consideration its state of repair, maintenance, and cleanliness; the design, comfort, decor, and furnishing of public areas; recreational and fitness facilities; meal quality and dining room service; entertainment, activities, and shore excursions; cabin comfort, decor, furnishings, and spaciousness; and hospitality, courtesy, and responsiveness of officers and crew.

We have opted for numerical ratings because some of our colleagues in the travel press have hopelessly muddled the more familiar star ratings. Traditionally, ships have been rated one to five stars. This system was easily understood by the cruising public and provided a quick way to compare critics' opinions. Several years ago, however, some writers changed the scale to one to six stars, precluding meaningful comparison. Although those guidebooks are no longer published and the writers are deceased, the practice continues, mainly because the cruise lines perpetuate it. We believe a standardized rating system helps consumers. But so long as the star system remains corrupted, we elect to abandon the star business.

VALUE RATINGS There is no consideration of cost in the quality ratings. If you want the finest cruise available and cost is no issue, look no further than the quality ratings. If, however, you seek both quality and value, consult the value rating, expressed in letters. All value ratings are based on brochure rates. Any discount you obtain will improve the value rating for a ship. Value ratings are defined as follows:

A	Exceptional value, a real bargain.
B	Good value.
C	Absolutely fair. You get exactly what you pay for.
D	Somewhat overpriced.
F	Significantly overpriced.

A WORD ABOUT NEW SHIPS

WE DO NOT EVALUATE OR RATE new ships until they have been in service for at least one year. This allows the new ship to work out any kinks and settle into normal operation. If you are considering a cruise on a new ship, check our ratings and descriptions of other ships in the same line for a good idea of what to expect. If a ship has not completed a year of service at press time, it will be marked as a "preview" in the ship's ratings box.

American Canadian Caribbean Line

461 Water Street, Warren, RI 02885
☎ 401-247-0955 or 800-556-7450
fax 401-247-2350
www.accl-smallships.com

TYPE OF SHIPS Small, no-frills, budget.

TYPE OF CRUISES Light adventure, destination-oriented, unhurried pace.

CRUISE LINE'S STRENGTHS
- innovative, small ships
- imaginative itineraries
- homey ambience
- friendly, diligent staff
- moderate prices
- no-cost or low-cost shore excursions

CRUISE LINE'S SHORTCOMINGS
- minimal service
- spartan cabins with small bathrooms
- limited shipboard facilities
- sparse pre-cruise information

FELLOW PASSENGERS Mature, experienced travelers ages 55–85; retired couples, seniors; teachers. Not all are sporty, but all are good sports; friendly and unpretentious, most with moderate means, college-educated, well-traveled. Even affluent passengers who care little for luxury and ostentation, are keenly interested in history, wildlife, and ecology. They are avid readers and play bridge and Scrabble. Most come from the northeast United States, Florida, and California.

Recommended for Travelers seeking friendship, companionship, light adventure in unusual destinations; budget-conscious travelers favoring a small ship with family atmosphere. Those who abhor large ships.

Not recommended for Swingers, hyper super-achievers, snobs, or night owls.

CRUISE AREAS AND SEASONS Spring–fall, U.S. coastal and intercoastal waterways between New England and Florida; Chesapeake Bay, Hudson River and Erie Canal, Maine, New England and Canada; small mid-America rivers and Great Lakes from Chicago. Winter, Bahamas and Caribbean.

THE LINE Shipbuilder and adventurer Luther Blount designed and built his first small ship in 1964 for cruising the Hudson River, Erie Canal, and Canada's inland waterways with his friends. A loyal following developed, and his hobby became a business that pioneered innovative itineraries and ship design.

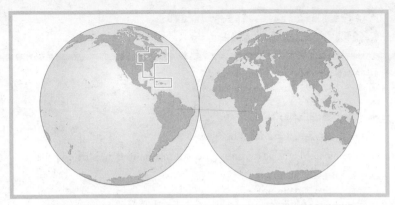

CRUISE AREAS AND SEASONS FOR AMERICAN CANADIAN CARIBBEAN LINE

With slightly larger ships, he expanded to the Bahamas, Virgin Islands, and small islands of the Eastern Caribbean, added "Caribbean" to the line's name, and again pioneered unusual itineraries in Central America, the Southern Caribbean, and other U.S. waterways.

Each vessel, built at Blount's shipyard in Warren, Rhode Island, had design improvements, larger cabins, and better public space. Blount was a hands-on president, designing every aspect of the ships (with design concepts adopted by many small cruise ships), supervising the building, and scouting new itineraries until his retirement at the age of 84 in 2001.

Before his death in September 2006 at age 90, Blount, in an unprecedented move, gave the M/V *Niagara Prince* to three New England schools: Rhode Island College (Providence), Roger Williams University (Bristol, Rhode Island), and Wentworth Institute of Technology (Boston), Blount's alma mater. He said he chose schools that need funds; the gift is divided into equal parts. The schools are to obtain a purchaser or operate her for a semester at sea. The *Niagara Prince,* which sailed for ACCL for ten years, is U.S.-flagged and SOLAS-certified and carries up to 90 passengers and crew.

ACCL remains a family enterprise. Daughter Nancy Blount, who took over when her father retired, is company president. The gift of the *Niagara Prince* corresponds with ACCL's decision to return to its roots, concentrating on North American itineraries with the line's two other ships and adding the Bahamas and Caribbean during the winter season.

THE FLEET	BUILT/RENOVATED	TONNAGE	PASSENGERS
Grande Caribe	1997	94	100
Grande Mariner	1998	97	100

STYLE Adventure at budget prices. Leave your Guccis at home—no one here would be impressed. Since its inception, ACCL has maintained an informal, unpretentious atmosphere with limited service and planned entertainment. Passengers receive an intimate look at places they visit.

The ships' shallow drafts enable them to cruise small tributaries. Bow ramps, a Blount innovation, allow access to inaccessible places. The ships carry a glass-bottom boat, small sailboats, and snorkeling equipment for use in warm climates.

ACCL cruises, staffed by American officers and crew, are run like a family outing. Surprisingly good food is served family style in a folksy atmosphere conducive to friendships. Limited table service is provided by cheerful, hardworking staff who are always ready to bring beverages or second helpings and deal with special requests.

New itineraries are offered every year, tapping pristine areas strong in natural beauty and history and providing frequent opportunities for exploring, particularly in ports where large ships cannot go.

DISTINCTIVE FEATURES Bow ramps; retractable pilothouse allowing vessels to sail under low bridges and the length of Erie Canal.

	HIGHEST	LOWEST	AVERAGE
PER DIEM	$327	$151	$246

Per diems are calculated from a cruise line's nondiscounted *cruise-only* published fares on standard accommodations and vary by season, cabins, and cruise areas.

RATES Port charges are additional.

Special fares and discounts 10% discount on certain cruises when two cruises are booked back to back; up to 15% discounts or more periodically on special promotions.
- **THIRD PASSENGER:** 15% discount for each occupant of cabin.
- **SINGLE SUPPLEMENT:** 175% for certain cabins, depending on season and time of booking. On select cruises, a single's willing-to-share program offers double-occupancy rates.

Packages
- **PRE/POST:** New Orleans, Maine.

PAST PASSENGERS Loyalty is rewarded; after ten cruises, a passenger gets one free. Advanced mailings on new itineraries and special discounts.

THE LAST WORD Up to 68% of passengers are repeat, suggesting that ACCL has found the right formula for a certain type of passenger: one who doesn't want or need pampering and appreciates small-ship cruising, preferring conversation and friendship to chorus lines and casinos. New itineraries usually sell out quickly. ACCL reflects the owners' hands-on philosophy and personal touch with customers. Passengers who understand the limitations of a small ship and the nature of these cruises enjoy themselves immensely; those who do not may discover they're on the wrong ship.

In the past, we complained about the dearth of information on itineraries and ports of call, but we are pleased to report that ACCL's new cruise brochure includes quite a lot of information on itineraries and ports. The only thing missing now is information on shore excursions sent to passengers before their cruise. Tours are not published in advance because, ACCL says, they are so often decided by the interests of the passengers and are subject to demand and weather conditions; however, experience shows they do not change that much. It is difficult to understand why ACCL handles such information haphazardly, particularly when its cruises and passengers are destination-focused. It's even more puzzling when you know that ACCL is one of the few cruise lines that does not profit on shore excursions. They're sold at cost—one of many reasons ACCL cruises are a truly good value.

ACCL Standard Features

Officers American.

Staff Dining, Cabin, Cruise: American.

Dining facilities One dining room with open seating; meals served at specific hours: breakfast, 8 a.m.; lunch, noon; dinner, 6 p.m.

Special diets Cruise line needs notice at booking, but chefs can accommodate basic requests.

Room service None.

Dress code Casual at all times; men never need a tie. Gentlemen might bring a jacket and women a dress in case they want to try a fancy place in a port.

Cabin amenities Air-conditioning/heat; upper-deck cabins have windows that can be opened. Very small bathroom with handheld shower. Reading light; plug for hair dryers. Limited drawer and closet space.

Electrical outlets 110 AC.

Wheelchair access No designated cabins; motorized chair between main and sun decks.

Recreation and entertainment Lounge with bar setup, books, and videos; informal entertainment, occasional lectures; bridge and parlor games. No casino, swimming pool, gym, or theater.

Sports and other activities Glass-bottom boat, Sunfish, kayaks, and snorkeling equipment on board for warm-weather charter.

Beauty and fitness No facilities. On request, cruise director will provide information about beauty/barber salons in ports.

Other facilities Ships have no doctors; "BYOB" policy.

Children's facilities None. Children under age 14 not accepted.

Theme cruises Fall foliage.

Smoking No smoking inside ships; allowed only in outside open areas.

ACCL suggested tipping $10–$15 per person per day. All tips are pooled and shared.

Credit cards None onboard. Passengers may use traveler's checks or personal checks. Visa or MasterCard to book a cruise.

Grande Caribe	QUALITY 2	VALUE A
Grande Mariner	QUALITY 2	VALUE A
REGISTRY United States	LENGTH 183/182 feet	BEAM 40 feet
CABINS 50	DRAFT 6.6 feet	SPEED 12 knots
MAXIMUM PASSENGERS	PASSENGER DECKS 3	ELEVATORS Chairlift
100/96	CREW 15/17	SPACE RATIO NA

THE SHIPS Built at Blount Marine in Warren, Rhode Island, the *Grande Caribe* and her near twin, *Grande Mariner*, are designed for coastal cruises. Like ACCL ships of the past, they have shallow drafts and bow ramps to guarantee access to areas large cruise ships cannot reach. They also have a retractable pilothouse for passage under low bridges and a chairlift for passengers who have trouble negotiating stairs. On warm-weather cruises, the ships can carry a Blount-designed glass-bottom boat, kayaks, snorkel equipment, and Sunfish.

Although the *Grande Caribe* is only slightly larger than earlier ACCL ships, her layout varies in several ways. The dining room is on the main deck; the lounge, with wraparound windows, is on the top deck. A new feature is a stern swimming platform.

The retractable pilothouse is lowered to pass under bridges by lifting off its roof, folding down its three sides, and disconnecting all the equipment. The captain's chair, console, steering mechanism, and equipment are then lowered to the promenade deck and reconnected so the ship can resume operation. It's quite a scene to watch, leaving you with an I-had-to-see-it-to-believe-it feeling.

The *Grande Mariner*, which made her debut in 1998, has more comfortable cabins than *Grande Caribe*, as well as unique features such as an acoustical "floating deck" between the engine room and main-deck cabins. This special deck is meant to reduce engine noise, along with sound-deadening enclosures for the ship's main generators. (We did not find the ship quieter than her earlier sisters. In fact, our cabin, 44A, was actually noisier from the sound of the generators.)

In another first for ACCL, the hull of the *Grande Mariner* is ice-strengthened for cruising in the Canadian subarctic waters of Labrador, Newfoundland, and parts of the St. Lawrence River. Incidentally, the ship's 24-passenger glass-bottom boat and shore launch are built with the same foam-based materials found in a life raft.

The *Grande Mariner*'s "vista view" lounge, a multifunctional room located forward on the upper deck, has wraparound windows to showcase passing scenery. The room has a bar, piano, and large projection screen; it can be used for lectures by visiting experts, historians, and naturalists, or for business seminars. A self-service bar has storage shelves for passengers' liquor and a fridge for chilling wine and beer. Nightly, the chef prepares hors d'oeuvres for the cocktail hour.

ITINERARIES *See* Itinerary Index.

CABINS Small, spartan, but functional cabins have twin beds on metal frames. Storage space is limited to four drawers, about one square foot of counter space, and a cabinet for hanging clothes; luggage goes under the beds.

Bathrooms, ingeniously designed by Blount, are small but utilitarian; they're a deluxe version of a "head" on a sailboat or RV. A small sink with spring taps lets water run for only a few seconds at a time. The handheld shower is very efficient and can be left in its wall mount when showering. The toilet has a fill-and-flush system that works very well.

The *Grande Caribe* has a third, lower deck with six cabins fitted with upper and lower berths and no windows. There are three similar inside cabins on the main deck. These nine are the least expensive of the *Grande Caribe*'s 50 cabins.

All other cabins are on the Main and Sun decks and have two beds, either side by side or in an L shape. Two cabins have double beds. Six cabins on the sun deck have doors that open to the outside promenade; others have large sliding windows—a pleasant feature on U.S. waterways when fresh, cool air fills the room.

Cabins are cleaned daily; linens are changed weekly. Bath towels are replaced every second day or as needed. (The ship does not have laundry facilities.) There is no room service.

On the *Grande Mariner*, each cabin has its own air conditioner with air circulated outside through ducts. Unlike many other ships where air is recirculated, the Blount-designed system supplies fresh air continuously to the cabins, and stale air is removed.

Also, *Grande Mariner*'s cabins are ACCL's most comfortable. Bathrooms, particularly, show marked improvement over earlier ships in the fleet. Gone is the hole in the floor from which odors escaped. Toilets operate on the standard principle, but the design is more streamlined. Cabin doors can be locked from the inside. However, passengers are not issued keys, and they don't need them.

Specifications 50 cabins (*Caribe* 9, *Mariner* 7 inside/no window; *Caribe* 8, *Mariner* 9 open onto promenade); all have private facilities and twin lower beds (except *Mariner* has 2 cabins with double bed); some convert to doubles. *Caribe* 8, *Mariner* 10 have upper and lower berths; 1 cabin has 1 double and 1 single. Standard dimensions, 80–110 square feet.

DINING A big advantage on a small ship is its fresh food and homemade bread and pastries. Aboard these ships, well-prepared American fare is much better than expected for the ship's category and better than on more expensive lines.

Menus are posted daily. One of two entrées available is lighter, healthful fare. This reflects past passengers' criticism of the ship's tendency to serve high-cholesterol foods. New menus are an improvement, but we would prefer more salads and green vegetables, and less gravy and sauces.

The main course of the hearty breakfast—eggs, pancakes, and so on—varies daily. Lunch usually includes a freshly made soup (the best we've had on any ship), salad, and dessert. Dinner features fish, chicken, or other meat; vegetables; and dessert. Meals are family style; staff serves dessert, beverages, and second helpings. Coffee, tea, and cookies are always available in the dining room.

The dining room, which has an open kitchen, has tables for four, six, eight, and ten. The square tables for four are also used for card games. Passengers bring their own liquor and wine, and ACCL provides storage, setups, and ice. For the captain's dinners, ACCL supplies wine and an open bar. Likewise, for Celebration Night, when passengers collectively celebrate birthdays, anniversaries, and so on, the line supplies wine. Make-Your-Own-Sundae, with many varieties of ice cream and toppings, is another popular event.

SERVICE The young and energetic crew members, most from Rhode Island and neighboring states, are outstanding. They are hardworking, smiling, and unfailingly polite. The same teams that clean the cabins also attend the dining room. They seem eager to please and are particularly accommodating to their mostly older passengers.

FACILITIES AND ACTIVITIES There is no evening entertainment of the usual cruise variety. Passengers gather in the lounge for informal, predinner cocktails. After dinner, some may linger for card or parlor games or to watch a film. The lounge has a television monitor for videotapes, and visiting lecturers or local talent may appear at ports of call. Most passengers are in bed by 10 p.m.

Although the ships have some paperbacks, avid readers should bring their own books. ACCL's captains are very knowledgeable about places the ships visit and often provide running commentary.

The ships have no shops, but the cruise director does open his "boutique" to sell signature shirts, caps, and jackets at least once during each cruise.

SPORTS AND FITNESS On board, a mile walk on the promenade deck usually starts the morning fitness activity for most passengers. Ashore, sports activities depend on the itinerary.

SHORE EXCURSIONS On the cruise's first day, the cruise director distributes descriptions of tours. Excursions vary with itineraries, cost $4–$45 each, and often are subject to demand and weather conditions. ACCL uses local operators specializing in small special-interest groups. The line says it continuously checks tours and books the most appealing choices.

POSTSCRIPT ACCL's ships' best features are their staff, itineraries, and the camaraderie among passengers—the latter not found on a large ship. The ships are basic (at times, you feel you're camping), but passengers appear to be happy and having a good time. Clearly they are the type more interested in destinations than in creature comforts.

Note that no liquor is sold on board ACCL vessels; BYOB basics with setups are offered.

Carnival Cruise Lines

3655 NW 87th Avenue, Miami, FL 33178-2428
☎ **305-599-2600, 800-438-6744, or**
800-CARNIVAL
www.carnival.com
.

TYPE OF SHIPS New, mod superliners and megaliners.

TYPE OF CRUISES Casual, contemporary mass market. "Fun Ships" hallmark makes the ship the destination—as central to the cruise experience as the ports of call.

CRUISE LINE'S STRENGTHS
- lavish recreational and entertainment facilities
- new fleet with unusual, innovative interiors
- value
- clear, easy-to-use literature
- variety of dining venues
- quality of cuisine for price category

CRUISE LINE'S SHORTCOMINGS
- megaliner size
- little relief from crowds and glitz
- lack of outdoor promenade deck on some ships
- long lines for facilities and services

FELLOW PASSENGERS From all walks of life, ages 3 to 93. Although Carnival's image has been that of a shipload of young swingers partying day and night (an image Carnival once cultivated to attract young people to cruising), the mix now is more likely to range from Joe Sixpack and his Nike-shod kids to Lester and Alice celebrating their 50th wedding anniversary. The cruises lend themselves to families with or without kids, honeymooners, married couples, singles, and seniors. Average age: 43. On a typical cruise, 40% are ages 35–55; 30% younger than 35 (including 575,000 kids annually); 30% older than 55. Fifty percent are repeat cruisers, and of those, 70% are Carnival repeaters. Most have middle to upper-middle income.

Recommended for First-time cruisers who want an active, high-energy, party atmosphere; families, young singles, and couples; young-at-heart of any age; those who enjoy Las Vegas glitz or similar ambience.

Not recommended for Small-ship devotees; sophisticated travelers who prefer ultraluxury and individual travel; anyone seeking a quiet or cerebral travel experience; those who consider Martha's Vineyard their ideal vacation spot.

CRUISE AREAS AND SEASONS Bahamas, Caribbean, Mexican Riviera, and West Coast, year-round. Alaska, Bermuda, Europe, Mediterranean, Greek Isles, Hawaii, and New England/Canada, seasonally.

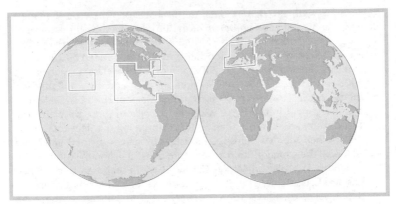

CRUISE AREAS AND SEASONS FOR CARNIVAL CRUISE LINES

THE LINE In 35 short years, Carnival Cruise Lines went from one ship that ran aground on its maiden voyage to becoming the largest, most influential company in the cruise business, having revolutionized the nature of cruises along the way. Its story is the stuff of legends.

The late Ted Arison, a cruise executive in Florida, and a maverick travel company in Boston bought the *Mardi Gras* (formerly the *Empress of Canada*) in 1972. After three years of losses and near bankruptcy, Arison took over the company, assumed its $5 million debt, bought the assets—*the Mardi Gras*—for $1, and created the "Fun Ship" concept, turning a profit in his first year and adding two more ships.

Arison's aim was to take the stuffiness out of cruising, abandon the elitist image on which classic ocean liners had thrived, and make cruises fun and available to everyone, particularly to middle America, who never dreamed of a holiday at sea. He hit the right button. Through the 1970s, Carnival ships broke occupancy records while traditional companies were sinking all around.

Carnival continued to defy conventional wisdom. In the late 1970s, with spiraling shipbuilding costs and the oil crisis putting the future of cruising in doubt, Carnival ordered a new ship, *Tropicale*, whose technology set new industry standards, changed ship profiles, and enhanced Carnival's Fun Ship concept. Then, a decade after its inauspicious beginning, Carnival added three radically new ships—*Holiday, Jubilee,* and *Celebration*—which became trendsetters of the 1980s and beyond. These 1,800-passenger superliners were not the largest passenger ships ever built, but their design and madcap decor were profoundly different from ocean liners of the past.

To prepare for the 21st century, Carnival added eight megaliners, each for over 2,600 passengers, and lifted eyebrows with such names as *Fantasy* and *Ecstasy*. They were followed in 1996 with the 101,000-ton, 3,400-passenger *Carnival Destiny*, the world's largest ship at the time. Carnival was so pleased with her performance and passenger response that it ordered four more like her, each costing $450 million or more.

Along with the *Destiny* class, Carnival started a new class of ships with the 88,500-ton *Carnival Spirit* in 2001, followed by three more of the group. Another new class of 110,000-ton ships started with the *Carnival Conquest* in 2002, with another three of them added by 2005, and a fourth, *Carnival Freedom,* in 2007. Still other new classes will begin in 2008 with the 112,000-ton *Carnival Splendor* and two 130,000-ton ships—*Carnival Dream* in 2009 and *Carnival Magic* in 2011. Carnival's new ship investment in the 1990s exceeded $5 billion; those so far for the 21st century added more than $3 billion, bringing the fleet total to 22 ships. When the new ships for its sister companies—a total of 15—are added in, the expenditure reaches more than $8 billion by 2009.

Under Arison's son Micky—Carnival Corp.'s chairman since 1990— Carnival Cruise Lines' young, aggressive team has marketed cruises as the universal dream vacation for everyone. The line carries about 3.6 million passengers a year.

A publicly held company since 1987, Carnival Corp. broadened its base (and buffed its image) by acquiring the classic Holland America Line and the upscale Windstar Cruises (sold in 2007) in 1989. In the 1990s, it acquired ownership of ultraluxurious Seabourn Cruise Line, Costa Cruises (Europe's largest line), and Cunard Line. More recently, it outmaneuvered Royal Caribbean for the purchase of P&O Princess Cruises, adding six brands to its inventory. These acquisitions give Carnival a total of 85 ships and a huge share of the world cruise market. All 11 lines operate as separate companies, each with a sharp focus; together, they give Carnival Corp. tremendous clout.

In 1999, Carnival became the first major cruise line to launch direct booking on its Web site. In recent years, the line has introduced departures from new gateways, particularly new U.S. ports such as Jacksonville, Florida, and Mobile, Alabama, advancing the "close-to-home" trend following the 9/11 attacks. For 2007, the line is using 18 North America home ports. It launched its first Mediterranean cruise in 2005 and has followed it with a longer season in each subsequent year. Now, it appears, Carnival is getting even more involved in Europe with a new joint venture with the Spanish cruise line Iberojet Cruceros in which Carnival Corp. will own 75% and Orizonia Corp., Iberojet Cruceros' owning company, will have a 25% stake. Iberojet currently operates the 834-passenger *Grand Voyager* and the 1,196-passenger *Grand Mistral,* which are to be transferred to the new joint venture whose fleet is expected to grow over the next several years.

At the same time, Carnival has expanded its focus on families, adding a second children's playroom to all *Fantasy*-class ships and extensive children's facilities on its newest ships. The line carries 575,000 children a year, and its children's program, Camp Carnival, employs one of cruising's largest staffs of trained personnel—more than 100 child counselors spread over 22 ships on a full-time basis, with additional personnel hired during peak periods. Camp Carnival has a reading program, youth fitness and spa programs, hands-on science, education, and art programs, and a kids' dining program. The line added fleetwide the Club O2 teen program developed with The Coca-Cola Company and featuring expanded facilities, a dedicated teen counselor on each ship, and a variety of new activities focusing on art, reading, science, geography, and physical fitness for younger cruisers.

Vacation Guarantee, a Carnival innovation, allows a dissatisfied passenger, after notifying the purser's office, to leave a cruise at the first non–U.S. port of call and get a prorated refund. Another Carnival first is a 24-hour, toll-free hotline—☎ 877-TVL-HTLN (885-4856)—for passengers who encounter a travel emergency (such as severe weather or an airline strike) en route to or returning from their cruise. Passengers outside the United States can call collect: ☎ 305-406-4779. Since 2001, Carnival has had a more flexible dining program along with lighter cuisine.

It offers Internet access for passengers and recently added wireless in the public areas fleetwide; some of the newest ships have wireless from stem to stern, including in cabins. In a joint venture with Wireless Maritime Services, Carnival is outfitting its fleet with technology that enables guests with any cell phone service to make or receive calls as they do on land, no matter how far out to sea they are. Calls are charged at international roaming rates as determined by the carrier and billed directly to passengers' cell phone bills. The technology also enables passengers to send and receive text messages on their phone and wireless devices like Blackberrys.

Not to be outdone by its competitors in the fun-and-games category, Carnival is the first cruise line to offer Water Wars, a popular attraction found in amusement parks in 22 countries. Created by Minnesota-based Water Wars, the units consist of two custom-built "battle stations" in which participants propel water balloons through the air via catapults in an effort to splash their opponents. Located adjacent to the main pool area, the new feature will have been installed fleetwide by summer 2007. The redesigning of the pool deck is part of an ambitious $250 million upgrading and refurbishing of the eight *Fantasy*-class ships to be fully implemented by 2009.

THE FLEET	BUILT/RENOVATED	TONNAGE	PASSENGERS
Carnival Celebration	1987/2000/03/06	47,262	1,486
Carnival Conquest	2002	110,000	2,974
Carnival Destiny	1996	101,353	2,642
Carnival Dream	2009	130,000	3,652
Carnival Ecstasy	1991/2000/06	70,367	2,052
Carnival Elation	1998	70,367	2,052
Carnival Fantasy	1990/2000/03	70,367	2,056
Carnival Fascination	1994/06	70,367	2,052
Carnival Freedom	2007	110,000	2,974
Carnival Glory	2003	110,000	2,974

THE FLEET	BUILT/RENOVATED	TONNAGE	PASSENGERS
Carnival Holiday	1985/94/98/2000	46,052	1,452
Carnival Imagination	1995	70,367	2,052
Carnival Inspiration	1996	70,367	2,052
Carnival Legend	2002	88,500	2,124
Carnival Liberty	2005	110,000	2,974
Carnival Magic	2011	130,000	3,652
Carnival Miracle	2004	88,500	2,124
Carnival Paradise	1998	70,367	2,052
Carnival Pride	2002	88,500	2,124
Carnival Sensation	1993	70,367	2,052
Carnival Spirit	2001	88,500	2,124
Carnival Splendor	2008	112,000	3,006
Carnival Triumph	1999	102,000	2,758
Carnival Valor	2004	110,000	2,974
Carnival Victory	2000	102,000	2,758

STYLE Youthful and casual, Fun Ships have so much action and diversions that the ship itself is the cruise experience. The emphasis on fun aims to get people out of their cabins and into public spaces to become part of the action. The variety of activity and entertainment attracts a range of passengers, but the basic appeal is to the young and young at heart—at reasonable prices.

An important part of creating Carnival has been Joe Farcus, an interior architect and decorator, unique in his role among the cruise lines. He believes people go on vacation to have fun, and his job is to create the surroundings and atmosphere for it. If you accept his flamboyant decor as entertaining, you will find it ingenious. But sometimes, so much bombards the senses that the impact is more exhausting than exhilarating.

Another characteristic: perhaps more than any line, Carnival has standardized features on its ships. If you see a waterslide on one ship, you can count on its being on the others. A menu with four desserts on one ship will be on others. Even deck names are the same. The uniformity helps keep down costs, and consistency is reassuring to passengers—and to their travel agents.

Among Carnival's latest innovations is a new Comfort Bed sleep system with plush mattresses, luxurious duvets, high-quality linens, and comfortable pillows, including a "suite pillow" menu for guests in suite accommodations. The items can be ordered on a special Web site, **www.carnivalcomfortbed.com.** Other new features are children's water parks and Serenity adults-only deck area on the open decks on eight *Fantasy*-class ships. Part of Carnival's $250 million refurbishment, upgrading and enhancement for these ships, the expanded outdoor recreation areas will be added initially to *Inspiration* and *Imagination* in fall 2007 and to the other ships in 2008 and 2009. Carnival has continued to improve its cuisine by hiring renowned French master chef Georges Blanc to create gourmet menus for the line's restaurants fleetwide. Blanc also trained Carnival chefs at his restaurants in France and aboard the line's ships.

Carnival's revamped and enhanced Web site has new and expanded features, including an interactive destination map, virtual tours, a close-to-home cruise locator, and **www.carnivalconnections.com,** an online community where family and friends can meet to plan and manage their cruise. Shore excursions can also be booked on the new Web site. A number of new adventure excursions in Alaska were added recently.

DISTINCTIVE FEATURES Ships' design and decor, children's programs, 24-hour pizzerias, miniature golf, free ice-cream and yogurt stations, sushi bars fleetwide, steakhouse supper clubs, fitness centers, tuxedo rentals, vacation guarantee, golf program, travelers' hotline, self-service digital photo printing kiosks, Internet cafes fleetwide, wireless Internet access, cell phone facilitation, water parks.

	HIGHEST	LOWEST	AVERAGE
PER DIEM	$467	$125	$286

Per diems are calculated from cruise line's nondiscounted *cruise-only* published fares on standard accommodations and vary by season, cabins, and cruise areas.

RATES All include port fees.

Special fares and discounts Super Savers early-bird program provides discounts ranging from up to $860 per cabin on three-day cruises to $2,200 on seven-day cruises.

- **CHILDREN'S FARE:** Same as deeply discounted third-/fourth-person rates. Passengers younger than age 21 must be accompanied by a parent, grandparent, or legal guardian 25 years old or older in the cabin. Exceptions apply to married couples and to children traveling with parents in a separate cabin.
- **SINGLE SUPPLEMENT:** 150% or 200%, depending on category.

Packages
- **CRUISE/AIR ADD-ON WITH TRANSFERS:** Yes.
- **PRE/POST:** Yes. Wedding and vow-renewal packages in U.S. home ports and eight Caribbean ports year-round, plus Vancouver.
- **OTHERS:** Yes.

PAST PASSENGERS Carnival Concierge Club is the line's newly introduced loyalty program, exclusively for "platinum" cardholders—that is, passengers who have sailed on Carnival ten or more times. The program provides cardholders with a staffed concierge desk at the purser's station, dedicated phone line on all Carnival ships, priority embarkation and debarkation and tender boarding, guaranteed supper club reservations and dining times, personalized stationery and custom-designed Carnival logo items, canapés one evening delivered to cabin, $20 entry fee into blackjack tournament, spa priority reservations and complimentary treatment upgrade, complimentary wash-and-fold laundry service, special luggage tags, and welcome letter from Carnival's president. After their first cruise, all passengers receive a two-year subscription to *Currents,* the line's onboard magazine, which includes discounts. A repeater's party is offered on five-day or longer cruises.

THE LAST WORD Carnival has had an enormous impact on cruises, particularly those aimed at the mass market. The line wrote the book on marketing. Yet despite its success, a Carnival cruise isn't for everybody. The ships have more glitter than glamour. Some people love them; others think they redefine tacky. For the generation that grew up with shopping malls and Las Vegas–style glitz, Carnival's gargantuan, flashy ships may feel like home. But if big and boisterous is not your style, Carnival is probably not for you. Everyone should take at least one Carnival cruise to see for themselves, though. The ships are eye-popping and the atmosphere infectious. Even the most staid, buttoned-down party poopers are often turned on by the Carnival neon and end up having the time of their lives.

Note: Carnival Cruise Lines now prohibits passengers from bringing alcoholic and nonalcoholic beverages onboard, including bottles of water. Carnival's policy allows passengers to bring one bottle of wine or Champagne per person (21 years and older) on board only during embarkation at the beginning of the cruise. Any additional quantity of wine, Champagne, alcoholic, and non-alcoholic beverages will be confiscated and discarded without compensation.

Carnival Standard Features

Officers Italian.

Staff International.

Dining facilities Two main dining rooms with four seatings (except *Spirit* class, one dining room). Breakfast and lunch cafeteria-style and Seaview Bistro dinner service in Lido restaurant; midnight buffet. Lido restaurant is four-in-one: pizzeria, Asian, trattoria, American grill. New York–style deli, sushi bars; steakhouse restaurants ($30 surcharge) on newest ships.

Special diets Low-salt, diabetic, vegetarian.

Room service 24 hours, upgraded menu.

Dress code Casual; no shorts in evening; two formal nights on 7-day; tuxedos not required, semiformal dress is acceptable.

Cabin amenities Closed-circuit television; safe. Bath with shower; international direct-dial phones. Hair dryers on *Destiny* and *Spirit* class; other ships on request. Terry robes in outside cabins on most ships.

Electrical outlets 110 AC.

Wheelchair access 14–28 cabins, depending on ship.

Recreation and entertainment Casino, bingo, dance club, library; 10 bar/ lounges (16 on *Spirit* class; 18 *Destiny* class; 22 *Conquest* class); two-deck show lounges (three-deck on *Destiny, Conquest,* and *Spirit* classes).

Sports and other activities Three or four outside swimming pools, shuffle-board, jogging tracks (*Fantasy, Destiny, Spirit* classes), table tennis, volleyball and basketball on some ships.

Beauty and fitness Beauty salon, sauna. Spas on all ships; full gym, exercise classes, body treatments. Spa fare on menus.

Other facilities Boutiques, tuxedo rentals, infirmary, video of cruise souvenir ($39), and coin-operated laundry facilities; Internet cafes fleetwide.

Children's facilities Camp Carnival, year-round, with supervised activities for toddlers to teens. Video arcades, waterslides, playroom, teen club/disco, children's menus, high chairs. Babysitting, 10 p.m.–3 a.m., $6 per hour for first child, $4 for each additional child in same family; children under age 2 also welcome. Passengers under age 21 must be accompanied by adult older than age 25 in same cabin.

Theme cruises Some.

Smoking Smoke-free dining room, main show lounge, selected lounges, and certain areas of the ships.

Carnival suggested tipping $10 per person per day added automatically to passenger's onboard account, which can also be prepaid when booking the cruise; 15% added to wine and bar bill.

Credit cards Cruise and shipboard charges: American Express, MasterCard, Visa, Discover, Optima.

Carnival Ecstasy/ *Carnival Fantasy*	**QUALITY 4**	**VALUE B**
Carnival Elation	**QUALITY 5**	**VALUE B**
Carnival Fascination/ *Carnival Imagination*	**QUALITY 6**	**VALUE A**
Carnival Inspiration	**QUALITY 6**	**VALUE A**
Carnival Paradise	**QUALITY 7**	**VALUE A**
Carnival Sensation	**QUALITY 4**	**VALUE B**
REGISTRY *Ecstasy/Elation/*	**LENGTH 855 feet**	**BEAM 118 feet**
Fantasy/Paradise **Panama;** *Fascination/Imagination /Inspiration/Sensation* **Bahamas**		
CABINS 1,026/1,028	**DRAFT 26 feet**	**SPEED 21 knots**
MAXIMUM PASSENGERS	**PASSENGER DECKS 10**	**ELEVATORS 14**
2,610/2,606	**CREW 920**	**SPACE RATIO 34**

THE SHIPS　Billed as ships for the 21st century, Carnival's eight megaliners were already dazzling passengers of the 1990s. Their flashy decor and high-energy ambience are Las Vegas, Disneyland, and *Starlight Express* all in one. Atrium lobbies ascend seven decks at the heart of the ship and contain huge, specially commissioned art. Throughout the vessels, there are so many imaginatively decorated bars, lounges, and entertainment and recreation outlets that they can't be absorbed in one cruise. On these ships, the senses work overtime.

Except for decor—each ship is themed—the vessels are identical, and as with all Carnival ships, even the deck names are the same. The *Carnival Fantasy*, first of the group, is dazzling with its towering atrium awash in lights. *Fantasy* was given a multimillion-dollar refurbishing in 2005.

The second megaliner, *Carnival Ecstasy,* is designed as a city at sea. Carnival watchers declared her the fleet's most elegant and sophisticated vessel, reflecting an effort to upgrade the style. But there's no mistaking this for anything but a Carnival ship. *Ecstasy's* decor takes inspiration from Manhattan's cafe society, showcasing exotic woods, Italian marbles, rich carpets, sumptuous fabrics, and a vintage Rolls-Royce on the lounge-lined City Lights Boulevard. The promenade's highlights are the **Neon Bar,** a piano bar with vintage neon signs, and **Chinatown Lounge,** guarded by huge lion-headed Foo dogs.

Carnival Sensation, third in the series, resembles *Ecstasy* with decor slightly more sophisticated than her mates'. Light, sound, and color create a "sensual" environment. Public rooms range from elegant to kitschy. Among them, the **Touch of Class Lounge** is a "hands-on" experience, with gigantic hands cupping the entrance, hands supporting tables, and chairs and bar stools shaped like hands.

After being chartered by the U.S. government for Hurricane Katrina relief efforts, *Ecstasy* and *Sensation* (and *Holiday*) were renovated extensively. Both ships got new nine-hole miniature golf courses, spa, gym, art galleries, conference rooms, and enlarged children's play areas. *Ecstasy* got new lighting, flooring, and wall coverings, and dessert stations were added to the Panorama Bar & Grill poolside restaurant. On *Sensation's* promenade, a patisserie and new photo gallery were installed and a redesigned Internet cafe moved to the Empress Deck.

Carnival Fascination takes Hollywood of the 1930s, 1940s, and 1950s as its theme, mixing homage and spoofs—and kitsch galore. On the entertainment promenade, Hollywood Boulevard, are **Puttin' on the Ritz Lounge, Bogey's Café,** and the **Passage to India Lounge**. Purple neon dramatically edges each of the seven decks rising from the Grand Atrium's lobby.

In September 2006, *Fascination* underwent a multimillion-dollar renovation that included a new nine-hole miniature golf course on Sun Deck, a patisserie on Promenade Deck, art gallery, atrium bar, and an enlarged children's play area on Verandah Deck. Other new features include a teen club, part of Carnival's ongoing expansion of its Club 02 teen program; a newly designed Internet cafe and a new conference room. The ship's spa was renovated with new treatment rooms and updated exercise equipment, among other enhancements.

Architect Joe Farcus's fertile imagination worked overtime creating the decor of the bars and lounges for *Carnival Imagination*. The ship's 24-hour pizzeria is now a feature on all Carnival ships. Favorite nightspots include **Shangri-La**, for music and dancing, and **Mirage**, a sing-along piano bar.

Farcus's concept for the *Carnival Inspiration* was drawn from the arts. Decor incorporates musical icons, themes, and motifs—from a larger-than-life replica of Elvis's guitar in the disco to the elegant **Chopin Lounge** and its piano. The ship offers the *Fantasy* group's multideck, glass-domed atrium and dramatic centerpiece, a promenade of lounges and bars, and sports and recreation features. In 2007, *Imagination* and *Inspiration* were renovated and got new features and enhancements similar to those on *Fascination*.

Carnival Elation boasts significant improvements over her *Fantasy* sisters and incorporates some of the best design elements, including the atrium lobby bar copied from *Carnival Destiny* and now a feature of many *Fantasy*-class ships. *Elation* was the first cruise ship with the Azipod propulsion system, which dramatically reduces engine noise and vibration. The system, now installed on many cruise ships, pulls rather than pushes the ship, eliminating the need for rudders or stern thrusters and increasing maneuverability and fuel efficiency.

Elation, the most sophisticated of the *Fantasy*-class ships, has a broader appeal than her older, glitzier sisters, although there is still plenty of glitter. *Elation*'s theme is the mythological Muses. The ship's noticeably more elegant decor uses copper tones and inlaid woods. Prisms and fiber-optic lights create subtle lighting and mood changes. Among new features are a sushi bar, Carnival's largest children's center, a patisserie and coffee bar, a redesigned Lido cafe area, a casino bar, and a conference center.

The eighth member of the group, *Carnival Paradise* was the world's first and only smoke-free cruise ship, with a bright red no-smoking emblem painted on the hull. But when the ship was home-ported on the West Coast, this distinction was dropped. Your first view on boarding *Paradise* is likely to be the atrium, centered by a large circular bar—a feature copied from *Carnival Destiny,* where it has been very popular. Immediately, you notice foot-tall Fabergé-like eggs. Used in decor throughout the ship, they have tiny lights to suggest the diamonds and rubies on Fabergé originals. From the bar, a stairway decorated with three kinds of wood winds upward to the Atlantic Deck, where every lounge recalls maritime history. *Paradise* immortalizes famous steamships in maritime history and evokes the era when travelers boarded famous vessels en route to foreign lands.

The open decks on all eight *Fantasy*-class ships are being transformed with the addition of a children's water park and Serenity adults-only deck area. The expanded outdoor recreation areas are being added first to *Inspiration* and *Imagination* in fall 2007 and to the other ships in 2008 and 2009. The new features are part of Carnival's $250 million refurbishment, upgrading, and enhancement for these ships.

As noted earlier, many enhancements have already been completed on the *Fantasy, Ecstasy,* and *Fascination* and partially executed on the

Sensation, Elation, and *Paradise.* Among them are remodeled cabins and suites, including new bathrooms, flat-screen televisions, atrium lobby bars, updated sound and lighting systems, coffee bars, nine-hole miniature golf courses, new art and photo galleries, New York–style delis in the Lido restaurants, and purpose-built conference facilities. By 2009, the entire *Fantasy-*class fleet will be completed, including the transformation of open deck areas

ITINERARIES *See* Itinerary Index.

CABINS As with all Carnival ships, the 12 cabin categories include some of the largest standard cabins and junior suites of any ship in their price category. They are finished in light oak, and although color schemes vary among ships, the furniture and decor are essentially the same— basic and comfortable.

Almost all cabins have twin beds that convert to king-size—a Carnival innovation quickly copied by other cruise lines. All, too, have the new Comfort Beds, an upgraded set of bed linens, duvets, and pillow menu (in suites only). In the recent *Fascination* refurbishment, cabins and suites got flat-screen televisions, new decor and remodeled bathrooms; *Sensation*'s suites got similar treatment. All *Ecstasy* cabins and suites were completely refurbished. Cabins have international direct-dial phones; a desk/dressing table; television with channels for movies, cartoons, and satellite programs (depending on ship's location); stereo music; and wall safes. Outside cabins have picture windows. Bathrooms are well designed and have roomy shower stalls. They have soap and some toiletries; hair dryers are available on request. Closet space is adequate for short, warm-weather cruises. All ships have self-service laundry rooms with washers, dryers, irons, and ironing boards—a big plus for families traveling with children.

Specifications 389 inside cabins, 564 outside; 54 suites with verandas (28 suites with bathtub Jacuzzi). Standard dimensions, 183–190 square feet; 953 with twins convertible to doubles; 19 inside with upper and lower berths; no singles. All ships have wheelchair-accessible cabins.

DINING Each ship has two dining rooms with two seatings for breakfast and lunch, and four seatings for dinner at 5:45 p.m., 6:15 p.m., 8 p.m., and 8:30 p.m. The rooms are on an upper deck and have large windows with good views.

Restaurants have round tables for eight people in the center of the room; the sides are lined with rectangular tables, which are sometimes difficult to get in and out of. The *Ecstasy*'s **Wind Star** and **Wind Song** and *Elation*'s **Imagination** and **Inspiration** dining rooms get more kudos for stylish decor than their older sisters. All earn criticism for high noise levels. The ships no longer have wine stewards; wine is served by waiters often unfamiliar with the selections.

Breakfast, lunch, and midnight buffet are served cafeteria-style on the Lido Deck. *Fantasy*'s **Windows on the Sea** is one of the group's most attractive restaurants, with pastel parasols, brass highlights, and etched glass. On the *Ecstasy,* the **Panorama Bar and Grill** has floor-to-ceiling windows and a playful ambience with signal flags and blue neon lighting. *Fascination's* **Coconut Grove Bar and Grille** has imitation palm trees as columns and a bamboo bar and tables.

Seaview Bistros, an alternative casual dinner service available fleetwide, offers specialty salads, pastas, steaks, and desserts in a cafe setting. They operate each evening from 6 to 9:30 in the Lido restaurant. Tablecloths, preset silverware, and flowers on tables set the tone. Service is buffet style, but waiters refill drink orders and food requests. Another winner is the around-the-clock pizzeria, offering delicious pizzas with varied toppings, fresh Caesar salads, and warm garlic rolls. All ships have sushi bars.

Carnival initially was not known for its cuisine, but recent efforts to upgrade the quality, selection, and variety have yielded outstanding results. The line has further improved its cuisine by adding gourmet selections created by French master chef Georges Blanc to restaurant menus fleetwide and training its chefs at Blanc's restaurants in France. The line now also offers menus with lighter, more contemporary cuisine and an expanded wine list. On a typical dinner menu there are three juices; four appetizers; three soups; two salads; two fish choices; three entrées of beef, chicken, or turkey; five desserts; and a variety of ice cream and sherbet, cheese, and beverages. At least one item per course is marked as spa fare, which has lower calories, sodium, fat, and cholesterol.

SERVICE Dining staff generally earn good marks, but cabin attendants get mixed reviews. Cruise directors and their staff are very professional, but the cruise director on ships of this size is in little evidence except when he or she is on stage. Recent passengers on *Fantasy* reported that contacting their room steward or the purser's desk by phone was nearly impossible. They also complained that they encountered orientation problems on boarding. Rather than being escorted to their cabins, they were handed ship diagrams and directed to find their cabins on their own. The bottom line: megaliners offer many wonderful facilities and options, but personal service is not among them.

FACILITIES AND ACTIVITIES The ships' array of activities include bingo, a singles party, a newlywed game, a passenger talent show, horse racing, ballroom and country line-dance classes, masquerades, wine and cheese parties, and sing-alongs. There are first-run movies daily and abundant boutiques. The library/lounge—especially the mahogany-paneled **Explorer's Club** on *Ecstasy*—is one of the loveliest rooms in the Carnival fleet.

The *Fantasy* group's most distinctive feature is an indoor promenade that serves as an "entertainment boulevard" of bars, lounges, disco, casino, and nightclubs. Called the Century Boulevard on the *Fantasy,* the promenade has the **Cats Lounge,** with decor inspired by the long-running Broadway show, and **Cleopatra's,** a piano bar with every conceivable cliché in ancient Egyptian art.

At one end of the boulevard, the spectacular two-deck **Universal** show lounge stages nightly entertainment on the scale of a Las Vegas extravaganza. It's outstanding. At the stern is the opulent **Majestic Bar,** with a king's ransom in marble and onyx. Through the bar is the flamboyant **Crystal Lounge,** where red and white lights nearly blind you. Here, you can catch the naughty comedy acts. The casinos, each with more than 200 slot machines, blackjack tables, roulette, and other games, are among the largest afloat.

The most amusing place in the *Fascination*'s nighttime array is **Club 88,** a piano bar named for the 88 keys on a piano and decorated with huge neon-lit keys at the door and on the columns between piano-shaped tables. At the **Passage to India Lounge,** two life-size elephant figures are a prelude to the interior draped with elaborate Indian ceremonial cloth. Furnishings include British Colonial–style mahogany chairs, a statue of a multiarmed Hindu deity, a domed shrine holding a Buddha, mosaic ceiling tiles, and floral carpets. The **Puttin' on the Ritz Lounge,** with decor inspired by Fred Astaire's top hat, offers late-night comedy acts and a vocalist.

Fascination's **Palace Lounge** shimmers in golden beige and silvery pink, with painted clouds decorating the walls. After her recent renovations, the ship has two new production shows: *Fiesta Latina* and *Far From Over: the 80s*—two lavish revues featuring fast-paced musical numbers and elaborate costumes and sets. To accommodate the extensive technical capabilities of these two new shows, the Palace Lounge was completely overhauled and a new revolving turntable, orchestra pit, and recessed speaker system, along with new stage lighting and a computerized audio/visual communications network, were added.

On the *Sensation*, the popular **Michelangelo Lounge** combines soft gray, yellow, and black in its furnishings and uses classic features, such as Ionic columns, Greek designs, and ceiling frescoes. The bar and dance floor are marble. Passengers have a range of new entertainment options on board with a fresh Vegas-style show with music that harkens back to the 1980s. The **Polo Lounge** was designed for those seeking a quiet spot—all the ships have at least one such lounge.

The *Elation*'s **Mikado** showroom (named after the Gilbert and Sullivan operetta) strikes a Japanese theme with large fans, rice-paper shoji walls, Japanese-motif upholstery, and gold-leaf bamboo and chrysanthemum designs sandblasted onto black fossil stone walls and tables. **Duke's** piano bar evokes Manhattan in the Jazz Age, paying tribute to Duke Ellington. Decor includes replicas of famous New York sights. A bar encircles a white baby grand piano on a turntable. The **Jekyll and Hyde Dance Club** has eight-foot-tall sculptures of Robert Louis Stevenson's fictional character with split faces, meant to convey benevolence and malice. The heads swivel to the music's tempo, and monitors set into the sculptures show live pictures of dancing guests and music videos.

On the *Paradise*, all public rooms are named for ocean liners. The **Blue Riband Library,** namesake of the international prize awarded for the fastest transatlantic crossing, pays tribute to the ships of yore in miniature models and old photographs. It contains a full-scale reproduction of the gold and onyx Hales Trophy, models of ships that won the prize, and memorabilia, including a signed photo of the Duke and Duchess of Windsor on Cunard's *Queen Elizabeth*.

In eye-popping contrast, the **America Bar** across from the library is named for the SS *America* and all but screams U.S.A. with its red, white, and blue color scheme, starred carpet, and stars and stripes on the walls. At the stern, the 1,300-seat, two-story **Normandie** show lounge carries an Art Deco theme and celebrates the French liner considered by some to be the best ship ever built. Another showroom, the **Queen Mary Lounge,** uses funnels from the great ship as the motif to line the bar and walls, frame the seats, and serve as table bases. From the Italian liner *Rex,* designer Farcus took the Latin meaning of *rex* (king) and conjured up the king of the jungle, giving the **Rex Dance Club** a jungle theme.

SPORTS AND FITNESS   Three swimming pools (one with a slide), Ping-Pong, shuffleboard, and volleyball are available, and pool games are staged almost daily. On Caribbean and Mexican cruises, depending on ports, you can play golf, sail, ride horseback, bike, hike, snorkel, scuba dive, and windsurf.

The sports deck has a fully equipped gym with trained instructors, separate locker rooms, dressing rooms, showers for men and women, six whirlpools, saunas, and steam rooms. Or one can choose from an array of exercise and aerobics classes, and a 500-foot outside jogging track—all included in the cruise price. Instructors will also create a fitness regimen for you to follow at home. Most Carnival ships have a secluded deck area for topless sunbathing.

Carnival's golf program provides play at 50 courses in the Bahamas, Caribbean, Hawaii, Europe, and Mexico. It offers one-on-one, 30- or 60-minute instruction from PGA teaching pros aboard ship and on golf excursions. Shipboard lessons are in a netted driving range where golfers' swings are videotaped and computer-analyzed. A take-home video with voice-over instruction and stop-action/slow-motion analysis is provided with each lesson. Golf packages include greens fees, instruction, cart rental or caddie, and transportation to and from courses. Prices range from $50 for onboard lessons to $225 for golf excursions. Equipment rentals include Nike-brand clubs and "soft spike" golf shoes and apparel.

SPA AND BEAUTY   The beauty salon and spa, operated by the Steiner Group, a British-based company, has nine private rooms for body and facial treatments—including facials, pedicures, massage, and herbal packs. Any of them can become an expensive indulgence. The spas on all ships in the group have been or are being expanded. During its recent renovations, *Sensation* got a totally new spa and gym on the Sports Deck, with body and facial treatments for women and men and ranging from a couples massage to the highly popular Gentle Touch Tooth Whitening ($199 for 40 minutes). The adjoining fitness center has Life Fitness equipment along with a full-body workout circuit and an aerobics studio with yoga, Pilates, or spinning classes. The facility is staffed from 7 a.m. to 8 p.m. Similar spa renovations are being done to all the *Fantasy*-class ships.

CHILDREN'S FACILITIES   Camp Carnival, which handles 575,000 kids fleetwide annually, is a year-round program with a wide array of activities supervised by trained counselors for children in four age groups: toddlers (ages 2–5), juniors (ages 6–8), intermediate (ages 9–11), and teens (ages 12–14). Young children enjoy puppet making, finger painting, and learning the alphabet and numbers; older kids have pizza parties, scavenger hunts, and lip-synch contests and play bingo, charades, and Twister. Teens can participate in the new Club O2 program with activities ranging from disco parties and star-search contests to evening deck parties. All ships have video arcades, wading pools, waterslides, playrooms (two on *Fantasy* class), teens' club/discos, children's menus, and high chairs.

One playroom is designed for kids ages 6–11 and is stocked with age-appropriate toys, games, and puzzles, including such popular pastimes as air hockey, foosball, and "pop-a-shot" basketball, along with the latest video games. The other playroom is geared toward toddlers.

Elation and *Paradise* have among Carnival's largest children's facilities, which are divided into three sections. One features an educational computer lab and computer games. The arts and crafts section has spin art, sand art, jewelry-making machines, easels for painting and drawing, and a gallery for displaying participants' creations. The third is an indoor play area with a climbing maze, toys, games, and a video wall where kids can watch movies, music videos, and cartoons. The outdoor play area has a schooner-shaped playhouse and a wading pool for toddlers. Teens get special attention, too, with **Virtual World**, photography workshops, late-night movies, and disco parties.

The latest additions include a youth fitness and spa program, introduced on *Carnival Miracle* and now available fleetwide, allowing kids ages 12–14 and their parents to have body and beauty treatments together on port days at discounted rates. Also featured is ExerSeas, a recreational fitness program designed to encourage kids to enjoy a diversity of fun physical activity from obstacle courses and basketball to popular games. A-B-Seas is a new reading program in which the youth counselors read popular children's books to parents and kids in the ships' libraries, followed by parents and kids presenting their own creative interpretations of the stories through puppet shows, skits, and other group activities. A science program, H2Ocean, offers a variety of fun, hands-on science projects, allowing kids to make their own ice cream or miniature hovercrafts. The EduCruise program has been expanded to include more interactive projects focusing on the cultures, landmarks, history, and geography of the ships' destinations. Kid-friendly dining options include special children's menus in the main dining rooms and a program that enables kids to dine with the youth counselors on Lido Deck. Recently, the line added new teen shore excursions and Club O2 teen clubs on most ships.

On *Sensation*, Camp Carnival, with bright blue, orange, yellow, red and green kid-size tables, cabinets, bench sofas and cushy carpeting, is now relocated to the Verandah Deck's atrium area overlooking the main pool. Club O2 for teens ages 15–17 on the Promenade Deck also was refurbished.

Camp Carnival operates 9 a.m.–10 p.m. At 10 p.m., babysitting is available in the form of slumber parties for $6 per hour for the first child, $4 for each additional child. Carnival has a Fountain Fun-Card for those younger than age 18, good for unlimited sodas from the bars and costing $12 on a 3-day cruise, $28 on a 7-day cruise. For those 18 and older, the card costs $16.50 and $38.50, respectively.

More custom-designed spaces geared toward 12- to 14-year-olds are also planned, and more than 50 interconnecting cabins are being added to several *Fantasy*-class ships.

SHORE EXCURSIONS Passengers can review shore excursions and make reservations online at **www.carnivalcruises.com** after paying for their cruise. Recently, Carnival has greatly expanded the quality and variety of shore excursions it offers. Nonetheless, dockside in almost all Caribbean ports are plenty of vans with drivers/guides eager for your business and ready to design a tour to your liking. Prices depend on your ability to bargain and the driver's eagerness, but always agree on a fee before the tour begins.

An air/sea package is recommended for cruises departing from Port Canaveral combined with Orlando attractions because the Orlando International Airport, where most passengers arrive, is about an hour's drive from Port Canaveral, where the ships depart. There is no public transportation between the two; those traveling on their own must hire a taxi or rent a car. Or, those booking cruise-only can buy Carnival's transfer package. Also, if you buy the Orlando package, plan to take the Spaceport USA bus tour on the day you sail. That way, the full morning can be spent at Spaceport USA, about 20 minutes from Port Canaveral. A late lunch is available aboard ship until 3:30 p.m. In Alaska, the line offers excursions for teens, along with nearly 100 tours for all ages.

Carnival Destiny	**QUALITY 8**	**VALUE A**
Carnival Triumph	**QUALITY 8**	**VALUE A**
Carnival Victory	**QUALITY 8**	**VALUE A**
REGISTRY *Destiny*/	**LENGTH 893 feet**	**BEAM 125 feet**
Triumph Bahamas; *Victory* Panama		
CABINS 1,321/1,379	**DRAFT 27 feet**	**SPEED 22.5 knots**
MAXIMUM PASSENGERS	**PASSENGER DECKS 12**	**ELEVATORS 18**
3,400/3,470	**CREW 1,050/1,100**	**SPACE RATIO 37/38**

THE SHIPS The *Carnival Destiny* was the largest cruise ship ever built when she made her debut in 1996 and was the first one too wide to transit the Panama Canal. When the ship was being planned six years earlier, Carnival employees were asked to submit their wish lists for enhancing the new vessel. Apparently, they got most of their wishes.

The *Destiny* had Carnival's first double-deck dining room; a show lounge spanning three decks; a double-width promenade lined with lounges and bars; a mall-style shopping area; a 9,000-square-foot casino; 18 bars and lounges; four swimming pools and an expansive spa; a retractable glass dome over the pool area; and sports and recreation facilities similar to the *Fantasy*-class ships. The pool area has a stage for entertainment and teak decks cantilevered in an amphitheater. **Virtual World** is a high-tech virtual reality game center. In 2005, after a multi-million dollar renovation, an expansive new teen club was added.

Destiny's configuration was a departure for Carnival at the time. Entertainment and recreation decks are between accommodations decks. The two lowest passenger decks have only cabins, followed by three decks of public rooms, then five decks of cabins and suites with balconies. To avoid big rooms and long corridors that would make the ship's huge size obvious, public rooms span two or three levels. The layout is often confusing, however.

Despite her size—nearly three football fields in length—*Destiny* does not seem as large from the inside as some of her *Fantasy*-class cousins. This is primarily because of the layout and the decor, which is softer and toned down—sometimes even tony—a change from Farcus's flamboyant creations on other Carnival ships.

The Rotunda (**Capital Lobby** on *Triumph*; **Seven Seas Atrium** on *Victory*), a nine-deck atrium with four glass elevators and a glass dome, is the ship's focal point. An enormous marble and onyx mural of geometric forms suggesting skyscrapers decorates the walls. The atrium has an attractive lobby bar at its base, creating a meeting place that helps humanize the huge space.

The *Carnival Triumph,* which debuted in 1999, built on *Destiny*'s success but incorporated new features, including an extra deck of cabins. Sixty percent of cabins have ocean views with a sitting area, and more than 60% of those have verandas. The ship celebrates the world's great cities, with such venues as **Underground Tokyo** video arcade, the **Rome Theater, Vienna Café** coffee bar, and **Oxford Bar.** A huge golden globe dominates the atrium; it's inlaid with glittering fiber optics that mark the world's metropolises. Smaller globes are part of the decor shipwide. The new Panorama Deck, one level above the Lido Deck, has 42 ocean-view cabins, most with verandas, and 24 inside ones, adding capacity for 132 guests. *Carnival Victory,* whose theme is the seven seas, arrived in August 2000.

ITINERARIES *See* Itinerary Index.

CABINS The group's standard cabins are the largest and the most attractively furnished in the Carnival fleet. All have hair dryers and safes; some have interactive television. Cabin numbers pinpoint your deck and location (forward, aft, or midship). Each section has its own elevators. Sixty percent of standard outside cabins have small balconies, all with clear panels for unobstructed ocean views. Unfortunately, they do nothing to absorb sound. This and insufficient soundproofing make the cabins noisy. Particularly to be avoided are cabins on Deck 6 forward, which are directly above lounges that operate most of the night. Ocean-view cabins have a sitting area with sofa and coffee table. Family cabins are near the children's play facilities. In the 2005 renovations, *Destiny*'s suites were upgraded.

Specifications 515 inside cabins, 432 outside with verandas; 48 suites with verandas, some with bathtub whirlpools. Standard dimensions, 220–260 square feet; all cabins with twins convertible to kings; 4 inside with upper and lower berths; no singles; 25 *Destiny,* 27 *Triumph, Victory* wheelchair-accessible cabins.

DINING Carnival's first bi-level dining rooms feel roomy, and the additional space allows wider separation between tables. But the restaurants are noisy. Both dining rooms enjoy ocean views.

The two-deck **Sun & Sea (South Beach Club** on *Triumph;* **Mediterranean** on *Victory*), the casual Lido restaurant, is dressed in shades of green with yellow, hand-blown Murano glass and hand-painted ceramic tile decorating walls and countertops. Different settings create dining options: Trattoria for pasta and made-to-order Italian dishes; Happy Valley for Chinese cuisine, stir-fried to order; and The Grille for hamburgers and hot dogs. Service has also been upgraded; waiters carry dishes and beverages to tables. The **Seaview Bistro** alternative dinner service in the Lido restaurant offers specialty salads, pastas, steaks, and desserts—plus a daily special—in a cafe setting. The bistro operates 6–9:30 each evening. Also open are a 24-hour pizzeria and, on the Promenade deck, a patisserie appointed with cherry wood counters and windowed banquettes. *Carnival Victory* has a New York–style deli.

FACILITIES AND ACTIVITIES In the evening, you are likely to run out of energy before you run out of choices. The flashy **Millionaire's Club (Club Monaco** on *Triumph;* **South China Sea Club** on *Victory*), is one of the largest casinos afloat, has more than 200 slot machines and 23 table games. In the lavishly decorated **Apollo Bar,** the piano revolves, enabling the pianist to shine a spotlight on anyone eager to test the microphone on each table.

At the whimsically decorated **Downbeat,** where a 20-foot trumpet and French horn are suspended above the bandstand, patrons sit on clarinet-shaped barstools or at glass tables supported by oversize sections of horns.

In the **Point After Dance Club,** tricolor neon lights snake across the ceiling above a bi-level floor, and more than 500 video monitors flash pictures and computer-generated graphics around the room. A staircase by the dance floor leads to the elegant **Onyx Room,** a more sedate club where backlit alabaster panels glow softly beside a neon-and-glass dance floor.

The three-deck **Palladium** show lounge, the venue for Vegas-style production shows, is one of the most technologically sophisticated afloat. The additional deck below seating levels allows the orchestra pit to be retracted, and the space above enables backdrops, lighting equipment, and performers to be "flown" offstage via cables. A Venetian glass chandelier hangs from the dome; at show time, it goes high-tech with fiber optics.

To achieve three decks of seats for 1,400 people, some sacrifices were made. The main floor is almost level, making viewing more difficult the farther back one sits. Also, balcony rails partially block some views. The big production shows are top-notch.

Yet more entertainment is offered in **Virtual World,** a game center with virtual-reality and electronic games, and **All Star Bar,** decorated with celebrity memorabilia, including tables bearing autographs of sports stars, and featuring seven big-screen televisions broadcasting sporting events.

SPORTS, FITNESS, AND BEAUTY *Destiny* has four pools, including a children's pool, and seven whirlpools. One has Carnival's trademark waterslide—but here, it is three decks tall and 214 feet long. A retractable dome covers the aft pool.

The 14,500-square-foot spa and health club is on two levels, one with a beauty salon, massage rooms, whirlpools, and sauna and steam rooms, the other with an aerobics room. The spa offers hydrotherapy baths, aromatherapy, and other body treatments. There is also a "Nouveau Yu Health Environment Capsule," an egglike temperature-controlled capsule designed to induce relaxation. The gym has an array of equipment, including bikes, treadmills, step and rowing equipment, and 16 Keiser or Life-Fitness machines. Instructors lead exercise classes and can be hired as personal trainers. An eighth-mile jogging track is on the sun deck. On the *Triumph*, more open space was provided on the Lido Deck for deck chairs, and the forward and aft pools were enlarged and bordered by "wading" areas.

CHILDREN'S FACILITIES The two-deck-tall, 1,300-square-foot indoor and outdoor play center includes a jungle gym and pool. See the *Fantasy* profile for information on Carnival's children's program.

Carnival Legend	QUALITY 8	VALUE A
Carnival Miracle	QUALITY 8	VALUE A
Carnival Pride	QUALITY 8	VALUE A
Carnival Spirit	QUALITY 8	VALUE A
REGISTRY Panama	LENGTH 963 feet	BEAM 105.7 feet
CABINS 1,062	DRAFT 25.7 feet	SPEED 22 knots
MAXIMUM PASSENGERS	PASSENGER DECKS 12	ELEVATORS 15
2,667	CREW 930	SPACE RATIO 40

THE SHIPS *Carnival Spirit*, the first of a new class of ships for Carnival, entered service in 2001, followed by triplets: *Carnival Pride* and *Carnival Legend* in 2002, and *Carnival Miracle* in 2004. They are among the longest ships in the Carnival fleet, but they still can pass through the Panama Canal. The ships have a number of environmentally friendly technical enhancements, and their technologically advanced Azipod propulsion system enables them to reach a maximum speed of 24 knots, and thus sail on innovative itineraries. The ships boast an exceptional space ratio of 40 (the *Fantasy* class is 34, *Destiny* class, 37) with the usual array of Carnival amenities and facilities, and some new ones, such as the first Carnival ships with a wedding chapel, and more recently, self-service digital-photo printing kiosks, now available fleetwide.

The theme of *Carnival Spirit* is design, particularly architectural design (which makes for an eclectic mix of decor), while that of *Carnival Pride* is icons of beauty, which gave Farcus's active mind neverending inspiration—from architecture and artistic masterpieces to athletic achievement and the human body. The beauty icons start with Renaissance inspiration in the atrium lobby, elevator, and stairwell areas, where huge reproductions of murals by Botticelli, Raphäel, and other Italian painters adorn the walls. Here, too, the craftsmanship of the Italian Renaissance is reflected in rich details of wood and bronze moldings, and it's dominated by gold, sienna, and burnt-red tones.

Carnival Legend's motif is inspired by great legends of history, from the ancient Greeks in the atrium, to modern jazz in the New Orleans design of **Satchmo's Club,** and the Art Deco of **Billie's Piano Bar,** named for blues legend Billie Holiday. *Carnival Miracle* has fictional characters as its theme—but Harry Potter is not among them. *Carnival Miracle* has Tampa as her home port year-round.

The ships' interior promenade meanders through public rooms on two consecutive decks, linking the ship's two atriums with its dining rooms, more than a dozen bars, lounges and entertainment venues, and a shopping arcade that includes a tuxedo rental and flower shop. The ships also have a wraparound outdoor promenade on Atlantic Deck—the first for a Carnival ship in two decades. All the *Spirit-* and *Conquest-*class ships have an upscale supper club located atop a towering 11-deck-high atrium, and a large percentage of balconied cabins. They have a two-level dining room; large poolside food courts offering casual breakfast, lunch, and dinner; a 24-hour pizzeria; and a sushi bar. *Spirit-*class ships have 16 lounges, ranging from an elaborate, multilevel showroom for Vegas-style revues, to an intimate piano bar, a casino, shopping mall, wedding chapel, video game room, and Internet cafe. There are several swimming pools—including one with a spiral waterslide—a spa and gym, a Camp Carnival program for kids ages 2–15, and a comprehensive golf program.

CABINS   The ships have several levels of suites with private balconies and set a new standard for outside cabins, 80% of which have private balconies. Many cabins can accommodate up to four guests; other are interconnecting and are ideal for large families.

Specifications   213 inside cabins, 99 outside, 624 outside with balconies, 68 with French doors; 52 suites, 6 penthouses, 16 wheelchair-accessible.

DINING   Each ship has three restaurants. *Pride*'s main dining room, the **Normandie Restaurant,** (**Empire** on *Spirit;* **Golden Fleece** on *Legend*), spanning two decks with wraparound windows, has elegant decor based on the famous ocean liner *Normandie,* one of the most beautiful passenger vessels ever built.

Spirit's unusual **Nouveau Supper Club,** Carnival's first alternative restaurant (reservations only; $30 charge), is situated topside with one end bordering the ship's huge red-glass smokestack and the other extending out over the top of the ship's multideck atrium. Menu specialties are prime aged beef, seafood, and other gourmet selections. The restaurant's counterpart on the *Pride* is **David's Supper Club,** with a full-size replica of the famous Michelangelo sculpture, *David,* celebrating the beauty of the human body.

The **Mermaids' Grille,** the ship's Lido restaurant, has a variety of food stations, each offering a different type of cuisine and including a 24-hour pizzeria.

FACILITIES AND ACTIVITIES The ships seem to have a dance floor at every turn. From the **Beauties Dance Club** to the **Starry Night** jazz club and the grand **Taj Mahal** show lounge. On the *Pride,* a famous Van Gogh painting was the inspiration for the Starry Night jazz club (**Club Cool** on *Spirit*). The beauty of ideas and intellectual achievement is enshrined in the **Nobel Library,** with a portrait of Alfred Nobel, who created the famous prize. The room also houses the Internet cafe. The beauty of experience is represented in the **Perfect Game** sports bar and the **Winner's Club** casino. **Butterflies Lounge** draws on natural beauty with faux windows decorated with colorful transparent fabrics that resemble butterfly wings. The fabrics disappear under special lights that illuminate the flocks of butterflies behind. Four different butterfly patterns are seen in the upholstery. Architectural beauty is celebrated in the Taj Mahal show lounge (**Pharaoh's Palace** on *Spirit*), filled with intricate Indian designs and stonework sparkling with small jewels pressed into decorative designs. Infrared listening devices for hearing-impaired passengers are available in the main lounge on most *Spirit*-class ships.

Other highlights include a chapel suitable for weddings or religious services, ice-cream/frozen yogurt bar, and a large conference center.

SPORTS, FITNESS, AND BEAUTY The ships' **Spa Carnival** is a two-level health and fitness facility, along with huge open decks and three swimming pools, one with a two-deck-high waterslide plus a children's wading pool. One of the pools is heated and has a sliding glass roof, known as a magrodome—ideal for Alaska, where *Carnival Spirit* spends her summers. A golf program, managed by Elite Golf Cruises of Florida, includes private lessons, digital teaching technology, and packages for shoreside play with priority tee times; it's $45 for excursions or $50 for a half-hour lesson and video. Equipment rental is available for an additional fee. Advance tee times can be made at ☎ 800-324-1106.

CHILDREN'S FACILITIES A variety of new and expanded family-friendly amenities have been added fleetwide to the Camp Carnival and include choices from fun, educational geography classes and candy-making machines to special family activities on a private island, teens-only shore excursions, and "just-for-kids" port lectures. **Fun Club,** located forward on Upper Deck 5 and decorated with a colorful undersea motif, is divided into three areas. The first area houses an arts and crafts center, the second has a computer lab, and the third has a playroom stocked with toys and games, a video wall displaying movies and cartoons, and kid-sized tables and chairs. An outdoor play area has a mini-basketball hoop and other playground equipment. **Real Virtuality,** a high-tech game room housing video and arcade games, is one deck below Camp Carnival.

A turndown service offering freshly baked chocolate chip cookies on formal nights is available. So too is the fleetwide Fountain Fun Card, a soft drink program for unlimited sodas, costing from $12 for three-day cruises to $28 for seven-day cruises for those under age 18 (18 and over, $16.50 and $38.50, respectively); and there are kids' menus. Babysitting is available 10 p.m.–3 a.m. in the children's playroom for $6 per hour for the first child and $4 for each additional child in the same family. Strollers are available for rent at $6 per day and $25 for the week.

Carnival Conquest	QUALITY 8	VALUE A
Carnival Freedom	PREVIEW	
Carnival Glory	QUALITY 8	VALUE A
Carnival Liberty	QUALITY 8	VALUE A
Carnival Valor	QUALITY 8	VALUE A
REGISTRY Panama	LENGTH 952 feet	BEAM 116 feet
CABINS 1,486	DRAFT 27 feet	SPEED 22.5 knots
MAXIMUM PASSENGERS	PASSENGER DECKS 13	ELEVATORS 15
3,700	CREW 1,160	SPACE RATIO 37

THE SHIPS *Carnival Conquest,* which made her debut in New Orleans in 2002, kicked off delivery of the largest class of vessels in the fleet. She also was the first to have her interior decor tied directly to her home port. Using the ship's interiors as a huge canvas, designer Joe Farcus created something of an ode to Impressionist and Postimpressionist art and the Big Easy's French legacy.

The main atrium, called the **Atelier,** has Impressionist paintings on the central ceiling dome and wall; the **Artists' Lobby** is dominated by a large hand-painted mural collage of famous paintings. The collage effect is picked up in the promenade and in other public areas throughout the ship.

Her sister ship, *Carnival Glory,* which arrived in 2003, takes colors as a theme, with each public room done in different shades of the rainbow and reflected in their name and decor. The kaleidoscope of colors begins in the Colors lobby, **Color Bar,** and the main atrium, named **Old Glory** after the United States flag. Each deck was given a different color; looking up through the atrium, it's easy to see the color definition of each deck. **Kaleidoscope Boulevard** has one-square-meter light fixtures subdivided into geometric modules that are backlit with strips of color. The result is thousands of tones in a slow-moving kaleidoscope.

Carnival Valor, inspired by its name, has heroes and heroism—real and imagined—as its theme. *Carnival Liberty,* launched in 2005, celebrates artisans and their craft. She debuted the line's first Mediterranean and Greek Isles summer with 12-day cruises round-trip from Rome (Civitavecchia).

Carnival Freedom, scheduled to be launched in Europe in 2007 with a series of Mediterranean cruises, has design as her theme and takes passengers on a journey of styles through the centuries—from ancient Babylon to the heyday of disco, from the 19th-century Victorian era to the contemporary style of the 1990s. In an unprecedented promotion, nine watercolors and pencil murals by Massachusetts-based artist Joan Barber, commissioned for *Carnival Freedom* and part of the ship's multi-million-dollar art collection, were on display at Flomenhaft Gallery in Manhattan four months prior to the ship's debut. *Freedom's* itineraries include the line's first-ever visit to the Greek Isles and Turkey.

The ships of the *Conquest* group have 22 lounges and bars, four swimming pools, a 214-foot-long waterslide, an Internet cafe, a 13,300-square-foot health club, a comprehensive golf program, and four restaurants, including an upscale reservations-only supper club, two bi-level main dining rooms, a sushi bar, a patisserie, and a 1,200-seat casual poolside restaurant.

Carnival Valor also scored a first—the first cruise ship to offer 100% stem-to-stern wireless Internet access, enabling passengers to surf the net from every public room, the pool decks, and any cabin. *Carnival Liberty* and *Carnival Freedom* have this technology as well.

ITINERARIES   *See* Itinerary Index

CABINS   By Carnival standards, the cabins are exceptionally low-key and understated, dressed in soft pastels and lovely rich wood that blends with the soft colors. They are also large for ships in this category, ranging from 185 square feet for a standard inside cabin to 220 square feet for a deluxe balcony cabin. A wall unit has a dresser/desk with drawers and cabinets; safe; minifridge; television with CNN, BBC, Discovery Channel, and other channels such as ABC, CBS, and NBC when available; and three closets that should be ample for most people on a week's cruise. All outside cabins have a sofa; most are sofa beds. The bathroom with a rather tight shower stall has a dispenser for shampoo and shower gel. All outside cabins get terry robes. There are a larger number of cabins with a small balcony with space for two chairs—and that's about all.

Specifications   10 penthouse suites, 42 suites, 504 outside with balcony, 343 outside without balcony, 18 outside with glass wall, 570 inside cabins, 28 wheelchair-accessible.

DINING   Each ship has two bi-level dining rooms. On *Conquest,* the **Monet** and **Renoir** dining rooms (**Platinum** and **Golden** on *Glory*) are identical architecturally and have panels of wood-veneered images of the Eiffel Tower in the walls and ceiling. The fabrics and colors are based on works by the two painters. *Glory's* dining rooms take their decor from their colors and are elegant in their simplicity—resembling, somewhat, the uncluttered lines of Japanese decor, with only a touch of color from a few hand-painted bonsai and cherry-blossom trees on the walls and ceiling. The rooms are the most crowded of any dining rooms we've experienced on any Carnival ship. Off to each side of *Glory's* Golden dining room is a private dinning room, **Copper** (for 28 people) and **Silver** (for 36 people), which are among the most handsome rooms on the ship. *Conquest's* Renoir Restaurant was inspired by *Lunch at the Restaurant Fournaise,* a tranquil scene of boaters relaxing at a cafe overlooking the Seine, featured in the wall-covering fabric. In the Monet Restaurant, one of the artist's famous *Water Lilies* series sets the motif.

Freedom's **Chic** and **Posh** dining rooms reflect the styles of the 1990s. The mood of the restaurants can be changed dramatically through innovative lighting strips that meander around the rooms and create a sparkling effect through the use of embedded color-changing lightbulbs. The poolside **Freedom Restaurant** incorporates the style of the 1980s with various replications of the Statue of Liberty in the decor. The bi-level **Restaurant Cezanne** (**Red Sail** on *Glory*, **Rosie's** on *Valor*) on the Lido Deck has the atmosphere of a 19th-century French cafe. In addition to Carnival's standard variety of Italian, Chinese, and other food stations, there are hamburgers and hot dogs, a 24-hour pizzeria, and a self-service ice-cream and frozen yogurt station. The restaurant is also the venue for an upscale seafood station on the second level of the Lido restaurant. **Café Fans** (**Creams** on *Glory*) on Promenade Deck is a patisserie serving a variety of coffees and rather pricey desserts; next door is a sushi bar. And there's 24-hour room service with new, expanded menus.

The Point, high on Panorama Deck, is *Conquest*'s reservations-only supper club, named for the style of Georges Seurat, known as pointillism, which renders images through thousands of individual dots, or points, of color. *Glory*'s **Emerald Room** has light fixtures resembling giant emeralds and a huge medallion on the wall made up of hundreds of these light fixtures. *Liberty*'s Harry's, named for famed jeweler Harry Winston, is bedecked with jeweled decor; *Freedom*'s **Sun King Supper Club,** named after Louis XIV, reflects the opulence of the 18th century with elaborate tapestries, antique mirrors, an impressive chandelier, and a large mural depicting the royal court. For structural reasons, the club is divided into two separate rooms (rather than the large open space by the funnel as on the line's *Spirit* class). **Scarlett's,** inspired by *Gone With the Wind,* is *Carnival Valor*'s alternative restaurant, with a small combo that plays music for dancing. The cost is $30 per person. In our experience, Carnival's alternative restaurants are excellent, with food and service top-notch and well worth the extra charge. Reserve early in your cruise, as they are very popular and fill up fast.

FACILITIES AND ACTIVITIES The **Toulouse-Lautrec Lounge,** the main show lounge, takes its inspiration from the painter's sketches, which were drawn from the subjects he saw in the cabarets, circuses, and brothels of Paris's Montmartre. To the sides of the stage are the famous windmill signs of the Moulin Rouge cabaret; the windmill motif is repeated in the carpet. *Glory*'s **Amber Palace,** the most extravagant room on the ship, is named after Russia's famous Amber Room (now reconstructed and open to the public) in the palace of Peter the Great. The wall covering, for example, replicates the mosaics of amber as they are on the palace walls; hanging from the ceiling is an enormous crystal chandelier, with smaller ones at the sides of the room. The Russian eagle is designed into the room's carpet, and the cut velvet covering on the seats would suit any czar's palace. *Freedom*'s **Victoriana** show lounge, named after Britain's Queen Victoria, is designed to evoke theaters in London's West End, with ornate moldings, fancy marble, and gold leaf. For those who take a backstage tour, the state-of-the-art stage and equipment is on par with the latest of Broadway.

The two shows on *Glory, Livin' in America* and *Rock Down Broadway,* are in keeping with the Carnival tradition of fast-paced Vegas-style revues that blend choreography with elaborate sets and costumes. *Rock Down Broadway* is one of the best shows we have ever seen on any cruise ship—or on Broadway, for that matter. *Carnival Valor* has *Far From Over: the 80s,* a tribute to the music and the movies of the 1980s, and *Nightclub Express,* a rollicking tour—hosted by a talking, singing sofa!—of ten famous cabarets and nightspots (with different sets, costumes, and music appropriate to each). The shows were produced by Carnival Productions, the line's in-house entertainment group. The show lounges of this group boasts the latest in shipboard technology, such as "fly-in" scenery capabilities; a turntable stage with built-in lifts allowing for multiple sets; a multimillion-dollar sound and lighting system, including laser pods; and a rising orchestra pit.

Conquest's **Tahiti Casino** and **Gauguin's Bar,** a sports bar, recall Postimpressionist Paul Gauguin's paintings of Polynesia. **Henri's Dance Club** takes its theme from the exotic jungle paintings of Henri Rousseau. Painted metal cutouts, meant to look like the coarse grass of Rousseau's paintings, are mounted on the wall, with occasional three-dimensional animal heads, similar to those lurking in the artist's works. *Glory's* **Camel Club Casino** is a bit incongruous. The camel color inspired Farcus to install statues of reclining camels (which kids love to climb, despite a sign reading "No one under 18 years of age is allowed in the Casino"), but from the camels it's a stretch to the main decor, meant to reflect the age of European rediscovery of ancient Egypt and the Orient. *Freedom's* **Babylon Casino** takes its theme from the famed Hanging Gardens of ancient Babylon. A reproduction of the legendary Ishtar Gate is done in blue-glaze brick with mythological animals, flowers, and geometric designs, and columns with Babylonian winged figures are placed throughout the casino.

On *Glory,* the **White Heat Dance Club** has gigantic white candles, 12 to 18 inches in diameter, in silver candelabra bases from two to five feet tall and giving off imaginary white heat. One deck below, the multipurpose **Ivory Club** has an Indian theme set off with elephant tusk replicas, and the bar stools and table bases replicate elephant feet. Across the way, the **Burgundy Bar** is a wine bar; **Cinn-a-Bar,** a piano bar; and the **Bar Blue,** taking its "blue" from giant peacock feathers in the motif, is the ship's jazz bar. The **Ebony Cabaret,** a multifunction showroom with African decor, is one of *Glory's* most successful rooms, using ebony wood, African textiles, and handsome authentic wooden masks in the decor. **On the Green,** the sports bar, celebrates golf with memorabilia from the game's legends

Carnival Liberty's **Seaside Theatre** has one of the largest LED screens (12 feet by 22 feet) ever installed on a cruise ship. Located poolside on Lido Deck, the facility shows movies, sporting events, concerts, and other programs, including the ship's "Morning Show," hosted by the cruise director.

On *Freedom,* **Player's Sport Bar,** with giant plasma screen televisions, shines with chrome, sports medallions, and memorabilia highlighting the 1950s, often referred to as the "golden era of sports"; **Studio 70** is an updated version of the famed Studio 54 disco in New York; **Bar Nouveau** on the promenade is a step back in time to the 1890s with its Art Nouveau style. There's also the 1940s **Habana Cigar Bar;** the 1770s **Monticello Library;** the 1910s **Scott's** piano bar, named for ragtime piano master Scott Joplin; and the 1930s **Swingtime** jazz club.

Daytime activities range from a Jazz *&* Bloody Mary Party to a Sing-Along or a Men's Hairy Chest Contest; art auctions, trivia quizzes, game shows, and adult comedy shows in the evening round out the offerings. They also have libraries, multipurpose conference centers, boutiques, infirmaries and Internet cafes—$0.75 per minute, or packages of 30 and 60 minutes for slight savings. Cruise e-mail is available for a one-time activation fee of $3.95. Local calls from passengers' cabins are $6.99 per minute within the United States; international calls, $9.99. Cell phone service is available fleetwide; international roaming fees apply.

SPORTS, FITNESS, AND BEAUTY   Each ship has a spa with a large variety of treatments, sauna and steam rooms, a very small indoor pool with a most unusual half-moon-shaped Jacuzzi, a gym with state-of-the-art equipment, and a beauty salon. There are four swimming pools, including one with Carnival's signature slide; seven whirlpools (although that number is often halved because of all the kids in them, even though they're not supposed to be); and a jogging track. You can start your day in the gym as early as 6 a.m. and be treated to classes in aerobics or abs or (for $10 extra per session) yoga, Pilates, or seminars on body care, diet, or cellulite. Sports include basketball, volleyball, and golf.

CHILDREN'S FACILITIES   The newest feature on the *Conquest*-class ships is the expanded teen recreation center, called Club O2, that houses a large, high-tech video-game room and teen dance club with a DJ spinning the latest hits, a bar serving nonalcoholic specialty drinks, and a video wall, along with new activities and shore excursions for teen groups.

For younger children, the *Conquest* group has the largest play areas in the Carnival fleet. The Camp Carnival program offers an arts and crafts center with spin and sand art and candy-making machines; an all-ages playroom with toys, games, and puzzles; a video room showing kids' movies and cartoons; and children's library, along with the latest PlayStation games. Babysitting is available nightly in the playroom from 10 p.m. to 3 a.m. for $6 per hour for the first child and $4 per hour for the second child in the same family.

There is also an outdoor play area and a wading pool and access to Carnival's trademark waterslide. Strollers rent for $6 per day and $25 per week and are available fleetwide.

Kids can make their own culinary creations through cake-decorating and pizza-making sessions, part of a full schedule of morning-to-night activities for children ages 2–14. Children receive their own printed activities program daily. Sample activities include storytelling, sing-alongs, and

Play-Doh Fun for younger cruisers, and disco parties, scavenger hunts, and pool parties for older kids. The ships offer a variety of kid-friendly dining choices and a daily junior special in the main dining rooms. Kids are also provided with freshly baked chocolate chip cookies on formal nights; youth counselors host children's-only meals poolside with a different cuisine featured each night. WaterColors, which debuted on *Carnival Valor,* is an art program that has been expanded fleetwide, teaching kids the techniques employed by professional artists in papier-mâché, oil paintings, and watercolors. SeaNotes is a music program that introduces kids to different musical instruments and genres.

Carnival Celebration	QUALITY 4	VALUE B
Carnival Holiday	QUALITY 4	VALUE B
REGISTRY *Holiday* Bahamas;	LENGTH 727/733 feet	BEAM 92 feet
Celebration Panama		
CABINS 726/743	DRAFT 25 feet	SPEED 21 knots
MAXIMUM PASSENGERS	PASSENGER DECKS 9/10	ELEVATORS 8
1,800/1,896	CREW 660/670	SPACE RATIO 32

THE SHIPS When the *Holiday* was unveiled in 1985, her decor was called zany. Micky Arison, Carnival's chairman, called it a "Disney World for adults." For those accustomed to the sleek lines of traditional ships, the boxy look of *Holiday* took some getting used to, but it was the innovations inside that revolutionized cruising, making the ship, with its four decks for recreation and entertainment, as much the destination as its ports of call. The most startling change was the main promenade deck. Instead of circling the ship, as had been typical, the deck runs double-width down only one side—a feature that became standard on all Carnival megaliners. Called Broadway on the *Holiday* with as much glitter as its namesake, it's both a meeting place and a thoroughfare, with bars, nightclubs, casinos, a disco, and reminders of Broadway: a traffic light, street lamps, an authentic 1934 bus, and Times Square.

A decade later, after larger and more flamboyant ships had been added to Carnival's fleet, the *Holiday* is regarded as traditional. That may be pushing credibility, but it's amazing how quickly passengers became comfortable with the new ideas the *Holiday* introduced. What's more, the innovations continue. The promenade was redesigned, and **Doc Holiday's** (a country-and-western lounge) was added. A separate section contains **Cyber City,** a virtual reality and game center. The fitness center was expanded, the casino renovated, and the Lido restaurant remodeled, adding another dinner option, a 24-hour pizzeria and deli counter. In 2006, more renovations created a redesigned lobby area to make it more comfortable and provide a relaxing atmosphere. In addition to other enhancements throughout the ship, a new nine-hole miniature golf course was added to Verandah Deck.

The *Holiday's* sister ships, *Jubilee* (since transferred to P&O Australia, a Carnival Corp. acquisition resulting from the purchase of Princess Cruises) and the *Celebration,* were identical in almost all aspects except decor. Each was themed and had a generous use of wood. The trio set the course for Carnival for the decade and had an incalculable impact on cruising. Zany, yes. Successful? You bet.

The *Celebration* pays tribute to New Orleans and Mardi Gras, complete with Bourbon Street, an outdoor cafe, bistro, and a New Orleans streetcar named, yes, Desire. But the most dramatic art is by San Franciscan Helen Webber, whose sculptured aluminum kites hang on wires the full six decks of the stairwells. The *Celebration,* like the other ships, has its own quiet corner—**Admiral's,** a library and writing room dedicated to great ocean liners of the past. *Celebration* recently completed a major refurbishment of all cabins, public areas, dining rooms, purser's lobby, stairs, and elevators.

Holiday set another course in 2004, being the first ship to depart from Mobile, Alabama, year-round.

ITINERARIES *See* Itinerary Index.

CABINS For all the unconventional elements on the ships' activity decks, cabins on the *Holiday* duo are downright sane and larger than most on other ships in the same price category. Outside cabins have picture windows; inside have backlit windows of the same size, making the cabin seem larger and less closed in.

Cabins are furnished with twin beds that can be converted to kings and have ample closet and drawer space in cabinets of genuine wood. Artwork decorates the walls and adds a touch of class.

Specifications 279 *Holiday/Celebration* inside cabins, 437/443 outside; 10 suites with whirlpool bathtubs. Standard dimensions, 180/185 square feet. 683/709 with twin beds convertible to kings; 27/16 inside, 10/8 outside with upper/lower berths. No singles. 15/14 wheelchair-accessible.

DINING The ships offer the same menus as other Carnival ships, with two dining rooms serving three meals. Carnival has upgraded and expanded Lido-area food service on all its ships to meet passengers' preference for casual breakfast and lunch choices. Specialties are offered in addition to standard favorites, such as scrambled eggs, hot dogs, and hamburgers. Particularly popular are the made-to-order pasta stations and expanded salad bars. Ice cream and frozen yogurt are available all day (cookies in the afternoon) in the Lido. Wine bars have been added on the promenade decks.

FACILITIES AND ACTIVITIES The Lido Deck has acres of open space and a swimming pool with a 114-foot-long spiral waterslide, a signature on Carnival ships. A more secluded pool is at the stern; a kids' pool is a deck below. The ships have spas with separate facilities for men and women. Decks are covered with Burmese teak.

Activities are numerous, ranging from wine tastings to surviving a "Survivor" game, inspired by the popular television show. In the evening, there's bar-hopping and people-watching on Broadway or Bourbon Street, and action in the casino or electronic game room. A favorite spot is the piano bar, but *Celebration's* **Red Hot Piano Bar** wins the award for novelty. Red walls glow under red lights, and the bar is shaped like a red piano with the ivories as the bar counter. And the music is . . . red hot. A spiral staircase leads directly to the casino a deck above.

The ships have huge theaters spanning two decks, where Broadway-style musicals and Las Vegas–type shows are staged twice nightly. Seats are terraced on six levels, giving all 1,000 patrons unobstructed views.

The year-round children's program, Camp Carnival, offers supervised activities for four age groups. **Cyber City** incorporates cutting-edge electronic game technology. For details on Carnival's children program, see *Fantasy* profile.

SHORE EXCURSIONS All Carnival ships offer similar shore excursions at common rates. They can be booked on Carnival's Web site. Many are off-the-shelf tours you often could take on your own. The main reason to book excursions through the cruise line is convenience. Carnival added a group of sports-oriented shore excursions for teenagers, such as horseback riding in Cozumel, biking in Key West, and cave tubing in Belize; these are discounted 20% off the regular price. The line has also expanded the shore excursions offered by its ships on Alaska cruises.

Carnival Splendor	PREVIEW	
REGISTRY Panama	LENGTH 952 feet	BEAM 116 feet
CABINS 1,503	DRAFT 27 feet	SPEED 21 knots
MAXIMUM PASSENGERS	PASSENGER DECKS 13	ELEVATORS NA
3,006	CREW NA	SPACE RATIO NA

THE SHIP The 112,000-ton *Carnival Splendor,* under construction in Italy, will be the line's largest ship when she enters service in spring 2008 and will represent a new class of ship for the line.

The 3,006-passenger ship will have an innovative new design with the largest spa and children's facilities in the Carnival fleet. The 17,800-square-foot spa covers two forward decks and will have an elaborate thermal suite, health and beauty treatment rooms, and Carnival's first thalassotherapy pool. The upper level of the spa will be encircled by a winter garden with a ceremonial teahouse. A 5,500-square-foot children's playroom, located midship, will have a water play area—a first for the line—on the level above.

A new sports deck aft will feature arena-style seating for games and other events, while a reservations-only supper club will be located atop the poolside Lido restaurant. The midship pool—one of four on board—will be enclosed by two full decks of glass walls. The area will be covered with a two-deck-high retractable dome that can be closed during inclement weather. A large balcony will encircle the upper deck of the pool area.

Of the ship's 1,503 cabins and suites, 60% will be outside and 60% of those will have balconies.

Carnival Splendor will be followed in 2009 and 2010 by even larger, as-yet-unnamed 130,000-ton ships.

Celebrity Cruises

1050 Caribbean Way, Miami, FL 33132-2096
☎ 305-539-6000 or 800-646-1456
fax 800-437-511; www.celebritycruises.com

TYPE OF SHIPS Stylish superliners and megaliners.

TYPE OF CRUISES Moderately priced deluxe; ample activity at comfortable pace; emphasis on quality.

CRUISE LINE'S STRENGTHS
- cuisine
- well-designed, stylish, spacious ships
- dining room service
- children's program
- value for money

CRUISE LINE'S SHORTCOMINGS
- lack of outside, wraparound promenade deck
- excessive promotion of onboard shopping
- boarding procedures
- loud deck music on some ships

FELLOW PASSENGERS Moderately affluent, ages range from late 30s to 60s in high season; ages lower in off-season. Typical passenger is age 48, married, with a household income of $50,000+. He/she tends to be an educated, experienced traveler who understands quality, owns a house in a relatively affluent suburb, and has college-age children. Fifty percent have cruised before, and of this group, 20–30% are repeaters with Celebrity. Due to the line's regular departures from the northeast United States in summer, a majority of passengers live on the East Coast; the balance come from the Midwest and West Coast.

Recommended for Middle- to upper-middle-income travelers in their 40s and older, whether first-timers or experienced cruisers, who appreciate good service and cuisine and want the recreation and entertainment of a large ship at an easy pace. Those with children during the holidays.

Not recommended for Small-ship devotees (except *Celebrity Xpedition*); those seeking a party atmosphere.

CRUISE AREAS AND SEASONS Caribbean in fall–winter; Alaska, Baltic, Bermuda, Canada and New England, Mediterranean in summer; Europe, Hawaii, Mexico, Panama Canal, South America, West Coast, spring, winter, and fall; Galápagos, year-round; Australia and New Zealand, winter.

THE LINE From its inception in 1989, Celebrity Cruises' objective has been to offer deluxe cruises for experienced travelers at affordable prices. The plan was greeted with skepticism, but in less than three years, Celebrity achieved its goal and did better than anyone imagined.

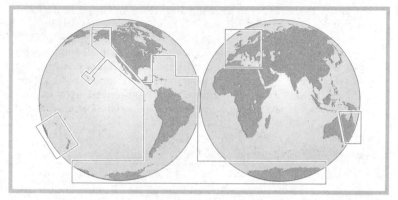

CRUISE AREAS AND SEASONS FOR CELEBRITY CRUISES

Quickly, it became apparent that Celebrity Cruises was more than just a new cruise line. It was a completely new product with a new generation of ships designed for today's travelers and new standards of service and cuisine in its price category. To their admirers, Celebrity's first vessels defined the ideal size of a cruise ship and balanced contemporary design and decor with traditional cruising.

Starting in 1992, Celebrity built a new class of cruise ships for the 21st century. Once again, Celebrity's ships were winners. The *Century* series of ships—*Century, Galaxy,* and *Mercury*—accommodated 26% more passengers in 48% more space than Celebrity's first generation of ships and had the latest in entertainment and interactive communications systems. The addition of these ships enabled Celebrity to expand beyond the Caribbean to Alaska and Europe. Celebrity was purchased by Royal Caribbean Cruises in June 1997 but operates as a separate brand.

No sooner were the *Century* ships in service than Celebrity added another new class of ships, the 91,000-ton *Millennium* group. The first of the French-built ships, *Millennium,* made her debut in 2000, followed by three more in 2001 and 2002. Then in 2006, it announced construction of three ships in yet another new class. The first, *Celebrity Solstice,* is to be launched in 2008 and the next two ships are slated for 2009 and 2010.

In 2004, Celebrity took a big leap into adventure cruises with a series in the Galápagos onboard the 296-foot *Celebrity Xpedition.* More recently, as a result of Royal Caribbean Cruises' 2006 acquisition of Pullmantur (the Spanish tour and cruise operator), a ship switch took place. Pullmantur's *Blue Dream* (originally Renaissance's *R6*) moved to the Celebrity Expedition brand and was renamed *Celebrity Journey,* while Celebrity's *Zenith* went to Pullmantur, and later in the year, Pullmantur's *Blue Moon* (originally Renaissance's *R7*) was also moved to the Celebrity Expeditions fleet, and renamed *Celebrity Quest.*

If this is not confusing enough, in May 2007, Royal Caribbean announced the creation of a new brand and a new category, Azamara Cruises, to be operated by Celebrity Cruises. Its category is meant to be "deluxe," that is, between premium and luxury, and it will be a specific competitor to the popular Oceania Cruises. The name Azamara was created from "aza," meaning blue, and "mar," meaning sea in several European languages. Two Celebrity ships have been renamed and form the new branch: *Celebrity Journey* became *Azamara Journey,* and *Celebrity Quest* (scheduled to join the fleet in October) has been renamed *Azamara Quest.* The short-lived Celebrity Expeditions brand has been retired (at least for the time-being), and its ship, *Xpedition,* has rejoined the Celebrity fleet.

THE FLEET	BUILT/RENOVATED	TONNAGE	PASSENGERS
Azamara Journey	2000/2006	30,277	710
Azamara Quest	2007	30,277	710
Celebrity Century	1995/2006	71,545	1,814
Celebrity Constellation	2002	91,000	1,950
Celebrity Eclipse	2010	118,000	2,850
Celebrity Equinox	2009	118,000	2,850
Celebrity Galaxy	1996	77,713	1,870
Celebrity Infinity	2001	91,000	1,950
Celebrity Mercury	1997	77,713	1,870
Celebrity Millennium	2000	91,000	1,950
Celebrity Solstice	2008	118,000	2,850
Celebrity Summit	2001	91,000	1,950
Celebrity Xpedition	2001	2,842	94

STYLE From the handsome, deep-blue-and-white exteriors with their signature stacks to the elegant interiors, Celebrity ships have style, combining the glamour of traditional cruising with a contemporary look. An example: famous contemporary artists, such as David Hockney and Roy Lichtenstein, are displayed alongside ancient Greek artifacts. On its first ships, introduced when atriums were becoming standard on cruise ships, Celebrity chose instead to make more space for public rooms, giving passengers entertainment and recreation options similar to those on megaliners, but without the glitz. Small lounges, each with its own ambience and entertainment, appeal to a broad range of tastes.

The ships were also designed for passenger comfort and flow. For example, the **Rendezvous Lounge** amidships provides a place where passengers can mingle before and after dinner, reducing crowds waiting for the restaurant or show lounge to open.

Celebrity distinguished itself from competitors by giving top priority to superior cuisine, hiring as food consultant Michel Roux, an award-winning master French chef who operates a Michelin three-star restaurant and other food enterprises in England. Roux helped design the ships' kitchens, trained its chefs, and guided food suppliers to ensure year-round quality. He created a sophisticated but unpretentious cuisine for refined palates, emphasized quality over quantity (although quantity is there, too), and established a new standard for competitors. Celebrity and Roux parted ways in 2006, but his influence on Celebrity Cruises is likely to be felt for many years to come.

Celebrity is the first cruise line to offer Acupuncture at Sea, now available fleetwide. The line also features the Savor the Caribbean series on *Millennium,* featuring some of the nation's hottest chefs. Celebrity Discoveries, the line's enrichment program, has been expanded with up to four lecturers on every cruise. The number of ConciergeClass cabins increased from 100 to 228 on all *Millennium*-class ships. *Azamara Journey* and *Azamara Quest* offer butler service and concierge amenities in every stateroom and suite.

DISTINCTIVE FEATURES Computer room on *Galaxy;* shipboard passenger-service manager. Children's program and specially priced shore excursions. Martini bars; ice bar on *Century.* Advance bookings for **AquaSpa.** Robes in all cabins. Butler service in suites. Alternative restaurant for casual dining; sushi cafes, made-to-order pasta and pizza bars; 24-hour room service. Internet cafes. Unique restaurants, music libraries, conservatories, and concierge service. LeapFrog SchoolHouse™ programs.

	HIGHEST	LOWEST	AVERAGE
PER DIEM	$686	$62	$195

Per diems are calculated from cruise line's nondiscounted *cruise-only* published fares on standard accommodations and vary by season, cabins, and cruise areas.

RATES All published rates include port fees.

Special fares and discounts Early-bird discounts, called Five Star rates, represent some of cruising's best values. Advance-purchase fares offer up to 50% discounts on cruise-only rates (deluxe cabins and suites excluded). Base rates for seven-day cruises offer upgrades for a low fee. Two itineraries—such as Eastern and Western Caribbean—can be combined at a special rate.

- THIRD/FOURTH PASSENGER: Yes.
- CHILDREN'S FARE: None
- SINGLE SUPPLEMENT: 150%–200%, depending on category. Guaranteed single rate.

Packages
- CRUISE/AIR ADD-ON WITH TRANSFERS: Yes.
- PRE/POST: Yes.
- OTHERS: Anniversary, honeymoon, weddings, family, vow renewal.

PAST PASSENGERS The Captain's Club is open to all passengers after their first Celebrity cruise. The club's benefits are determined by the number of times you cruise. For Classic level (one to five cruises): one-category upgrade, custom air arrangements, presailing specialty restaurant reservations, priority embarkation/debarkation (where available) for Founder Classic members, exclusive party, welcome amenity gift with purchase at AquaSpa, certificates for Celebrity casino, golf clinic and special rate for simulator, wine tasting, reunion cruises, quarterly newsletter with exclusive offers. Select level (six to ten cruises): private event for members, behind-the-scenes tours, priority status for shore excursion wait list, preferential debarkation (where available), plus all Classic benefits. Elite level (11 or more cruises): private shipboard departure lounge with continental breakfast, plus all Classic and Select benefits.

THE LAST WORD Celebrity Cruises has been one of the industry's true success stories. It created the right formula at the right time: classic cruising updated for contemporary lifestyles and available at reasonable prices. Its immediate success resulted from exceeding everyone's expectations and reflected the extensive planning and testing that went into the ships. The line has maintained high standards for its price range and continues to enhance the product by adding new deluxe amenities as well as value items like reduced rates for children. Almost anyone would enjoy a Celebrity cruise, but first-timers with cultivated tastes and experienced cruisers who seek greater comfort and service than is common in this price range will be most appreciative of the value.

Celebrity Cruises Standard Features

Officers Greek.

Staff Dining: European; Cabin: International; Cruise: European and American.

Dining facilities One main dining room with two seatings for breakfast and lunch; midnight buffet; indoor/outdoor Lido buffet breakfast and lunch. *Century* and *Millennium* classes, two-level dining room. Alternative restaurants. AquaSpa cafe on *Millennium* class and *Century*. Two dining venues on Celebrity Expedition ships.

Special diets Request at time of booking.

Room service 24-hour menu; butler service in suites.

Dress code Casual but not sloppy during the day; informal in evening, with two nights formal or semiformal.

Cabin amenities Direct-dial phone; bath with shower; suites with marble bathrooms. Robes in all cabins. Television with CNN and music channels. Hair dryers, safes, minibars, on *Century* and *Millennium* classes.

Electrical outlets 110/220 AC; 110 AC only on *Horizon* and *Zenith*.

Wheelchair access See Cabin section for each ship.

Recreation and entertainment Card room/library, casino, three-deck show lounge, bars/lounges, disco, video game room. Bingo, lotto, horse racing, culinary demonstrations, wine tasting, fashion show, dance lessons, art auctions, floral demonstrations on *Millennium*. High-tech entertainment center on *Century* class.

Sports and other activities Two outside swimming pools; exercise classes, walks, golf putting, table tennis, deck and pool games. Golf simulators on *Century* and *Millennium* classes; volleyball, basketball on *Millennium* class.

Beauty and fitness Barber/beauty salon; health club, gym, and sauna; jogging track on sun deck; elaborate spa with beauty treatments.

Other facilities Boutiques, hospital, laundry and dry cleaning services, meeting facilities on *Century*, *Millennium* classes; Internet on all ships. No passenger-operated washers or dryers.

Children's facilities Playroom; teen disco; babysitters; age-specific programs with counselors year-round.

Theme cruises Occasionally.

Smoking Not permitted in dining room or theater. Other public rooms have designated areas.

Celebrity suggested tipping Per person per day: waiter, butlers (suites only), $3.50; assistant waiter, $2; restaurant, 15% service charge added to all beverage checks.

Credit cards Cruise/onboard charges: American Express, MasterCard, Visa, Discover.

Celebrity Century	QUALITY 8	VALUE B
Celebrity Galaxy	QUALITY 8	VALUE B
Celebrity Mercury	QUALITY 8	VALUE B
REGISTRY Bahamas	LENGTH 815/866 feet	BEAM 105/105.6 feet
CABINS 907/935	DRAFT 25/25.5 feet	SPEED 21.5 knots
MAXIMUM PASSENGERS	PASSENGER DECKS 10	ELEVATORS 9/10
1,750/1,870	CREW 860/909	SPACE RATIO 40

THE SHIPS Celebrity got a jump on the millennium with the 1995 debut of the *Celebrity Century,* first of a new fleet designed for 21st-century cruising. *Celebrity Galaxy* followed in 1996 and *Celebrity Mercury* in 1997. More than ten teams worked with *Century*'s builders to achieve a comfortable, inviting, integrated design. With 48% more space than the first ships but only 26% more passengers, this spacious trio has one of cruising's highest passenger-to-space ratios in their category. Public rooms range in style from an elegant wood-paneled bar to a futuristic disco. Sony Corporation of America designed a sophisticated, interactive communications and entertainment system, and the company's music, pictures, and electronic publishing divisions provide products and expertise.

Century's focal point is a three-deck **Grand Foyer** encircled by a staircase and topped with a painted glass dome lit as if by sunlight during the day and as a starlit sky at night. The piazza has marble floors, burled woods, brass trim, suede furniture, and a waterfall with changing fiber-optic images. Nearby are boutiques and the **COVA Café de Milano,** a floating version of Pasticceria Confetteria COVA, the Milan-based pastry shop famous for its exquisitely handmade chocolates, pastries, and signature coffees

The *Galaxy* is slightly larger than *Century* with improvements over her sister ship, including the atrium, with a 40-foot-tall video panel projecting changing images, and a high-tech computer center offering classes. The atrium has been improved further on *Mercury*, with a spiral staircase leading to the promenade deck, where the port side has the COVA Café (now found on all Celebrity ships).

The *Galaxy*'s best new feature was a retractable glass dome covering a swimming pool and the surrounding deck. The **Oasis,** one of the ship's most popular areas, has an indoor/outdoor grill and bar that in the evening offers alternative casual dining, now available fleetwide.

The ships have multilevel, multipurpose observation lounges that become discos in the evening. One of the ships' two atriums, positioned aft and spanning three decks, opens onto the casino, **Rendezvous Lounge,** the dining room's foyer, and a Champagne bar.

Century-class vessels, like their predecessors, have multimillion-dollar art collections that are virtually contemporary art museums at sea. The focus for *Century* is contemporary masters; for *Galaxy*, the avant garde; and for *Mercury*, works by artists who emerged after pop art in the 1960s and 1970s. The collections were assembled by Christina Chandris, the ships' curator and former fine art adviser, in collaboration with the Marlborough Gallery of New York. The line provides information for a self-guided art tour.

In spring 2006, *Century* emerged from a $55 million remake that transformed the decade-old ship into one closer to the line's newer *Millennium* class. The most important changes are the addition of 314 large, new balconies to cabins throughout the ship and 24 new cabins and suites (2 handicapped-accessible) on the stern of Deck 12. A sushi cafe and an alfresco dining area were added on Deck 12. Another big addition is a specialty restaurant with tableside cooking. The spa was expanded and a cafe added. A new sports deck was added on Deck 14—complete with basketball court and table tennis. Cabins were given new decor, new bedding, new mattresses, duvets, and luxurious Egyptian cotton linens, accented with colorful throws and shams, and flat-screen televisions.

On Deck 7, the sports bar became a martini bar. The computer station became a High Seas Computing learning center with newly dedicated space for courses ranging from basic computer use to Web site creation to digital photography. On Deck 4, six cabins were removed to enlarge the children's area and add a new teen area and video arcade. The remade *Century* sails on short cruises from Miami, the first time Celebrity has a ship departing regularly from Miami.

In spring 2007, *Mercury* was the next to get a makeover that included the addition of 14 new verandas to aft cabins and a transformation of the ship's shopping area. The latter has a new **Boutique C,** an appointment-only jewelry store; a destinations store featuring merchandise reflective of the region in which the ship is sailing; and Celebrity's **Blue Collection,** a line of upscale, casual apparel. It also has **Beauty,** Celebrity's first "cosmeceutical" (pairing science with cosmetics) store, offering brands such as Dr. Brandt, DermaNew, Freeze 24/7, L'Occitane, and others. A skin-care specialist is available by appointment. Other improvements included upgraded gym equipment, each with individual televisions; new bedding similar to that of Century; and refurbished pool deck, bars, and other public areas.

ITINERARIES *See* Itinerary Index.

CABINS Each deck has its own color scheme, with cabins on each using complementary colors for carpeting and bedspreads. Windows in the spacious cabins are framed in rosewood, conveying luxury and comfort. All cabins in *Century* class have built-in vanities; generous closet and drawer space; large bathrooms with showers, hair dryers, and terry robes; telephones, safes, and minibars; radios and flat-screen televisions; and Internet access and wireless facilities. Interactive cabin television enables passengers to order breakfast or room service, book spa appointments, buy shore excursions, gamble (charged to the room), order merchandise from shops, and watch pay-per-view movies (including adult selections). Interactive televisions located throughout the ship provide information and entertainment.

Cabins on *Galaxy* were modified to accommodate more features. Some storage space was lost, particularly drawer space. All have minibars, and upper-category cabins have VCRs. The ships have penthouse and royal suites, and all suites have marble bathrooms, whirlpool tubs, verandas, and butler service. In her recent remake, the number of ConciergeClass cabins and suites was expanded to 178. *Galaxy* and *Mercury* have the service, too.

Specifications Celebrity Century, 304 inside cabins, 581 outside; 66 suites, 314 suites and deluxe cabins with verandas. 806 with twin beds; 10 wheelchair-accessible. *Celebrity Galaxy/Mercury,* 305 inside cabins, 615 outside; 48 suites and 170 (184 Mercury) minisuites with verandas; 877 with twin beds; 10 wheelchair-accessible. All three ships: Standard dimensions, 172 square feet; all twins convertible to doubles; third/fourth persons available; no singles.

DINING *Century*'s stylish **Grand Restaurant,** the main dining room, was Celebrity's first two-tiered dining room; a majestic staircase leads to a colonnaded center aisle reminiscent of the Karnak Temple in Egypt. Each of two galleys prepares food for half of the dining room, thus providing speedier service, consistent temperatures, and freshness. The **Orion Restaurant** aboard *Galaxy* has a larger second tier to accommodate the ship's greater capacity, and decor is lighter and contemporary. The room's focal point is an enormous, backlit ceiling panel of a hemisphere with continents superimposed. The *Mercury*'s **Manhattan Restaurant,** with a backdrop depicting the Big Apple skyline, is completely different from those of its sisters. Food, however, is the same on all three ships and meets the line's high standards. Celebrity eschews themed nights for dinner—common on other lines and often more show than authenticity. Rather, themes are given to the lunchtime buffets, when chefs are better able to do justice to ethnic cuisine. A popular nightly feature is the presentation of Captain's Bites, a chef's sampling provided in public rooms and available fleetwide.

In its recent remake, *Century* got a new, luxurious specialty restaurant, **Murano,** offering elegant dining in the style similar to the reservations-only restaurants on the *Millennium*-class ships, and with a special menu designed by Michel Roux. The venue offers tableside cooking, carving, and flambéing. There is a surcharge.

The Casual Dining Boulevard on the Lido Deck has been expanded to include a sushi cafe, a made-to-order pasta and pizza bar, and a small ice-cream parlor. The venue also serves buffet breakfasts, themed lunches, and dinner service with a casual dress code. Here, too, an afternoon tea buffet is served in addition to Celebrity's traditional **Elegant Tea.** *Galaxy's* **Oasis** (**Palm Springs Grill** on *Mercury*) is a casual-dining alternative restaurant. The outdoor section has a small swimming pool in a garden setting and is covered by a dome (particularly appealing on Alaska itineraries). Celebrity was the first line to offer complimentary pizza delivered to cabins—a service now available on many cruise ships.

SERVICE European-style service has distinguished Celebrity from other midprice cruise lines in the past and has been one of the ships' best and most rewarding features. However, recent reports indicate that service has slipped. We hope the cruise line is doing something about it.

FACILITIES AND ACTIVITIES   The two-deck **Celebrity Theater** used for Broadway-style revues and cabaret shows has a sloping orchestra section and canti-levered balconies providing unobstructed sight lines. The venue has a re-volving stage, the ability to handle multiple backdrops, an orchestra pit with adjustable height, sophisticated lighting, and other special effects.

The Art Deco **Crystal Room** (**The Savoy Nightclub** on *Galaxy;* **Pavilion** on *Mercury*), a low-key nightclub for evening dancing, has etched-glass panels, a luminous alabaster dome ceiling, rotating bronze globe, and a chic color scheme of red, black, and gold that recalls 1930s New York. The Savoy employs a jungle motif in its late-night cabaret, and **Fortune's Casino** has the full roster of games. **Rendezvous Square,** next to the dining room, is a lively place for cocktails or socializing before and after dinner.

High atop *Century*, **Hemisphere** (**Stratosphere Lounge** on the *Galaxy* and **Navigator Club** on *Mercury*) is an airy, sunlit observation lounge by day transformed into a futuristic "disco under the dome" at night, when window blinds lower automatically, etched-glass room dividers illuminate one by one, and a special table "glows." The hemi-sphere then rises—casting light from within—and the dance floor appears. Telescopes are placed around the room's edge for stargazing. On *Galaxy*, the Stratosphere has three sections. The outer one next to the floor-to-ceiling windows is a quiet zone for reading and daytime viewing of scenery. The middle level is ideal for cocktails at sunset, and the innermost can accommodate meetings during the day as pull-down screens separate it from other areas of the lounge. In the evening, the inner room becomes the disco, as sophisticated equipment transforms it and provides a terrific laser light show.

Century's new **Martini Bar** has the first "ice bar" at sea with a liquid wall that freezes to form a sparkling crystalline surface and a bar counter that freezes into ice-cold stone, while a solid block of ice displays bottles of liquor behind the bar. To complement the cool design, kinetic lighting was installed throughout the room and regularly changes the venue's color and appearance. The bar offers Celebrity's menu of more than 30 versions of martinis. The sister ships have martini bars, too. *Century's* outdoor **Sunset Bar** on the top deck aft is a tapas bar dressed in teak, stone, and stainless steel, topped with an arched-glass canopy. There also is a new bandstand with live music, offering a romantic setting at sunset. *Century's* other clubs and lounges include the fleetwide favorite, COVA Café, serving pastries and a menu of coffees, teas, and other beverages by day. At night, the cafe is transformed into a romantic, lamp-lit wine bar with live music. All other clubs and lounges on *Century*—**Crystal Lounge, Michael's Club** jazz/piano bar, **Rendezvous Lounge,** and **Hemispheres**—have been refurbished. Flexible walls fold into pillars in a conference center, allowing it also to serve as a cinema, meeting room, library, or card room. Keypads in the armchairs can be used for responses to questions or for interactive movies.

Activities are numerous and varied to appeal to a range of passengers and include exercise and dance classes, contests, singles' parties, honeymooners' Champagne party, and karaoke. Informational seminars also may be scheduled. First-run movies, older films, and adult pay-per-view movies are shown daily on cabin television; a schedule is provided in your cabin. High Seas Computing has a new home in a dedicated space and offers Internet access and courses ranging from basic computer use to Web site creation to digital photography.

SPORTS, FITNESS, AND BEAUTY   The spacious ships have 62,000 square feet of open decks that allow for a variety of sports, including simulated golf, Ping-Pong, volleyball, basketball, darts, and jogging. The *Century's* two swimming pools have cylindrical waterfalls and are rimmed with teak benches.

AquaSpa, the ships' health and fitness center, is among the most popular feature on all three ships. It's one of the best-equipped gyms at sea, with a hydropool, saunas, steam rooms, cardiovascular machines, and weight stations. Personal trainers are available to create individualized training programs. Aerobics classes are ongoing. The spa offers a variety of beauty and health treatments. The most unusual is rasul, based on an Asian ceremony, with a seaweed soap shower, medicinal mud pack, herbal steam bath, and massage. Not to be missed on *Mercury* and *Galaxy* is the tranquilizing thalassotherapy treatment taken in a 115,000-gallon pool with water-jet massage stations. Spa treatments are expensive; they may be booked in advance of your cruise. During her renovation, *Century's* AquaSpa was expanded and a new Spa Café where spa cuisine is served was added. *Celebrity's* Acupuncture at Sea program, a feature now available fleetwide, was also added. The program offers acupuncture treatments, therapies, and lectures by licensed doctors of Asian medicine.

CHILDREN'S FACILITIES   With every new ship, Celebrity's children's facilities have been improved. The **Fun Factory** on *Galaxy* and *Mercury* is a

1,600-square-foot playroom, and there's also a kids' splash pool. In its recent renovations, *Century's* Fun Factory area was expanded, adding a new teen room and offering a variety of new activities geared exclusively to teenagers. During summer and major holidays, Celebrity ships offer supervised daily programs for four age groups: Ship Mates (ages 3–6), Celebrity Cadets (ages 7–9), Ensigns (ages 10–12), and Admiral T's (ages 13–17). Younger children enjoy painting, drawing, songs, dances, movies, and other age-appropriate activities.

Celebrity Summer Stock lets young actors participate in theatrical shows with dances and costumes. The Young Mariners program showcases the operations of the ship and provides the opportunity to meet the captain and learn navigation by the stars. Junior Olympics offer water volleyball and basketball, golf putting, Ping-Pong, and other games. At meals, kids can join their peers at the Celebrity Breakfast Club and at dinner, order from their own or the regular menu. The program also has family activities and a masquerade parade. Century's **X-Treme,** the new teen lounge and video arcade, is a dedicated space with a dance floor, juice bar, jukebox, and karaoke, along with computers offering Internet access.

In November 2006, Celebrity, working with LeapFrog SchoolHouse™, enhanced the onboard activities for kids of all ages by providing multisensory learning tools and instruction that align with Celebrity's travel itineraries around the world. Recognized for its interactive, electronic education programs and products for pre-kindergarten through eighth grade, LeapFrog has created on board a variety of its most popular products, plus six exclusive educational modules for children ages 3 through 9. The programs focus on such subjects as dinosaurs, science and space, sports, art and music, and wildlife. Also developed were activities tailored to specific Celebrity itineraries, such as the heritage, customs, crafts, art, and music of Alaska, Bermuda, the Caribbean, the Mediterranean, and Mexico—all regions where Celebrity generally attracts a high percentage of families traveling with children.

SHORE EXCURSIONS Passengers can review and make reservations online at **www.celebritycruises.com.**

Celebrity Constellation	**QUALITY 8**	**VALUE B**
Celebrity Infinity	**QUALITY 8**	**VALUE B**
Celebrity Millennium	**QUALITY 7**	**VALUE B**
Celebrity Summit	**QUALITY 8**	**VALUE B**
REGISTRY Bahamas	**LENGTH** 965 feet	**BEAM** 105 feet
CABINS 1,059	**DRAFT** 26 feet	**SPEED** 24 knots
MAXIMUM PASSENGERS	**PASSENGER DECKS** 11	**ELEVATORS** 10
2,038	**CREW** 999	**SPACE RATIO** 46.6

THE SHIPS When the *Celebrity Millennium* debuted in 2000, she launched a new class of ships for Celebrity—somewhat larger than her sister ships and with many of the same facilities, but even more spacious and with contemporary refinements sure to please maturing baby boomers. These included the line's largest spa, a unique specialty restaurant with a dine-in wine cellar, a large boutique of designer fashions, a music library, floral conservatories with full-service florists, and huge suites.

The *Millennium*, the first of four sister ships, also enabled Celebrity to expand its cruise horizons. *Celebrity Infinity*, which debuted in 2001, offered the line's first cruises to Hawaii; *Celebrity Constellation* entered service in Europe in 2002.

These ships are powered by environmentally friendly gas-turbine engines, which reduce exhaust emissions by up to 90% and lower noise and vibration levels considerably. The way these ships glide out of port is reminiscent of the smooth sailing aboard steam-driven classic liners from the past. The only vibration noticed was in the aft section when the Azipod propulsion system was altering the ship's course. That same propulsion system allows the ships to cruise at 24 knots, enabling them to sail to more destinations in shorter time. They are also able to transit the Panama Canal. Changes in the exterior design—a lean, chiseled profile with a new stack design and hull striping—make the group look like the faster ships that they are.

The interiors, created by some of the same design teams that worked on other Celebrity ships, are the line's most sophisticated and elegant to date. They have something of a back-to-the-future decor, blending the glamour and grandeur of turn-of-the-19th-century luxury liners with the amenities and state-of-the-art technology that passengers in the new millennium expect. The ships also boast Celebrity's signature features: museum-quality contemporary art collections, an enormous **AquaSpa, COVA Café, Michael's Club** piano bar, martini and Champagne bars, and cuisine by Michel Roux.

Passengers are introduced to the *Millennium* via the **Grand Foyer,** which has a translucent, backlit onyx staircase. Opposite the shore excursion desk is a bank of four glass elevators—the first external-facing ones ever built on a cruise ship—that capture panoramic views as they rise. One passenger, enjoying her elevator ride with Amsterdam views, said, "It was almost as good as a shore excursion." Next to the elevators, a paneled wall of wood and metallic vinyl rises from the entry to the top of the ship through a series of atriums.

Celebrity ConciergeClass is an enhanced level of accommodations with upgraded amenities and priority services with the notion that little extras make a big difference. The amenities include a bottle of chilled Champagne on arrival, fresh flowers and fruit, afternoon canapés, a leather key holder, personalized stationery, an oversized tote bag, and an umbrella to use during the cruise. In 2005, the number of cabins in ConciergeClass was more than doubled from 100 to 228.

Sleeping comfort is enhanced with pillow-top mattresses; lush duvets; pillow selections (such as goose down, Isotonic, and others); and a new room-service breakfast menu. In the bathroom, Concierge-Class passengers find oversized Egyptian cotton towels, Frette bathrobes, two hair dryers, a Hansgrohe shower head, and a selection of fine toiletries. On the veranda, they have a table for alfresco dining, cushioned chairs, and high-powered binoculars.

Priority service gives them priority luggage delivery, dining time and seating preferences, shoe-shine service, VIP invitations to exclusive shipboard events, priority shore excursion bookings, early embarkation and debarkation privileges, and a one-touch phone button direct to a ConciergeClass desk representative.

Unique to the ships are their floral conservatories and the silk floral displays by Emilio Robba of Paris, renowned for his silk floral artistry. The floral conservatories—the first at sea—provide an attractive botanical environment, ideal for romantic occasions and reflective moments. Designed by Robba, they combine natural flora with his silk creations. The floral boutiques are operated by full-time florists who produce flower arrangements and corsages for passengers and hold classes in flower arranging several times a week. Following the facility's success on *Infinity*, a small conservatory and boutique were added to *Millennium*, replacing the little-used teen center. On the three newer ships, larger conservatories replaced *Millennium's* sports bar. The *Millennium*-class ships also have **Online@Celebrity Cruises** Internet cafe, a computer training and education program, Acupuncture at Sea, and meetings space with a business center.

ITINERARIES *See* Itinerary Index.

CABINS Of the 1,059 cabins, 80% are outside, and of those, 74% (or 56% of the total) have verandas. All cabins have air-conditioning, minibar, safe, telephone with voice mail, shower, hair dryer, and multifunction interactive television. Standard cabins are furnished with twin beds that are convertible to queen size. *Infinity, Summit,* and *Constellation* have Connect@Sea and in-cabin Internet access. The spacious cabins are well appointed and beautifully finished. Added touches, such as a silver carafe of fresh water replenished regularly, heighten the level of service. There are no self-service launderettes—particularly missed on long sailings.

The Penthouse suites, measuring 1,690 square feet with veranda, have marble-floor foyers, separate living and dining rooms, baby grand piano, butler's pantry, master bedroom with generous closets, exercise equipment, dressing room with vanity, marble master bath with twin sinks, whirlpool tub, separate shower, toilet and bidet area, powder room, motorized draperies, lights and security system, two interactive audio/visual entertainment systems with flat-screen TV, fax machine, veranda with whirlpool, wet bar, and lounges.

The Royal suites have floor-to-ceiling glass doors, separate living room with dining and sitting area, two entertainment centers with flat-screen TVs and VCRs, walk-in closet, bath with whirlpool tub and stall shower, and a veranda with whirlpool tub. There are also Celebrity suites, each with themed decor and floor-to-ceiling windows; and Sky suites (including six wheelchair-accessible) also with floor-to-ceiling glass doors, sitting area with sofa bed and lounge chair, entertainment center, minibar, walk-in closet, and bathroom with whirlpool tub. All but a few suites have verandas, and all have butler service.

Specifications 853 outside; 206 inside. 2 Penthouse suites; 8 Celebrity suites; 8 Royal suites; 32 Sky suites (6 wheelchair-accessible)—all with verandas. 5 inside and 4 outside cabins are wheelchair-accessible and have flat floor entrances and 35-inch-wide cabin bathroom doorways. Public elevator doorways are 39 inches wide.

DINING The **Metropolitan Restaurant,** the main dining room spanning two levels, features bold, geometric motifs in reds, blues, and golds based on French designs from the late 1940s and early 1950s, which the designers describe as "restrained exuberance." At night, panels with dramatic architectural scenes are lowered onto the room's expansive windows, with a quintet providing quiet, elegant accompaniment. It's called **The Trellis** on *Infinity* and has an 18th-century-garden theme.

The **Olympic,** Celebrity's first specialty restaurant, is the *Millennium's* showstopper. It takes its name from a rare maritime treasure—a section of the original Edwardian carved-wood paneling from the *Olympic,* sister ship of the *Titanic.* First discovered in a private English residence, the exquisite French walnut paneling ornamented with gold leaf in Louis XVI style was bought at auction at Sotheby's. Seating only 134 people, the intimate dining room uses an Edwardian decorating theme to convey nostalgia for the elegant golden days of steamship travel. The Olympic restaurant had the cruise industry's first demonstration galley (an open kitchen where guests can see their meals being prepared). The reservations-only restaurant (surcharge, $30 per person) has its own menu of gourmet cuisine, and to make the dining experience even more memorable, some dishes are finished and presented tableside. One treat is Waldorf pudding—a re-creation of an original dessert from the *Olympic.* There is piano and violin entertainment. Memorabilia from the *Olympic* includes White Star Line china and the ship's bell, which is on exhibit in the foyer.

Adjoining the room is a separate wine cellar, which can be used as a private dining room for small groups of eight persons or so. The wine list has almost 200 international selections, some of them quite prestigious. Passengers may also order recommended wines by the glass with each of the four courses. Wine and after-dinner espressos can increase the tab to $100 or more for a couple.

The same theme of honoring a different liner from the past, with superb design and decor re-creating the first-class dining experience of a past era, is found on *Millennium's* sister ships. *Infinity's* **S.S. United States** restaurant has etched glass panels from the famous American liner's first-class ballroom. The French liner *Normandie* is featured in *Summit's* alternative restaurant; **Ocean Liners** on *Constellation* salutes the classic ships of the past with memorabilia and paintings of famed liners and original lacquered panels from the *Ile de France.*

At the entrance to each restaurant, glass cases containing memorabilia from the famous ships invite a close look. The ambience of the great liner era is enhanced by cutlery and china reproduced from classic ship designs and the style of music performed throughout the evening.

The three-hour dining experience is a unique opportunity to enjoy fine dining in the style of a bygone age. It is certainly worth the $30-per-person service charge added to your shipboard account when booking these restaurants.

The **Ocean Café** (**Seaside Café** on *Constellation*), an indoor/outdoor restaurant designed to resemble a Portuguese outdoor cafe, is the casual dining venue for breakfast and lunch buffet, while the **Ocean Grill,** with a separate entrance, is an alternative dining venue featuring steak, fish, rotisserie chicken, pizza, and pasta. There is no fee for this by-reservation, partial-waiter-service restaurant. Fleetwide, Celebrity's Casual Dining Boulevard on the Lido Deck, with its sushi café and pizza-and-pasta bar, is a nightly alternative to the more formal atmosphere in the main dining rooms. Savvy travelers discover the **AquaSpa Café,** where they can select light, healthy food and fruit plates, whole-grain cereals and breads and yogurt at breakfast, and cold poached salmon and chicken and crudités at lunch. Smoothies and fresh vegetable and fruit juices are available for an extra charge.

During her Caribbean winter season, the *Millennium* features her Savor the Caribbean series with well-known guest chefs. As part of the program, passengers can participate in a hands-on cooking class with the featured chef on each cruise. Two classes are offered per cruise with a class size limited to eight. The two-hours-long class cost $59 per person. Guests also may participate in a Bacardi-sponsored class that teaches them to make specialty drinks such as mojitos. As part of the program, the cruise line offers a series of culinary-inspired shore excursions. For example, in San Juan, guests can enjoy a private cooking demonstration with Chef Robert Trevino at his highly acclaimed Parrot Club, known for its Puerto Rican fusion fare.

SERVICE Service in the main dining rooms is very attentive and up to Celebrity's high standards. In the buffet-style cafe, you never have to carry your tray; waiters are ready to assist you. The alternative dining rooms have the highest level of service of any ship of this category and price range.

FACILITIES AND ACTIVITIES The Celebrity Theater is the line's first three-tiered show lounge, seating 900 passengers in a classically inspired but contemporary setting with a full circular balcony. Designed by premier theater designers, the stage, orchestra pits, and lighting can accommodate most any Broadway-style show at sea. Sight lines are excellent and seats extremely comfortable with room between rows. The use of dazzling laser and lighting effects, movable stage levels, and the big-screen video is stunning, but they are frequently more remarkable than the quality of entertainers.

The ever-popular **Rendezvous Lounge,** an elegant cocktail lounge that leads to the dining room, has music for dancing, and the **Platinum Club,** on a balcony overlooking the lounge, is a martini and Champagne bar. **Michael's Club,** another Celebrity tradition, is a richly appointed piano bar with traditional English Georgian decor and natural cherry paneling. **Extremes,** at the top of the ship overlooking the pool deck, was Celebrity's first sports bar.

High above the ship on Sunrise Deck is a glass-sheathed observation lounge for panoramic viewing by day. It is transformed into an early evening cabaret and piano bar with a dance floor and a late-night disco. The richly decorated **Fortune's Casino** has 228 slot machines, 23 game tables, and a huge selection of video casino games. Overlooking the Grand Foyer is a card and games area; the **COVA Café,** with a separate tearoom and well-attended classical music performances each evening; The cafe quickly becomes a favorite hangout for many, especially non-American travelers who enjoy the European flair of this onboard version of the classic Milan coffeehouse. Passengers are served a variety of coffee drinks, Champagne cocktails, and morning and afternoon pastries, often accompanied by music from a harpist or pianist.

Words is a two-level library where passengers can check out books and rent iPods. **Online@CelebrityCruises,** the line's Internet cafe, has 18 individual stations enabling passengers to check e-mail and other services. The charge is a flat $2 per message, incoming or outgoing, or $.75 per minute. There are reduced-rate packages of $70 for 100 minutes; $120 for 200 minutes; and $250 for 500 minutes. If you want to use your laptop, there is a $10 daily charge for rental of the Connect@Sea kit plus the above charges for minutes. Computer classes are available for $20 an hour. Similar facilities have been added fleetwide.

Another innovation was the Acupuncture at Sea program, in which two to four doctors offer treatment for pain management, smoking cessation, weight loss, and stress management; present lectures about acupuncture, feng shui, nutrition, and healing with herbs; and diagnose and treat specific syndromes with medicinal herbal formulas. The acupuncture program is available on *Constellation* and *Summit.*

The ship's conference room is designed to hold more than 300 people in auditorium-style seating and offers the latest audiovisual technology, including seat voting/interactive systems and full control booth. The center also can double as the ship's cinema. Five flexible rooms, each offering television, monitors, computers, teleconferencing, Internet connections, fax machines, and private satellite telephones, are available for meetings and other functions.

The **Emporium,** the *Millennium*'s European-style shopping arcade, has designer boutiques, an art gallery, a signature Celebrity shop, and COVA Café store.

SPORTS, FITNESS, AND BEAUTY   The Resort Deck has the Riviera pool with four freshwater whirlpools and plenty of areas for sunbathing as well as shaded spots. The deck also houses an entertainment area with a canopied stage and bandstand, a teakwood dance floor, two outdoor bars and the **Grill.** Forward is the **AquaSpa, Aqua Dome,** and the fitness area. The Sunrise Deck overlooking the pool area has a running track and golf simulator (reserve at the Purser's Deck), and the Sports Deck holds a full-size basketball court, paddle tennis, volleyball, and quoits, a game similar to horseshoes.

The 25,000-square-foot AquaSpa, which Celebrity says is the largest and most extensive spa on any cruise ship, is an impressive facility that includes a large fitness area; a gym with an enormous array of equipment (rowers, exercise bikes, recumbent bikes, treadmills, steppers) and an aerobics area; and an indoor hydropool with air beds, whirlpools, sauna, steam, and tropical showers. The Persian Garden is a tranquil, aromatherapy oasis that can be booked by the hour. The AquaSpa has a beauty parlor and 16 treatment rooms, including a dry float room with shower, Alpha Massage Capsule, a disabled-accessible, full-body treatment room, and other specialty rooms.

The spa offers Celebrity's water-oriented treatments of Middle Eastern, Asian, and European origin, as well as such specialties as thalassotherapy, hydrotherapy, a new aromatic bath, and first-at-sea treatments such as hot-stone therapy. Fitness consultants are on hand to assist with programs and assessments. In addition to the equipment in the fitness area, there are four daily classes, two of which, such as yoga and spinning, carry a $10 fee. Four decks down, the promenade does not completely circle the ship, as the lower level of the main dining room takes up the aft portion of Promenade Deck. Still, the long and wide promenade is a fine place for walkers and passengers for whom being on deck, close to the sea, is one of the great joys of cruising.

CHILDREN'S FACILITIES The **Fun Factory,** for children ages 3–12, offers a variety of activities with an ocean-travel and exploration theme. Children enjoy a puzzle wall, movie room, and colorful play area under the supervision of experienced counselors. A separate arts and crafts room is available for younger children, whereas the older ones have their own broadcast room (though sometimes used by the younger children), video game arcade, dance floor, and CD jukebox.

SHORE EXCURSIONS A variety of tours from adventure activities to cultural experiences are available. They can be reviewed and booked on Celebrity's Web site.

Celebrity Solstice	2008	
Celebrity Equinox	2009	
Celebrity Eclipse	2010	
REGISTRY Bahamas	LENGTH 1,033 feet	BEAM 121 feet
CABINS 1525	DRAFT NA	SPEED NA
MAXIMUM PASSENGERS	PASSENGER DECKS NA	ELEVATORS NA
2,850	CREW NA	SPACE RATIO NA

THE SHIPS In 2006, Celebrity Cruises ordered three 118,000-ton ships, a new class of ships for Celebrity dubbed "Solstice class." All three are being built in Germany by the well-known shipbuilder Meyer Werft, who has built most of Celebrity's previous ships.

The first ship, Celebrity Solstice, is to be delivered in fall 2008; the second ship, *Celebrity Equinox,* is scheduled for summer 2009; and the third, as-yet-unnamed ship is to be launched in 2010.

The new ships will measure 1,033 feet in length and 121 feet in width and carry 2,850 passengers, based on two passengers per cabin. Celebrity says their larger size will allow for larger standard cabins and a significant range of services and amenities inspired by input from past passengers and travel agents. Approximately 90% of the accommodations will be outside, and 85% of those will have balconies. According to Meyer Werft, the new ships will incorporate Celebrity's tradition of breakthrough design and innovations. Celebrity estimates the cost of the ships will be approximately $245,000 per berth, based on current exchange rates.

Celebrity Xpedition	PREVIEW	
REGISTRY Ecuador	LENGTH 292 feet	BEAM 48 feet
CABINS 50	DRAFT NA	SPEED 15 knots
MAXIMUM PASSENGERS 94	PASSENGER DECKS 10	ELEVATORS none
	CREW 64	SPACE RATIO NA

THE SHIP Celebrity's *Xpedition,* added in 2004, is completely different from the rest of the fleet. Small and deluxe, it is used for year-round sailing in the Galápagos Islands. But even eco-focused travelers appreciate fine cuisine, wine, and modern amenities, and indeed, Celebrity Cruises uses as a tag line for *Celebrity Xpedition*'s Galápagos cruises: "Where the untamed meets the indulged."

Celebrity is able to offer these cruises by having purchased an Ecuadorian tour operator that held the necessary government permits for Galápagos sailings and ensuring that the 100-passenger *Xpedition* (formerly the *Sun Bay*) was Ecuadorian-flagged and crewed. The German-built vessel is headed by an experienced Royal Caribbean or Celebrity captain, assisted by Ecuadorian and international officers. Most of the staff are experienced in cruise service but have been retrained by Celebrity.

The cruise includes all meals, naturalist guides, folkloric entertainment, enrichment program, shore excursions, gratuities, and Zodiac rides, as well as bottled water, soft drinks, and alcoholic beverages (except premium brands) on board. On cruise-tour packages, passengers fly to Quito for a two-night stay at the luxurious J. W. Marriott hotel and a city tour by bus and on foot. In addition, the package includes airport transfers, round-trip flights between Quito and Baltra via Guayaquil, Galápagos entry fee; one or two nights' hotel stay in Quito on return, and some meals in Quito.

Despite its small size, *Xpedition* feels spacious. The **Discovery Lounge** includes a large bar, comfortable seating, and a library with books and games. Here, passengers attend folkloric presentations, lectures, and naturalist discussions about each day's program. The ship also has a small exercise room with sauna, several bars, outdoor deck lounging space, and a small boutique.

The open seating **Darwin Dining Room** is elegant but not stuffy. It serves breakfast and luncheon buffets with cooked-to-order dishes including omelets and pastas, and full-service dinner. Waiters eagerly bring drinks and special sandwiches or entrées beyond the regular menu choices. Guests can also dine alfresco on many occasions at the **Beagle Grill.**

Cabins and suites have television, telephone, fluffy cotton bathrobes, Egyptian cotton towels, safe, and hair dryer. Standard cabins (145 square feet) have a large rectangular window and are furnished with two twin beds or one queen bed, a small sofa, desk area with minifridge, and mirror. There is ample closet space and a well-appointed bathroom. The one penthouse suite (460 square feet) has two single beds and one double bed as well as two verandas. Other suites measure 230 square feet.

Xpedition does not have a passenger elevator and is not equipped to accommodate wheelchair passengers or those who can't climb two or three flights of stairs. The ship has a doctor onboard for every voyage, but it does not have Internet access. The ship has a modern waste management system that Celebrity upgraded further.

Passengers enter and leave the ship via a platform incorporated into the vessel's structure. To explore ashore, they are tendered via Zodiac craft and proceed on foot. The ship stops at several islands for wildlife viewing. Snorkeling and swimming are included on several excursions; a dive trip can be booked for an additional charge. As on all Galápagos cruises, naturalist guides or the ship's staff accompany all excursions, providing commentary and discussions.

Azamara Journey	PREVIEW	
Azamara Quest	PREVIEW	
REGISTRY Bahamas	LENGTH 593 feet	BEAM 95 feet
CABINS 355	DRAFT NA	SPEED 22 knots
MAXIMUM PASSENGERS	PASSENGER DECKS 8	ELEVATORS 4
710	CREW 390	SPACE RATIO NA

THE SHIPS In 2006, Celebrity Cruises acquired two ships after Royal Caribbean, Celebrity's owner, purchased Pullmantur, the Spanish tour and cruise operator. The 30,277-ton *Blue Dream* (formally Renaissance's *R6*) was renamed *Celebrity Journey,* and her sister ship, *Blue Moon* (formerly Renaissance's *R7*), renamed *Celebrity Quest.*

Then in May 2007, Royal Caribbean created Azamara Cruises, to be operated by Celebrity Cruises, as a new brand to fill the deluxe category, meant to be between premium and luxury and a competitor to the popular Oceania Cruises. Azamara's name stems from *aza,* meaning blue, and *mar,* meaning sea in several European languages. The two ships have been renamed: *Celebrity Journey* became *Azamara Journey,* and *Celebrity Quest* (scheduled to join the fleet in October 2007) becomes *Azamara Quest.*

After being acquired by Celebrity, each ship had a month-long drydock when facilities and attractions were added to make them more consistent with the Celebrity fleet. These included the addition of two specialty restaurants, 34 junior suites (by taking three cabins and making them two), a variety of Celebrity's most popular signature elements, and Celebrity's first wine bar, where fine wines by the glass are offered and wine and Champagne tastings, seminars, and mini-pairings of food and wine are held. Concierge services were also expanded.

The ships offer 15 classes of accommodations, all providing butler service and such amenities as fresh-cut flowers, fresh fruit, Elemis toiletries, Frette cotton robes, slippers, plasma television, and European bedding.

The ships have open seating in the main dining room and do not require formal attire. Passengers in suites receive one night of complimentary dining in one of the specialty restaurants.

The ships' AquaSpa facilities offer spa treatments not available on any other ships in Celebrity's fleet. Passengers in suites can have certain spa services in their room. The ships also offer an outdoor spa relaxation lounge and an aesthetics suite offering Acupuncture at Sea, laser hair removal, and microdermabrasion.

Azamara Journey entered service in May 2007, taking over the Bermuda summer program of Celebrity's former *Zenith*, sailing on seven-night cruises from Cape Liberty, New Jersey. Then from October 2007 through April 2008, she moves south for a series of 12- to 18-night cruises to Brazil, Antarctica, the Chilean Fjords, and other areas of South America.

When *Azamara Quest* enters service in October 2007, she will introduce a series of 12- to 14-night Caribbean cruises, followed by a series of 14-night eastbound and westbound Panama Canal itineraries.

Azamara passengers will benefit from a loyalty program with three levels, depending on how many cruises they have taken. Azamara's cruise rates will be higher than Celebrity's, perhaps by as much as 40%.

Costa Cruise Lines

Venture Corporate Center II
200 South Park Road, Suite 200, Hollywood, FL 33021-8541
☎ 954-266-5600 or 800-462-6782; fax 954-266-2100
www.costacruises.com

TYPE OF SHIPS New modern superliners.

TYPE OF CRUISES Mass market, designed for Europeans as much as North Americans—hence, more European in service and ambience.

CRUISE LINE'S STRENGTHS
- Italian style and service
- friendly, attentive crew
- itineraries

CRUISE LINE'S SHORTCOMINGS
- noise level in dining rooms
- excessive announcements on European-based ships
- language problems

FELLOW PASSENGERS Costa has two seasons: Caribbean (and South America for its European clients), from late fall to early spring, and Europe, mainly from spring through fall, although some European cruises are now year-round. This results in two sets of passengers. In the Caribbean, up to 70% of passengers are North Americans, depending on the cruise; average age is 54 years, with annual household income of $50,000+. A bevy of Italian-American fans and newlyweds are attracted by the line's Italian style. Most have cruised before.

In Europe, 80% or more are Europeans likely to have traveled abroad, probably even cruised before. Among the North Americans, average age is about the same as Caribbean cruisers, but they would be inclined to rent a car and drive through Europe on their own instead of taking an escorted tour. They enjoy traveling with and meeting people from other countries.

Recommended for Italophiles; first-time cruisers and less experienced travelers who want to sample European ambience, but with facilities typical of a large ship; and repeat cruisers who want to try something different.

Not recommended for Those who like small ships as well as an all-American atmosphere, or those who prefer to travel with Americans.

CRUISE AREAS AND SEASONS The Baltic Sea, Black Sea, Caribbean, Dubai, Far East, Greek islands, the Holy Land, Mediterranean, Northern Europe, Norwegian fjords, Russia, South America, and transatlantic cruises.

THE LINE Genoa, Italy–based Costa Crociere, parent company of Costa Cruise Lines, had been in the shipping business for more than 100 years and in the passenger business for almost 60 years when it was bought

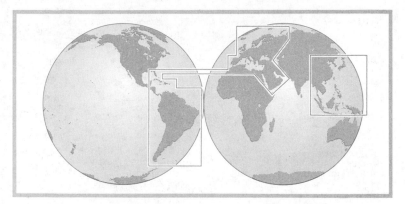

CRUISE AREAS AND SEASONS FOR COSTA CRUISE LINES

jointly by Carnival Corporation and Airtours, a European tour company, in 1997. (Three years later, Carnival acquired Airtours' shares as well.)

Costa, Europe's largest cruise line, was among the earliest lines to offer one-week Caribbean cruises from Miami (1959) and the first to introduce an air/sea program (late 1960s). Despite its long Florida-Caribbean association, Costa changed course in the 1990s to become more Europe-focused. Of its 12 ships, only two sail from U.S. ports, and they sail only in winter. The others are positioned in Europe and one in Asia.

Costa launched the 1990s with four new ships costing more than $1 billion and intended to serve a broad spectrum of passengers. The ships combined modern and classic qualities with new design features. The line added the larger *Costa Victoria* in 1996, followed by the even larger *Costa Atlantica* in 2000; the latter's sister ship, *Costa Mediterranea,* came in 2003. With the arrival of two 105,000-ton ships, *Costa Fortuna* and *Costa Magica* in 2003 and 2004, another billion-dollar expansion continued. The last three ships alone doubled the line's passenger capacity. Costa's largest ship to date, the 112,000-ton *Costa Concordia,* and now the line's flagship, debuted in 2006 and remains in Europe, while her twin, *Costa Serena,* was scheduled to follow in 2007.

But Costa is not finished. In 2006, the company ordered two more ships for delivery in 2009: a third sister ship to the *Concordia* and a 92,700-ton vessel, *Costa Luminosa,* with an option for a sister ship for 2010. These new ships, including the *Costa Serena,* amount to almost a 2 billion euro investment for Costa and are part of a nearly 4.5 billion euro investment made by the company for its fleet expansion and upgrade program since 2000. These ships will bring the Costa fleet to a total of 15 by 2010.

Also in 2006, *Costa Marina* was stationed in Asia for the winter season, sailing from Singapore; and *Costa Classica* was based in Dubai. The line moved the *Costa Allegra* to the Far East, becoming the first European mass-market line to base a ship in Asia permanently to serve the Chinese market. However, it is also being marketed to Europeans and others.

THE FLEET	BUILT/RENOVATED	TONNAGE	PASSENGERS
Costa Allegra	1990/2001	28,430	1,000
Costa Atlantica	2000	85,619	2,114
Costa Classica	1991/2001	52,926	1,356
Costa Concordia	2006	112,000	3,300
Costa Europa	1986/90/2002/03	54,800	1,494
Costa Fortuna	2003	102,600	2,720
Costa Luminosa	2009	92,700	2,260
Costa Magica	2004	102,600	2,720
Costa Marina	1990	25,600	1,000
Costa Mediterranea	2003	86,000	2,114
Costa Romantica	1993/2003	53,049	1,356
Costa Serena	2007	112,000	3,300
Costa Victoria	1996/2004	75,166	1,928
Unnamed	2009	112,000	3,300
Unnamed	2010	92,700	2,260

STYLE In the early 1980s, Costa coined the phrase "cruising Italian style" to celebrate its Italian basis in everything from design to cuisine. Its fleet is designed and built in Italy by Italians, with floors and walls of Italian marble, splendid wood cabinetry, designer fabrics and linens, and Italian art throughout. The ships reflect the sophisticated architecture and decor of modern Italian designers rather than the classic Italian look. The Finnish-built *Costa Atlantica* was the first to depart somewhat from the Italian style, and subsequent ships have come to resemble Carnival ships more and more, as Joe Farcus, Carnival's well-known designer, has been responsible for the last four ships.

Life on board is made to seem *molto Italiano,* from the pasta and espresso to Italian language lessons, Italian cooking classes, Italian ice cream, pizzas in the pizzerias, and toga parties. Theme nights such as the Festa Italiana feature an Italian street festival with boccie ball games, tarantella dance lessons, pizza dough–tossing contests, Venetian mask making, and more. Yet for all the trimmings, the Italian ambience has been diluted, mainly because Costa ships no longer have all-Italian crews.

The ships are modern, with gyms, spas, and fitness programs, and Costa's Caribbean shore excursions emphasize outdoor activities. One of Costa's most popular innovations is its private beach on Isla Catalina off the Dominican Republic. The island is near the sprawling resort of Casa de Campo, which, among its many facilities, has a tennis village, four of the Caribbean's best golf courses, and a marina village with restaurants and shops, enabling Costa's ships on Eastern Caribbean cruises to spend the day at the island and the evenings at the marina.

All dining and public rooms on Costa ships are nonsmoking, but that doesn't mean passengers, especially European ones, don't light up. The ships do not have self-service launderettes, a much-appreciated amenity available on most new large ships. Laundry and pressing services are available from the ships' facilities, but these are costly.

DISTINCTIVE FEATURES Free hot pizza throughout the day. On Caribbean cruises, couples can renew their wedding vows in a shipboard ceremony. Alternative dining on the newest ships, unusual private Caribbean island, fiesta nights, toga party. Grand Prix driving simulator and spa cabins and suites on *Concordia/Serena*.

	HIGHEST	LOWEST	AVERAGE
PER DIEM	$538	$86	$161

Per diems are calculated from cruise line's nondiscounted *cruise-only* published fares on standard accommodations and vary by season, cabins, and cruise areas.

RATES Port charges are included.

Special fares and discounts Early booking fares offer up to 45% savings. Ask about ProntoPrice, the line's new pricing policy for early bookers.

- **CHILDREN'S FARE:** Same as third/fourth passenger fares (works for single parents, too); also $199 or "Kids Sail Free" for children ages 17 and younger on some cruises.
- **SINGLE SUPPLEMENT:** 180%–200%.

Packages
- **AIR/SEA:** Discounts for groups.
- **PRE/POST:** Available for most cities where cruise begins and ends.
- **OTHERS:** Various discounts available; inquire.

PAST PASSENGERS Costa Club is the line's passenger club, which passengers can join after their first cruise. With each subsequent Costa cruise, you receive points based on the number of days of the cruise and expenditures charged to your cruise card. The Costa Club card is valid for three years. Depending on your category, members receive discounts in the beauty salon, fruit basket, free dinner in an alternative restaurant that has a charge; and discounts on cruise fares, ranging from 5–18%, among others. Past passengers also receive mailings announcing new itineraries and a Costa magazine.

THE LAST WORD Costa prefers to be number one in Europe, where it has a strong base and years of experience, rather than struggle in the fierce competition of the Caribbean. The strategy virtually guarantees that when you take a Costa cruise in Europe, the experience will be European rather than catering to American tastes.

Some Americans welcome the opportunity to take a European vacation with Europeans. Others are turned off by cliques in lounges and bars and the steady stream of announcements—for bingo, shopping talks, and shore excursions—in five languages, even though English-speaking hostesses are aboard to cater to North Americans. Fortunately, the multilingual announcements on Caribbean cruises are kept to a minimum and normally are used when matters of safety are being broadcast.

Areas are designated as smoking or nonsmoking on Costa ships, but some European smokers flout the restrictions—defiantly.

Costa Cruise Lines Standard Features

Officers Italian.

Staff Dining: Italian, European, Asian, and others; Cabin: International; Cruise: International.

Dining facilities One main dining room (two on *Costa Victoria;* five on *Costa Concordia, Costa Serena*), two seatings for breakfast and dinner, one for lunch, midnight buffet featuring Italian cuisine; indoor/outdoor buffet breakfast and lunch. Alternative dining; *Atlantica, Concordia, Fortuna, Magica, Mediterranea, Serena, Victoria* (extra charge). Pizzerias and pastry cafes on most ships.

Special diets Should be requested four weeks in advance.

Room service 24 hours, limited menu; butler service in suites with full service for meals from dining room menus.

Dress code Casual; informal, evenings; two nights formal/semiformal.

Cabin amenities Phone, radio, private shower, hair dryer, safe, television; suites have whirlpool bath, minibar, and veranda.

Electrical outlets 110/220 AC; adapters available on board.

Wheelchair access 6 cabins on *Classica, Romantica, Victoria;* 8 on *Allegra, Atlantica, Mediterranea;* 24 on *Magica, Fortuna;* 29 on *Concordia, Serena.*

Recreation and entertainment Casino, bars and lounges with nightly entertainment, showrooms, disco, dance and Italian language lessons, bingo, bridge, horse racing, library, card room. *Concordia/Serena:* Grand Prix driving simulator, giant video screen on Pool Deck.

Sports and other activities Three swimming pools, *Atlantica, Concordia, Fortuna* (one for children); *Mediterranea, Magica, Serena;* two, *Classica, Romantica, Victoria* (plus one inside); one, *Allegra, Marina, Riviera.* Exercise classes, snorkeling lessons, paddle tennis, table tennis, deck and pool games. *Victoria, Atlantica, Mediterranea, Magica, Fortuna,* tennis/basketball.

Beauty and fitness Barber shop and beauty salon, spa, sauna, European beauty treatments, fitness centers, jogging track, whirlpools.

Other facilities Boutiques, medical facility, laundry and dry cleaning services, meeting room, chapel. Internet access on all ships.

Children's facilities Costa Kids year-round; babysitters. (No babysitting service in cabins.) *Concordia/Serena,* computer games for kids.

Theme cruises Golf, food and wine, health, music, others.

Smoking Smoking in designated public areas; all dining and public rooms are nonsmoking.

Costa suggested tipping Costa debits passenger shipboard account as follows: $3 per person per day each for cabin steward/stewardess, waiter; $1.50 per person per day for waiter's assistant and $1 per person per day for head waiter. Passengers may change the amounts by contacting Guest Relations desk; 15% gratuity added to all beverage bills (including mineral water in dining room).

Credit cards For cruise payment and onboard charges: American Express, Carte Blanche, Diners Club, Discover, MasterCard, Visa.

Costa Atlantica	QUALITY 7	VALUE C
Costa Mediterranea	QUALITY 7	VALUE C
REGISTRY Italy	LENGTH 960 feet	BEAM 106 feet
CABINS 1,057	DRAFT 19.5 feet	SPEED 24 knots
MAXIMUM PASSENGERS	PASSENGER DECKS 12	ELEVATORS 12
2,680	CREW 920	SPACE RATIO NA

THE SHIPS Costa Atlantica and her twin, Costa Mediterranea, were the largest, fastest ships in the fleet when they entered service in 2000 and 2003. After Costa came under the Carnival umbrella, and with interior design in the hands of architect Joe Farcus, who is known for creating the flamboyant decor of Carnival ships, there was considerable concern that he would "Carnivalize" these Costa ships. Farcus's imprint is unmistakable, but he has combined touches of his trademark fantasy and glitter with European elegance that seem to work and delight most—but not all—of the North Americans and Europeans who have sailed on them. It's safe to say that Farcus's decor is the antithesis of the modern, spare interiors created by Italian designers for some of Costa's other ships.

Atlantica, because of her balconies and large windows, has a more open, lighter appearance than Costa Victoria, which recently had balconies added to 246 of her cabins. Most of the public rooms are on decks 2 and 3, anchored by a spectacular glass-ceiling atrium. The decor of Atlantica, including the use of Murano glass and inlaid mosaic, is flamboyant, with such features as the Alice in Wonderland–style red-leather chairs with extremely high backs in the atrium bar.

The Farcus touches are everywhere—the red-leather benches near the theatrical multilevel fitness room have little boots on them. Whimsical or fantastic motifs are worked into the carpets, the banquettes, and the tables with subtlety and taste.

Atlantica is dedicated to Federico Fellini, the great Italian filmmaker, with her 12 passenger decks named for movies directed by him and huge blow-ups from his work placed in public rooms. (Although, as one passenger pointed out to us on a recent cruise, none of Fellini's movies are to be found among the ship's movie selections.) Besides the impressive large public spaces, there are intimate quiet areas, like the small Italian garden by the chapel. The ship also pays homage to Venice with Caffe Florian, a replica of the 18th-century landmark in St. Mark's Square, with a menu and music taken from the original. Traditionalists will probably find these rooms to be the ship's most attractive area. *Costa Mediterranea* is dedicated to the history, art, and architecture of Italy and the Mediterranean. The decks, for example, are named for mythic and historic figures—Medea, Pandora, Cleopatra, etc. Recently, *Costa Mediterranea* completed a multimillion-dollar refurbishing at the Grand Bahamas Shipyard in Freeport, Bahamas.

Atlantica was the first Costa ship to offer Internet access, available in a center that doubles as the library and in some cabins and suites, where guests can bring their own laptop computer or rent one. The cost is a steep $0.50 per minute.

The ships are equipped with a dual Azipod propulsion system, technology that contributes to smooth sailing. They have received the Green Star from the Italian Register of Shipping for innovative environmental protection design.

ITINERARIES *See* Itinerary Index. In 2007, *Costa Atlantica* was marketed exclusively to Europeans.

CABINS The ships have 13 categories of cabins, most on decks 1 and 4–8. Of the total 1,057 cabins, 78% are outside. The 678 cabins, or almost 65% of cabins and suites, have verandas with clear acrylic barriers in front, enabling passengers to lie in bed and look out at the port of call or the sea. Another 68 cabins have French balconies, but these have views obstructed by the lifeboats, as noted in the deck plan.

Cabins are stylish in decor and very well designed, with an unusual amount of polished hardwood floors as well as carpets and fine leather. All cabins have direct-dial telephone, television, minibar, safe, hair dryer, amenities, and ample storage. In the suites, the bedside lamps have exceptionally attractive Murano glass shades with smaller, concentrated lights attached for nighttime reading. The suites also have plush robes, marble baths, double sinks, and Jacuzzi tubs. In standard cabins, showers are much larger than on the line's previous vessels.

Specifications 824 outside cabins; 233 inside; 678 cabins (including 58 suites) with verandas. Cabins with verandas measure 210 square feet; inside cabins, 162 square feet; suites with verandas, 360 square feet. 8 are wheelchair-accessible.

DINING The ships have several dining venues. The two-level **Tiziano Restaurant** (**Degli Argentieri** on *Costa Mediterranea*) is the main dining room serving undistinguished continental cuisine with some Italian specialties; the **Botticelli Buffet** offers breakfast and lunch in an informal setting with a rather limited, repetitive selection; and the **Napoli Pizzeria** serves a variety of fresh, hot pizzas throughout the day. Surprisingly, there are no pasta stations in either the dining room or the Lido buffet, as on Costa's other ships.

The dining rooms are comfortable, but the noise level is high, depending on where you sit. Healthful menus with low-fat, low-carb, low-calorie, and low-cholesterol courses are available in the dining rooms for lunch, dinner, and at the informal breakfast. A generous number of vegetarian dishes is offered, and there is a separate children's menu.

Club Atlantica by Marchesi (**Club Medusa** on *Mediterranea*), the alternative, by-reservation restaurant, is located at the top of the ship, above the Lido restaurant. It is modeled after its namesake in Venice and has an extra charge of $23 a person—and worth every penny. It offers two appetizing single-choice menus and wines served amid candles, flowers, and live musical entertainment. If you come only once, you might want to mix and match selections from both menus. The cuisine here is so outstanding that it shows up the dining room's mediocre results and makes one wonder why there is such a marked difference.

SERVICE Not everyone agrees about the service. Some say it's excellent, warm, and efficient; others say it's often haphazard. But for sure, long-time Costa fans will miss the verve of an Italian crew, as now the only Italians in the restaurants are the maître d'hôtel and his assistant. On a recent cruise, we found service throughout the *Costa Atlantica* to be excellent and its top attraction. There are no wine stewards in the dining room.

FACILITIES AND ACTIVITIES Daytime diversions include dance, gaming and golf lessons, port and shopping talks, the ubiquitous art auctions, health and beauty workshops, bridge, handwriting analysis, tennis singles, arts and crafts, and quizzes. The cruise staff is one of the most active this writer has ever encountered, keeping passengers busy with games, dancing, and other activities, and creating an atmosphere that reminded me of traditional cruises of the past. The library and card room are handsome and well used, but the multinational nature of the passengers means a somewhat limited number of books in English. The Internet center, which is part of the library, has five terminals. **Via della Spiga** is the ship's shopping promenade, and there's a full-service conference center.

Evening entertainment is designed for the multinational nature of the passengers, with more dance, music, and magic than comic routines. The **Caruso Theater** (**Osiris** on *Mediterranea*), the impressive three-level main show lounge at the front of the ship, has very few columns to interrupt sight lines. En route to the theater, passengers pass the **Paparazzi Lounge** with bigger-than-life, black-and-white photographs of celebrities, such as Joe DiMaggio.

Caffe Florian, replicating the famous St. Mark's Square landmark, serves afternoon tea, coffees, liqueurs, and aperitifs with background music evoking the romance of the Venetian legend that captivated such luminaries as Vivaldi, Dickens, Stravinsky, and others. The **Madama Butterfly Grand Lounge** is a large multifunction room and bar used for activities throughout the day and evening. The **Coral Lounge,** used for seminars and special entertainment, has an underwater quality, with blue walls and huge white coral trees behind etched glass.

The glittering **Fortuna Casino** (**Grand Canal Casino** on *Mediterranea*) is well laid out, with comfortable access to slots, roulette, and blackjack tables. It has its own bar—one of 12 on the ship—and is adjacent to the Madama Butterfly Grand Lounge.

Dancing in the evenings ranges from disco to swing, and bands playing for guests waiting to enter the dining room inspire impromptu dance sessions in the lounges. The bi-level **Dante's Disco,** with an outstanding sound system, is positioned on the bottom two passenger decks—a good choice because the action tends to go to the wee hours of the night.

Theme nights are offered in the Costa tradition and include Fiesta Italiana and Notte Mediterranea, street festivals at sea with boccie ball and tarantella dance lessons, costumes, music, and finger food from Spain, France, Greece, and Turkey. Then, too, the last night is the always popular Toga Party-at-Sea, when passengers show their ingenuity—or lack thereof—creating a toga out of a bedsheet that the ship supplies.

SPORTS, FITNESS, AND BEAUTY   Each ship has three outdoor pools plus Jacuzzis. One pool has a retractable roof that converts the central pool deck into an 11,000-square-foot solarium, thus providing all-weather swimming. At the top of the ship is a stand-alone waterslide that does not empty into a pool. The **Aurora Pool,** the third pool located in the rear of the ship, is a quiet hideaway. It adjoins the dramatic two-level **Ischia Spa and Gym,** which has thalassotherapy and a broad range of other treatments, as well as well-used sauna, steam, and whirlpools. Costa has full- and half-day spa packages as well as à la carte, all of them pricey. Above the spa is a tennis court, where undersized racquets are used; it converts to a basketball or volleyball court.

The workout area is theater style, with a main floor and balcony; it has an array of Technogym equipment like that found in a major health club, plus sophisticated electronic aerobic monitoring equipment. Exercise classes are offered for all fitness levels, including children's jogging and aerobics.

CHILDREN'S FACILITIES   The large and well-fitted **Pinocchio's Children's Room** is the center of children's activities. Costa Kids, a year-round program available on Caribbean and European cruises, offers daily activities geared to two age groups: Costa Kids Club, 3–12 years, and Costa Teens Club, 13–17 years. Two youth counselors are aboard each ship year-round; counselors are added when there are more than 12 children on a cruise. **Youth Center** activities include video-game competitions, bridge and galley tours, arts and crafts, a treasure hunt, Italian lessons, bingo, board games, karaoke contests, pizza parties, ice-cream socials, face painting, cartoons, and movies.

At sea, Kids Club hours generally are 9–11:30 a.m., 2–5:30 p.m., and 8–11 p.m. On Caribbean cruises, group babysitting for ages 3 and up (children must be out of diapers) is available on request from 6:30–11 p.m. In port, hours are 8:30 a.m.–12:30 p.m. and 2:30–6:30 p.m. There is a charge. Costa also offers Parents Night Out. On two different nights, parents can enjoy evenings alone while their children have the evening with their peers at a supervised buffet or pizza party with activities designed especially for them.

European cruises have three clubs: Baby Club, 3–6 years; Junior Club, 7–12 years; and Teens Club, 13–17 years. Baby Club offers a story hour, crafts, games, and ice-cream parties. Junior Club has aerobics, puppet theater, mini-Olympics, and team treasure hunts. Teens Club offers sports and fitness programs, guitar lessons, video productions, and a rock-and-roll hour. In Europe, free group babysitting for ages 3–6 is available, subject to staff availability. A disco and teen club offer a dance floor, video games, four computer stations, and a large television monitor.

SHORE EXCURSIONS On Eastern Caribbean cruises, the ship stops at Isla Catalina, where Costa developed facilities for a fun day at the beach with games and water sports. The ship also offers tours to **Casa de Campo,** one of the Caribbean's largest resorts, for tennis, horseback riding, and golf on world-famous Pete Dye courses. You must buy the ship's shore excursion to go to Casa de Campo; cruise passengers are not allowed to venture there on their own during the day. The ship docks at Isla Catalina for the day and the Casa de Campo marina for the evening, enabling passengers to enjoy the resort's elegant dining and nightlife. The ship offers diving and snorkeling at selected ports.

In Europe, shore excursions generally are as varied as the cruises and range from a glacier walk in Norway to a visit to Egyptian pyramids. Itineraries are port-intensive, rarely including more than one or two days at sea during a week.

Costa Fortuna	QUALITY 8	VALUE C
Costa Magica	QUALITY 8	VALUE C
REGISTRY Italy	LENGTH 890 feet	BEAM 124 feet
CABINS 1,358	DRAFT NA	SPEED 20 knots
MAXIMUM PASSENGERS	PASSENGER DECKS 13	ELEVATORS 18
3,470	CREW 1,068	SPACE RATIO NA

THE SHIPS If the name is any indication, then good fortune showered Costa with the *Fortuna,* launched in late 2003, followed by her twin, *Magica,* in 2004, as part of the line's enormous expansion program that added four big ships in four years.

Costa Fortuna and *Costa Magica* were the largest ships in Costa's history and the largest ships in Italian maritime history when they were launched. They were also the first post-Panamax ship (a ship too wide to transit the Panama Canal) for a European cruise line and the first post-Panamax ships to sail in Europe year-round.

Although the ships are not quite as large, their "footprint" is similar to *Carnival Destiny's*, with a three-story show lounge, two main dining rooms, a casual Lido restaurant, large spa and fitness facilities, three swim-ming pools, shops, a chapel, Internet cafe, and children's and teen's areas. But there are differences, too. For example, the casino was made smaller to accommodate the **Grand Bar** with a large dance floor because Costa's Italian and European passengers like to dance more than gamble. Also, in place of the sports bar on the Carnival ships, the ships have cigar bars.

Costa Fortuna's interiors pay tribute to the great Italian liners of yesteryear; public rooms are named for these classic ships and the year they entered service. The **Michelangelo 1965 Restaurant** has a 20-foot-long model of the liner *Michelangelo* in its foyer. Exhibited for years in Milan's central railway station, it is believed to be the second-largest ship model in the world.

Inverted scale models of Costa vessels, past and present, glide across a blue ceiling over the bar of the *Costa Fortuna*'s nine-deck atrium. The mod-els are among 38 found on the vessel, which is awash in art and memora-bilia, including a collection of antique nautical objects and antique globes. *Costa Magica*'s theme is the magic of Italy's enchanting small villages.

ITINERARIES *See* Itinerary Index. *Costa Fortuna,* marketed exclusively to Euro-peans, sails from Italy to South America during the winter season

CABINS More than half (853) of the 1,358 cabins are outside. Of those, 522 cabins and 64 minisuites and suites have balconies. All come with hair dryer, safe, and stocked minibar. Standard cabins have showers only, but minisuites have bathtubs, and suites are equipped with whirlpool tubs. Minisuites and suites also have butler service.

Specifications 474 inside cabins (160 square feet); 335 outside standard (174–190 square feet); 458 outside with balcony (210 square feet); 64 suites (360–650 square feet); 27 wheelchair-accessible (220 square feet).

DINING Italian specialties like homemade pastas are highlights in the bi-level main restaurant, **Michelangelo 1965** (with big windows in the stern), and **Raffaello 1965** at midship (**Costa Emerald** and **Portofino** on *Costa Magica*). Casual meals and pizza are served in the spacious **Cristoforo Columbo 1954** buffet restaurant; and perched high on Deck 11 is the **Conte Grande 1927** supper club (**Vicenza Club** on *Magica*), a reservation-only venue where you dine on dinnerware by Versace and eat Italian cuisine by Zeffirino, the famous Genoa restaurant with a branch in Las Vegas. The cover charge is $23.

FACILITIES AND ACTIVITIES The ships' main gathering spot, morning and night, is the centrally located **Conte di Savoia 1932 Grand Bar** named for Italy's most elegant ocean liner (**Grand Bar Salento** on *Magica*). People gather here from early morning for cappuccino until late into the night, when a live band plays for dancing. The room has a huge parquet dance floor, sweeping black granite bar, and gilded fabrics in yellow, blue, and green. At 11,000 square feet, it may be the largest bar afloat.

In the **Vulcania 1927 Disco,** a glass wall surrounds the upper level, enabling gamblers in the casino one deck up to look down on the dancers. Named after the liner *Vulcania,* the disco has a large mechanized figure of Vulcan, the mythical god of fire, who pounds out fiber-optic sparks on an anvil in time to the music.

Other appealing rooms are the **Leonardo da Vinci 1960 Lounge,** displaying reproductions of masterpieces like the *Mona Lisa* etched onto large glass canvases. The room has a combo for dance music and becomes the venue for late-night cabaret. A more intimate bar/dance venue is the **Conte Verde 1923 Lounge.** Inspired by the grand ballroom of the *Conte Verde* liner, the room sports an emerald-green ceiling and large malachite vases of Murano glass that sprout topiary trees ("verde" means *green* in Italian). The **Conte Rosso 1921 Piano Bar** pays tribute to *Conte Verde*'s sister ship and is colored red ("rosso" means *red* in Italian).

The Rex Theater 1932, (Urbino Theater on *Magica*) where big production shows are staged, is an enormous room stretching over three decks and seating 1,100 passengers. The stage is flanked by towering funnels to recall the powerful *Rex*, which held the transatlantic speed record from 1933 to 1935. The *Rex* was Italy's fastest and most famous ocean liner. Along the corridor to one theater entrance is a display case containing a historic model of the *Rex*, which was built at the same yard as the liner. Outside another entrance is a case of bejeweled theatrical costumes and masks from famous plays like *Macbeth*.

POSTSCRIPT Although these ships are designed for European cruisers, Americans who want to cruise the Mediterranean on a very large ship with all the latest amenities will find the facilities, activities, and entertainment to be similar to those on mainstream U.S. lines like Carnival. There's plenty of action for children, teens, and adults, from games and sports contests to classes, shopping, shows, and dancing from ballroom to hip-hop—plus, an international flair and very active nightlife centered around dancing and dining on Italian cuisine.

Costa Concordia	PREVIEW	
Costa Serena	PREVIEW	
REGISTRY Italy	LENGTH 951 feet	BEAM 116 feet
CABINS 1,500	DRAFT 24 feet	SPEED 20.5 knots
MAXIMUM PASSENGERS	PASSENGER DECKS 11	ELEVATORS 13
3,780	CREW 1,110	SPACE RATIO NA

THE SHIP Costa's new flagship, *Concordia*—a symbolic name connoting concord or peace—is the largest cruise ship built for an Italian company and the European cruise ship with the largest passenger capacity. Built in Italy and costing 450 million euros, she entered service in 2006 and is sailing the Mediterranean year-round.

Costa Concordia is the first of three sister ships Costa is building for a total investment of almost 1.5 billion euros. The second ship, *Costa Serena,* made her debut in May 2007 and the third, *Costa Luminosa,* will be launched in 2009.

Among *Concordia*'s special features are the **Samsara Spa,** which claims to be the largest spa at sea, extending over two decks with 55 cabins and 12 suites that come with special and exclusive privileges for passengers who reserve them. It also has the **Ponte Francia** pool deck—spanning two decks and including two swimming pools with retractable glass roofs—making it the largest enclosable pool area on any cruise ship, according to Costa. The deck has a huge movie screen and a multilingual audio system for watching movies day and night. But the ship's most unusual feature of all is the Grand Prix (Formula One) race car simulator, identical to the cars in which real champions train. Race car aficionados can drive like the pros and even get a recording of their performance. *Costa Serena* will have these special features too.

Concordia is the fifth Costa ship to be designed by Joe Farcus, the well-known interior designer for Carnival Cruises. For this ship, he drew inspiration from European architectural styles up to the 1900s, such as Irish gothic, Belgian Art Deco, Austrian baroque, and Italian postmodern, among others. The public areas on the ship are named after some of Europe's most beautiful and famous cities—Dublin, Lisbon, London, Paris, Prague, Stockholm, Vienna, etc. In 2007, *Costa Concordia* was sailing from Italy on Mediterranean cruises year-round.

ITINERARIES *See* Itinerary Index.

CABINS *Costa Concordia* has 1,500 cabins, including 70 suites and 501 cabins (or about 40%) with verandas.

Specifications 586 inside cabins, 343 outside; 501 cabins with balcony; 29 wheelchair-accessible.

DINING *Concordia* has five restaurants. The ship's reservation-only specialty restaurant, **Club Concordia,** features cuisine by renowned chef and creator of Italian molecular cuisine, Ettore Bocchia, executive chef of the Michelin-star restaurant of Villa Serbelloni in Bellagio, Italy. By studying the physical and chemical properties of food, Bocchia focuses on enhancing the flavor of ingredients while creating new textures for his cuisine.

FACILITIES AND ACTIVITIES *Concordia* has 13 bars, including one cognac and one cigar bar; a show lounge spanning three decks; a casino and nightclub, an Internet cafe and library, shops, and a giant movie screen on the Pool Deck. For kids, the Children Squok Club has its own splash pool; teenagers have **Mondovirtuale,** a computer game area.

On the Grand Prix race car simulator, passengers 16 years of age and older can learn how to drive like the pros. Located on one of the top decks, the simulator has real-time vehicle modeling (the same technology used by Grand Prix champion drivers in training). Passengers can compete virtually in a Grand Prix race at speeds of more than 200 miles per hour and can record their performances throughout the week to compete with other guests. The simulator has four levels of difficulty, ranging from a test mode for three minutes on the track without other drivers, up to championship mode with one qualification and seven racing laps for a maximum of 13 minutes.

SPORTS, FITNESS, AND BEAUTY *Concordia* has three pools, of which two are under retractable magrodomes, enabling their use in the Mediterranean in any weather, even in midwinter. There are also five Jacuzzis and an outdoor jogging track.

The ship's pride is its 20,500-square-foot **Samsara Spa,** which extends over two decks. Elements in the spa's design and treatments were inspired by the meaning of "Samsara," which is associated with the path to spiritual enlightenment and balancing of life energies. The spa offers a full menu of treatments based on Ayurvedic principles, an ancient Indian holistic healing method. The spa is centered by an indoor pool where passengers can enjoy thalassotherapy sessions; other facilities include a state-of-the-art fitness center, sauna, Turkish bath, solarium, and a treatment room for couples.

The ultracomfortable Samsara cabins and suites, adjacent to the spa or nearby, have an Asian atmosphere typical of Samsara and were designed specifically for passengers who want to immerse themselves in the spa and wellness program. They have direct access to the spa via private elevators and stairs not available to other guests, and such exclusive amenities as flat-screen televisions, Elemis bath amenities, and exclusive access to the **Ristorante Samsara,** with a full menu of wellness cuisine served in private surroundings.

Passengers staying in Samsara accommodations receive a Welcome Ritual package (included in the cruise price). It includes unlimited access to the spa and thalassotherapy pool, two complimentary fitness classes, personalized consultation with a spa expert, two treatments, two sun-lamp sessions in the solarium, and an invitation to a special spa tea ceremony. Other passengers have free access to the fitness center, but for access to some spa amenities, they must purchase a day pass for 35 euros or a weekly pass for 199 euros. Spa accommodations (directly connected to the spa) have been so popular on *Costa Concordia,* that the number of spa accommodations on *Serena* has been increased from 66 to 99 (87 cabins and 12 suites).

Costa Victoria	QUALITY 5	VALUE C
REGISTRY Italy	LENGTH 828 feet	BEAM 105 feet
CABINS 964	DRAFT 24 feet	SPEED 23 knots
MAXIMUM PASSENGERS	PASSENGER DECKS 10	ELEVATORS 12
2,394	CREW 800	SPACE RATIO 38.9

THE SHIP Costa's first megaship made her debut in 1996. Designed by well-known naval architect Robert Tillberg, she was the largest passenger liner built in Germany when she was launched. Despite her large size, her shallow draft provides exceptional maneuverability and gives the ship access to smaller ports and the Suez Canal. Her size also made possible more choices in dining and entertainment.

Ultramodern and sophisticated, the circular **Planetarium Atrium** spans seven decks and has four glass elevators connecting the lobby with the pool deck above. It's capped by a large glass dome admitting sunlight that reflects off a colored glass sculpture by Milanese artist Gianfranco Pardi on the Boheme Deck (Deck 5). Deck 5 also has the purser's office, shore excursion desk, and a piano bar. All but one of the ten passenger decks are named after Italian operas.

The most dramatic room is the **Concorde Plaza,** an observation lounge at the bow. It spans four decks; a floor-to-ceiling glass wall provides spectacular ocean views. Opposite the windows is a marble dance floor adjoining a center stage; its backdrop is a waterfall inspired by Leonardo da Vinci's drawings of the moon eclipsing the sun. Decorated in blues, silver, and gold, the lounge serves as an elegant area for socializing, special events, and evening entertainment, including cabaret shows, games, bingo, and port lectures.

ITINERARIES *See* Itinerary Index. *Costa Victoria* sails from Italy on Mediterranean cruises year-round.

CABINS The majority of cabins are on the upper decks. Sixty percent are outside cabins with a porthole or large, square window. Cabins are small compared with those on *Costa Romantica*. Originally, the ship had no cabins with balconies, which was definitely a drawback for the ship, but in 2004, full balconies were fitted to 246 cabins. *Victoria* was the line's first ship to have a minibar, safe, hair dryer, and interactive television in every cabin. All cabins have direct-dial telephones and sliding doors that separate the living area and bathroom. Circular bathrooms have rounded showers and vanity areas.

The six top suites and 14 minisuites, forward on the pool and sports decks, are decorated with Laura Ashley fabrics and trimmed with pear wood. They have sitting areas, whirlpool baths, walk-in closets, and queen beds, plus one upper berth and a Murphy bed, thus accommodating up to four people. Butler service is provided.

The *Victoria*'s unique fan coil system allows each cabin to be refreshed with its own recycled air or outside air. Thus, nonsmokers' air isn't mixed with smokers'. The ship does not have self-service laundries for passenger use.

Specifications 391 inside cabins, 553 outside; 20 suites; 250 cabins with balcony; 6 wheelchair-accessible. Standard cabins range from 120 to150 square feet.

DINING *Costa Victoria* was the first Costa vessel to have two dining rooms: **Sinfonia Restaurant,** aft, and **Fantasia Restaurant,** amidships. Both are decorated with marble and pine walls and glass chandeliers from Murano. Their picture windows are transformed from ocean views by day to Italian scenes by night by murals that drop in place like window shades.

Dinner menus have fewer selections than are offered on some ships in Costa's price group, but choices are ample and of good quality, balancing Italian and European dishes with American favorites. A different pasta is featured at lunch and dinner; American audiences rave over them. A typical dinner menu offers three appetizers, two soups, two salads, three pastas, four entrées (one vegetarian), three or more desserts, ice cream, sherbet, cheese, and fresh fruit. The presentation is always attractive.

Ristorante Magnifico by Zefferino, the ship's reservations-only alternative restaurant, is modeled after the famous Zefferino's in Genoa. Passengers pay an extra charge of $23 per person, but it's worth it and has proven to be popular. Walls are hung with ten paintings of earlier Costa passenger ships by artist Stephen Card and contribute to the cozy atmosphere created by the addition of candlelight, flowers, soft music, and excellent service.

Passengers dine informally at an indoor/outdoor buffet serving breakfast and lunch. **Bolero,** the indoor buffet, is surrounded by glass windows and furnished with rattan chairs and marble tables. The outdoor **Terraza Café,** similar to one on *Romantica* but much larger, is protected by a large white canopy made by Canobbio, an Italian firm specializing in circus tents and sports arena coverings. Other dining options include two buffets, a pizzeria, ice-cream bar, and grill.

FACILITIES AND ACTIVITIES Daytime diversions include lessons in dance, Italian, and gaming; bingo; bridge; backgammon; culinary demonstrations; port and shopping talks; horse racing; and the Not-So-Newlywed Game. The teen center has a video game room, and there's a library, card room, and Internet center. Movies are shown on the in-cabin televisions.

The two-deck **Festival Show Lounge** is decorated in rich reds with Tivoli lights twinkling in the ceiling. The stage can be raised for variety and production shows or lowered for dancing.

The **Grand Bar Orpheus,** with a bar trimmed in rare blue Brazilian marble, is popular for cocktails and after-dinner espresso. It's connected by a curved glass stairway to the big, bright **Monte Carlo Casino.** Just outside the casino is **Capriccio Lounge,** an intimate piano bar decorated with floor-to-ceiling mosaics by Italian painter Emilio Tadini.

Theme nights may include Notte Tropical, the lively Festa Italiana, and the rollicking Roman Bacchanal. The full-service conference center offers meeting space, audiovisual equipment, movable leather chairs equipped with flip-top desks, and a board room for 20. The center has its own front desk, which meeting planners applaud.

SPORTS, FITNESS, AND BEAUTY The **Solarium,** a top-deck viewing and sunning area, has pipes that continuously emit mists of cool water. The two outdoor pools are surrounded by six whirlpools and two shuffleboard courts. Nearby is the **Wimbledon Tennis Court,** a miniature court using smaller racquets and balls. It can be converted to a basketball or volleyball court.

In addition to the beauty salon, the **Pompei Spa** has an indoor swimming pool centered with a large mosaic and surrounded by Roman columns and teak lounge chairs. The spa offers a Turkish bath, saunas, massage, thalassotherapy, hydrotherapy, and other beauty treatments. A 1,312-foot jogging track connects the spa to the gymnasium, which is equipped with weight-training equipment and an aerobics room. This is the first ship to carry products from Tuscany's chic Terme di Saturnia.

CHILDREN'S FACILITIES Costa Kids Club for children ages 3–12 is further divided by age group depending on the number of children on a particular sailing. See *Costa Atlantica,* above, for details on the children's program.

Costa Classica	QUALITY 7	VALUE C
Costa Romantica	QUALITY 7	VALUE B
REGISTRY Italy	LENGTH 722/610 feet	BEAM 102 feet
CABINS 654/678	DRAFT 24 feet	SPEED 18 knots
MAXIMUM PASSENGERS	PASSENGER DECKS 11	ELEVATORS 10/8
1,680/1,697	CREW 650/722	SPACE RATIO 41.5/40

THE SHIPS *Costa Romantica* and *Costa Classica* are almost identical. These spacious ships with public rooms on the upper four decks have ultra-modern Italian interiors using a king's ransom in marble, dramatic window walls, futuristic sculptures, clean lines, angular shapes, and fine art. The result reflects modern Italian design and is a radical departure from traditional Italian ocean liners of the past.

Passengers are introduced to the ship in its dramatic **Grand Lobby,** set low on the Copenhagen Deck, which is dedicated entirely to cabins, as are the deck below and the two decks above. White-gloved room stewards escort passengers to their cabins. The background music of Vivaldi and other Italian composers is meant to underscore the start of a week of "Cruising Italian Style." The ships' layouts are easy to follow, with one lounge or public space flowing to the next, creating openness and harmony. Decks are named after European cities.

The dramatic centerpiece of *Romantica's* lobby is a moving sculpture by Japanese artist Susumu Shingu. Installed in 1992 to commemorate the Columbus quincentennial, it's a mobile with panels that move continuously and change color against the area's Carrara marble walls and floors.

Romantica's heart and social center is the **Piazza Italia** on the Verona Deck—an atrium furnished as a lounge, with a small bandstand and dance floor on one side and a bar on the other. The lounge is the favorite gathering spot for pre-lunch and pre-dinner drinks, as it's a short walk from the dining room. Forward are meeting rooms, the library, chapel, card room, and the ground floor of **L'Opera,** the bi-level show lounge. From the Piazza, a double stairway leads up to the Vienna Deck and the popular **Romeo's Pizzeria** and **Juliet's Patisserie.** Forward are shops on the Via Condotti, named for Rome's fashionable shopping street.

ITINERARIES *See* Itinerary Index. *Costa Classica* is based in Dubai for the winter season; *Costa Romantica* sails from Italy to South America.

CABINS Spacious and well designed, cabins are these ships' best feature. Standard cabins are fitted in cherry furnishings, including a dresser and desk unit with large mirror; bedside tables; a control panel for lights by the bed; ample closet space; and two chairs, one of which opens into a bed suitable for a child.

Elegant touches are the white curtain spanning the room, which can be raised and lowered to cover the oversized porthole; designer amenities; and high-quality bed and bath linens. All cabins have television, radio, safe, direct-dial satellite phone, and hair dryer. The 24-hour room service offers sandwiches and beverages.

Specifications *Costa Romantica,* 216 inside cabins, 428 outside, no singles. 16 suites, 18 minisuites. Standard dimensions, 175 square feet inside, 200 square feet outside. 242 take third and fourth persons. *Costa Classica,* 216 inside cabins, 688 outside; 4 grand suites, 16 with verandas. Standard dimensions, 175–200 square feet. 359 cabins take third and fourth persons. 6 singles. 6 wheelchair-accessible.

DINING *Romantica's* **Botticelli Restaurant,** similar to *Classica's* counterpart, **Tivoli,** is beautifully laid out almost entirely in off-white and brown Carrara marble with coffered ceilings. Elegantly designed wicker-backed chairs encircle round tables, most seating eight, dressed in starched white cloths, fine china, glassware, and flowers. Movable side panels faced with a variety of scenes—a European city, landscapes, or Italian gardens—are changed each evening. They were designed by Giorgio Cristini, set designer for Milan's famous La Scala opera house.

The lovely room lacks carpeting or wall coverings, causing an extraordinarily high noise level that hinders conversation. Acoustical material was added, particularly in the ceiling, which helped—but not enough. Side tables toward the back of the room get less noise.

Il Giardino, the Lido cafe for indoor breakfast and lunch buffets, is among the ship's prettiest informal settings; its rattan chairs are dressed in English country fabrics against aquamarine glass walls and wood floors. At least two evenings per cruise, a dinner buffet is offered. The midnight buffet's setting changes depending on weather and the theme.

Adjacent to the Lido cafe, the **Terrazza Café** reproduces the *Classica's* popular **Al Fresco Café,** the ship's most pleasant location from dawn to dusk. Set with wicker chairs and tables under a high-peaked canvas canopy, it provides a cool, inviting outdoor setting for breakfast and lunch.

The other big hit is **Romeo's Pizzeria,** where pizza is served throughout the day. It's free, but you might want to buy a glass of wine or beer to wash it down. Romeo's neighbor, **Juliet's Patisserie,** open from 9 a.m. to midnight, serves pastries (without charge) and espresso. It's also the **Martini Bar.**

Afternoon tea, with fabulous desserts, is served daily; a cart dispenses Italian ice cream from 10 p.m. to midnight, and **Notte Tropical** is an outdoor tropical buffet.

FACILITIES AND ACTIVITIES Lessons in dance, Italian , and gaming; bingo. Bridge, backgammon, and culinary demonstrations are some of the daytime diversions. Evening entertainment is designed to appeal to the multinational passenger mix. *Romantica's* main show lounge, the **L'Opera Theater** (**Colosseo** on *Classica*), is a modern interpretation of a classic, horseshoe-shaped concert hall. Creating a glamorous setting are red and royal-blue carpets, blue-velvet seats against a wall of blue mosaics, and brass accents. Most seats have good sight lines, and back-pain sufferers will like the hard, stiff balcony seats. L'Opera has shows nightly.

Romantica's casino is spectacular, with stucco walls inlaid with gold accents and a large crystal chandelier. **The Tango Ballroom,** a multipurpose lounge with large dance floor, becomes a high-energy nightclub with live music. The room has window walls and is a lovely daytime retreat. The **Diva Disco** atop the ship, a daytime observation and cocktail lounge with floor-to-ceiling windows, is the late-night hot spot. Everyone's favorite is the toga party, when passengers create Roman garb from sheets provided by the ship. It's remarkable how many ways passengers find to make togas, and almost all passengers join in and have a great time.

SPORTS, FITNESS, AND BEAUTY Two outdoor pools are separated by Costa's distinctive yellow stacks. One has four Jacuzzis and is surrounded by three terraces of teak decks with lounge chairs. The second is inlaid with ceramic tiles; suspended above it is a Susumu sculpture in red metal, which changes shape in the wind.

The **Caracalla Spa** on the *Classica* has floor-to-ceiling windows. *Romantica*'s smaller spa is beside the stack. In addition to weights, life cycles, and treadmills, the spa has sauna, steam, and massage rooms, plus a beauty salon offering personalized hair and body treatments. A partial deck above the swimming pools has a jogging track and sunbathing space.

CHILDREN'S FACILITIES *See Costa Atlantica section.*

Costa Europa	QUALITY 7	VALUE B
REGISTRY Italy	LENGTH 798 feet	BEAM 101 feet
CABINS 747	DRAFT 75.5 feet	SPEED 24 knots
MAXIMUM PASSENGERS	PASSENGER DECKS 9	ELEVATORS 7
1,773	CREW 650	SPACE RATIO 36.4

THE SHIP The *Costa Europa*, the former *Westerdam* of Holland America Line, joined the Costa fleet in 2002. She is not a superliner, but she fits well with the fleet. She is longer, narrower, and has fewer decks than the newer ships, and a lower space-to-passenger ratio, but she's a spacious ship nonetheless. (Moviegoers saw her in *Out to Sea*, the 1997 comedy starring Jack Lemmon and Walter Matthau.)

When she debuted in 1989, she was hailed as one of the decade's most magnificent ships. She combines the style and refinement of great liners with state-of-the-art facilities. To increase her capacity from 1,000 to 1,494 passengers and update her facilities, the ship was stretched. A 130-foot section was added, providing space for a two-tiered show lounge, more bars, a sports deck, fitness facilities, library, larger restaurant, and second buffet. Before entering service for Costa, the ship got another face-lift.

Comfortable, classy, and contemporary, the *Costa Europa* is dressed in pastels with lovely woods and interesting art and antiques. Most public rooms are on the Promenade Deck, anchored by the casino and several lounges forward and a bi-level lounge aft.

The dining room is on the lowest passenger deck. The main section has an interesting wood and Plexiglas dome. Dining is elegant and menu choices extensive; linen-covered tables are set with fine china, silver tableware, and fresh flowers.

The *Costa Europa* has two Lido restaurants, where buffets are available. You can have breakfast and lunch—as well as alternative dining several nights—in the pleasant settings of the veranda by the Sun Deck pool or the Lido restaurant by the Upper Promenade pool.

ITINERARIES *See* Itinerary Index. *Costa Europa* sails from Italy on Mediterranean cruises year-round.

CABINS The ship has 13 cabin categories and boasts standard cabins with comfortable sitting areas. Minimum cabins are only slightly smaller, and suites are more than double average size. Most are fitted with twin beds; more than a third can be converted to queens. All have ample drawer and closet space. The comfortable decor employs the same soothing colors of public rooms. All cabins have telephone, closed-circuit television, multichannel music system, and fine toiletries; all outside cabins (except a few lower-priced ones) have bathrooms with a tub and shower.

Specifications 326 inside cabins, 421 outside. Standard dimensions, 200 square feet for outside cabins. Some upper/lower berths; no singles; 4 wheelchair-accessible.

FACILITIES AND ACTIVITIES The theater on Sun Deck is particularly pretty, with gray-velour seats and deep-blue carpets and walls. Current films are shown daily. The space is also used for religious services, meetings, and lectures. Other daytime activities include bridge tournaments, dance lessons, karaoke, and bingo.

Entertainment and activities are similar to those on her sister ships. Promenade Deck has a cluster of lounges and bars. In one, an orchestra plays for predinner cocktails. Later, the space becomes a disco. Next door is a sports bar, and across the way, another bar with a small dance floor.

The Book Chest is a delightful spot for those who like to read in quiet comfort. The nearby **Ocean Bar,** where every table has a sea view, is the best for people-watching, because everyone passes en route to the main lounge, a multipurpose room with evening entertainment. The ship has a children's facility.

SPORTS, FITNESS, AND BEAUTY The Sports Deck has an unobstructed 40-by-40-foot jogging track, glass windbreaker walls, and two tennis practice courts. A retractable roof protects the Sun Deck swimming pool, two Jacuzzis, and bar. The fitness center on Navigation Deck offers exercise equipment, saunas, and massage rooms. The beauty salon and barber shop are on Promenade Deck.

POSTSCRIPT *Costa Allegra* is now based in Asia, catering to the Chinese market and thus is outside the scope of this book. Costa's European portfolio includes Aida Cruises, which specializes in cruises for the German market.

Cruise West

2301 Fifth Avenue, Suite 401, Seattle, WA 98121-1856
☎ 888-851-8133; fax 206-441-4757
www.cruisewest.com

TYPE OF SHIPS Small, informal, coastal cruising vessels; small, deluxe ocean-going ships.

TYPE OF CRUISES Casual, close-up, light adventure, with emphasis on scenery and wildlife in coastal areas.

CRUISE LINE'S STRENGTHS
- innovative itineraries
- enthusiastic crew
- itinerary flexibility allows extra time for wildlife viewing
- small-ship experience
- exploration leaders on board

CRUISE LINE'S SHORTCOMINGS
- small cabins; noisy lower-deck cabins on older ships
- small bathrooms with handheld showers on older ships
- limited shipboard facilities and evening activities

FELLOW PASSENGERS Mature, physically active; mid-40s to mid-80s. Retired couples and seniors. Passengers somewhat older on Columbia River cruises; younger on Alaskan cruises. Up to 70% have college degrees or some college education; passengers are well traveled and more curious about nature, history, and ecology than typical passengers on mainstream cruise ships.

Passengers are outgoing; most would rather rise early to catch the sunrise than party late. Most are from California, Florida, New York, the Great Lakes region, Pacific Northwest, and Texas; some are from Canada. About 40% are repeaters. Regardless of age, they like the intimacy of a casual cruise to places larger liners cannot reach.

Recommended for Small-ship devotees; people looking for light adventure, to experience a region up close; those preferring wildlife to nightlife.

Not recommended for Travelers who: need to be entertained; seek a lavish, resortlike experience with emphasis on nightlife; prefer facilities and activities of large ships; gamblers.

CRUISE AREAS AND SEASONS Alaska and western Canada, spring–summer; Aleutian Islands and Bering Sea, summer; Atlantic Coast, Canada, Great Lakes, Japan, New England, summer–fall; Columbia and Snake Rivers, Pacific Northwest, spring and fall; California, fall; Caribbean, Costa Rica, Panama, Gulf of California, South Pacific, Vietnam/China, winter.

THE LINE After flying "The Hump" in the China-Burma-India theater in World War II, Charles B. "Chuck" West moved to Alaska to become a bush pilot. Flying over the northern wilderness, he recognized Alaska's

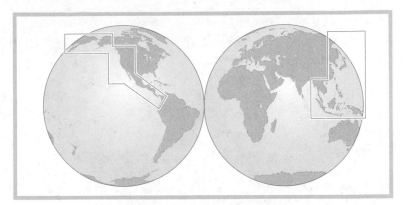

CRUISE AREAS AND SEASONS FOR CRUISE WEST

great tourism potential. In 1946, he organized, sold, and piloted the first all-tourist air excursion north of the Arctic Circle. From that, he built the largest tour company in Alaska—Westours—which he sold to Holland America Line in 1971.

Starting over again at age 60, West built the tour company that became Cruise West, beginning in 1986 with a luxury cruiser for day tours on Prince William Sound. In 1990, adding its first overnight coastal cruising vessel sailing from Juneau to Glacier Bay, and six vessels in seven years, the line became America's largest small-ship cruise company. Other ships followed as the company expanded its operations. In 1997, *Spirit of Endeavour*, the line's most luxurious ship to date, began offering more upscale cruises. In 1998, the line took another major step, sending two ships to cruise Mexico's Gulf of California for the winter, thus becoming a year-round operator. The line's American-built and -flagged vessels are subject to Federal Maritime Commission bonding and strict U.S. Coast Guard inspections.

In 2001, Cruise West added *Spirit of Oceanus* and launched a new era for the line, enabling it to develop new worldwide itineraries and attract new audiences. The all-suite ship, formerly *Renaissance V*, was the line's first oceangoing vessel and the most luxurious ship in the fleet by far. In the same year, it added the *Pacific Explorer* (formerly *Temptress Explorer*), offering cruises in Costa Rica and Panama. One of its biggest moves was the purchase in 2006 of two former Clipper Cruises ships: *Nantucket Clipper*, renamed *Spirit of Nantucket* (a sister ship to *Spirit of Endeavor*), and the slightly larger *Yorktown Clipper*, renamed *Spirit of Yorktown*. These ships boosted the line's capacity by 25% and enabled Cruise West to venture east, adding New England, Canada, the Atlantic seaboard, and the Caribbean.

In 2006, Cruise West introduced cruises to Japan, the South Pacific, and the Kuril Islands, and for 2007 the line expanded in Asia with new itineraries in Japan, Grand Asia, and Vietnam. Meanwhile, the cruise line was recently awarded nearly 80% more entries into Glacier Bay National Park, further enhancing its role as the leading small-ship line in Alaska.

THE FLEET	BUILT/RENOVATED	TONNAGE	PASSENGERS
Pacific Explorer	1995/98	575	100
Spirit of Alaska	1980/95	97	78
Spirit of Columbia	1979/95	98	78
Spirit of Discovery	1976/92	94	84
Spirit of Endeavour	1983/99	95	102
Spirit of Nantucket	1984/95	95.8	102
Spirit of '98	1984/95	96	96
Spirit of Oceanus	1991/2001	1,263	120
Spirit of Yorktown	1988/97	97	138

STYLE Cruise West believes that responsible travel means having enriching experiences that cause minimal impact on the environment. The company encourages environmental education and understanding through unusual, up-close experiences, while respecting wildlife and natural habitats.

The small, shallow-draft vessels can nose into shore for close views of scenery and wildlife and navigate intricate waterways, narrow locks, and small marinas inaccessible to larger ships. Their size and casual atmosphere inspire instant friendships not always possible on larger ships.

Two of the vessels have bow-landing capabilities, enabling them to pull up to wilderness beaches or shoreside parks. En route, narration and occasional talks by park rangers, historians, and other specialists inform passengers of the history, geology, and wildlife of areas they're visiting. Otherwise, onboard style is unstructured.

Passengers entertain themselves by immersion in the scenery and wildlife, reading, playing cards and games, or socializing with other passengers and the crew.

Cruise West's young, mostly college-age crew is recruited primarily from the Pacific Northwest and Alaska. Their caring attitude and enthusiasm are some of the line's strengths. Also notable is the cuisine, which is more sophisticated than is normally associated with small-ship, light-adventure cruising.

DISTINCTIVE FEATURES Bow ramp on *Spirit of Columbia;* bow stairs on *Spirit of Alaska.* Open bridge. Dib launches (inflatable, Zodiac-like motorized launches with covers, seats, and railings) and Zodiacs for adventure cruises.

	HIGHEST	LOWEST	AVERAGE
PER DIEM	$850	$207	$491

Per diems are calculated from cruise line's nondiscounted *cruise-only* published fares on standard accommodations and vary by season, cabins, and cruise areas.

RATES Port charges included.

Special fares and discounts Look for early-bird discounts and refundable/changeable air on seven-day or longer cruises when booked by specific deadlines.

- **SINGLE SUPPLEMENT:** Varies from 125% to 200%; single cabins on *Spirit of '98* and *Spirit of Discovery*. A twin rate is available for singles on select cruises and all inside "B" and "C" cabins.

Packages

- **AIR/SEA:** Air add-ons available from up to 75 gateways.
- **PRE/POST:** Variety of cruise-land-tour Alaska packages with up to nine days of land touring into places like Denali National Park and remote lodges accessible only by floatplane.

PAST PASSENGERS The Quyana Club (the name means "thank you" in Yu'pik Eskimo) offers passengers newsletters, shipboard credits, and 5% savings on all cruises and pre/post packages.

THE LAST WORD The company remains faithful to its founder's vision that small groups maximize travelers' enjoyment without overwhelming villages, small ports, and wilderness areas they visit, and that the focus should be outward, on nature and culture, rather than inward, on nightclubs and gambling. By focusing on wildlife—passengers are likely to see whales, bears, seals, and eagles—and the wilderness, Cruise West says it is increasing awareness and support for protection of natural treasures. And now, Cruise West has a whale of a guarantee: On any of its Wilderness Inside Passage Cruises, you are given a guarantee that whales will be sighted—if not, Cruise West will refund $250 of your cruise price after your return home.

Most passengers try an Alaskan cruise first. If they like it, they graduate to cruises elsewhere. Costa Rica, Mexico, or Panama give Cruise West alumni a complete contrast to Alaska or the Northwest. Yet, the Gulf of California offers similar attractions—wildlife, beautiful scenery, and interesting culture—and much the same appeal. Cruise West's Web site is particularly useful regarding cabins. There are diagrams with precise measurements of each cabin category and readable deck plans.

Cruise West Standard Features

Officers American.

Staff Dining, Cabin, Cruise: American.

Dining facilities One dining room with open seating; meals served at specific hours. Early continental breakfast and 6 p.m. appetizers in forward lounge. Coffee, tea, fresh fruit available throughout day. Occasional buffet on open deck or picnic on shore.

Special diets Vegetarian, low-fat, low-salt, and other heart-healthy requests accommodated; notice required at time of booking.

Cruise West Standard Features (continued)

Room service None, except for owner's suite on *Spirit of '98*.

Dress code Casual at all times. Most passengers wear jeans, chinos, and layer with shirts, sweaters, and light jackets in cooler climates.

Cabin amenities Air-conditioning/thermostat; upper-deck cabins have windows that open. Most bathrooms on older ships are small, some with handheld showers; some have sink and vanity in room, separate from bathroom. Reading lights over bed; limited closets, storage on older ships. *Spirit of Endeavour, Spirit of '98,* and *Spirit of Oceanus* have television and VCR, satellite phone, Internet access, minifridge, safe, hair dryer.

Electrical outlets 110 AC.

Wheelchair access *Spirit of '98* and *Spirit of Oceanus* have elevators.

Recreation and entertainment Forward lounge with bar setup, television, small library with reference books of area, informational videos, movies; informal entertainment by crew; briefings by exploration leaders, occasional talks by historians, park rangers, and other experts. Bridge, other card and board games. Ships stock binoculars, but it's wise to bring your own. Musical entertainment on **Gulf of California** cruises.

Beauty and fitness Some fitness equipment, such as stair steppers and exercise bicycles. No beauty/barber shop.

Other facilities Doctor on **Gulf of California** cruises and on *Oceanus;* at least one crew member on each vessel is trained in First Response. Satellite phone, e-mail, and Internet access on *Spirit of '98, Spirit of Oceanus, Spirit of Endeavour.* E-mail access on *Spirit of Yorktown* and *Spirit of Nantucket.*

Children's facilities None.

Theme cruises Occasionally on American history, culinary.

Smoking Not allowed in public rooms or cabins; smoking allowed only in designated outside area.

Cruise West suggested tipping No tipping is expected or required for either cruise or land-based service. Any tips offered are pooled and shared by nonofficer staff.

Credit cards For cruise payment and onboard charges: American Express, Visa, MasterCard.

Spirit of Oceanus	QUALITY 6	VALUE C
REGISTRY Bahamas	LENGTH 295 feet	BEAM 50 feet
CABINS 57	DRAFT 13.25 feet	SPEED 14.5 knots
MAXIMUM PASSENGERS 120	PASSENGER DECKS 5	ELEVATORS 1
	CREW 64	SPACE RATIO NA

THE SHIP Built in 1991 as the *Renaissance V*, the *Spirit of Oceanus* was acquired by Cruise West in 2001 and named the line's flagship. Prior to that she had been the *Sun Viva* of Sun Cruises, and *MegaStar Sagittarius* under Star Cruises, from which Cruise West purchased her.

The deluxe *Spirit of Oceanus* was Cruise West's first oceangoing vessel and, as such, opened up new horizons for the line, from new destinations worldwide to newer, more upscale cruises that would appeal to a completely new market. In addition to Alaska in summer, she sails on long voyages to the Bering Sea from Anchorage or Nome. In winter, she sails to the South Pacific and Japan, and now, for the first time, she is sailing to Vietnam and China in November 2007.

Registered in the Bahamas—another first for Cruise West—the ship has American officers, an onboard naturalist guide, and an English-speaking crew whose numbers constitute the highest crew-to-guests ratio in the line's fleet. In 2005, the ship was refurbished with two additional suites, new carpeting, mattresses, upholstery, window treatments, and passenger phone and Internet access.

ITINERARIES *See* Itinerary Index.

CABINS *Spirit of Oceanus* has spacious, all-outside suites, each with a large picture window or porthole, ranging in size from 215 to 550 square feet. The 15 suites on the Sun and Sports decks have private teak balconies—another first for Cruise West ships. Other cabin amenities include a walk-in closet, marble-topped vanity, and a lounge area separated from the bedroom by a curtain. All suites can be configured with two twin beds or a queen-size bed and have a television/VCR, safe, minibar, satellite telephone, and private bathroom with a marble sink and shower and hair dryers.

Recently, the ship introduced its new posh 550-square-foot Owner's Suite, which has a foyer with Italian limestone tile; a spacious bathroom with jetted whirlpool tub; a state-of-the-art living room with a flat-screen television, Bose stereo system, and dining, gaming, meeting, and library areas; a teak sun deck. The master bedroom is furnished with a king-size bed and decor details from Ireland and Italy.

Specifications 57 cabins, from 215 to 550 square feet; 15 suites with teak balconies.

FACILITIES AND ACTIVITIES The handsomely appointed *Spirit of Oceanus* has marble and polished hardwood interiors, sumptuous fabrics, and fine art. There are two large lounges (one with a grand piano) and several elegant bars, providing havens for conversation, reading, or playing board games. Among other features passengers enjoy on a Cruise West ship for the first time are a hot tub on the aft Sports Deck, a health facility, a patio bar, and a pool in warm climates.

The ship has a library, an elevator providing access to all five passenger decks, and spacious outside viewing areas and walkways on four of the five guest decks. The elegant dining room accommodates all guests at a single seating. Among the changes in the latest renovations, the casino was removed to make room for more public space, and a small room with exercise equipment was added. The ship has a small clinic staffed by a doctor.

Spirit of Endeavour	QUALITY 3	VALUE C
REGISTRY United States	LENGTH 217 feet	BEAM 37 feet
CABINS 51	DRAFT 8.5 feet	SPEED 12 knots
MAXIMUM PASSENGERS	PASSENGER DECKS 4	ELEVATORS None
102	CREW 28	SPACE RATIO NA

THE SHIP Built in 1983 in Jeffersonville, Indiana, *Spirit of Endeavour* (formerly *Newport Clipper* of Clipper Cruise Lines) was launched for Cruise West in 1996 after a $5 million refurbishing. She was Cruise West's most luxurious ship at the time and added a new level of comfort to the line's fleet until the *Spirit of Oceanus* was acquired. One of the more deluxe small vessels sailing in Alaska and the Gulf of California, *Endeavour* has teak decks, a wide companionway, and comfortable lounges.

In the renovations, passenger phone and Internet access were added; safety features were updated, and new engines and bridge electronics were installed. New bow and stern designs increase the ship's fuel efficiency by more than 22%. A bulbous underwater bow extension reduces the bow wake and water resistance. A stern fairing forces water to flow closer to the surface, reducing drag.

The *Spirit of Endeavour*'s clean lines and raked bow make it look most like a small cruise ship. Viewing breathtaking scenery in Alaska is a major activity on this ship, which appeals to those looking for quiet social life and a relaxed itinerary; in the Gulf of California, there are daily excursions that appeal to those eager for light adventure.

Passengers give high marks to the ship's educational programs, and they appreciate finding two pairs of high-powered binoculars and umbrellas in their cabins. The ship does not have an elevator. The decor throughout is understated and pleasing. *Endeavour* does not have a promenade deck completely surrounding the ship.

ITINERARIES *See* Itinerary Index.

CABINS Cabins are large compared with the line's older sister ships and have wide picture windows. They're equipped with phone, television/ VCR, and tiled baths with showers. Refurbishing in 1999 added new closets, lighting and window treatments, wall coverings, artwork, and furniture; bathrooms were upgraded as well.

Cabins are on three decks and of four types: The 100 series on the Main Deck includes eight of the AAA category, measuring 109 square feet, and four A cabins of about the same size. The Lounge Deck has As that open onto the outside deck, 12 AAAs, and 2 deluxe cabins measuring 155 square feet. Upper Deck has 20 AAs and one deluxe cabin, all opening to an outside veranda. The A and AA have twin or double beds, and some cabins accommodate three passengers; most have large picture windows.

Specifications 51 cabins. The cruise line's brochures show precise layouts of each category.

DINING   The **Resolution Dining Room** accommodates all passengers at a single open seating; most tables seat six or eight persons, none are for two. Mealtimes may vary depending on the itinerary, but generally, breakfast is served at 7:30 a.m., lunch at 1 p.m., and dinner at 7:30 p.m. The food gets high praise from passengers, and there's a good selection of wines. An unusual custom on board: the chef personally introduces the evening menu and invites passengers to dinner. As with most small ships, there is a great deal of camaraderie among passengers and friendly interaction with the ship's staff.

FACILITIES AND ACTIVITIES   The spacious **Explorer Lounge** is a multipurpose room and the heart of the ship's activity, beginning with continental breakfast in the morning and coffee, tea, and cocoa available throughout the day. It is also used for most of the lectures. A wide selection of videos and magazines is available in the library, along with a good selection of books and reference works pertaining to the area of the cruise.

The main activity on an Alaska cruise is sightseeing, which Alaska offers like no other place in the country. A Baja California and Gulf of California cruise during the winter months offers more sports activities, such as hiking, swimming, snorkeling, and kayaking, as well as sightseeing and spotting wildlife. Among the highlights are an opportunity to swim with sea lions, watching dolphins play, and photographing a colony of blue-footed boobies, but the most anticipated activity of all is whale-watching. From about mid-January to mid-March, large numbers of California gray whales assemble in the lagoons of Bahia Magdalena, which passengers visit.

Spirit of Nantucket	QUALITY 5	VALUE C
Spirit of Yorktown	QUALITY 5	VALUE C
REGISTRY United States	LENGTH 207/257 feet	BEAM 37/43 feet
CABINS 51/69	DRAFT 11.5/12.5 feet	SPEED 7/10 knots
MAXIMUM PASSENGERS	PASSENGER DECKS 4	ELEVATORS None
102/138	CREW 29/42	SPACE RATIO NA

THE SHIPS   United States–built and flying the American flag, the *Spirit of Nantucket* and the slightly larger *Spirit of Yorktown* are almost identical. They were acquired by Cruise West from Clipper Cruises in early 2006; the ships' staff were rehired by Cruise West.

Spirit of Nantucket has three passenger decks and *Spirit of Yorktown* four, including a spacious top Sun Deck aft of the bridge—a comfortable place for watching the passing scene. With shallow drafts, the ships glide into small places as easily as they tie up in small ports, sailboat-filled harbors, and coves. Lounges and cabins are decorated with high-quality furnishings. No glitter, no glitz.

Both ships have a single forward observation lounge and bar on the center deck that serves as a social center. Three sides of the cheerful room have large windows trimmed with light wood. Textured fabric and neutral colors give the lounge a warm, contemporary look. During cruises, the room has the air of a club, with passengers conversing, reading, writing postcards, or simply watching scenery. It is also the scene for lectures, early breakfast buffet, afternoon cookies, and hors d'oeuvres at cocktail time.

ITINERARIES *See* Itinerary Index.

CABINS All six categories of cabins are outside, and all but the lowest category have picture windows.

Cabins on the promenade deck open onto an outdoor, wraparound deck (as on river steamboats). Although these have an airy feel, some passengers might prefer cabins that open onto a central corridor. On the *Yorktown,* four cabins on the Sun Deck are the largest and most private.

The cabins are small but adequate, well lighted, offer ample storage, and appear more spacious because of a large wall mirror. Beds are parallel or at right angles; the latter provides more floor space. The furnishings have a clean, modern look, with closets and dressers in light wood, and landscape paintings on the wall. Bathrooms have showers only and are small, with limited shelf space. In an effort to let passengers get away from it all, cabins have neither telephones nor televisions. Radios, however, provide wake-up calls, ship information, and music. Some cabins get noise from the hydraulic lift that raises and lowers the gangplank in port.

There is no room service. Laundry, beauty shop, and barber shop are usually available in port. The ships carry no nurses or doctors except on specific cruises. However, the vessels are almost always near shore in case of medical emergency. Lack of medical staff and the difficulty of walking on steep gangways make the ships unsuitable for many physically disabled persons.

Specifications All outside cabins; no suites. Standard dimensions range from 122 to 139 square feet on *Yorktown,* 106–123 square feet on *Nantucket.* All have 2 lower beds, some with pull-down third bunk; no singles. None are wheelchair-accessible.

DINING The dining room, on the lower deck, has large windows and pleasant decor reflecting fine quality. Passengers dine at a single, open seating at round or square marble-topped tables, which are covered with cloths for dinner. The food is American cuisine overseen by a chef trained at either the prestigious Culinary Institute of America or at Johnson & Wales University. Meals feature excellent soups, good-quality beef, fresh seafood, vegetables, and fruit. They're presented in a straightforward manner by the young, cheerful staff. Selections are not as extensive as on larger ships—dinner menus offer four entrées—but all menus include a regional specialty. A small but moderately priced selection of wines is available.

An early light breakfast is served in the lounge; lunch buffets are offered on the Sun Deck, weather permitting. Snacks, including fresh fruit, are available throughout the day. In the afternoon, freshly baked chocolate chip cookies are set out in the lounge, welcomed by passengers who have gathered in anticipation. The bar is open from 11 a.m. to midnight.

SERVICE The clean-cut staff of young American men and women are cheerful, attentive, friendly, and unfailingly polite. Most are college students from the U.S. heartland, who sign on for a year of employment. They take care of the restaurant, bar, and cabins, working 12 hours a day, six days a week, and smile through it all.

FACILITIES AND ACTIVITIES The cruise director briefs passengers daily about upcoming adventures. Daily seminars by naturalists, historians, or other experts on places visited on the cruise precede follow-up discussions after the visits. The naturalist also acts as guide for nature walks, bird-watching, and study of the local environment. Afternoons at sea, a movie plays in the dining room. A local folklorist or other interesting characters may come on board for a lecture, discussion, or entertainment. Activity centers on the destination, whether it's a tour of a historic town, a golf game, or a forest hike. There are no organized fun and games. Deck space is adequate for a destination-oriented ship, and most people use it to sunbathe, read, or watch the scenery—often through binoculars. Evenings in port enable passengers to explore local nightlife. Otherwise, passengers gather in the lounge after dinner to visit, or they retire to the dining room to watch videos. Most are in their cabins by 10 p.m.

SPORTS AND FITNESS Walkers can circumnavigate the Promenade Deck, and when the ships tie up at night, as they often do, passengers walk into town. Depending on itinerary and weather, snorkeling directly from the ship is available, and scuba diving, windsurfing, deep-sea fishing, golf, or tennis can be arranged. The ships have no pools, whirlpools, exercise equipment, or fitness centers.

SHORE EXCURSIONS Cruises usually call at ports seldom visited by other ships and often tie up at small, out-of-the-way marinas and yacht harbors, enabling passengers to explore remote islands and coastlines on foot. Where *Nantucket* cannot dock, passengers go ashore by Zodiac boat; *Yorktown* has dib launches. In urban areas, ships often tie up within walking distance of cultural attractions and offer above-average tours at reasonable costs.

POSTSCRIPT Although the adventures are light and seldom far from civilization, many itineraries entail walking, wet landings, and climbing in and out of Zodiacs in remote areas. Some involve traversing open sea, and with the ships' shallow drafts, passengers may have a bumpy ride for several hours. Because the ships do not carry doctors and do not have elevators, they are not able to handle passengers with serious health or physical limitations.

SPIRIT OF '98	QUALITY 3	VALUE C
REGISTRY United States	LENGTH 192 feet	BEAM 40 feet
CABINS 49	DRAFT 9.3 feet	SPEED 13 knots
MAXIMUM PASSENGERS	PASSENGER DECKS 4	ELEVATORS 1
96	CREW 26	SPACE RATIO NA

THE SHIP Added to Cruise West's fleet in 1993, *Spirit of '98* previously sailed as the *Pilgrim Belle, Colonial Explorer,* and *Victorian Empress.* The handsome vessel has the profile and interior of a turn-of-the-19th-century riverboat (she had a role in the 1994 movie *Wyatt Earp*).

Built in 1984, *Spirit of '98* has decor that recalls a Victorian country hotel. Accenting a handsome mahogany and mirrored bar in the forward observation lounge are fanciful wall lamps and wood columns trimmed with strip mirrors. Continuing the theme on her four decks are extensive use of wood, wingback chairs, leaded glass, and old-fashioned brass lamps. The ship has one elevator operating between Main and Upper decks.

ITINERARIES *See* Itinerary Index.

CABINS All cabins are outside and have varied arrangements. They're roomy, with closet and storage space adequate for a casual cruise. All are decorated in rich Victorian-style colors and fabrics. All have TV/VCR combinations, are air-conditioned, and have windows that open—a welcome feature.

Cabins on Lounge and Upper decks open onto promenades. On Main Deck, lower-priced cabins have windows on the outside hull, a benefit for those who like privacy but want to keep their curtains open.

The ship has an amazingly large, two-room owner's suite on the top deck with picture windows on both sides. The only cabin on the deck, just behind the bridge, it has a sitting area, a game and meeting area, complimentary bar, television, VCR, king-size bed, and bathroom with full-size tub. Occupants may have their meals served en suite.

Specifications 48 outside cabins; 1 suite. Standard dimensions, 100–120 square feet. 40 with twins; 2 with upper/lower bunks; 4 with queen, 6 with doubles. 2 singles.

DINING The **Klondike Dining Room** provides seating at a variety of table configurations, including booths next to the picture windows. One open seating is offered at each of three meals. The cuisine is better than expected for this type of cruise. It's mostly Pacific Northwest fare encompassing fresh seafood, local produce, and Northwest wines and local specialty beers. In Mexico, meals have Mexican choices. Bread and pastries are baked on board. Coffee, tea, cocoa, and fruit are available all day.

An early continental breakfast is available in the forward lounge; full breakfast is at 7:30 a.m. in the dining room. Lunch features soups, salads, and sandwiches. Appetizers served between 6 and 7 p.m. may include Alaskan Dungeness crab and artichoke dip or baked Brie.

Entrées at dinner are attractively presented and surprisingly sophisticated. They may include fresh halibut in Dijon sauce, veal piccata with white wine and capers, or Oregon razor clams grilled with garlic aioli.

SERVICE   The young, enthusiastic crew are friendly, caring, and especially considerate of older passengers. These "customer service representatives" perform a variety of duties, including cleaning cabins and serving in the dining room.

FACILITIES AND ACTIVITIES   Unusual in coastal cruise ships, **Soapy's Parlor** is a second, quiet lounge with wraparound windows at the stern, a good spot for watching the vessel's wake. Tea is served in the afternoon. The Bridge Deck has ample space for sunning, viewing scenery, or lounging. A barbecue lunch is offered in good weather. A small area serves as a gift shop, where caps, mugs, and similar items are sold. A shuffleboard court and huge checkerboard are on the Bridge Deck, along with two exercise machines.

The forward lounge is the ship's social center at night. Most entertainment is provided by the passengers interacting with each other in conversation, cards, or board games in the lounge or dining room. Absent are a pool, casino, aerobics class, bingo, midnight buffet, or napkin-folding classes. The crew provides informal talent and lively entertainment on Crew and Casino nights. Vegetable races are amusing, and can be lucrative for those who wager correctly on such entries as Percy Potato or the Lemon Sisters. A television shows evening movies. Guest lectures, talks by the cruise coordinator/naturalist, and entertainment from the old-style player piano are offered.

Spirit of Discovery	QUALITY 2	VALUE D
REGISTRY United States	LENGTH 166 feet	BEAM 37 feet
CABINS 43	DRAFT 7.5 feet	SPEED 13 knots
MAXIMUM PASSENGERS	PASSENGER DECKS 3	ELEVATORS None
84	CREW 21	SPACE RATIO NA

THE SHIP   Built in 1976 as the *Independence* and renamed *Columbia,* the vessel cruised the East Coast and Puget Sound before being acquired by Cruise West in 1992 and renamed *Spirit of Discovery.* The forward lounge of this three-deck vessel is the ship's social center and cool-weather retreat. Nicely decorated in blue, soft grays, teals, and mauves, it has a bar with standard spirits plus Pacific Northwest wines and specialty brews. Furniture is arranged in conversational groupings. These, along with mirrored ceiling and chrome accents, give it the look of a private yacht or small, European-style hotel.

The lounge offers good views to both sides and over the bow through vertical windows at the front. Passengers at the bow can almost touch the vegetation when the ship noses up to shore. The bridge has a wraparound viewing area and is open to passengers at most times. A stair stepper, exercise bicycle, and rowing machine are available.

ITINERARIES *See* Itinerary Index.

CABINS Cabins on all three decks are outside with large windows. Most are small but adequate and furnished with a vanity, desk, and chair. Bathrooms have showers. Closets could use more hangers. Two sought-after smaller cabins, sold as singles, are amidships on the Bridge Deck.

Four spacious, deluxe cabins on the top level have a queen-size bed, desk and chair, television/VCR unit, and fridge/minibar. All Bridge Deck cabins and most Lounge Deck cabins open onto a promenade. The two lowest-priced cabins are on the lower Main Deck forward, reduced in size to fit the hull's curvature.

Specifications 43 outside cabins; no suites. Standard dimensions, 64 square feet (single cabin) to 127 square feet. 34 with twins, 1 with double, 4 queens, 2 with upper/lower berths, 2 singles.

DINING The **Grand Pacific Dining Room,** aft on the main deck, is pleasant and airy, but a bit noisy because it's over the engine room. The food is imaginative and quite good, encompassing Pacific Northwest versions of classic American fare with fresh local produce and seafood. All passengers dine in one open seating; table configurations vary.

A continental breakfast is available for early risers. Sit-down breakfast, lunch, and 6 p.m. appetizers are served. Two entrées are offered at dinner; they may include lingcod baked in parchment or a superb rack of Ellensburg lamb roasted with Dijon rosemary crust.

SERVICE Customer service, galley and engine crew, and deckhands are young Americans, most from the Pacific Northwest. They're attentive, enthusiastic, and outgoing. Friendships form between crew and passengers, and many crew members receive holiday greetings from passengers for years after they meet.

Spirit of Alaska	QUALITY 2	VALUE D
Spirit of Columbia	QUALITY 2	VALUE D
REGISTRY United States	LENGTH 143 feet	BEAM 28 feet
CABINS 39/38	DRAFT 7.5/6.5 feet	SPEED 12/10 knots
MAXIMUM PASSENGERS	PASSENGER DECKS 4	ELEVATORS None
78	CREW 21	SPACE RATIO NA

THE SHIPS *Spirit of Alaska* and *Spirit of Columbia* are identical in size, similar in layout, and are smaller versions of their sister ships. *Spirit of Alaska,* built in 1980 as the *Pacific Northwest Explorer,* was extensively renovated when acquired by Cruise West in 1991, and she was renovated again in 1995. *Spirit of Columbia* (formerly *New Shoreham II* of American Canadian Caribbean Line) joined in 1994 after being refitted in a Western national park lodge theme.

Both ships have four decks, with most cabins on the lower and upper decks and a forward lounge and dining room amidships on the Main Deck. The lounge is the center of social life and site of briefings. It has a small bar, gift shop, reference library focused on the cruise area, television, and movie videos. The upper deck has an unobstructed walking and jogging circuit and several exercise machines.

On *Spirit of Alaska,* the Bridge Deck provides open and covered seating and a good-weather venue for buffet lunches. Bow ramp stairs enable passengers to walk directly onto shore; some complain the stairs are steep and difficult to negotiate.

Besides decor, *Spirit of Columbia* differs in having a large owner's suite with windows overlooking the bow, three additional suites, a raised wheelhouse with 360-degree viewing, and an unusual bow ramp. A hinged, V-shaped segment of the bow can be lowered to form a ramp, giving direct access to shore from the forward lounge.

ITINERARIES *See* Itinerary Index.

CABINS Cabins on both ships range from roomy—for ships of this size—to very small. *Spirit of Alaska*'s suites and deluxe cabins have small sitting areas and are open to promenades. Three Bridge Deck suites have oversized double beds and windows on two sides and accommodate a third person.

Spirit of Columbia's 11 suites and deluxe cabins have a television/ VCR, refrigerator, side tables, and a chair. Suites have a double bed; deluxe rooms, twins. The owner's suite has a queen-size bed, tub/ shower, and complimentary bar. Upper- and Bridge Deck cabins open directly onto promenades.

On both ships, Main Deck cabins are on the short passage between the dining room and forward lounge, a high-traffic area but convenient for those who want easy access to activities and facilities. Windows in these cabins are on the outside hull, ensuring privacy. Lower-deck cabins have portlights high on the bulkhead and not for viewing. Baths are small units with handheld showers and curtains on tracks. Most cabins have twin beds; all have reading lights, closets, and under-bed storage. They're just above the engine room and can be noisy when the ship is under way, but they are a good buy for budget watchers.

Specifications Alaska, 12 inside cabins; 24 outside; 3 suites. Dimensions range from 81 to 130.5 square feet. 26 with twins; 13 with doubles; 7 cabins accommodate third persons; no singles. *Columbia,* 12 inside cabins; 20 outside; 7 suites. Dimensions range from 73.5 to 176 square feet.

DINING Meals are served at a single open seating. Cuisine is good American fare, emphasizing fresh Pacific Northwest and Alaskan seafood and local produce. The *Spirit of Alaska*'s Grand Pacific Dining Room has small round and square tables with upholstered banquettes running bow to stern underneath side windows.

SERVICE The young American staff helps set the friendly ambience and, despite the considerable workload, remains courteous, enthusiastic, and helpful, especially to seniors. Most retain a sense of awe about the magnificent region the vessel sails, often sharing passengers' excitement for wildlife sightings or glacier calvings, when enormous pieces of a glacier break off and crash into the sea.

Pacific Explorer	QUALITY 3	VALUE C
REGISTRY Honduras	LENGTH 185	BEAM NA
CABINS 50	DRAFT 12 feet	SPEED 12 knots
MAXIMUM PASSENGERS	PASSENGER DECKS 4	ELEVATORS None
100	CREW 33	SPACE RATIO NA

THE SHIP Built in 1995 and remodeled in 1998, the *Pacific Explorer* specializes in cruises of Costa Rica and Panama. More recently, the historic Panamanian port of Portobello, dating from 1502, was added to its itinerary. The ship is staffed with English-speaking Costa Ricans and guides. A lounge and dining room are on the lower of four decks; cabins and a forward lounge are on Main and Upper decks. The bridge, sunning area, and outdoor bar are on the Sun Deck.

All cabins have picture windows and are air-conditioned. They have television/VCR and private baths with showers. There are three types of cabins—deluxe (152 square feet), AAA/AA (122 square feet), and A (107 square feet)—and they are furnished with either twin or double beds. International cuisine and Central American specialties are served, along with breads and desserts made on board by the pastry chef.

POSTSCRIPT Readers considering a cruise on any Cruise West ship should read the entire section for a more complete picture of the cruise experience the line offers.

Crystal Cruises

2049 Century Park East, Suite 1400, Los Angeles, CA 90067
☎ **310-785-9300 or 888-799-4625; fax 310-785-3891**
www.crystalcruises.com

TYPE OF SHIPS Modern, luxury superliners.

TYPE OF CRUISES Modern version of glamorous, traditional cruising with a touch of California glitz, for upscale, sophisticated travelers.

CRUISE LINE'S STRENGTHS
- service
- beautifully designed ships
- alternative restaurants
- globe-roaming itineraries
- interesting, unusual, and varied shore excursions
- enrichment program

CRUISE LINE'S SHORTCOMINGS
- two seatings in main dining room
- some cabins with restricted views, except on *Serenity*

FELLOW PASSENGERS Professional, retired or semiretired, experienced travelers; likely to be business owners, entrepreneurs, and executives rather than staff; ages 45–70. Typical passenger is affluent, active, friendly, fashion-conscious, and often a 55- to 60-year-old couple or mature single. Approximately 53% are repeaters.

Recommended for Quality-conscious travelers who appreciate style with flash and want large-ship facilities; urbane first-time cruisers who can afford it.

Not recommended for Anyone uncomfortable with or uninterested in sophisticated ambience.

CRUISE AREAS AND SEASONS Caribbean, Central America, Mexico, Panama Canal, fall and winter; South America and world cruise, January–March; Asia, March–May; Arctic Circle, Baltic, Europe, Mediterranean, and North Cape, April–September; New York/New England/Canada, fall. Antarctic, South Africa, West Africa, Dubai, Egypt, seasonally.

THE LINE Two years before her first ship debuted in 1990, Crystal Cruises promised it would return grand ocean liner elegance and personalized service to modern cruises for the "upscale mass market"—an apparently inconsistent term. The line not only delivered on its promise, but *Crystal Harmony,* its first ship, was even better than its advance billing. It quickly became the ship by which others in her class—or aspiring to be in her class—were measured.

And therein lies the tale. There were no other ships in her class. Crystal Cruises created a niche all its own: a ship the size of most superliners but carrying a third fewer passengers (some comparably sized ships carry

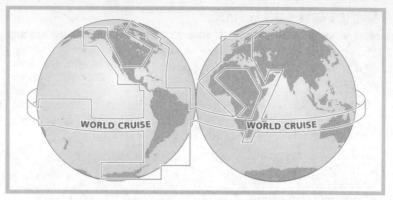

CRUISE AREAS AND SEASONS FOR CRYSTAL CRUISES

twice as many passengers) and offering the best of all worlds—the facilities of a large, spacious ship with the personalized service of a small vessel.

Crystal Cruises' first ship was built in Japan by its owners, Mitsubishi Heavy Industries, a subsidiary of Nippon Yusen Kaisha, the Japanese shipbuilding giant known for its technologically advanced ships. The ship incorporated state-of-the-art engines, radar, and navigational equipment. Comfort and amenities went far beyond the norm. (*Crystal Harmony* left Crystal Cruises in late 2005 to join the new cruise line created by its owners for the Japanese market.)

Ironically, Crystal's second ship, *Crystal Symphony*, was built in Finland, for cost-saving reasons. *Crystal Serenity*, a third ship which debuted in summer 2003, was built in France. Somewhat larger than her sister ships, *Serenity* set a new direction for Crystal Cruises, with facilities for greater focus on enrichment programs and enhanced onboard amenities. Between 2004 and 2006, in a two-stage effort, *Crystal Symphony* was given a major makeover that brings her facilities closer to *Crystal Serenity*.

THE FLEET	BUILT/RENOVATED	TONNAGE	PASSENGERS
Crystal Serenity	2003	68,000	1,080
Crystal Symphony	1995/2004/06	51,044	940

STYLE Exceptionally spacious ships with superliner facilities and Rodeo Drive style are designed for affluent travelers willing to pay for luxury and personal attention and who appreciate high quality in details. The cruises provide fine food and service in a gracious atmosphere; stimulating enrichment programs, a year-round roster of celebrity and expert speakers, and varied itineraries with more structure than ultraluxurious lines but less formality than luxury ships of old. Itineraries generally include more days at sea than is the norm, so passengers have time to fully enjoy the luxury and pampering that Crystal offers. A new trend is the ships occasionally remaining in ports for two days.

Not one to rest on its laurels—Crystal consistently sweeps the awards ratings—the line continues to add enhancements and interesting options and, thus, value to its cruise experience. Crystal has an incredible range of interesting and unusual shore excursions, enabling passengers to go canoeing in Croatia or climb Kilimanjaro. There are more and more adventure-type shore excursions, additional programs in the onboard Creative Learning Institute, an expanded roster of theme cruises; and a series of extended land programs. On board, there are such added attractions as wine tastings, Pilates and yoga class, laundry, and shuttles to town in ports free of charge.

Following installation of wireless service aboard its ships, Crystal recently added cell phone service in partnership with SeaMobile. The wireless service allows text messaging and the use of such equipment as a Blackberry. International roaming fees apply to all shipboard cell phone calls or messages and will appear on the passenger's home cell phone bill.

In response to the growing trend in multigenerational travel, Crystal has created a special area on its Web site to offer advice and guidance for families seeking to design a family reunion vacation. Responding to another trend, in January 2007, Crystal became the first line to remove trans fats from its ships' galleys and replaced them with transfat-free oils, incorporating the changes in all ships' menus and restaurants.

DISTINCTIVE FEATURES Computer University@Sea, Creative Learning Institute. Two specialty restaurants at no extra cost; gentlemen hosts; close-captioned television for hearing-impaired passengers; free self-service laundry on each deck; business center with audiovisual equipment, fax machines, and office equipment; secretarial, translation, and e-mail services; takeout laptops; air-conditioned tenders with toilets. Wireless and cell phone service.

	HIGHEST	LOWEST	AVERAGE
PER DIEM	$1,594	$271	$840

Per diems are calculated from cruise line's nondiscounted *cruise-only* published fares on standard accommodations and vary by season, cabins, and cruise areas.

RATES Port charges additional. Crystal has added a fuel surcharge of $5 per person per day on all 2007 cruises.

Special fares and discounts Crystal has promotional discounts ranging from 10% to 30% and more, depending on the cruise; they may or may not be used with other promotional rates and Crystal Society savings. Another group marked with a V in Crystal's brochure offers two-for-one savings.

- **THIRD PASSENGER:** Ages 12 and older: minimum fare for cruise.
- **CHILDREN'S FARE:** Younger than age 12, half-fare with two full-paying adults and free on certain cruises.
- **SINGLE SUPPLEMENT:** Crystal's single's fare begins at 125% of the double-occupancy rate for the lowest categories and is applicable to advance-purchase discount rates (130% for World Cruises).

Packages
- **AIR/SEA:** Yes.
- **PRE/POST:** Yes.
- **OTHERS:** Honeymoon; extended land programs.

PAST PASSENGERS Crystal Society past-passenger club offers amenities that increase with the number of cruises. These include business- and first-class air upgrades, confirmed stateroom and penthouse upgrades, shipboard credits, free cruises in staterooms and penthouses, limousine transfers, prepaid gratuities, and private luncheon and dinner parties.

Passengers are automatically enrolled after their first Crystal cruise and receive financial bonuses with every subsequent cruise. The higher reward levels are 5–30 cruises, 50, 70, and 100 cruises, but all members receive a 5% cruise discount, an additional 5% savings for reservations made while on a cruise, priority check-in, a Crystal Society travel bag, membership card, recognition pin, quarterly newsletter, and, beginning with the tenth cruise, a complimentary bottle of wine and fresh flowers on every cruise. Several cruises, including the annual president's cruise, are Crystal Society Sailings (marked with a *C* in the compendium) and feature a personal escort, exclusive events, and special gifts.

THE LAST WORD Crystal Cruises identified a market of experienced travelers (but not necessarily experienced cruise passengers) who weren't being served by other cruise lines and created a product that set new standards of luxury for large ships. Those who can afford the cruises get quality all the way. Compare Crystal's quality and extra amenities with those of other lines in the same price bracket, and you find Crystal's cruises are among cruising's best values.

Crystal Cruises Standard Features

Officers Norwegian captains and international officers

Staff Dining: European; Cabin: International; Cruise: American.

Dining facilities One main dining room, two seatings for dinner with open seating for breakfast and lunch; buffet breakfast and lunch on Lido Deck; alternative dinner restaurants; cocktail hour; midnight buffet; tea.

Special diets Requests should be made when reservations are confirmed (or at least one month in advance). Kosher, 90 days advance notice. Low-carb selections are available on menus in all dining venues.

Room service 24-hour menu; butler service on Penthouse Deck.

Dress code Casual by day; casually elegant in the evening, with two formal evenings per week of cruising.

Cabin amenities Direct-dial phone with voice mail; television with CNN and ESPN, DVD; stocked minibar; safe; bathroom with tub, two hair dryers, robes; suites with marble bathrooms and whirlpool tubs.

Electrical outlets 110/220 AC.

Wheelchair access 8 *Serenity*; 4 cabins on *Symphony*.

Recreation and entertainment Casino, disco, nightclub, show lounge, piano bar, coffee and wine bar, cinema/theater, six lounges, observation lounge, card game and meeting room, video game room, smoking room. Guest lecturers, area specialists, celebrities. Bingo, bridge, dancing, and crafts classes. Computer classes.

Sports and other activities Two outdoor swimming pools, one with retractable roof; two Jacuzzis; teak deck for walking or jogging; paddle tennis; table tennis, golf clinics, and practice corner; deck and pool games.

Beauty and fitness See text.

Other facilities Boutiques, concierge, hospital, laundry and dry cleaning, valet service, launderettes, photo processing center, video camera rentals, meeting facilities, business service center, e-mail facilities.

Children's facilities Playroom, babysitters, youth programs.

Theme cruises Food and wine; golf, film and theater; Crystal Comedy Club at Sea; Big Band & Ballroom dance; Cabaret at Sea; Mind, Body & Spirit; Sotheby's and Smithsonian; and others.

Smoking Dining rooms, nonsmoking; public rooms, smoking in designated areas.

Crystal suggested tipping Per passenger per day: cabin stewardess, $4; butler, $4; senior waiter, $4; waiter, $3; $5 for single travelers; $6 or $7 per person per dinner in specialty restaurants; 15% added to bar bills.

Credit cards For cruise payment and onboard charges: all major credit cards, cash, and traveler's checks. Ship uses a charge system, with the bill settled at the end of the cruise.

Crystal Symphony	QUALITY 9	VALUE B
REGISTRY Bahamas	LENGTH 790/781 feet	BEAM 105/99 feet
CABINS 470	DRAFT 25 feet	SPEED 20 knots
MAXIMUM PASSENGERS	PASSENGER DECKS 8	ELEVATORS 9
94	CREW 575	SPACE RATIO 52.6/54.3

THE SHIPS Gleaming white inside and out, Crystal Cruises' ships are a symphony of Japanese technology and artistry, European service and tradition, and American flair for fun and entertainment. The elegance is in their simplicity, clean lines, and extraordinary attention to details. The line's quality, luxury, and spaciousness—one of the highest ratios of passenger-to-space of any ships—are immediately evident. The decor—a bit glitzy but always in good taste—was created by Swedish, Italian, and British designers influenced by Japanese artistic understatement. Quiet colors and well-made furnishings harmonize. Fine fabrics and textures set off marble and woods accented with brass and stainless steel. The generous use of glass gives interiors an airy ambience.

Passengers' introduction to *Crystal Symphony,* which debuted in 1995, is the **Crystal Plaza,** an atrium lobby with a spiral waterfall and cascades of Lucite lights, stairways, and railings that appear to float in space. They're outlined with brass fixtures against white marble walls. Fresh greenery, hand-cut glass sculpture, and a waterfall provide accents. Summing up the feeling of opulence is—what else?—a crystal piano. The beautiful vessel has lounges for many purposes and moods. The **Palm Court,** one of the most handsome lounges afloat, is an airy space in white and mint green with graceful palms under skylights. It wears the atmosphere of a traditional palm court in the afternoon when tables are set for tea with crisp linens and gleaming silver, and a harpist strums. Forward of the Palm Court is the fabulous **Vista Lounge,** a tri-level observation room with white leather chairs on sky-blue carpets and floor-to-ceiling windows that frame a 270-degree view. The lounge is designed in accordance with the principles of feng shui, the ancient practice of balance and harmony. All cabins are outside—about half have verandas, and all have large, well-designed bathrooms.

In 2004, Crystal invested $12 million to renovate the *Crystal Symphony* with a completely new feng shui–minded spa and fitness center, an expanded Computer University@Sea, redesigned specialty restaurants, and a new **Vintage Room,** as well as a refurbished dining room, library, and penthouse suites and cabins. In 2006, Crystal spent $23 million more to complete *Symphony*'s makeover. In just two weeks, nearly 1,300 people worked around the clock at the BAE Shipyard in Norfolk, Virginia, on more than 150 separate projects to create what Crystal says is essentially a new ship. With a new sophisticated and contemporary style, the comprehensive undertaking transformed all staterooms and much of Tiffany Deck, the ship's main entertainment area. There, the renovation included boutiques, shops, and a cafe, as well as a new casino and new nightclub and dozens of behind-the-scenes improvements.

ITINERARIES *See* Itinerary Index.

CABINS Large, comfortable, and handsomely appointed with fine fabrics and high-quality furnishings, the well-equipped cabins have sitting areas. *Symphony*'s standard cabins are roomy. All are outside, and 214 have verandas and overall dimensions of 246 square feet. Other standard cabins cover 202 square feet and have large windows. All have a sitting area with two chairs, large bathrooms with two sinks in a six-foot counter, bathtubs plus showers, and large closets. In the 2006 renovations, all of *Symphony*'s deluxe and standard cabins were completely redesigned with the minimalist look of today's boutique hotel. Ultra-luxury notes are found in the new Murano glass bedside lamps, Rubelli fabrics, and handsome leather headboard, along with special LED reading lights and new 20-inch flat-screen televisions that carry CNN and ESPN (when available). Bathrooms also have a new look, with oval glass sinks atop granite countertops. Large down pillows (there's a pillow menu) and comforters on beds, plush robes, fluffy towels, fine toiletries, and voice mail on the direct-dial telephone reflect attention to detail. All cabins have fresh flowers, two hair dryers, and Internet access.

More than half of all cabins have private verandas. Lifeboats obstruct views from some cabins, but Crystal's literature notes them as "limited" or "extremely limited" views and prices the cabins accordingly.

The ship's ultimate luxury is on the all-suite, concierge-attended Penthouse Deck. Suites have large bedrooms, large sitting areas, and luxurious marble bathrooms with Jacuzzi bathtubs. The four most extravagant suites encompass 982 square feet, including verandas. In *Symphony*'s 2004 renovations, all penthouse cabins were updated with new decor of Italian-made fabrics in blues, peaches, and lavenders. CD players and DVD televisions were added. All Penthouse Deck suites have verandas.

The suites are attended by European-trained, white-gloved butlers and Scandinavian stewardesses. The young men, dressed in formal attire (some find this pretentious) are as competent as they are eager to serve. They will unpack your bags (and repack them at cruise's end), arrange a party or a dinner in your suite, and attend to other special requests. Nightly at cocktail time, they serve hors d'oeuvres and pour drinks from your fully stocked bar.

During a day at sea, passengers are given a ship tour on which they visit other cabin categories—a useful sales gimmick! Should the impulse seize you to book your next Crystal voyage right there, a "cruise consultant" is aboard to make the arrangements—at a discount.

Specifications *Symphony,* 411 outside cabins, including 65 penthouse suites with verandas and 214 deluxe cabins (246 square feet) with verandas; 197 deluxe cabins (202 square feet) without verandas; 7 wheelchair-accessible. No singles. All twins convert to queens or kings.

DINING Super in quality and stunning in presentation, cuisine is one of Crystal ships' best features, on par with top restaurants in New York and Los Angeles. Food is served on fine china by waiters who are as polished as the silver. The spacious dining rooms with floor-to-ceiling windows and modern chandeliers are elegant and well designed. More space than usual is allowed between tables, helping keep noise down. Tables for two are more numerous than usual.

In the 2004 renovations, *Symphony*'s **Crystal Dining Room** was redesigned with rich, dark paneling offsetting a bronze, maroon, and peach color palette. Along with the new decor came new lighting, window treatments, and an acoustically designed, elegant ceiling. Also added was **The Vintage Room,** a classic boardroom with access to the ship's extensive wine cellar—a copy of the one on *Crystal Serenity*. It is located in a newly constructed space at the heart of the ship's entertainment area on Deck 6. Designed for the line's exclusive winemaker's dinners, The Vintage Room accommodates 12 in a luxurious setting of deep green colors and rich polished woods. The charge is $180 per person for the special menu paired with fine wines.

Dinner menus, placed in cabins in advance, are greatly varied during a cruise. Typically, they include a choice of four appetizers, three soups, two salads, pasta, five entrées of fish, poultry, and meat, vegetables, and an array of desserts. Low-salt, low-fat, low-carb, and low-sugar choices are available. As of late January 2007, all transfats had been removed from galleys on both ships and replaced with transfat-free oils.

The maître d'hôtel often asks passengers for their favorite dishes, which the kitchen will prepare with advance notice. The wine list has more than 250 varieties. The ships' most innovative features—the first for cruising and starting the trend—were the intimate, alternative dinner restaurants, available at no extra cost to all passengers. The alternative restaurants have a hidden charm: Dining in the same surroundings on a long cruise can sometimes become boring. The two additional restaurants offer a change of ambience and cuisine—a great bonus. One of the alternative restaurants, **Jade Garden,** serves Japanese specialties and other Asian cuisine, while **Prego** features Italian dishes. Each restaurant has its own kitchen; dishes are cooked to order. Reservations are required. Make yours early because both are enormously popular.

Symphony's Prego has a waiting list almost every night and probably ranks as the ship's main attraction. Decorated to suggest Venice, the room has banquettes and high-backed chairs around tables seating four or six. Dishes are outstanding. The Jade Garden stresses Asian simplicity of design. Light-hued screens with bamboo patterns cover the windows and multicolored carpeting and upholstery provide an upbeat and modern look to this popular restaurant. Food is excellent, prepared to order by an Asian chef and relies heavily on seafood, but beef and chicken entrées are also available.

The level of service and cuisine in the dining room and alternative restaurants is meant to compensate for the lack of the single-seating dining room traditional on luxury ships. (Diehards consider this Crystal's unforgivable sin. However, two seatings accommodate the many passengers who like to eat early. What's more, it has not had an adverse effect on Crystal's success.) The indoor/outdoor **Lido Cafe** serves breakfast, midmorning bouillon, and lunch. Luncheon and themed buffets set up around the pool are very popular. The **Trident Bar,** an extension of the Neptune Pool swim-up bar, offers hot dogs, hamburgers, and other snacks, and there's a bar for ice cream and frozen yogurt.

Crystal ships serve a late-risers breakfast from 10 a.m. to noon, as well as a Sunday brunch in the **Crystal Cove** on Sundays at sea. The line also offers casual dining with an informal menu on deck on select evenings, usually after a day in port; passengers dress as they like in slacks, jeans, or shorts, and eat when they wish.

A sumptuous tea is served daily in the **Palm Court,** and the Crystal Plaza is the setting for a weekly dessert extravaganza set to the music of Mozart. Should you still suffer hunger pangs, the fruit basket in your cabin will have been replenished, or your cabin attendant will bring any item on the extensive 24-hour room service menu. You also may dine in your cabin, with courses served one by one.

The attractive **Bistro Café** serves coffee and pastries for late risers and wine and cheese, coffees, teas, and desserts during the day. It now has a new look enhanced with new decorative tiles, new wall finishings and fresh upholstery—all in a warm palette of russets and earth tones. On several sailings, a wine and food festival features guest chefs and wine experts.

SERVICE The ships have among the highest crew-to-passenger ratios in cruising. The well-trained staff is young, cheerful, and eager to please; service is thoroughly professional and consistently excellent. Dining room staff primarily are European; cabin attendants, European and Filipino; and the cruise and entertainment staff, American. A European-style concierge and purser service are available around-the-clock.

FACILITIES AND ACTIVITIES Cultural and destination-oriented lectures by experts, political figures, and diplomats are a regular afternoon or after-dinner feature. Daytime pursuits include card and other games, dancing classes, golf clinics, and arts and crafts. The well-stocked library has videos, DVDs, books, and periodicals.

The **Computer University@Sea** was doubled in size in 2004 to accommodate the increased demand for the line's programs, and in 2006 it was outfitted with all new equipment and wireless facility, including cell phone service. Depending on cruise length, classes range from "PC Basics" to "Digital Video Editing;" The newest courses are Windows Vista operating system and Office 2007. The classroom aboard *Symphony* has 25 computer workstations and hands-on lab sessions. Passengers may also schedule private instruction in their cabins. Rental laptop computers are available. Crystal was among the first to introduce e-mail service on its ships. Passengers have their own e-mail address, which they receive with their cruise ticket. There is an initial $5 set-up fee and a range of charges thereafter, depending on use. The line also offers a selection on packages based on the number of days used. Internet access is available in all cabins. The **library,** with more than 3,000 titles, is located in a new facility in the ship's atrium amidship. A door with brushed-bronze finish opens to an inviting room of warm woods and Andrew Martin leather chairs. The VHS tape collection was replenished with DVDs. The **Hollywood Theatre,** with high-definition video projection and hearing-aid headsets, runs films each afternoon and evening. Films and other programs also are available on cabin televisions. For further diversion, pricey temptations with designer names are sold in the pretty shops on **Avenue of the Stars.** The area was recently transformed into a more elegant space with dramatic white marble, black accents, clean stone finishes and stunning chandeliers. **Facets** has a new private area for passengers to consider high-end jewelry purchases, and **Apropos** continues to offer the line's logo items and resort wear. Tiffany Deck (Deck 6), the main entertainment area and the hub of social activity, shopping, and casually elegant dining, has been transformed from stem to stern with new color schemes, new construction, and new contemporary lighting that will create different moods as day moves into night.

Pre-dinner options include cocktails in the **Vista Lounge** or wood-paneled **Avenue Saloon** or a classical concert by a harpist or trio. The **Connoisseur Club,** adjacent to the Avenue Saloon, is a cigar and cognac lounge with private club atmosphere.

A cabaret show in **Starlite Club** and two Broadway-style, full-scale, high-quality productions in the **Galaxy** show lounge are offered at night. Local entertainers may perform at ports of call. One evening is a masquerade party.

Repertory Theatre at Sea is a delightful innovation for entertainment. It includes well-known comedy and light drama performed by professional actors on every cruise. The diverse roster offers up to 91 scenes, excerpts, or reading from larger works as varied as Shakespeare, Edgar Allen Poe, and Henry James. In the Starlite Club, centrally located midship on Tiffany Deck, the walls were removed and a dramatic round bar has become its centerpiece. With window walls sparkling with Swarovski crystals, the new Starlite Club now provides a stylish, open environment with panoramic sea views where lectures are featured by day and dancing by night.

Galaxy Lounge, the main show lounge, offers an array of first-rate productions that might range from classical ballet to a Broadway revue. Crystal has its own production team, Gretchen Goertz and Kathy Orme, who create all the production shows, which are original and very good. The talented show troupe includes former dancers from the Bolshoi Ballet and London's West End. The shows usually have spectacular costumes—some valued at $10,000 apiece—and sets by award-winning designers. The ship's casino was reduced in size and completely redesigned with black flooring and a sophisticated new black and silver color palette. In addition to blackjack, roulette, and baccarat, new offerings include The Ultimate Texas Hold-em and state-of-the-art slot machines. Before sailing, passengers receive an application for credit at the casino, if they care to have it. Reducing the casino's size made room for a new late-night nightclub, **Luxe,** with the sophisticated contemporary look of polished aluminum, Philippe Starck bar stools, glass Bizzaro mosaics, and a dazzling new lighting system that flashes electric color off shimmering finishes and shades of black, silver, and white.

SPORTS, FITNESS, AND BEAUTY A lap pool has adjacent whirlpools, and an indoor/outdoor swimming pool has a swim-up bar and a retractable roof. There's generous sunning space on deck, plus table tennis, shuffleboard, pool games, golf, and the only full-scale paddle tennis court at sea. Deck 7 offers a wraparound, unobstructed route for walking or jogging.

On *Symphony,* the enlarged spa was completely reconstructed following the design principles of feng shui. The new facility, with sweeping ocean views, has eight treatment rooms, a relaxation area, a private canopied teak sun deck, a state-of-the-art steam shower and sauna area, and custom-designed manicure/pedicure areas with sunken foot bowls. A dry float-bed suite, appropriate for singles or couples, has a sensory bed to create a feeling of weightlessness, ideal for Aroma Spa and other treatments. The **Fitness Center** has a separate room for yoga, Pilates, aerobic and personal training instruction, and a gym with state-of-the-art fitness equipment, all with heart-rate sensors.

Crystal's alliance with TaylorMade showcases its prestigious r7 Super-quad driver and other TaylorMade equipment. Crystal's golf program includes right- and left-handed clubs for men and women, golf clinics, instruction by PGA golf pros, a putting green, practice cage, and driving ranges aboard the ships. A golf pro is generally on board offering lessons and tips and the line schedules several golf cruises during the year.

CHILDREN'S FACILITIES Supervised youth programs are provided only when the line knows in advance that a sizable number of children will be aboard. **Fantasia,** a children's playroom, is more of an entertainment center, with video games for children ages 3–16. In-room babysitting can be arranged with crew members for $7.50 per hour for one child, $10 per hour for two children, and $12.50 per hour for three children.

SHORE EXCURSIONS Shore excursions are sold on board, but they can also be booked in advance online. Crystal's efficient tenders have air-conditioning—a much-appreciated amenity. Crystal provides good maps and information about each port. The concierge and excursion desk helpfully suggest and arrange independent port programs.

Crystal continues to add interesting and ambitious excursions. They range from hiking and kayaking to rafting, horseback riding, and wildlife viewing. One exotic option is a wildlife tour in dugout canoes on a Botswana safari offered on the occasional Africa cruises.

Crystal Serenity	QUALITY 10	VALUE C
REGISTRY Bahamas	LENGTH 820 feet	BEAM 105.6 feet
CABINS 550	DRAFT 25 feet	SPEED 22 knots
MAXIMUM PASSENGERS	PASSENGER DECKS 9	ELEVATORS 8
1,080	CREW 655	SPACE RATIO 63

THE SHIP *Crystal Serenity,* built at Alstom Chantiers de L'Atlantique in France, made her debut in July 2003. The ship combines the best features of her sister ship with new ones added, including more dining venues, more penthouse suites, more cabins with verandas and butler service, more entertainment lounges, and more fitness options, among others. The new ship is almost 20% roomier and is richly decorated in refined taste, incorporating soft, muted colors that complement the beautiful crystal-glass signature touches throughout the vessel.

Some of the new features are an alternative Asian restaurant and sushi bar (the third evening alternative), a boardroom with a wine cellar for special dinners and wine tastings at an extra charge, a second paddle tennis court, a new learning center for creative and educational hands-on classes, and a club lounge off the atrium for Crystal Society members, making *Serenity* one of the first ships to have a room dedicated specifically to its past passengers.

The familiar favorites from previous Crystal ships include a contemporary rendition of the **Palm Court,** a spacious observation lounge with potted palms set into hexagonal skylights, the clubby **Avenue Saloon,** and the **Connoisseur Club.** The **Computer University@Sea** classroom is more than 50% larger than the facility on the earlier ships and has a 24-hour Internet center, plus a private area for one-on-one computer instruction. The *Serenity*'s spa and fitness center, approximately 40% larger than the one on her sister ship, are quite lavish. Located high up and aft, the two sections have separate entrances and good sound-proofing—hence the thumping of exercise machines does not intrude upon the serenity of the treatment room or the **Lido Cafe** below.

Crystal Serenity has an even greater space ratio (63) than her sister ship, with 34% more public space and one deck more than *Crystal Symphony*. The ship was designed by an international team headed by well-known Swedish naval architect Robert Tillberg, who worked on Crystal's other ship. Tillberg says *Serenity* is a sister, not a twin, to *Symphony*. His team was responsible for most of the public rooms and all passenger and staff accommodations. Other firms designed the specialty lounges and restaurants, spa, and retail shops.

ITINERARIES   *See* Itinerary Index

CABINS   Like *Crystal Symphony,* the ship has no inside cabins, and approximately 85% of the outside cabins and suites have private verandas. None have obstructed views, as the lifeboats are stowed below the cabin decks. One and a half decks of *Serenity* are devoted to 100 penthouse accommodations with verandas (56% greater than on *Crystal Symphony*). Of those, the most lavish are four Crystal Penthouses, each measuring 1,345 square feet—or 37% larger than those on the sister vessel.

In addition to the suites, there are 468 outside cabins with verandas and 80 outside staterooms with large picture windows. The eight wheelchair-accessible cabins are found in various categories: two penthouses, two veranda cabins, and four cabins with picture windows.

The deluxe cabins with veranda (Categories A and B) are virtually identical to the penthouse cabins with veranda (Category PH), all being 269 square feet, but the former do not have butler service. The cabins are furnished with a comfortable sofa with a pop-up coffee table for in-cabin dining; queen or twin beds with two night tables and lamps rather than reading lights. The entertainment center has a remote-control television and DVD player. The minibar and refrigerator are stocked with complimentary soft drinks and bottled water. All cabins have a data port for laptop computer hookup. The veranda is furnished with two white plastic chairs and a table; chaise lounges can be requested. The bathrooms have full-size tubs and showers and twin sinks.

DINING   Passengers on *Serenity* have the choice of five evening dining venues: the main **Crystal Dining Room** (two seatings); **Tastes,** an indoor/outdoor poolside area for casual evening dining; and three specialty restaurants: **Prego** for Italian fare; a sushi bar, a first for Crystal; and **Silk Road** for Pan-Asian cuisine. The latter features eclectic creations by famous master chef and Crystal consultant Nobuyuki "Nobu" Matsuhisa, known for his innovative blend of classic Japanese dishes with Peruvian and European influences. Two of the alternative restaurants operate on a reservations-only basis for no extra charge. No reservations are needed for the sushi bar. In general, service seems better and a bit less harried in Silk Road, perhaps because the menu is less extensive.

Serenity's Prego is entirely different in style than on her sister ship. It is a long, two-level room located aft on the starboard side, decorated in white and gold with bas-relief urns filled with fruit on the bulkhead pilasters. The decorative panels show Tuscan city scenes using two-dimensional depictions: the front panel low in height and the rear one in full height, with indirect lighting between to brighten the settings and create depth. Two Italian favorites on the menu are pumpkin ravioli flavored with apricot, and filet of Angus beef topped with gorgonzola. The restaurant also offers mouthwatering blends of seafood and pasta.

Among the Nobu selections on Silk Road's pan-Asian menu are lobster with truffle yuzu sauce, black cod with miso, and chicken with teriyaki balsamic. The airy portside setting is executed in lime green and soft blue lighting, with the sushi bar at the entrance.

During the day, passengers have choices similar to her sister ship, plus some new ones. Permanent hot-food stations aft of the ship's second pool serve luncheon buffets with a theme. The ship also offers stylish versions of its popular **Bistro,** a coffee and wine bar for morning and afternoon snacks such as cold meats, salads, cheeses, and desserts; the **Lido Cafe** for breakfast and lunch; the **Trident Grill** for casual, poolside lunches throughout the afternoon; an ice-cream/frozen yogurt bar; and 24-hour room service. Crystal expanded its healthy breakfast options at **Tastes** with gluten-free, lactose-free, sugar-free, fat-free, and whole-grain selections.

FACILITIES AND ACTIVITIES The **Galaxy Show Lounge** is the main entertainment venue for production shows and has improved sight lines and state-of-the-art sound and lighting systems. It's truly a showroom for the 21st century. Several new shows are being offered. A second cabaret lounge, the **Stardust Club,** provides a venue for daytime activities, such as dance classes and wine tasting, as well as for evening dancing and cabaret entertainment.

The **Palm Court,** with floor-to-ceiling 270-degree panoramic windows, is a splendid, roomy top-deck lounge in blue-gray with rattan seating, used for afternoon tea with a menu of about a dozen regular and herbal teas. It's also a good spot for evening dancing and entertainment, special events, and for simply enjoying the changing scenery. New room extensions offer unusual views of the glass-enclosed bridge wings one deck below. Other public facilities include the **Crystal Plaza** and **Crystal Cove,** the lobby area with a two-story atrium and **Crystal Piano Bar;** the **Avenue Saloon,** Crystal's clubby signature piano bar; the **Connoisseur Club,** a cigar lounge for after-dinner drinks; a casino; **Pulse,** a disco/nightclub for late-night dancing and karaoke; **Hollywood Theater,** a cinemaconference center with theater-style seating for day and evening movies, lectures, and religious services; a staffed library with books and DVDs—and even a great selection for kids—and comfy reading bays; a card room for Crystal's avid bridge players; and a gallery of high-end retail shops.

Passport to Music is a partnership with Yamaha to offer a program of music instruction as part of the line's new **Creative Learning Institute** (CLI), perhaps the most original experiential and interactive "edutainment," as Crystal calls it, offered at sea. Music instruction is offered in **The Studio,** *Crystal Serenity*'s handsome, high-tech facility created expressly for CLI programs.

The Studio is outfitted with 15 portable grand-piano keyboards—Yamaha's newest state-of-the-art model—and supported with the Clavinova digital piano. Certified Yamaha music teachers are aboard to teach groups of 12 to 15 guests. Depending on the length of the cruise, the average curriculum offers six 60-minute sessions; guests receive a certificate at the program's completion. A selection of software created by Yamaha enables guests to continue their musical journey at home.

Other Crystal partnerships for the Creative Learning Institute allow well-known organizations and schools, such as Berlitz, the Cleveland Clinic, Society of Wine Educators, Pepperdine University, and Tai Chi Cultural Center, among others, to bring experts aboard to share their knowledge in a classroom setting. The CLI curriculum offers progressive levels of instruction on a single subject or several one-class sessions of related topics. The main categories are Arts and Entertainment, ranging from Asian woodblock printing to acting workshops; Business and Technology, estate planning to fundraising to patent applications; Lifestyle, dealing with topics such as book clubs, candle making, or menu planning; Wellness, with health and fitness topics and serious medical subjects, such as prostate cancer, led by an expert from the Cleveland Clinic; and Wine and Food. The CLI is very popular—a kind of Elderhostel at sea. Thus, when the ship is full, it's wise to sign up early. There is no charge for any of the courses.

Repertory Theatre at Sea, similar to that on *Crystal Symphony*, features well-known comedy and light drama performed by professional actors. The diverse roster offers scenes, excerpts, or reading from larger works as varied as Shakespeare, Edgar Allen Poe, and Henry James.

SPORTS, FITNESS, AND BEAUTY *Serenity*'s 8,500-square-foot spa and fitness centers are approximately 40% larger, with more treatment rooms and a larger gym and aerobics studio than her sister ship, with state-of-the-art equipment. In response to passenger feedback, the ship has a second paddle-tennis court, an outdoor lap pool flanked by two whirlpools, a second indoor/outdoor pool covered by a sliding roof, a full promenade around the exterior of the ship for walking, jogging, and shuffleboard, and a Sports Deck with two golf driving ranges, putting green, and table tennis.

CHILDREN'S FACILITIES *Crystal Serenity* has a **Fantasia** children's and teen center with video games, both small and located high up and aft of the Palm Court foyer. Programs apply when there are children aboard, which is not often on long cruises. Holiday cruises bring out families. Then, too, Crystal, like most cruise lines, is seeing a steady increase in multigenerational as well as family cruising.

POSTSCRIPT The *Crystal Serenity* is an evolutionary ship for the line. The recent refurbishment of the *Crystal Symphony* reflects the newer ship's lead. Roominess is probably the most obvious improvement, enabling Crystal to expand where the line excels, such as in the expansive and spectacular Palm Court, the Creative Learning Institute, Computer Learning Center, standard cabin size, more accommodations with butler service, and additional seats in the alternative restaurants. All in all, *Crystal Serenity* has gone a long way to keep Crystal Cruises ahead of any competition.

Cunard Line

24303 Town Center Drive, Suite 200, Valencia, CA 91355-0908
☎ 661-753-1035 or 800-7-CUNARD
www.cunard.com

TYPE OF SHIPS Large, traditional ship; deluxe megaship.

TYPE OF CRUISES Wide range of destinations and durations, from warm-weather vacations to transatlantic spring-to-fall service for affluent, demanding travelers; distinctively British pedigree.

CRUISE LINE'S STRENGTHS
- name recognition
- distinctive ships
- itineraries
- accommodations and service
- single cabins on older ship

CRUISE LINE'S SHORTCOMINGS
- mixed products on ships

FELLOW PASSENGERS Cunard attracts a broad spectrum of passengers—from first-timers eager to visit many ports to veterans who seldom leave the ship—but most are upscale, mature, experienced travelers. Depending on time of year, the makeup is about 50-50 American and British, with large contingents of Europeans and repeaters. QE2's world cruises attract a crowd—affluent and older, taking long winter vacations—very different from that on other itineraries. QM2 passengers may be all ages, incomes, and professions, as well as families with children, and people eager to take an ocean voyage on the famous ship.

Recommended for Those who enjoy a certain amount of formality and tradition and are accustomed to luxury and willing to pay for it.

Not recommended for Those uncomfortable with elegance, who prefer a casual or nonstop party atmosphere.

CRUISE AREAS AND SEASONS Around the world in winter; transatlantic, April–November; Europe, spring–fall; Baltic, Caribbean, Mediterranean, New England and Canada, Panama Canal, and South America, seasonally.

THE LINE Cunard Line, with a history stretching back to 1840, sailed into the new millennium with new owners, new management, and a new direction. But reinventing itself is nothing new for Cunard. With the postwar birth of the jet age and the demise of transatlantic passenger service, traditional steamship companies like Cunard had to adapt to the new realities to survive. Some converted their ships for modern cruising, some built new ships, and some bought or merged with other cruise lines. Cunard took all these steps and more.

During the era of the grand ocean liners, Cunard Line was best known for its queens—the *Queen Mary* and *Queen Elizabeth*—which set

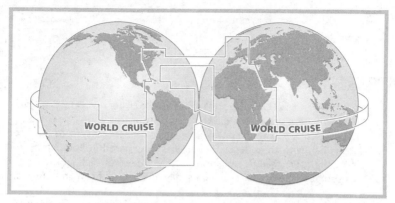

CRUISE AREAS AND SEASONS FOR CUNARD LINE

the standard of elegance at sea for decades. *Queen Elizabeth 2* made her debut in 1969, when the future of transatlantic service was uncertain.

In 1971, Cunard was acquired by Trafalgar House, a multinational conglomerate headquartered in London, but doubts persisted throughout the decade as to whether the line would survive. Having the only ocean liner on regular transatlantic service helped keep her going. In 1982, the *QE2* was pressed into Her Majesty's service during the Falkland Islands War. For Cunard and the *QE2*, it was a blessing in disguise, giving the ship a new lease on life with the publicity and a much-needed refurbishment by the British government before her return to passenger service.

In 1998, Cunard was sold to Carnival Corporation, and the following year, Cunard's other ships were moved to other lines, leaving only the *QE2* and *Vistafjord*, renamed *Caronia* under the Cunard brand. The new owners spent millions renovating the *QE2* and rebuilding Cunard with new ships.

The first, *Queen Mary 2*, christened by Her Majesty Queen Elizabeth II on January 8, 2004, was billed as the "grandest and largest passenger liner ever built" according to Cunard. She is intended to evoke a bygone era of seagoing luxury while representing the next era of ocean liner evolution, to create "a new golden age of sea travel for those who missed the first." After the *Queen Mary 2* entered service, the *QE2* was transferred to England to serve primarily the British market. Later in the year, Cunard's offices were integrated with Princess Cruises and moved to the West Coast for back-office economies. The new *Queen Victoria* is scheduled for delivery in December 2007.

In June 2007, Cunard Line sold *QE2* to Dubai World for US $100 million and will deliver her to her new owners in November 2008. Then, she will cease being a cruise ship, and after being refurbished and adapted for her new home, will become a tourist destination in Dubai at The Palm Jumeirah, the world's largest man-made island. From 2009, the *QE2* will be berthed at a specially constructed pier to create a luxury floating hotel and retail and entertainment destination.

THE FLEET	BUILT/RENOVATED	TONNAGE	PASSENGERS
Queen Elizabeth 2	1969/87/94/96/9/01/04	70,327	1,791
Queen Mary 2	2004	150,000	2,592
Queen Victoria	2007	90,000	2,014

STYLE The legendary *Queen Elizabeth 2* has a style all her own, and the *QM2* is developing a similar yet different style, too. Today, *QM2* is the only passenger ship sailing the Atlantic on a regular schedule, from April to November, with three levels of service. Now based in Southampton, England, the *QE2* sails on an annual world cruise from January to April. Both ships offer shorter cruises, usually in the Caribbean and Europe, that fill the weeks between.

To many, the *Queens* are the ultimate cruise experience—both cities at sea that dwarf all but the newest mega liners. The *Queens* are proud, elegant, formal, and as British as—well, yes—the Queen. Throughout its history, Cunard has been an innovator in response to changing lifestyles. *QE2* was the first ship to have a full-fledged spa, and now *QM2* has Canyon Ranch's first spa at sea. Recognizing the impact of the electronic revolution, Cunard installed the first computer learning center, satellite editions of world news, and an electronic library on the *QE2*.

DISTINCTIVE FEATURES Year-round gentlemen hosts, computer learning centers, British nannies, driving range and putting green, florist, tuxedo rental, electronic library, bookshop. *QM2*: **Canyon Ranch Spa Club,** Royal Academy of Dramatic Art performances, and **Illuminations,** the only planetarium at sea, largest ballroom and largest library at sea.

	HIGHEST	LOWEST	AVERAGE
PER DIEM	$596	$266	$431

Per diems are calculated from cruise line's nondiscounted *cruise-only* published fares on standard accommodations and vary by season, cabins, and cruise areas.

RATES Most port charges are included.

Special fares and discounts

- **EARLY-BOOKING DISCOUNTS:** Approximately 20% off brochure fares with extra 5% off for past passengers.
- **THIRD/FOURTH PASSENGER:** Specific fares listed in chart in brochure.
- **CHILDREN'S FARE:** If the child is the third or fourth person, third/fourth person fare applies.
- **SINGLE FARES:** Single-occupancy cabins listed in brochure. Supplement for single occupancy of double cabin is 140%–200%, depending on cabin.

Packages

- **AIR/SEA:** Yes.
- **PRE/POST:** Yes.
- **OTHERS:** Yes.

PAST PASSENGERS Cunard World Club, the past passenger program, has three levels: Silver (after one cruise); Gold, third through seventh voyage; and Platinum, seven cruises or completion of 48 consecutive days. Benefits include savings on sailings, onboard club representative, special mailings with savings offers; access to a members-only Web site, and more. Platinum members get priority check-in and an onboard invitation to a Senior Officers' Party.

Look for Cunard to introduce a new guest loyalty program in the near future that will add a new level of status and upgrade some benefits to its present silver, gold, and platinum levels, such as priority check-in, special disembarkation lounges, wine tastings, and preferred dining reservations. Cunard World Club has already added diamond status. To achieve diamond class, members must have sailed with Cunard at least 15 times or logged 150 sea days. Diamond benefits include all platinum-level services plus complimentary Internet packages with additional hours, priority luggage delivery, complimentary lunches in the specialty restaurants aboard Queen Mary 2 and Queen Victoria.

THE LAST WORD Cunard has long been known for luxury, but if you don't understand the differences in the levels of luxury, it can be somewhat misleading. For example, the popular image of the QE2, and now for QM2, is glamour, grand luxury, and haute cuisine. For those who buy the highest-priced suites and deluxe cabins and dine in the grills, this picture is accurate—but that's less than 30% of passengers. On her transatlantic run, QM2 has four levels of service, including the new Britannia Club, determined by cabin category, which is a polite way of saying four classes based on price. Each category is assigned specific restaurants, and entry by the others is restricted accordingly. The redeeming factor is that all entertainment, sports, recreational facilities, and shops are available to everyone, regardless of their cabin location.

A new Britannia category, Britannia Club, launched in April 2007, offers a new level of exclusive service for those passengers booked in deluxe balcony cabins. Britannia Club guests will enjoy their own separate, small single-seating restaurant, where tableside preparation and an enhanced wine list and a sommelier is meant to impart the atmosphere of a private salon. Located at one end of the Britannia Restaurant, passengers in the exclusive dining venue enjoy Cunard's White Star Service[SM] from a dedicated maitre d'hôtel and the same waitstaff throughout the voyage. Britannia Club cabin amenities include a bon voyage bottle of sparkling wine and strawberries, daily shipboard newspaper (or abridged newspaper), complimentary bottled water, bathrobes and slippers, pillow menu and duvets, and fresh fruit daily on request.

In March 2005, Cunard launched White Star Service, a training program for officers and staff focusing on three pillars: the legendary, the elegant, and the memorable. Each member of the ship's crew wears a black enamel pin on which the three words are inscribed. Named for the White Star Line with which Cunard merged back in 1934, the new service is intended to acquaint the ship's crew with Cunard's long history, and through it instill in them the pride and high level of service that is the Cunard tradition.

Although Cunard has been carrying passengers for 165 years, just now it has to be called a work-in-progress as it reinvents itself once again. The years prior to the launch of the QM2 were ones of change and setting the line's new direction. That mission is still in development and probably will be for several years as new ships are added to its fleet. Stay tuned.

Cunard Line Standard Features

Officers British and international.

Staff British and international.

Dining facilities QE2, single seating in five dining rooms for three meals, except Britannia, two seatings; informal Lido cafe for three meals and midnight buffet; snack bar. Casual indoor/outdoor cafe for breakfast and lunch buffets. QM2, Queen Victoria, Todd English restaurant, 4 dining rooms, pub, and a Lido-style King's Court with an Asian section, one featuring Italian specialties plus the carvery, salads, and such. QM2, Britannia Club.

Special diets Diabetic, low-calorie, low-cholesterol, low-salt, and vegetarian.

Room service 24-hour room service.

Dress code Formal/informal, for dining, depending on evening.

Cabin amenities Radio, direct-dial telephone, 20-channel television with CNN. Bathroom with tub and shower in suites. Refrigerator, walk-in closet, TV/VCR, bathrobes, hair dryer, safe, fruit baskets, nightly turndown service, and verandas.

Electrical outlets 220/110 AC.

Wheelchair access QM2, 30 cabins; QE2, ramps; four cabins; bathtubs with grab bars, wide doors, low sills, two elevators designed for the handicapped. Queen Victoria, 20 cabins.

Recreation and entertainment Casino, cabaret, revues. enrichment seminars, guest lectures. Lounges, bars, disco, bingo, dance lessons, gentlemen hosts, computer learning center, planetarium (QM2).

Sports and other activities Indoor/outdoor pools, deck sports, putting and driving net, jogging track, paddle tennis, table tennis.

Beauty and fitness Spa, fitness center, gym, barber/beauty salon, exercise class. See text for more details.

Other facilities Cinema/theater, launderette, laundry/dry cleaning service, library, bookshop, shops, hospital. QE2, tuxedo rental shop, foreign exchange, Harrods, florist, boardroom, synagogue. QM2, Hermes, Chopard, kennels.

Children's facilities Teen center, video, supervised children's playrooms, nursery, British nannies, babysitting; special children's evening meal served daily in the Lido at 5:30 p.m.

Theme cruises None.

Smoking Designated areas in public rooms.

Cunard suggested tipping $11–$13 per day added to bill, depending on cabin category. Both ships include 10%–15% gratuity for bar and salon services.

Credit cards For cruise payment and onboard charges: American Express, Diners Club, Discover, MasterCard, Visa.

Queen Mary 2	QUALITY 8	VALUE B
REGISTRY Great Britain	LENGTH 1,132 feet	BEAM 135 feet
CABINS 1,296	DRAFT 32 feet	SPEED 30 knots
MAXIMUM PASSENGERS	PASSENGER DECKS 14	ELEVATORS 22
3,090	CREW 1,253	SPACE RATIO 57.25

THE SHIP *Queen Mary 2,* Cunard's new flagship, was not only the biggest, widest, longest, and most expensive ship ever built when she was launched, but her debut gave birth to a new Cunard cruise line.

The ocean liner is meant to be reminiscent of great transatlantic steamships and, in Cunard's words, "relaunch the golden age of travel for those who missed the first one." Designed as an ocean liner for the 21st century and intended to appeal to baby boomers who Cunard sees as the ship's main market, the overall impression is one of quiet grace, conservative and a bit formal in a British manner without being stuffy. The refined interiors successfully combine contemporary elegance with a classic liner look.

The spacious *QM2,* costing upward of $800 million and constructed at Alstom Chantiers de L'Atlantique in Saint-Nazaire, France, was christened by Her Majesty Queen Elizabeth II on January 8, 2004. The slick-hulled 150,000-ton vessel, with a height of 237 feet from keel to funnel top, travels at speeds of up to 30 knots, making her one of the fastest cruise ships and able to undertake unusual itineraries. She can carry up to 3,090 passengers in a quasi-class system similar to that on *QE2,* with the cabin category determining restaurant assignments.

QM2 has the first and only spa at sea operated by the world-famous Canyon Ranch health resorts; the world's first and only planetarium at sea; the largest ballroom at sea; the largest library at sea; the largest wine cellar at sea; and ten dining venues, including the first shipboard restaurant by popular American chef Todd English.

There are 14 lounges and bars, a two-story theater, a casino, five indoor and outdoor swimming pools including a children's pool, an adults-only pool, another pool with a magrodome, hot tubs, boutiques, and a children's facility complete with British nannies. The learning center offers a variety of lecturers from a range of industries, disciplines, and academic backgrounds. The ship's $5 million art collection includes more than 300 original works of art.

On departing the ship at ports of call, passengers use four lounges—**Kensington, Chelsea, Knightsbridge,** and **Belgravia**—named for

London's best-known upscale neighborhoods and tube stops; those in wheelchairs are transferred to tenders or docks by a hydraulic platform.

QM2 is following the pattern the *QE2* had for many years, sailing on regularly scheduled transatlantic crossings between New York and Southampton from spring to November and longer worldwide cruises at other times. As a result of her unprecedented publicity and instant popularity, the number of her transatlantic cruises was doubled and in 2007 included calls at Hamburg, Germany, and Le Havre, France.

ITINERARIES *See* Itinerary Index. For the 2007–2008 season, *QM2* has offered an expanded season of transatlantic crossings, as well as six new four-day Getaways and twelve 10-day Caribbean voyages from New York

CABINS The main cabin categories correspond to the ship's dining rooms—**Britannia, Princess**, and **Queen**. Britannia offers 17 cabin levels ranging from standard (about 194 square feet) to deluxe (248 square feet). Princess accommodations are 381-square-foot junior suites, while Queen encompasses five levels of suites, ranging from 506 square feet to two-story Grand Duplex apartments at 2,249 square feet each.

Seventy-five percent of the 1,296 cabins have eight-foot-deep balconies. Thirty cabins for disabled passengers are available in various categories. The cabins are well laid out and very comfortable. The decor throughout has a quiet, tony quality, using light apricot, beige, and other soft pastels. All have interactive television with multilanguage film and music channels, direct-dial phone, hair dryer, 110/220-volt outlets, and bathroom with tub and/or shower.

The five duplex apartments (**Balmoral, Windsor, Holyrood, Buckingham,** and **Sandringham** suites) are two stories high and cover from 1,500 to 2,250 square feet. They have two-story glass walls at the ship's stern, providing great sea views. The lavish suites have their own exercise area, veranda, two full bathrooms with tub and shower, a walk-in closet, a separate sitting area, and refrigerator. Occupants in duplex apartments are pampered by butler service and room-service dining prepared by chefs from the **Queen's Grill.** Apartments can be connected to a penthouse to create a 2,220-square-foot suite.

Four deluxe penthouses (Queen Mary, Queen Anne, Queen Elizabeth, and Queen Victoria suites) overlooking the ship's bow measure between 861 and 1,076 square feet. Each features a marble bathroom with tub and shower, walk-in closet, refrigerator, separate dining area, and sitting area with large picture windows.

Suite amenities include two plasma flat-screen televisions, an entertainment system, a bon voyage bottle of Champagne, personalized stationery, a bar with selected spirits or wine and soft drinks, plush terry cloth bathrobes, slippers, and daily fresh fruit and predinner canapés. Penthouses can also be connected with two of the suites to create more than 5,000 square feet of living space. In addition to dining at the Queen's Grill restaurant, suite passengers have an exclusive lounge for afternoon tea, cocktails, and an after-dinner aperitif. Several suites have a private elevator entrance.

Specifications Duplex apartments, 5; deluxe penthouses, 4; penthouses, 6; suites, 82; outside standards with veranda, 782; outside standards, 138; inside standards with atrium view, 12; inside standards, 281. 30 wheelchair-accessible.

DINING Seating in the main restaurants corresponds to the category of the passenger's accommodation. The elegant Queen's Grill is reserved exclusively for luxury penthouses, duplexes, and suites, and the **Princess Grill** for passengers in junior suites. Both have single-seating dining and operate much like an upscale à la carte restaurant. If there has been any disappointment voiced with the ship, it's with the Queen's Grill. Given the exclusivity of the venue, the quality of the service is not convincing for the price. Aware of the criticism, however, Cunard has worked to improve it and recent reports are very favorable.

The **Britannia Restaurant** accommodates all other cabin categories with 1,347 seats and offers open seating for breakfast and lunch and two seatings for dinner. The three-deck-high room spans the width of the ship, with a dramatic central staircase meant to recall the grand dining rooms of past Cunard liners. Despite the large number of passengers being served at one time, the food and service get high marks. In 2007, Cunard added the Britannia Club, a private room within the restaurant for the exclusive use of passengers booked in the 46 AA deluxe accommodations. This single-seating clublike restaurant offers the Britannia Restaurant menu, plus à la carte options and table-side flambé service.

Another vast space is the **King's Court,** the Lido restaurant serving buffet breakfast and lunch and four casual dining alternatives for dinner. At lunch, there are regional specialties and carved meats. In the evening, King's Court is transformed into sit-down restaurants: **La Piazza** for Italian specialties, **Lotus,** offering Chinese and Asian cuisine, the **Carvery,** serving carved meats, and **Chef's Galley** for chef's selections. Here, passengers can watch and learn the preparation of their meal from Cunard or guest chefs. .

Other dining options include **Todd English,** featuring the innovative Mediterranean cuisine of its renowned namesake, open for lunch (surcharge, $20) and dinner (surcharge, $30) with indoor seating overlooking the aft pool terrace. Reservations are required. The cuisine is outstanding, and indeed the restaurant was so popular that Cunard added the surcharge in order to handle the demand. The **Golden Lion** and **Boardwalk Café** are casual venues for pub grub or fast food, offering hot dogs, hamburgers, and other grills, a daily specialty, soups, and salads. Afternoon tea is served in the **Queens Room** or in the Queens Grill Lounge.

FACILITIES AND ACTIVITIES In a six-day transatlantic crossing, the *QM2* offers a roster of more than 200 activities. Some are traditional cruise-ship fun and games, but many are designed especially for this ship. The **Royal Court Theatre,** the main showroom with tiered seating for 1,100 passengers, boasts concert-hall acoustics, a hydraulic proscenium stage, and sophisticated lighting and sound equipment. The theater is the venue for full-scale West End– or Broadway-type productions and other entertainers. The **Empire Casino** offers blackjack, roulette, and slot machines. The **Queen's Room** is truly the most elegant ballroom at sea.

Illuminations, the first-of-its-kind planetarium at sea, has stadium-type seating where passengers are entertained with celestial shows, movies, lectures, and other programs. In 2007, in partnership with the American Museum of Natural History's Hayden Planetarium, Cunard added two space shows in Illuminations. Four shows are presented daily, including the Hayden Planetarium's new productions, *Cosmic Collisions,* narrated by Robert Redford, and *Passport to the Universe,* narrated by Tom Hanks. A third show, *The Search for Life: Are We Alone?,* is narrated by Harrison Ford. It was developed by the AMNH in collaboration with NASA. Outside the entrance to Illuminations, new plasma screens present the AMNH's AstroBulletins, showcasing new developments in astrophysics, tapping the latest images from NASA satellites and other observatories.

ConneXions, with the latest electronic equipment and Internet access, has seven function rooms to use as classrooms or meeting rooms; they can be separated or joined to adjust for class sizes. The ship's enrichment programs range from wine appreciation and cooking to seamanship and navigation, and are taught by expert guest instructors, some from Oxford University. Computer classes and business services are also available. The facility has the latest electronic equipment and Internet access. Also on tap are the plays and workshops being presented by members of England's famous Royal Academy of Dramatic Art, which supplies the actors and conducts the workshops.

The *QM2*'s 8,000-volume library, the largest at sea, and the **Bookshop,** similar to those on the *QE2,* are furnished with comfortable leather sofas and armchairs and directed by a full-time librarian. The library also has books on CD. Mayfair Shops, a shopping gallery, offers a myriad of items from sundries to fine leather goods and formal wear for sale and rental. Also in this area is the elegant **Champagne Bar,** created by the famous Champagne house Veuve Clicquot Ponsardin, its first and only venture on a cruise line. In addition to a variety of Champagne, the bar has a menu that includes caviar and foie gras.

SPORTS, FITNESS, AND BEAUTY The *QM2* boasts the largest spa afloat, designed by the famous Canyon Ranch, which also operates it. The **Canyon Ranch SpaClub®,** covering 20,000 square feet on two decks, has a staff of 50 to provide treatments and lead classes in yoga and tai chi as well as health-related workshops. The spa has 24 treatment rooms, an aqua-therapy center, whirlpool, saunas, reflexology, an aromatic steam room, a gym with state-of-the-art equipment, a juice bar, and men's and women's locker rooms. The spa is very popular. You should book your treatments early as it fills up fast.

The *QM2* proves that passengers are willing to pay extra for many shipboard amenities—in this case, *QM2*'s fitness facilities and Canyon Ranch Spa. The spa issues a Canyon Ranch SpaClub® Passport, covering the locker rooms and aquatic center for these charges: one-day Passport, $35; three consecutive days, $55; five consecutive days, $85. The fee is the same for at-sea or in-port days. The Passport is issued free with the booking of a spa treatment. Appointments can be made 21 days or more prior to sailing. To book, call reservations: ☎ 866-860-4662 for U.S. residents; +1-(702) 414-6279 for all other nationalities, who can call collect and reverse charges. Another option: e-mail the ship at qmhspa2@cunard.com.

CHILDREN'S FACILITIES The **Play Zone** for small children and **The Zone** are located all by themselves on Deck 6 aft. The area has a small splash pool and toddlers are supervised by nannies. Older children have a separate facility with computer terminals and activities.

PET FACILITIES Cunard has a long tradition of carrying and caring for passengers' pets aboard its ships. To our knowledge, *QM2* is currently the only ship that has kennels. The ocean liner has 12 kennels and a full-time kennel master who manages the kennel program and daily pet care such as feeding, walking, and cleaning. Recently, Cunard enhanced its Pets on Deck program by adding amenities such as fresh-baked biscuits at turndown and a choice of beds and blankets. Pets receive a complimentary gift pack with a *QM2*-logo coat, Frisbee, name tag, food dish and scoop, a complimentary portrait with pet owners, a crossing certificate, and a personalized cruise card. Other perks include pet toys, cat posts and scratchers, and premium pet foods. The kennels and adjacent indoor and outdoor walking areas are open throughout the day, enabling guests to spend time with their pets. Kennel reservations may be made at time of booking and are based on availability. The fee ranges from $300 to $500.

Queen Elizabeth 2	QUALITY 7	VALUE C
REGISTRY Great Britain	LENGTH 963 feet	BEAM 105 feet
CABINS 950	DRAFT 32 feet	SPEED 28.5 knots
MAXIMUM PASSENGERS	PASSENGER DECKS 12	ELEVATORS 13
1,791	CREW 921	SPACE RATIO 36

THE SHIP In September 2007, the *QE2* celebrated her 40th anniversary with a commemorative voyage around the British Isles. Until the arrival of *QM2*, *Queen Elizabeth 2* had been the lone survivor of Cunard's long, rich history of ocean travel. Extensive face-lifts between 1995 and 1999 helped her retain her uniqueness: a grand ocean liner with the flexibility to provide a modern cruise experience.

Major remodeling of most public areas was directed by John McNeece, Britain's leading cruise-ship interior designer, and MET Studio, an architectural and design firm that worked with James Gardner, the *QE2*'s original designer. They improved passenger flow and added new decor, facilities, and ambience that address today's lifestyle while retaining the ship's distinctive character. By integrating *QE2* and Cunard history into the decor, the designers created a floating museum display, named Heritage Trail, as well as a ship as modern as the 21st century. Escorted tours of the 24 exhibits underscore her traditions.

Public rooms are on three decks—Quarter, Upper, and Boat—with new links and stairways to let traffic flow naturally and to reflect passengers' activities at different times of day. Promenades echo the earlier *Queens*. Passengers enter the *QE2* through the Midships Lobby, a two-story atrium on Deck 2 elegantly decorated in mulberry and green against honey-colored cherry wood trimmed in bronze, where a harpist is usually in residence during embarkation. A four-part mural by Peter Sutton depicting the history of Cunard and the *QE2* covers the atrium's circular walls. The bell from the first *Queen Elizabeth* and the *Spirit of Atlantic* statuette are displayed.

ITINERARIES *See* Itinerary Index.

CABINS Comfortable and convenient, all cabins were refurbished, and their bathrooms retiled and given new fixtures in recent renovations. Two new Grand suites (QS category), including one that is wheelchair-accessible, and two Princess Grill cabins were added.

The *QE2*'s complex arrangement of cabin categories is different for the world cruise and the transatlantic service. Because dining assignments are determined by cabin category, it's important to understand precisely what you're buying. In principle, when you pay more, you get more.

The top 6 among 23 categories—plus the 4 named suites—dine in the Queen's Grill. The next group, ultradeluxe, is split between the Princess and Britannia grills. Assignments continue on down the line.

Categories don't completely reflect the variety of configurations. The top two decks, Signal and Sun Boat, have the largest, most luxurious suites with verandas and penthouse service, which includes butlers whose duties range from planning parties to arranging priority disembarkation. Ultra-deluxe cabins are amidships on Sun Deck, Deck 1, and Deck 2; other categories are fore and aft on Decks 2 and 3 as well as the two lower decks.

All cabins have television with 24-hour CNN, information, and movies. Cabins in grill and deluxe class have refrigerators, VCRs, and bathrooms with tub and shower; premium class has bathrooms with shower only. Bathrooms of 55 penthouse suites are in marble. *QE2* has a total of 136 single cabins covering five categories.

Specifications 97 single and 222 double inside cabins; 39 singles and 592 doubles outside; 700 with 2 lower beds; 7 ultraluxury suites. Some wheelchair-accessible cabins. Standard dimensions not available.

DINING Four of the dining rooms have single seating for each meal. The **Mauretania Restaurant** has an early and a late seating. Named for an early Cunard ship, this restaurant has as the centerpiece *White Horses,* a sculpture by Althea Wynne that depicts four horses riding waves, emblematic of the British sailors' term for whitecaps. On transatlantic service, this restaurant has two seatings.

The **Caronia Restaurant,** named for another Cunard ship of legendary opulence, is now one of the ship's most attractive rooms. At the entrance is a 15-foot model of the *Mauretania* (one of the Heritage Trail's largest items). In the style of an English country house, the restaurant has rich mahogany-paneled walls and columns and a white-painted ceiling with Murano glass chandeliers in a spreading leaf design. On the back wall behind the captain's table is a lovely Italian hill-country scene.

The **Princess** and **Britannia** grills have their own separate entrances from the **Crystal Bar.** The latter's name honors Cunard's first ship, *Britannia,* a model of which is displayed in the Heritage Trail group entitled "Samuel Cunard and the Paddle Steamers." The **Queen's Grill** is reserved for passengers booked in Queen's Grill class only. Among its latest additions were etched glass doors and a completely new galley.

Menus are identical in all restaurants, except the Queen's Grill, where cuisine is meant to be of the highest gourmet standard and patrons enjoy tableside preparations. The rooms' sizes and ambience differ more than the food. Fare includes hors d'oeuvres, three soups, sorbet, five entrées, two salads, four or five desserts, cheese, ice cream, sherbet, and fruit. A spa menu is available.

The **Lido** is the ship's most obvious bow to current lifestyles. It was transformed into a buffet-style restaurant, providing an informal setting for breakfast, lunch, dinner, and the midnight buffet. Coffee and drinks are served all day. From our experience, with the exception of the Queen's Grill, the food—and certainly the service—are the best aboard, surpassing even the Princess Grill. Floor-to-ceiling windows open to the outside deck, making the room light and airy. White, beige, and mint decor is set off by two murals by Italian artist Giancarlo Impiglia depicting the *QE2* cruise experience. Stairs lead from the cafe to the Deck 1 Lido area and the **Pavilion** bar and grill.

SERVICE Officers are British, but most hotel and cabin staff are European, many of them women. The level of dining room service rises with the dining room and price. In Grill class, service is meant to be luxurious. For other passengers, it's, well, British. Most passengers say it's friendly and attentive. Unless you're in a top suite, do not expect cabin and dining service to be any different or better than most mainstream ships.

FACILITIES AND ACTIVITIES Varied lounges and public rooms provide an array of activities. A day could begin with exercise in the fitness center or jogging, progress to a lesson in the computer center, and move to a seminar or workshop in the theater. The latter also functions as a lecture hall, conference room, and cinema. There is also a business center, where passengers can send and receive e-mail and faxes at more than a dozen computer stations. Enrichment programs offer seminars, workshops, and lectures by experts. Bingo, a horse-racing game, arts and crafts, and beauty demonstrations are available.

The *QE2* and her sister ship have the only libraries at sea with full-time professional librarians. Doubled in size with a bookshop, the *QE2* library has more than 6,000 books, hundreds of videos, and a multimedia reference library. Red-leather seats and desks are provided, but the library is so popular there's often no place to sit.

Lifestyle updates were central to the ship's renovations as evidenced in the **Golden Lion,** a large, classic English pub decorated in mahogany and plaid. It's the ship's informal social center, with an upright piano, television, karaoke, and darts. Many lagers, stouts, and draught beers are served. The classy **Grand Lounge** showroom has a fully equipped curtained stage, dance floor, a new audio system, and improved sight lines. The latest addition brings fledgling Broadway and West End shows for development aboard ship. Passengers may attend rehearsals, workshops, and improvisation sessions performed by the cast that may appear on opening night.

The popular **Yacht Club,** aft, with handsome, nautical decor and America's Cup memorabilia, is a lounge and bar by day and a sophisticated nightclub in the evening. The **Chart Room** on Quarter Deck showcases Cunard's nautical antiques. A piano from the *Queen Mary* plays for cocktails and after dinner. A bust of Queen Elizabeth II decorates the blue and gold **Queen's Room,** which has retained its dignified best with royal-blue carpeting interwoven with gold Tudor roses. The royal connection is showcased in exhibits of the Queen's Standards, presented to the ship by Queen Elizabeth.

The room is the setting for afternoon tea with live music and evening ballroom dancing. (Gentlemen who forget their formal attire may visit the *QE2* tuxedo rental shop.) Gentlemen hosts are on board to dance with the unescorted ladies. Lounges offer varied dance music and celebrity performers, who have included Bill Cosby and Dick Clark, among others.

SPORTS, FITNESS, AND BEAUTY The ship has indoor and outdoor pools. Deck sports include golf (putting and driving area), shuffleboard, table tennis, and jogging on a track. Exercise classes are available daily in the fitness center and gym on Deck 7. The European-style spa on Deck 6 offering sauna, massage, and beauty and body treatments is operated by Steiner of London; the barber shop and beauty salon are located on Deck 1.

Among her extensive facilities, the *QE2* has one of the largest, best-equipped hospitals afloat.

CHILDREN'S FACILITIES **Club 2000** teen center is on Quarter Deck, and a supervised children's playroom and nursery are available high up on Sun Deck.

Queen Victoria	PREVIEW	
REGISTRY Great Britain	**LENGTH 964.5 feet**	**BEAM 106 feet**
CABINS 1,007	**DRAFT 26.2 feet**	**SPEED 23.7 knots**
MAXIMUM PASSENGERS	**PASSENGER DECKS 12**	**ELEVATORS 12**
2,206	**CREW 900**	**SPACE RATIO NA**

THE SHIP Past Cunard passengers will feel at home on the new *Queen Victoria,* which keeps Cunard traditions, reinforcing Cunard's commitment to its British heritage, and borrows from her sister ships—even public rooms mostly carry the same names as on *QM2* and *QE2*. The elegant new ship presents an inviting, gracious ambience of yesteryear, with a grand lobby three stories high with a sweeping staircase, mosaics and marble floors, sparkling chandeliers, plush carpets, large artworks, and rich fabrics. Designers incorporated the latest technology in her contemporary interiors elsewhere.

Due to debut in December 2007, she will first be seen on America's shores in January 2008, at the start of her maiden world cruise. Departing Southampton on January 6, *Queen Victoria* will be joined by *QE2* sailing in tandem for a historic transatlantic crossing and arriving in New York on January 13. There, they will meet *QM2* for a three-*Queens* landmark event. But that's not all.

QE2 and *Queen Victoria* will continue their tandem sailing to Fort Lauderdale, Florida, where they will arrive two days later. From there, they will go their separate ways. *Queen Victoria* will sail around the world in a westerly direction, visiting 37 ports in 23 countries. *QE2* will go around South America and cross the Pacific via Easter Island to Auckland and Sydney, Australia. Then, in Sydney on February 24, the two ships will meet again. At that meeting, passengers will have another unique opportunity. As part of their world voyage, passengers can sail part of the way on one *Queen* and part on the other.

ITINERARIES   *See* Itinerary Index.

CABINS   Of *Victoria's* 1,007 cabins and suites, approximately 86% are outside and 71% of them have balconies. In Cunard tradition, the choice of accommodation determines your dining venue. Passengers of the high-end suites with marble bathrooms and butler service dine exclusively in the **Queens Grill.** Those one level down dine in the **Princess Grill** at a reserved table in a single seating. All other passengers dine in the **Britannia Restaurant.**

The standard amenities for all passengers include 24-hour room service, satellite television, direct-dial telephone, refrigerator, safe, and hair dryer, bathrobe and slippers, nightly turndown service with pillow chocolate, shoe-shine service; daily fresh fruit (on request); and daily shipboard newspaper (additional charge).

The top categories—Princess, Queen, Penthouse, Master, Grand—of suites range in size from 342 to 2,131 square feet (measurements include balcony). In addition to the standard amenities for all passengers, those exclusive to Queens Grill suites include priority embarkation and luggage delivery, pillow menu, fresh fruit daily, Champagne and strawberries on embarkation, butler and concierge service, personalized stationery, atlas, and books, whirlpool bathtubs, refrigerators stocked to passengers' preferences, complimentary bottled water, bar stocked with spirits, wines, and soft drinks, access to the Queens Lounge and private deck area, in-suite dining, flower arrangement, board games and computer games console, priority disembarkation and tender service, and DVD player. Princess Suites have most, but not all, of these amenities; butler service, priority embarkation, and luggage delivery, for example, are not included.

Britannia category includes balcony, oceanview, and inside cabins that measure from 242 to 472 square feet including balcony; oceanview cabins, 180–201 square feet; and standard inside cabins, 152–243 square feet. Passengers dine at a reserved table for either early or late seating in the Britannia Restaurant. Sparkling wine awaits them at embarkation.

Specifications 864 outside cabins, 143 inside; 718 with balconies. Queens Grill suites: Grand 4, Master 2, Penthouse 25, Queens 35; Princess suites 61; Britannia cabins: balcony 591, oceanview 146, inside 143; wheelchair-accessible 20.

DINING The Queens Grill and Princess Grill, limited to passengers booked in the Queen and Princess suites, offer à la carte menus and service meant to be the ultimate dining experience of the ship. Both restaurants have one seating. These passengers have exclusive use of the Grills Lounge, accessed by a private elevator. It opens onto the **Grills Terrace,** where pre-dinner cocktails, canapés, and Champagne are served. They also have exclusive use of the Courtyard for afternoon tea and dining alfresco, and the Grills Terrace and **Grills Upper Terrace,** outdoor areas that offer deck service.

The two-tiered Britannia Restaurant on Decks 2 and 3 serves early and late dining with assigned seating. Next door, the **Chart Room** is an elegant pre-dinner cocktail lounge and bar with a nautical theme.

Dining alternatives include the **Todd English Restaurant,** which undoubtedly will be as popular as the one on *QM2.* The reservations-only restaurant has a surcharge ($20 for lunch, $30 for dinner). The **Lido,** the venue for casual eating, has a bright and airy ambience by day and night. The **Golden Lion** offers an impressive selection of beer and cider and a hearty pub menu. **Café Carinthia** specialties are teas, coffees, and pastries. Then, too, room service is available around the clock.

FACILITIES, ENTERTAINMENT, AND ACTIVITIES *Queen Victoria'*s elegant public rooms offer a variety of lounges to cater to the different interests and moods of passengers. These include the **Midships Lounge,** a wine bar; **Churchill's Cigar Lounge,** featuring a worldwide selection of cigars; a casino; the **Commodore Club,** an observation lounge on Deck 10, which should be popular for watching sunsets as the ship travels around the world; and **Hemispheres,** the nightclub with contemporary decor and a spectacular setting with its domed glass roof.

The ship's main show lounge, the splendid **Royal Court Theatre,** rises three levels and has the first private boxes at sea. The boxes are open to anyone on the ship and can be reserved. If there's space at the start of the show, boxes will be available on a first-come, first-serve basis. For passengers using the boxes, there's a private lounge where they can have after-dinner or preshow drinks with items such as Champagne and chocolates. The theatre will feature star performances and West End–style productions.

Cunardia is a museum at sea with maritime memorabilia and artifacts from the company's former grand liners. The museum will have rotating exhibitions featuring a particular period of the company's history, complete with "amusing anecdotes." Nearby, the stylish **Royal Arcade,** with its wood paneling, wrought iron, green marbles, and white stone, was inspired by London's Burlington and Royal arcades.

ConneXions™ Conference Centre hosts guest lecturers, celebrity speakers, and other enrichment programs. **ConneXions™ Internet Centre,** just off the **Grand Lobby,** offers Internet and e-mail access and classes to improve your computer skills. Charges apply for Internet and e-mail access. The library, with 6,000 titles, is set on two levels connected by an ornate spiral staircase. Its warm mahogany interiors, leather sofas, and huge windows that face the sea make an inviting quiet corner for reading or daydreaming. The **Winter Garden,** a sun-dappled conservatory filled with greenery, has a retractable glass roof that enables passengers to feel the warm sunshine without going outside.

The **Queens Room** is meant to evoke an ambience reminiscent of that enjoyed by Queen Victoria in her much-loved home. Here, passengers are treated to a white-glove service for a traditional afternoon tea. Cantilevered balconies, ornate frescoes, and backlit glass panels rising two decks in height create an unmistakable sense of occasion. In the evening, the elegant room becomes the setting for another fine Cunard tradition—ballroom dancing. It also makes an ideal setting for the captain's cocktail parties, themed balls, and a host of social occasions.

SPORTS, FITNESS, AND BEAUTY The **Cunard Royal Spa and Fitness Club** offers aerobics classes and a gym with state-of-the-art cardiovascular fitness equipment, including treadmills and bikes complete with their own personal LCD television screens. The spa, which has a hydropool and thermal suite, offers a range of therapies and beauty treatments. The ship has two outdoor pools.

CHILDREN'S FACILITIES *Queen Victoria* has dedicated facilities inside as well as outside areas for children ages 1 to 12.

Disney Cruise Line

P.O. Box 10210, Lake Buena Vista, FL 32830
☎ 407-566-3500 or 800-DCL-2500; fax 407-566-7417
www.disneycruise.com

TYPE OF SHIPS Modern ocean liners with classic steamship lines.

TYPE OF CRUISES Family-oriented mainstream cruises combined with a Walt Disney World vacation, designed for all ages.

CRUISE LINE'S STRENGTHS
- Disney name recognition
- innovative ships
- dining venue variety and presentation
- friendly, conscientious staff
- outstanding private island
- children's facilities
- family cabins

CRUISE LINE'S SHORTCOMINGS
- intrusive, loud public announcements
- Disney overdose
- overregimentation of children's programs
- uneven cuisine
- unnecessary pressure to vacate ship on disembarkation

FELLOW PASSENGERS A cross-section of the nation—similar to patrons at Disney theme parks.

Recommended for Families with children or grandchildren. But, like the Disney parks, a Disney product for kids of all ages.

Not recommended for Anyone who isn't enraptured by Disney.

CRUISE AREAS AND SEASONS Bahamas, Caribbean year-round; Europe; Mexican Riviera, summer 2008.

THE LINE When Disney does something, it does it big, in a spare-no-expenses way. So we were ready for the Disney Cruise Line to make a huge splash when its first ship, *Disney Magic,* was launched in 1998. What you see here and on her twin, *Disney Wonder,* is the result of three years of intensive planning by cruise industry veterans, Disney creative talent, and dozens of the world's best-known ship designers. Their task was to design a product that makes every adult feel the vacation is intended for them, while at the same time giving every child the same impression. The results may surprise people, including adults without children.

   The ships are both classic and innovative. Exteriors have traditional lines, reminiscent of great ocean liners. Inside, they're up-to-the-minute technologically and full of novel ideas in dining, entertainment (both productions and facilities), cabin design. Even Disney's exclusive cruise terminal at Port Canaveral, Florida, is part of the overall strategy,

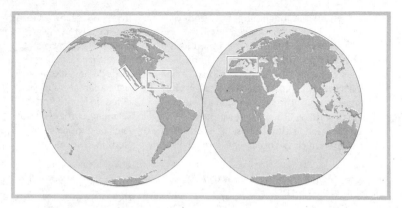

CRUISE AREAS AND SEASONS FOR DISNEY CRUISE LINE

aiming to make enjoyable even embarkation and disembarkation.

Disney offers a "seamless vacation package," that enables you to combine a three- or four-day stay at Walt Disney World with a three- or four-day cruise on *Disney Wonder*, or seven-day cruises on *Disney Magic*. Disney Cruise Line passengers are met at the airport by Disney staff and transported to the terminal in easily identifiable buses. During the hour's ride, they watch a cruise video. When your cruise is packaged with a stay at most Disney hotels, you check in once. The key that unlocks your hotel room door also opens the door to your cruise cabin.

The major innovation is in dining. Each evening on board, you dine in a different restaurant with a different motif, but your waiters and dining companions move with you.

To cater to varied constituencies, some facilities, services, activities, and programs were designed specifically for adults without children, seniors, and honeymooning couples. For example, in addition to the themed restaurants, each ship has an alternative restaurant, swimming pool, and nightclub for use by adults only, as well as entertainment for all the family. Disney continues trying to enhance the adult experience with such facilities as an adults-only cafe, an adults-oriented sports bar, and an area for teens. The line also has kept up with technology by providing advanced online check-in for passengers and wireless access (at a cost) for those who bring their computers.

Overcoming the hassle of tendering passengers was an important consideration when Disney selected its private Bahamian island visited on all its cruises departing from Port Canaveral; deep water enables ships to pull dockside. In 2000, the line inaugurated a seven-day Eastern Caribbean itinerary, and two years later, it added an alternating Western Caribbean one.

In 2005, *Disney Magic* ventured to the West Coast, in conjunction with Disneyland's 50th anniversary celebrations, sailing from Los Angeles to Mexico. Disney followed that venture with its biggest leap to date—a series of European cruises in 2007 with transatlantic positioning cruises as the beginning and end of the European season. More recently, Disney announced it will return to the West Coast in 2008.

In February 2007, Disney announced it would be building two ships scheduled to be launched in 2011 and 2012, and more than doubling the line's capacity. The 124,000-ton ships will be two decks taller than the line's present ships and have 1,250 cabins. The post-Panamax ships (too large to transit the Panama Canal), measuring 1,115 feet in length and 121 feet in width, will be built at Meyer Werft yard in Germany. Disney has not released details about the ships except to say they will be a modern interpretation of classic ocean liners, much like the present fleet.

THE FLEET	BUILT/RENOVATED	TONNAGE	PASSENGERS
Disney Magic	1998/2003/05	83,000	2,700
Disney Wonder	1999/2004/06	83,000	2,700
Unnamed	2011	124,000	NA
Unnamed	2012	124,000	NA

DISTINCTIVE FEATURES Three themed restaurants with "rotation" dining, sports bar in a funnel, children's facilities, cabin design, port terminal. Pagers for adults with children participating in youth activities. Online check-in.

	HIGHEST	LOWEST	AVERAGE
PER DIEM	$650	$123	$348

Per diems are calculated from cruise line's nondiscounted *cruise-only* published fares on standard accommodations and vary by season, cabins, and cruise areas.

RATES Price includes port charges.

Special fares and discounts Early booking can save on three-, four-, and seven-night cruises and packages; consult Disney's brochure or its Web site for details.

- **CHILDREN'S FARES:** Prices vary depending on the length of the cruise. Consult Disney's brochure or its Web site for details.
- **SINGLE SUPPLEMENT:** 175%.

Packages Weeklong packages pair a visit to Walt Disney World in Orlando with unlimited admission to the theme parks and a three- or four-night cruise. A seven-day cruise-only package is available. Consult the Disney brochure for these prices.

- **AIR/SEA:** Yes.
- **PRE/POST:** Yes.
- **OTHERS:** Honeymoon.

THE LAST WORD The vessels are complex and innovative, breaking the mold of traditional cruise ships. Initially, cruise experts questioned whether

Disney could fill its ships when kids are in school, but Disney estimated that if 1% to 2% of the estimated 40 million annual visitors to Disney's resorts and parks bought a Disney cruise vacation, the ships would sell out. Disney was right and now, after almost a decade of success, no one is questioning them any longer.

Disney Cruise Line Standard Features

Officers European, American, and international.

Staff Cabin and Dining: International; Cruise: American and International.

Dining facilities Three themed family restaurants with "rotation" dining; alternative adults-only restaurant; indoor/outdoor cafe for breakfast, lunch; pool bar and grill for burgers, pizza, and sandwiches; ice-cream bar.

Special diets Request at the time of booking for low-sodium, kosher, and other dietary requirements.

Room service 24 hours.

Dress code Casual by day; resort casual and informal in the evenings. Jacket requested for men in Palo, Lumiere's, Triton's in evening; one formal and one semiformal night on *Magic* seven-night cruises.

Cabin amenities Direct-dial telephone with voice mail; tub and shower, two-in-one bathrooms; television, safe, hair dryer. Beachside massages on private island for a fee.

Electrical outlets 110 AC.

Wheelchair access Yes.

Recreation and entertainment Theater with Broadway-style musicals, movie theater, family nightclub, adult nightclub, pub, lounges.

Sports and other activities Sports Deck, basketball, paddle tennis, family sports, adult, family and kids' pools, table tennis, shuffleboard, biking and water sports on Castaway Cay (extra charge).

Beauty and fitness Spa with sauna, steam rooms; beauty salon, newly expanded fitness center.

Other facilities Self-service launderettes; digital photographic services; dry cleaning; satellite phone services; medical facilities; guest services desk; 24-hour front-desk service; fax conference facilities on *Disney Wonder*.

Children's facilities Age-specific supervised children's program, year-round youth counselors; teen club; nursery for ages 12 weeks to 3 years.

Smoking Smoking not allowed except in designated areas.

Disney suggested tipping Per guest per cruise for a 3-, 4-, 7-, 10-, 11-, and 14-night cruise: dining room server, $11, $14.75, $25.75, $36.75, $40.50,$51.50; assistant server, $8, $10.75, $18.75, $26.75, $29.50, $37.50; head server, $2.75, $3.75, $6.50, $9.25, $10.25, $13; cabin host/hostess, $10.75, $14.50, $25.25, $36, $39.75, $50.50. 15% service charge added automatically to bar, beverages, wine, and deck service bills.

Credit cards For cruise payment and onboard charges: all major credit cards.

Disney Magic	QUALITY 8	VALUE C
Disney Wonder	QUALITY 8	VALUE C
REGISTRY Bahamas	LENGTH 964 feet	BEAM 106 feet
CABINS 875	DRAFT 25 feet	SPEED 21.5 knots
MAXIMUM PASSENGERS	PASSENGER DECKS 11	ELEVATORS 12
2,700	CREW 950	SPACE RATIO 35.4

THE SHIPS *Disney Magic* and *Disney Wonder* are modern cruise ships with long, sleek lines, twin smokestacks, and styling that recalls classic liners but with instantly recognizable Disney signatures. Colors—black, white, red, and yellow—and the face-and-ears silhouette on the stacks are clearly those of Mickey Mouse. Look closely and you'll see that *Magic*'s figurehead is a 15-foot Goofy (Donald Duck on *Wonder*) swinging upside down from a boatswain's chair, "painting" the stern.

Interiors combine nautical themes and Art Deco inspiration, but Disney images are everywhere, from Mickey's profile in the wrought-iron balustrades to the bronze statue of Helmsman Mickey (Ariel on *Wonder*) at the center of the three-deck Grand Atrium. Disney art is on every wall, stairwell, and corridor. Some works are valuable old prints of Disney cartoon characters. A grand staircase sweeps from the atrium lobby to Deck 4, where there are shops selling Disney Cruise–themed clothing, collectibles, jewelry, and sundries, classic Disney toys, and souvenirs. (The shops are always full of buyers; some people speculate that the cruise line derives as much revenue here as other lines do from their casinos, which the Disney ships do not have.)

The ships have two lower decks with cabins, three decks with dining rooms and showrooms, then three decks of cabins, and two Sports and Sun decks with separate pools and facilities for families and for adults without kids. Signs with arrows point the way to lounges and facilities, and all elevators are clearly marked forward, aft, or midship. (More deck plans mounted on walls would help newcomers get their bearings.) Daily in your cabin, you receive Your Personal Navigator, listing onboard entertainment and activities separated into options for teens, children, adults, and families, plus shore excursions.

Following the renovation of *Disney Magic* in 2003, *Disney Wonder* got similar treatment in 2004. Three new, age-specific venues to appeal to adults and older teenagers—**Aloft** (**The Stack** on *Magic*) a teen haven, **Cove Café,** and **Diversions,** a sports bar—were added. Then in 2005 and 2006, the ships got further renovations when even more new adult options were added, along with new features to appeal to kids and families.

ITINERARIES *See* Itinerary Index.

CABINS Cabins and suites are spacious with generous wood paneling throughout. About three-fourths are outside, almost half with verandas. The 12 cabin categories range from standard to deluxe, deluxe with veranda, family suite, one- and two-bedroom suite, and royal suite. Categories are similar to those at Walt Disney World hotels. The cruise cabin category passengers selected are matched with a comparable category for their three or four days' stay at a Disney hotel.

Note: If you're staying at a Disney resort before your cruise, be sure to complete and return your cruise forms at the hotel. By showing your shoreside room key card at the cruise terminal, you can bypass lines and board directly. Cruise-only passengers may encounter a wait at check-in.

Cabin design reveals Disney's finely tuned understanding of the needs of families and children and offers a cruise-industry first: a split bathroom with bathtub/shower and sink in one room and toilet, sink, and vanity in another. This configuration, found in all but standard inside cabins, allows any member of the family to use the bathroom without monopolizing it entirely. All bathrooms have both tub and shower. *Note:* For added convenience, couples or families should pack two of essentials like toothpaste, providing one for each sink.

All cabins sleep at least three; many accommodate four or five and some up to seven. In some, pull-down Murphy beds provide additional daytime floor space. Storage space is generous. Bureaus are designed to look like steamer trunks.

Cabins have direct-dial telephone with voice mail, television, hair dryer, and cooler. The room key also opens the safe. All cabins on both ships have new Sealy Posturepedic Premium Plush Euro-top mattresses, new pillows, and finer linens. The concierge-level suites were given new duvets, and their occupants have a choice of pillows as part of Disney's Pillow Talk program. In the bathrooms, passengers will find new deluxe bath towels and bath sheets and upgraded products by H2O Plus spa—all in specially designed bottles with the Disney logo and Mickey's picture.

Specifications 256 inside cabins, 621 outside. Two Walt/Roy Disney suites (sleeps up to 7); 2 two-bedroom suites, 18 one-bedroom suites, 80 family cabins—all sleep up to 5; 282 deluxe cabins with verandas (up to 3 or 4); 237 deluxe outside cabins (up to 4), 96 deluxe inside cabins (up to 4) and 160 standard inside cabins (up to 4). 16 wheelchair-accessible, including 4 one-bedroom suites, 6 deluxe cabins with verandas, 2 deluxe outside cabins, and 4 standard inside cabins.

DINING Disney's most innovative area is dining. Ships have three different family restaurants, plus an alternative restaurant for adults only. Each night, passengers move to a different family restaurant, each with a different theme and menu, taking along their table companions and waitstaff. In each restaurant, tableware, linens, menu covers, and waiters' uniforms fit the theme.

On *Magic,* **Lumiere's**—named for the candlestick character in *Beauty and the Beast*—is a handsome venue serving continental cuisine. A mural depicts Beauty and the Beast (the equivalent restaurant on *Wonder* is called **Triton,** themed after *The Little Mermaid*). **Parrot Cay** dishes up Caribbean-accented food in a fun, tropical setting and seems to be the most popular for breakfast. But it's **Animator's Palate** that reflects the creative genius of Disney animation. Diners are given the impression they have entered a black-and-white sketchbook. Over the course of the meal, the sketches on the walls are transformed into a full-color extravaganza. Waiters change their costumes from black and white to color. The first course is a montage of appetizers served on a palette-shaped plate, and one of the desserts—a tasteless mousse in the shape of Mickey—comes with a parade by waiters bearing trays of colorful syrups—mango, chocolate, and strawberry—used to decorate it. It's entertaining, but the food is, at times, less than inspired, and hot dishes are likely to arrive cold, but no ones seems to care—they are too absorbed in watching Disney perform its magic.

Palo, the Italian restaurant named for the pole gondoliers use to navigate Venetian canals, is the intimate, adults-only restaurant. It's the best aboard. The lovely, semicircular room has a sophisticated ambience with soft lighting, Venetian glass, inlaid wood, and a backlit bar. Northern Italian cuisine is featured. Food and presentation are excellent. More than two dozen kinds of wine are available by the glass at reasonable prices. There's a $10 per-person cover charge. Reservations are required and can be booked in advance online. Otherwise, make them as soon as you board, as the restaurant is very popular and reservations go fast. Other dining options include **Topsiders** (**Beach Blanket Buffet** on *Wonder*), an indoor/outdoor cafe serving breakfast and lunch; a pool bar and grill for hamburgers and hot dogs; **Goofy's Galley** for sandwiches, wraps, paninis, and ice cream; **Pinocchio's Pizzeria;** for brick-oven pizza. The free soda fountain outside the buffet is very popular. In the adults-only Cove Café, located next to the Quiet Cove pool, passengers can enjoy gourmet coffees, specialty drinks, and lighter fare, along with a supply of popular magazines. The ships also have 24-hour room service.

On seven-night cruises, the dining options are expanded. They include a Captain's Gala dinner with wine and French continental cuisine, and a Til We Meet Again dinner as a final-night farewell, featuring some of the best dishes of the cruise. On four- and seven-night cruises, there's also a Champagne brunch ($10 per person) on sea days, high tea, and character breakfasts hosted by Chip and Dale, the latter offering kids a chance to meet and pose for pictures with popular Disney characters in Caribbean attire.

SERVICE Passengers lavishly praise Disney cast members, as cruise and park staff are called. Staff are among the most accommodating you will encounter in travel, and they try hard to smooth your way. More than once when I stopped to get my bearings, a staff member was beside me in seconds to help.

FACILITIES AND ACTIVITIES Disney diversions are geared to children, families, and adults. A day at **Castaway Cay,** Disney's 1,000-acre private island, is meant to be the ultimate escape. The natural environment has been preserved. Miles of white-sand beaches are surrounded by beautiful water. A pier allows access without tendering. A four-car open tram (like those at Disney World) conveys passengers from the ship to **Scuttle's Cove** family beach. The shuttle runs every five minutes. You could walk the quarter mile to the beach, but it's inadvisable in the blistering heat. (Bring sunblock and wear a hat.) Strollers are available, as are rental bikes, floats, and kayaks. Lounge chairs under pastel umbrellas are plentiful, and some hammocks swing under the palms, but otherwise there's very little shade.

Disney Imagineers have created shops, restrooms, and pavilions that give the impression they have been there for years. A supervised children's area includes a "dig" at a half-buried whale skeleton replica. Water sports are offered in a protected lagoon. One snorkeling course is near shore; the other, farther out, requires more endurance. Lifeguards watch snorkelers all around the courses. The cruise line has also planted several "shipwrecks." On one in about ten feet of water, snorkelers can see a Mickey Mouse statue. There's also a treasure chest, its contents guarded by large fish. Snorkel equipment rents for a pricey $25 for adults and children 10 years and older, $10 for ages 5–9. The Gateway Package, a combination of snorkel equipment and float for the day plus a one-hour bicycle rental is also available for $6 more for children; $7 more for adults. Nature trails and bike paths are provided. The main beach offers kids' activities, live Bahamian music or DJ, and shops. **Cookie's BBQ** serves a buffet lunch of burgers, pork ribs, hot dogs, baked beans, slaw, corn on the cob, fruit, and potato chips.

A second tram connects to **Serenity Bay,** the adult beach on the island's opposite side. The adult beach is a long sweep of sugary sand. A bar serves drinks, and passengers can enjoy a massage in one of the private cabanas with shuttered doors opening on the sea. The latest addition to Castaway Cay is the *Flying Dutchman,* the pirate ship seen in the successful film, *Pirates of the Caribbean: Dead Man's Chest.* The 175-foot "ghost ship," anchored off the island, provides a scenic photo op; passengers who rent boats on Castaway can get a closer look at the ship.

Nightly entertainment is unlike any other cruise line's and features good-quality, Disney-produced shows. The 977-seat **Walt Disney Theater** stages a different musical production each night, with talented actors, singers, and dancers. These family musicals are on the level of Disney theme parks' live entertainment rather than Broadway and may appeal more to children than to adults.

Disney Dreams has about every Disney character and song ever heard and offers a light plot wherein Peter Pan visits a girl who dreams of Disney's famous characters. Recently, the show got a sprinkling of its own pixie dust with new laser effects that give the impression of real pixie dust falling from the ceiling of the theater. Other new effects have given the show more life and color. It's pure schmaltz, but audiences give it a standing ovation. Another night offers *Hercules, The MUSE-ical* (*Wonder* only), a comedy that's the least saccharine of the lot.

In the smaller **Buena Vista Theater** with full-screen cinema, passengers watch first-run movies and classic Disney films. Now on *Wonder* and *Magic,* movies are also playing poolside on a brand-new, state-of-the-art giant 24-by-14-foot LED screen affixed to the forward funnel on Deck 9 in the Goofy Pool area. Passengers watch not only Disney movies on the screen, but also other features, such as major sporting and broadcast events.

Another fun evening is the "Pirates IN the Caribbean" deck party, when passengers are transformed into pirates for the night and treated to a special dinner with selections presented on a parchment menu. This is followed by a deck party with classic Disney characters in pirate garb, stage performances, fireworks, and the original *Pirates* movie airing on the jumbo screen. Passengers join a conga line with the cruise staff, Goofy, and his seafaring friends to learn special dance steps. Then suddenly, the mood of the party changes as Captain Hook, Mr. Smee, and a gang of "bad" pirates take over the party with special effects including black lighting, skull-and-crossbone projections, and an invasion of pirates rappelling from the funnel. The music changes from light pop to lightly sinister hard-rock classics—reminiscent of earlier days for the adults. Just in time, and before Captain Hook can enlist audience dads to join his gang of pirates, Captain Mickey appears and saves the day, ridding the ship of the evil buccaneers with a swashbuckling finish.

The seven-night cruises also have a show that includes variety acts, musical performances, and a cavalcade of Disney characters. The show tells the story of a young cruise passenger trying to achieve his dream of becoming a seafaring captain. Mickey, Minnie, and the rest of the Disney characters help the boy realize that if he believes in his dream, it can come true. Woven into the show is an overview of the events, activities, venues aboard the ship, and an introduction to the officers, along with tips to make the cruise more enjoyable, such as the best time to meet the Disney characters.

Two other recent additions are *The Golden Mickeys*, a character-filled musical revue using all the glitz and glamour of an awards show to honor the great animated films and characters that Disney has produced for more than 75 years. The passengers, too, are treated as celebrities, given red-carpet treatment, and taken on a journey to celebrate comedy, romance, heroes, and the characters we love to hate—the villains of Disney films. *Twice Charmed: An Original Twist on the Cinderella Story (Magic only)* is the newest addition. **Studio Sea,** modeled after a television- or film-production set, is a family-oriented nightclub offering dance music, cabaret acts, passenger game shows, and multimedia entertainment. The Art Deco **Promenade Lounge** is a daytime haven for reading and relaxation and a nightspot for cocktails and piano music. A pub, formally in the sports bar in the ship's forward, decorative funnel, was moved to Deck 3 to make way for **Aloft,** the teen center.

Beat Street on *Magic* (**Route 66** on *Wonder*) is an adult-oriented evening entertainment district with shops and themed nightclubs: **Rockin' Bar D,** (**Wavebands** on *Wonder*) with live bands or DJ playing rock and roll, top 40, and country music; **Diversions,** a sports pub and casual hangout with flat-screen plasma televisions where passengers can watch sports or play games; and **Sessions,** on *Magic* (**Cadillac Lounge** on *Wonder*), a casual yet sophisticated place to enjoy easy music. Disney ships have no casinos. (Research showed its target markets weren't interested in gambling at sea, Disney says.) They don't have libraries, either.

Unlike *Disney Magic, Disney Wonder* has three conference rooms on Deck 2. In its more recent innovations, the rooms were upgraded with state-of-the-art presentation tools and LED flat-screen television. The meeting space has a business center, individual computer stations, and a refreshment bar. Both ships provide wireless connections for passengers who come with wireless-ready laptops. The hot spots are in several public areas and lounges and all open areas on Decks 9 and 10. Rates for wireless access start at $0.75 per minute, or $55 for 100 minutes and $100 for 250 minutes. Those without laptops can use computers in the ship's Internet cafes in the **Promenade Lounge, Cove Café, Aloft** (*Disney Wonder*) and the **Stack** (*Disney Magic*).

SPORTS, FITNESS, AND BEAUTY Of three top-deck pools, one has a Mickey Mouse motif and waterslide and is intended for kids. Another is set aside for families; the third is for adults. At night, the family pool area can be transformed for deck parties and dancing.

The ocean-view **Vista Spa and Salon,** above the bridge, is an area reserved exclusively for adults. In the ship's most recent renovations, the spa got three specifically designed, ocean-view spa villas, complete with an indoor spa treatment suite connected to a private outdoor veranda with a hot tub, open-air shower, and chaise lounge. The fitness center offers Life Fitness exercise equipment, exercise instruction, thermal-bath area, saunas, and steam rooms. It's supervised by a qualified fitness director. Along with the spa expansion, the fitness enter was doubled in size, providing space for more exercise equipment, spinning classes and Pilates instruction, and personal beauty and fitness consultations. The spa, run by the British-based Steiner group, offers pricey beauty treatments along with a sales pitch for Steiner products. Despite high prices, the spa is very popular; it's generally booked for the entire cruise within hours of embarkation. Adult passengers can make spa appointments on the Disney Cruises Web site. The Sports Deck has paddle tennis and a basketball court. A full promenade deck lures walkers and joggers and shuffleboard players. *Wonder's* Quiet Cove adult pool, adjacent to the Vista Spa, got a makeover with a teak deck, more deluxe lounge chairs, and two hot tubs with waterfalls.

CHILDREN'S FACILITIES Playrooms and other kids' facilities occupy more than 15,000 square feet. Programs of age-specific activities are among the most extensive in cruising. They include challenging interactive activities and play areas supervised by trained counselors. Also offered is a children's drop-off service in the evening at the **Oceaneer's Club**. This service is available from 9 a.m. until midnight or 1 a.m. and is included in the cost of the cruise. Children in the drop-off program are taken to dinner at Topsiders or Beach Blanket Buffet.

The ships' expanded **Flounder's Reef Nursery** was improved with enhanced lighting that creates the look of being under the sea. The toddler area, doubled in size, has toys from Hasbro, Disney's partner, and a special porthole for parents to check on their kids without the little ones seeing them. The ships provide parents with pagers. Passengers can register their children for the nursery online at Disney's Web site up to three days prior to vacation, and in the nursery on sailing day between 1:30 p.m. and 3:30 p.m. Availability is limited and on a first-come, first-serve basis. The nursery holds up to 30 children (10 infants and 20 toddlers). The child/counselor ratio is one babysitter to four children (ages 12 weeks to 1 year); one babysitter to six children (ages 1–2 years); and one babysitter to 11 children (2–3 years). On embarkation day, the nursery is open 1:30–3:30 p.m. to take reservations for the cruise. In *Wonder*'s most recent renovations, the Mickey Pool on Deck 9 was extended to provide a pool with interactive fountains and splash zones for children not yet toilet trained and in swim diapers.

Group babysitting in Flounder's Reef Nursery is available for select hours every day. (Guests should check with programming once on board for the exact times, as the hours change daily in accordance with daily activities, ports of call, etc.) Flounder's Reef is open 5:45 p.m. to midnight, nightly. Cost is $6 per child per hour; $5 per hour for each additional child. A two-hour minimum is required; maximum ten hours per child, based on demand and availability.

The Oceaneer's Adventure program encompasses Oceaneer's Club (ages 3–7), themed to resemble Captain Hook's pirate ship, with plenty of places for activity. Its Neverland theme has been expanded and the Captain's Closet dress-up area revamped. There's more space for hands-on, interactive activities along with additional PlayStation and computer stations. **Oceaneer's Lab** (ages 8–12), offers high-tech play, including video games, computers, lab equipment, and a small room for listening to CDs.

On *Wonder*, Oceaneer's Lab has a new computer simulator enabling children to try their hand at steering the ship in and out of ports. The simulator, fashioned as a replica of the ship's bridge, has giant video screens that provide a panoramic view of the ports similar to the actual view from the ship's bridge. Kids wear ID bracelets, and parents receive pagers for staying in touch with their playing children. Both parents and children give the youth programs high marks.

Aloft (The Stack on *Magic*) sits high on Deck 11 in the ornamental smokestack with lots of space and nooks and crannies. The program also has organized activities, including volleyball at Castaway Cay. The teen program seems to be a hit, as teens enjoy having an area to themselves in the evenings as well as having their own area apart from the kids. Aloft, with eclectic decor that's a cross between a college dormitory and a trendy coffee shop, features beanbags and a soda bar. It's a teen haven for socializing with newfound friends and offers high-tech diversions such as a big-screen television, MP3 players, computers, and video-game systems, some of which have wireless controllers. While the room succeeds in its hardware, the activities—apparently too juvenile for teens—appear to need some work; on a recent cruise, one passenger reported that only a handful of teens hang out at any one time there, often munching on snacks, sometimes watching movies. Passengers can register their children for youth activities on Disney Cruise's Web site.

SHORE EXCURSIONS On some itineraries, the ships dock in Nassau for 15 hours—ample time to explore the island, enjoy a sport, visit Atlantis Resort on Paradise Island, shop, and take in a show and casino. The ship offers at least 12 excursions for Nassau, most of them fairly standard tours. Among choices are the Glass Bottom Boat Tour, $25 adults/$17 children; Snorkel Tour, $37/$27; Discover Atlantis, $39/$26; Historic Nassau city tour, $23/$18; a Powerboat ride for teens, a ride on a custom-built speedboat, $41/$31. A similar ride for families and children costs $39/$29. Children's prices apply to ages 3 through 9. Booklets on excursions for the Eastern and Western Caribbean itineraries are also available. Shore excursion descriptions, including those for Disney's new European cruises, are available on the line's Web site, and can be booked in advance of your cruise.

POSTSCRIPT The Disney Cruise Line attracts a high percentage of first-time cruisers, thanks to Disney's reputation for quality, service, and entertainment, which helps dispel doubts about cruise vacations. At the same time, great effort is made to ensure that the ships appeal to adults—with or without children—as much as to families with an extensive menu of adult activities. The presence of hundreds of children onboard does not diminish the adult experience.

More difficult to escape than children, however, is Disney's sugary, cute entertainment, which permeates every cruise. Expressed differently, you don't need to adore children to enjoy a Disney cruise, but you'd better love Disney.

Our main criticism of the ships' design is that all outdoor public areas focus inward—toward the pools rather than seaward, as if Disney wants you to forget you're on a ship. There's no public place on any deck where you can relax in the shade and watch the ocean (at least not without a Plexiglas wall separating you). If this quintessential cruise pleasure ranks high with you, book a cabin with private veranda.

Some bothersome areas could quickly be improved. Examples: Public announcements are intrusive. Bar bills include a 15% gratuity, *then* have an empty space marked "gratuity" below the total. This amounts to a second tip. Guest Services says the space enables passengers to reward "extraordinary" service with something "extra." But most passengers, especially first-timers, won't know that or may be too shy to ask and will add a second tip. At Palo, food is excellent, but service is slow. At Topsiders, food is mediocre, selections limited, and tables very crowded, but service is outstanding.

On the plus side, passengers departing from Port Canaveral booked on airline flights can check in for most flights shoreside. (Too bad all cruise lines can't provide this service.)

Holland America Line

300 Elliott Avenue West, Seattle, WA 98119
☎ 206-281-3535 or 877-SAILHAL (724-5425); fax 800-628-4855
www.hollandamerica.com

TYPE OF SHIPS Modern superliners.

TYPE OF CRUISES Traditional yet modern, high-quality premium cruises.

CRUISE LINE'S STRENGTHS
• tradition and experience
• easy-to-like ships
• consistent quality and style
• worldwide itineraries
• impeccable condition of ships

CRUISE LINE'S SHORTCOMINGS
• show lounge entertainment
• shore excursion cancellation policy
• communication problems with dining staff due to language

FELLOW PASSENGERS Experienced travelers and families who seek comfort and consistency, quality, a refined environment, and and those who choose cruises by their destinations. Many are retired business owners with some college education and professionals, but the range includes secretaries on their first cruise, affluent seniors who cruise often, honeymooners, young families, multigenerational families, and some disabled travelers. They're social-minded, well mannered, and outgoing, but not loud. They enjoy traveling with old friends and making new ones. They're conservative and seek good value. They often cruise to celebrate a special occasion, such as an anniversary or a family reunion.

The average age varies by cruise length and itinerary. A seven-day Alaska and seven-day Caribbean cruise on the same ship attract different ages and incomes. More than 55% are couples; 50% are groups—as different as business or tour groups, or square-dancing and stamp-collecting clubs.

Recommended for Those who enjoy cruise traditions and want a high-quality experience in a refined environment, but like the facilities of superliners. Small-ship devotees open to trying a larger ship. Budget cruisers able to move up to higher quality, families, and multigenerational vacationers.

Not recommended for Swingers, party seekers, late-night revelers, trend seekers, or pacesetters.

CRUISE AREAS AND SEASONS Africa, Asia, Caribbean, Hawaii, Mexico, Pacific Coast, Panama Canal, South Pacific, fall to spring; Alaska, Canada, Europe, New England, transatlantic, summer/fall; Antarctica, South America, world cruise, winter.

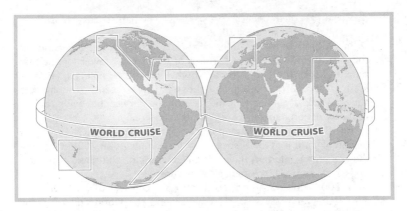

CRUISE AREAS AND SEASONS FOR HOLLAND AMERICA LINE

THE LINE Holland America has carried passengers since 1872. It's among the few lines to make a successful transition from a classic steamship company to a modern cruise line, and it did so better than most, managing to keep its identity and traditions intact while developing a fine mainstream product.

One turning point came in the early 1980s when the line introduced the *Nieuw Amsterdam* (sold in 2000), a forerunner of today's superliners. She was revolutionary because of such features as a square stern that provided 20% more open deck, two outdoor heated pools, a fully equipped gym, spa, and whirlpool, coded cards rather than keys for cabins, and cabin television—all features that quickly became standard on new ships.

In 1988, HAL acquired the unusual Windstar Cruises, and the following year, Holland America, Windstar, and Seattle-based Westours, which pioneered Alaska tours and cruises, were acquired by Carnival Corp. The marriage proved to be brilliant, enabling Holland America to continue its expansion (four stunning new ships in the 1990s, and another four early in the new millennium) and allowing the line to expand in Alaska, return to Europe after nearly two decades, and increase its number of longer cruises. All were factors critical to HAL's retaining its many loyal fans.

The *Statendam*-class ships, the first HAL ships to have private verandas, combine classic elegance with state-of-the-art technology, offering such features as multideck atriums, fountains, whirlpools, and treadmills. The faster *Rotterdam* and her sister ship, *Amsterdam*, with top cruising speeds of 25 knots, gave the line new flexibility in creating itineraries. They were followed by slightly larger twins, *Volendam* and *Zaandam,* and another new class of 82,000-ton cruise ships, dubbed the Vista series, arrived between 2002 and 2006. Altogether, the line introduced ten new ships in ten years—a challenge for any cruise line. And now, the first of the new 2,044-passenger Signature-class ships, *Euro-dam,* will debut in summer 2008.

In 1998, to widen its audience and meet the market's demand for short vacations, HAL offered cruises of five days or fewer for the first time. In 2001, the line introduced wheelchair-accessible tenders and Internet access for passengers fleetwide. More recently, the line has added wireless connection and cell phone service fleetwide, and a shore-excursion booking facility on its Web site.

But these enhancements pale compared with the extensive, $225 million Signature of Excellence program completed in 2006, updating the line for the modern traveler while continuing to uphold the traditions that are Holland America's signature.

In 2008, Holland America will mark its 50th year of world cruising with four grand voyages: 114 days around the world and a 65-day Pacific cruise on the *Amsterdam;* and 68 days to South America and Antarctica, followed by 73 days around Africa on the *Prinsendam.* The line's first world cruise in 1958 sailed out of Hoboken, New Jersey, on the *Statendam.*

THE FLEET	BUILT/RENOVATED	TONNAGE	PASSENGERS
Amsterdam	2000/06	61,000	1,380
Eurodam	2008	85,000	2,044
Maasdam	1994/2006	55,451	1,258
Noordam	2006	85,000	1,848
Oosterdam	2003/06	81,769	1,848
Prinsendam	1988/93/96/99/2002/04	38,000	793
Rotterdam	1997/2005	59,652	1,316
Ryndam	1994/2004	55,451	1,258
Statendam	1993/2005	55,451	1,258
Veendam	1996/2006	55,451	1,258
Volendam	1999/2006	60,906	1,432
Westerdam	2004/05	81,769	1,848
Zaandam	2000/04	60,906	1,432
Zuiderdam	2002/06	81,769	1,848
Signature-class/Unnamed	2010	85,000	2,044

STYLE HAL cruises are classic but contemporary, blending Old World traditions with modern lifestyles. They offer the full range of activities expected on large, mass-market ships. The pace is leisurely, designed for experienced, mature travelers and families.

To attract younger passengers, the line has progressively expanded onboard sports and fitness facilities; added sports bars with ESPN programming, alternative dining, Internet access, sports and adventure shore excursions for active passengers on Alaska and Caribbean cruises; and beefed up its children's program. Now, with the completion of Signature of Excellence, most ships have special teens-only areas, as well.

In 1997, Holland America bought the uninhabited 2,400-acre Bahamian island of Little San Salvador, renamed it Half Moon Cay, and developed it as HAL's private island destination on Caribbean itineraries. Located between Eleuthera and Cat Island, less than 100 miles southeast of Nassau, the 45-acre facility fronts a gorgeous white-sand beach. Three areas, connected by walkways and a tram, are an arrival marina and plaza built to resemble ruins of a Spanish fort, a shopping area styled as a West Indian village, and a food pavilion. In 2005, the aqua park was expanded to include slides and other new features.

The market has shops, an ice-cream parlor, coffee shop, bar, and art gallery. There is a playground, wedding chapel, and post office selling Bahamian stamps—including one issued to commemorate the island. Passengers get a barbecue lunch of West Indian selections. The sports center offers snorkeling and diving on nearby reefs, Sunfish sailing, other water sports, volleyball, and basketball, and there's horseback riding and swimming with dolphins. Nature trails feature a bird sanctuary designated by the Bahaman National Trust. Passengers can debit the cost of all services and sports to their cabins; cash is required for island stamps; craft vendors take credit cards.

Holland America's vessels feel like ships, not floating hotels. The fleet shares characteristics that reinforce the line's traditions: art and antiques reflecting Holland's association with trade and exploration in the Americas; Dutch officers and Indonesian crews, linking Holland's historical ties to Asia; and the **Crow's Nest,** an observation bar inspired by the lookout on the main mast of the company's old sailing ships. Now passengers can view the multimillion dollar collections with a free self-guided tour using an iPod, introduced on the *Westerdam* in July 2006.

With the new Signature of Excellence program, the line has aimed for an even more youthful look and ambience with enhancements to cabins, dining, spa, and children's facilities, and the introduction of new features throughout the fleet, such as early boarding from 11:30 a.m. on the day of departure, four evening dining times, and the addition of the **Pinnacle Grill,** a steak and seafood specialty restaurant. New activities and shore excursions stress active sports. The goal has been to make the HAL experience more relevant to today's and tomorrow's traveler (read baby boomers). All Holland America ships have been outfitted with cell phone capability. Passengers can make and receive calls and send text messages on their own cell phones and PDAs, so long as they are activated for international dialing with the passengers' home provider. International roaming fees apply and appear on their home cell phone bill.

Ever-mindful of their longtime loyal fans, Holland America has worked to strike a balance between the pace and nature of the changes needed to attract a broader, younger audience, while keeping the traditions that older passengers cherish.

One of Holland America's most important initiatives has been On-Deck for the Cure, an onboard, noncompetitive 5K fitness walk to raise money for the Susan G. Komen Breast Cancer Foundation. Rolled out in 2006 and offered fleetwide, the program invites passengers to participate, suggesting a $15 donation. Up to 250 passengers per cruise are participating, raising $350,000 in the first year.

DISTINCTIVE FEATURES Escalators; self-service laundries on some ships, good libraries, fresh flowers shipwide; fruit basket, robes in cabins, hot hors d'oeuvres at cocktails, chimes played by a uniformed steward to announce dinner, private Bahamian island, alternative dining, Internet centers, cell phone capability; Culinary Arts program, Explorations Café powered by the *New York Times*. Self-guided art tour with iPod; Greenhouse Spa.

	HIGHEST	LOWEST	AVERAGE
PER DIEM	$911	$88	$371

Per diems are calculated from cruise line's non-discounted *cruise-only* published fares on standard accommodations and vary by season, cabins, and cruise areas.

RATES Port charges are included.

Special fares and discounts Save up to 45% for early booking under the Caribbean Savings program. A similar Alaska program offers 25% off. Membership Rewards, a program with American Express, offers mileage redeemable for upgrades and discount dollars.

- THIRD/FOURTH PASSENGER: Low rates.
- CHILDREN'S FARE: Reduced rates for ages 2–18; specific rates for younger than age 2. Ages 19 and older are billed as third/fourth persons sharing parents' room.
- SINGLE SUPPLEMENT: 150%–190% of double rate or specific rate on certain cruises; guaranteed share program.

Packages
- AIR/SEA: Yes.
- PRE/POST: Yes.
- OTHERS: Renewal of vows and other pricey packages for special occasions. Just for Us includes couple massage and chilled Cordon Rouge Champagne at embarkation, a guarantee of table for two in the dining room, framed photo, and more. Romantic Voyage offers bon voyage flower bouquet upon arrival, Champagne, private card lesson with $25 in chips, chocolate truffle dessert after farewell dinner, and spa day for one.

PAST PASSENGERS Mariner Society members receive discount and upgrade offers about five times a year, amenities, recognition, theme cruises, and occasional cruises with HAL's president. Enhancements include baggage tags, separate check-in, party hosted by the captain, and certificates for third to tenth cruise, based on the number of cruises.

THE LAST WORD Holland America puts itself in the premium category, between luxury and economy, but it's at the high end of premium, a hair's breadth from luxury, and deluxe by any standard. The refinements and thoughtful touches it offers are unavailable on many comparably priced ships. HAL's consistency—even the names of most public rooms are the same fleetwide—has built a large, loyal following that doesn't find the predictability boring—rather, it's reassuring.

We are happy to report that Holland America has dropped its ambiguous "no tipping required" policy. Now, $10 per person per day is added to your shipboard bill. You can add to, reduce, or delete it.

Holland America Line Standard Features

Officers Dutch, British, Norwegian.

Staff Dining: Dutch and Indonesian supervisors, Indonesian and Filipino staff; Cabin: Indonesian and Filipino; Cruise: American, others.

Dining facilities One dining room, four seatings. Indoor/outdoor Lido restaurants for casual buffet breakfast, lunch, and alternative dining; taco, pasta, and ice-cream bars.

Special diets Kosher; low-sodium, low-cholesterol, low-fat; vegetarian; sugar-free desserts; baby foods. Request 30 days in advance.

Room service hours; dining room menu during dining hours.

Dress code Casual with two formal/semiformal nights per week of cruise. Tuxedo rental service available.

Cabin amenities Television with CNN, TNT, ESPN, TCM, CNBC, Discovery, and children's channel, multichannel music system, hair dryers, and direct-dial telephone. Suites and deluxe cabins have DVD players, whirlpool bath, and minibar.

Electrical outlets 110 AC.

Wheelchair access 21 cabins on *Amsterdam, Rotterdam;* 22 on *Volendam, Zaandam;* 28 on Vista class; 4–6 on others.

Recreation and entertainment Theater for movies and lectures, show lounge, nightclub, casino, bars, and lounges, karaoke, masquerades, crew show, culinary demonstrations, kitchen tours, bingo, card games, bridge, pool games, dance classes, library. Sports bars with ESPN.

Sports and other activities Two outdoor pools, tennis, golf putting, volleyball, table tennis, shuffleboard.

Beauty and fitness Beauty/barber shop, saunas, massage, fitness program, gym with professional instructors, treadmills, bikes, stair climbers, practice tennis. Spa treatments and fitness programs.

Other facilities Religious services, medical facilities, laundry/dry cleaning service, self-service launderettes on some ships, meeting room. Credit-card phones. Wedding ceremony and amenity packages for vows renewal, honeymoons, and anniversaries at additional charge. Internet centers or Exploration Cafés.

Holland America Line Standard Features (continued)

Children's facilities Club HAL year-round youth program with counselors and age-specific activities for three age groups. Teens ages 13–18 have their own areas with sun deck, waterfall, lounge, and other features.

Theme cruises See specific ships.

Smoking Designated smoking areas in public rooms; some, such as dining rooms, card room, library, and theater, are designated nonsmoking.

Holland America suggested tipping A $10 per person per day gratuity added to passenger's shipboard account; 15% added to bar bills.

Credit cards Cruise and onboard charges: American Express, Discover, Master-Card, Visa; no cash.

Maasdam	QUALITY 8	VALUE B
Ryndam	QUALITY 8	VALUE B
Statendam	QUALITY 8	VALUE B
Veendam	QUALITY 8	VALUE B
REGISTRY Netherlands	LENGTH 720 feet	BEAM 101 feet
CABINS 629	DRAFT 24.6 feet	SPEED 22 knots
MAXIMUM PASSENGERS	PASSENGER DECKS 10	ELEVATORS 8
1,258	CREW 557	SPACE RATIO 44

THE SHIPS The *Statendam* and her sisters introduced a new class of ships in the 1990s that set the style and standard for Holland America into the next century. They combine Old World tradition with state-of-the-art technology and provide an imposing yet inviting ambience. The spacious ships differ in decor but are identical in layout and offer almost identical facilities and activities.

Interiors of the Italian-built ships were designed by De Vlaming, Fenns, and Dingemans (VFD), the Dutch firm responsible for earlier HAL ships, and which helped establish the line's signature look. In the group's public areas, designers drew from Holland America's history to capture the golden age of Dutch shipping, but in a contemporary context. Multimillion-dollar collections of art and artifacts from the 17th to 19th centuries are integrated into the decor. These combine with contemporary art to enhance the ships' modern image. Together, they make the ships floating art galleries. In materials, the world was VFD's emporium. Designers used woolen fabrics from Holland; leathers from Germany, France, and England; glass from Italy. Cabins were made in Finland, a Danish company supplied teak, and furniture was built in Slovenia. Galley equipment came from the United States.

Public rooms span two decks on the Promenade and Upper Promenade in an asymmetrical pattern, allowing for bars and lounges of different sizes.

The *Maasdam*, fifth ship in the company's history with that name, is a far cry from the first *Maasdam*—a double-masted iron steamship that carried eight first-class and 288 steerage passengers. It sailed the Atlantic monthly from 1872 to 1884 at a speed of ten knots. Today's computer-piloted *Maasdam* has only one class and moves at more than twice that speed.

Passengers are introduced to the *Maasdam* by a three-deck atrium on the Lower Promenade Deck. Under a ceiling of mirrors and fiber-optic lights, the atrium sparkles with a 30-foot glass sculpture, *Totem*, by Italian artist Luciano Vistosi. The sculpture contains thousands of pieces of glass that catch the light and cast specks of color on nearby surfaces.

Atrium sculptures on *Statendam* and *Ryndam* are classic in style but out of scale with their setting. On *Statendam*, it's a huge fountain with a bronze statue of three enormous mermaids rising from the sea. On *Ryndam*, it's a tribute to sea legends in marble (five tons!). An oversized sea dragon twines around the sculpture's top and an undersized boat at the bottom, an improbable mermaid on its bow. The decor of the *Statendam*, also the fifth HAL ship to bear the name, is more baroque than the other ships' and often eclectic. Interiors range from conservative to bizarre, blending textures and earth tones with classic European and exotic Indonesian motifs. The *Veendam* is the most stylish of the group, with different color schemes, furnishings, and art. The atrium features a glass sculpture, as on *Maasdam*. Adjacent is the Crystal Terrace.

Ryndam was the first to receive the Signature of Excellence makeover and now sports new public rooms with brighter decor, cabin improvements, dining enhancements, and children's facilities, among others.

ITINERARIES *See* Itinerary Index.

CABINS Comfortable, contemporary furnishings in light wood are combined with continental touches. Standard cabins are almost 30% larger than comparable ones on ships of similar category. Large mirrors lighten the rooms, and in many, curtains separate the sleeping and sitting areas. Seventy-seven percent are outside cabins.

All cabins in all categories fleetwide have new custom-designed Sealy Posturepedic Premium Euro-top mattresses (called Mariner Dream beds) and a pillow menu. Now they have a modern, very different look for HAL, with a light bed and a display of pillows. The cabins also have upgraded bed linens, towels, and terry robes, flat-screen televisions with DVD players, massage showerheads, and lighted magnifying mirrors.

All cabins have hair dryers, direct-dial telephone with automated wake-up service, multichannel music system, and closed-circuit television. Full-length double closets and deep chests of drawers—nice features for long cruises—provide ample storage.

Standard cabins have sofas, of which 70% are sofa beds. All outside cabins have a bathtub and shower. Suites and deluxe cabins have a veranda, minibar, DVD player, and whirlpool bath. Each suite also has a small private dining area; laundry and dry cleaning is free.

Passengers in suites have a concierge to assist with appointments and other needs, plus the comfortable **Neptune Lounge** for the private use of Penthouse and Deluxe suite passengers only. It has its own library, television, and bar.

Specifications 144 inside cabins, 485 outside (including 120 deluxe cabins and 29 suites with verandas). All with twin beds convertible to queen. Standard dimensions are 186 square feet, inside cabin; 196 square feet, outside cabin. 16 deluxe/36 standard outside have connecting doors for family suites. Some upper/lower berths and single cabins; 6 wheelchair-accessible cabins.

DINING   The ships' crowning glories are their dazzling **Rotterdam Dining Rooms.** Surrounded on three sides by floor-to-ceiling windows that embrace the scenery and span the Promenade and Upper Promenade decks, the rooms are a harmony of elegant tradition and modern technology. An impressive curved staircase connects the two levels.

On the *Maasdam,* a fountain of antique Argentine marble is the lower level's centerpiece. A ceiling canopy of a thousand morning glories is made of blown glass from Murano, Italy. Between the decks is a border of fiber-optic florets programmed to change color, altering the room's mood. Four large, colorful linen screens depicting day and night cover the walls on both decks.

One passenger's verdict: "The room is so beautiful, it takes your breath away." The room is large but remarkably quiet; diners can converse in normal voices and hear chamber music playing on the balcony. The secret: glass ceilings look spectacular—and absorb sound.

Dining here and on all Holland America ships is more elegant, and menu choices more extensive, than on most mainstream cruise ships. A typical dinner menu offers a choice of seven appetizers (six cold, one hot); three soups (two hot, one cold), and three salads (five dressings); six entrées, including a vegetarian selection and a light and healthy one, plus selections of cheese and fruit, six desserts, pastries, ice cream, and light and sugar-free desserts. Tables are set with white Rosenthal china bearing a gold HAL logo, silver tableware, wine coolers, and fresh flowers on starched tablecloths. Many tables have either window or balcony seats. A microphone at the captain's table on the main floor allows him or other speakers to address the room; upper-level guests view the speaker on television monitors.

An important element of the Signature of Excellence program has been the fleetwide addition of the **Pinnacle Grill.** The venue replaces the former private King's Room off the main dining room. Sterling beef is the grill's major draw; you can choose your cut from the display tray, including a 20-ounce porterhouse steak. Recently, the menus have been enhanced with a new selection each day. The food is superbly prepared, presented, and served. Reservations are required, and there is a charge: $15 for lunch (served usually on sea days only), and $30 for dinner.

Responding to passengers' preference for casual, flexibly timed breakfast and lunch—and alternative dining in the evening—Holland America has worked to perfect the Lido buffet, outdoing competitors in quality, choice, and presentation. More lunch choices—hot dogs, hamburgers, pasta, satay, and tacos—are available by the Lido pool. A free ice-cream bar is open daily. Sandwiches, desserts, coffee, and tea are available here around the clock. Hot hors d'oeuvres with Indonesian tidbits are served in public rooms before dinner, and a weekly Indonesian Lido buffet is popular. And should you still be hungry, the 24-hour room service menu has been expanded, and your cabin's fruit basket is freshened daily.

On all ships now, the Lido restaurant has been reconfigured into food stations, replacing the cafeteria design. Entrées from the dining room are served as part of the casual dinner option—a handy alternative after a busy day ashore.

One of the main ingredients that Signature of Excellence added to the fleet is the new Culinary Arts program and **Culinary Arts Center,** presented by *Food and Wine* magazine. It has a state-of-the-art show kitchen where cooking demonstrations, tasting events, and cooking classes take place. Some cruises offer presentations by guest chefs. Passengers in the audience get an up-close view of the cooking action on large plasma screens, while broadcast capabilities provide all guests the opportunity to watch from their cabins. In addition to the onstage kitchen, the centers have portable cooking stations where up to 16 guests can participate in hands-on classes that often feature regional cuisine reflecting the ship's itinerary.

The one-hour demonstrations by the executive or guest chefs are free. The daily classes, limited to a dozen or so participants sharing six cooking stations, run one-and-a-half hours, during which an appetizer, entrée, and dessert are prepared. There is a charge of $29 per person for Holland America chefs and $39 per person for guest chefs. A set of recipes is included, plus a 10% discount at the Pinnacle Grill or complimentary admission to a wine-tasting event.

Integral to the program is Holland America's culinary adviser, master chef Rudi Sodamin, who has been instrumental in developing the centers and instructional programs. Sodamin, who emphasizes high-quality ingredients and creative presentation, has added a number of his signature dishes to the menus.

Replacing the Java Café is the **Gourmet Shop** and wine-tasting area. It sells culinary items, china and silverware from the Pinnacle Grill, and Rudi Sodamin's cookbooks.

SERVICE   HAL's efficient Dutch officers and the friendly Indonesian and Filipino crew are a good combination. Unobtrusive service by a gracious and attentive staff is a hallmark—and a reason the line has so many loyal fans. Dining room supervisory personnel are officers; many crew members have been with Holland America for many years.

Unlike most cruise ships, HAL has retained a tradition its fans love: a uniformed steward passes through the ship playing chimes to summon passengers to dine. (Older passengers are reminded of the page boy in old Philip Morris cigarette ads.)

FACILITIES AND ACTIVITIES The *Maasdam* and her sisters each have five lounges, often with the same names and similar entertainment. The Promenade Deck is anchored by the two-deck main show lounge designed by Joe Farcus, who is known for his innovative, flamboyant ship interiors for Carnival Cruise Lines. Daytime activities include lectures, bridge tournaments, dance lessons, bingo, putting contests, kite flying, movies (with popcorn), religious services, and—the most unusual—guided tours of the ship's art and antiquities.

The ships have large, comfortable card and puzzle rooms, a shopping arcade, and libraries with floor-to-ceiling windows. The ships hold auctions of contemporary art. Be wary of the sales pitch. If the bargain sounds too good to be true, it probably is.

In the *Maasdam's* **Rembrandt Show Lounge,** delft ceramic tiles are set against brocade, gold-tinted mirrors, and mahogany paneling that recall the 17th-century Dutch master whose portrait is etched into glass doors at the entrance. The **Vermeer Lounge** on the *Ryndam* honors the 17th-century Dutch master Jan Vermeer. It's Art Nouveau in style, reminiscent of great movie palaces of the 1930s, with lacy mahogany woodwork and silver columns amid dozens of luminescent tulips.

For the **Van Gogh Lounge** on the *Statendam,* the artist's *Starry Night* is the inspiration for computerized special effects, fiber-optic lighting, and curtain drawing. Staircases frame the stage, whose revolving platform facilitates set changes. The *Veendam's* **Rubens Lounge** is named after the celebrated 16th-century Flemish painter Peter Paul Rubens and features glass sculptures in his style. The lounges offer Broadway-style shows similar to entertainment on many mainstream cruise ships. The **Ocean Bar** on the Upper Promenade showcases music by a combo. Here Matthys Roling, one of Holland's best-known artists, created her signature "drapery" art, decorating ceilings and walls in beige and red fabric. The oddly shaped **Piano Bar,** adjacent to the casino and popular for sing-alongs, is designed around a piano, with two semicircles of tables and curving sofas. Lights are programmed to change, altering the cozy room's ambience. The **Explorer's Lounge** has traditionally been passengers' favorite spot for after-dinner drinks.

The casino offers blackjack, Caribbean poker, roulette, dice, and slot machines. Outside, kinetic artist Yaacov Agam created a computer display wall that shows thousands of constantly changing images.

Another Signature of Excellence initiative is **Explorations Café** powered by the *New York Times,* a new concept, not only for Holland America, but for the cruise world. The new venue is a combination 2,000-book library, puzzle corner, Internet center, music-listening area, DVD library, and Torrefazione coffee bar. Located on Upper Promenade Deck 8, it replaced the card room, which was moved down the hall to the former Queen's Room section of the dining room.

Designed to replicate the comfort of a living room, it is operated in co-operation with the *New York Times* and has *Times* crossword-puzzle tables with write-on, wipe-off tops, plus cases of memorabilia from the *Times* archives. The electronic edition of the *New York Times* is downloaded to the room's computers. The daily quiz and crossword puzzle can be picked up at the desk. The area also includes a huge globe, educational programs on interactive flat screens, and Discovery Channel programming on a larger screen. There's a DVD library in the Explorations Café, where passengers can choose from 1,000 titles for $3 per day. Internet access ranges from $0.40 to $0.75 per minute; wireless hot spots are located in various lounges around the ship for use with your own laptop.

The best java on board is found at the coffee bar in the Explorations Café (or **Windstar Café** on some ships) that serves Torrefazione, Starbucks' premium brand. A free snack is included with the purchase of a drink, which costs $1.50 for an espresso, cappuccino, caffe latte, or hot chocolate, or $2.25 for specialty sodas.

The **Crow's Nest,** traditionally a sedate observation lounge by day and disco by night, got a big Signature of Excellence makeover and has a lively nightlife, thanks largely to the venue's design changes. *Ryndam's* lounge is now outfitted in shocking pink and other bold colors, and private seating areas are cordoned off by soft curtains. There are disco lights, a dance floor, a high-tech video wall, and a striking new bar of backlit onyx.

SPORTS, FITNESS, AND BEAUTY   The ships' upper decks cater to active passengers. At the center of a teak expanse on Navigation Deck is one of two outdoor swimming pools. On the Lido, a second swimming pool, with whirlpools and wading pool, has a retractable glass roof for use in cool weather—a great asset on Alaskan cruises. A tiled wall with a bronze sculpture of dolphins frames the area.

The topside Sports Deck has two practice tennis courts (on *Statendam,* the space is a jogging track). A teak deck encircling the Lower Promenade Deck has space for deck chairs, walkers, and joggers (four laps equal one mile). The fleetwide Passport to Fitness program awards points for daily exercises and activities that can be redeemed for prizes, such as a belt pack or T-shirt.

The *Ryndam* now has a **Greenhouse Spa and Salon,** a brand exclusive to Holland America with features developed in the Texas-based Greenhouse Spa chain, such as a Strawberry Herbal Back Cleanse, a hydrotherapy pool (day use, $20, and a thermal suite, $20 for the day). Inaugurated on the Vista-class ships, the Greenhouse Spa has been added fleetwide as part of the Signature of Excellence program. Operated by Steiner, the larger, more sophisticated facility has new treatment rooms, steam and aromatic room, a new relaxation room with heated ceramic lounges and a wide range of skin, body, and hair treatments, and couples' massage rooms, reflecting a change in the demands of today's passengers. The ocean-view gym is equipped with treadmills, step machines, rowing machines, stationary bikes, and a Hydra fitness circuit with ten resistance machines. In front of the spa is an outside deck for exercise classes.

At **Half Moon Cay,** HAL's private island, which is a stop on most Caribbean itineraries and Panama Canal cruises, passengers have new activities to enjoy as a result of the Signature of Excellence program. These include a horseback riding and swimming excursion, a stingray adventure, a guided personal watercraft tour, and an aqua park with large water toys in the shapes of whales, octopuses, sharks, and dolphins. The new activities augment the island's array of excursions—scuba diving, catch-and-release deep-sea fishing, eco-tours by glass-bottom boat, kayaking, and parasailing. The island has a water-sports center, a playground, volleyball, basketball, nature trails, and a bird reserve. Passengers can have a beachside massage or rent a private, air-conditioned beachfront cabana for the day ($249).

CHILDREN'S FACILITIES All ships have year-round, full-time youth coordinators (one for every 30 children, more during holidays and summer). They organize and supervise programs for three age groups: generally, 5–8 years, 9–12 years, and teens. On some ships, Club HAL accepts children as young as 3 years old.

Daily activities for children ages 5–8 may include storytelling, candybar bingo, games, arts and crafts, charades, and ice-cream parties. Those ages 9–12 might learn to putt, have dance lessons or theme parties, or participate in deck sports or scavenger hunts, table tennis, or karaoke. Older children have a teen disco, dance lessons, arcade games, sports, card games, trivia contests, bingo, and movies. All have pizza and Coke-tail parties and ship tours. The ships have wading pools, activity rooms with video games, and children's menus listing such favorites as hamburgers, hot dogs, fish and chips, chicken fingers, and pizza.

On the first night of each cruise, kids and their parents meet the youth coordinator, who outlines the program. At sea, there is at least one activity in the morning, afternoon, and evening; none are scheduled on port days. Babysitting by staff volunteers (availability isn't guaranteed) costs $8 per hour for the first child and $5 more per hour for additional children from the same family.

One of the main objectives of the Signature of Excellence program—to appeal to the growing market of multigenerational vacationers—can be seen in the new and expanded Club HAL facilities. Teens now have their own area, which is supervised but off-limits to adults. The **Loft** lounge has a dance floor, lights, music videos, and DVDs. Upstairs is the **Oasis,** the teens' new private sun deck, complete with its own waterfall, covered snack areas, and hammocks. Two rooms loaded with games and toys for ages 3 to 7 accommodate 20 children each, with additional areas available as needed. For the 8- to 12-year-olds, entertainment includes PlayStations, Internet access, arcade games, and karaoke. Among other enhancements is a Port Day program, allowing parents to place kids in Club HAL from 8 a.m. to 5 p.m., including a boxed lunch. Mom and Dad are then free to go off the ship and enjoy the destination. From 10 p.m. to midnight, parents can take advantage of Club HAL's After Hours program, which runs $5 per child per hour.

SHORE EXCURSIONS It's almost hard to believe, but Holland America offers more than 2,500 shore excursions in 296 ports of call in 60 countries. They range from active, exotic, cultural, historic to nature and adventure tours, and from a few hours to a full day, and include those suitable for families as well as unusual experiences like Formula One racing in Barcelona. The 106 Medallion Collection, intended for those who want something more than a typical tour, offers extraordinary adventures and exclusive events; group size is limited. Part of the Medallion series is the Signature Collection, personalized tours with private luxury vehicle, professional driver, and English-speaking guide. The custom-designed tours are available in four- and eight-hour segments and best for parties of two to eight.

Holland America has been a leader in Alaska travel and offers programs ranging from cruising near glaciers on day boats to rail travel on the domed McKinley Explorer. In Ketchikan, you can have a half-day sightseeing/flight-seeing combination, or you can kayak, fish, or pan for gold. Every Glacier Route cruise visits Sitka's Alaska Raptor Rehabilitation Center, dedicated to returning injured bald eagles to the wild.

In the Caribbean, in addition to standard offerings, there are environmentally sensitive eco-tours focusing on the islands' nature, history, and culture, which are designed to help passengers better understand the islands. They range from guided rain-forest hikes to air tours to view archaeological sites. European shore excursions can be expensive on any cruise line, but HAL's seem to cost more than its closest competitor. Save money by taking standard city tours on your own and buying the cruise line's excursions that are unique or that visit attractions difficult to reach.

Note: Shore excursions can be booked on Holland America's Web site. Be very sure of your tour choices before you buy. In addition to the industry's standard policy of no refunds for cancellations 24 hours before a tour, Holland America charges a 10% fee for any cancellation made ten days prior to the cruise sailing. There are other, rather complicated cancellation fees and credits for such items as a private car or minivan; you should inquire before making a commitment.

Amsterdam	QUALITY 8	VALUE C
Rotterdam	QUALITY 9	VALUE C
Volendam/Zaandam	QUALITY 8	VALUE C
REGISTRY Netherlands	LENGTH 780/781 feet	BEAM 105.8 feet
CABINS 690/658/716	DRAFT 29.8/24 feet	SPEED 25/23 knots
MAXIMUM PASSENGERS	PASSENGER DECKS 10	ELEVATORS 12
1,380/1,316/1,432	CREW 647	SPACE RATIO 44/47/42

THE SHIPS The *Rotterdam,* the line's sixth ship bearing that name, upholds Holland America's tradition in contemporary style but little resembles *Rotterdam V.* She's more like the *Statendam* quartet, with almost the same layout and with many of their most popular features. Both she and her slightly larger sister, *Amsterdam,* were designated as the line's flagships and introduced new features. Their speed gives HAL more flexibility in designing itineraries. Each has more deluxe cabins with verandas, an alternative restaurant, extensive facilities for the handicapped, and a private lounge and concierge desk for suite passengers.

The *Volendam* and *Zaandam,* built in Italy, created a new generation of luxury cruise ships that combined features from the *Statendam* group and the *Rotterdam.* The twins are about as long and wide as *Rotterdam,* but their tonnage is greater because they have more passenger cabins—1,432 compared with *Rotterdam's* 1,316 passengers.

The principal architect for all four ships, Frans Dingemans, created interiors in keeping with HAL's tradition and passenger preferences. He describes *Rotterdam's* interiors as an evolution from the *Statendam* group. The enhancements are a three-story atrium (oval instead of octagonal), a larger Lido restaurant, and a dome over the Lido pool. But *Rotterdam* differs from *Statendam*-class ships in other ways, too: She's longer, wider, and more spacious, as well as faster. Because she's designed to be speedier, the hull is longer and more tapered. Like *Rotterdam V,* she has two funnels aft. Three stairwells put passengers never farther than about 125 feet from access to the public rooms. The layout of the public rooms on the *Volendam* and *Zaandam* is the same as that of *Rotterdam. Rotterdam's* interior was inspired by (not a replica of) her predecessor, though some of her namesake's rich interiors and 1930s Art Deco style have been incorporated. More woods and darker colors were used to achieve a classy as well as classic ambience.

A huge sculpture fills the *Rotterdam's* three-deck atrium. More a curiosity than a work of art, it represents a Flemish clock tower with 14 timepieces and is embellished with mermaids, dolphins, and snakes. All HAL ships have valuable art collections, but *Rotterdam's* is the most varied, with museum-quality antiques that evoke the Dutch maritime tradition. The most memorable are life-sized replicas of the terra-cotta warriors found at Xi'an, China.

In the *Volendam's* three-deck-tall atrium is a monumental crystal sculpture by Luciano Vistosi, one of Italy's leading contemporary glass artists. He also created the towering atrium sculptures of the *Maasdam* and *Veendam.* The centerpiece of the *Zaandam's* atrium is an impressive pipe organ with mechanical figures of dancing musicians. The organ may be played by hand or operated automatically. Both ships showcase multimillion-dollar art collections, including works created specifically for the vessels by world-class artists.

The theme of *Volendam's* decor is flowers—from the 17th to 21st centuries—which are featured in public rooms' fabrics, art, doors, and other design elements throughout the ship. Music is the *Zaandam's* theme, with music-related decor throughout.

HAL invested $1 million to add a closed-loop system for the hearing impaired, Braille directories and directional buttons in the elevators, and large-print menus for the visually impaired. In cabins, light-flashing telephones and bed-shaker alarm systems are available.

The atrium centerpiece of *Amsterdam* is an ornate astrolabe clock tower with a carillon in its base and four faces: an astrolabe, world clock, planetary clock, and astrological clock. On display near the **Crow's Nest Lounge** is *Four Seasons,* a gold-plated sculpture of four pieces, originally created for the *Nieuw Amsterdam* of 1938 and bought from a private collector. At the Lido pool, passengers will see a trio by British sculptor Susanna Holt—two brown bears fishing, their cub nearby.

ITINERARIES *See* Itinerary Index.

CABINS Standard cabins, a roomy 185–195 square feet, are similar to those in the *Statendam* group. On the *Rotterdam,* another 120 deluxe cabins at 245 square feet have whirlpool baths, DVD players, minibars, refrigerators, and verandas with chaise lounges.

Navigation Deck 7 has 40 suites, all with verandas, a private lounge, and concierge station where passengers may settle accounts, book shore excursions, and make special requests. The area's glass walls overlook the corridor, but when privacy is wanted, an electric current makes the high-tech glass opaque. Each of four penthouse suites offers living room, dining area and kitchen, bedroom, dressing areas, and steward's entrance. Two suites are wheelchair-accessible. The *Amsterdam* has 15 more suites than her sibling.

The *Volendam* and *Zaandam* have more deluxe veranda cabins than their sister ships. The penthouse, 28 deluxe suites, and 168 Verandah minisuites and deluxe cabins have large verandas, DVD players, whirlpool bath, and minibar. All cabins have a sofa, hair dryer, telephone with voice mail and automated wake-up service, music system, and television. They are furnished with twin beds, convertible to a queen size.

Specifications Rotterdam/Amsterdam, 139/135 inside cabins, 358/383 outside, 36/50 suites, 161/172 cabins with verandas, some adjoining cabins. 498 standard cabins with twin beds, 618 with convertible twins or queen beds, 284 with third and fourth berths. No singles. 21 wheelchair-accessible (*Amsterdam,* 23); four have connecting doors for accompanying companions. *Volendam/Zaandum,* 1 penthouse and 28 suites with verandas, 168 deluxe cabins (120 deluxe minisuites) with verandas, 383 standard outside cabins, 136 standard inside, 21 wheelchair-accessible cabins.

DINING *Rotterdam's* elegant, bi-level **La Fontaine Dining Room** spans the Promenade and Upper Promenade decks. Decor mingles Venetian, contemporary, and baroque designs. Panoramic windows overlook the stern. The ceiling represents a star-filled night sky broken by circles of colored glass. Around the balcony are hundreds of individually lighted Venetian-glass morning glories. On the back wall are two giant murals of waterbirds, recalling *Rotterdam V's* famous Ritz-Carlton room.

In the large, informal **Lido restaurant,** passengers can enjoy a full breakfast and lunch, including hot dogs and hamburgers grilled to order or make-it-yourself tacos. An ice-cream-sundae bar, tea, and coffee are available all day. Alternative evening dining is offered several days of every cruise.

The *Volendam's* impressive, bi-level **Rotterdam Dining Room** at the stern has huge windows and an elegant staircase connecting the two levels.

Overhead, six large wrought-iron chandeliers designed by Italian artist Gilbert Lebigre hang from the ceiling; they are lighted by fiber optics.

FACILITIES AND ACTIVITIES   The *Rotterdam*'s **Ambassador Lounge and Tropic Bar** (Upper Promenade Deck) has a movable wall allowing different configurations. After dinner, the lounge is a large room for dancing; in late evening, it's an intimate piano bar with the piano on a turntable.

Repeat passengers will recognize the ships' traditional collection of small public rooms. The adjoining **Half Moon** and **Hudson** rooms accommodate up to 115 people for meetings or parties. **Ocean Bar** has replicas of items from the old Holland America building in Rotterdam; a copy of the sculpture of Henry Hudson's ship, *Halve Maen* ("half moon"), crowns the roof. The larger **Explorers' Lounge** focuses on the maritime heritages of Italy and Holland in a large mural of Renaissance Venice. The dance floor is made of Italian marble in a floral pattern.

The Crow's Nest Lounge has floor-to-ceiling windows around three quarters of this delightful daytime observation lounge. The room has three sections. To one side is a **Tea Area** decorated with porcelain and silver. To the other is a **Captain's Area,** with leather chairs and old ship models. At center is a circular bar and dance floor that become the nighttime disco.

Queen's Lounge, the two-level main show lounge, has state-of-the-art sound and lighting equipment, a rotating stage, hydraulic lifts, and a dance floor. Deep red, burgundy, and orange decor reflects the opulent age of sea travel. Huge, gold-etched Murano glass chandeliers resemble upside-down umbrellas. Along the room's sides, statues of Moorish guards hold large candelabra. The theater curtain is hand-painted satin in maroon, gold, and black.

Volendam's main show lounge, the two-level **Frans Hals Lounge** in Art Deco design, was inspired by the city of Amsterdam's famous Tuschinski Theater. The multicolored ceiling and colonnades contrast with dark wood walls and huge, colorful ceramic vases. The **Casino Bar,** the ship's sports bar, showcases cinematic memorabilia. On *Zaandam,* the **Casino Bar** spotlights music. The ship also has the cruise line's traditional **Explorer's Lounge, Ocean Bar, Piano Bar, Library, Half Moon Room,** and **Hudson Room,** the last of which serves as a card or meeting room; and Crow's Nest, which doubles as an observation lounge and nightclub. The **Wajang Theater,** equipped with writing tables and headphones for meetings, has become the venue for the **Culinary Arts Institute** as part of the Signature of Excellence program.

On the *Volendam,* the Navigation Deck was extended aft to accommodate additional cabins, and the outdoor swimming pool moved to the Lido Deck. The arrangement provides direct access between indoor and outdoor swimming pools and the **Lido restaurant.** For *Volendam*'s Lido pool area, British artist Susanna Holt created a bronze sculpture of arcing dolphins, similar to those found on other HAL ships.

Another change on these ships that frequent HAL passengers will notice is the funnel design that more closely resembles those of the old *Noordam* rather than the *Rotterdam* or the *Statendam* group.

Volendam was the first of the fleet to have an Internet center with eight computer terminals and a printer. (It's now part of the Explorations Café powered by the *New York Times.*) Open 24 hours, it is staffed from 9 a.m. to noon, 2 to 6 p.m., and 9 p.m. to midnight. There is a one-time activation fee of $3.95 and basic charge of $0.75 per minute with a five-minute minimum; bulk pricing packages start at 100 minutes for $55. Instructions for use are posted on each computer terminal. Internet centers and wireless Internet service are available fleetwide. Laptop rental is $20 per day; wireless card, $10 per day. CruisE-mail is a new service offering passengers an e-mail address, if they are unable to access their own. There is a $3.95 charge to send a CruisE-mail (in addition to the basic time charges), but passengers only pay the time charge to receive incoming messages.

SPORTS, FITNESS, AND BEAUTY The ships now have a new **Greenhouse Spa.** (See *Statendam* group for details). The Lower Promenade Deck is a wraparound teak deck, ideal for walking or cooling off in the line's traditional wooden deck chairs.

All Holland America ships that call at the line's private island, Half Moon Cay, benefit from Signature of Excellence enhancements, such as the new horseback riding and swimming excursion, the stingray adventure, and aqua park with large water toys in the shapes of whales, octopuses, sharks, and dolphins. The new activities augment the cay's array of excursions—scuba diving, fishing, eco-tours, kayaking, and its water-sports center, playground, volleyball, basketball, nature trails, and bird reserve.

CHILDREN'S FACILITIES The Sports Deck has a playroom with craft-making areas, video games, and a teen disco. As part of the Signature of Excellence program, they got the new facilities of Club HAL (see "Children's Facilities" under the *Statendam* group for details).

Prinsendam	QUALITY 7	VALUE C
REGISTRY Netherlands	LENGTH 669 feet	BEAM 95 feet
CABINS 398	DRAFT 23.5 feet	SPEED 21.8 knots
MAXIMUM PASSENGERS	PASSENGER DECKS 9	ELEVATORS 4
793	CREW 443	SPACE RATIO 48

THE SHIP The *Prinsendam* comes to the line with an illustrious history as the *Seabourn Sun* and *Royal Viking Sun,* having been the prize of Cunard's purchase of Royal Viking Line in 1994. The *Sun* was given a $15 million renovation, renamed, and moved to Seabourn, which turned out to be a mismatch.

When the ship was transferred to Holland America Line in 2002, Swedish architect Thomas Tillberg, the vessel's original interior designer, and Frans Dingemans, HAL's main architect, were engaged to oversee major renovations that transformed her into a HAL ship. The ship emerged with a redesigned interior, new decor, and renamed decks and public rooms to correspond with the other ships in the HAL fleet. Artwork was added, including a frosted and sculptured glass cylinder and wall murals by Bolae for the circular atrium. The *Prinsendam* was named for a sentimental favorite that was lost after an accident in Alaskan waters several years ago.

The sleek vessel has a sharply raked bow and a beautiful profile, which distinguishes her from the rectangular shape of newer ships. The Finnish-built *Prinsendam* is a spacious ship. Penthouse and deluxe veranda suites are palatial; standard cabins are as large as other ships' suites. Treats include walk-in closets, comfortable lounges, a swim-up bar in the main pool, a lap pool, a spa, and a golf simulator of famous courses, plus some unusual features like a same-level gangway for easy access to docks or tenders; air-conditioned tenders with lavatories and catamaran hulls for stability; and two high-speed man-overboard boats. Fine wood and high-quality fabrics are used throughout. Public rooms and facilities are on three center and two top decks.

In early 2005, the *Prinsendam* received some Signature of Excellence enhancements, including a Culinary Arts Center and flat-screen televisions in all cabins and suites. The ship already operates a Greenhouse Spa and a Pinnacle Grill. Since *Prinsendam* sails longer voyages around the globe and attracts a mature audience, it did not receive expanded youth facilities. Due to space limitations (she is half the size of the Vista-class ships), the *Prinsendam* also does not have the Explorations Café.

ITINERARIES *See* Itinerary Index.

CABINS Cabins are spread over eight decks. Seventeen categories offer four accommodation types: suites, deluxe veranda outside, outside with a large window, and standard inside cabins. All suites and deluxe cabins (more than a third of accommodations) have verandas. HAL spent millions of dollars upgrading cabins and giving them a new, more modern look in the Signature of Excellence style. Bathrooms received new sinks, tile, and plumbing repairs, while verandas got new doors, teak decks, and rattan furniture. In fall of 2007, all the ship's bathrooms are being renovated and upgraded.

All cabins have flat-screen televisions with CNN, TNT, ESPN, TCM, Discovery, and ship's programming, phone, minifridge, locking drawers, safe, hair dryer, refrigerator, and walk-in closets (cruising's first, but not found in wheelchair-accessible cabins). Most bathrooms have tub and shower. All but a few have twin beds convertible to kings, and most have a small sitting area with love seat, table, and chair. Two decks have launderettes. Room service is available 24 hours a day.

The largest, most luxurious suites are on the top two decks. Dividers separate the bedroom and sitting areas. Additional amenities for deluxe cabins and suites include bathrobes, extra-luxurious towels, DVD and video library access, personalized stationery, veranda, and floor-to-ceiling windows. In addition, penthouse and deluxe veranda suites have the private Neptune Lounge, staffed by a concierge, for their exclusive use. They receive afternoon tea and hors d'oeuvres before dinner upon request; a private cocktail party with the captain; an exclusive Indonesian rijsttafel luncheon hosted by the captain and hotel manager; and complimentary corsages and boutonnieres on the first formal night, among other amenities The sole penthouse veranda suite was one of the first on a cruise ship to have a whirlpool bath surrounded by picture windows facing the sea. Promenade Deck has lanai cabins complete with private deck area and whirlpool—a new concept for HAL.

Specifications 25 inside cabins, 373 outside including suites; 68 suites; 1 penthouse suite; 151 with verandas; 82 deluxe. Standard dimensions, 191 square feet. 344 outside cabins and suites with 2 lower beds, convertible to kings; 19 suites with 2 lower beds convertible to kings and a sofa bed; 3 single cabins (2 outside, 1 inside); 8 wheelchair-accessible.

DINING *Prinsendam's* dining room on Lower Promenade Deck has large windows on three sides, providing a panorama of sea and scenery. Passengers are served in two seatings with assigned tables for dinner, and in open seatings for breakfast and lunch. Tables seating two, four, six, or eight are set with fresh flowers, fine china, crystal, and silverware. Menus are similar to those on other HAL ships, with specialties added from the region of the cruise.

A major change that HAL made with her acquisition was the switch from one- to two-seating dining, which means the main dining room no longer needs to seat all passengers at once. However, the Lido restaurant required expansion. As a result, the forward dining room was reconfigured to include the Ocean Bar, an art gallery, an Internet center, and the **Pinnacle Grill at the Odyssey,** the handsome alternative restaurant featuring steaks, seafood and Pacific Northwest wines. Entrées are prepared on a hot grill to guarantee tenderness and taste. Reservations are required, and the service carries a charge of $30 for dinner and $15 for lunch (sea days only).

The **Lido restaurant** is the venue for casual buffet breakfast, lunch, dinner, and late-night snacks. The variety of food here is impressive and includes a salad bar, soups, hot entrées, carvery, pizzeria, cafe, taco bar, ice-cream bar, and dessert area; 24-hour coffee and tea are available. The restaurant, located aft on Lido Deck, has been expanded to both sides of ship with two service lines. A wall of windows overlooks the deck and sea. There's outdoor seating on the terrace, which resembles a sidewalk cafe with a teak floor. The **Terrace Grill** serves hot dogs and hamburgers poolside.

FACILITIES AND ACTIVITIES Promenade Deck holds most of the public rooms, including a casino, the **Explorer's Lounge,** a movie theater showing first-run films, a card room, the library, boutiques, shore excursions office, the 24-hour front desk, and the show lounge. *Prinsendam* offers a program of port and theme lectures similar to those on other HAL ships and has Signature of Excellence's new **Culinary Arts Center** (see *Ryndam* for details).

The redesigned **Queen's Lounge** showroom was given a new stage and state-of-the-art sound and light to bring the facility up to par with newer HAL ships. Production shows feature a cast of seven top-notch entertainers. In front of the stage is a sizable dance floor. Typical of ships built in the 1980s, the lounge has a low ceiling and poor sight lines from seats in the rear. The Ocean Bar, with bandstand and dance floor, is action central in the evening. Forward of the Ocean Bar is the new **Internet Center,** with 11 flat-screen computer stations; and an art gallery.

The casino offers slot machines and roulette, craps, and blackjack tables. Just outside the casino is the **Java Bar and Café,** one of the ship's most popular spots. It leads to the handsome **Oak Room,** reminiscent of a men's club, with leather chairs in a wood-paneled setting. It's a cozy daytime retreat and popular for after-dinner drinks.

The busy Explorer's Lounge, opposite the casino, is one of the *Prinsendam*'s loveliest rooms. It has a wall of windows with sea views and is decorated with Dutch etchings. In keeping with the Holland America fleet, there is a massive painting of 17th-century Dutch ships—in this case, being given a royal send-off on a voyage of exploration. Classical music is piped in during the day, and a trio plays classical favorites every evening. The lounge's comfortable leather chairs are popular with passengers who want to read, since the nearby **Erasmus Library** seats only four. Stairs lead to the dining room below. Above the bridge is an observation lounge with 180-degrees of wraparound windows facing the bow. It's a favorite perch for watching the world go by wherever the ship may roam. A pianist plays here in the evenings.

SPORTS, FITNESS, AND BEAUTY   A wind-sheltered swimming pool on Lido Deck has a whirlpool and swim-up bar and is ringed by a sunning area. Outdoors are shuffleboard, table tennis, and quoits. A teak deck for walking wraps the Lower Promenade Deck, and an Astroturf jogging track encircles the Sports Deck. The wood-paneled **Golf Club and Pro Shop** on Deck 5 is a cozy hangout for golfers, with comfortable seating and magazines. It has a sophisticated golf simulator of 22 courses, including many on the PGA tour (similar to the high-tech simulator on the *Zuiderdam*). A large golf cage is found on the Sports Deck (12), but the putting area on that deck has been replaced by a versatile sports court for volleyball, basketball, and tennis.

The **Greenhouse Spa** has a lap pool with two whirlpools and a glass-enclosed fitness facility with toning and cardiovascular equipment. The spa boasts nine treatment rooms and an array of treatment choices. Also available are sauna and beauty salon.

Noordam	QUALITY 9	VALUE B
Oosterdam	QUALITY 8	VALUE C
Westerdam	QUALITY 8	VALUE B
Zuiderdam	QUALITY 8	VALUE C
REGISTRY Netherlands	LENGTH 935 feet	BEAM 105.8 feet
CABINS 924	DRAFT 24 feet	SPEED 22 knots
MAXIMUM PASSENGERS	PASSENGER DECKS 12	ELEVATORS 14
1,848/1,918	CREW 800	SPACE RATIO 46

THE SHIPS With the arrival of the *Noordam* in 2006, Holland America has completed the Vista-class 85,000-ton cruise ships that it built. The ships take their names from the "vista" points of the compass: *Zuiderdam*, south; *Oosterdam*, east; *Westerdam*, west; and *Noordam*, north. The "-dam" suffix follows the line's century-old tradition for its passenger ships.

The Vista-class name, selected from an employee contest, is meant to represent the ships' forward-looking design and HAL's future direction with ships that are the most advanced and most luxurious Holland America has ever built. Constructed at the Italian shipyard Fincantieri Cantieri Navali, these ships have more than doubled Holland America's passenger capacity in less than four years. *Noordam* came with Signature of Excellence facilities and amenities, and *Oosterdam* got its makeover in late 2006. *Westerdam* and *Zuiderdam*, which already have some of the amenities, such as the Pinnacle Grill, the Greenhouse Spa, and the Euro-top mattresses, will have the others added in the next few years. Those ships also will receive new aft cabins, increasing their passenger capacity to 1,918, matching that of *Noordam. Oosterdam* will get aft cabins in 2009.

Zuiderdam was the line's determined effort to attract younger passengers, broaden its base, and lower the average age of its customers. The ship offers a more contemporary image—with the use of bright colors (orange, purple, and magenta), suede walls, and jazzy patterns in Holland America's first disco—and such 21st-century amenities as data ports in cabins and a high-tech golf simulator.

Zuiderdam definitely is a departure from past Holland America ships. Reactions have been mixed. Some people see in it the influence of Carnival Cruises and say it was time for updating the HAL look; others prefer the line's traditional style. Yet, on balance, there's no mistaking that the ship is a Holland America product.

The traditional fresh flowers are still everywhere, and so is the multi-million-dollar art collection and signature HAL rooms like the Explorers Lounge, Half Moon, Hudson Room, and Ocean Bar. There's also a three-deck-high atrium with Art Deco styling and a fascinating Waterford crystal sea horse suspended from the ceiling. In a cruise-ship first, Holland America introduced on the *Westerdam* in July 2006 a free self-guided tour of the ship's outstanding art and antiques collection using an iPod. By 2007, all its ships will offer its passengers the new high-tech device for tours of the ships' multimillion dollar art collections.

This quartet are HAL's largest ships but carry only 25% more passengers. Passengers benefit by having bigger cabins and more (but not necessarily larger) lounges and other public areas in an asymmetrical layout that reduces the impression of an immense ship.

The vessels' propulsion system includes a full-scale diesel-electric power plant, backed up by a gas turbine as an additional power source. The ships use the Azipod propulsion system, allowing for greater maneuverability, operating efficiencies, and environmental benefits. Installed on both sides of the vessels are innovative exterior elevators serving ten decks and providing passengers with panoramic sea views.

Other new features include a cabaret-style show lounge as well as a new three-deck main show lounge; a casual around-the-clock cafe, an Internet cafe and data ports in all cabins, the largest spa facilities in the fleet, an extensive **Club HAL** children's facility with inside and outside play areas, two interior promenade decks, an exterior covered promenade deck encircling the entire ship, a large Lido pool with a retractable dome, and the signature Crow's Nest observation lounge.

CABINS   One of the most significant differences in the Vista ships is their large number of veranda cabins. Eighty-five percent of the accommodations are outside, and two-thirds have balconies. (By comparison, on the *Statendam*-class ships, only suites have verandas.) The deluxe veranda outside cabins, the largest category, have 200 square feet, plus a roomy, 54-square-foot veranda. All cabins are furnished with sofas, minibars, hair dryer, safe, and telephone with voice mail and data port. Most cabins have tubs, an amenity normally found in more costly suites on other lines. There is a Neptune Lounge with a concierge for the exclusive use of penthouse and deluxe veranda suite passengers. In addition to 28 wheelchair-accessible cabins, there is a dedicated elevator for wheelchair users, assistance with tender embarkation, and two tenders equipped with wheelchair-accessible platforms.

Specifications   924 cabins, 623 with verandas. 2 penthouse suites (1,318 square feet), 60 deluxe suites (510–700 square feet), 100 superior suites (398 square feet), 461 deluxe outside (254 square feet). 165 standard outside cabins (185 square feet), 136 inside (170–200 square feet). 28 wheelchair-accessible cabins.

DINING   The two-story **Vista Dining Room,** the main restaurant, has floor-to-ceiling windows on three sides and two grand staircases. Each level has its own galley, which makes for faster service. On the *Westerdam,* the dining room ceiling is made up of colorful Chihuly-designed glass around the light fixtures.

The large, bright **Lido restaurant** has been expanded and designed in food-court style, with specialty areas offering made-to-order omelets, deli sandwiches, Italian and Asian specialties, salads, etc. Outside, the large Lido pool area is covered by a retractable dome; a sculpture of polar bears is a reminder of Holland America's role in Alaska cruising.

The **Pinnacle Grill** is the ship's specialty, reservations-only restaurant and is twice the size of those on her sister ships, but the decor with elaborate silver chairs and overhead lights is in keeping with their rococo style. The tables are set with Bulgari china for dining on the featured Pacific Northwest cuisine. There is a $30 per-person charge for dinner and $15 for lunch (sea days only).

SERVICE   The *Noordam* has received especially good reviews, particularly for the friendly and gracious Indonesian and Filipino crew for their unobtrusive, attentive service.

FACILITIES AND ACTIVITIES   The ships' new additions are the **Queen's Lounge,** a versatile venue where cabaret-style shows are staged and movies shown; the **Windstar Café,** which is open 20 hours a day, offering specialty coffees, smoothies, pastries, and snacks; HAL's first disco; and the three-tier, bright red **Vista Lounge,** with a bar near the entrance, an orchestra pit, and $10 million of the latest sound and light equipment, where big production shows are staged. Currently playing are *Stage & Screen* (based on movie musicals) and *Under the Boardwalk.*

Passengers on the *Oosterdam* see *Tommy Tune's Paparazzi,* a multi-million-dollar musical extravaganza created by the nine-time Tony award–winning director, choreographer, dancer, and singer, Tommy Tune; it was the first show he created specifically for a cruise ship. The show, which pays homage to our fascination with celebrities and the photographers who chase them, was added to the *Westerdam* in 2004. As popular as ever is the Crow's Nest, the topside observation lounge where passengers escape for quiet by day and dancing by night.

SPORTS, FITNESS, AND BEAUTY The **Greenhouse Spa,** operated by the Steiner Group, is more than twice the size of the spas on the original *Statendam*-class ships. It has 11 treatment rooms (including one for couples), a large hydrotherapy pool, and offers features such as a unisex thermal suite with aromatic steam and sauna chambers.

As noted earlier, all Holland America ships that call at Half Moon Cay already benefit from some Signature of Excellence initiatives, such as the new horseback riding and swimming excursion and the stingray adventure. The new activities augment the island's array of excursions—scuba diving, fishing, eco-tours, kayaking, and its water sports center, playground, volleyball, basketball, nature trails, and bird reserve.

CHILDREN'S FACILITIES **Club HAL,** enhanced with Signature of Excellence features, has new and expanded facilities like those on the *Ryndam* and other ships in the fleet. Teens have their own area with a lounge for dancing and hanging out, and the **Oasis,** their own private sun deck, complete with its own waterfall, covered snack areas, and hammocks. Among other enhancements is a Port Day program, allowing parents to place kids in Club HAL from 8 a.m. to 5 p.m., including a boxed lunch, while their parents go off the ship. Club HAL's After Hours program, from 10 p.m. to midnight, provides babysitting for $5 per child per hour.

Eurodam	2008	
Unnamed	2010	
REGISTRY Netherlands	LENGTH 935 feet	BEAM 106 feet
CABINS 1,022	DRAFT 24 feet	SPEED 22 knots
MAXIMUM PASSENGERS	PASSENGER DECKS 13	ELEVATORS 14
2,044	CREW 820	SPACE RATIO 44

THE SHIPS Holland America has ordered two 86,000-ton, 2,044-passenger Panamax ships as part of its Signature of Excellence program, and designated them as Signature class. Each ship will cost $450 million. The first is due in summer 2008 and another in spring 2010 and will represent a 22% increase in the line's capacity. The name *Eurodam* breaks with the Holland America tradition of reusing the name of a previous vessel (there has never been a *Eurodam*), but "Euro" certainly reflects the line's heritage and "-dam" retains the suffix used for all its vessels.

The Signature class ships will have 1,022 double cabins, of which more than 67% will have verandas and 86% will be outside. They will offer more decks and 63 more cabins than the line's Vista class; 57 of them will be veranda cabins and 10 will be a new style of cabin with floor-to-ceiling, wall-to-wall panoramic windows.

New concepts for the ships' interior include a topside 144-seat pan-Asian restaurant and 50-seat lounge, an Explorer's Lounge Bar, a premium wine-tasting lounge, a new Italian specialty restaurant adjacent to the Lido area, a luxury jewelry boutique, a new atrium bar area, an enhanced and reconfigured show lounge, and a new photographic and imaging center. The Explorations Café will be relocated to the starboard side of the Crow's Nest Lounge, providing a new scenic pleasure for passengers who want to relax with a book, listen to music, or surf the Internet.

The ship will also have Signature of Excellence upgraded amenities and facilities, including a Culinary Arts Center (presented by *Food and Wine* magazine), an expanded Greenhouse Spa with thermal suite and hydro-pool, HAL's largest gym, and extensive youth facilities.

MSC Cruises

6750 North Andrews Avenue, Fort Lauderdale, FL 33309
☎ **800-666-9333 or 954-772-6262; fax 908-605-2600**
www.msccruises.com

TYPE OF SHIPS New, modern superliners and megaliners and classic ocean liners.

TYPE OF CRUISES Mass market, designed for Europeans as much as North Americans—hence, more European in service and ambience.

CRUISE LINE'S STRENGTHS
- Italian style and service
- friendly, attentive crew
- itineraries
- value for money
- entertainment
- new, spacious ships

CRUISE LINE'S SHORTCOMINGS
- Uneven cuisine
- Some service glitches

FELLOW PASSENGERS MSC has two seasons: Caribbean from late fall to early spring, and Europe from spring through fall, although some European cruises are year-round. This results in two sets of passengers. In the Caribbean, up to 85% of passengers are North Americans, depending on the cruise; average age is 50 years and older, with annual household income of $50,000 or more. Italian American fans and newlyweds are attracted by the line's Italian style. Most passengers have cruised before.

In Europe, most are Europeans in a wide range of ages; a large number are families. Among the North Americans, average age is about 40 years and older.

Recommended for Italophiles, first-time cruisers, and less experienced travelers who want to sample European ambience, but with large-ship facilities; those looking for a real bargain; repeat cruisers who want to try something different.

Not recommended for Anyone who likes small ships as well as an all-American atmosphere or those who prefer to travel with Americans only.

CRUISE AREAS AND SEASONS Caribbean, Mediterranean, Northern Europe, South Africa, South America, and transatlantic seasonal positioning cruises.

THE LINE Starting in 1995, a Swiss group operating a global fleet of 250 container ships and 36 fast ferries, Mediterranean Shipping Company (MSC) acquired three cruise ships in less than four years. In 2005, the new line added another four ships, including two ships from bankrupt First European (Festival) Cruises. The purchase increased its fleet from

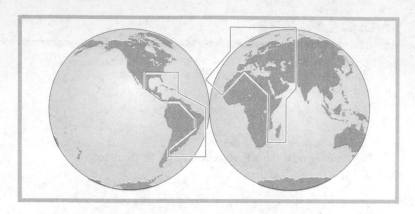

CRUISE AREAS AND SEASONS FOR MSC CRUISES

three to seven ships almost overnight and launched the line's bid to be a major player in Europe and North America. To underscore its intentions, MSC expanded its presence in North America with new offices in Fort Lauderdale, Florida, and hired one of the cruise industry's best-known executives, Rick Sasso, to head up the operation.

MSC continues to expand at a breathtaking pace. The 89,600-ton, 3,013-passenger *MSC Musica* was added in June 2006. Her twin, *MSC Orchestra,* debuted in spring 2007, to be followed in 2008 by another sister, *MSC Poesia,* and a fourth, *MSC Magnifica,* in 2010. MSC is also building two larger, post-Panamax ships (too large to transit the Panama Canal), *MSC Fantasia* and *MSC Splendida* at Aker Shipyard in France. Both are 133,500 tons and will carry 3,300 passengers; they are scheduled to be delivered in 2008 and 2009, respectively. These builds will bring MSC Cruises' fleet to 12 ships by 2010.

One of the largest cruise lines in the Mediterranean, MSC also sails to South Africa and South America and recently has expanded in northern Europe. Drawn by the extraordinary boom in European cruises, MSC decided to have only one ship—*MSC Lirica*—in the North American market for the 2007–2008 winter season, but the cruise line has committed a second, larger, new ship to it in 2009.

THE FLEET	BUILT/RENOVATED	TONNAGE	PASSENGERS
MSC Armonia	2003	58,625	1,556
MSC Fantasia	2009	133,500	3,300
MSC Lirica	2003	59,058	1,560
MSC Magnifica	2010	89,600	2,550
MSC Melody	1982/92/97	35,143	1,062
MSC Musica	2006	89,600	2,550

THE FLEET	BUILT/RENOVATED	TONNAGE	PASSENGERS
MSC Opera	2004	59,058	1,712
MSC Orchestra	2007	89,600	2,550
MSC Rhapsody	1977/95/97	17,095	774
MSC Splendida	2009	133,500	3,300
MSC Poesia	2008	89,600	2,550
MSC Sinfonia	2002	58,625	1,556

STYLE MSC Cruises is Italian in heart and spirit from design to cuisine to personnel. In fact, it's tagline, "Beautiful. Passionate. Italian." suits it well. The ships reflect classic cruising updated for today's travelers and are very much "today," with gyms, spas, and fitness programs. In the Caribbean, MSC has made changes to appeal to American tastes. For example, prices are in dollars rather than euros; cabin television carries American movies; announcements are given first in English, breakfast and lunch buffets offer choices that American passengers prefer.

All dining and theaters on MSC ships are nonsmoking, but don't be surprised to see some passengers, especially European ones, light up. Laundry and pressing services are available from the ships' facilities, but the ships do not have self-service launderettes, a much-appreciated amenity available on most new large ships. Throughout the season, MSC has promotions—for baby boomers, seniors, baseball fans, golfers—with substantial reductions and Kids Sail Free.

DISTINCTIVE FEATURES Sophia Loren is spokesperson and godmother for several ships; pizzerias and sushi bars on newer ships; golf simulators, Internet cafes; WiFi hot spots on the newest ships.

	HIGHEST	LOWEST	AVERAGE
PER DIEM	$521	$124	$275

Per diems are calculated from cruise line's non-discounted *cruise-only* published fares on standard accommodations and vary by season, cabins, and cruise areas.

RATES Port charges are included.

Special fares and discounts
- **CHILDREN'S FARE:** Special children-sail-free rates are often available; inquire.
- **SINGLE SUPPLEMENT:** Varies with sailing; consult MSC brochure for details.

Packages
- **AIR/SEA:** Available for both Europe and Caribbean.
- **PRE/POST:** Yes.

PAST PASSENGERS MSC Club, the past-passenger program, has three levels based on one point accrued for each night sailed on any MSC Cruise worldwide. Passengers may join by completing the form in their cabin and can begin accumulating points on their current cruise. They may also write to the club at mscclub@msccruisesusa.com. Passengers begin at the Classic level; at 22 points they move to the Silver level; and at 43 points they reach the Gold level. The rewards include a welcome cocktail and discounts on shore excursions, in onboard boutiques, and on future cruises. As a passenger's level increases, so do the benefits.

MSC Cruises Standard Features

Officers Italian.

Staff Dining: Italian, other European, Asian, Central American; Cabin: international; Cruise: international.

Dining facilities Two main dining rooms on newest ships; one on older ships; two seatings for lunch, midnight buffet; buffet breakfast and lunch. *Musica*-class have 4 restaurants, sushi bar, and alternative dining (extra charge). Pizzerias on most ships.

Special diets Should be requested at time of reservations.

Room service 24 hours.

Dress code Casual, informal; formal/semiformal—1 night on 4- to 6-night cruise, 2 nights on 7- to 10-night cruise, 3 nights on 11- to 14-night cruises, and four nights on 15-night or longer cruises.

Cabin amenities Phone, radio, private shower or bathtub, hair dryer, safe, television; minibar and veranda in higher categories.

Electrical outlets 110/220 AC; adapters available on board.

Wheelchair access *MSC Musica, MSC Orchestra* 17 (2 outside, 3 with balcony, 12 inside); *MSC Opera* 5; *MSC Lirica, MSC Sinfonia, MSC Armonia* 4 inside; *MSC Melody* 4; *MSC Rhapsody* 1.

Recreation and entertainment Casino, bars and lounges with nightly entertainment, showrooms, disco, dance lessons, bingo, library, card room, video arcade. Cigar room on *MSC Musica* and *MSC Orchestra.*

Sports and other activities 2 swimming pools on newest ships. Exercise classes. Golf simulators, volleyball, shuffleboard.

Beauty and fitness Beauty salon, spa, sauna, fitness centers, jogging track.

Other facilities Boutiques, medical facility, laundry and dry cleaning services, meeting room, Internet access on all ships. Internet cafes, WiFi in select public areas on newest ships.

Children's facilities Supervised Mini Club Kids program year-round; babysitters; children's pools.

Theme cruises Art, music, well-being, golf, culinary, hobby, dance, singles, astrology, bridge.

Smoking Smoking in designated public areas; no smoking in dining rooms and main show lounges.

MSC Cruises suggested tipping Gratuities, which may be adjusted, added to passenger onboard accounts. Normally, 6 euros per person per day in the Mediterranean; $12 per person per day in the Caribbean. Gratuities are included in the price of beverages on bar bills.

Credit cards For cruise payment and onboard charges: American Express, MasterCard, Visa.

MSC Musica	PREVIEW	
MSC Orchestra	2007	
MSC Poesia	2008	
REGISTRY Panama	LENGTH 964/961 feet	BEAM 106/108 feet
CABINS 1,275	DRAFT NA	SPEED 23 knots
MAXIMUM PASSENGERS	PASSENGER DECKS 13	ELEVATORS 13
3,013	CREW 987	SPACE RATIO 35

THE SHIPS MSC Cruises' newest flagship, *MSC Musica,* constructed at Aker Shipyard (formerly Chantiers de l'Atlantique) in France, debuted in spring 2006. The Panamax vessel is part of the line's $3 billion expansion program launched in 2003 with the introduction of the *MSC Lirica* and followed by *MSC Orchestra* in spring 2007, and *MSC Poesia* in spring 2008.

MSC Musica, the largest member of the MSC Cruises' fleet, comes with plenty of wow. If Sophia Loren as godmother isn't enough of a wow, then the ship's three-deck atrium has plenty more with a waterfall and a see-through piano suspended over a transparent floor above the waterfall. Or a three-deck show lounge with red walls, red carpets, and red seats—there's even red (and black) in the cabins—or the four restaurants, a wine bar, and a sushi bar all adding to the wow.

Genoa, Italy–based De Jorio Design International, designers of the *Lirica* and *Opera,* had the 1930s in mind when they created the *MSC Musica*'s interiors. They blended Art Nouveau and Art Deco geometric 1930s designs with high-tech and contemporary styles, along with Italian touches.

ITINERARIES *See* Itinerary Index.

CABINS In response to passengers' preference for outside cabins, more than 80% of the cabins are ocean-view accommodations and 65% of them have balconies.

DINING Dining venues include the elegant **Garden Restaurant,** with columns and fresco ceilings, a sushi bar with a Zen garden, a self-service pizzeria, and a large grill cafeteria.

FACILITIES AND ACTIVITIES The ship has a lounge that can be used as a theater, concert, or conference room; a music hall equipped for orchestras, cabaret performances, and dancing; a panoramic disco with plasma screens; a well-equipped stage in the pool area; and locations throughout the ship for musical performances such as small jam sessions and karaoke. There are numerous bars and lounges: **Cyber Cigar Room, Wine Tasting Bar, Piano Bar,** and **Cozy Bar** for an after-dinner aperitif or cappuccino; a 46-foot-long bar in the casino; and a **Well-Being and Fitness Center Bar** in the spa.

Entertainment venues include a three-deck theater, an elegant 7,000-square-foot casino, a panoramic disco at the ship's stern, and numerous locations throughout the ship for additional entertainment. There's also a shopping mall, card room, library, art gallery, virtual games room, and children's playroom.

SPORTS, FITNESS, AND BEAUTY The 13,000-square-foot spa/beauty facility offers aerobics, yoga, and such treatments as aromatherapy, thalassotherapy, chromotherapeutic hydro-massage, and a purifying Turkish bath.

In addition to the spa, the Sports Deck has two large swimming pools, a kids' wading pool, four hot tubs, tennis and volleyball court, golf simulator, minigolf and golf training, and a jogging track.

MSC Poesia has a somewhat different interior design from her sisters, especially in the entertainment areas. A sports bar will replace the wine bar and instead of a Chinese restaurant, passengers will find a Mediterranean-themed specialty restaurant with nightly changing menu that will coincide with the ship's Mediterranean ports of call. When *Poesia* enters service, she will sail in the Mediterranean and Adriatic.

The *Musica*-class ships have 17 wheelchair-accessible cabins (3 ocean view with balcony, 2 ocean view without balcony, 12 inside).

MSC Lirica	QUALITY 8	VALUE B
MSC Opera	QUALITY 8	VALUE B
REGISTRY Panama	LENGTH 824 feet	BEAM 94 feet
CABINS 795	DRAFT 25 feet	SPEED 19 knots
MAXIMUM PASSENGERS	PASSENGER DECKS 9	ELEVATORS 9
1,756	CREW 800	SPACE RATIO NA

THE SHIPS The first of MSC's new ships, the *Lirica* (or "Lyric" in English) debuted in 2003, with Sophia Loren doing the christening honors. *Lirica* was followed by a sister ship, *MSC Opera,* in 2004, the first phase of the line's expansion plans. The ships are powered by an advanced propulsion system to reduce engine noise and increase comfort levels.

The *Lirica*'s decor is more subdued than the *Opera*'s, with her public rooms in quieter colors and low lighting but with lots of windows to connect passengers to the sea and keep the atmosphere cheerful. The *Lirica* has eight bars and lounges and a disco that doubles as an observation lounge during the day.

ITINERARIES *See* Itinerary Index.

CABINS All cabins are furnished with twins that convert to queens, vanity and chair, satellite television, minibar, safe, radio, hair dryer, and 24-hour room service. The bathrooms are small but provide adequate storage space. Some cabins come with upper bunks for triples or quads. Only suites have private balconies, bath with tub, a sitting area with a love seat that converts to a third bed, coffee table, and chair. There are two two-room family suites (237 square feet).

Specifications *Lirica/Opera,* 795 cabins, 387 standard outside, 272 inside (140 square feet); 132 suites with verandas (250 square feet); *Lirica* 4, *Opera* 5, inside cabins for disabled passengers (226 square feet).

DINING Each of the sister ships has two dining rooms—**La Bussola** and **L'Ippocampo**—that serve authentic Italian cuisine as well as international selections. Both restaurants have two seatings for dinner with assigned seating. Breakfast and lunch are open seating.

Le Bistrot Cafeteria is another option, and hot dogs, hamburgers, and pizza are available at the poolside grill for lunch and in the evening. The *Lirica* serves afternoon tea and the traditional midnight buffet. There's an ice-cream bar (extra cost) on Lido deck and a 24-hour room service menu. The **Coffee Bar** serves real Italian espresso ($1.60), which is also available at most of the ship's bars.

Wines are reasonably priced, with house wine costing about $4 per glass. Wine, beer, and soda packages are available for purchase.

FACILITIES AND ACTIVITIES Typical of MSC's ships is lots of activity during the day and evening. Throughout the ship, one of the "animators" (entertainers dressed in various costumes) is likely to surprise you with some light-hearted antics. **The Lyric Lounge** is the setting for games and contests when the cruise staff manages to get passengers to participate—Europeans seem to get with the fun more readily than American passengers do. There's music nightly in the various lounges, especially for dancing, which, again, Europeans seem to enjoy most. The **Broadway Theater,** the main show lounge, stages two Las Vegas–type shows or dance productions, magicians, and comics every evening.

Each ship has two swimming pools separated by two hot tubs. There and on the sun decks, you can relax on a lounger with its own shade attached. The ships have spas, fully equipped gyms, saunas, and jogging tracks. They are equipped with a **Virtual Reality Center** and an Internet cafe with 16 terminals and WiFi hot spots on the pool decks and in select bars, cafes, lounges, and a shopping gallery. Internet access costs $5 for the first ten minutes and $0.50 each additional minute. For those with their own wireless laptop, prepaid packages for Internet access costs from $15 for 30 minutes to $100 for 250 minutes.

Passengers can pass their time inside with Italian cooking and language lessons, trivia, bingo, dance lessons, and arts and crafts or outside with minigolf, Ping-Pong, and shuffleboard tournaments.

CHILDREN'S FACILITIES The I Pirati Mini-Club, open for three hours in the morning and afternoon and two hours in the evening, has a full-time staff. Children under age 3, when accompanied by an adult, may use the space. Babysitting is available for a fee. An MSC Junior Card for kids for sodas costs $28.

POSTSCRIPT For the winter 2007–2008 season, the *Lirica* will be MSC's only ship serving the U.S. market, sailing on 7-, 10- and 11-day cruises in the Caribbean and Panama Canal, departing from Fort Lauderdale, Florida.

MSC Armonia	QUALITY 7	VALUE B
MSC Sinfonia	QUALITY 7	VALUE B
REGISTRY Panama	LENGTH 824 feet	BEAM 94 feet
CABINS 777	DRAFT 22 feet	SPEED 21 knots
MAXIMUM PASSENGERS	PASSENGER DECKS 9	ELEVATORS 9
2,087	CREW 700	SPACE RATIO NA

THE SHIPS *MSC Sinfonia,* the former *European Stars,* was launched in 2002 by the now-bankrupt First European (Festival) Cruises and began sailing for MSC in 2005, after she had been purchased at auction in 2004 for 220 million euros. *MSC Sinfonia,* as the name indicates, has been inspired by the great symphonies of classical composers from Beethoven and Mozart to Debussy and Tchaikovsky. Both *Sinfonia* and her sister ship, *Armonia* (the former *European Vision*), were constructed at Aker Shipyard in France. The *Armonia* has most of the same facilities as her sister ship, but her interior architecture is different.

Each ship has six bars, a showroom, dining room, indoor/outdoor restaurant, pizzeria, grill, spa and fitness center with gym and sauna, beauty salon, disco, cabaret, casino, Internet cafe with 16 terminals, two outdoor swimming pools, jogging area, two whirlpools, children's club, minigolf, golf simulator, video arcade, shops, and conference room.

ITINERARIES *See* Itinerary Index.

CABINS All accommodations have air-conditioning, satellite television, telephone, minibar, safe, radio, bath, hair dryer, and 24-hour room service. Suites feature a bedroom with a king-size bed, bath with bathtub and shower, private veranda, sofa bed, Internet connection (extra fee), and floor-to-ceiling windows. Standard outside and inside cabins are furnished with a convertible king-size bed and bath with shower.

Specifications 371 outside, 272 inside cabins (140 square feet); 132 suites with private balcony (237 square feet); 2 family suites without balcony (140 square feet); 4 inside cabins for disabled passengers (226 square feet).

MSC Melody	QUALITY 5	VALUE B
REGISTRY Panama	LENGTH 671 feet	BEAM 99 feet
CABINS 532	DRAFT 26 feet	SPEED 19 knots
MAXIMUM PASSENGERS	PASSENGER DECKS 8	ELEVATORS 5
1,492	CREW 535	SPACE RATIO NA

THE SHIP *MSC Melody,* formerly the *Star/Ship Atlantic* of Premier Cruise Lines, was acquired in 1997 by MSC. She has several lounges, a showroom, six bars, including a piano bar, sushi bar, and wine-tasting bar, disco, casino, two dining rooms. Other facilities include a cinema, Internet cafe, conference room, library, card room, cigar room, art gallery and shopping area, video arcade, children's playroom, teens' club, and medical center.

The fitness center and beauty salon has two saunas and two steam rooms, plus a gym offering yoga and aerobics classes. For outdoor diversions, there are two swimming pools and solarium, two whirlpools, minigolf and golf simulator, tennis court, and jogging track.

ITINERARIES *See* Itinerary Index.

CABINS The cabins and suites are moderate in size; all have radio, direct-dial telephone, air-conditioning, satellite television, radio, and private bathrooms. Suites have a living room/sitting area, sofa bed, minibar, a bedroom with a king-size bed, safe, and a full bath. Minisuites are furnished with a king-size bed, bath, and minifridge. Outside and inside standards have a two lower beds, bathtub or shower.

Specifications 303 outside, 151 inside cabins; 6 suites, 72 minisuites; 4 for disabled passengers.

MSC Rhapsody	QUALITY 5	VALUE B
REGISTRY Panama	LENGTH 541 feet	BEAM 76 feet
CABINS 382	DRAFT 20 feet	SPEED 19 knots
MAXIMUM PASSENGERS	PASSENGER DECKS 7	ELEVATORS 2
812	CREW 370	SPACE RATIO NA

THE SHIP Built in 1977 as the *Cunard Princess, MSC Rhapsody* was first refurbished in 1995 after being purchased by MSC, and once again in 1997. Facilities include a swimming pool, whirlpool, fitness center, sauna, conference room, library, cafe, bars, casino, card room, video arcade, jogging track, disco, cinema, boutique, beauty and barber shops, children's playroom and medical center. Laundry services are available.

A comfortable ship enhanced by a friendly atmosphere, she offers international cuisine with an Italian emphasis. Passengers dine in the window-lined **Meridian Dining Room** at two seatings. In her most recent renovation, the original buffet area was replaced by an extensive indoor/outdoor casual dining area.

ITINERARIES *See* Itinerary Index.

CABINS The cabins are small with limited storage space and thin walls; all have air-conditioning, television, telephone and radio, and private bathrooms. The suites feature a living room/sitting area, sofa bed, refrigerator, a bedroom with a king-size bed (convertible into two single beds). Standard outside and inside cabins are furnished with a two lowers convertible king-size bed, bath with tub or shower.

Specifications 233 outside, 127 inside cabins; 20 suites, 2 deluxe suites; 1 for disabled passengers.

Norwegian Cruise Line/
NCL America

7665 Corporate Center Drive, Miami, FL 33126
☎ 305-436-4000 or866-234-0292; fax 305-436-4120
www.ncl.com

TYPE OF SHIPS Modern superliners and new megaliners.

TYPE OF CRUISES Contemporary, mainstream, emphasizing "Freestyle Cruising."

CRUISE LINE'S STRENGTHS
- sports activities
- Freestyle Cruising options and flexibility
- variety of dining venues
- nonsmoking cabins
- innovative ships

CRUISE LINE'S SHORTCOMINGS
- loud deck music
- small bathrooms on some ships
- family accommodations and offerings
- unusual luxury accommodations
- Hawaii-only itineraries

FELLOW PASSENGERS Norwegian Cruise Line is the everyman's cruise line, with attractive ships where anyone can feel comfortable. Passengers, mostly from the United States and Canada, represent all walks of life, including young professionals, families, and seniors. Average household income ranges from $50,000 to $70,000.

Recommended for First-time cruisers, active travelers of all ages who want a fun vacation and like the facilities of a large ship. Middle-income travelers and multigenerational vacationers. Those who seek an unstructured atmosphere.

Not recommended for Snobs with five-star pretensions. Seasoned or sedentary travelers who want to be catered to for every whim.

CRUISE AREAS AND SEASONS Bahamas, Caribbean, Hawaii, New York–Caribbean, year-round; Mexico, South America, winter to spring; Alaska, Bermuda, Europe, Mediterranean, spring to fall; New England/Canada, fall; Panama Canal, April and September–October.

THE LINE On December 19, 1966, the Sunward sailed from Miami with 540 passengers on the first three- and four-day cruises to be offered year-round by Norwegian Caribbean Line between Miami and the Bahamas. With this voyage, NCL was born and so was modern cruising. Those cruises—the first packaged for the mass market—are credited with launching cruising as we know it today. Since then, NCL, renamed Norwegian Cruise Line, has played a major role in shaping today's cruises.

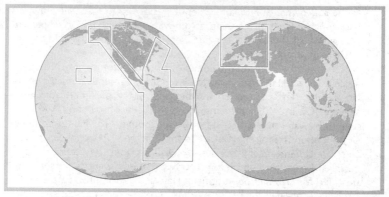

CRUISE AREAS AND SEASONS FOR NORWEGIAN CRUISE LINE/NCL AMERICA

Within five years of start-up, NCL had acquired three brand-new ships, pioneered weekly cruises to many Caribbean destinations, and introduced a day on a private island in its itineraries—a feature quickly copied by its competitors.

Yet for all these innovations, nothing equaled in excitement and impact NCL's purchase of the *Norway* in 1980. After buying her as the *France* for $18 million, NCL spent $100 million to transform her from a great ocean liner to a Caribbean cruise ship, setting in motion trends that transformed cruising completely.

Later in the decade, a series of costly expansion decisions, including the acquisition of Royal Viking Line and Royal Cruise Line, weakened NCL's debt-encumbered parent company, opening the way for more aggressive lines to take over its pacesetting role. However, by the 1990s, NCL had reinvented itself with a fleet of new, innovative ships that made NCL a trendsetter once again. Among the most notable were alternative dining, sports bars with broadcasts of ESPN and major sporting events, and separate sitting areas in standard cabins—an amenity that usually had been reserved for deluxe accommodations. These innovations soon became standard on new large ships.

In 1997, NCL became the first line to base a ship in Houston for year-round cruises to the Western Caribbean. The following year, it became the first mainstream cruise line to base a ship in southern South America for the winter season, sailing between Chile and Argentina. NCL took over two ships of the defunct Majesty Cruise Line, then ordered a 2,000-passenger ship, bought an unfinished hull intended for Costa Cruises (since completed as the *Norwegian Sky* and now is NCL America's *Pride of Aloha*), stretched three ships, streamlined the fleet with new names, and bought Orient Lines.

At the dawn of the new millennium, a bidding war between Carnival Cruises and Star Cruises (Asia's major cruise line) ended with Star Cruises as the sole owner of NCL and Orient Lines. By 2001, NCL's new owners had launched Freestyle Cruising, an innovative concept providing passengers with flexibility and challenging many cruise traditions, added a series of megaships, and started new, year-round cruises of Hawaii.

Now number three in the lineup of big cruise companies, NCL once again astonished the cruise world by acquiring Project America's unfinished ships (left abandoned by the bankruptcy of American Classic Voyages Co. in 2001), agreeing to finish their construction. With the help of Hawaii's powerful Senator Daniel Inouye, NCL gained congressional exemption to reflag NCL's foreign-flagged *Norwegian Sky* to U.S. ship registry and sail it year-round in Hawaii under the American flag—all in exchange for completing the two Project America vessels, also destined for U.S. flag operations in Hawaii. In turn, NCL created NCL America as its new brand to operate the new U.S.-flagged ships and itineraries within Hawaii.

As a next step, NCL locked up the deal even more completely by buying the two remaining U.S.-registered cruise ships—the *Independence* and the *United States*—saving the latter from the scrap yard for potential U.S. flag operations after a total reconstruction of the vessel that had sat idle for almost two decades. NCL is undertaking a comprehensive evaluation to decide if it is feasible to rebuild the *United States,* a major job costing as much as building a new ship.

Meanwhile, NCL expanded its Homeland Cruising program with more new U.S. departure ports, such as seasonal cruises from Philadelphia, Baltimore, and Charleston, South Carolina, and year-round cruises from New York. The 78,500-ton *Norwegian Sun* and 91,000-ton *Norwegian Star,* which inaugurated the Freestyle Cruising concept, were added in 2001, and *Norwegian Dawn,* built specifically for the new concept, came the following year. *Norwegian Spirit* (formerly Star Cruises' *SuperStar Leo*) was added in 2004, while the smaller *Norwegian Sea* departed for Star Cruises. The 93,500-ton ship *Norwegian Jewel* arrived in 2005, her sisters, *Norwegian Pearl* in 2006, and *Norwegian Gem,* to follow in October 2007—all built at Meyer Werft in Papenburg, Germany.

Even with all these developments, NCL has not finished. In 2006, NCL marked its 40th anniversary by ordering two (with an option for a third) 150,000-ton megaships, dubbed F3, as the third generation of Freestyle Cruising ships. Costing approximately $2.8 billion, they are to be built at Aker Yards S.A. (formerly Chantiers de l'Atlantique) in France, with the first two ships to be delivered in 2009 and 2010. Based on a new design with a host of new features, the Freestyle Cruising megaships each carrying 4,200 passengers, will be NCL's first post-Panamax ships. Among their most significant new amenity will be all outside cabins with private balconies.

Since Star Cruises took control of NCL in 2000, it has added nine new ships to the NCL fleet—an investment of almost $7 billion. NCL plans to transfer all her ships under 70,000 tons to Star Cruises by 2009, while adding a megaliner a year. Two ships departed in 2007: *Norwegian Wind* in April and *Norwegian Crown* in October.

THE FLEET	BUILT/RENOVATED	TONNAGE	PASSENGERS
Norwegian Dawn	2002/05	92,250	2,244
Norwegian Dream	1992/98/2005	50,764	1,747
Norwegian Gem	2007	93,000	2,380
Norwegian Jewel	2005	92,502	2,376
Norwegian Majesty	1992/99/2004	40,876	1,462
Norwegian Pearl	2006	93,530	2,394
Norwegian Spirit	2000/05	75,338	1,966
Norwegian Star	2001	91,000	2,240
Norwegian Sun	2001	78,309	1,936
F3/Unnamed	2009	150,000	4,200
F3/Unnamed	2010	150,000	4,200
NCL AMERICA FLEET			
Pride of Aloha	1999/2004	77,104	2,002
Pride of America	2005	81,000	2,138
Pride of Hawaii/ Norwegian Jade	2006	93,000	2,466

STYLE NCL has always been at the heart of mainstream cruising with attractive ships reflecting contemporary lifestyles and offering a variety of activities for all ages almost around the clock. NCL ships have thoughtful amenities and signature items, including a full luncheon buffet served on embarkation, expanded room-service menus, ice-cream parlors, and alternative restaurants; the Chocoholic Buffet, a weekly dessert extravaganza; and pool and beach attendants to provide spraying and mist machines on Jewel and Pearl's warm-weather cruises. All dining rooms are nonsmoking. In some casinos, some blackjack tables are reserved for nonsmokers. On the newest ships, facilities for disabled passengers have been substantially enhanced, including cabins and show lounges equipped for the hearing-impaired and for wheelchairs. An extensive, year-round children's program includes supervised activities for four age groups.

Fitness centers—open 24 hours/7 days a week fleetwide—offer fully equipped exercise facilities, aerobics classes, basketball/volleyball courts, and golf practice facilities. Water sports instruction is combined with experiences in ports. All ships have a Dive-In snorkeling program and can arrange scuba excursions for certified divers—even in Alaska. Great Stirrup Cay, NCL's private Bahamian island, offers varied activities.

Under its new owners, NCL introduced Freestyle Cruising to replace some of cruising's time-honored traditions with flexibility and options. The goal has been to broaden cruising's appeal. Gone are rigid dining hours, assigned seating, and dress codes. Instead, NCL ships' dining venues (the newest ships offer ten or more restaurants) have open seating and open dining with continuous service as in a restaurant. Passengers can dine when, where, and with whom they want. The dress code is also optional, from casual to formal, depending on the venue. Other elements of Freestyle Cruising include increased service, with a ratio of almost one crew member per cabin, upgraded cabins, more relaxed disembarkation at the end of a cruise, enhanced enrichment, from computer classes to yoga and mountain biking, and a simplified gratuity system. Wireless access, introduced in 2004, and cell phone service is available fleetwide. The Freestyle Cruising program has been phased in throughout the fleet.

One of NCL's best innovations, rolled out on *Pride of America* in 2005, and now available on all the newest ships, makes selecting a dining venue easier and more convenient. Flat-screen televisions situated in easy-to-see locations around the ship list all the restaurants and indicate availability and waiting time for dinner. If passengers prefer not to wait, the staff at each restaurant can make reservations in another restaurant, or passengers can be given a pager to be buzzed when space becomes available. Another bow to the electronic age, NCL has gone to etickets. Passengers now receive their tickets and other documents via email, unless they or their travel agent requests otherwise.

DISTINCTIVE FEATURES Freestyle Cruising, Chocoholic Buffets, dive program and offbeat excursions in Alaska, single/open seating for many meals, alternative dining and dining-availability monitoring screens, full-scale Broadway shows, and sports bars. Nonsmoking cabins, cabins for the hearing-impaired. 24/7 fitness centers, Internet centers, including wireless access. Children/teen programs. Bowling and climbing wall on *Norwegian Pearl* and *Norwegian Gem*. Ship-within-a-ship luxury suites, some with restricted access.

	HIGHEST	LOWEST	AVERAGE
PER DIEM	$297	$76	$167

Per diems are calculated from cruise line's nondiscounted *cruise-only* published fares on standard accommodations and vary by season, cabins, and cruise areas.

RATES Port charges are included.

Special fares and discounts NCL's LeaderShip fares, available through travel agents, are capacity-controlled with discounts up to 50%. Other early-booking fares are also available. NCL's Premium Air Service handles requests for upgrades, stopovers, and flights on specific airlines and air/sea bookings. Requests for deviations must be written or faxed 60 days in advance and they carry a nonrefundable service fee, plus fare differential, if applicable.

- **CHILDREN'S FARE:** Children under age 2 free, charged only taxes and port charges. At certain times of the year, NCL offers family fares that provide a 10% discount on the cruise fare for the second stateroom when booking a minisuite (second can be in any category); inquire.
- **SINGLE SUPPLEMENT:** Based on double occupancy rate.

Packages
- **AIR/SEA:** Yes.
- **PRE/POST:** Yes.
- **OTHERS:** Yes.

PAST PASSENGERS Latitudes, NCL's past passenger program, was recently enhanced with benefits based on the number of cruises passengers have taken. The program is divided into four tiers: Bronze (1–4 completed cruises), Silver (5–8), Gold (9–13), and Platinum (14 or more). All levels have access to a Latitudes customer service desk, subscription to *Latitudes,* a quarterly members-only magazine, exclusive pricing on all sailings, Polo Club benefits when sailing on Orient Lines, Latitudes check-in desk at pier, Latitudes ship pin, members-only cocktail party hosted by Captain, and Latitudes onboard liaison.

Additionally, Silver members receive treats delivered to their cabin twice during the cruise; Gold receives VIP service, including priority boarding, a welcome-aboard basket, priority restaurant reservations, tender tickets and disembarkation, and an invitation to the Captain's VIP cocktail party. Platinum gets all of the above plus complimentary dinner in Le Bistro restaurant. Membership is automatic and free. Members can call ☎ 800-343-0098 or 305-436-4872 or visit **www.ncl.com.**

THE LAST WORD In the 1990s, NCL had a litany of problems and financial woes that caused its competitors to outpace it in expansion and innovations. But thanks to Star Cruises' purchase and the deep pockets of its new owners, NCL has been able to reinvent itself and can look ahead to a bright future once again, as a trendsetter with its new direction and new ships with many additional features.

Norwegian Cruise Line Standard Features

Officers Norwegian.

Staff Dining and Cabin: international; Cruise: American and British.

Dining facilities *Majesty* and *Dream,* 6; *Star* and *Sun,* 11; *Spirit,* 9; *Dawn,* 11; *Jewel, Pearl, Gem,* 10; *Pride of America,* 9, *Pride of Aloha,* 6, *Pride of Hawaii,* 10—all with open seating, some with charge ($10–$20). Embarkation lunch; Chocoholic, midnight buffets; Sports Bar & Grill; ice-cream parlors; pizzerias; French, Italian, Spanish, Asian, and steak house specialty restaurants.

Special diets Vegetarian, low-salt/calorie, kosher; must be requested 14 to 30 days in advance.

Room service 24 hours.

Dress code Casual by day, informal in evening. Optional formal/semiformal attire one night on short cruises, two on seven-day.

Cabin amenities Phone, refrigerator, some bathrooms with tub, sitting areas in standard cabins on newest ships; television with CNN and ESPN, safe, hair dryers. *Majesty,* ironing board. *Jewel*-class ships, coffeemakers, espresso in suites, terry robes.

Norwegian Cruise Line Standard Features (continued)

Electrical outlets 110 AC.

Wheelchair access *Dream, Majesty* 7 cabins; *Spirit,* 4; *Sun, Star,* 20; *Dawn,* 24; *Jewel, Pearl, Gem,* 27. All have cabins with bathtubs with grab bars. Newer ships: Braille indicators for elevator buttons and cabin numbers, electrical hoists for pools and Jacuzzis, tender boats accessible via wheelchair. Older ships: barriers to wheelchairs removed, ramps built. For details on each ship's facilities, contact NCL.

Recreation and entertainment Up to 11 lounges, sports bars; Broadway shows, Las Vegas–style revues, comedy, nightclub, disco, casino, library. Wine tastings, singles, honeymooner parties, video arcade. Martini, wine-tasting bars on newest ships.

Sports and other activities Sports Afloat program with golf practice, basketball, volleyball, table tennis. Snorkeling; scuba for certified divers. Private island with water sports rental equipment. Most ships, two swimming pools (*Jewel,* three pools); jogging track. *Pearl* and *Gem,* four bowling alleys ($5 with shoes), climbing wall and full-dimension tennis court and viewing stand.

Beauty and fitness Aerobics, fitness center, sauna, jogging track, barber/beauty salon. Spa on *Dream, Spirit, Jewel*-class, *Sun.*

Other facilities Medical, dry cleaning/laundry. Meeting facilities; 24-hour Internet cafe and wireless access fleetwide—$0.75 per minute, packages available; laptop rental, $20 per day; WiFi network card, $10 per day.

Children's facilities New and enhanced year-round program for ages 2–17 in four age-specific levels with youth counselors. Children's menus, fares, babysitting. *Dawn, Star, Spirit,* kids' splash pool, playroom; *Dream, Majesty, Spirit, Jewel*-class, unlimited soda packages, $16, backpack with unlimited soda program, $39.50; teen passport, $34.50.

Theme cruises See text.

Smoking Nonsmoking dining rooms; nonsmoking sections in public rooms.

NCL suggested tipping NCL automatically applies a service charge to passenger's shipboard account: $10 per passenger per day for those ages 13 and older, $5 per day for children ages 3–12; no charge for children under age 3. Charges can be adjusted; 15% added to bar tabs and spa services.

Credit cards For cruise payment and onboard charges: American Express, Visa, MasterCard, Discover.

Norwegian Dawn	QUALITY 8	VALUE B
Norwegian Gem	PREVIEW	
Norwegian Jewel	QUALITY 9	VALUE B
Norwegian Pearl	PREVIEW	

Norwegian Star	QUALITY 8	VALUE B
REGISTRY Panama	LENGTH 965/935 feet	BEAM 105 feet
CABINS 1,112–1,197	DRAFT 27/28 feet	SPEED 22.5/25/24 knots
MAXIMUM PASSENGERS	PASSENGER DECKS 10–15	ELEVATORS 10–12
2,224/2,376/2,240	CREW 1,100–1,154	SPACE RATIO 38.3/38.8/40.5

THE SHIPS The $400 million, 91,000-ton megaliner *Norwegian Star* (formerly slated for Star Cruises) was a prototype for future NCL ships. In 2001, she joined the *Norwegian Sun* for the first-ever dual cruise-ship christening in Miami. Her name, *Norwegian Star,* was meant to signify the link between NCL and its owners, Star Cruises. Her sister ship, *Norwegian Dawn,* was delivered in December 2002. The third ship, *Norwegian Jewel,* made her debut in Europe in August before arriving in the United States in September 2005; and to mark its 40th anniversary, NCL launched its most innovative ships to date, *Norwegian Pearl* in December 2006 and *Norwegian Gem* in October 2007.

Built at the maximum size to pass through the Panama Canal, these ships are NCL's largest and fastest ships to date. They have been fitted with pod drives, which greatly improve maneuverability. While all the ships are meant to be similar, each has introduced new features that subsequent sister ships have enhanced or expanded. The trendsetting *Star* was the first to have NCL's trademark of decorative artwork splashed along her hull—a burst of colorful stars and streamers in green, red, yellow, purple, and aqua running from bow to midship. The design is meant to evoke the longtime cruise tradition of passengers throwing streamers from the bow of the ship as the vessel pulls away from the dock to embark on its voyage. Other *Jewel*-class ships have similar artwork; for example, the *Norwegian Gem* will come with colorful gems tumbling down her sides. Yet, none has taken its innovative role quite as far as the new *Norwegian Pearl,* which is loaded with wow! For starters, it has cruising's first bowling alley, NCL's first climbing wall, a full tennis court, Chihuly sculpture in the **Crystal Atrium,** buffet "action stations" for *à la minute* food preparation, new "romance" suites, three spa treatment rooms for couples, and sexy, wide lounging beds in quiet corners around the ship.

ITINERARIES *See* Itinerary Index.

CABINS The ships have set new cruise industry standards in their cabins, with rich cherrywood finishing, tea- and coffeemakers in every cabin, and larger bathrooms than in the line's other ships, with toilet, shower, and washstand compartments separated by sliding doors, television, safe, and hair dryer. Sixty-five percent of cabins are outside, and more than 70% of these have balconies. Cabins are furnished with two beds that convert to queen, and most cabins have a sofa bed or pop-up trundle bed for a third lower bed; some have a fourth pull-down berth. A large number of cabins (including suites and minisuites) interconnect to create a two-, three-, four-, or five-bedroom area suitable for families.

A steel-and-glass structure on top of the ships, aft from the main sun deck, is a fantasy world, unlike anything on any other vessel today. Meant to create a ship within a ship, two six-room Garden Villas on *Star* and *Dawn* each cover 5,750 square feet (*Pearl*, 4,390 square feet), and each have a roof terrace and private garden and offer open-air dining, Jacuzzis, and totally private sunning and relaxing areas—all yours for a mere $26,000 per week. In addition, these ships have two Owner's Suites, two honeymoon suites, 30 penthouse suites, and an entire deck of spacious minisuites with balconies; and on *Pearl*, a new category of romance suites at the stern with floor-to-ceiling glass doors to enjoy sea and sunset views. Cabins for disabled passengers are available in various categories.

The ship-within-a-ship concept on *Norwegian Jewel* and *Norwegian Pearl*, has somewhat different configurations, demonstrating the enhancement and expansion of earlier NCL innovations. On Deck 14, a block of ten suites (which NCL calls villas) is grouped around an open courtyard with a small swim-against-the-current lap pool at the center. It also has a hot tub, men's and women's steam rooms, and a small fitness area. Eight of the villa suites have separate children's bedrooms. Both ships have two large three-bedroom garden villas with ultramodern decor. Each bedroom is furnished with a king- or queen-size bed and a luxury bath. One of the baths has a whirlpool tub and separate shower.

The *Pearl* has even more Owner's Suites and at the very top of the ship on Deck 15, two new Deluxe Owner's Suites with private patios and fabulous views. All the top category suites have butler service and access to an exclusive concierge. Accommodations throughout the *Pearl* are brightly decorated in orange, fuchsia, and teal, and if you have trouble remembering the direction of fore and aft, the carpeting in the corridors is designed with fish swimming forward.

Both *Jewel*'s and *Pearl*'s facilities for the handicapped are particularly outstanding. The 27 wheelchair-accessible cabins are available in various categories, including suites; all have collapsible shower stools mounted on shower walls and toilets with collapsible arm guards and lowered wash basin. Hearing-impaired kits are available on request. Cabin equipment includes such items as vibrating alarm clock, a light that flashes when there's a knock on the door, television with closed captioning, fire alarm flashing light, and permanently lit emergency lights. Cabins and elevators have Braille text. In public rooms, there are dedicated wheelchair positions in the Stardust Theater, which is equipped with hearing-impaired induction systems, and an electrical hoist for access to the pools and hot tubs. An NCL crew member will tour the ship with passengers on the first day to help them get oriented.

Specifications Dawn/Star 360 standard cabins with balconies; 242 outside, 355 inside; 107 minisuites with balconies; 4 Owner's, 4 romance suites, 30 penthouse suites on *Dawn*, 26 on *Star*; 2 multiroom Garden Villas; 20 wheelchair-accessible on *Star*, 24 on *Spirit*.

Jewel/Pearl/Gem 360 standard cabins with balconies (205 square feet); 243 outside (161 square feet), 412 inside (143 square feet); 134 minisuites with balconies (284 square feet); 2 Garden Villas with 3 bedrooms (4,390 square feet); 2 Deluxe Owner's Suites (928 square feet), 5 Owner's Suites (750 square feet); 24 penthouse suites (572 square feet); 4 romance suites (288 square feet); 10 Courtyard Villas (572 square feet); 27 wheelchair-accessible.

DINING   In keeping with the line's trendsetting Freestyle Cruising, enabling passengers to dine where, when, and with whom they wish, the ships have up to 11 (*Pearl,* 11 or 14, depending on how they're counted) different restaurants offering different menus every night—the most dining options of any other ship in the North American market. In 2006, to beef up its cuisine (excuse the pun!), NCL hired three new corporate chefs to develop "dynamic new menu concepts" and implement them on board the fleet by the end of the year. Initial reports are good.

Versailles (**Venetian** on *Dawn*) is an ornate main dining room with floor-to-ceiling windows, offering the traditional five-course cruise dining experience with the same waitstaff for the cruise or opening seating. *Jewel's* **Tsar's Palace** and *Pearl's* **Summer Palace,** inspired by palaces of the Russian czars, have white and gold ceilings, green marbled pillars and 24-karat-gold-coated chandeliers. **Aqua** (**Indigo** on *Pearl*) is a contemporary-styled second dining room with a lighter menu. Both rooms are open 5:30–10 p.m. On *Star,* **Endless Summer** (**Salsa** on *Dawn*), set around the second level of the central atrium, is a Tex-Mex and tapas-style restaurant, offering sangria, tamales, black bean soup with chorizo, enchiladas, and quesadillas. On *Dawn,* it's **Impressions,** with a 1900s French bistro style. These restaurants do not have a surcharge. *Pearl's* Tex-Mex cafe faces a 24-hour bistro on the atrium's second level.

The *Star's* **Soho,** (*Jewel's* **Chin Chin;** *Pearl's* **Lotus Garden**) a high-end Pacific Rim group of restaurants, features California fusion and Asian cuisine with such specialties as Mongolian Hot Pot. **Ginza,** the Japanese restaurant ($10) has an à la carte section, a sushi bar (all you can eat for $12.50), and a teppanyaki room ($20; reservations required). On *Dawn,* the Japanese/Chinese/Thai complex is called **Bamboo,** with similar outlets.

The handsome **Cagney's Steakhouse,** with a 1930s theme, has become the line's signature restaurant and is featured on all *Jewel*-class ships ($20 per-person cover charge; reservations required). **Le Bistro**, a French restaurant, serves nouvelle cuisine and French classics ($15 per person; reservations required).

For the restaurants that require reservations, it's wise to reserve early. Cagney's is particularly popular. Checking availability has been made easy with NCL's new electronic system. Seventeen screens, placed strategically around the ship, show the status of seat availability and/or waiting time in each restaurant. Passengers who select a specific restaurant are given a beeper that buzzes them when their table is ready.

The Market Café on *Star* (**Garden Cafe** on *Jewel;* redesigned **Garden Café** on *Pearl* and *Gem*) offers "action stations" preparing made-to-order omelets, waffles, fruit soups, ethnic specialties, and pasta, as well as an extensive buffet and grills, including hamburgers, fish and chips, potpies, and wok dishes. On the *Pearl*, the indoor/outdoor buffet has a new layout and extends over a third of the deck, with a large area of outdoor seating at the stern. To one side in the Garden Café is the kids' cafe, with small seats and low tables. In another corner, **La Trattoria** (**La Cucina** on *Pearl*), which opens in the evening and provides table service, offers popular Italian fare, including an antipasto cart for passengers to make their own selections. The ships also have an outdoor grill, an ice-cream bar, and a coffee shop, plus 24-hour room service.

SERVICE The downside of NCL's otherwise terrific ships is service in the dining room and Le Bistro and in some bars, which is often very slow and haphazard. In contrast, cabin attendants are good, often very good.

FACILITIES AND ACTIVITIES One of the ships' most distinctive attractions is the show lounge, spanning three decks without obstruction and seating up to 1,042 people. One of the *Pearl*'s several new shows, entitled *Tubez,* is an edgy (some might say over the edge) musical interspersed with daredevil stunts on bikes, skateboards, and in-line skates against a hip-hop set.

The **Star Club Casino** (**Pearl Club** on *Pearl*) offers blackjack, baby baccarat, roulette, three-card poker, Caribbean stud poker, and craps, as well as some games other lines don't have, such as pai-gow poker, pai-gow tiles, and even a big baccarat table (available only by special request prior to sailing). Also available is a new electronic player tracking system that logs each passenger's play and rewards him for it. The card records players' earnings and offers various rewards, including onboard amenities, credit applied to their onboard account, reduced rates for future cruises, and even a complimentary cruise if the level of play is high enough.

On *Dawn,* passengers are treated to two shows. *South Beach Rave!,* meant to reflect the energy and excitement of Miami's hot South Beach, has DJs from the popular Miami television show *Deco Drive* manning the controls, plus red-hot radio personality Nikki Night from Miami's Y-100 FM. *Rave!* rocks as musicians appear from every corner of the theater, together with horn players, guitarists, and drummers, combining for a pastiche of Latin sounds. *Bollywood* is a celebration of India's traditional film culture, founded on spontaneous song and dance. Bombay nights come alive when the audience enters the theater as the scents of spices, incense, and perfumes fill the air. Bright sarongs and turbans combine to create a tapestry of color as stilt walkers, magicians, and jugglers assemble to present the story. Aerialists wrapped in silks, belly dancers, and snake charmers perform against the Taj Mahal in the background. The Broadway-type shows that passengers enjoy on *Jewel* are *Band on the Run* and *Cirque Bijou.*

Under an exclusive partnership with the famed Second City improv troupe, six performers stage a comedy revue aboard *Norwegian Dawn* on each of her round-trip sailings from New York City. In addition to performing one night each sailing, the inventive and hilarious Second City ensemble hosts onboard workshops introducing the art of improvisation to *Dawn* passengers, exploring their artistic voices and providing the techniques needed to express those voices. The troupe also gives workshops designed especially for children. Second City also appears on *Norwegian Jewel, Norwegian Spirit,* and *Norwegian Pearl* when the ships are in the Caribbean.

The *Star* has a cabaret lounge, karaoke bar with a large screen, a cigar lounge, wine cellar, Champagne bar, a beer garden, an atrium cafe for coffee and pastries, an English pub, an attractive card room and library, and an Internet cafe with 17 stations. There is also a cinema/auditorium, four adjoining meeting rooms, gift shop and department store, and a wedding chapel.

Norwegian Dawn has these attractions, too, but its most distinctive feature is the high-quality art on loan from Star Cruises Chairman Tan Sri Lim Kok Thay's personal collection. These include paintings by Henri Matisse, Claude Monet, and Pierre-Auguste Renoir—all of which have been exhibited in such famous museums as the National Gallery of Art in Washington, D.C., and the National Museum in Stockholm.

A distinction for the *Norwegian Gem* when she enters service in autumn 2007 and takes over *Norwegian Dawn*'s home port in New York, will be that she is the only ship offering seven-day cruises from New York to the Bahamas and the Caribbean on a year-round basis.

The *Pearl*'s Deck 7 is action central for the ship, centered by the colorful **Crystal Atrium,** which is dominated by a floor-to-ceiling big-screen television and bright, cheerful decor of aqua and strawberry. It houses the reception, concierge, cruise consultant, shore excursions offices, and to one side, Java Café. Nearby stands a large Dale Chihuly glass sculpture and overhead, the crystal ceiling by this artist resembles hundreds of icicles. Off to one side of the atrium is **Bar Central**—actually three connected but very different bars—a martini bar, a Champagne and wine bar, and a beer and whisky pub. A circular stairway from the atrium leads to Deck 8, where there are two casual restaurants: **Blue Lagoon,** serving snacks, burgers, and a variety of light fare around the clock, and **Mambo's Latin,** offering tapas and Tex-Mex specialties.

On your way aft on Deck 7, you pass the Internet cafe on the port side and the photo gallery on starboard, to reach the *Pearl*'s most distinctive feature—**Bliss Ultra Lounge & Nightclub.** During the day, Bliss is a sports bar with the cruise world's first shipboard bowling alley ($5 including shoes for a ten-frame game) with flat-screen televisions tuned to the day's top games or sports events and foosball and other arcade games. In the evening, Bliss is completely transformed into a hip, high-energy ultralounge, complete with plush turquoise, purple, and red velvet banquettes and sexy daybeds. The plasma screens blare with hot music videos spun by ship's Vibe Master, the bar and dance floor gather crowds, and mood-lit bowling adds to the unusual experience— all decadent enough that you might imagine walking into Hugh Hefner's bedroom or Paris Hilton's playpen.

While it may be surprising to find a four-lane, ten-pin bowling alley on a cruise ship, placing it in a sports bar and nightclub was brilliant.

Bowling immediately creates camaraderie and fun. It's a great place to meet people and it sure beats just going to a bar. The bowling alley also gives NCL a leg up on other cruise ships' breakthroughs such as climbing walls, boxing ring, and racing car simulators because bowling can be enjoyed by all ages, from kids to seniors. Not everyone can climb a rock wall, and boxing and race car simulators have age limits.

Among the *Pearl*'s other 11 bars and lounges is the **Corona Cigar Club,** offering hand-rolled cigars, cognacs, and spirits, and a small **Sake Bar** with a selection of sake and Asian beers. On Deck 13, the **Spinnaker Lounge** is a large observation lounge with horizontal windows in the floor allowing views of the bridge. The lounge has a dance floor and stage for entertainment, with colorful decor and unusual mod chairs and sculpted settees. It's the venue for bingo, dance lessons, and similar activities by day and cabaret in the evening.

NCL was the first cruise line to offer WiFi (wireless Internet access) fleetwide. Passengers who bring their laptops can rent a wireless network card for $10 a day; laptops can be rented for $20 a day. Wireless Internet access costs $0.75 per minute, though buying minutes in bulk—100- or 250-minute packages—can bring the cost down to $0.40 per minute. The wireless service functions best in certain areas of each ship, but it normally enables poolside surfing as well as access in meeting rooms and some other public areas. Now, too, NCL offers the use of cell phones at sea. The *Pearl* has meeting facilities with three breakout rooms, including a boardroom, a library, card room, and chapel. The shops, which appear aft on Deck 7 on the earlier *Jewel*-class ships, were moved to the Crystal Atrium area to make way for Bliss.

SPORTS, FITNESS, AND BEAUTY   The *Star*'s main pool is located amidship on Deck 12. Aft is the bi-level spa and fitness center, with a waterfall in the atrium of its reception area and an indoor pool that is said to be the longest on any cruise ship. The fitness center has state-of-the-art cardiovascular workout equipment, aerobic and boxercise area with a sprung wooden floor, steam and sauna rooms, a jet-current exercise pool, whirlpool, and hydrotherapy facilities. NCL's spas are operated by Mandara, one of the world's leading operators of resort spas, and feature an array of exotic treatments combining Asian and Eastern techniques.

On the *Dawn*, the 11,302-square-foot **El Dorado Spa (South Pacific** on *Pearl*) has 15 treatment rooms, with one designed exclusively for couples. There are private hydrotherapy baths, a lap pool, a Jacuzzi, two Japanese pools, sauna, and a steam room in both the men's and women's areas. The *Pearl* has NCL's first thalassotherapy pool and 17 treatment rooms, of which three are designed for couples. Passengers may also have spa treatments in their cabins, poolside and on-deck massages on port days, and massage and de-stress treatments on secluded beaches during private island visits. Deck 12 of the *Jewel* and *Pearl* has two swimming pools, a three-tiered slide, and a kid's wading pool.

The Sports Deck has an outside jogging track, golf driving range, and volleyball, tennis, or basketball court. This deck on the *Pearl* sports

NCL's first climbing wall and a large sports area that includes a multi-function court for regulation tennis, volleyball, and basketball, complete with a spectator stand. To complement the ships' sports facilities, NCL offers an array of active shore excursions, including mountain biking, sailing, and scuba diving.

CHILDREN'S FACILITIES The ships have huge children's centers, complete with a playroom, outdoor pool, movie theater, computer rooms, teen center, video arcade, a nursery, and toddlers' nap room. There is even a special children's area in the buffet restaurant, where kids have their own low-level serving counter and kid-size tables and chairs. *Norwegian Dawn*, constructed with families in mind, also has the **T-Rex Kid's Center**, a supervised facility with a jungle gym, a playroom, **Flicks theater, Clicks,** a computer learning center equipped with five terminals, **Doodles** arts and crafts area, and **Snoozes** sleeping area. A highlight is the **T-Rex Pool**, a Jurassic-themed children's pool with dino-riffic waterslides, a kids-only Jacuzzi, and a paddling and wading pool for the little ones.

The **Teen Club** is a disco strictly for teens, with a video wall showing the latest music video hits, a cinema, and **Video Zone,** a huge arcade with 23 of the latest video games. On the *Pearl*, teens get the New York–inspired **Metro Center** teen's club complete with graffiti. NCL has a special kids' menu, including kid-size hamburgers, hot dogs, spaghetti, chicken fingers, and ice-cream sundaes.

In NCL's year-round Kid's Crew, program coordinators plan and supervise daily activities for four age groups: Junior (ages 2–5), First Mates (6–9), Navigators (10–12), and Teens (13–17). At sea, the hours are 9 a.m.–noon; 2–5 p.m., and 7–10 p.m.; first evening of cruise, 8–10 p.m.; port days, 7–10 p.m. Group-sitting in port is available from 9 a.m. to 5 p.m.for a nominal charge. Children under age 2 sail at a substantially reduced fare. For babysitting, inquire from cruise line prior to departure.

Activities include dances and arts and crafts. There are races, treasure hunts, and games planned for the day at the beach. The ship publishes *Kids' Cruise News* and *Teen Cruise News* daily. Also available are an ice-cream bar and children's menus. The Kids' Soda package gives unlimited soda-fountain access for $16 for seven days. A Kids' Backpack provides baseball cap, luggage tags, T-shirt, and more for $39.50, depending on cruise length. Teen Passport for teens ages 13–17 enables them to purchase a coupon book for $34.50 to be used for up to 20 nonalcoholic specialty drinks, as well as enjoying exclusive dance and pizza parties and a farewell Frat Party.

SHORE EXCURSIONS NCL's Web site lists the shore excursions, together with prices. The excursions can be booked online. Frequently, the ships on Caribbean itineraries stop at Great Stirrup Cay, NCL's private island in the Bahamas—an idea originated by NCL in 1977 and copied by many other cruise lines. The island has two main beaches and several others that are not maintained. It has two bars, food service, restrooms, beach chairs and umbrellas, and a straw market. A wide variety of water sports is available, including snorkeling, sailing, and kayaking, as well as volleyball, table tennis, and walking and jogging paths. A live calypso band provides music for listening and dancing throughout the day.

Norwegian Spirit	QUALITY 8	VALUE B
Norwegian Sun	QUALITY 8	VALUE B
REGISTRY Panama/Bahamas	LENGTH 882/853 feet	BEAM 105 feet
CABINS 998/968	DRAFT NA/26 feet	SPEED 24/23 knots
MAXIMUM PASSENGERS	PASSENGER DECKS 12/11	ELEVATORS 13/12
1,966/1,936	CREW 882/968	SPACE RATIO 38.3/40

THE SHIPS *Norwegian Sun's* handsome interior, created by Swedish marine architects Tillberg Design, is one of cool elegance. In the glass-domed, eight-deck atrium and throughout the ship, there is no glitz or bright lights, but rather an airy, refined setting with a multimillion-dollar art collection integrated into the decor.

The reception and purser's desks, concierge, and shore excursion offices are on Atlantic Deck. **Neptune's Court,** a second atrium, has a grand staircase just outside the **Seven Seas Dining Room,** connecting Atlantic Deck to Promenade and International decks with the main show lounge.

The *Norwegian Sun* was the first of the fleet to have NCL's Freestyle Cruising elements included during the construction. Among them are more dining options—11 restaurants (some with surcharge or pay as you go). They include three dining rooms, an outdoor buffet, an indoor garden buffet, pizzeria, and wine bar, the NCL signature **Sports Bar & Grill, Le Bistro,** an ice-cream bar, and Champagne and cigar bars.

Among other new features, *Norwegian Sun* has a "lifestyle area" for classes in computers, financial planning, yoga, and so on, a wedding chapel, a larger gym and spa than NCL's earlier ships, and larger cabins. She was the first to have the new cabin category of minisuites with balconies, now available on all the newest *Jewel*-class ships.

At the **Internet cafe,** passengers can go online 24 hours a day. Ship's photographers have digital cameras, enabling passengers to e-mail photos home (for an additional fee). A Skycam on the bridge is downloaded onto a Web site so family members ashore can track the voyage. Other facilities include the Atrium Room, available for small private functions, and a medical center.

In a joint venture, **dutyfree.com** and Colombian Emeralds International manage *Norwegian Sun's* gift shops. Passengers view jewelry patterns and designs at a kiosk, with home delivery available. Liquor selections, displayed in the shopping arcade, can be ordered through room service.

Norwegian Spirit (formerly Star Cruises' *SuperStar Leo*), added to the fleet in 2004, is not a twin of the *Sun,* but a close relative in her features and facilities. She has similar Freestyle Cruising elements, such as nine restaurants, a large spa and fitness center, and a 24/7 Internet cafe, among others.

In October 2006, *Norwegian Sun* was the first cruise ship to home-port in New Orleans after Hurricane Katrina, at the city's new $37 million Erato Street Terminal, designed to accommodate larger cruise ships. For the 2007 winter season, *Norwegian Sun* moves to Miami, being replaced in New Orleans by the *Norwegian Spirit*.

ITINERARIES   *See* Itinerary Index.

CABINS   Cabins are similar to those on other NCL ships and are furnished with two lower beds that convert to a queen, a sitting area, dressing table, refrigerator, safe, television, radio, and telephone. Those on the *Sun* have bathrooms with bidet. Other than the penthouses and owner suites, all cabins are uniform in size and efficiently laid out. Closet space is adequate. All cabins have Internet hookups. Sixteen penthouses with teakwood-furnished balconies have butler service and an exclusive room service menu for breakfast, lunch, and dinner.

The *Sun,* with more outside cabins (64% total) than NCL's earlier ships, has larger cabins and 52 suites, including 30 minisuites with balconies, measuring 267–301 square feet. Four Owner's Suites, located forward above the ship's bridge, have 828 square feet each.

Specifications   *Norwegian Spirit,* 591 outside cabins, 374 with balconies; 374 inside; 16 penthouse suites; 4 wheelchair-accessible. *Norwegian Sun,* 675 outside (145–221 square feet), 325 inside (167–176 square feet); 52 suites with balconies (436 square feet); 16 doubles, 185 triples, 779 quads; 20 wheelchair-accessible.

DINING   Both the *Spirit* and *Sun* reflect the Freestyle Cruising's concept with their dining options. On a seven-day cruise, passengers never need to eat dinner in the same restaurant more than once if they care to pay extra in some of the eateries. Among their choices, they can enjoy either of two main dining rooms, **Four Seasons** and **Seven Seas** on the *Sun,* with open seating from 5:30 to 10 every evening; a more formal Italian restaurant, **Il Adagio** ($10), by reservation; French fare at **Le Bistro** ($15); a Pacific Rim restaurant complex with a sushi bar and teppanyaki room ($15–$20); a Asian restaurant ($10); a 24-hour indoor/outdoor cafe with food stations serving hamburgers, hot dogs, soups, and salads; and a "healthy living" restaurant with a lighter, more contemporary menu, including selections from *Cooking Light* magazine and spa menus. Note, however, that some of these restaurants have a surcharge, and some are pay as you go.

Shogun, *Spirit*'s Asia complex ($10), has a show kitchen at the entrance where passengers are visually introduced to traditional styles of preparation. At **Cagney's,** a traditional steak house ($20), they can enjoy certified Angus beef, veal, pork, lamb, seafood, and grilled chicken.

The casual **Great Outdoor Café** and **Garden Café (Raffles Terrace and Buffet** on *Spirit*) have "food action stations" serving up paella, sushi, Norwegian waffles, pasta, and more, intended to eliminate long buffet lines. Both cafes offer breakfast, lunch, and snack specialties that vary daily. There is a pizzeria and **Sprinkles Ice Cream Bar.** The 24-hour room-service menu offers pizza, too. **Blue Lagoon Café** on *Spirit* is a 24-hour food court serving hamburgers, fish and chips, potpies, and wok dishes and includes a buffet for kids with small seats and tables.

Passengers give the ship's cuisine, especially the alternative dining options, good reviews. The only dining disappointment is breakfast and lunch in the Pool Deck cafe for the lack of variety.

FACILITIES AND ACTIVITIES   The ships have similar bars, including a **Champagne Bar,** by the atrium with large glass windows and a view of the lobby area, serving Champagne and premium vodkas along with caviar and pâté de foie gras. A modest but respectable half bottle of Veuve Clicquot with pâté de foie gras accompaniment is a mere $40–$50; if you go for the works, a bottle of Dom Perignon with sevruga caviar and pâté will run you about $150.

Nonsmoking guests can select from the martini menu in the **Windjammer Bar** on *Sun,* and cigar connoisseurs enjoy freshly hand-rolled stogies and premium brandy behind the glass walls of the adjoining but segregated **Cigar Club** with humidor. The **Java Bar** (*Sun*) and **The Café** (*Spirit*) coffee bar have a great selection of coffees, tea, and liqueurs at fair prices, and serve pastries and cookies. *Spirit* also has the **Bier Garten Grill** offering beer and cocktails and Bavarian food, such as weisswurst and pretzels.

Sun Club Casino offers blackjack, roulette, Caribbean poker, and slot machines. Now playing in the golden, two-deck **Stardust Lounge** with a proscenium stage is *Hey Mr. Producer: The Musical World of Cameron Mackintosh,* which highlights the legendary musicals Mackintosh produced, including *Cats, Miss Saigon, Les Miserables,* and *The Phantom of the Opera.* With the venue's sound, lighting, and audiovisual facilities, the lounge can be easily transformed into a disco.

Dazzles Lounge has what NCL claims is the longest bar at sea. Passengers can see cabaret acts, illusionists, and comedians. The entertainment is uniformly of high standard, in keeping with the NCL tradition.

The *Sun* also has a wedding chapel for ceremonies in port, a library, and the **East Indies Conference Center,** which seats 100 and can be divided into three smaller rooms.

On the Pool Deck, the **Topsider's Bar** is a long poolside bar with stools and outdoor tables; on the Sports Deck, the **Sports Bar** offers televisions with videotaped and live broadcasts of sporting events. The **Observation Lounge** has floor-to-ceiling windows overlooking the bow. Roaming the decks is a Skymobile beverage cart making drink deliveries to passengers. When the ships sail in the Caribbean, pool attendants provide Evian water, suntan lotion, cold face towels, and fresh fruit.

NCL racked up another first in 2004 when it began offering onboard cell-phone service on the *Norwegian Sun.* The new technology is now available fleetwide. Consumers are charged by their cellular wireless providers at the roaming rates set by their carriers.

SPORTS, FITNESS, AND BEAUTY   The two swimming pools are connected by steps and a central wading platform to four hot tubs and set off by dark-wood decks and dark-green lounge chairs. Also on the enormous Sun Deck is a spa with therapists trained in a wide range of treatments. It has a unisex beauty salon and a gym/aerobics area with exercise equipment; exercisers can enjoy ocean views through floor-to-ceiling glass walls.

On *Sun*'s Sports Deck, passengers will find a golf driving net, a full-size basketball/volleyball court, a batting cage, and shuffleboard. A walking and jogging track circles the Promenade Deck. *Spirit*'s Sports Deck is similar, with four golf driving nets.

CHILDREN'S FACILITIES Kids Korner playroom on International Deck offers Kid's Crew, a year-round, supervised program divided into four age groups. (See "Children's Facilities" in the *Norwegian Dawn/Gem/ Jewel/Pearl/Star* section for details.) A kids' splash pool is on Sports Deck. Teen Passport, for teens ages 13–17, enables them to purchase a coupon book for $34.50, to be used for up to 20 nonalcoholic specialty drinks, as well as enjoying exclusive dance and pizza parties and a farewell Frat Party. *Spirit*'s **Teen Club** includes a disco for teenagers; the video arcade has 70 of the latest video machines. Its children's **Pirate** theme pool area has a wading pool and two small slides. (See *Norwegian Dawn/Gem/Jewel/Pearl/Star* for details of children's program.)

SHORE EXCURSIONS In Alaska, NCL offers some of mainstream cruising's best offbeat excursions, such as glacier hiking, mountain biking, forest trekking, a six-hour hike outside Skagway, and three hours of sea kayaking from Juneau (you're likely to see a whale close enough to feel its spray). Flight-seeing from Juneau to a remote lodge showcases vast ice fields. The more exotic tours have few slots; book early. Among the most popular is Dive Into Adventure, for snorkeling and scuba diving. It's active and attracts a variety of passengers. Plus, few people can say they have been diving in Alaska. At excursion's end, participants shiver out of wet suits and jump into the heated pool on Sun Deck.

Note: Alaska shore excursions are expensive on every cruise line because of the very short season in which operators have to make money and the very high costs of operating tours in Alaska.

Norwegian Dream	QUALITY 5	VALUE C
REGISTRY Bahamas	LENGTH 754 feet	BEAM 94 feet
CABINS 834	DRAFT 23 feet	SPEED 21 knots
MAXIMUM PASSENGERS	PASSENGER DECKS 10	ELEVATORS 11/10
1,747	CREW 721	SPACE RATIO 29

THE SHIP *Norwegian Dream* (her twin, *Norwegian Wind*, left the fleet in April 2007) was designed for people who want to know they're on a ship at sea. At almost every turn, glass walls frame the ocean and connect with the outdoors—a link that many modern cruise ships have lost. But this ship, breaking the mold on design, has unusual features inside and out. All five upper decks are open and slant downward to create a more sleek profile than those of most large new ships.

The comfortable, contemporary settings are the work of well-known Norwegian designers Petter Yran and Bjorn Storbraaten. High-quality fabrics, fine woods, marble, and brass trim translate to casual elegance. Windows and use of glass bring the outdoors into the indoor decor. Light floods the interiors, giving them a lively atmosphere.

In early 1998, *Dream* was stretched 130 feet, and all cabins and most public rooms refurbished. Lengthening resulted in a sleeker, more hydrodynamic profile, one captain says. The new section added 251 cabins and increased the ship's length to 754 feet and its passenger capacity from 1,246 to 1,747, but the space ratio decreased, surrendering some of the ship's spaciousness.

Lengthening also resulted in a new entrance and lobby and 12 new Owner's Suites, expansion of the **Four Seasons Dining Room,** a larger casino and nightclub, an enlarged fitness center and spa, playroom, coffee bar and lounge, splash pool, wet bar, and two whirlpools, outdoor cafe and pizzeria, and three new passenger elevators. Show lounges and bars received additional seating, and the shopping arcade nearly doubled.

The striking entrance on the Promenade Deck has a Nordic motif in blue and gray with wood blinds, marble accents, and Art Deco lighting. Here are a 24-hour reception desk, information and concierge desks, the purser's office, and shore excursion and Dive In desks. The ship's most innovative feature is the dining rooms—four instead of the traditional one or two. The rooms have multiple tiers, creating more intimate settings and enabling all diners to enjoy panoramas through acres of windows. Topside, the tiered Sun Deck becomes an amphitheater for evening entertainment.

ITINERARIES *See* Itinerary Index.

CABINS The ship offers 15 categories; almost all are on the lower five of the vessels' ten decks. All portside cabins are nonsmoking; 34 cabins are equipped for the hearing-impaired, and 13 are wheelchair-accessible.

In a departure from the usual midprice ships, 80% of cabins are outside with large windows; standard cabins are larger than average; all have a sitting area with table and sofa chair or love seat that converts to a third bed; a curtain separates sleeping and living areas.

There are some trade-offs. Bathrooms are small, particularly the shower stall, and storage space is insufficient. Space around beds is tight, but separate sitting and sleeping areas compensate. Almost all cabins have twin beds that convert into a queen, television with CNN and ESPN, radio, telephone, and hair dryer.

Passengers in International Deck cabins, added when the ships were lengthened, must access them through the Four Seasons Dining Room, which was expanded across the ship's width. Otherwise, these passengers must detour up or down a deck.

Owner's Suites measure 336 square feet and accommodate up to five people. Located on the Sun Deck, each has a separate bedroom and living room with convertible double sofa, television, stereo system, refrigerator, and balcony. Bathrooms have a tub and shower and entrances from both hall and bedroom. Other top-category suites also have balconies; most have refrigerators and floor-to-ceiling windows. They're served by an attentive concierge who provides complimentary amenities, including wine and hors d'oeuvres.

Specifications 181 inside cabins, 695 outside; 12 Owner's Suites; 6 penthouse suites with balcony; 62 balcony cabins. Standard outside dimensions, 160–176 square feet. Most cabins have 2 lower beds convertible to queen; some have third and fourth berths. 1 single; 13 wheelchair-accessible; 34 hearing-impaired.

DINING Both of the main dining rooms have their own personality and setting. They have the same menus and food comes from a central kitchen. The diverse, distinctive settings make dining more fun and interesting, and open seating enables passengers to meet.

The three levels of **Terraces** are separated by greenery and connected by twin stairways. Some passengers say the arrangement suggests a supper club in vintage Hollywood movies. A mural covers the back wall, and a wall of glass allows splendid views.

The Four Seasons Dining Room, extending side-to-side in the ship, is the largest dining room. Floor-to-ceiling bay windows extend over the water and offer spectacular views. Four terraced areas provide excellent sight lines. **Sun Terraces,** the smallest dining room, is casually appointed in light wood and wicker. It's set on three narrow terraces with walls of glass on three sides that extend overhead. Shades protect diners when the sun is above. The view is across the aft swimming pool to the sea.

Le Bistro, the alternative restaurant, is open to all passengers on a first-come, first-served basis. The cozy, informal cafe offers a daily pasta dish prepared tableside and other light fare. Wine by the glass is available. The former Sports Bar was replaced with a buffet restaurant as part of the ship's transformation to Freestyle dining. The **Coffee Bar** is designed as a coffee house, with such memorabilia as antique coffee machines on display. Coffee and coffee-flavored drinks are served. The area, with curved walls and quiet niches, incorporates the ship's library and card room.

Free ice cream and frozen yogurt are available poolside each afternoon. The Sun Deck splash pool has a semicircular "wet bar." Nearby, the casual **Topsiders** serves breakfast and lunch buffets and snacks. If you aren't watching calories and are willing to stand in long lines, you can pig out at the one-night **Chocoholic Buffet.**

SERVICE The ships are praised for good cabin service, but complaints about service in dining areas are not uncommon.

FACILITIES AND ACTIVITIES Daytime activities include art auctions, bingo, dance classes, bridge tours, culinary demonstrations, and pool and parlor games. We repeat our warning: At art auctions, know what you're buying. Bargains are rare, despite the sales pitch. A conference center on Sun Deck accommodates 60 people and can be divided into two spaces. An Internet cafe with computer terminals is available on the International Deck; fees apply.

Fabulous entertainment is the cruise highlight. Passengers often give the shows standing ovations. *Dreamgirls* was the opener for the *Norwegian Dream,* and the ship has featured 42nd Street in the **Stardust Lounge,** the main showroom. On alternate nights there are Las Vegas–style variety shows. The room is well laid out in four tiers, providing comfortable seats and clear sight lines. The lounge has a dance floor, and dance music may be provided.

The **Monte Carlo** casino, dressed in hot magenta and black, offers blackjack, Caribbean stud poker, craps, roulette, Let It Ride, and 133 slot machines. Adjacent to the casino is **Dazzles** nightclub, which has a circular granite bar, a circular dance floor, and curved sofas in velvet harlequin patterns. **Lucky's** piano bar has a dance floor and is popular after the show.

Other nighttime action takes place on the Sports Deck, anchored forward by the **Observatory Lounge** with floor-to-ceiling windows—an ideal spot for viewing Caribbean sunsets. Open decks are sometimes used for outdoor parties. The informal **Rendezvous Bar,** next to Four Seasons Dining Room, is a good meeting spot.

SPORTS, FITNESS, AND BEAUTY Sports and fitness programs are offered year-round. The Sports Deck is a mecca for active passengers. Golf instruction and a driving range, plus two outdoor pools, are available on Sun Deck. Upstairs on Sky Deck is the basketball and volleyball court. The International Deck offers a small pool.

The **Spa and Fitness Center** on the Sports Deck has been enlarged to accommodate a full-service spa with eight treatment rooms for massage therapy, herbal wraps, and facials. A weight room has Cybex training equipment. Aerobics and other exercise classes balance excesses at the Chocoholic Buffet. A wide walking/jogging track wraps around Promenade Deck. The beauty salon is next to the Observation Lounge.

Tiered teak decks, separated by decorative greenery, are a sunbathers' and people-watchers' delight at the forward pool. It's an innovative design, but it's noisy. On some evenings, the area hosts outdoor events and dancing. Snorkeling instruction is offered at sea, and hands-on experience is available in ports of call.

CHILDREN'S FACILITIES Kids Korner playroom is the base for NCL's fleetwide, year-round Kid's Crew program. (See *Norwegian Star* for details.)

Norwegian Majesty	QUALITY 5	VALUE C
REGISTRY Panama	LENGTH 680 feet	BEAM 89 feet
CABINS 731	DRAFT 20 feet	SPEED 20 knots
MAXIMUM PASSENGERS	PASSENGER DECKS 9	ELEVATORS 6
1,462	CREW 661	SPACE RATIO 28

THE SHIP *Norwegian Majesty,* which was built in 1992, was lengthened in 1999 by 112 feet through insertion of a prefabricated midsection that added 202 new cabins, plus new public areas and facilities. The lengthening also increased the ship's capacity from 1,056 to 1,462 passengers. The work added a second pool, second dining room, new casino, another outdoor bar, **Le Bistro** restaurant, coffee bar, and substantially more deck space. Crew cabins were expanded to accommodate increased staff. Two new elevators and a third stair tower were incorporated.

The lengthening also gave *Norwegian Majesty* a sleeker, more hydrodynamic profile, enabling the ship to maintain its 20-knot speed with the same power plant, despite increased size. New buoyancy reduced the ship's draft, allowing her to call at some ports that were previously inaccessible because of shallow waters.

In 2003, the ship started a series of cruises from Charleston, South Carolina, to the Western Caribbean. The homeporting in Charleston reflected a continuing expansion of NCL's Homeland Cruising program, aimed particularly at the drive markets in nearby states.

Norwegian Majesty debuted as Majesty Cruises' *Royal Majesty* with an understated elegance intended to appeal to affluent passengers. Stylish interiors create a refined, harmonious environment of simplicity and clean lines. Contemporary decor employs soft colors, natural wood, leather sofas, glass, mirrors, and fresh foliage. The ship is well laid out with many quiet corners; forward lounges have walls of sloped windows.

Passengers step almost directly into the two-deck atrium that serves as the main lobby and contains the front desk and shore excursion office. Called **Crossroads,** the circular area has white marble floors and stairs to a white marble island centered with a baby grand piano and furnished with banquettes.

The Atlantic Deck is devoted entirely to public areas. Off the lobby is the **Four Seasons Dining Room;** beyond, the **Seven Seas Restaurant.** Forward are boutiques, library, card room, and meeting room. Small lounges border **Rendezvous,** a large V-shaped piano bar connecting to **Royal Fireworks,** a lounge with panoramic windows.

Norwegian Majesty is an attractive ship, but it's had an unusual amount of technical problems, indicating perhaps that it's time to give it a major overhaul.

ITINERARIES *See* Itinerary Index.

CABINS The 14 categories range from Owner's Suites to inside cabins with lower and upper berths. About 65% are outside. Standard cabins are modest in size. They have clean, uncluttered lines and are finished in natural wood. Most have twin beds separated by a chest of drawers. A desk unit has drawer space and a dressing mirror, and three closets add to storage. Each cabin has a television carrying CNN, cable sports, shipboard notices, and movies. Bathrooms have showers and a large sink, with ample counter and shelf space and a hair dryer. All cabins have a built-in ironing board.

Upper-category suites and cabins have a minibar, queen beds, and large windows. Forward on Majesty Deck, a group of cabins spans an unusual half-moon contour overlooking the bow. The two Owner's Suites on Norway Deck have marble baths and 24-hour butler service.

Specifications 202 new deluxe or standard outside and standard inside cabins. 250 inside, 481 outside; 20 suites. Standard cabins, 108–145 square feet. 680 cabins with 2 lowers (617 convert to doubles); 51 with double beds; 198 with 3 berths; 174 with 4 berths; 20 suites accommodate 3 persons; 4 wheelchair-accessible.

DINING   The impressive **Seven Seas Restaurant** has wraparound, full-length windows. A white baby grand piano plays on a small island at the center. Most tables are set for four or six, contributing to the room's intimate feeling. Seven Seas was the first smoke-free dining room on a major cruise ship.

The **Four Seasons Restaurant** also offers ocean panoramas through floor-to-ceiling windows. Adjacent is the 62-seat Le Bistro alternative restaurant ($15), which serves light Italian and continental cuisine during flexible dining hours.

Breakfast and lunch buffets are served inside the casual **Café Royale** on Sun Deck; outside space overlooks two pools. The room is attractively furnished in light wood and wicker chairs. It's tight for buffet lines. Buffets are average, offering a range of hot and cold dishes, daily specialties, and cakes, pastries, muffins, and breads. The cafe is connected to the **Royal Observatory,** a handsome observation lounge/bar below that doubles as a sports bar. **Piazza San Marco Grill,** a second Sun Deck serving area, is partially covered. Burgers, hot dogs, pizza, ice cream, snacks, and late-night buffets (different from the nightly midnight buffet) are offered.

SERVICE   The crew encompasses 46 nationalities. Except, at times, for the dining room, service shipwide has received generally good reviews until recently, when they have been less than stellar.

FACILITIES AND ACTIVITIES   Daytime offerings include bridge tours, table-tennis tournaments, bridge and Scrabble, fruit- and vegetable-carving demonstrations, poolside fashion shows, napkin-folding classes, wine tasting, and dance. The ship has a card room, well-stocked library, and small boardroom. The Internet cafe is also in the card room; fees apply.

The **Palace Theater** show lounge is on one level with a steeply tiered floor. Sight lines to the circular stage are excellent from almost every seat. The ship's midsection has the **Monte Carlo Casino,** offering blackjack, Caribbean stud poker, roulette, and slot machines. Next door, the attractive **Polo Bar** has piano music nightly. One deck below, a small coffee bar and lounge offers coffees, teas, and coffee-flavored drinks, plus bar service. **Royal Fireworks** is a quiet area or meeting space by day and a dance lounge before and after dinner.

In summer, when the ship is in Bermuda, she isn't allowed to stage big productions or open the casino. Instead, the ship offers excursions to local nightclubs. An evening cocktail cruise along Bermuda's pretty shores is another option.

SPORTS, FITNESS, AND BEAUTY   Fitness fans pair workouts and ocean views in the gym. Equipment includes Life Circuit machines and a Nordic Track.

Exercise and dance classes are held in a mirrored studio. The spa on Promenade Deck has saunas for men and women and offers massage. A small beauty parlor also offers facials and spa treatments. A jogging track circles Promenade Deck.

The top decks were transformed by the addition of a second swimming pool and the **Topsider's Bar,** a second open-air bar. Sky Deck above the Sun Deck provides more sunning area while shading the two pools and whirlpools below. It has lounge chairs, restrooms, and showers.

CHILDREN'S FACILITIES Supervised program; see "Children's Facilities" in *Norwegian Dawn/Gem/Jewel/Pearl/Star* section for details. **Kids Korner** play area has a kiddies' pool, playground rides, ball slide, and a puppet theater. Bathrooms have lowered kiddies' sinks. Older children have a video arcade.

SHORE EXCURSIONS The ship spends four days in St. George's, in front of King's Square. Nearby are shops, historic St. Peter's church, and motor-scooter rentals (the island's most popular transport; no car rentals are available). The picturesque town is ideal for walking and convenient to beaches, but to reach Hamilton, a town at the island's opposite end, you need to take a taxi or bus or rent a moped. Hamilton is, however, included in some shore excursions. Among other excursions available is a visit to the Bermuda Aquarium Museum and Zoo. The ship's sports program offers sailing, snorkeling, scuba diving, and deep-sea fishing.

NCL AMERICA

IN MAY 2003, NCL CORP. surprised the cruise world when it announced that it would have a U.S.-flagged ship in Hawaii by summer 2004, employing an all-American crew, and subject to all American laws. The announcement came soon after Congress passed a federal spending bill that included an exemption to the Passenger Services Act. As a result, NCL, in exchange for completing two former Project America vessels (now *Pride of America* and *Pride of Hawaii*) to sail in Hawaii under the U.S. flag, was also given an exemption to reflag one existing, foreign-flagged NCL ship that would sail under the U.S. flag within Hawaii (but not Alaska or the Caribbean). The U.S.-flagged ship does not have to make at least one foreign port call on any itinerary, as all foreign-flagged ships are required to do by law. That avoids long ocean journeys and multiple days at sea.

Under the exemption, NCL's *Norwegian Sky*—the first ship to offer Freestyle Cruising when it debuted in 2000—was reflagged to the U.S. ship registry in July 2004. As the renamed *Pride of Aloha*, it launched NCL America's first Hawaii cruises with all-American crews on July 4, 2004. *Pride of Aloha* passengers enjoy up to 96 hours of port time, all within Hawaii on a weeklong cruise.

Pride of America, constructed at the Lloyd Werft shipyard in Germany, is the first new oceangoing passenger ship built in nearly 50 years to sail under the American flag. She began service in Hawaii in 2005, offering seven-night, inter-island cruises round-trip from Honolulu. The third Project America ship, *Pride of Hawaii*, debuted in Hawaii in 2006.

On the heels of its Project America purchase, NCL Corp. bought the only two existing U.S.-built oceangoing cruise ships, the *United States* and the *Independence*, and says it plans to completely rebuild the 50-year-old vessels. To rebuild the two U.S.-built ships, the minimum the law requires is to maintain the hull and superstructure as 100% U.S., so all the steel and structural work is done in a U.S. shipyard. Beyond that, NCL can choose a U.S. or European shipyard, or both, for interior work. NCL says renovations are likely to take several years. According to NCL, the purchase was a practical way for NCL to expand its three-ship U.S.-flagged fleet; others say it was a shrewd move to protect its Hawaii position from competition.

Pride of Aloha	QUALITY 6	VALUE B-
Pride of America	QUALITY 8	VALUE B
Pride of Hawaii (to Feb. 08)	QUALITY 8	VALUE B
REGISTRY United States	LENGTH 853/921/965 feet	BEAM 105 feet
CABINS 1,001/1,069/1,233188	DRAFT 26//26.3/27 feet	SPEED 23/22/25 knots
MAXIMUM PASSENGERS	PASSENGER DECKS 12/10/15	ELEVATORS 12/10/15
2,138/2,002/2,466	CREW 920/921/1,021	SPACE RATIO 38.5/37.7/37.3

THE SHIPS From the ship's exterior with a floral lei painted on her hull to the interior brightened with murals of the South Pacific, blue carpets with tropical fish, birds, flowers and shells, *Pride of Aloha* sings Hawaii. After a multimillion-dollar makeover in San Francisco, the former *Norwegian Sky* was reflagged and on July 4, began her new life of year-round cruises of the Hawaiian Islands.

The focal point of the ship is the eight-deck-high atrium awash with colorful Hawaiian art and motifs. Everywhere in the public areas, bright colors glow, monkeys peer out from columns, and the **Longboard Bar** honors renowned Hawaii surfer Duke Kahanamoku. At the impressive **Kumu Cultural Center,** passengers can watch a multimedia presentation on volcanoes or view historic movie posters, menus from vintage cruise ships, and pieces of surfing memorabilia.

Pride of America has as her theme the "Best of America," reflected in the decor and names of public rooms—you can't miss it, starting with the design of the atrium, called the **Capitol Atrium,** inspired by the U.S. Capitol and the White House. The nine dining outlets and many lounges have such names as **Liberty Restaurant, Lazy J Steakhouse, Cadillac Diner,** and **Napa Wine Bar,** among others. In keeping with NCL's new signature, painted on the hull of *Pride of America* is a vibrant, artistic interpretation of the Stars and Stripes and the bald eagle.

In addition to an abundance of public rooms, the ship has state-of-the-art entertainment venues, two pools, extensive children's facilities, and large meeting facilities. It also sports several NCL firsts, including a conservatory, a new category of family suites, a tennis court, and an art gallery—all named and decorated to reflect America's diversity.

Pride of Hawaii, a twin of the *Norwegian Jewel,* was the sixth new Freestyle Cruising ship to be added to the NCL fleet in only five years. The theme of her decor is Hawaii's culture and history. The ship has ten restaurants, including **Cagney's Steakhouse, Blue Lagoon,** and **Le Bistro,** as well as the line's typical Asian complex with a sushi bar, teppanyaki table, and a Pacific fusion restaurant. The ship also has one top-deck Garden Villa and ten Courtyard Villas with private courtyard and sundeck. The ship has another new NCL concept—**Bar Central**—three connected but very different venues: a martini bar, a Champagne and wine bar, and a beer and whiskey pub.

In February 2008, NCL plans to withdraw *Pride of Hawaii* from Hawaii cruising temporarily and deploy her in Europe as a result of the steep increase in competition in Hawaii during 2007. The ship will undergo a short wet dock when a casino will be added, her name changed to *Norwegian Jade,* and she will be re-flagged to Bahamas registry. As *Norwegian Jade,* she will sail on 12- to 14-day Eastern and Western Mediterranean cruises from Barcelona, Istanbul, and Athens, and later reposition to Southampton for a series to the North Cape, Europe, and British Isles intended primarily for the British market.

ITINERARIES *See* Itinerary Index.

CABINS All *Aloha's* cabins have a refrigerator, small desk, telephone, coffeemaker, in-room safe, and television. Bathrooms have nice storage nooks, but except for suites, all are shower-only. There are several suite categories, including ten penthouse suites at 364 square feet and up, and four Owner's Suites at 650 square feet.

Pride of America's extensive choice of cabins is highlighted by a grand Grand Suite, as well as NCL's new concept—family suites. The six Owner's Suites, each with 870 square feet, are named after Hawaiian flowers; each of six deluxe penthouse suites cover 735 square feet, and 28 penthouse suites range from 504 to 585 square feet. The suites are furnished with a king-size bed and walk-in closet, a bathroom with a separate shower and Jacuzzi bath, dressing area, and flat-screen television; a separate living room has a Bang & Olufsen entertainment center, television with a DVD player and CD/DVD library, and computer access with Internet connection.

Each of the eight new family suites covers 360 square feet and has a living room furnished with a double sofa bed and entertainment center, separate den with a single sofa bed, a private bedroom with twin beds convertible to a queen, and a private balcony. Four additional family suites (330–356 square feet) are interconnecting cabins sleeping up to eight people. The larger of the two cabins is an oversize outside cabin with two single beds that can be combined for a queen-size bed, plus a sitting area with a double sofa bed. The cabin interconnects with another outside cabin that has two single beds and two upper berths. The eight-person family suites have two bathrooms.

The 1,400-square-foot Grand Suite, positioned high atop the ship forward of the main sundeck, offers sweeping views of the ocean and an impressive assortment of amenities. It has a large living room with a Bang & Olufsen entertainment center with television, CD, stereo, DVD player, CD/DVD library, computer access with Internet connection, and a wet bar. The suite also has a dining room with a polished teak table seating six, plus a private butler. The master bedroom has a king-size bed and bathroom with separate shower and Jacuzzi bath, a dressing area with a flat-screen television and a large walk-in closet, and a separate powder room. On the large wraparound veranda, suite occupants and their guests can enjoy open-air dining, a Jacuzzi for up to six people, and private areas for sunbathing and for entertaining up to 50 visitors.

Pride of Hawaii's cabins come with NCL standards, including cherrywood finishing, refrigerators, tea- and coffeemakers in every room, large bathrooms with separate shower and washbasin separated by sliding doors. The ship also has a large number of interconnecting cabins, including suites and junior suites, to create a two-, three-, or more bedroom area suitable for families, as well as expanded kids' and teen centers.

Specifications Pride of Aloha, 983 cabins, including 572 outside, of which 243 have balconies; 10 penthouse uites; 4 Owner's Suites. *Pride of America,* 1,069 cabins, of which 660 have balconies; 250 family accommodations; 1 Grand Suite; 34 Penthouse suites; 6 Owner's Suites; 12 family suites. *Pride of Hawaii,* 1,233 cabins; 783 outside with balconies; 405 inside; 27 wheelchair accessible.

DINING   On *Aloha,* Freestyle Dining gives passengers the option of dining in two open-seating main dining rooms, **Crossings** and the **Palace Restaurant,** as well as the 24-hour buffet-style **Hukilau Cafe,** and other casual venues, for no charge. The three excellent specialty restaurants have a $10 charge—**Pacific Heights** for Asian fusion, **Kahili Restaurant** for high-end Italian fare, and the **Royal Palm Bistro** for French Mediterranean cuisine. Outdoor barbecues are nicely presented. Room service is available around the clock.

Pride of America offers nine restaurants and nine different menus every night. These include two main restaurants and alternative gourmet, ethnic, and casual eateries. *Pride of Hawaii* has ten restaurants, similar in variety to NCL's *Jewel*-class ships. As part of its ongoing effort to improve the line's cuisine, in 2006, NCL hired three new corporate chefs to develop "dynamic new menu concepts" and implement them on board the fleet, including the NCL America ships. Among the changes, the chefs are out of the galley and positioned at the serving islands to prepare items such as pasta, sushi, and stir-fry *à la minute* or carving to order.

On *Pride of America* the **Skyline,** a main restaurant, has decor inspired by the architecture and skyscrapers of the 1930s; **Liberty,** the second main restaurant one deck up, has Colonial design featuring

America's Founding Fathers and large paintings depicting important moments in American history. Both offer traditional dining.

Also on Deck 5, **East Meets West,** an elegant Pacific Rim/Asian fusion restaurant, has a sushi and sashimi bar and a teppanyaki room with two tables accommodating 32 people and offering Japanese-style dining with food prepared in front of guests. **Jefferson's Bistro,** NCL's signature restaurant, has an à la carte menu of nouvelle and classic French cuisine and decor inspired by Thomas Jefferson's home, Monticello. (Jefferson was the U.S. ambassador to France from 1785 to 1789.)

On Deck 6, the **Lazy Jay Steakhouse** is an upscale steak house with Texas decor and art depicting the Houston Space Center, Texas Rangers, and Dallas Cowboys. It serves Angus beef and other grilled meat, seafood, and chicken. The indoor/outdoor **Cadillac Diner,** a 24-hour diner, has decor of 1950s pop stars, complete with Cadillac seats and a video jukebox. The fare includes hamburgers, fish and chips, potpie, and wok dishes.

On Deck 11, **Little Italy,** a casual Italian eatery inspired by New York's Little Italy, serves pasta, pizza, and other Italian specialties. **Aloha Café/Kids Café,** the indoor/outdoor buffet with a Hawaiian theme, including outrigger canoes and Polynesian carvings and artifacts, has food stations for prepared-to-order omelets, waffles, fruit, soups, and ethnic specialties. It also includes a buffet with small chairs and tables to accommodate 36 kids.

SERVICE When NCL America started its Hawaii operation, it was bombarded with complaints about service. However, the cruise line tackled the problems and worked hard to correct them with an extensive crew training program and other measures. Approximately 65% of the crew is from Hawaii; after they had proper training, the service complaints have dropped considerably.

FACILITIES AND ACTIVITIES In *Pride of Aloha's* **Stardust Theater,** passengers can enjoy several Las Vegas–style shows. Enhancing the ship's Hawaii-themed activities are lectures and classes on how to create tropical jewelry, husk a coconut, or do the hula.

The **Capitol Atrium,** the heart of *Pride of America,* carries her all-American theme with a decorative stone floor, water feature, and a stunning backlit glass dome. Her nine lounges and bars are designed to reflect the diversity of the country, such as the **Mardi Gras Cabaret,** the ship's nightclub, the **Gold Rush Saloon,** and two outdoor pool bars, **Key West Bar & Grill** and the **Waikiki Bar.**

The **Soho Art Gallery** offers original works of art, while Newbury Street resembles New England shops in the early 1900s. There is NCL's first conservatory, with a tropical landscaped garden and live exotic birds; the **S.S. America Library,** honoring the famous ship; and the **Hollywood Theater,** with large golden statues adorning the walls. The ship has WiFi capability and an Internet cafe. Passengers can obtain an Internet access card for their laptops or rent a laptop with wireless Internet capability.

Pride of America's meeting facilities—among the largest at sea—encompass six meeting rooms ranging from boardrooms for 10 people to an auditorium that can accommodate more than 250 people. Five of the meeting rooms—named for Hawaii and her islands—can be used individually or combined. The **Diamond Head Auditorium** is a multi-level circular room that boasts a state-of-the-art audiovisual system with multiple screens that lower from the ceiling to be viewed by all participants. The auditorium also splits into two amphitheater-style presentation rooms. The conference area has a business center, a separate large gathering and break area, and the **Lanai Bar and Lounge** for group cocktail parties and other purposes.

Pride of America's meeting facilities should appeal to the business market on several accounts. Meetings on board the only large U.S.-flagged ships regularly sailing the Hawaiian islands and visiting only U.S. ports qualify for corporate and individual tax deductions for meetings expenses.

SPORTS, FITNESS, AND BEAUTY *Pride of Aloha*'s **Body Waves Fitness Center** has a good selection of machines and a spacious aerobics studio. As with NCL's other ships, the spa is operated by Mandara Spa and offers facials, massages, manicures, and hairstyling services. The ship also has a basketball/volleyball court, two golf driving nets, two swimming pools, four whirlpools, and a kids' pool.

Pride of America's **Santa Fe Spa and Fitness Center,** a tranquil area decorated with natural elements such as stone, wood, and artifacts from New Mexico, offers an exotic menu of spa and beauty treatments. The fitness center has Cybex exercise equipment and Life Fitness cardiovascular machines, each with its own flat-screen television, an aerobics room for yoga, power walking, and other fitness classes, and saunas and steam room.

The Sports Deck has a basketball and volleyball court. The large South Beach sunning and swimming area, inspired by Miami's Art Deco district, has some novel distractions and activities capturing the energy and fun of Ocean Drive and Lincoln Road.

Pride of Aloha has the first golf pro shop at sea along with a comprehensive shoreside golf program. The ship features top-of-the-line golf equipment such as Callaway clubs and Adidas shoes for rent, guaranteed tee times, and NCL Golf Hawaii logo items for purchase. The shop offers onboard clinics with local golf pros and three practice nets and play at some of Hawaii's leading courses along the cruise route. Prices start at $95 per person. Transportation is included in all rounds of golf.

CHILDREN'S FACILITIES *Aloha* has a modest **Kids Korner** facility and teens can hang out at The Club. On *Pride of America,* the **Rascal's Kids Center** and pool offers supervised facilities designed around an animal theme. All three ships have NCL's age-specific children's program to keep the little ones busy throughout their cruise. (See *Norwegian Dawn/Gem/ Jewel/Pearl/Star* for details.)

SHORE EXCURSIONS All three ships offer dozens of shore excursions, as varied as golf and rain-forest walks to kayaking and helicopter rides over lava flows. All are listed on the cruise line's Web site, together with their prices. For the night the ships spend at Kauai, the highlight is a luau and show that NCL America has newly created in partnership with the 35-acre Kilohana Plantation, NH Productions, and Gaylord's Restaurant, one of the island's top restaurants. Kilohana Plantation also offers additional activities for passengers, including a train ride on the Kauai Plantation Railway or a vintage carriage ride through the estate. They can play traditional Hawaiian games or have a Hawaiian arts and crafts lesson. The new show, produced by a local company and entitled *Kalamaku,* tells the story of one family's journey from Tahiti to Kauai and is performed by a cast of 40. It is staged on Monday, Thursday, and Saturday evenings to coincide with NCL America's ships being in port.

Another new feature is giving passengers a taste of the real Hawaii in *Ho'okipa Aloha,* a 45-minute show with real Hawaiian students of hula performing as they would for each other. The show is staged on embarkation day from Honolulu on each ship. NCL America has partnered with several halau, a hula school for young and old, to present the hula in a form most visitors never see. To NCL's credit, it is an ongoing effort to give passengers an authentic look at the Hawaiian culture and heritage.

Oceania Cruises

8300 NW 33rd Street, Suite 308, Miami, FL 33122
☎ 305-514-2300 or 800-531-5658; fax 305-514-2222
www.oceaniacruises.com

TYPE OF SHIPS Midsize deluxe ships.

TYPE OF CRUISES Upscale cruises with a casual ambience on worldwide, destination-oriented itineraries, usually ten days or longer.

CRUISE LINE'S STRENGTHS
- medium-size ships, newly renovated and refurbished
- diverse foreign home ports and itineraries
- overnights in interesting ports
- gourmet dining in specialty restaurants
- choices of four open-seating restaurants
- casual onboard atmosphere; no formal dress code
- affordable fares, value-added deals

CRUISE LINE'S SHORTCOMINGS
- lack of facilities for children
- few cruise departures from U.S. ports
- no short cruises to sample the product
- limited nightlife
- crowded tables in main dining room

FELLOW PASSENGERS Oceania Cruises attracts a mix of first-time cruisers eager to try a premium cruise line and experienced travelers who simply enjoy the line's longer, destination-focused itineraries. Average passenger age is 55. Many are former Renaissance Cruises fans; others are likely to be experienced travelers who have sailed on other premium and even luxury lines attracted by the value Oceania's prices represent. Oceania passengers prefer smaller ships and savor international travel.

Recommended for Travelers who want to visit far-flung lands; those who appreciate extra time in ports. Intellectually curious couples and mature singles who appreciate a good value and enjoy touches of luxury cruising. Those who prefer medium-size ships.

Not recommended for Families with children; those who seek the party atmosphere of some large cruise ships or seek lots of nightlife and entertainment.

CRUISE AREAS AND SEASONS Europe, spring/summer/fall; Asia, Caribbean, South America, winter/spring; transatlantic, spring/fall.

THE LINE A privately held company built from scratch, Oceania Cruises was founded in 2003 by two cruise industry veterans—Frank Del Rio, former president and CEO of now-defunct Renaissance Cruises, and Joe Watters, former president of Crystal Cruises. The Oceania team—Del Rio as president and CEO and Watters as chairman—brought complementary talents to the new cruise line. Del Rio, who knows the ships well, hav-

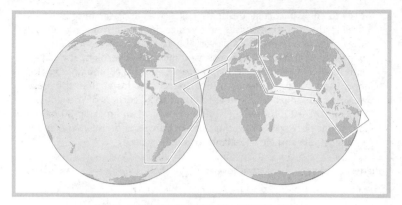

CRUISE AREAS AND SEASONS FOR OCEANIA CRUISES

ing previously operated them with Renaissance, had been running Oceania's day-to-day operations until he took over as chairman; Watters, until his recent retirement, focused on developing the onboard product, designated as premium with luxury touches—an effort to set the line apart from its competitors in the premium cruise category.

Oceania Cruises was launched with the 684-passenger *Regatta,* the former *R2.* Her identical sister, *Insignia,* the former *R1,* was added the following year, and a third copy, *Nautica,* the former *R5,* debuted in 2005. Oceania selected these three specific ships—of all the available R-class ships on the market after Renaissance's demise—because they had the most high-end suites, an important asset in attracting sophisticated travelers. In addition, Oceania got a great deal for leasing the vessels from the banks that repossessed the ships after Renaissance's collapse, thus avoiding incurring a big debt and enabling the new cruise line to provide its product at very competitive prices.

In 2006, Oceania was able to purchase the three ships for $375 million—the cost to build even one ship today. Then in early 2007, Apollo Management, a New York–based $12 billion private equity firm, acquired majority interest in Oceania Cruises for approximately $850 million. The line's founding management team remains stakeholders in the cruise line. Soon thereafter, Oceania placed a billion-dollar order with Italy's Fincantieri shipyard for two 1,260-passenger, 65,000-ton ships to be delivered in the fall of 2010 and summer of 2011, and an option for a third vessel to be delivered in 2012. The new midsize vessels represent a new class of ships for the line, dubbed Oceania class, and defined as upper-premium cruising. Among their many new features, the ships will have six open-seating restaurants and larger, more luxurious cabins and suites with more amenities than the present fleet.

Oceania's destination focus first centered on Europe, South America, and the Caribbean; new destinations such as North Africa have been added as the line builds its passenger base. Many itineraries have been tailored to include overnight port stays to allow passengers more time to enjoy particular destinations, such as St. Petersburg, Russia, on the Northern Europe cruises, and Venice on Mediterranean ones. With the arrival of *Nautica*, Oceania was able to chart a different course, with winter and spring in the Far East and including overnight stays in such cities as Beijing, Dubai, Hong Kong, and Mumbai (Bombay), to name a few. The new ships with a cruising speed 20% faster than the present *Regatta*-class ships, will be able to cruise to all corners of the globe.

For 2007–2008, the line's itineraries have an amazing 80 or more overnight port stays in destinations in Europe and elsewhere, and will visit Australia and New Zealand for the first time.

THE FLEET	BUILT/RENOVATED	TONNAGE	PASSENGERS
Insignia	1998/2004/05/07	30,277	684
Nautica	2000/05/07	30,277	684
Regatta	1998/2003/05/07	30,277	684
Oceania I	2010	65,000	1,260
Oceania II	2011	65,000	1,260

STYLE Oceania's goal has been to create a fine product focused on cuisine, service, and destination-oriented itineraries, and to offer it at reasonable prices. The line's relaxed onboard atmosphere resembles the casual elegance of a country club, neither stuffy nor pretentious. Formal wear is never a requirement for dinner; passengers dress stylishly but comfortably to enjoy their evenings. Oceania's ships—small compared to today's more typical megaships—provide the intimate atmosphere of a small ship, and at the same time have the facilities of larger ships. For example, each ship has several lounges, a spa, and four restaurants with open seating, enabling passengers to dine when, where, and with whom they choose.

Recently, Oceania added two innovations—Cruise Planner and Guest Referral Network—to its Web site, **www.oceaniacruises.com,** enabling passengers to plan and book a cruise online 24/7 with complete access to live inventory and prices. They can also customize their vacation with regard to pre- and postcruise hotel options, shore excursions, and insurance. With the Cruise Planner, passengers can plan and save information on their cruise and build a day-by-day planning journal to take on their cruise.

DISTINCTIVE FEATURES Medium-size ships. An upper-end premium product with deluxe touches. Tranquility Beds. Four restaurants, open-seating dining, destination-focused itineraries. Affordable pricing; many special deals.

	HIGHEST	LOWEST	AVERAGE
PER DIEM	$1,040	$400	$665

Per diems are calculated from cruise line's nondiscounted *cruise-only* published fares on standard accommodations and vary by season, cabins, and cruise areas.

RATES Gratuities and port charges are additional.

Special fares and discounts Oceania's early-booking policy is to open most new itineraries with two-for-one pricing or free economy air, and then close on the promotions as the ships fill. Guests who book early can realize tremendous savings.

- **THIRD PASSENGER:** Fares vary by individual sailing.
- **CHILDREN'S FARES:** None.
- **SINGLE SUPPLEMENT:** 200%.

Packages

- **AIR/SEA:** Yes. First- and business-class upgrades for additional charge.
- **PRE/POST:** Yes. Most air/sea packages include one to three nights in a hotel in the departure city.
- **OTHERS:** Yes.

PAST PASSENGERS After passengers sail once, they automatically become a member of the Oceania Club, the line's past-passenger club. Then, the more they sail, the higher their level of rewards. All members receive an *Oceania Club Journal* and an invitation to the captain's cocktail party for members. Other awards, depending on level of membership, might include complimentary gratuities, spa or onboard credits, and discounts on future cruises. A dedicated page for the club at **www.oceaniacruises.com** includes information, news, and fun behind-the-scenes information.

THE LAST WORD Oceania Cruises has developed a substantial following in less than three years. The line is well run, and passengers have favorably responded to its consistent product. They like the line's midsize ships, their country-club-casual atmosphere, the cuisine, and unusual itineraries. Oceania appears to be doing well financially, but because it is both new and privately held, it would be prudent to buy third-party travel insurance. Actually, we could say that's a good idea for any cruise.

Oceania Cruises Standard Features

Officers Italian, Croatian, and other Europeans.

Staff Dining and Cabin: European; Cruise: British, North American, and European.

Dining facilities Four restaurants include a main dining room, two alternative restaurants, and a casual buffet-style eatery.

Special diets Request at booking or no later than 30 days prior to sailing.

Room service 24 hours with cabin menu. Top suites may order from any of the four restaurant menus.

Dress code By day, resort-casual attire. Evenings are business casual or smart casual. No jackets, ties, or fancy dress. Each cruise has two gala evenings, but formal wear is not required.

Oceania Cruises Standard Features (continued)

Cabin amenities Direct-dial telephone, television with CNN and ESPN, cabin music, hair dryer, safe, deluxe toiletries, and bathrobes. Concierge level and higher cabins and suites: DVD players and minifridge; Owner's and Vista suites: full entertainment system. *Insignia:* Concierge Level, Veranda and Penthouse suites, flat-screen televisions.

Electrical outlets 110/220 AC

Wheelchair access Three inside staterooms.

Recreation and entertainment Several lounges have live music by ship's orchestra or musical trio. Entertainment, typically low key, features cabaret acts, soloists, jugglers, comedians, and dance music. One to two small production shows staged on every cruise.

Sports and other activities Outdoor pool, golf cage, shuffleboard, deck sports, and jogging track.

Beauty and fitness Men's and women's steam rooms, full-service Mandara Spa with treatment rooms, beauty salon, exercise facility, aerobics, and fitness classes. Massages on deck in private cabana.

Other facilities Library with 1,000 books, card room, two boutiques, Oceania@Sea 24-hour Internet cafe, medical center, self-service laundry, dry cleaning and laundry services, four elevators. Nondenominational Sunday services; Jewish Sabbath observance led by crew member or passenger.

Children's facilities None.

Theme cruises None.

Smoking Smoking is permitted only in two designated areas of the ship: forward starboard on the Pool Deck, and aft port corner on Horizon Deck. Smoking is prohibited in all other areas, including within cabins and on cabin or suite balconies.

Oceania suggested tipping An $11.50 per person per day and $3.50 per person per day gratuity (for private butlers if in Penthouse, Owner's, and Vista) added automatically to onboard account. It may be adjusted at the passenger's discretion. Also, 18% added to spa services and bar purchases.

Credit cards For cruise payment and onboard charges: American Express, Diners Club, Discover, MasterCard, and Visa.

Insignia	QUALITY 9	VALUE A
Nautica	QUALITY 9	VALUE A
Regatta	QUALITY 9	VALUE A
REGISTRY Marshall Islands	LENGTH 593.7 feet	BEAM 83.5
CABINS 342	DRAFT 19.5 feet	SPEED 18 knots
MAXIMUM PASSENGERS	PASSENGER DECKS 9	ELEVATORS 4
684	CREW 410	SPACE RATIO NA

THE SHIPS Because the *Regatta*, *Insignia*, and *Nautica* are practically identical, the new line has been able to create a consistent product across its fleet. Despite the young age of all three ships—seven years or less—Oceania Cruises gave each of the former Renaissance ships a major renovation prior to entering them in service. These included adding new teak decks on the Pool Deck, the aft dining terrace, and private balconies. The old patio furniture was replaced with more classy-looking lounges, and the pool and whirlpool area resurfaced with an attractive marble-and-tile look.

Oceania also revamped the decor and use of the interior public spaces, such as the observation lounge, martini bar, atrium and grand staircase area, and the alternative restaurants. Much of the gaudy, heavily patterned furnishings were replaced and toned down with a more elegant, muted look. Decor remains traditional, but some contrast was added with a $2 million contemporary art collection.

More enhancements were completed recently when all wooden furniture was replaced, brass handles added to cabin doors, and teak decks on balconies were replaced. Public areas, cabins, and the spa were refurbished.

The reception desk, destination services, the concierge, medical center, and an imposing grand staircase are found on Deck 4. One deck above, Deck 5, is totally dedicated to public spaces, including the casino, **Martini's Lounge,** the **Regatta** (or **Insignia**) **Lounge,** the **Grand Bar,** photo gallery, two boutiques, and the main dining room.

In 2006, *Insignia* was given a multimillion-dollar refurbishment from stem to stern with stylish new furnishings and new amenities, as well as a behind-the-scenes mechanical and technical upgrade. Among the enhancements, all teak decking and railings and all cabin doors and hardware were reconditioned. Throughout the ship, its rich wood paneling was restored and new carpeting was installed. **Horizons,** the ship's observation lounge and nightclub, got a new bar with a handcrafted granite top and a front of crackled, backlit Murano glass.

At the top of the ship on Deck 11, eight new private cabanas—said to be a first for cruising—were added along with teak decking. The luxury cabanas offer sweeping sea views through walls of glass and are furnished with a custom-made teak Balinese daybed, chic white privacy drapes, and a roll-back Roman-shade roof that affords optimum amounts of sun and shade. Cabanas may be reserved for a day or the full cruise and include the services of a dedicated attendant who provides drinks, snacks, and chilled towels. Passengers may also get meal service and spa treatments in their cabana. Cabanas cost $50 per day for port days and $100 per day for sea days. Passengers can book full-cruise packages and receive a discount and special amenities; discount varies from cruise to cruise based on length and number of port and sea days.

Insignia also got new state-of-the-art communication equipment to facilitate faster Internet speeds and the use of cell phones at sea. The ship has a new multimillion-dollar art collection, comprising antique nautical paintings and models along with contemporary and traditional pieces from renowned artists and masters. New pieces will be added throughout the year.

By spring 2007, *Regatta* and *Nautica* had undergone the same extensive upgrading with new carpets throughout the ships, new bedding in the cabins, deluxe cabanas and rich teak decking on the top deck, new rich decor in the **Polo Grill** and the **Grand Bar,** and rebuilt Owner's and Vista suites.

ITINERARIES *See* Itinerary Index.

CABINS Prior to entering service for Oceania, all cabins were upgraded with deluxe appointments: fine linens and bedding, including Tranquility Bed mattresses, silk-cut duvets and fluffy goose-down pillows, French-milled toiletries, and teak verandas. Passengers also enjoy plush cotton robes and slippers.

The roomy Owner's (aft) and Vista (forward) suites on Decks 6–8 have floor-to-ceiling glass doors with spectacular views from the living room, dining room, and master bedroom and lead to a private wraparound teak veranda. The suites have a separate guest bathroom and butler service. These suites are furnished with queen-size bed, whirlpool, two color TVs, and an entertainment center with DVD and CD players. DVDs are available from the reception desk.

On Deck 8, the Penthouse Suites offer a large living area with sliding glass doors, stylish furniture, and either twin or queen beds, space for in-suite dining, minibar, vanity desk, bath with tub, ample closet space, and butler service that includes arranging priority restaurant reservations and complimentary shoe shine, among other services.

To fill the gap between the more pricey suites and standard cabins, Oceania created a new category called Concierge Level. These 216-square-foot cabins with verandas occupy preferred locations on Deck 7. They have amenities similar to a Penthouse Suite, but the space is much smaller. Concierge Level passengers, however, get many perks, including priority embarkation with a dedicated check-in desk and priority luggage delivery, welcome bottle of Champagne, minibar, 20-inch color television and DVD player, personalized stationery, Hansgrohe hand-held massaging showerheads; and Caswell-Massey toiletries.

Concierge Level cabins as well as deluxe balcony cabins are furnished with cherrywood furniture and dark-wood accents, and dressed in blue and gold decor. Located on Deck 6, the deluxe balcony cabins have a queen or two twin beds, comfortable seating area with sofa, breakfast table, vanity desk, and spacious closets.

Deluxe ocean-view cabins on Decks 4, 6, and 7 have a queen or two twin beds and large panorama windows. Standard ocean-view cabins have either a porthole or panorama window with obstructed views. Inside cabins on Decks 4, 6, 7, and 8 have a comfortable seating area, vanity desk, ample storage space, and a queen or two twin beds.

During the recent renovations, all cabins and suites fleetwide got new third-generation Tranquility Beds with Imperial mattresses. They also were redecorated in warm jewel tones of gold and deep sapphire. Sleek new glass-topped cocktail tables custom-made in Italy lend a chic yet functional element. The Owner's and Vista suites have been completely rebuilt from the bottom up under the direction of renowned shipboard architect Petter Yran. The suites were lavishly fitted with new Empire-style furnishings and couture fabrics of claret and gold, a wide-screen plasma television, a Bose® surround-sound audio system, and wide-screen laptop computers. The Vista Suites, using a palette of gold, meadow, and sage, project an ambience of understated elegance. All Concierge Level Veranda and Penthouse suites have new flat-screen televisions.

Specifications 342 cabins and suites, of which 314, or 92%, are outside and almost 70% have verandas. Six Owner's Suites (962 square feet); 4 Vista Suites (786 square feet); 52 Penthouse Suites (322 square feet); 171 cabins (216 square feet), all with balconies; 83 ocean-view cabins (150–165 square feet) and 26 inside cabins (158 square feet); 3 inside wheelchair-accessible cabins.

DINING The **Grand Dining Room**—open for breakfast, lunch, and dinner—is elegantly appointed with a domed ceiling adorned with hand-painted frescoes, soft lighting, and dramatic ocean views. The decor is similar to the room's look during its Renaissance days. Unfortunately, tables are crowded next to each other, often making it difficult for waiters to serve.

While the service is decidedly white glove—and in the evening, waiters wear tuxedos—passengers dine in a relaxing atmosphere in casual attire. The dress code never requires jacket and tie, although many gentlemen do wear jackets with a sport shirt for dinner. On gala nights, passengers might dress more elegantly, if they choose to do so. A classical string quartet or concert pianist usually provides background music during dinner.

The ship's menus have been crafted by master chef Jacques Pepin, the line's executive culinary director and one of America's best-known chefs via his numerous television appearances, food columns, and cookbooks. He has also served as the personal chef to three French heads of state, including Charles de Gaulle. The line offers a selection of more than 150 wines.

The ships have two alternative dining venues, **Polo Grill** and **Toscana;** both are very good and outshine the main dining room in cuisine and service. Reservations are required, but there is no extra charge. Resplendent with rich, dark woods and elegant furnishings, they have floor-to-ceiling windows affording views of the seascapes. Polo Grill is a classic steak house with an extensive menu of aged prime beef, lamb, pork, and fresh seafood. Desserts might include New Orleans pecan pie or a traditional New York cheesecake, among other choices.

In Toscana, diners enjoy an Italian ambience and may select from such Italian specialties as gnocchi in creamy pesto sauce, risotto with porcini mushrooms, caramelized shallots and fresh thyme, or sautéed medallions of veal tenderloin with roasted bell peppers in Gorgonzola cheese and Marsala wine sauce—all served on fine china and crystal. Great service enhances the ambience.

According to Oceania's policy, all suite and Concierge Level passengers may make two reservations at each of the alternative dining venues (total of four nights), while standard-cabin passengers may make one reservation in each venue (total of two nights). After that, the venues are open to more reservations as space permits.

For a more casual dining experience, the buffet-style **Terrace Café**— where casual breakfast and lunch are available—is transformed at dinner into **Tapas on the Terrace.** Passenger serve themselves at a buffet, but the atmosphere is enhanced by linens and upgraded dinnerware and glassware on the table, and service by waiters who often carry plates to the tables and bring drinks. Menus vary but are decidedly Mediterranean in flair, along with different chef's specials nightly.

Waves, the poolside bar and grill, is a lunchtime option offering grilled meats, seafood, salads, and made-to-order deli sandwiches. All passengers can order room service from a cabin menu 24 hours a day. Those in Penthouse Suites and above may also order room service from the four restaurant menus.

As part of the recent fleetwide upgrading, all the restaurants were replenished with new tableware of Versace china, Reidel crystal, and Christofle silver, which Oceania has dubbed the Perfect Table.

SERVICE Passengers praise the service as warm and attentive. The high staff-to-guest ratio of more than one crew member per cabin facilitates a high degree of personalized service.

FACILITIES AND ACTIVITIES The **Regatta** (or **Insignia** or **Nautica**) **Lounge,** dressed in royal blue and gold decor, is furnished with curved couches, upholstered chairs, and cocktail tables. During the day, enrichment lectures might be held here. When the sun goes down, the lounge features entertainment that might include a soloist, comedian, or juggler, and a revue-style production show once or twice during a cruise.

Martini's, reminiscent of a private gentlemen's club, is the place to relax with friends for martinis and live piano music. In the **Grand Bar**, just outside the main restaurant, you can enjoy a rare vintage or a grappa. **Horizons,** a convivial bar on Deck 10, offers live entertainment and sweeping views to enjoy along with your favorite cocktail. Later in the evening, it becomes the venue for dancing.

Before the ship visits a port, the cruise director provides a talk with historical background and information on the culture, traditions, and language of that destination. The line also offers culinary demonstrations by its executive chef and his staff. Passengers might take a dance lesson, participate in an arts and crafts class, take a golf or bridge lesson, or enjoy bingo or a wine-tasting session. The **library** is stocked with more than 1,000 volumes. Oceania@Sea is the line's 24-hour Internet center.

SPORTS, FITNESS, AND BEAUTY Deck 9 has the **Oceania Spa** operated by Mandara, plus a hair salon, fitness center, an outdoor pool, and two whirlpools. The large, airy fitness center has new exercise equipment, a large aerobics area, and offers a variety of fitness classes led by personal trainers. One deck up, on Deck 10, passengers can walk, jog, or run along the fitness track (13 laps equal one mile). The Deck 11 Sun Deck is the place for a tranquil respite on a cozy lounge chair. Here, golfers can practice their swing in a golf cage.

CHILDREN'S FACILITIES Oceania cruises are not designed for families with children. Given the nature of the cruises, most children would probably be bored to tears. The line's passengers—mostly couples and mature singles—are not likely to appreciate rambunctious kids, either. The ships have no children's facilities, no babysitting, no video arcades, no climbing walls, and no youth activity programs.

SHORE EXCURSIONS Oceania offers two sets of shore excursion packages online: Discovery, for those new to the ports of call, and Explorers, for experienced cruisers who may have already visited the ports. Prebooking a shore package can bring peace of mind for some, saving having to stand in line at the shore excursion office onboard ship. Others prefer to wait until they get on board to book shore excursions individually. Prearranged packages provide a 10% discount—a good value. However, these packages are nonrefundable and cannot be changed nor substitutions made. Purchasing excursions on board costs more, but there's often a wider selection from which to choose. Also, booking on board offers greater flexibility, as passengers often change their mind about excursions after they board the ship.

Also to be considered in making a selection are the ports where the ships overnight. For example, when *Nautica* sails in Asia, her itineraries feature overnight stays in such cities as Bangkok, Beijing, Dubai, Hanoi, Ho Chi Minh City, Hong Kong, Kyoto, Luxor, Mumbai (Bombay), and Shanghai. Passengers are able to enjoy two full days and an evening in each of these ports and enjoy the local culture, dining, and sightseeing.

Oceania has also developed pre- and postcruise hotel stays and extended land tours of three to nine days to such locales as Beijing and the Great Wall, Chiangmai, Guilin, Myanmar, Siem Reap, Xian, and the Yangtze River.

POSTSCRIPT For former Renaissance Cruises fans, Oceania was a dream come true. They could once again enjoy sailing on a deluxe midsize ship at an affordable price. Yet, today's Oceania has come a long way from the former Renaissance product. Oceania Cruises has attracted a new fan base that extends far beyond the former Renaissance cruiser. Most passengers never sailed with Renaissance; rather, they are experienced cruisers who have traveled on other high-quality cruise lines and are attracted by Oceania's itineraries, the ships and their fine onboard product, and the price.

Oceania I	2010	
Oceania II	2011	
REGISTRY TBA	LENGTH 825 feet	BEAM 105
CABINS 630	DRAFT 23 feet	SPEED 20 knots
MAXIMUM PASSENGERS	PASSENGER DECKS 9	ELEVATORS NA
1,260	CREW NA	SPACE RATIO NA

THE SHIPS   In March 2007, Oceania Cruises announced it was building two 1,260-passenger, 65,000-ton ships to be delivered in the fall of 2010 and summer of 2011, and an option for a third vessel to be delivered in 2012. The new midsize vessels, to be built at Italy's Fincantieri shipyard and each costing a half-billion dollars, represent a new class of ships for the line. Dubbed Oceania class and being defined as upper-premium cruising, the ships will have six open-seating restaurants and larger, more luxurious cabins and suites with more amenities than the present fleet, among other new features.

Designed by the renowned marine architectural firm of Yran & Storbratten, public areas and accommodations will be dressed with rich wood paneling and granite accents, opulent furnishings, and a museum-quality art collection that will include rare nautical antiques. Four specialty restaurants will feature the line's signature **Polo Grill** and **Toscana** along with two new specialty venues—a French bistro and a pan-Asian restaurant.

The Oceania-class vessels will be 825 feet long and 105 feet wide and accommodate 1,260 guests. The ships will have 630 staterooms and suites—almost double what Oceania ships have currently—and on average will be 50% larger than the *Regatta* class. Approximately 96% of all accommodations will have ocean views and 93% will boast large, private teak verandas. The ships will be powered by diesel-electric engines and operate with twin screw propellers, with a service speed of 20 knots. They will be designed to cruise the world, boasting a cruising speed 20% faster than the present *Regatta* class. They will be equipped with two bow thrusters to enhance maneuverability and will be "green ships," employing the most advanced environmental systems and technology.

Orient Lines

7665 Corporate Center Drive, Miami, FL 33126
☎ **305-436-4000 or 800-333-7300; fax 305-436-4120**
www.orientlines.com

TYPE OF SHIPS Midsize ocean liner.

TYPE OF CRUISES Affordable, destination-intensive, light adventure with first-class amenities, fine cuisine, and refined ambience.

CRUISE LINE'S STRENGTHS
- service by attentive crew
- itineraries
- singles policy
- price
- dock-level gangway door
- expert lecturers on longer voyages
- precruise information

CRUISE LINE'S SHORTCOMINGS
- limited room service
- entertainment

FELLOW PASSENGERS Orient Lines attracts mature, experienced, inquisitive passengers who are friendly and interested in the line's off-the-beaten-track itineraries. On longer cruises, passengers range in age from 50 to 70, have average annual incomes of about $75,000, and are retired or semiretired, business owners, managers, or professionals. Most are North Americans, but some cruises might include Brits and other Europeans, Australians, and South Africans, depending on the itinerary. Many are veteran cruisers, but several are first-timers who have traveled frequently and are drawn to an Orient cruise by its strong destination focus.

Recommended for Orient Lines has two seasons, each with a different appeal. On longer, winter cruises, passengers tend to be seasoned travelers, not necessarily experienced cruisers, who have the curiosity to appreciate exotic destinations, seek a learning experience, but like to travel in comfort. Also, small-ship devotees wanting to sample a cruise on a larger ship but not a megaliner. From April to October, passengers tend to be first-time cruisers, families, and honeymooners, those wanting a land and sea vacation in Europe.

Not recommended for Unsophisticated or inexperienced travelers and those seeking a high-energy, holiday-at-sea, party atmosphere.

CRUISE AREAS AND SEASONS Africa, Antarctica, and South America, including the Amazon, Caribbean, and Panama Canal, winter. Greek Isles, Mediterranean, Northern Europe, Russia, and Scandinavia, spring and summer.

THE LINE Orient Lines originated in 1991, when its former CEO, Gerry Herrod, a British entrepreneur and tour and cruise line veteran, bought the Russian

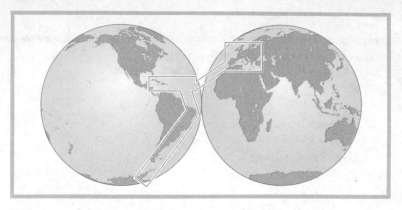

CRUISE AREAS AND SEASONS FOR ORIENT LINES

liner *Alexandr Pushkin* for about $25 million. It had been in a Singapore yard for minor repairs, and the Soviets couldn't pay their bills. The ship, built in East Germany in 1965 for the Soviets, was one of four sister ships with ice-strengthened hulls. They served as Soviet troop ships.

At the cost of $75 million, Orient Lines transformed the vessel into a luxury liner and named her *Marco Polo*. At this time, the cruise line was launched to offer upscale voyages for experienced travelers to exotic destinations at reasonable prices. In its second year, the mission changed when the line found success in a summer Mediterranean program.

Orient Lines was purchased by Norwegian Cruise Line in 1998, but continues to operate as a separate entity. Subsequently, NCL, including Orient Lines, was purchased by Star Cruises. The Marco Polo's last sailing with NCL will be March 2008, when she will be acquired by new owners.

THE FLEET	BUILT/RENOVATED	TONNAGE	PASSENGERS
Marco Polo	1965/1993	22,080	826

STYLE "Adventure in elegance" is one way Orient Lines' cruises have been described. From the start, Orient differed from most mainstream cruise lines by focusing on destinations, giving as much weight to developing unusual itineraries as to providing all the comforts and fine cuisine of a deluxe ship.

Meant to be an all-encompassing experience, the line's cruises include detailed port briefings, lectures by distinguished guest speakers (except on Mediterranean cruises) and experts on destination areas, and extended pre- and postcruise hotel stays with sightseeing. Some itineraries feature shipboard performances by local groups to showcase the culture of regions visited.

DISTINCTIVE FEATURES Gentlemen social hosts (except on Mediterranean cruises), local cultural performances, helicopter and topside helipad, videotaping of lectures for replay on ship's television, a low single supplement, Antarctic cruises.

	HIGHEST	LOWEST	AVERAGE
PER DIEM	$659	$155	$357

Per diems are calculated from cruise line's nondiscounted *cruise-only* published fares on standard accommodations and vary by season, cabins, and cruise areas.

RATES Port charges are additional.

Special fares and discounts Advance-purchase discounts of up to 50%, 120 days before departure, depending on itinerary and cabin. Savings up to 28% for two or more cruises in sequence.

- **SINGLE SUPPLEMENT:** 125% on all cabin categories except A and suites. For Mediterranean sailings, 50% for categories D–K, 75% for B and C, 100% for A and suites. The line frequently waives the supplement in special promotions.
- **SINGLE GUARANTEE:** Guaranteed share program in some cabin categories.

Packages

- **AIR/SEA:** Yes.
- **PRE/POST:** Cruises are designed as cruise/tours with one- to three-day pre- and postcruise hotel stays in gateway cities. Several Mediterranean itineraries also include two- to six-day escorted motor coach tours.
- **OTHERS:** Yes.

PAST PASSENGERS After their first cruise, passengers are enrolled in the Polo Club and receive information on new itineraries, the club magazine, cruise discounts, up to $175 onboard credit (depending on cruise length), a bottle of wine in their cabin, a private VIP party with the captain, and certain benefits when sailing on NCL ships as well.

THE LAST WORD The *Marco Polo* is midsize by today's standards, yet she is among the largest ships cruising to exotic destinations regularly. Her size enables her to provide upscale comfort and a full range of facilities, and her capacity provides a larger passenger base over which to spread costs. Hence, the line can offer cruises at prices considerably lower than its competitors with smaller deluxe ships.

Orient Lines cares about single travelers. As well as having gentlemen hosts to dine and dance with unaccompanied women passengers, the line offers one of cruising's lowest single supplements and occasional singles promotions. Also, it's fastidious in matching participants in its guaranteed-share program. Children are rare aboard the ship but are treated like royalty.

Orient Lines Standard Features

Officers European.

Staff Dining, Cabin: Filipino; Cruise: American and British.

Dining facilities One dining room with open seating for breakfast and lunch and two seatings for dinner with assigned tables; Lido restaurant for buffet breakfast, lunch, tea, and specialty dinners.

Orient Lines Standard Features (continued)

Special diets Sixty days advance notice.

Room service Continental breakfast, cabin attendants on call.

Dress code Casual by day; several formal/semiformal nights.

Cabin amenities Direct-dial telephone, safe, television with CNN when available, movies and ship programs, radio, hair dryer, toiletries. Bathrobes and slippers in upper-category cabins; small refrigerators in suites. Deluxe suites with sitting room, marble bathroom with tub and shower, and minibars.

Electrical outlets 110/220 AC.

Wheelchair access Two cabins.

Recreation and entertainment Four lounges, port/country lectures by experts, piano and/or string trio at cocktails and after dinner, folkloric dancers in port; library, card room.

Sports and other activities Small outdoor swimming pool; table tennis.

Beauty and fitness Beauty salon/spa, massage, aerobics studio, exercise equipment, saunas.

Other facilities Medical unit. Zodiacs; helicopter and landing pad; meeting room. Internet access.

Children's facilities No special facilities.

Smoking None in dining room; smoking permitted in designated wing of main lounge bar during shows, but not during lectures and briefings.

Orient suggested tipping Per day per person, $9; 15% of bar and wine bills and spa services are added to passenger's shipboard account. All tips are pooled and divided.

Credit cards For cruise payment and onboard charges: American Express, MasterCard, Visa, Diners Club, Discover.

Marco Polo	QUALITY 7	VALUE A
REGISTRY Bahamas	LENGTH 578.4 feet	BEAM 77.4 feet
CABINS 425	DRAFT 27 feet	SPEED 20.5 knots
MAXIMUM PASSENGERS	PASSENGER DECKS 8	ELEVATORS 4
826	CREW 350	SPACE RATIO 27.6

THE SHIP A lovely vessel with classic lines, *Marco Polo* has been enhanced by handsome Art Deco interiors created by A. and M. Katzourakis of Athens. Reminiscent of grand liners of the 1920s, pastel furnishings are set against etched and beveled glass, brass, chrome, and rich wood accented by Thai and Burmese antiques and prints, plus modern paintings.

Marco Polo is a comfortable ship designed for long cruises. Built for Arctic service, her hull is strengthened for icy waters and ice floes, with many extra frames added. A gangway door enables passengers to enter the ship at the same level as most docks and piers, averting a long walk up a steep gangway. A significant advantage is *Marco Polo*'s superior stability. Twelve-foot waves and rough seas, particularly in such notorious waters as Drake Passage on an Antarctica cruise, are hardly noticeable.

Most cabins are on the main deck, one level below Belvedere Deck, which accommodates most public rooms and includes the lobby, three of four entertainment lounges and bars, the casino, and a library with more than 1,000 volumes.

Outside vantage points—especially on the upper deck forward and Promenade Deck aft—are numerous for viewing scenery and wildlife or watching sunsets.

ITINERARIES *See* Itinerary Index.

CABINS Being an older vessel, *Marco Polo* has a variety of cabin sizes and configurations. Almost 70% are outside; those in upper A–D categories have picture windows.

Cabins are light and handsomely appointed with light-wood furniture and pastel bedspreads, curtains, and carpeting. Most are comfortably sized for long cruises, with ample storage space, dressing table with pull-out writing desk, and good reading lights. All have a telephone with international direct-dialing, radio, television with CNN in some areas, two channels for movies, and one for ship programs, safe, and a bathroom with shower, built-in hair dryer, and complimentary toiletries. Upper-category cabins provide bathrobes, slippers, and safes. Deluxe suites have a large sitting room, separate bedroom, large marble bathroom with tub and shower, and stocked minibar, replenished without charge. Junior suites and some deluxe cabins have a sitting area and bathroom with tub and shower. Family cabins have curtain-divided sleeping areas.

Views from accommodations on Sky Deck, including junior suites and deluxe cabins and ten cabins on the upper deck, are partially obstructed by lifeboats. These are noted on the deck plan in the line's brochure. Two deluxe suites and some upper-deck and Promenade Deck cabins have windows facing deck areas; however, one-way glass prevents outsiders from seeing in.

Specifications 129 inside cabins, 290 outside; 6 suites. Standard dimensions, 140–180 square feet. 388 cabins with 2 lower beds (42 convertible to double beds); 28 accommodate a third passenger, 10 accommodate 4 passengers. Suites and some upper-category cabins have double or queen-size beds, some have twin beds convertible to doubles; 2 wheelchair-accessible.

DINING Fine cuisine and exemplary service in elegant surroundings with tables set in fine china, crystal, and fresh flowers make dining one of the ship's best features. The **Seven Seas Restaurant** is a large, formal room dressed in mauves and grays. Breakfast and lunch have open seating, but the two dinner seatings have assigned tables with seating for four, six, or eight.

Entry is from the central foyer graced with large abstract paintings and Asian statues. A central, raised area with an Art Deco circular ceiling is separated from lower sides by etched-glass partitions. Floor-to-ceiling mirrors on inside walls help create a spacious feeling. Booths and tables for two to ten people are by windows at either side of the room. The room is designated nonsmoking.

Dinner menus offer three appetizers, two soups, four entrées, and two or three desserts, cheeses, and fruits. Lighter, low-fat, low-salt, or vegetarian selections are indicated. Wines from Argentina, Australia, California, Chile, Europe, and South Africa are offered at reasonable prices.

Raffles serves casual breakfast and lunch buffets, plus Asian food on some evenings; at lunch its aft corners have cooked-to-order pasta and specialty stations, and outside, there's a deck grill and an ice cream and dessert bar. Its large windows overlook the Pool Deck. Chairs and tables with umbrellas are set around the pool. Afternoon tea is served here and in the small **Palm Court.**

Twice weekly in the evenings, Raffles becomes an elegant, very popular bistro for 90 passengers (reservations required) with a changing menu of Chinese, Thai, and other Asian cuisines. A $15 charge per person includes wine and gratuities. On more casual Mediterranean sailings, Raffles' capacity increases to 370, and Italian and regional specialties are served all but one night of the cruise, when the Asian menu is featured.

Surprisingly for a deluxe ship, room service is unavailable, except for continental breakfast and in case of illness. The line maintains that the ship's fine-dining experience is best enjoyed in the dining room. Some passengers might disagree after a long, tiring day on tour. Despite the official policy, most cabin stewards will bring food to the cabin on request. Another point: on tour days, dress for dinner is casual, and the dining room atmosphere more relaxed.

SERVICE *Marco Polo*'s tone is set by its friendly, service-oriented officers; lively British and American cruise staff; and most of all, its well-trained, hard-working Filipino crew, who win high praise for their attentiveness and cheerful dispositions. The dining staff seems to anticipate every need, and the restaurant managers must have eyes in the back of their heads, always observing and rushing to correct even the simplest error. Cabin staff know passengers' names minutes after their arrival and address them by name throughout the cruise. This courtesy makes an indelible impression. Overall, the service on the *Marco Polo* is as fine as any we've had on a cruise ship, including the most luxurious ships at triple the price.

FACILITIES AND ACTIVITIES Lectures by experts on the cruise region are well attended. Lectures are not presented on Mediterranean cruises because of itineraries' port-intensive nature. Among other diversions are bridge tours, origami, art classes, bridge and backgammon lessons and tournaments, workshops on magic, white-elephant sales, passenger talent shows, service club meetings, fashion shows, and joke contests.

The **Ambassador Lounge** showroom features local entertainment brought on board in various ports. These presentations and Filipino crew show are highlights of the cruise and much better than the mediocre musical revues and variety shows staged on other nights. Other entertainment might include a classical concert or a piano recital. The lounge, divided into three curved sections, slopes gently toward the stage. Sight lines are good except behind pillars or when the room is completely full. Large windows span both sides of the room, and a marble-topped bar flanked by mirrors is at the rear. Diamond-shaped lighting fixtures, blue carpets and curtains, and pink decor give the room a 1930s look.

The **Polo Lounge** piano bar, with a cream-colored baby grand piano encircled by a bar, is popular for predinner cocktails and late-evening relaxing and sing-alongs. It's also used for afternoon bridge games. The casino offers roulette, blackjack, and slot machines. To one side is an elegant white-marble bar, black-leather swivel chairs, and photos of famous entertainers. Off the casino are a small card room and a well-stocked library with comfortable leather armchairs and big windows. Guidebooks for the many countries visited by Marco Polo are provided. The **Palm Court,** a small room with marble-topped tables and wicker chairs, is a pleasurable retreat for afternoon tea or quiet conversation. Opposite are two small boutiques. Tucked away in a small area is the Internet center.

The **Charleston Club,** one of several multipurpose lounges, is used for bingo, painting lessons, cocktails, late-evening music and dancing, and midnight pizza. Glass doors open onto a lounge with a white baby grand piano and small bandstand, marble-topped bar, and dance floor. The lounge is a popular late-night gathering spot, though most passengers retire early.

SPORTS, FITNESS, AND BEAUTY   On the Pool Deck is a 15-foot-long swimming pool with teak benches on three sides. Table tennis and shuffleboard are available. A fitness center on the upper deck has a small, mirrored exercise room with treadmills, stationary bicycles, rowing machine, stair steppers, weight machines, and free weights. Aerobics and exercise classes are offered. Separate saunas for men and women and three outside Jacuzzis are available. The beauty salon, operated by Mandara Spa, offers a full range of services, including facials, massage, and hydrotherapy.

An upper-deck jogging track ringing the ship consists mostly of a narrow, rubberized path behind the lifeboats. For walkers, Promenade Deck has a one-fifth-mile course between the Charleston Club and bridge gangway. It's all on teak decks with sea views.

SHORE EXCURSIONS   All cruises feature pre- and postcruise packages and are particularly popular given the distances most passengers travel to the ship. Most cruises also include an unusual highlight ashore. Having the helipad is reassuring in case of an emergency in remote areas and for scouting ice conditions in Antarctica.

Note: Shore transport in some remote/primitive locations is not top of the line. Because of this, some shore excursions are inappropriate for passengers with limited mobility. Also, a fee may be charged for upgraded shore accommodations, but it is worth the cost in some out-of-the-way locations.

POSTSCRIPT Writing in 1298, Marco Polo opened his famous *Travels* with the words: "Ye kings, princes, nobles, townsfolk and all who wish to know the marvels of the world, have this book read unto you." If he were writing today, he might say, "All ye who wish to know the marvels of the world, take a cruise on the *Marco Polo*."

Princess Cruises

24305 Town Center Drive, Santa Clarita, CA 91355-4999
☎ 661-753-0000 or 800-PRINCESS; fax 661-753-1535
www.princess.com

TYPE OF SHIPS New superliners and megaliners.

TYPE OF CRUISES Modern, mainstream, worldwide, moderately upscale.

CRUISE LINE'S STRENGTHS
- worldwide itineraries
- Caribbean private island
- ScholarShip@Sea enrichment program
- spacious cabins, many with verandas
- 24-hour restaurant on most ships
- traditional or anytime dining
- scuba certification

CRUISE LINE'S SHORTCOMINGS
- congestion in 24-hour restaurants
- uneven cuisine in 24-hour restaurants

FELLOW PASSENGERS Princess passengers are difficult to characterize because their ages and incomes vary with the ships, seasons, and destinations. Basically, passengers are ages 45 and older with annual incomes of $40,000 and up. They tend to be experienced travelers who cruise frequently and enjoy Princess's mainstream vacations, but they can range from a California schoolteacher or a Midwestern computer systems analyst on a first cruise to affluent retirees on their 20th cruise. On longer cruises and those to "exotic" destinations, the average age is 55 or older; on one-week Caribbean cruises, the average age is younger.

Recommended for Modestly affluent first-timers, frequent cruisers who want easy-paced travel and prefer a balance between sea and land time, and those who understand *The Love Boat* was only a TV show.

Not recommended for Swingers or first-time cruisers in search of the Love Boat; small-ship devotees.

CRUISE AREAS AND SEASONS Caribbean, year-round; Africa, Amazon, Antarctica, Australia/South Pacific, Hawaii/Tahiti, Holy Land, Mexico, Orient, Panama Canal, Southeast Asia, winter; Alaska, Baltic, Bermuda, Canada/New England, Europe, Mediterranean, Scandinavia, summer.

THE LINE Princess marked its beginning in 1965 when a small, one-ship line called Princess Cruises sailed to the Mexican Riviera, using a 6,000-ton ferry vessel named *Princess Patricia*. In the intervening years, the company has grown from a pioneer of modern-day cruising with a focus on the West Coast to a worldwide fleet of 15 modern ships sailing to all seven continents. From its inception, Princess Cruises helped create the relaxed, casual atmosphere that typifies today's cruises.

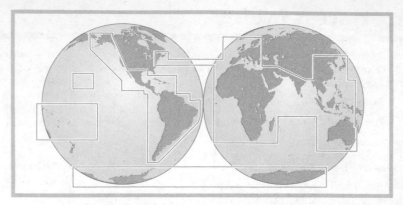

CRUISE AREAS AND SEASONS FOR PRINCESS CRUISES

In 1974, P&O (Peninsular and Orient Steam Navigation Company), a British firm and one of the world's oldest and largest steamship companies, which had been in the cruise business since August 1844, bought the American company Princess Cruises. It acquired its first *Island Princess* and first *Sun Princess*. The following year, P&O bought *Island Princess*'s sister, *Sea Venture,* and renamed her *Pacific Princess,* better known to TV viewers as the Love Boat.

In the early 1980s, Princess became a trendsetter for modern mainstream cruising when it launched the *Royal Princess.* She was hailed as the most stylish ship of the day, setting new standards in comfort and amenities. (Much to the sorrow of her loyal fans, *Royal Princess* was transferred to P&O Cruises in 2005.) In 1988, Princess almost doubled its capacity when it acquired Los Angeles–based Sitmar Cruises, another cruise pioneer, and integrated the Sitmar ships into its fleet. The line continued to benefit from its involvement in *The Love Boat* television series, which had an incalculable impact on modern cruising, popularizing it for a generation of television viewers—those who make up most of cruise passengers today—and helping dispel cruising's elitist image.

In the 1990s, Princess launched $3 billion worth of dazzling megaships. *Sun Princess* ushered in the *Grand*-class concept and the line's largest vessel when it entered service in 1995. She was followed by triplets over the following four years—all with the architect, Njal Eide, who designed the *Royal Princess,* and, like her, with significant new features, including cruising's first 24-hour restaurant, two atrium lobbies, and two show lounges.

The 109,000-ton, $400 million *Grand Princess,* the largest cruise ship ever built when she debuted in 1998, was the first of the Princess fleet too large to transit the Panama Canal. The expansion tripled the line's capacity. Two more like her followed in 2001 and 2002.

That was only the beginning. Two more ships, the 92,000-ton *Coral Princess* and *Island Princess,* made their debut in 2003 and ushered in a new class of ship. They were the best yet, combining the best features of the *Sun-* and *Grand*-class ships. They came with innovative power generation technology, combining diesel engines and gas turbines (the latter placed in the ship's funnel), and only 10% inside cabins and 80% of outside ones with balconies. In 2004, Princess saw its largest expansion to date with its largest ships: the 116,000-ton *Sapphire Princess* and *Diamond Princess* and the 113,000-ton *Caribbean Princess*. *Crown Princess,* a sister ship and slightly larger version of *Caribbean Princess,* arrived in 2006, and their sister ship, *Emerald Princess,* in 2007, inaugurating the line's first ship to homeport in Rome's seaport, Civitavecchia.

In spring 2007, Princess added the 710-passenger *Royal Princess* (formerly *Minerva II* of Swan Hellenic) for a series of European cruises to new destinations, particularly along the Dalmatian Coast—some of the ten new ports the line added in the 2007–08 season. More new ports are being added when Princess returns to world cruising for the first time in more than five years with a 102-day voyage on *Pacific Princess,* departing Fort Lauderdale, Florida, in January 2008.

Already a major player in Alaska and the Panama Canal, in the last few years, Princess has increased its Caribbean presence by 75%, added itineraries throughout Asia and the Pacific, expanded in Europe, added safaris in Kenya and South Africa, sailed on its first Antarctic cruise, expanded its ScholarShip@Sea program, and opened Internet cafes fleetwide.

Princess's Alaska role was enhanced in 1997 with the opening of the handsome Mount McKinley Princess Lodge, featured on the line's cruise tours. The lodge sits on 146 acres inside Denali State Park and has a spectacular view of 20,320-foot Mount McKinley and the Alaska Range. Princess has four other Alaskan properties. In 2007, Princess added the *Pacific Princess* in Alaska for a small-ship alternative to its typical megaliners that sail on Alaska cruises.

On Caribbean cruises, the line offers Princess Cay, its private island in the Bahamas. Princess has one of the industry's best and most extensive selections of shore excursions. Almost all can be booked in advance of your cruise. Princess is also a leader in seasonal savings, deeply discounted advance-purchase fares, and two-for-one promotions. Just about everything you ever wanted to know about Princess Cruises is available on its Web site, one of the most extensive of any cruise line.

In 2003, the hard-fought battle between Carnival Corp. and Royal Caribbean to buy Princess/P&O Cruises ended in Carnival's favor. All of Carnival's 11 cruise lines, including Princess, continue to operate separately under their own brands.

THE FLEET	BUILT/RENOVATED	TONNAGE	PASSENGERS
Caribbean Princess	2004	113,000	3,070
Coral Princess	2003	92,000	1,970
Crown Princess	2006	116,000	3,070
Dawn Princess	1997	77,000	1,950

THE FLEET	BUILT/RENOVATED	TONNAGE	PASSENGERS
Diamond Princess	2004	116,000	2,670
Emerald Princess	2007	116,000	3,070
Golden Princess	2001	109,000	2,600
Grand Princess	1998	109,000	2,600
Island Princess	2003	92,000	1,970
Pacific Princess	1999/2002	30,277	680
Royal Princess	2007	30,277	710
Ruby Princess	2008	116,000	3,070
Sapphire Princess	2004	116,000	2,670
Sea Princess	1998	77,000	1,950
Star Princess	2002	109,000	2,600
Sun Princess	1995	77,000	1,950
Tahitian Princess	1999/2002	30,277	670

STYLE California modern in the mainstream, sedate but not staid, a Princess cruise is the essence of mass-market cruising: warm, inviting, and comfortable, suitable for a broad spectrum of people. The fleet has British officers, with their steamship tradition, Italian officers, with their natural charm, and a multicultural dining and hotel staff. Often trendsetters in facilities and amenities, the ships have the look of a well-bred, middle- to upper-middle-class environment (that is, nothing too flashy or exaggerated) where almost anyone can feel at home. The line has worked hard to improve its entertainment and food, with menus featuring fresh, contemporary selections, and now offers some of the best cuisine in its category and superior to most in its alternative Italian restaurant. Shipboard activities are varied and numerous. Ships fleetwide have gyms, saunas, and spa services and offer fitness and sports programs on board and in port. Princess's newest ships have telemedicine technology, giving ships' doctors worldwide access to medical specialists.

The New Waves scuba diving program, associated with PADI (Professional Association of Diving Instructors), offers snorkeling and scuba certification. All Princess ships have Internet access and alternative dining options. Personal Choice Dining and Anytime Dining are flexible dining room options, available on *Sun*- and *Grand*-class ships. With it, an automatic gratuity system for the staffs is in effect on board, adding $10 per person per day to a passenger's shipboard account. FlightChoice provides passengers with information on their flight schedule 60 days prior to sailing with the option to choose a customized air schedule. Cruise Personalizers is an online service that enables passengers to book shore excursions, make special occasion arrangements, and tell staff about dietary requirements before their cruise.

One of Princess's newest facilities, which the line dubbed Direct to the Wilderness, enables passengers to extend their cruise to tour Alaska, to board their train right at the new Princess terminal in Whittier. From there, they are whisked off to one of Princess' two Denali lodges, arriving the same afternoon. The new facility slashes travel time and the number of transfers, and thus gives passengers more time at Denali. Another new amenity, available on four of the newest ships, is Movie Under the Stars—the first on a cruise ship—in which the top deck becomes an open-air theater, showing popular films and major sporting events on a huge screen.

Princess's latest innovation, Chef's Table, was launched on the *Emerald Princess* along with the debut of the new ship in April 2007 and will be introduced gradually fleetwide. It's an opportunity to join the executive chef in the ship's galley for predinner cocktails and hors d'oeuvres with Champagne, followed by a multicourse tasting dinner especially created for participants by the chef at their special table in the dining room. For the dessert course, the chef rejoins the group. Each couple receives an autographed copy of Princess's cookbook, *Courses, A Culinary Journey,* and a complimentary photo with the chef. *Chef's Table* can be reserved for up to ten passengers on select nights at a cost of $75 per person.

In spring 2007, Princess Cruises debuted a series of enhancements to its food service meant to reflect changing trends and passenger preferences. Introduced first on the new *Emerald Princess* and *Royal Princess,* it includes new menus and presentation in dining rooms, alternative restaurants and buffets, as well as some special touches such as an afternoon "cookies and milk break" and cabin delivery ($3 service charge) of homemade pizza.

Princess has been among the first to offer Luggage Valet, an advance home-to-cabin shipping service (provided by DHL Worldwide Express). First available for Europe-bound travelers on four Princess ships in summer 2007, the program is being expanded to other destinations. Prices start at $90 per bag one way for domestic shipments, and vary internationally depending on weight and destination. Bags are insured up to $2,000; additional insurance is available for purchase. Reservations can be made up to 30 days prior to sailing date. Package Valet, enabling passengers to ship home items purchased at the ship's boutiques, is to follow.

DISTINCTIVE FEATURES Scuba certification, 24-hour restaurants, terry robes and fresh fruit in cabins on request, fresh flowers in suites. Self-service launderettes, private Bahamian island, Alaska lodges. Telemedicine technology, wedding chapels, wedding Webcam on *Grand* class, Personal Choice and Anytime Dining on *Sun* and *Grand* classes, balcony breakfast/dinner, wireless Internet capability fleetwide, Movie Under the Stars, Chef's Table, Luggage Valet.

	HIGHEST	LOWEST	AVERAGE
PER DIEM	$365	$78	$188

Per diems are calculated from cruise line's nondiscounted *cruise-only* published fares on standard accommodations and vary by season, cabins, and cruise areas.

RATES Port charges included.

Special fares and discounts Frequent two-for-one fares; savings and upgrades on combining consecutive cruises.

- **THIRD/FOURTH PASSENGER:** 50% of fare for suites to 30% of fare for inside cabins.
- **CHILDREN'S FARE:** Same as third/fourth passenger.
- **SINGLE SUPPLEMENT:** 150%–200%, Love Boat Savers discounts.

Packages
- **AIR/SEA:** Yes.
- **PRE/POST:** Yes.
- **OTHERS:** Wedding, honeymoon, anniversary, renewal of vows, and grand occasion.

PAST PASSENGERS In 2007, Princess introduced new features to its Captain's Circle loyalty program. Among them was the ability for members to qualify for awards either by the number of cruises completed or the total number of days sailed. Captain's Circle offers three membership levels: Gold (one cruise), Platinum (five cruises or 50 cruise days), and Elite (15 completed cruises or 150 cruise days). Some of the other perks, depending on the passenger's level, are a free minibar setup, free Internet access, free laundry services, priority tender embarkation, complimentary wine tasting, a boutiques discount, upgraded stateroom amenities, and priority embarkation and disembarkation, which enables Elite passengers to choose the time they prefer to leave the ship. Captain's Circle past-passenger club members are invited to a captain-hosted cocktail party and to participate in activities, such as a photo contest with prizes. Members receive a membership number to use when booking a cruise or corresponding with Princess, ensuring that they receive club benefits. Recognition pins are given and fine-quality gifts are presented at onboard parties to passengers who have sailed the most days with Princess. Members receive newsletters reporting new itineraries, new ship plans, staff profiles, chef's recipes, special discounts, and coupons for specific sailings and members-only sailings.

THE LAST WORD For millions of Americans, the popular image of cruising is a Princess cruise. It's perhaps not as luxurious or glamorous as the television image, but it's apparently close enough for the line to attract more than a million passengers a year. Princess's strength is in its consistency, new fleet, itineraries, and well-executed shore excursions. Little changes from ship to ship. Your ship will be comfortable, your cruise enjoyable, and you will get a lot for your money, if you have realistic expectations and plan ahead to take advantage of the line's heavily discounted fares.

To its credit, Princess integrated seven enormous ships in four years smoothly—a gigantic job—and has been able to maintain the high standards, particularly of cuisine and service, that has gained the line its loyal following.

Princess Cruises Standard Features

Officers British and Italian.

Staff Dining: Italian, European, Filipino; Cabin: Filipino; Cruise: American, British.

Dining facilities One main dining room, two seatings for three meals (*Sun* and *Coral* groups, two dining rooms; *Grand* group, three; *Diamond, Sapphire,* five); Personal Choice/Anytime Dining, on *Sun, Coral,* and *Grand* groups; alternative bistro on *Sun, Grand* group: Italian, Sterling Steakhouse; *Coral,* Italian and New Orleans. Informal buffet breakfast, lunch in Lido restaurant, pizzeria, patisserie. *Grand, Coral,* and *Sun* groups, 24-hour dining. Balcony breakfast or dinner. *Royal Princess,*traditional dining, Sabatini's and Sterling Steakhouse, balcony dining.

Special diets Diabetic, low-calorie/cholesterol/salt, vegetarian.

Room service 24-hour room service with light menu.

Dress code Casual during day, evenings vary; usually there are two smart casual, three informal, and two formal in week's cruise.

Cabin amenities CNN, ESPN, Discovery/Learning channels, and movies on television, fresh fruit daily and terry robes in cabins on request, direct-dial telephone, minifridges, hair dryers.

Electrical outlets 110/220 AC.

Wheelchair access 25–28 cabins on *Grand* group; 20 on *Coral* group; 19 on *Sun* group; 3 on *Pacific, Tahitian.*

Recreation and entertainment Las Vegas– and Broadway-style revues, music and dancing, casino, disco, wine and caviar bar, karaoke, theater, dance classes, bingo, bridge. *Grand* group, virtual reality center, three show lounges. *Coral* group, two show lounges, one with three revolving stages; demonstration kitchen. ScholarShip@ Sea courses.

Sports and other activities Two or three outdoor pools on all ships; *Grand* group, five. Paddle tennis, jogging, scuba program, golf practice. *Grand* group, swim-against-current lap pool.

Beauty and fitness Spa, saunas, beauty/barber salon, fitness program.

Other facilities Library, hospital, boutiques, self-service laundry, meeting facilities, religious services; *Grand* group, wedding chapel, wedding Webcam, Internet cafe.

Children's facilities Princess Kids, Princess's youth program on all ships, has special facilities and full-time youth coordinators: *Grand Coral,* and *Sun* groups. *Royal, Pacific,* and *Tahitian,* no dedicated spaces but youth counselor runs planned activities when there are 20-plus kids. Group babysitting available 10 p.m.–1 a.m. for children ages 3–12 for a $5 per hour charge. No in-cabin babysitting. See text.

Smoking No smoking in dining rooms and main showrooms; other public rooms have designated areas.

Princess Cruises Standard Features *(continued)*

Princess suggested tipping Gratuities automatically added to passenger's account at $10 per person per day for dining and cabin service. Passengers can add or reduce amount at pursers' desk; 15% is added to bar bills.

Credit cards For cruise payment and onboard charges (settled at the end of the cruise): American Express/Optima, Carte Blanche, Diners Club, MasterCard, Visa, Discover; traveler's and personal checks; U.S., Canadian, and British currency.

Dawn Princess	QUALITY 8	VALUE C
Sea Princess	QUALITY 8	VALUE C
Sun Princess	QUALITY 9	VALUE B
REGISTRY Bermuda	LENGTH 856 feet	BEAM 106 feet
CABINS 975	DRAFT 26 feet	SPEED 21 knots
MAXIMUM PASSENGERS	PASSENGER DECKS 14	ELEVATORS 9
1,950	CREW 830	SPACE RATIO 39.5

THE SHIPS Before its launch, *Sun Princess*—at the time, the largest cruise ship ever built—was described by Princess as offering an intimate feel. Skeptics scoffed.

But guess what? Princess did it. Well, "intimate" is perhaps a stretch, but it certainly managed to diminish the interiors of this big ship to a human scale. The Italian-built ship made her debut in December 1995, the first of Princess's new class of ships. Her mates, *Dawn Princess, Sea Princess,* and *Ocean Princess,* arrived between 1997 and 2000. (*Ocean Princess* left the fleet in September 2002 to join P&O Cruises.) From the outside, the gleaming white liners look colossal, towering 14 decks and stretching nearly three football fields in length. But inside, clever design has created a welcoming, accessible ambience.

The ships are spacious without being overwhelming. Warm colors and refined decor enhance the inviting atmosphere. The group set new standards for megaliners. Their layout is innovative in many ways. Rather than one cavernous atrium, these ships offer two. Instead of one enormous show lounge, there are two main show lounges. Two dining rooms are on different decks, and their layout, decor, and table arrangements help create an intimate ambience. Five dining outlets, including cruising's first 24-hour restaurant, provide options. Small bars and lounges capture the intimacy of a small ship while giving passengers choices. Although other ships offer multiple lounges and dining alternatives, few developed the concept to the extent of Princess's *Sun*- and *Grand*-class ships. Whatever you choose to do, you can do, and whatever you miss one night, you can catch the next night.

The four-deck **Grand Plaza** is the ships' main atrium and social hub. It's a showcase of the exquisite Italian craftsmanship evident throughout the vessels and sets the tone for each ship. On the *Sun Princess,* in the elegant space, golden marble suggests the sun, and beige, bronze, and brown accents hint at shade. Sunbursts are set in the marble floors at every level of the atrium, and a backlit stained-glass dome overhead conveys an abstract underwater scene in aqua and turquoise. Glass elevators and a circular, floating staircase connect the decks and provide a stunning setting for the captain's parties.

Among the amenities are five swimming pools, a huge health center and spa, children's and teen rooms, a shopping arcade, computerized golf simulator, library and reading room with "audio chairs," each with its own bay window looking out to sea, and a business and conference center for up to 300 people. Each ship has a $2.5 million collection of paintings, sculptures, ceramic tiles, and Murano glass.

Another significant feature of the ships is their connection with the sea. A wraparound teak promenade lined with canopied steamer chairs provides a peaceful setting to read, daydream, or snooze.

ITINERARIES *See* Itinerary Index.

CABINS About two-thirds of cabins are outside; 70% of those have private balconies. There are 28 cabin categories. Nineteen cabins—among the most on any cruise ship—were designed to Americans with Disabilities Act specifications. Lifeboats obstruct views from 28 outside cabins on Promenade Deck. All standard cabins have a queen-size bed convertible to two singles, refrigerator, safe, ample closet, and bath with shower, terry robes, and hair dryers. All are well appointed and decorated in light, eye-pleasing colors.

Category A minisuites with private balcony are lavish in comfort, decor, and size—almost 400 square feet, plus the balcony. A marble-floored foyer with a mirror gives the illusion of a large apartment. Tastefully decorated in beige and butter tones accented by light woods and fine fabrics, each has a separate sitting area with leather chairs and a sofa that converts to a queen-size bed, and an entertainment console with television and music channels. A bar includes a refrigerator.

The bedroom, separated by a curtained archway, has a queen-size bed, vanity/desk, and second television. Drawer space is ample, and the small walk-in closet has a safe. Sliding doors in the sitting area and bedroom lead to a balcony extending the length of the suite. Two lounge chairs and a table make it ideal for breakfast or napping. Etched glass divides the whirlpool tub from a shower stall, and a door separates the toilet and washbasin.

As on all new Princess ships, there are self-service launderettes with washers, dryers, irons, and ironing boards at no charge. You pay for soap, bleach, and dryer sheets from a dispensing machine.

Specifications 372 inside cabins, 603 outside (410 with verandas); 32 minisuites and 6 suites with verandas. Standard dimensions, 135–173 square feet. All with 2 lower beds, convertible to queen; 300 with third berths; no singles; 19 wheelchair-accessible.

DINING Here are the choices: two dining rooms, cruising's first 24-hour restaurant, pizzeria, grill, patisserie, ice-cream bar (there's a charge), 24-hour room service, and the newest addition, a steak house ($15 surcharge). And now passengers have the option to dine where and when they want with Personal Choice and Anytime Dining.

The two main dining rooms are on Emerald Deck and Plaza Deck. They have an asymmetrical seating layout and small table groups in various sizes separated by etched-glass dividers. The design gives each group of tables a certain privacy. Separate galleys and service stations in every corner reduce traffic and help ensure that food reaches tables at the proper temperature. The walls are decorated with lovely scenic murals, adding to the gracious surroundings. Lunch and dinner menus offer a selection of appetizers, soups, salads, entrées, and desserts. A pasta special is offered every evening, although it is no longer prepared tableside. Healthy Choice selections, included on the regular menu, provide low-cholesterol, low-fat, and low-sodium alternatives. Wine list choices are reasonably priced, some under $20. Wines are also available by the glass.

Horizon Court on Lido Deck is an innovative 24-hour cafe with 270-degree ocean views through floor-to-ceiling windows, with seating on a trio of terraces. By day, buffets are served at two stations; at night, the center of the room becomes a restaurant with table service and a dance band. Reservations aren't needed, and there's no extra charge.

Breakfast choices range from fresh fruit to hot dishes, with a different special daily. At noon, entrées include ravioli, roast beef, and a salad bar, but selection and preparation do not match the quality or variety in the dining room.

The pizzeria offers a sidewalk cafe setting with marble-top tables and wrought-iron chairs on the balcony overlooking the atrium. It's open for lunch, and from 6 p.m. to 2 a.m. it serves pizza hot from the ovens. Waiters take orders for drinks and pizzas. There's no charge for the pizza, but diners usually tip the waiters. The outdoor **Grill** serves cooked-to-order hamburgers and hot dogs; the patisserie on the Plaza Deck has espresso, cappuccino, and pastries. **Sundaes** is a poolside ice-cream parlor; there's a charge per scoop.

SERVICE Officers are British and Italian, dining staff European, bar and cabin stewards Filipino, and reception and cruise staff American and British. Most of the crew are friendly and well trained, especially the dining staff, which consistently garners high praise. Service at the reception desk is uneven, and sometimes brisk; individual cabin stewards, ever smiling and eager to please, occasionally get mixed reviews, often the result of insufficient training.

FACILITIES AND ACTIVITIES The cruise staff presents an enormous variety of entertainment. You might start your day's activities with bridge or dance lessons, or a craft demonstration. In the afternoon you might play golf or table tennis, take a lesson in the casino, join a word or trivia game, or watch a culinary demonstration or horse races. Movies are shown three or four times daily. And then there's bingo.

The wood-paneled library has a large selection of books, plus audio chairs with built-in headsets that are set by large bay windows over-looking the water. The **Card Room** is also used as a meeting room or for private parties. The ships offer a full schedule of daytime diversions, from art auctions and dance lessons to bridge tournaments and bingo. Internet cafes with 20 or more computers are available on all Princess ships. Internet access costs 35 cents per minute.

Note: Art auctions have become ubiquitous on major cruise ships. Most of the art is terrible and terribly overpriced, despite claims to the contrary. One Sea Princess passenger recently wrote:

. . . the tacky, in-your-face display of art for auction [is] everywhere on the ship from embarkation to disembarkation—and it grew day by day . . . on easels, hanging on walls, and even stacked up around the casino lobby, Atrium piano bar, and Wheelhouse and Horizon Court. Tacked on to many were auction announcements with the time and location highlighted in thick orange magic marker. Flyers also appeared in cabin mailboxes almost daily, and, after the "final" auction, another notice appeared announcing the "requested FINAL 'Rocky IV, Death Wish' absolutely final auction." Frankly, Princess has too much class to be using this sort of revenue-generating scheme in the first place, but the carnival hawker's atmosphere and the total lack of knowledge or finesse exhibited by the auctioneer were almost comical. Sea Princess, like her sisters, is an elegant ship with lovely decor, but even the "legitimate" artwork in many passageways and some elevator lobbies was obscured by the easels and announcements of art for sale.

We couldn't agree more.

The Grand Plaza is the ship's hub. The Promenade Deck contains only public rooms and is anchored by the two showrooms. Forward is the **Princess Theatre,** with an enormous stage for Broadway-style pro-ductions. Graduated theater seating and an absence of pillars ensure fine sight lines.

Aft is the marble-walled **Vista Lounge** with tiered seating and floor-to-ceiling ocean views. Dancing and cabaret-style entertainment are of-fered. To one side, a large, free-form bar encourages mingling. Shows in both lounges are repeated—four performances each for early and late seating over consecutive days. The ship's program suggests that passen-gers attend according to their dining room seating, but some passengers prefer to return to one show for an encore. This hasn't created seating problems because not all passengers attend all performances.

The **Grand Casino** has slot machines, video poker, blackjack, roulette, and craps. The stained-glass ceiling, lighted to simulate a spinning roulette wheel, is visible on the deck below, from where passengers access the casino via a staircase in the second atrium. On the Sun, a bronze tubular sculpture by Arizonan Lyle London decorates the lower level.

Flanking the ships' second atrium are the disco and the romantic **Ren-dezvous Lounge.** The disco's entrance glitters with fiber-optic lights and a video dance floor, rather than video wall. Rendezvous Lounge, an elegant refuge, serves caviar, imported wines, and Champagnes by the glass. The

Atrium Lounge, with a white baby grand piano and dance floor, is particularly popular for predinner cocktails and late-night sing-alongs. Afternoon tea is also served there as well as in the **Horizon Lounge.**

The **Wheelhouse Bar** near the Princess Theatre is one of the ship's most attractive, inviting rooms. Resembling a British men's club, it's decorated in rosewood and dark burgundy with sumptuous, sprucegreen leather chairs. Ship models and P&O memorabilia adorn the walls. Live dance music seems a jarring note in this room that could be ideal for quiet conversation. Yet passengers seem to enjoy the lively atmosphere, packing the dance floor before dinner and late into the night. On the *Sun,* a gallery outside the bar displays costumes worn by opera diva Dame Joan Sutherland.

Before the *Sea Princess* returned to Princess Cruises, after a two-year tour of duty with P&O Cruises, her top deck was outfitted with a special 300-foot Times Square–type outdoor screen for Princess' new, popular Movie Under the Stars. Passengers can enjoy first-run movies, concerts, and sporting events. Generally, reservations are required.

SPORTS, FITNESS, AND BEAUTY   Some of the most innovative architectural designs benefit sports and fitness activities. One of the ship's pools is open to the sky, though set between two decks. On Riviera Deck are the main pools and the ocean-view spa. Half of this large area is a well-equipped gym; the other half is a mirrored room where aerobics classes are held. The spa has 11 massage and beauty treatment rooms, saunas, showers, changing facilities, and an ocean-view beauty salon. Next door, a computerized golf center simulates play on a half-dozen top courses ($20 per half hour for up to four players).

The **Lotus Spa** program features daily exercise and well-being classes as well as traditional and exotic spa and salon services. Start your day with a Lotus Walk on Promenade Deck, followed by a spinning class or aerobics and stretch classes. More leisurely classes include Aqua Aerobics, Pathway to Yoga, and the use of visualization, meditation, and relaxation techniques in the Mind, Body, and Soul classes.

Sunbathing areas are spread across three top decks with a pool and bar (live band during daytime) on one; another pool, whirlpool, and grill on another; and a splash pool, bar, and paddle tennis, volleyball, basketball court on the third. A one-sixth-mile jogging track girdles the top deck; a broad teak promenade encircles the ship. (Three times around equals a mile.)

CHILDREN'S FACILITIES   Princess Kids, Princess's fleetwide youth program provides age-specific activities for three groups: Princess Pelicans (ages 3–7), Shockwaves (ages 8–12), and Remix (ages 13–17). It also includes in-port programs with lunch, running from 8 a.m. to 5 p.m. at no charge, and learning opportunities through a partnership with the California Science Center and the use of National Wildlife Federation educational materials on wildlife and conservation. The program includes studies of the stars, oceans, and coral reefs, and building and racing sailboats, among others, and complements Princess's junior ranger program in Alaska and the fleetwide Save our Seas environmental program. Participants take home a "Pete's Pals" booklet reflecting endangered species, including white pelicans, manatees, sea turtles, and panda bears in areas Princess sails. Group babysitting for ages 3–12 is available from 10 p.m. to 1 a.m. for $5 per hour per child. Children can now travel on most itineraries at six months.

Sun Princess's **Fun Zone** is one of the most enchanting playrooms at sea. Here, kids romp in a splash pool, play in a castle and big-as-life doll's house, and perform in a little theater. Next door, **Cyberspace** (**Wired** on *Sea Princess*), the teen club, offers video games, a disco, and refreshments.

POSTSCRIPT Of all the megaliners launched since the mid-1990s, *Sun Princess* and her siblings have best reduced behemoth interiors to human scale. They also prove that big can be beautiful, in large part due to their fine Italian craftsmanship. With choices 24 hours a day—in dining, activities, entertainment, and relaxing—anyone seeking less regimented cruising should find happiness on these ships.

Caribbean Princess	QUALITY 8	VALUE B
Crown Princess	QUALITY 9	VALUE A
Diamond Princess	QUALITY 8	VALUE B
Emerald Princess	2007 (PREVIEW)	
Golden Princess	QUALITY 8	VALUE B
Grand Princess	QUALITY 8	VALUE B
Sapphire Princess	QUALITY 8	VALUE B
Star Princess	QUALITY 8	VALUE C
REGISTRY Bermuda/Britain	LENGTH 951 feet	BEAM 118/159
CABINS 1,300–1,557	DRAFT 26 feet	SPEED 22 knots
MAXIMUM PASSENGERS	PASSENGER DECKS 13	ELEVATORS 16
2,600–3,100	CREW 1,200/1,110	SPACE RATIO 37/42

THE SHIPS Saying the 109,000-ton, $450 million *Grand Princess* was the largest, most expensive cruise ship built when she debuted doesn't say much. But comparisons clarify the image: *Grand Princess* is about four times the length of New York's Grand Central Station. She's 28 feet taller than Niagara Falls, 49 feet taller than the Statue of Liberty, and too wide by 43 feet to transit the Panama Canal.

And what does "most expensive" mean? *Grand Princess's* price tag was almost twice the cost of the Pathfinder mission to Mars. Happily, there's plenty on this ship to suggest that Princess got its money's worth. Of the ship's 928 outside cabins, 710 have balconies—the most on any other cruise ship at the time. She was the first with three main dining rooms and three main show lounges, each with a different show nightly. Her 13,500-square-foot casino was the largest afloat.

Get the picture? She's big, expensive, and has plenty of wow! But *Grand Princess* also comes with innovations even more exciting than those of the *Sun* group. For starters, she has cruising's first wedding chapel (Princess is, after all, the company of the Love Boat); the first virtual-reality arcade with a motion-based ride for up to 18 people, car races, and skiing; a blue-screen video production facility that lets passengers star in their own videos; and the first swim-against-the-current lap pool at sea. She was the first cruise ship with a southwestern restaurant (one of three alternative restaurants) and the first to have 28 wheelchair-accessible cabins. At the time she debuted, *Grand Princess* was one of few cruise ships with duplicate operational and technical systems to ensure continued operation in emergencies. Her sisters have similar features.

Grand Princess's most unusual and noticeable design feature is the **Skywalkers Nightclub,** an aluminum structure suspended 18 decks above the water at the stern like a skybox at a stadium. Accessed by a glass-enclosed moving walkway, it's an observation lounge by day and a disco by night. On the *Crown Princess,* Skywalkers was moved forward, freeing up space for **The Sanctuary,** a new premium amenity for adults only, a nonsmoking outside area with lounges for sunning and some pampering for a small fee of $15 for a half day. Special attendants offer cold towels, beverages, and snacks. There are also two private cabanas for spa treatments.

The ship's enormous interior is diminished by being divided into many small spaces offering dozens of activities—so many choices that a week of cruising isn't enough time to try them all. The myriad options should be a comfort to first-time cruisers fearful of feeling confined or having nothing to do.

Among other distinctive features is the bridge, which extends beyond both sides of the ship. It's glass-enclosed to protect the computerized navigational instruments. A bow observation area gives passengers nearly the same view that officers have from the bridge. Balconies, outlined in blue glass, are built out from the ship's body in stair-stepped tiers. The design opens all balconies to the sun, but the negatives are a loss of privacy (cabins above overlook lower spaces) and noise traveling upward.

In spring 2004, the *Grand* class more than doubled in cabin count when three more super megaliners were added: the 113,000-ton *Caribbean Princess* in April, the 116,000-ton *Diamond Princess* in May, and the 116,000-ton *Sapphire Princess* in June. The count jumped again when two more ships similar to the *Caribbean Princess* were added—the *Crown Princess* in 2006 and the *Emerald Princess* in 2007.

The *Crown Princess* introduced a new itinerary for Princess Cruises, sailing from the new Brooklyn, New York, Terminal Port facility on alternating nine-day Eastern and Western Caribbean cruises, including Grand Turk in the Turks & Caicos. *Crown Princess* was one of the first cruise ships to call at Grand Turk at the island's new port and terminal. Princess is also making it easier for passengers from the Northeast sailing on its ships from the Brooklyn Cruise Terminal to get to and from their ship with a new transportation option. Begun in May 2007, the pre- and postcruise motor coach transfer service is available from all major metropolitan areas, including Baltimore/Washington, D.C., eastern Pennsylvania, Massachusetts, and Connecticut/Providence, Rhode Island.

The *Caribbean Princess* is a slightly larger version of the *Grand Princess*, with most of the same features—three dining rooms, three show lounges, several alternative restaurants, a wedding chapel, Lotus Spa, nine-hole putting course and golf simulator, library, and Internet cafe. But she has 261 more cabins, in all categories. As with her sister ships, 80% of all outside cabins, or 881 cabins, have balconies. The *Sapphire* and the *Diamond* are larger versions of the *Grand* as well, with only minor differences.

Caribbean Princess introduced Movie Under the Stars, a great way for passengers to enjoy the latest movies under the heavens as they relax on deck. The movies and special sports events play on a giant, Times Square–style screen built into the superstructure of the vessel at the midship pool. The feature has been so popular that Princess has installed it on *Grand Princess, Sea Princess,* and *Crown Princess.* The screen can also be used for the Caribbean night parties held during every cruise. And true to any movie-watching venue, popcorn and other snacks are available. Another new feature is a Caribbean-themed alternative restaurant.

As noted before, Princess is the Love Boat and now, on *Crown Princess,* it provides an opportunity for an "Engagement Under the Stars by video." Just before the outdoor evening movie, a guest can propose to another person (presumably his unsuspecting love) by video while passengers watch the big screen in anticipation of the answer. The package includes a special romantic dinner, amenities, and the creation of keepsakes to remember the occasion long after they return home. If the couple wants to marry aboard ship, Princess has a complete program for that also.

ITINERARIES *See* Itinerary Index.

CABINS These Princesses each have 35 cabin categories! (*Crown Princess* has only 13 cabin categories.) Most cabins are on Decks 8–12, with a few on Decks 5 and 14, and of the outside cabins, 80% have verandas. The majority range from 215 to 255 square feet, a spaciousness generally available only in deluxe suites. The pastel decor renders a pleasant ambience. Closet and shelf space is generous; drawers are limited but adequate.

The ships' balconies offer several benefits. First, they entice passengers to spend more time in their cabins, reducing crowds in public areas. Second, with so many available in standard cabin, the amenity is affordable for a wider audience. The ships' wheelchair-accessible cabins are also available in all main categories.

Cabins are more traditional in layout than those on the *Sun* group. Suites have tiled (not marbled) bathrooms and do not have Jacuzzi tubs. The two 800-square-foot Grand Suites (one on *Golden*) are aptly named. Each has a large balcony with whirlpool, a living room with fireplace, wet bar, three televisions, and walk-in closets.

New amenities have been added for passengers in suites, including expedited embarkation and disembarkation, packing and unpacking service upon request, free Internet access, dry cleaning, laundry, and even shoe polishing. On formal nights, they'll receive a complimentary corsage and boutonniere. They can enjoy tea served in their suites and schedule a private portrait sitting with a shipboard photographer.

Specifications *Caribbean/Crown* 1,557 cabins, 1,105 outside, 452 inside; 25/28 suites with balconies; 2 interconnecting family suites; 180/186 minisuites with balconies; 674/532 standard with balcony; 25 wheelchair-accessible. *Golden, Star/Grand,* 1,301 cabins, 935/928 outside, 366/372 inside (160 square feet); 205/208 suites with balconies (325–800 square feet); 502 outside with balconies (215–255 square feet); 228/218 standard outside (165–210 square feet); 28 wheelchair-accessible, including 18 outside/10 inside (240–385 square feet); 609 with upper berths. *Diamond, Sapphire,* 1,337 cabins, 960 outside, 377 inside; 28 suites with balconies; 2 interconnecting family suites; 186 minisuites with balconies; 532 standard with balcony.

DINING   Each ship has eight dining venues and offers the line's Personal Choice dining options. This enables passengers to choose between Traditional Fixed Seating dining with assigned seats and Anytime Dining, thus providing passengers more flexibility in deciding when, where, and with whom they dine, as in a restaurant.

The main dining rooms, named for famous Italian artists—**Botticelli, Da Vinci,** and **Michelangelo** (on the *Star,* the rooms are named for famous Italian places: **Portofino, Amalfi,** and **Capri**)—have low ceilings and clusters of tables in a serpentine layout that breaks the space, so guests don't feel they're dining in a large room with many people. At least one of the three dining rooms is designated for traditional dining; one for Anytime Dining; and the third for either arrangement, depending on demand. Generally, it is wise to make a reservation if you want to dine at a specific time. Otherwise, you can just show up.

Horizon Court, the 24-hour Lido cafe, has its own galley and a terrace for outdoor dining. The layout is different from that on *Sun Princess* and causes crowding and confusion. Open for brunch (on sea days only) and dinner by reservation are the popular **Sabatini's Trattoria,** an Italian specialty restaurant ($20 surcharge), and the **Sterling Steakhouse** ($15 surcharge). *Crown Princess's* Sabatini's was moved to Deck 16, expanded in size and menu, and made more elegant. The ship's steak house is now **Crown Grill** on Deck 7 and much larger, although the decor continues to be traditional steak house. Another new feature on *Crown Princess* is **Vines,** a wine bar where sushi and finger food are served.

The *Sapphire Princess* expanded the Personal Choice dining concept with a new twist—five main dining rooms, four with a different decor and theme, along with a dish to go with the theme. Passengers on the Anytime Dining plan can choose the one traditional seating dining room or smaller restaurants, each with its own menu—**Vivaldi** (Italian cuisine), **Sterling** (steak house), **Santa Fe** (southwestern) and **Pacific Moon** (Asian). They also have the option of ordering from each restaurant's themed dishes in addition to each day's menu. Those in the traditional dining room are not left out; they have changing menu options, including items from the themed restaurants.

Another new feature is Balcony Dinner, $50 per person, and Balcony Breakfast, $25 per couple, with cocktails, fresh flowers, Champagne, special menus, and in-room service. (The breakfast is terrific indulgence and offers a vast amount of delicious food and at $25 for two is a real bargain. Try it. You'll love it.) For now, the breakfast is served on sea days and is available fleetwide, but the dinner is an amenity on *Grand*-class ships only.

Outdoors are **Prego,** where pizza is served all day, **Trident Grill,** providing hot dogs and burgers, and an ice-cream bar where a scoop costs $2. The **Promenade Bar** overlooking the atrium on Deck 7 doubles as a patisserie and serves a light breakfast of croissants and espresso, as does the **Lobby Bar** on Deck 5 on *Golden* and *Star. Crown Princess* has a somewhat different take on its atrium, known as the **Piazza** and used for daytime entertainment, such as a mime or stilt walkers, that can be enjoyed by the whole family. On the sides of the atrium are **Crooner's,** the lobby bar, **International Café,** a patisserie and coffee bar. Room service is available 24 hours. Because dining is available at all times, passengers do not need to plan shore time around mealtimes. The many dining options also reduce lines and crowds.

Emerald Princess, launched in spring 2007, was the first of the fleet to have the line's series of enhancements to its food service. Meant to reflect changing trends and passenger preferences, it included new menus and presentation in dining rooms, alternative restaurants and buffets, as well as some special touches such as an afternoon "cookies and milk break" and cabin delivery ($3 service charge) of homemade pizza. Princess expects to introduce the program fleetwide over the next year.

FACILITIES AND ACTIVITIES The *Grand Princess's* **Voyage of Discovery,** the $2.5 million virtual reality center, is an eyepopper. The room has interactive games and a cyber bar, but its main attraction is a wild, motion-based virtual-reality ride that seats 18 people. Passengers buy a Voyager card for $20, which they use to start machines, and the cost of play ($0.75–$3) is deducted. At the blue-screen **Limelight Studio,** passengers can star in their own video, inserted into an existing scene from a popular movie or historical event. Neither the virtual-reality center or blue-screen studio are found on *Golden Princess* or *Star Princess.* Rather, *Golden* has a digital studio that provides a face-replacement computer program. *Star* (and other ships) have a blue-screen-portrait type of computer with which subjects can be photographed against a variety of backgrounds (similar to the Limelight system). It's a portable system operated off a laptop computer.

Standard diversions are plentiful: bingo, karaoke, cards, board games, spelling bees, and dance classes. The small business center has phone, fax, and computer facilities. (There's a charge to use the equipment.) In the 36-seat wedding chapel, couples can be married or renew their vows with the captain presiding. All eight ships have Webcams in their chapels, enabling folks at home to watch an onboard wedding live.

Shops sell sundries, clothing, jewelry, perfumes, and souvenirs. All are convenient to the **Grand Atrium,** the heart of the ship. In the **Art Gallery,** reproduction and original prints are for sale; the ubiquitous auctions are held almost daily and, unfortunately, often obscure the multimillion-dollar museum-quality collection of contemporary art on all ships. The ship's library, **A Quiet Corner,** boasts an extensive book collection and the ever-popular private reading and listening chairs. The newest addition is the **Internet Café,** which is open 24 hours daily; and a florist, who prepares fresh floral arrangements for purchase. Introduced on the *Coral Princess,* Princess Cruises has now extended the innovative Scholar-Ship@Sea fleetwide. On the *Crown Princess,* a wide range of courses are offered each sea day. For some there is a small fee, usually about $10.

The ships offer a great variety of entertainment. Each of three showrooms has its own shows nightly. **Vista Show Lounge,** the midsize theater, presents cabaret-style entertainment that's quite varied. On Deck 16, across from Sabatini's, *Crown Princess* has a delightful, living room–style piano bar, **Adagio Lounge,** that has proven to be very popular for dessert or after-dinner drinks into the wee hours, particular when Sammy Goldstein is tickling the ivories.

Princess Theatre, a two-deck showroom, stages large-scale production shows and revues and has the best sight lines and most comfortable seats of any shipboard theater we have experienced. The shows, all created by Princess's production department, are outstanding. The **Explorer's Lounge** nightclub features soloists and bands playing a variety of music. The **Casino,** designed by the architects who created Caesars Palace Forum in Las Vegas, has one of the world's largest examples of holographic art. It also has 260 slot machines, 17 blackjack/poker tables, roulette, and craps.

The ships have many other small entertainment venues, some with music and dancing. The **Wheelhouse Bar,** with the ambience of a private club, offers music for dancing; **Snookers** sports bar (although not on *Crown*) has a bank of television monitors that broadcast sports programs, also available in cabins (the system can show events on Princess Theatre's big screen, too). **Calypso Bar** and **Oasis Bar,** outdoors and poolside, are frequently the scene of special events, including the Captain's Party. A retractable dome can be closed in bad weather. **Center Court Bar** is near the sports facilities; **Sea Breeze** and the **Mermaid's Tail** are middeck bars. **Alfresco's** bar overlooks the aft pool, which can be covered and converted into a stage for live concerts.

On *Sapphire Princess,* the signature **Skywalkers Lounge** has been moved a bit farther forward than on other *Grand-* class ships, providing 35% more space and a new 125-foot balcony. **Club Fusion,** a multipurpose, high-tech venue, is ideal for dancing or for use as a theater with its 42 high-definition television screens. On *Crown Princess,* the new balcony is given over to **The Sanctuary,** meant to be a "pocket of tranquillity."

SPORTS, FITNESS, AND BEAUTY Each of the *Grand-*class ships has five swimming pools—including one for children and one for crew—and nine whirlpools. The **Princess Links** computerized golf simulator lets passengers try some of the world's top courses. A landscaped putting green is available, as are paddle tennis, basketball, and volleyball courts. A swim-against-the-current lap pool is the centerpiece of the **Lotus Spa.** The gym has treadmills, Stairmasters, Lifecycles, weight machines, an area for exercise and aerobics classes, and trainer-led options (for a charge) such as yoga, kickbox press, pulse group cycling, and Pilates. There are changing rooms and saunas (no charge) for men and women and an outside jogging track. The beauty spa, operated by Steiner, has 11 massage rooms offering a range of pricey treatments, such as aromatherapy massage, mud and seaweed wraps, and reflexology. Also featured are Asian-influenced treatments, such as chakra stone therapy, a massage with hot, oiled stones. On *Star Princess,* the Lotus Spa is even larger than on her sister ships, with more treatment rooms and a thermal suite with steam rooms, heated lounge chairs, cool showers, and an ice bath for use by spa clients only, before or after treatments. A teak promenade encircles the ship; five and a half laps is just shy of a mile.

CHILDREN'S FACILITIES The two-level **Shockwaves** offers a whale-shaped splash pool, life-size dollhouse, children's theater, ball jump, games, and more. Programs are age-specific and supervised. The **Remix Teen Center,** also bi-level, has a video disco, refreshment bar, video games, and private whirlpool. See "Children's Facilities" in the *Sun* group for Princess Kids' new expanded program. *Crown Princess* and other ships have added the Youth Security Patrol—specially trained young adults wearing easily identifiable bright yellow shirts walk around the ship to help keep an eye on kids.

SHORE EXCURSIONS Princess shore excursions are well organized, particularly given the size of ship and number of people touring. Excursions on Mediterranean cruises cover the most important attractions; we recommend them, especially for first-timers. Passengers familiar with the ports may want to arrange their own activities. During calls in Mexico, Princess has a variety of adventure-type tours, such as Dolphin Encounters and kayaking, certified scuba diving, and excursions in all-terrain vehicles, at a range of prices. Descriptions of shore excursions and prices are available on the Princess Web site; once you have booked your cruise, you can also book shore excursions.

Princess's latest Web site innovation is interactive eBrochures, said to be the cruise industry's first. It offers a clickable table of contents, interactive deck plans, a built-in search function, custom printing of selected pages, the ability to zoom in on maps and deck plans, and direct links to detailed content on **www.princess.com.** In November 2006, Princess added the facility to enable passengers to access their boarding passes and review information on their cruise, air, transfers, pre- and post-hotel packages, shore excursion reservations, and spa appointments in one place.

POSTSCRIPT Even with Princess's many innovations and attractions, passengers who have sailed with the line before will recognize these super-megaliners as very much Princess ships. They appeal most to those who see their size as a positive thing, providing options every hour of the day. They are sure to be popular with first-time cruisers. A big dividend of their size is a smooth ride. Those with health problems will be comforted to know the ships have a two-way video system (the first cruise ships to have it) that allows the ships' doctors to confer live with medical specialists and top hospitals ashore and in the United States. *Crown Princess, Golden Princess* and *Star Princess*'s telemedicine facilities are even more state-of-the-art and include a digital X-ray machine, defibrillators positioned around the ship as well as in the ship's hospital, and other high-tech equipment.

Coral Princess	QUALITY 9	VALUE B
Island Princess	PREVIEW	
REGISTRY Bermuda	LENGTH 964 feet	BEAM 106 feet
CABINS 987	DRAFT 26 feet	SPEED 21.5 knots
MAXIMUM PASSENGERS	PASSENGER DECKS 16	ELEVATORS 12
2,566	CREW 900	SPACE RATIO 44.6

THE SHIPS   In 2003, the 92,000-ton *Coral Princess* made her maiden voyage and was christened in the Panama Canal by the president of Panama—the first cruise ship ever to have such an honor; and her sister, *Island Princess,* debuted in Vancouver, also marking a milestone as the first cruise ship ever christened in the Canadian port city.

These twins were a new class of ships for Princess, built specifically to transit the Panama Canal, and they reverse the line's recent trend of building megaships of more than 100,000 tons. Despite their smaller size, they are very spacious and include most amenities and services found on Princess's largest vessels, such as a wedding chapel, alternative dining options, a 24-hour restaurant, **Internet cafe,** and a substantial number of balcony cabins. Indeed, the duo appear to combine the best features of the *Sun* and *Grand* classes, plus having some great attractions that even the bigger ships can't boast.

Constructed at Chantiers de l'Atlantique, the ships are Princess's first French-built vessels. They are very well laid out, making it easy for passengers to get oriented quickly. Their refined and pleasing decor is sophisticated yet comfortable, interesting in detail, and easy on the eyes. Among their newest features are the unusual high-tech facilities in the aft show lounge and their innovative power-generation technology—a gas turbine/diesel engine combination, with the gas turbines placed in the ships' funnels. The configuration not only has environmental advantages, but also allows for additional space inside the ships used for enhanced passenger facilities. Then there are the unique features: the first-ever cruise ship kiln—yes, a kiln—and a television-style demonstration kitchen. Emeril would feel right at home.

ITINERARIES   *See* Itinerary Index.

CABINS   Nearly 90% of the ships' cabins are outside, and most of these—83%—have private balconies. Although there are 33 price levels, mostly resulting from location, season, and length of cruise, essentially there are only five types of cabins: suites with balconies (468–591 square feet), minisuites with balconies (323 square feet), outside standard with balconies (214–257 square feet), outside standard (168 square feet), and inside standard (160 square feet). The best value for the money are the outside standards with balconies, rightly called affordable balconies. The wheelchair-accessible cabins range from 217 to 374 square feet and are available in most categories.

Throughout, the cabins are decorated in easy-to-live-with warm colors and mellow wood. All cabins have twin beds that can be converted to a queen, television with CNN, CNBC, ESPN, TNT, Discovery Channel, movies, and several radio channels, minifridge, ample closet and drawer space, two hair dryers, safe, telephone with voice mail, and bathroom with shower. Further amenities are added in the pricier categories: minisuites have a queen-size bed, separate sitting area with sofa bed, balcony, two televisions, bathroom with tub and shower, and robes (can be requested in standard cabins). Suites enjoy a larger balcony, walk-in closet, a wet bar, and bath with whirlpool tub. The pebbly non-slip surface of the bathroom floor is a welcome safety feature. There's a self-serve laundry on every cabin deck—another appreciated amenity.

Specifications   879 outside cabins (527 with balconies), 108 inside; 16 suites and 184 minisuites with balconies; 8 minisuites; 616 upper berths; 20 (16 outside/4 inside) wheelchair-accessible.

DINING   The ships' Personal Choice Dining lineup offers two main dining rooms, **Provence** and **Bordeaux,** which passengers can choose for either Traditional Fixed Seating (Provence Dining Room at either first or second seating each evening) or Anytime Dining (Bordeaux Dining Room, 5:30–10 p.m., or by reserving a specific time). Passengers may change from Traditional to Anytime Dining during the cruise, if they prefer. Further options are the 24-hour **Horizon Court** for breakfast, lunch, and bistro dinner for casual evening dining; the **Pizza Bar,** where the specialties are varied and excellent; and the patisserie.

Two alternative restaurants carry a surcharge. The new **Bayou Café and Steakhouse,** the first New Orleans–style dinner restaurant at sea ($15 per person, which includes a hurricane cocktail), offers Cajun specialties and live jazz. Reviews on this eatery are mixed. Some thought the food was excellent; we did not, and considering that New Orleans is noted for fabulous cuisine and some of the best restaurants in the country, we were disappointed with the Bayou's menu. The best aspect of the cafe is the jazz music in the evening, but be sure to avoid the seating at the side tables behind the orchestra; the sound level there is deafening.

Sabatini's ($20 surcharge), the popular Princess signature Italian restaurant, is open for dinner only except on sea days, when it serves brunch. Dinner has a set menu of so many courses—all excellent—that it's almost too much food. The outstanding service is as good as the food. And if you are still suffering hunger pangs, there's a poolside hamburger grill, an ice-cream bar (extra charge) near the pool, and 24-hour room service.

SERVICE The service throughout the ship is excellent. The friendly staff greets passengers at all times of day in all parts of the ship, and they are eager to help. The **Sabatini** staff is wonderful, and our Filipino room steward was superb, going out of his way to be helpful. We have never had a more cheerful, attentive, and professional room steward on any ship, including the most luxurious ones. Other passengers have reported enthusiastically the same kudos for the staff of *Island Princess.*

FACILITIES AND ACTIVITIES The ship's design maximizes the public space for passenger activities, with some lounges spanning the ship from port to starboard. Most of the public rooms are on Decks 6 and 7. Just as on the larger vessels, this duo has three show lounges, but with an added dimension—the two-story interactive high-tech aft lounge. Known as the **Universe Lounge,** the decor was inspired by Jules Verne's classic, *20,000 Leagues Under the Sea,* and sports three revolving stages with integrated lifts, giant projection screens, and the latest in lighting technology, digital sound, and video systems. The stages are designed for a diverse slate of entertainment, from Vegas-style shows to movie screenings and full television productions to small classroom-style demonstrations.

The Universal Lounge is also home to Princess Cruises' fleetwide enrichment program, ScholarShip@Sea, which Princess calls "edutainment." Considering the courses available—cooking, photography, ceramic painting, decorating, visual arts, computers, health, finance, and lectures on a wide variety of topics—the term is accurate. Introduced on the *Coral Princess,* the lounge's demonstration kitchen can be moved into place for cooking classes by the ship's chef or visiting culinary experts. The room has network plug-ins for up to 50 laptop computers and an infrared headset system for the hearing impaired. Each cruise offers a slate of up to 20 courses, with six options offered each sea day. For some there is a small fee, usually about $10 to $25. Other daytime activities are standard cruise-ship fare (which pale by comparison to the edutainment) and include the ubiquitous art auctions, bingo, horse racing game, ice-carving demonstrations, and pool games.

Evening entertainment is as varied as the venues. *Coral Princess* has musical shows performed by a cast of 17 lively and very professional singers and dancers in the bi-level **Princess Theatre,** the main show lounge, or the multipurpose Universal Lounge. There is also a variety of music from jazz to country, singers, comedians, and novelty acts in other lounges and bars, as well as classical concerts on some days. The **Wheelhouse Bar,** which spans Deck 7, is one of the most handsome rooms on any cruise ship and is very popular with passengers for cocktails and dancing before and after dinner. Farther along the deck are some new gathering places, such as the **Churchill Lounge,** a cigar and spirits lounge with its own humidor, and the **Rat Pack Bar,** a 1960s retro martini bar—both firsts for Princess. One deck down is the casino, with London-style decor, and the Explorer's Lounge, which becomes the disco in the late evening. There's also a wedding chapel, an Internet cafe, a library and card room, duty-free shops, and an art gallery.

SPORTS, FITNESS, AND BEAUTY The Lido Deck (14) has a swimming pool, three whirlpools, and a poolside bar. In the **Lotus Spa,** meant to reflect the soothing aura of Bali, there is a swim-against-the-current pool, covered by a retractable glass magrodrome, and two whirlpools. Farther aft is the aerobics room and gym. Be prepared for a hard sell of the spa lotions and other products by the Steiner staff; your response should be equally firm if you have no interest in purchasing them. The new vessels offer a nine-hole putting course and golf simulator.

CHILDREN'S FACILITIES On Deck 12 aft is action central for Princess's supervised age-specific children's program. The outstanding facilities include **Off Limits,** the teen center with special activities for young adults ages 13–17, including video games and a teen disco. The **Fun Zone** is a special center for Princess Piloteers (ages 8–12), with regular activities designed for this age group. **Pelican's Playhouse,** the children's center for ages 2–7, is where **Youth Center** staff host a daily schedule of age-specific activities. The Pelican's Pool is a dedicated children's pool.

Pacific Princess	QUALITY 8	VALUE C
Royal Princess	PREVIEW	
Tahitian Princess	QUALITY 8	VALUE C
REGISTRY Gibraltar	LENGTH 594 feet	BEAM 83.5feet
CABINS 344	DRAFT 19.5 feet	SPEED 20 knots
MAXIMUM PASSENGERS	PASSENGER DECKS 9	ELEVATORS 4
680/710	CREW 373	SPACE RATIO 44

THE SHIPS *Tahitian Princess* and *Pacific Princess,* which joined the Princess fleet in late 2002, and the newly acquired *Royal Princess,* were the former *R3, R4,* and *R8* of the now-defunct Renaissance Cruises. The triplets are midgets compared with the other ships in the Princess fleet, but many of the line's passengers who lamented the departure of the former *Pacific Princess* have been pleased with these ships. In addition to their more intimate cruise environment, the ships are quite new, having entered service originally in 1999, and they come with many modern features.

The ships offer many of the Personal Choice Cruising options that have become Princess trademarks. These include four restaurant choices: the main dining room, **Sabatini's Trattoria, Sterling Steakhouse,** and the 24-hour **Lido cafe,** plus a poolside barbecue grill.

The ships each have a show lounge, eight bars, an observation lounge, casino, a library and card room, two shops, and a medical center. There is a swimming pool, a spa with two whirlpools and beauty salon, a fitness center, and jogging track.

Ninety-two percent of the cabins are outside, and more than two-thirds of these come with a private balcony. All have television with

CNN, ESPN, and first-run movies, VCR, personal safe, refrigerator, and hair dryer. Passengers have a self-service launderette.

Specifications 344 cabins, including 10 suites, 52 minisuites; 317 outside, 27 inside; 232 have balconies; 3 wheelchair-accessible.

POSTSCRIPT *Tahitian Princess* sails year-round in Tahiti and the South Pacific on the region's only ten-day cruises. The three different itineraries sail round-trip from Papeete, Tahiti, call at Bora Bora, Moorea, and Raiatea, and either the Cook Islands, Samoa, or the Marquesas. The *Pacific Princess* has operated on a split deployment, sailing half the year throughout French Polynesia and the wider Pacific region for Princess Cruises, and the other half for P&O Cruises.

In 2008, Princess Cruises will return to world cruising with *Pacific Princess* on a 102-day voyage traveling across six continents, visiting 42 destinations in 31 countries. Departing January 10, 2008, *Pacific Princess* sails westbound from Fort Lauderdale, Florida, to Southampton, England, via the Caribbean, South America, South Pacific, Australia, Asia, the Middle East, and Europe.

Royal Princess, formerly the *Minerva II* of the now-defunct Swan Hellenic Cruises, is named for a beloved former Princess ship. She joined the fleet in April 2007 after a refit that transformed her into a Princess and is sailing on a series of European cruises that have added some interesting new ports to the Princess roster, such as Ravenna, Italy; Split, Croatia; Kotor, Montenegro; and Canakkale (for Troy), Turkey—all UNESCO World Heritage Sites. Other destinations include Corsica and Sardinia.

Regent Seven Seas Cruises

1000 Corporate Drive, Suite 500, Fort Lauderdale, FL 33334
☎ 954-776-6123, 800-477-7500, or 800-285-1835; fax 954-772-3763
www.theregentexperience.com

TYPE OF SHIPS Small and midsize luxury vessels with big-ship facilities.

TYPE OF CRUISES Quiet, luxurious, destination-oriented cruises with personal service and sophisticated amenities.

CRUISE LINE'S STRENGTHS
• service
• itineraries
• cuisine
• single, flex-time/open-seating dining
• all-inclusive prices
• all-outside deluxe accommodations and amenities

CRUISE LINE'S SHORTCOMINGS
• limited, staid shipboard activities

FELLOW PASSENGERS Affluent, well educated, well traveled, 45 years and older, $150,000+ annual income; more than 75% are Americans. They cherish their individuality and shun group travel. Most are senior executives, professionals, and high-end resort vacationers; many own their company. They usually have cruised before on luxury liners, have sophisticated tastes, and care about elegance and service. Some are likely to be special-occasion celebrators and incentive awards winners.

Recommended for Upscale, independent, active, seasoned travelers accustomed to luxury and quality. Small-ship devotees who appreciate the advantages and accept the limitations of such vessels.

Not recommended for Joiners; people who need to be entertained, want a full day of shipboard activity, or thrive in a Vegas atmosphere.

CRUISE AREAS AND SEASONS Antarctica, Asia, Australia, Middle East, New Zealand, winter; Canada, Caribbean, Central and South America, Mexico, transcanal, U.S. East Coast, fall/winter/spring; Alaska, Bermuda, Europe, Mediterranean, spring/summer; Northern Europe, summer; South Pacific, year-round.

THE LINE In 1995, Radisson Diamond Cruises and Seven Seas Cruise Line merged to form Radisson Seven Seas Cruises. The deal represented an expansion into cruising by Radisson Hotels International, owned by Carlson Hospitality Worldwide.

Launched in 1990 by a wealthy Japanese businesswoman who established its high standards, Seven Seas Cruise Line's *Song of Flower* (sold in 2003) quickly made her mark by offering deluxe cruises at rates considerably lower than its competitors and winning accolades and awards

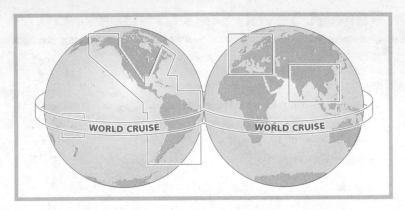

CRUISE AREAS AND SEASONS FOR REGENT SEVEN SEAS CRUISES

after only its first year. Radisson Seven Seas introduced the *Paul Gauguin* in 1998, and in a joint venture with Monte Carlo–based V. Ships, it debuted the all-suite luxury *Seven Seas Navigator* in 1999 and the larger, all-suite, all-balcony *Seven Seas Mariner* in 2001, and her sister ship, *Seven Seas Voyager,* in 2003. Each ship can boast some of cruising's highest space-to-passenger and crew-to-passenger ratios.

In a major reorganization of its hotel division in 2006, Carlson Hospitality brought Radisson Seven Seas Cruises into the Regent brand and changed the cruise line's name to Regent Seven Seas Cruises. Following the name change, RSSC began a multimillion-dollar investment to upgrade and refit all cabins and suites and public areas fleetwide.

The cruise line often charters deluxe exploration ships, such as the *Explorer II,* for adventure and Antarctic cruises. For 2008, the line has two Antarctic cruises, departing Ushuaia, Argentina, on January 21 (11 nights) and February 1 (15 nights) on *Explorer II.* Also in 2008, *Seven Seas Voyager* leaves from San Francisco on January 6, on a 115-night world cruise, with seven segments and calling at 51 ports in 26 countries on five continents with 11 overnight stays.

THE FLEET	BUILT/RENOVATED	TONNAGE	PASSENGERS
Paul Gauguin	1998/2006	19,200	320
Seven Seas Mariner	2001/06	50,000	700
Seven Seas Navigator	1999/2007	33,000	490
Seven Seas Voyager	2003/06	46,000	700

STYLE The size of the ships, their relatively small number of passengers, and price ensure the cruises a certain exclusivity. They also help define the high level of service and personal attention passengers expect—and receive.

Shipboard life is informal during the day but formal in style (though not necessarily in dress) in the evening. Surroundings are spacious and luxurious, the ambience sophisticated. The ships have loyal fans.

The affluent passengers on these ships are accustomed to a high level of service and comfort, which the ships deliver in their spaciousness, luxurious surroundings, and attentive staff. There is the usual array of shipboard staples—exercise classes, word and board games, bingo, the ubiquitous art auctions—but nothing too taxing. In fact, if there's a criticism to be made, it would be the need to provide passengers with more imaginative shipboard activities. The all-inclusive prices include select complimentary wine and spirits at all bars and restaurants fleetwide on every sailing.

RSSC offers NewspaperDirect across the fleet. With this service, passengers may receive daily printed editions of their favorite national or international newspapers, including *USA Today, Financial Times,* the *Wall Street Journal, Frankfurter Allgemeine Zeitung,* and *Le Monde,* among others. Recently, the line upgraded its Internet access and added digital satellite-fed television, WiFi hot spots in select public areas, shipboard cell phone service, and additional online capabilities. Internet access costs $0.35 per minute or $0.25 per minute when purchased in a package of 100 minutes. Now, too, passengers with deposited reservations can pre-reserve a table for dining at one of the line's reservations-only restaurants, as well as spa treatments.

RSSC has also launched a series of new programs and amenities called The Regent Experience. It includes Travel Concierge, meant to give passengers the tools to customize their travel based on their personal interests and preferences. Special à la carte tour and hotel arrangements can be prebooked through a dedicated toll-free number, or passengers may select from an array of exclusive Concierge Collection and other shore excursions and preregister on RSSC's Web site. Passengers confirmed in suites with butler service can e-mail their special requests in advance.

In 2007, as part of its Travel Concierge program, Regent introduced iJourneys: downloadable, personal iPod walking tours available for purchase for a variety of Mediterranean ports such as Barcelona. Each one-and-a-half-hour tour, compatible with iPod or MP3 players, comes with a map, commentary, historical context, a touch of humor, and tips such as back entrances and shorter lines at popular attractions. Additional tours are being developed for select ports worldwide.

Another new program to help passengers customize their cruises is an enrichment program, called Circles of Interest and featuring 12 "circles"—food and wine, performing arts, photography, history, archaeology and literature, the environment and marine life, antiques, jewelry and shopping, active exploration and wellness, art design and museums, families and friends, and romance—with ship and shore activities linked by theme. Passengers can step into the circle that interests them and enhance their cruise with a tailored program of onboard lectures and workshops.

DISTINCTIVE FEATURES No-tipping policy. Water sports platform and marina on *Paul Gauguin.* Extensive book/video libraries. Cordon Bleu–directed venues on *Mariner* and *Voyager.* WiFi hot spots. iPod music systems with Bose speakers preset with music in upper category suites.

Inclusive prices (see RATES below).

	HIGHEST	LOWEST	AVERAGE
PER DIEM	$1,267	$295	$771

Per diems are calculated from cruise line's nondiscounted *cruise-only* published fares on standard accommodations and vary by season, cabins, and cruise areas.

RATES Gratuities and wine with lunch and dinner included. Select complimentary wine and spirits at all bars and restaurants fleetwide on every sailing. Soft drinks and room bar setup included; nonalcoholic drinks restocked daily, depending on ship. Port charges are additional.

Special fares and discounts
- Between 25% and 50% savings on select voyages. Second-passenger savings of 50% savings off standard fares.
- **SINGLE SUPPLEMENT:** Specific amounts per cruise in brochure.

Packages
- **AIR/SEA:** Yes.
- **PRE/POST:** Yes.

PAST PASSENGERS Regent Seven Seas Society for repeat passengers offers members' sailings with incentives and special prices. Some sailings are hosted by the line's president. Members receive quality gifts based on the number of days they cruise. The programs has five tiers: SSS member (4 to 20 nights), Silver (21 to 74 nights), Gold (75 to 199 nights), Platinum (200 to 399 nights), and Titanium (400+ nights). Details on the benefits for each tier are available on Regent's Web site.

THE LAST WORD After the *Diamond* departed, RSSC was left with its newest ships more similar in size and style and has been able to focus on providing its passengers with the ultimate in luxury. Despite the intense competition in the luxury end of the market, not only from the established luxury lines but from new entries and from the new phenomenon of luxury adventure ships, the line has been able to maintain the lead it has enjoyed for several years.

Regent Seven Seas Standard Features

Officers *Mariner:* French and European; *Navigator/Voyager:* European, international, Italian; *Paul Gauguin:* French and international.

Staff Dining and Cabin: European and international; Cruise: American and British.

Dining facilities Two dining rooms on *Navigator;* four on *Mariner, Voyager* with open seating for three meals; informal indoor/outdoor cafe for buffet breakfast and lunch. Reservations-only alternative dining on *Navigator, Mariner, Voyager;* four choices.

Special diets Accommodated with advance notice.

Room service 24-hour service with full-meal, in-cabin dining.

Dress code Casual by day; smart casual most evenings; some evenings, jackets required for men. Formal or semiformal for Captain's parties. Visits in some ports of call may require women to cover heads, legs, and arms.

Cabin amenities Direct-dial phone, hair dryer, television, VCR/DVD, radio, stocked minibar, marble bathroom with tub and shower (except *Gauguin*). CNN, *Navigator,* all suites; *Mariner, Voyager* all suites, all verandas, robes, safe. Butler service in select cabins, iPod and Bose speakers in butler suites.

Electrical outlets 110 AC.

Wheelchair access *Mariner,* 6; *Navigator, Voyager* 4; *Gauguin,* 1.

Recreation and entertainment Nightly shows, nightclub, cabaret, and piano entertainment in two lounges, small casino, dancing, card games, backgammon, book/video library, lecture program.

Sports and other activities One outside pool. See text.

Beauty and fitness Beauty salon, small gym. Carita spas on all ships; see text.

Other facilities Boutique, hospital; *Mariner, Voyager,* Internet cafe, launderettes; *Navigator* and *Gauguin,* Internet access in library. Meeting space and business facilities.

Children's facilities Club Mariner children's program on select cruises; summer environment program on *Gauguin*.

Theme cruises Yes.

Smoking Smoking sections designated in public areas; no cigar or pipe smoking in dining room.

Regent Seven Seas suggested tipping Gratuities are included in cruise fare; therefore, no-tipping policy.

Credit cards For cruise payment and onboard charges: American Express, Diners Club, MasterCard, Visa, Discover.

Seven Seas Navigator	QUALITY 8	VALUE B
REGISTRY Bahamas	LENGTH 560 feet	BEAM 81 feet
CABINS 251	DRAFT 21 feet	SPEED 20 knots
MAXIMUM PASSENGERS	PASSENGER DECKS 8	ELEVATORS 5
490	CREW 345	SPACE RATIO 67.3

THE SHIP In a joint venture with Monte Carlo–based V. Ships, Regent Seven Seas Cruises launched its all-suite luxury ship, *Seven Seas Navigator,* in 1999 and renovated her in 2006. The Italian-built vessel, the fastest in the Regent fleet at the time, has an ice-strengthened hull, giving her the ability to operate virtually anywhere in the world. V. Ships, established in 1984, is a company of the Vlasov Group, one of the world's largest providers of ship management and related services.

A small ship with a big-ship feel, the spacious *Navigator* (with one of the industry's highest space ratios) has half a dozen lounges, superbly appointed outside suites (90% with balconies, walk-in closets, and well-appointed bathrooms), single-seating dining, an alternative restaurant, a wide teak deck surrounding the pool, and a slate of worldwide, port-intensive itineraries.

Designed by Norwegian architects Yran *&* Storbraaten, *Navigator's* public rooms are strikingly contemporary and minimalist. Yet unusual lamps, exotic chairs, and varied materials and textures provide visual interest. The entire ship is well integrated, with light-blue carpeting throughout and bold oil paintings (all for sale) decorating the corridors. A bank of glass elevators offers a bird's-eye view of the gracefully designed ship and a panoramic view of the pool area. Nonetheless, they seem out of place on a small luxury vessel, and the exposed machinery is jarring.

The ship blazed the trail for RSSC's first ventures to South America, Alaska, and a world cruise.

CABINS Particular attention was lavished on the accommodations. They range from roomy standard suites of 301 square feet plus veranda to Master Suites with 1,067 square feet plus a 106-square-foot balcony. All standard suites are identical; price varies by location. Ten suites are interconnected. Four suites are wheelchair-accessible with extra-wide doors and large, shower-only bathrooms.

The suites, like the rest of the elegant ship, are decorated in subdued colors with cherrywood accents. They have sitting areas, twin beds convertible to a queen, marble bathrooms with separate tub and shower, and walk-in closet with safe. Other amenities include a minibar with liquor setup, bathrobes, hair dryer, new flat-screen television, DVD players, and clocks. In the 2006 renovations, the layout of some suites was changed and big cabinets that had been built to hold a television were replaced with flat screens, which allows for more rooms in the suites. All accommodations fleetwide have new mattresses, down comforters, Egyptian cotton percale Anichini linens with satin-stitch embroidery, cashmere throws, and new linens and Regent luxury amenities in bathrooms. Upper category suites also have iPod music systems with Bose speakers preset with music content.

In standard suites, a coffee table rises to dining-table height with the touch of a button, and upper-level suites have proper dining room tables. Passengers can dine en suite, ordering from the dining room menu during meal hours, with dishes served course by course. The ship offers 24-hour room service.

Master and Grand suites, which come with butler service, have a foyer with a powder room, living/dining area, and a separate bedroom with bathroom that has a bidet. Two other top suite categories (A and B) also offer butler service—a posh touch that includes cocktails served daily.

Specifications 251 outside suites, 90% have balconies. Standard balcony suites, 301 square feet plus balconies; 10 Grand Suites, 538 square feet plus balconies; 4 Master Suites, 1,067 square feet plus balconies; 4 wheelchair-accessible.

DINING The open, single-seating **Compass Rose Restaurant** provides a gracious setting, with a small dance floor for occasional dinner dances. An alabaster compass rose skylight looks down on the pale yellow walls; draperies in soft pastels frame the picture windows; and potted plants are interspersed among the widely spaced tables.

Fine service, gracious ambience, and generous space between tables add to the luxury. Seating is open; neither times nor tables are assigned. Gourmet cuisine is the ship's most outstanding feature. Selections change daily and include fresh seafood and prime meats. Preparation and presentation are varied and sophisticated.

Passengers stroll across a parquet floor to enter the **Portofino II Ristorante,** the alternative restaurant with its own galley. It provides a gorgeous setting of linen-draped tables, blue-cushioned chairs, and filmy white curtains, imparting a true Mediterranean flavor; this venue serves the ship's best dishes. At breakfast and lunch, the indoor/outdoor Portofino provides buffet dining; at night a wing of the spacious room is transformed into an à la carte restaurant featuring northern Italian specialties. Tables must be reserved for dinner, but there is no service charge here or elsewhere on this gratuities-included ship. Complimentary wine is served in both dining venues.

FACILITIES AND ACTIVITIES The two-tiered **Seven Seas** show lounge hosts varied entertainment, ranging from Broadway revues to concert pianists. The **Stars Lounge** is the disco/after-hours club where sleek, deep-blue leather chairs backed in wood line up along a glass-topped bar.

A few steps away, cigar lovers gather in the **Connoisseur Club's** tobacco-colored leather armchairs near a granite-topped faux fireplace. Next door, the small **Navigator Lounge** serves coffee and cocktails throughout the day. At the large library stocked with books, periodicals, and 800 videos, there is a bank of nine computers where passengers can check their e-mail. Two boutiques sell designer wares.

A dark, rich-looking casino has tables for blackjack, stud poker, roulette, and craps; slots and poker machines are found in an adjacent room. High on Deck 11, passengers walk through a hall of marble and carpet to emerge in the light, attractive **Galileo's,** a piano bar and lounge with indoor/outdoor seating and a dance floor. One deck higher, forward, the **Vista Lounge** provides a hideaway of tambour chairs with thick yellow-and-green striped cushions (private parties welcome).

SPORTS, FITNESS, AND BEAUTY Adjacent to the Vista Lounge are the gym, aerobics rooms, and spa managed by Carita of Paris.

The large midship pool area offers a grill and two whirlpools, plus a venue for moonlight barbecues and dancing. Golfers get two driving cages and a putting green.

CHILDREN'S FACILITIES Club Mariner children's program is available on selected cruises. The program has two tiers: children ages 6 to 11 and 12 to 17. The activities focus on the destination's nature, heritage, and crafts. Special tours are offered and a children's menu is served in the dining rooms.

Seven Seas Mariner	QUALITY 8	VALUE B
Seven Seas Voyager	QUALITY 9	VALUE B
REGISTRY Wallis and Futuna/Bahamas	LENGTH 709/670 feet	BEAM 93/94.5 feet
CABINS 328/353	DRAFT 21/23 feet	SPEED 20 knots
MAXIMUM PASSENGERS	PASSENGER DECKS 8/9	ELEVATORS 8
700	CREW 445/447	SPACE RATIO 71.4/70

THE SHIPS   In another joint venture, Monte Carlo–based V. Ships and Regent Seven Seas built cruising's first all-balcony, all-suite luxury cruise ship. The *Seven Seas Mariner,* delivered in 2001, and her sister, *Seven Seas Voyager,* delivered in 2003, had the same architects and interior designer, Petter Yran and Bjorn Storbraaten, who have designed many luxury cruise ships. The stylish sisters are the largest ships in the RSSC fleet, with the greatest space ratio of any cruise ships to date. Both ships were renovated and upgraded in 2006, and *Mariner* was further refurbished in 2007.

The two ships, which were built at different shipyards—*Mariner* in France, *Voyager* in Italy—are sisters rather than twins, with some major differences. The latter ship improved over her sister ship by taking some of the best features from *Navigator,* particularly the larger size of its suites and the full bathtub and separate glass-enclosed shower stall, along with some extra marble touches in the bathroom. *Voyager*'s hull is wider than *Mariner*'s, and she has one additional deck. Two of the alternative restaurants, **Signatures** and **Latitudes,** were relocated to Deck 5 and are serviced by a single galley, and Latitudes was completely redesigned to have a show kitchen visible to passengers from their tables and used for cooking demonstrations and classes. Also, *Voyager* is the first ship to have two independent propulsion and power-generation systems in two separate areas of the ship—a significantly enhanced safety measure.

On both ships, most of the public rooms are located on the first three and top two passenger decks and have as their focal point an eight-deck-high atrium with three glass-enclosed elevators and stairways curving up through the atrium. For some, the lounges on *Mariner* are so spacious they lack atmosphere; for others, the spaciousness of her public areas is the very essence of the ship's luxury. Significantly, the area of the public rooms on *Voyager* was reduced by 23%; two lounges on *Mariner* were combined into one lounge on *Voyager.*

The ships' spaciousness and sparseness are immediately evident in the atrium, where the sculpture decor and visible elevator machinery give it a raw, unfinished look. The starboard side gallery leading off the atrium on Deck Six serves as a wide connecting boulevard running fore and aft past the open-plan library. The Promenade Deck windows provide natural light, and the generously proportioned space is furnished with wicker chairs, planters, and greenery. Art auctions take place here.

The ships' facilities include a spa, a bi-level main show lounge, a small nightclub lounge with a dance floor, a large forward observation lounge, a library, and an Internet cafe. There is a Club Mariner for children on select cruises. The ship has the standard RSSC features, such as all gratuities included in the fare, port-intensive itineraries, and single, open-seating dining with complimentary wine at dinner, but it's the choice of four restaurants that makes these ships different.

Also, the duo's innovative pod propulsion system eliminates the traditional shaft-and-rudder system, making the vessel up to 15% more efficient and reducing noise and vibration. The pods have forward-facing propellers that can be turned 360 degrees, which optimizes maneuverability, fuel efficiency, and speed.

ITINERARIES *See* Itinerary Index.

CABINS The cabins are spread over five center decks and come in 12 or 13 categories of outside suites, all with balconies. *Mariner* suites range from 301 square feet to 1,580 square feet including the veranda (*Voyager,* 356 to 1,403 feet). *Voyager* suites are paneled in light wood with fabrics in gold, orange-rust, and light green. The deluxe suites are the most numerous and have a slightly partitioned and curtained bedroom with king-size bed (convertible to twins) and lounge, walk-in closet and marble bathroom with a full tub and shower. Curiously, the bath and closet on *Mariner* are smaller than on the *Navigator,* something that was rectified on the *Seven Seas Voyager.* The ships now have new furnishings and linens similar to *Navigator.*

The Penthouse Suites, somewhat misnamed, are larger than the deluxe category at 449 square feet on *Mariner* (370 square feet on *Voyager*), but not all are located on the top deck as the name might imply. They feature a roomy, partitioned lounge with L-shaped couch, two lounge chairs, and a glass-top table. The 73-square-foot teak deck balcony on *Mariner* (50 square feet on *Voyager*) has rather ordinary white plastic chairs and a low table. Accommodations increase in spaciousness in the higher categories, which also offer butler service. Some suites will take a third person, and the two-bedroom master suites accommodate up to five.

All accommodations have satellite telephone, flat-screen television with 13 channels, including CNN and ESPN, DVD for American and European systems, and hookups for personal video cameras, safe, bathrobes, hair dryer, in-suite bar setup upon embarkation, and complimentary replenished bottled water, soft drinks, and beer. The suites are attended by European stewardesses.

An expandable tabletop makes in-cabin dining a pleasure and is very popular, especially at the end of a busy day ashore. A full meal may be ordered from the **Compass Rose Restaurant** or from an in-suite menu 24 hours a day. Valet dry cleaning, laundry service, and tailor service for minor repairs and small alterations are available. The self-service launderettes on cabins decks are complimentary.

Bose Wave music systems have been installed on *Voyager, Mariner,* and *Navigator.* In addition, all suites on *Mariner* and *Navigator* have DVD players and an extensive DVD movie library. *Voyager* has a DVD library and players in all suites. Some 47 of *Mariner's* suites now have new deluxe shower stalls, with rain showers and tile seating.

Specifications Mariner 328/Voyager 353 suites; 80 deluxe suites (356 to 1,403 square feet). Limited number of suites accommodate 3 persons; *Mariner,* 6/*Voyager,* 4 wheelchair-accessible. On *Voyager,* 24 suites are interconnecting.

DINING The choice of four dining venues gives the *Mariner* and *Voyager* their most distinctive quality, and all the venues offer a wide variety of high-quality cuisine. Two restaurants have open seating with no reservations necessary; two take reservations for specific tables; none have an additional charge. Complimentary wines are served with dinner in all four restaurants.

The spacious **Compass Rose Restaurant,** the main restaurant and the largest of the four, accommodates most passengers in open seating dining for three meals. The attractive room has a recessed arched ceiling and faux light-wood columns topped with a band of stainless steel capitals. The menu, changed daily, might offer homemade crab cakes as an appetizer, cream of asparagus soup, two salad selections, pasta dish, and main courses, such as sautéed jumbo prawns and Black Angus beef. The choices also include vegetarian dishes and a menu degustation (a sampler of dishes appropriate to the cruising region).

La Veranda, an indoor/outdoor venue, serves a buffet with sheltered outdoor seating aft at wooden tables and chairs set under an awning. There is also an outdoor grill here. Inside the room's etched glass doors, the stylish high-back wooden chairs are set around tables under a coffered ceiling; the walls are hung with alluring black-framed Cote d'Azur travel posters. The unusual chairs have vertical double rows of hollow squares cut into the high backs, reminiscent of the work of Scottish designer Charles Rennie Macintosh. In the evening, a portion of La Veranda becomes a Mediterranean bistro for casual dining, offering a tapas, mezze, or antipasti buffet, followed by table service for the soup of the day, salad, pasta, main course, and dessert.

Latitudes, the smallest of the four, is a reservations-only dinner restaurant with a set sampler menu and tableside presentations. Having started with a more Asian menu, the choices now might range from a foie gras mousse, crab and avocado in a light curry sauce, tomato bisque, pan-fried lobster in a lemongrass gravy, and beef tenderloin in salsa. The setting combines a South Seas and Asian decor with black lacquer chairs, walls decorated with wooden masks and headdresses, and large windows with slatted venetian blinds. The restaurant offers an "Indochine" menu with such exotic selections as Cambodian wafu salad and steamed fresh halibut in a matsutake mushroom broth with gingered vegetables.

Signatures was the first permanent dining venue aboard a cruise ship directed by chefs from Le Cordon Bleu, the famed French culinary institute. The reserved-table restaurant is repeated on *Voyager,* offering a wide choice of entrées and main courses and worth several visits on a long cruise. Marinated fillet of red snapper and roast breast of quail with turnips in a morel sauce are two examples from the list of six choices. The appetizing dessert list included warm chocolate tart with cinnamon ice cream. The sophisticated setting features rust-red chairs with gold tassels, an etched-glass divider between the serving and dining area, and black glass against the aft wall. The chefs take their talents a step further by offering Le Cordon Bleu *Classe Culinaire des Croisieres* on certain voyages. Workshops, conducted by Le Cordon Bleu–trained chefs, provide a hands-on introduction to the art of French cooking. Classes are limited to 16 guests in three two-hour sessions and cost $395 per person. Upon graduation, participants receive their own chef's apron and short toque, a tea towel, and a Le Cordon Bleu cookbook of classic recipes, as well as a certificate of participation. Inquire from the cruise line for future schedules. Both *Mariner* and *Voyager* have this program on select sailings.

FACILITIES AND ACTIVITIES Public rooms are varied in location from high up and forward to down low and aft. The **Observation Lounge,** located two decks above the bridge, offers comfy rust- and tan-colored seating to enjoy hot hors d'oeuvres and soothing piano music before dinner, while taking in a grand 180-degree view. From a perch along the horseshoe-shaped bar, the space takes on a magical quality at night.

The semicircular **Horizon Lounge,** facing aft on one of the lowest passenger decks, is the handsome setting for afternoon tea, with music and light after-dinner entertainment. Additional covered outdoor seating (little used) is a quiet spot for daytime reading. Nearby, the **Connoisseur Club,** with tan leather chairs and an electric fireplace, makes a sophisticated setting for smoking Cuban and Dominican cigars and sipping liqueurs and wines.

The liveliest venue is the **Mariner Lounge (Voyager Lounge** on *Voyager*), drawing a crowd before dining in the adjacent Compass Rose or Latitudes restaurants. *Mariner*'s curvy Art Deco design is highlighted by deep-blue fabrics covering the chairs and glass tabletops, embedded with a translucent star pattern and framed by raised wooden rims.

Stars nightclub-cum-disco, decorated with black-and-white photos of Fred Astaire, Ingrid Bergman, Katharine Hepburn, and other movie stars, is an oddly designed space with a spiral staircase in its midst that links to the midsize casino above. The semicircular two-level **Constellation Lounge,** with continuous brushed blue cotton banquette seating, is joined by staircases flanking the stage. Here, full shows and cabaret acts are presented under a starlit ceiling of changing colors.

In the past, production shows have not been a strength of this line, but to their credit, that changed with the two shows that debuted on *Voyager.* The shows are performed by four primary singers plus a production cast of six. One show on both *Mariner* and *Voyager* is entitled *Lullaby of Broadway* and highlights Broadway shows from the 1950s to today, with a multitude of numbers and costume changes. The second, a very innovative show, at least for a cruise ship, is entitled *On a Classical Note* and features opera, classical music, and light operettas; it is staged on the *Voyager.* The four lead singers have a real opportunity to shine, especially when three different Gilbert and Sullivan operettas were staged in one production. Both ships stage other enjoyable shows, as well. The ships also bring aboard local entertainment from destinations the ships visit, such as (on a South American cruise) a tango and folkloric show in Argentina and a troupe of Chilean folk singers and dancers in Valparaiso.

The open-shelf library offers a generous selection of hardbacks, reference books, and videos, with tables to spread out an atlas and comfortable seating for reading newspapers and magazines. The adjacent **Club.com** is the plainly decorated Internet center with more than a dozen terminals (three more in the library) and offers very low charges for sending and checking e-mail. Passengers may also browse and enjoy computer games. Computer instruction, free and very popular, is excellent. A long, rectangular card room also serves as a conference center.

Amidships on the same deck is a gallery of high-end shops, plus two specialty boutiques placed at two corners of the atrium landings.

SPORTS, FITNESS, AND BEAUTY   The ships' spas are operated by Carita of Paris, with trained therapists available for a variety of treatments that include thalassotherapy, aromatherapy, seaweed and mud wraps, and a variety of massages. Adjoining the spa is an indoor/outdoor fitness center with treadmills, aerobic benches, Nautilus machine, Lifecycles, Stairmasters, free weights, and other exercise equipment. The center also has a beauty salon.

Deck space centers on the Lido pool and three whirlpools, an outdoor bar, and a mezzanine/jogging track above. Outdoor sports include paddle tennis, shuffleboard, and golf nets.

CHILDREN'S FACILITIES   Club Mariner children's program is available on selected cruises. See *Navigator* for details.

POSTSCRIPT   *Mariner*'s roominess has pluses and minuses. The latter become evident in the public lounges and bars, where except for the cocktail hour before meals, the ship's spaciousness often makes it seem empty of life. After dinner, the show lounge is a draw, but otherwise, most passengers retire to their suites. Occasionally, when younger passengers are on board, they may enliven the bars. On the other hand, it's good to note that the European-modern public rooms are lovely and varied in atmosphere and function. Passengers can now select their shore excursions in advance at the cruise line's Web site.

Paul Gauguin	QUALITY 9	VALUE B
REGISTRY Bahamas	LENGTH 513 feet	BEAM 71 feet
CABINS 160	DRAFT 16.9 feet	SPEED 18 knots
MAXIMUM PASSENGERS	PASSENGER DECKS 7	ELEVATORS 4
330	CREW 215	SPACE RATIO 59

THE SHIP   Named for the French artist whose life and work embodied the romance of French Polynesia, the *Paul Gauguin* is the most deluxe ship of its size to cruise the South Seas year-round. Its space ratio is among cruising's highest, and its shallow draft allows access to small, rarely frequented ports.

The French-built vessel, which will mark her tenth anniversary in 2008, is owned by French investors and managed by Regent Seven Seas. *Gauguin's* clean lines, understated elegance, and attention to detail are immediately apparent. The yachtlike ship has an airy ambience with stylish touches, such as blond paneling and gray carpets. The ship underwent a $6 million refurbishment in 2006, which included the addition of a new piano bar, five suites at the stern with private balconies, a remodeled casino, and new fabrics and carpeting throughout the public areas.

ITINERARIES *See* Itinerary Index.

CABINS All accommodations are outside suites with separate sitting area; 50% have verandas. Each is furnished with a queen- or twin-size beds (convertible to queen), closed-circuit television and VCR, safe, direct-dial telephone, and refrigerator stocked with soft drinks, mineral water, and complimentary liquor on arrival. Interiors are enriched by crown moldings and wood accents. Finely crafted furnishings include a love seat and vanity/desk. Storage space includes two closets and built-in drawers. Marble bathrooms have a full-size bathtub and shower, plush towels and cotton robes, hair dryer, and assorted toiletries. Some passengers report being able to hear conversations next door. Cabins above the engine are noisy.

Specifications 160 outside cabins and suites; 80 with balconies. Cabins range from 200 square feet with picture window or portholes and 249 square feet with 56-square-foot veranda to the 531-square-foot Owner's Suite with 57-square-foot veranda; 1 wheelchair-accessible.

DINING Two restaurants offer single open seating. Both have ocean views on three sides. An outdoor bistro, **Le Grill,** provides casual dining throughout the day and evening. Dinner for about two dozen people features freshly prepared steaks and seafood. An espresso bar and 24-hour room service are other options. **Restaurant L'Etoile,** the main dining room, features French and continental cuisine. The smaller **La Veranda** is a reservations-only dinner restaurant offering an Italian and other selections. Complimentary wine is served at lunch and dinner; the ship has an excellent wine list. Guests with reservations enjoy predinner cocktails and hors d'oeuvres in the **Connoisseur Club** (open after dinner for drinks and cigars). Evening attire is "country club elegant" (no ties).

SERVICE The crew generally succeeds in its quest to provide outstanding service. A few glitches in the dining room and in cabin maintenance have been reported, but the overall experience is fine.

FACILITIES AND ACTIVITIES In tribute to Gauguin and French Polynesia, the **Fare** (pronounced "faray") Tahiti Gallery is a small library with books, videos, and other materials on the artist and region. A guest lecturer on every cruise discusses regional history and attractions. The ship has a card room and boutique stocked with Polynesian gifts.

Le Grand Salon is the main lounge for early-evening dancing, entertainment, and daily lectures. Indoor/outdoor **La Palette Lounge** is used for afternoon tea, cocktails, and late-night disco. The small casino has blackjack, roulette, and slot machines, but local regulations bar use of the slots. Nighttime entertainment is minimal. Movies are shown daily on the closed-circuit cabin system; the reception desk lends videos. A singer/pianist performs in La Palette before dinner, and the ship's Filipino band plays for dancing before dinner in Le Grand Salon and afterward in La Palette until 11:30 p.m., when the disco starts up.

In summer, the ship has a joint program with Jean-Michel Cousteau's Ocean Futures Society, called Ambassadors of the Environment, promoting ocean responsibility. The program engages children ages 9 to 15 with fun activities to educate them about marine and island ecosystems and traditional Polynesian culture. The program costs $199 per child and includes a variety of onboard and shoreside activities. Adult family members are encouraged to participate in the program's optional shore excursion.

SPORTS, FITNESS, AND BEAUTY   The fitness center offers free weights and exercise machines that are in use constantly. Aerobics, hydrocalisthenics, and a walkathon are held daily. A separate Carita of Paris salon and spa offers a steam room, massage, facials, and beauty treatments, such as aromatherapy. Three- to six-day spa packages are available.

Paul Gauguin has an outdoor pool and splash bar on an upper deck and a retractable marina at sea level where passengers indulge in sports, including diving and snorkeling. Windsurfing and kayaking equipment is available. Snorkeling gear can be signed out at the cruise's start. Diving is a major attraction. The ship provides PADI-certified instructors and dive boats, as well as courses for novices (PADI certification available) and excursions for certified divers.

SHORE EXCURSIONS   Many shore excursions are water oriented. Outings include a Jet-Ski tour of Bora Bora, outrigger/jeep combination tours, shark feeding, and helicopter tours. Weather permitting, a beach party is held on the line's private *motu*, a small islet.

POSTSCRIPT   Passengers concerned about seasickness should know that rough sailing isn't unusual for this ship, owing to her shallow draft and the sometimes rough Pacific waters. The redeeming feature: she travels mostly short distances between ports and is often at anchor in a sheltered bay at night.

Royal Caribbean International

1050 Caribbean Way, Miami, FL 33132
☎ 305-539-6000 or 800-327-6700; fax 800-722-5329
www.royalcaribbean.com

TYPE OF SHIPS Superliners and megaliners.

TYPE OF CRUISES Mainstream, mass market, modestly upscale, wholesome ambience.

CRUISE LINE'S STRENGTHS
- outstanding facilities and activities
- entertainment
- product consistency
- innovative amenities

CRUISE LINE'S SHORTCOMINGS
- small cabins on older fleet
- limited storage in cabins on older fleet
- impersonal nature of big ships

FELLOW PASSENGERS Moderately upscale couples, singles and families with household income of $40,000+ looking for wide variety in shipboard activities and destinations. Average age is 40s, slightly lower on three- and four-night cruises and slightly higher on ten-night or longer trips. In summer, the age drops because of large number of families traveling with children. About half have cruised at least once, and a quarter are Royal Caribbean repeaters. Genders split evenly, and nine in ten are North Americans. Up to 73% of men and 65% of women are married; 36% are professional, managerial, or proprietors. Educational level, occupations, and age differ on three- and four-night cruises, which are less expensive, shorter cruises appealing to younger people and first-timers.

Recommended for Almost anyone taking a first cruise. Those who like large ships, want an array of options, want to be active, sociable, and don't mind large crowds. Ideal for families, particularly several generations traveling together, because there's something for every age.

Not recommended for Small-ship devotees; those who seek a quiet or intellectual milieu, hate crowds, and have no patience for long lines.

CRUISE AREAS AND SEASONS Caribbean, year-round; Costa Rica, Mexico, Panama Canal, fall to spring; Alaska, Bermuda, Europe, Mediterranean, northeastern United States, spring to fall; Asia, Australia, New Zealand, South America, South Pacific, fall.

THE LINE Founded in 1969 as a partnership of three prominent Norwegian shipping companies, Royal Caribbean Cruises Ltd. was the first company to launch ships designed for year-round Caribbean cruising. The vessels proved to be so popular that within five years more capacity was needed. Two vessels were stretched—cut in half, then lengthened by

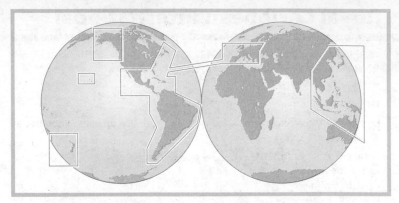

CRUISE AREAS AND SEASONS FOR ROYAL CARIBBEAN INTERNATIONAL

inserting prefabricated midsections, and more superliners with unique designs were added. In 1988, *Sovereign of the Seas* was the first of a new generation of megaliners and the largest cruise ship ever built at the time. On *Sovereign*'s arrival in Miami, traffic backed up for miles as people on shore tried to glimpse her. That year, too, RCCL merged with Admiral Cruises, a short-cruise specialist.

The line got a jump on the 21st century with Project Vision, a new generation of six megaliners. The first, *Legend of the Seas,* debuted in 1995 with acres of glass and cruising's first 18-hole miniature golf course. In 1999, RCCL launched *Voyager of the Seas,* the first of another new ship class and the industry's first 142,000-ton cruise ship. It came with cruising's first climbing wall and ice rink. The climbing walls proved to be so popular that they have been installed fleetwide.

In 2001, the *Radiance* group, another new class, was introduced with the 2,100-passenger, 90,060-ton *Radiance of the Seas;* she was followed by three more sister ships. And now, not to let any other cruise line get ahead of it in the "largest ship" category, RCCL introduced the 160,000-ton *Freedom of the Seas,* dubbed an ultravoyager, in 2006; a second sister, *Liberty of the Seas,* in 2007; and the third, *Independence of the Seas,* in 2008. Roughly 15% larger than *Voyager,* the *Freedom of the Seas* stands 18 stories high and can carry more than 3,600 passengers and 1,400 crew. In early 2006, RCCL ordered its largest ship yet, the 5,400-passenger, 220,000-ton ship, currently named *Project Genesis,* to be built by Aker Yards of Finland for a 2009 delivery. The new ship will measure 1,180 feet in length, 154 feet in width, and 240 feet in height—plenty of space for more innovations—and cost an estimated $230,000 per berth or $1.5 billion per ship. In 2007, Royal Caribbean exercised its option for a second Genesis ship.

In a surprise move in 1997, RCCL bought Celebrity Cruises—a deal worth $1.3 billion. Celebrity operates as a separate brand. In 2002, RCCL's attempt to buy Princess Cruises, one of its main competitors, was thwarted by Carnival, which won out in the end after a heavy bidding war. After two decades of focusing solely on the Caribbean, RCCL expanded to other parts of the world, such as Canada, Europe, and now Asia, Australia and New Zealand, and Latin America. They've also added more U.S. departure cities and built a cruise departure port in New Jersey named Cape Liberty Cruise Port. To reflect its growth, the line changed its marketing name to Royal Caribbean International. The line offers the option of advance shore-excursion booking and created Royal Celebrity Tours, a land-tour company in Alaska and the Canadian Rockies.

In 2006, RCCL made a major investment in Europe by buying Pullmantur, a well-established Spanish tour and cruise operator, and moving two of Pullmantur's ships to the Celebrity Expeditions brand. As further evidence of RCCL's expansion, the line will have seven ships in Europe in 2008 and will base its newest ship, *Independence of the Sea*, in England for her maiden summer season. Beginning in December 2007, the line will base *Rhapsody of the Seas* in Singapore for a series of nine Asian cruises. Meanwhile, Royal Caribbean is helping Jamaica with its plans to build a new cruise terminal at Ocho Rios, scheduled to be completed in 2008. It will also improve berthing and other facilities at Montego Bay. The new facilities are intended to accommodate the 220,000-ton *Project Genesis* ships.

RCCL teamed up with Wireless Maritime Services, a joint venture of Cingular Wireless and Maritime Telecommunications Network (MTN), to provide fleetwide cell phone service that enables passengers to make and receive calls on their own phones in international waters. WiFi hot spots are also available fleetwide. *Freedom* and the new *Liberty of the Seas* have wireless capability in cabins and throughout the ship.

Express Departure is an option available on all Royal Caribbean and Celebrity ships in their arrival ports in North and South America and Europe. The program enables passengers who are willing to carry their own luggage off the ship to keep their luggage in their cabin the night before departure. The next morning they listen for the announcement when they can depart the ship. Carrying their own luggage, they then pass through Customs and are on their way.

Another service, Luggage Valet, also facilitates your journey's end. You pay $10 per person (for up to two bags per person) for the service to the participating airlines—American, Continental, Delta, and United—and receive your airline boarding pass and luggage tags before you disembark the ship. After you clear Customs, you leave your luggage with the airline representative. At the airport, you can proceed directly to the security checkpoint. The service must be booked onboard the ship, and is offered at Los Angeles, Miami, Port Canaveral, Port Everglades, San Diego, San Juan, Seattle, Tampa, and Vancouver. The service is particularly convenient if you have a flight later in the day.

For all its firsts and innovative designs, RCCL is still a conservative company that built its success on a solid, consistent product. Royal Caribbean is a public company, traded on the New York Stock Exchange.

THE FLEET	BUILT/RENOVATED	TONNAGE	PASSENGERS
Adventure of the Seas	2001	142,000	3,114
Brilliance of the Seas	2002	90,090	2,100
Empress of the Seas	1990/98/2004	48,563	1,602
Enchantment of the Seas	1997/99/2005	80,700	2,252
Explorer of the Seas	2000	142,000	3,114
Freedom of the Seas	2006	160,000	3, 634
Grandeur of the Seas	1996/98	74,140	1,950
Independence of the Seas	2008	160,000	3, 634
Jewel of the Seas	2004	90,060	2,100
Legend of the Seas	1995	69,130	1,800
Liberty of the Seas	2007	160,000	3, 634
Majesty of the Seas	1992/97/2006	73,941	2,350
Mariner of the Seas	2003	142,000	3,114
Monarch of the Seas	1991/99	73,941	2,350
Navigator of the Seas	2002	142,000	3,114
Radiance of the Seas	2001	90,090	2,100
Rhapsody of the Seas	1997	78,491	2,000
Serenade of the Seas	2003	90,060	2,100
Sovereign of the Seas	1988/96/2003	73,192	2,250
Splendour of the Seas	1996/98	69,130	1,800
Vision of the Seas	1998	78,491	2,000
Voyager of the Seas	1999	142,000	3,114
Project Genesis	2009	220,000	5,400
Project Genesis	2010	220,000	5,400

STYLE RCI ships are big ships that hum with activities almost around the clock and are designed for high-volume, year-round, warm-weather cruises. That C in RCI could just as well stand for *consistency*. Whether you take a Royal Caribbean cruise in Europe or the Caribbean, the activities are many and varied and designed primarily for U.S. and Canadian passengers.

The ships have acres of sun decks, large pools, and lots of outdoor activity: games, competitions, the Vitality fitness program, and sports, like golf, that often combine with sports in port. The ships have contemporary decor with such themes as Broadway hits, operas, and the circus. All vessels have extensive programs for children, catering to the 330,000 kids that RCI carries annually.

Royal Caribbean was one of the first cruise lines to move toward removing trans fat from its menus and expects to have fully trans fat–free menus fleetwide by the end of this year. Its latest program catering to today's lifestyles is called Vitality, which is meant to bring together many elements—the onboard spa and fitness classes, shore-side activities, special menus, take-home workout plans, virtual personal trainers, and healthy cooking recipes—to create a total experience for passengers who participate in it.

DISTINCTIVE FEATURES **Viking Crown Lounge,** climbing wall, golf program, Labadee (RCI's private beach), and Coco Cay in the Bahamas, **Crown & Anchor** lounges in San Juan and St. Thomas. Room service from dining room menus during lunch and dinner, children's program. Internet centers. Miniature golf course on *Legend, Splendour, Radiance, Voyager, and Freedom* class; ice rink, *Voyager-* and *Freedom-*class; *Explorer's* Oceanography Center, *Freedom, Liberty's* surfing, boxing ring.

	HIGHEST	LOWEST	AVERAGE
PER DIEM	$675	$60	$218

Per diems are calculated from cruise line's nondiscounted *cruise-only* published fares on standard accommodations and vary by season, cabins, and cruise areas.

RATES Port charges are included.

Special fares and discounts
- **BREAKTHROUGH FARES:** Capacity-controlled discounts (up to 40%) that change daily; the earlier you buy, the better the discount.
- **THIRD/FOURTH PASSENGER:** Yes.
- **CHILDREN'S FARE:** Third/fourth person rates.
- **SINGLE SUPPLEMENT:** 200%
- **SINGLE GUARANTEE:** Category and cabin assigned by RCI.

Packages
- **AIR/SEA:** Yes.
- **CRUISE/AIR ADD-ONS WITH TRANSFERS:** Yes.
- **PRE/POST:** In departure ports and some vacation spots.
- **OTHERS:** Honeymoon, golf, family, wedding. Romance and Special Occasions packages (extra charge) designed for honeymooners or special occasion.

PAST PASSENGERS The Crown & Anchor Society has four membership levels based on how many cruises you take: Gold membership, one to four cruises; Platinum, five to nine; Diamond, ten or more. A Diamond Plus level recognizes passengers who have completed 24 cruise credits. They receive a cruise credit each time they sail, as well as extra cruise credits when they sail on a cruise/cruise-tour of 12 nights or longer and book a suite. The biggest benefit is personalized attention by shipboard personnel. Members get *Crown & Anchor,* a quarterly magazine with information on new programs, itineraries, and ships; special offers and coupons; a color-coded landing card sticker; wine tasting; members-only Web page, sweepstakes, and shoreside events; and on cruises of seven or more nights, a cocktail party. Gold members also receive special offers on future cruises. Platinum members get terry robes for use during the cruise, custom air arrangements, private departure lounge, special 800 number for reservations, and more.

Diamond customers can count on exclusive coupons, boarding privileges, concierge service on select ships, and priority dining room seating, shore excursions, spa services, and disembarkation. The Diamond Plus level, in addition to the benefits of other levels, gets behind-the-scenes tours, a personalized amenity delivered to their cabin, and a cabin upgrade. After 49 cruise credits, a member gets dinner with a ship's officer and a VIP theater experience, including a backstage tour. When one reaches 100 cruise credits, the member is treated to a free seven-night cruise in a balcony stateroom.

In 2007, Royal Caribbean introduced the first loyalty program specifically designed for passengers under the age of 18. The Crown & Anchor Society Youth Program was launched in May on the maiden voyage of *Liberty of the Seas* and will be extended to its other ships in due course. Members will automatically attain their parents' membership level—Gold, Platinum, Diamond, or Diamond Plus—when they enroll. Some of the program's benefits include onboard specials at venues like Ben & Jerry's and Y-spa, Royal Caribbean's teen spa. Parents can enroll their children in the program at **www.royalcaribbean.com/youth.**

THE LAST WORD RCI is a cruise line of megaliners. It targets 80% of people buying cruises; only budget and luxury customers are excluded. There's no denying that the huge ships are big and impersonal, and they have blurred and narrowed the quality that once separated RCI from the pack. If you don't like big ships, this isn't the line for you. But if you want a cruise vacation on ships that have everything, RCI offers good value.

Royal Caribbean International Standard Features

Officers Norwegian, international.

Staff Dining, Cabin: international; Cruise: American and British.

Dining facilities Two seatings for dinner plus midnight buffet; indoor/outdoor cafe with breakfast and lunch buffet; alternative dining for dinner with table service on all ships. *Voyager* and *Freedom* classes, three-level dining room; five alternative venues; *Radiance, Freedom* class, six venues. **Johnny Rockets,** *Freedom* and *Voyager* classes, *Majesty, Sovereign of the Seas.*

Special diets Low-fat, low-cholesterol, lean cuisine. Full vegetarian menus. Request kosher at time of booking.

Room service 24 hours with light menu; dining room menus for lunch/dinner.

Dress code Casual but neat by day, informal in evening; one or two nights formal/semiformal. Tuxedo rental available.

Cabin amenities Direct-dial telephone, radio, television, daily world news update, bathtubs in suites, suites with marble baths on *Majesty, Monarch*; Family Suites; *Voyager, Radiance, Freedom* classes: cyber-cabins.

Electrical outlets 110 AC.

Wheelchair access Ramps on all ships; 4 cabins on *Majesty, Monarch, Empress*, 6 cabins on *Sovereign*, 17 on *Legend/Splendour*, 15 on *Vision* and *Radiance*, 26 on *Voyager* class, 32 on *Freedom* class.

Recreation and entertainment Show lounge with entertainment nightly, disco, bingo, horse racing, movies, wine tastings, dance lessons. **Viking Crown Lounge,** bars/lounges, card room, library, Internet cafe.

Sports and other activities Two outdoor pools; sports deck with basketball, table tennis, shuffleboard. Miniature golf course on *Legend, Splendour, Radiance, Freedom* and *Voyager* classes. Climbing walls fleetwide. Ice rink on *Voyager* and *Freedom* classes; trampoline, 3 pools, *Enchantment*; boxing ring, FlowRider surf simulator, H20 Zone aqua park, 3 swimming pools, *Freedom* class.

Beauty and fitness Beauty/barber shop, massage, sauna, Vitality fitness program, jogging track, health club. Solarium, elaborate spa on *Vision, Voyager, Radiance,* and *Freedom* classes; cantilevered whirlpools, *Freedom.*

Other facilities Boutiques, medical facilities, laundry and dry cleaning services, meeting rooms, Internet and e-mail service, cinema/theater on *Monarch, Sovereign, Freedom* and *Voyager* classes; florist, chapel, ice-cream parlor (also on *Majesty*), karate room on *Freedom* class.

Children's facilities Year-round youth programs. Playrooms and teen centers on *Sovereign, Vision, Voyager, Radiance* and *Freedom* classes, plus *Empress of the Seas;* teen nightclub on *Majesty, Monarch,* and *Vision, Freedom* and *Voyager* classes. Fisher-Price program for infants and their parents.

Theme cruises Jazz, country music, variety of sports.

Smoking Public rooms are nonsmoking except in designated areas.

RCI suggested tipping Per person per day, cabin steward $3.50; dining room waiter, $3.50; assistant waiter, $2; 15% added to bar/wine bill.

Credit cards For cruise payment and onboard charges: American Express, Carte Blanche, Diners Club, Discover, MasterCard, Visa, JCB.

Enchantment/Grandeur	QUALITY 7	VALUE A
Legend of the Seas	QUALITY 7	VALUE C
Splendour/Rhapsody	QUALITY 7	VALUE A
Vision of the Seas	QUALITY 8	VALUE A
REGISTRY Bahamas	LENGTH 867–990 feet	BEAM 105–106 feet
CABINS 902–1,126	DRAFT 24–25 feet	SPEED 22–24 knots
MAXIMUM PASSENGERS	PASSENGER DECKS 10	ELEVATORS 9–11
1,804–2,435	CREW 735–784	SPACE RATIO 38.32

THE SHIPS *Legend of the Seas,* the first of six megaliners in the Project Vision series, arrived in 1995, and her five sisters followed over the next four years. Constructed in France and Finland, the megaliners were quickly labeled the ships of glass. Each has two acres of windows, glass windbreaks, skylights, and walls of windows in public spaces. The **Centrum,** the centerpiece atrium, rises seven decks—two more than on the *Sovereign*-class vessels—and is topped by the **Viking Crown Lounge.** Bubble elevators whisk passengers to the lounge. The ships embrace the sea and vistas through windows and glass. Natural light sparkles, and open space is abundant.

Each has distinguishing features. At the Centrum's base is the **Champagne Terrace and Bar,** where fine wines and Champagne are served by the glass. The elegant setting sets the tone for the ships. *Grandeur's* **Champagne Bar** covers the Centrum's entire lower level. A white baby grand piano stands next to a stairway to the second level. Decorative screens create conversation corners.

Works of art on *Splendour* were created by more than 50 artists and studios. The ship's atrium sculpture is the fleet's most dramatic. The work consists of three elements symbolizing the solar system. The dominant component, an 18-foot gilded disk representing the sun, hangs on a diagonal, silhouetted by rays from the skylight. Iridescent bulbs around the disk transmit and reflect colored light throughout the atrium. Hundreds of steel cords attached to the upper, outer rim of the disk gather at the top of the atrium and are illuminated, creating a glow.

On the Sun Deck is the Solarium, a landscaped indoor/outdoor area with a second swimming pool, whirlpools, and a cafe. Its Crystal Canopy provides cover in inclement weather. Unlike glass roofs on other ships, this one doesn't fold onto itself; instead, it moves intact. The design uses much more glass, admitting maximum light into the Solarium when the roof is closed. The most celebrated features on *Legend* and *Splendour* are the world's first full-scale floating miniature golf courses. The station where equipment and tee times can be obtained resembles a miniature clubhouse.

Enchantment of the Seas arrived in Boston after completing an extensive renovation. The ship was cut in two in Rotterdam and a 73-foot midship section constructed in Finland was inserted. It brought her overall length to 990 feet, displacement to 80,700 tons, and her cabin total to 1,126 with the addition of 151 new accommodations. But lengthening the ship was more than an engineering feat. It was a complete makeover, with some unusual features such as an ondeck trampoline complete with bungee cords.

One of the most striking additions to *Enchantment* are two suspension bridges on Deck 10, raising the walkway/jogging track and spanning more than 75 feet on each side of the Pool Deck below. Supported by dramatic arches, the bridges cross over two new areas of the Pool Deck, which jut out past lower decks to overhang the water. Each area is edged with 14-foot-high sheets of glass, offering great views. They also have peekaboo windows in the floor to see the water below. The overhanging space on the port side has a new bar; the starboard side houses a band shell that opens like an orange for poolside musical entertainment.

In total, the main pool area was expanded by nearly 50%, with two pools, four whirlpools, and a new, circular, kid-focused Splash Deck with 64 water jets. Forty of the jets are connected to an interactive touch-pad system, letting kids spray each other or create their own fountain effects. At night, the area closes to become a decorative fountain with a fiber-optic light show.

In addition to the signature climbing wall at the stern, *Enchantment* has four bungee trampolines at the stern on Deck 10. Participants strap into a harness connected to two bungee cords that help them head skyward, while keeping them safely centered when they come in for a landing on the trampolines. The jogging track also offers a new "vitality course" with four fitness stops. In between laps on the quarter-mile track, runners can pause to jump rope, work their arms, back, and stomach at the sit-up/push-up bars, strengthen their legs at a step-up station, and cool down with a series of suggested stretches. Another addition is **Grab and Go,** a fast-food restaurant on deck. The deck also has two ball zones, each with three basketball hoops of different heights to accommodate youth, teen, and adult shooters.

Enchantment's fitness center was expanded, and the **Day Spa,** one deck below, has five more treatment rooms, including a couple's massage room. New entertainment and shopping options were also added. The new **Boleros Latin Club,** a bar with a glass dome ceiling, serves specialty drinks such as mojitos and caipirinhas and features live Latin jazz in the evenings. The new **Latte'tudes** coffee and ice-cream shop serves espresso drinks from Seattle's Best Coffee and Ben & Jerry's ice cream. This new area also has computer terminals for Internet access. Next door, **Casino Royale** has been expanded with more slot machines, while the shopping area has new boutiques, including a Fossil watch store, a fine jewelry store, a photo electronics retail shop, an extended art auction gallery, and photo gallery with new digital photo kiosks.

New accessibility features were added throughout the ship, including ramps, pool and Jacuzzi lifts, access to the Splash Deck, and a lift to the bungee trampoline area.

ITINERARIES   *See* Itinerary Index.

CABINS   A major improvement in the *Vision* class was the size of standard cabins—153 square feet compared with 122 square feet in comparable *Sovereign*-class cabins. For two decades, Royal Caribbean said cabin size was unimportant because passengers spend so little time in their rooms, but in the *Vision* class, cabins are larger and more comfortable, with sitting areas and, for the first time, many balconies—one in four. Many more have bathrooms with tubs and showers, too. Pastels and light woods are used in decor. The Royal Suite has a baby grand piano, whirlpool tub, and veranda. Two new family cabins sleep six.

Specifications 327 inside cabins, 575 outside; 83 suites; 4 Family Suites; 231 with balconies; 388 third/fourth persons; no singles; 17

wheelchair-accessible. *Grandeur/Enchantment,* 399/463 inside cabins, 576/663 outside, 18 suites; 4 Family Suites; 72 deluxe outside; 212/248 with balconies; 403 third/fourth persons; no singles; 14/20 wheelchair-accessible. *Rhapsody/Vision,* 407 inside cabins, 593 outside; 18 suites; 72 deluxe; 4 Family Suites; 229 with balconies; 287 third/fourth persons; no singles; 14 wheelchair-accessible.

DINING *Legend's* **Romeo and Juliet Dining Room** (the **King and I** on *Splendour* and **Great Gatsby** on *Grandeur*) spans two decks and has 20-foot-tall glass walls on each side, offering spectacular views from every table. The walls are virtually all glass—the load-bearing function is handled by interior columns. A revolving platform with a grand piano is framed by curving stairways to the balcony.

Decor in *Splendour*'s King and I is noteworthy. A Thai temple facade has been replicated, and 16 historical paintings plus two epic murals were created by artists of Thailand's royal family. Each painting tells a story.

The nautical-motif **Windjammer Café** on Sun Deck is the indoor/outdoor area for breakfast and lunch buffets and alternative evening dining. Glass walls on three sides and a sloping skylight brighten the room. Each lunch has a theme, and ethnic food joins the regular array of hot dishes, salads, and sandwiches. Dinner, served 6:30 to 10:30 p.m., offers full table service. The cafe is a popular spot for reading, playing cards, and watching the water.

SERVICE Dining-room service and room stewards have received mixed reviews. Some workers know little English (although RCCL says it has a minimum requirement for all employees regarding English language proficiency, and all international employees are required to take the Marlin's English test to ensure minimum required language skills). They also lack training, probably because the line added so many large ships in a short time. With RCCL's ongoing training system, the problem should improve.

FACILITIES AND ACTIVITIES *Vision*-class ships are state-of-the-art at every turn. Computers helped design the bi-level **That's Entertainment Theatre** on *Legend* (**Palladium Theater** on *Grandeur* and **42nd Street Theatre** on *Splendour*) to ensure good sight lines for nightly, full-scale Broadway productions. The venue has a computerized system to move scenery, a device commonly used on Broadway, as well as an orchestra pit that can be raised and lowered.

The **Schooner Bar** is a piano lounge popular for its sing-along sessions. Decor includes authentic rigging and an aroma of tar. **Casino Royale** is next door. On *Grandeur*, passengers enter across a glass floor strewn with "sunken treasure" of jewels and gold coins. The cruise line has a beverage program for adults and kids for unlimited fountain soda and juice for $4 per day for ages 17 and under and $6 per day for over 18 plus 15% gratuity.

The spacious **Anchor's Away Lounge** on *Legend* (**South Pacific Lounge** on *Grandeur* and **Top Hat Lounge** on *Splendour*) spans the ship's stern. It's a second showroom, used for parlor games, art auctions, daytime dance activities, and late-night shows and dancing. Topside, the glass-sheathed **Viking Crown Lounge** is an observation lounge by day and a nightclub and disco at night. Nightclub action is away from the room's quieter piano bar. On all the ships, the lounge is accessible from the atrium by glass elevators. Aft of the show lounge (to entice you coming and going!) is a mall with varied shops in attractive settings. For example, the **Harbour Shop,** selling liquor and sundries, recalls an old English vintner's shop through aged timber, antique barrels, and stone floors. The casino offers blackjack, Caribbean poker, roulette, craps, and 178 slot machines.

The conference center can be divided into four rooms, each with full audiovisual support. Adjoining is an attractive lounge that also can be divided. A card room can be divided into two sections, and there is a 2,000-volume library that on the *Grandeur* has an amusing lifelike sculpture entitled *Snoozin.* **Explorers Court,** off the Centrum on the port side of Deck 8, is the place to relax, read, or converse. Starboard is the **Crown & Anchor Study,** a more formal gathering place.

SPORTS, FITNESS, AND BEAUTY The Sun Deck has an outdoor pool. Contrasting is the quiet Solarium, the second pool area. When the Windjammer Café and main dining room are closed, the Solarium's cafe serves snacks, alcoholic beverages, sodas, and juices. The area can be covered by a glass canopy. Beyond the Solarium, the **Fitness Center and Day Spa** contains a beauty salon, aerobics area, gym, changing rooms, saunas, steam baths, and seven massage rooms (treatments are pricey). A Sports Deck is at the stern. Each ship has a padded promenade circling most of the ship.

Legend's much-publicized golf course, **Legend of the Links** (**Splendour of the Greens** on *Splendour*), is above the spa. It was designed by Adventure Golf Services, whose other miniature courses include one at the Mall of America in Bloomington, Minnesota. Each hole of the 6,000-square-foot Links is surrounded by rough to simulate a shoreside layout. On *Legend,* the 17 holes (12 on *Splendour*) range in size from 155 to 230 square feet, tees are 5 feet wide, and the longest hole is 32 feet. There is no charge for play. The glass dome over the aft swimming pool can slide to the golf course, where it can be raised to provide almost ten feet of vertical clearance for golfers. A walkway along one edge of the course has benches to encourage spectators. Halogen lights illuminate nighttime play, and baffles redirect wind generated by the ship's motion. A jogging track surrounds the course. Tournaments and children's tee times are available.

CHILDREN'S FACILITIES Outstanding *Vision*-class facilities for children complement RCI's supervised youth program, Adventure Ocean, available year-round, day and evening, and in port. Activities target ages 3 to 17, split into five age groups. Daily schedules are delivered to cabins. Among the most distinctive activities is teacher-led Mad Science, which aims to make science entertaining and amusing. Group babysitting ($5 an hour per child) is available 10 p.m. to 1 a.m. In-room babysitting is also available for

$8 an hour per room for a maximum of two children (minimum age, one year). Family Suites have separate bedrooms for children.

Club Ocean is the children's center. On *Grandeur,* it's submarine-themed and includes a tunnel, slide, pool of colored balls, and writing wall. Nearby is **Fanta-SEAS** (**Optix** on *Legend*), the space-themed teen center. The ships also have video arcades.

Note: If you or your children consume a lot of soft drinks, consider buying the unlimited soda and juice package detailed earlier in this section.

Adventure of the Seas	QUALITY 8	VALUE C
Explorer of the Seas	QUALITY 8	VALUE C
Mariner of the Seas	QUALITY 8	VALUE C
Navigator of the Seas	QUALITY 8	VALUE C
Voyager of the Seas	QUALITY 8	VALUE C
REGISTRY Bahamas	LENGTH 1,020 feet	BEAM 157.5 feet
CABINS 1,900	DRAFT 29 feet	SPEED 23.7 knots
MAXIMUM PASSENGERS	PASSENGER DECKS 15	ELEVATORS 14
3,114	CREW 1,185	SPACE RATIO NA

THE SHIPS The $500 million *Voyager of the Seas* was the largest cruise ship ever built—142,000 tons—when she made her debut in 1999, and also the first of six similar ships launched over the following five years.

Voyager is awesome. She's twice the size of the largest aircraft carrier ever built, twice as wide as Broadway in New York, and taller than a 20-story building. She has six diesel engines, each the size of a locomotive, and they produce 15,000 horsepower—the equivalent of 150 cars.

A crew of 10,000 people worked 21 million hours to cut, shape, bend, and weld more than 300,000 pieces of steel into the vessel's hull. Her 14 passenger decks cover 646,000 square feet. Furnishings include 538,000 square feet of carpeting, 15,000 chairs, and a $12 million art collection.

Voyager is cruise ship as entertainment. In contrast to other mega-liners, where the goal has been to reduce the behemoth to human scale, RCI has made a virtue of *Voyager*'s enormous size, touting her many options and features that only a ship of this size could offer. These include an ice rink, climbing wall, inline skating track, five-story theater, and tri-level dining room.

Voyager also has a television studio, wedding chapel, and the largest youth facilities, largest spa and fitness center afloat at the time of her debut (since overtaken by *Freedom*-class ships). Fifty percent of cabins have balconies. Food and entertainment options and conference facilities rival those at major resorts.

At the heart of the ship, the **Royal Promenade** stretches the length of one-and-a-half football fields between a 10-story atrium at one end and an 11-story grand atrium at the other. Stores, an ice-cream parlor, Champagne bar, and pub border the tree-lined boulevard. Around-the-clock entertainment, including jugglers, magicians, and mimes, brings a street-fair atmosphere to the Promenade. Overhead lighting simulates day-to-night conditions outside. Three decks of inside cabins "with a view" overlook the boulevard. The rooms have window seats to watch the scene below, but the idea has not worked as RCI planned because the line failed to put one-way glass on the windows; hence, passengers in these cabins can see and be seen. To avoid being part of the peep show, they must keep their curtains closed.

Studio B is *Voyager's* pièce de résistance. It has a 40-by-60-foot ice rink with arena-style seating for 900 spectators and is available for passenger use during the day (skates may be rented at no additional cost) and for ice shows at night. Fifty television monitors and a broadcast studio are adjacent to the area, which can also serve as a show lounge or conference facility or be used for game and variety shows and musical concerts.

When we first heard about the ice rink for a ship cruising the Caribbean, we were puzzled, to say the least. But we were pleasantly surprised. The entertainment is wholesome, high-quality, and certainly a welcome alternative, particularly for families, to the stale Las Vegas shows that have become the staple of most cruise ships.

Explorer of the Seas, Adventure of the Seas, Navigator, and *Mariner* are almost identical to *Voyager* and have the same unusual attractions, including the ice rink and climbing wall, as well as the RCI standard features. *Explorer* was the first ship to boast an interactive, state-of-the-art atmospheric and oceanography laboratory. She was also RCI's first ship with Internet access in the cabins. *Navigator of the Seas* was the first of the fleet to get the cell phone service that enables passengers to make and receive calls at their personal numbers in international waters. Both amenities are now available fleetwide.

ITINERARIES   *See* Itinerary Index.

CABINS   Large by RCI standards, cabins are similar in size and decor to those aboard *Vision*-class ships. Enhancements include larger closets and beds with rounded corners to leave more floor space. All cabins offer telephone, television, electronic minibar, hair dryers, and twin beds convertible to queen.

Specifications   Standard inside cabins, including the 138 Category G with atrium views, 150 square feet. 757 cabins with private veranda (50% of the total) have 180-square-foot interiors plus 4.5-by-8.8-foot balcony; 26 wheelchair-accessible.

DINING   *Voyager's* main dining room is actually three: the **Carmen, La Boheme,** and **Magic Flute** (**Mozart, Strauss,** and **Vivaldi** on *Adventure;* **Columbus, De Gama,** and **Magellan** on *Explorer*) restaurants connected by a grand staircase. Decor includes a 15-foot crystal chandelier, an antique harp, and gilded marble pillars. Seats—enough for almost 2,000 people—offer views of the staircase and main floor or the ocean.

Other dining venues are **Portofino,** an upscale Italian restaurant for dinner (reservations only; $20 surcharge); **Windjammer Café,** the Lido restaurant for breakfast, lunch, and dinner; **Café Promenade,** for continental breakfast, all-day pizzas, and specialty coffees; **Island Grill,** with a display kitchen, for casual dinner; **SeaSide Diner,** a 1950s, 24-hour eatery with indoor/outdoor seating and jukebox music; and **Sprinkles,** with around-the-clock ice cream and yogurt. There's a **Johnny Rockets,** a wildly popular seagoing version of the fast-food chain. *Mariner* and *Navigator* also have RCI's steak house, **Chops Grille,** specializing in grilled steaks and other meats ($20 surcharge).

FACILITIES AND ACTIVITIES In addition to the ice rink and television studio, *Voyager* has one of the most impressive showrooms afloat. The 1,347-seat **La Scala Theater,** inspired by Milan's famous opera house, rises through five decks and has a stage trimmed with gold leaf, a dome with hand-painted murals, and boxes with satin bunting.

Voyager also offers the $1 million **Aquarium Bar** with 50 tons of water in four huge saltwater aquariums, **Spinners,** a revolving gambling arcade with an interactive roulette wheel that players sit in to play, and **Casino Royale,** one of cruising's largest casinos. Also aboard are a cigar and brandy lounge, Champagne bar, English pub, **Schooner Bar,** and a two-deck-tall library. The **Scoreboard** sports bar carries events live on large monitors. Alongside the glass bridge spanning the Royal Promenade is the **Vault,** a two-deck-high late-night disco. **Jesters,** the adults-only nightclub on *Adventure* (the **Chamber** on *Explorer*) is made to look like a gothic castle, with suits of armor, bats, and gargoyles. Sitting atop of *Voyager* is **High Notes,** a jazz club offering nightly performances. Also high on the ship is a chapel where weddings are performed.

Voyager's conference center seats up to 400 people and can be converted into six smaller rooms and a boardroom. Also available are a multimedia screening room, video conferencing, classrooms, and space for exhibition and trade shows. Business services provide typing, copying, and computer access.

SPORTS, FITNESS, AND BEAUTY The 15,000-square-foot health center offers exercise equipment. The Solarium and spa occupy 10,000 square feet. On the ship's funnel is cruising's first climbing wall. Novices and experienced climbers alike are well briefed in advance, and participants work in teams. For most passengers, it's their first rock-climbing experience, and they love it! Other facilities include a nine-hole golf course, driving range, golf simulators ($20 an hour), inline skating track, and basketball/volleyball court. Also available are **Sea Quest** dive and snorkel shop and the **19th Hole** golf bar. Little wonder that one passenger upon touring *Voyager* remarked, "This sure is a guy's ship."

CHILDREN'S FACILITIES **Adventure Ocean,** RCI's expanded children's facilities, provides age-specific programs: Aquanauts (ages 3 to 5), Explorers (ages 6 to 8), Voyagers (ages 9 to 11), Navigators (ages 12 to 14), and Guests (ages 15 to 17). The latter have a day/nightclub with computers, soda bar, DJ, and dance floor. **Paint and Clay** is a crafts area for young children; **Kids Deck** has deck checkers, shuffleboard, and tic-tac-toe; **Challenger's Arcade** is a virtual-reality game center; and **Virtual**

Submarine provides underwater virtual-reality entertainment for all ages. The **Computer Lab** has 14 stations with games for amusement and education. Adventure Beach, for families, has swimming pools, a waterslide, and water games and is convenient to **SeaSide Diner.** Adventure Ocean opens 30 minutes before the morning shore excursions depart to give parents some flexibility in planning for their day.

POSTSCRIPT Passengers have responded to *Voyager* and her sister ships enthusiastically, and almost anyone would enjoy a week on these ships. But you need to understand that it's not cruising in the traditional sense. The ship is the destination; her itinerary is almost immaterial. Like we said, these are cruise ships as entertainment.

Majesty of the Seas	QUALITY 5	VALUE C
Monarch of the Seas	QUALITY 5	VALUE C
Sovereign of the Seas	QUALITY 5	VALUE C
REGISTRY Bahamas	LENGTH 880 feet	BEAM 106 feet
CABINS 1,140–1,193	DRAFT 25 feet	SPEED 19 knots
MAXIMUM PASSENGERS	PASSENGER DECKS 11	ELEVATORS 11
2,744–2,852	CREW 833	SPACE RATIO 32.3/30.8

THE SHIPS When the *Sovereign of the Seas* was introduced in 1988, she was the largest cruise ship ever built and stirred unprecedented excitement and publicity. More important, she came with innovations that influenced the design of all superliners and megaliners that followed.

Her dramatic atrium, the **Centrum,** was a cruise-ship first. Located amidships and spanning five decks, the atrium opens the space to create a light and inviting environment. Stairs and balconies around the atrium and its glass-enclosed elevators seem suspended in air. A white piano set amid tropical foliage at the atrium's base plays soft music that carries to upper decks and sets the harmonious tone found shipwide. The atrium, similar to a hotel's lobby, provides a friendly focal point. Passengers are dazzled but not intimidated, and the notion of entering a behemoth dissipates. The atrium also separates the forward section of the ship, which contains the cabins, from the aft with all public rooms and dining, sports, entertainment, and recreation facilities.

The arrangement has several advantages. Cabins are quieter, distances among public areas are shorter, and the ship doesn't seem so enormous. The ship looks outward—few areas lack natural light or a view to the outdoors—a feature absent on many new ships. Together with an incredible array of facilities, they explain passengers' immediate acceptance of the megaliner. *Sovereign's* twins, *Monarch of the Seas* and *Majesty of the Seas,* arrived with few changes—a few more cabins, a Family Suite, and a redesigned **Windjammer Café** (which was recently redesigned on *Majesty* into the Windjammer Marketplace).

Many public rooms carry the same names. Throughout, contemporary elegance creates a warm, inviting ambience.

The ships are floating resorts, making the most of their size by providing spaces for varying tastes. These include the signature **Viking Crown Lounge** perched high on the stack, wide, outdoor promenades encircling the vessels, and sunny and shaded areas on three decks. They offer so many facilities and activities that even the most frantically active person can't participate in all the options.

Recently, *Sovereign* was given a stem-to-stern makeover with new decor and new and expanded facilities and amenities that bring her more in line with the newer *Voyager*-class fleet. Among the new amenities, the new Centrum area on Deck 5 now has **Latte'tudes,** a coffee bar and ice-cream shop serving Seattle's Best Coffee and Ben & Jerry's Ice Cream; and nearby **Wi-Fi,** the Internet center. Passengers can use their own or on-board rented WiFi laptops to try out the ship's wireless facility.

Monarch and *Majesty of the Seas* have also been given a complete renovation and refit, particularly to the dining facilities, spa, casino, and main Pool Deck, as well as adding similar *Voyager*-class features and wireless and cell phone capability.

ITINERARIES *See* Itinerary Index.

CABINS Each of the trio has 16 categories of cabins. Designed to make the most out of every inch of space, they're fitted with a vanity table, chair, and twin beds convertible to daytime couches. *Monarch's* and *Majesty's* cabins are similar to *Sovereign's* in size and decor, but came with major enhancements—verandas on 50 deluxe outside cabins, and suites and Family Suites sleeping up to six. In her recent renovation, balconies were added to 62 suites and junior suites on Deck 10, and bathrooms in these accommodations were completely renewed.

Family Suites have two bedrooms, a sitting room, two bathrooms, and veranda. *Majesty* has 146 cabins in the larger outside category, more comfortable than those on *Sovereign,* and the Bridge Deck contains only suites and deluxe cabins with private verandas. Bathrooms, though not large, are well designed with ample space for toiletries, thick towels, hair dryers, and excellent water pressure.

Specifications Sovereign, 427 inside cabins, 722 outside; 12 suites; 62 with balconies. Standard dimensions, inside, 119 square feet, outside, 122 square feet; 945 with twin beds (convertible to doubles); 401 third/fourth persons; no singles; 6 wheelchair-accessible. *Majesty* and *Monarch,* 444/1,048 inside cabins, 721/1,193 outside; 12 suites; 62/63 deluxe cabins and suites with verandas. Standard dimensions, 120 square feet; 917 with twin beds (convertible to queen); 260/299 third/fourth persons; no singles; 4 wheelchair-accessible.

DINING RCI ships don't serve gourmet fare and don't intend to. Rather, galleys produce ordinary food that's plentiful but not excessive, with ample variety. All ships have the same menus (consistency at work), although longer European and Asian cruises may feature local dishes. A typical menu offers five juices and appetizers, three soups, two salads, five entrées with a choice of pasta, fish, chicken, veal, and beef; three desserts, and a selection of cheeses and ice cream.

In keeping with its Vitality program, all menus have light selections annotated with nutritional information. You can also select vegetarian dishes or request the full vegetarian menu for an entire cruise. Wine lists include California, French, and other vintages. Prices are moderate.

Each ship has two dining rooms serving three meals, all with assigned seating. The *Sovereign's* **Kismet Dining Room** has elaborate columns and lighting fixtures; its twin, **Gigi Dining Room,** has columns styled after palm trees. *Monarch's* **Brigadoon Dining Room** has a Scottish tartan motif; the **Flower Drum Song Dining Room** has sophisticated Asian decor. Lunch and dinner can be ordered from dining-room menus through room service.

A noticeable difference on *Sovereign* is her **Windjammer Market-place,** where breakfast, lunch, and a casual alternative dinner are available. In the evening, it offers full table service and a menu that changes daily. Also added were **Johnny Rockets** (on *Majesty,* too), similar to the popular *Voyager*-class venue, and **Sorrento's,** a pizza parlor. After its recent renovation, *Majesty* got a pizza parlor and **Compass Deli.** On the *Monarch,* the **Windjammer Café** spans the ship's width and is wrapped on three sides by windows. The Café also has a mini-atrium with winter garden, waterfalls, and skylight.

SERVICE RCI's crews, from the Norwegian captains to the mini–United Nations of the cabin and dining-room staff, are courteous and eager to please. An affable, largely Filipino group of stewards tidies rooms twice daily and provides evening turndown service. Dining staff have many Europeans and provide attentive, efficient service. Indeed, the staff is so conscious of the constant evaluation of their work, as reflected in passengers' comment cards, that they sometimes overdo their attention. And it's likely that your waiter, when his supervisors aren't around, will all but beg you to praise him in your comments—his job may depend on it.

FACILITIES AND ACTIVITIES Among activities may be bingo, napkin folding, wine tasting, parlor games, dance classes, bridge, ice carving, parties for singles, children, and teens, a costume party, religious services, and a passenger talent show. The wood-paneled library resembles an English club; it can also be used for meetings. Two levels of Sun decks provide peace, privacy, and a place to read.

Almost 24 hours a day, there's music to suit every mood—including big band, steel band, Latin, country, rock, strolling violins, and classical concerts. The **Follies Lounge,** *Sovereign's* richly decorated bi-level showroom, stages two shows nightly. The rooms have video walls with 50 television monitors on movable banks of 25 screens each. Comfortable seats have excellent sight lines, with a few exceptions. Another lounge is *Sovereign's* and *Majesty's* **Boleros Nightclub,** the hot Latin-flavored nightspot with music and drinks to go with it.

Cantilevered from the funnel and encircling it is the extraordinary **Viking Crown Lounge.** The room, 12 stories above the water, provides a fabulous 360-degree view of the sea and sunset.

Among small lounges is the nautical-motif **Schooner Bar,** a favorite casual bar by day and a lively piano bar at night. **Casino Royale** next door offers blackjack, 170 slot machines, and American roulette. **Touch of Class** is a chic Champagne bar where 50 people can clink flutes and scoop caviar. Decor lives up to the lounge's name with two lifelike bronze statues of 1920s flappers. Other options include **Flashes** (the teen nightclub), karaoke, a shopping boulevard, and a movie theater.

SPORTS, FITNESS, AND BEAUTY Fitness enthusiasts have a one-third-mile outside deck encircling the vessel and a second jogging track. The well-equipped health club offers saunas and locker rooms, a large exercise room with ballet bars, an array of exercise equipment, and a high-energy staff. The Sports Deck has twin swimming pools, two whirlpools, and a basketball court. Vitality fitness activities start with a sunrise stretch class or water exercises, low-impact aerobics, and walkathons, basketball, and table tennis tournaments. Participants earn "dollars" for each activity, redeemable for T-shirts and visors. Vitality Unlimited is designed for senior citizens. All menus offer low-fat, low-calorie entrées, prepared to American Heart Association guidelines. The beauty salon/barber shop offers massage and beauty treatments at additional cost.

On *Sovereign* and *Majesty,* the spa and fitness center were moved to Deck 9 and redesigned and enlarged with 11 treatment rooms, including a couples massage room. There are also new state-of-the-art cardiovascular and resistance machines, free weights, and an aerobics center with free classes; yoga, Pilates, and spinning classes are available for $10 per session.

CHILDREN'S FACILITIES RCI was among the first lines to create a children's program with youth centers, playrooms, and counselors. *Sovereign*-class ships offer the program year-round. They also have video arcades and teen centers. *Majesty* and *Monarch* have teen nightclubs. Kids get their own daily agenda, slipped under the cabin door each night. Among the activities are ice-cream and pizza parties, dance classes, golf putting, face painting, midnight basketball, autograph hunts, talent shows, and shore tours. Babysitters (extra cost), cribs, and high chairs are available. Captain Sealy's Kids' Galley, a menu for children ages 4 to 12, offers such favorites as peanut butter sandwiches, hamburgers, and pizzas, along with salads, fruit, and alphabet soup.

The *Sovereign* and *Majesty* have an **Adventure Ocean and Teen Club** with learning and play areas with computers, toys, and books. **Fuel** is the teen's own disco and the **Living Room** is their place to chill out, watch large-screen televisions, or surf the Web. Teens also have a no-adults-allowed area, the **Back Deck**—it's a sun deck with an outdoor dance floor.

SHORE EXCURSIONS Except for its golf programs and cruises that include Labadee in their itinerary, RCI's shore excursions are similar to those of other lines cruising the Caribbean. They include island tours, beach trips, and snorkeling and diving. RCI's private resort, **Labadee,** created in 1987 on the north coast of Haiti, offers one of the best days at the beach of any line. Its setting is beautiful—lush mountains rise behind a lovely cove with a series of crescent-shaped beaches. There are pavilions for dining, entertainment, water sports equipment, and a marketplace with Haitian crafts, which are the Caribbean's best. Music, dancing, and performances by a local folklore group are provided.

Labadee has a pirate-themed water playground, sponsored by the Coca-Cola Company, and featuring a "sunken" pirate ship and a mascot, Labadee Luc, who appears on signage throughout the peninsula. The **Splash Bash,** a special play area for kids ages 3 to 5, has a central pipe that sends water into three play areas with dams, waterwheels, and other fun activities. Admission to the water playground is $5 per person for a two-hour period. Volleyball courts are new, and in March 2007, the Dragon's Flight, a 4,000-foot-long zip line, was added. It glides participants 200 feet above the ground, offering great views of the water around them.

Some itineraries call for a day at **Coco Cay,** a small Bahamian island. Diversions for a range of ages include beach games, pedal boats, shopping, steel-band music, visits to a shipwreck led by snorkeling instructors, a barbecue, palm-shaded trails, six sandy beaches for swimming, and hammocks and beach chairs for lounging. Children's programs are available.

Empress of the Seas	QUALITY 5	VALUE C
REGISTRY Bahamas	LENGTH 692 feet	BEAM 100 feet
CABINS 801	DRAFT 25 feet	SPEED 19.5 knots
MAXIMUM PASSENGERS	PASSENGER DECKS 9	ELEVATORS 7
2,020	CREW 685	SPACE RATIO 30.4

THE SHIP   A new look and a new name, *Empress of the Seas* (formerly *Nordic Empress*), were given to her in May 2004 and were meant to reflect the scope of the redesign that brought her facilities more in line with RCI's newer ships. Among the changes were new dining, entertainment and fitness areas, and a general face-lift to the lobbies, elevators, landings, corridors, and restrooms, and enhancements to the shopping areas and Pool Deck.

Even before the changes, the *Empress* dazzled, from light that streams in by day to nighttime glitter. Passengers board at the nine-deck-tall atrium called the **Centrum.** Two of four elevators are glass and overlook a waterfall and greenery. Most public rooms flow from here. Two center decks contain the dining room, showroom, casino, and lounges. The Sun Deck topside is an all-day center of activities—from sunning and swimming to entertainment and dancing under the stars. It also contains the fitness and kids' centers.

In March 2008, *Empress of the Seas* will be transferred to Pullmantur, the Spanish tour and cruise company that Royal Caribbean purchased in 2006.

ITINERARIES   *See* Itinerary Index.

CABINS   The dozen categories include many inside and lower-priced outside cabins. All are designed to be light and tropical in feeling. All have two lower beds, color television, three-channel radio, telephone, and private bath. Sixty percent are outside cabins with large windows. All suites and deluxe cabins have balconies. All cabins were renovated with new and upgraded bathrooms.

CABINS, including the Royal Suite; superior outside cabins were given new decor, while the Owner's Suites were completely redesigned with new furniture and finishes.

Specifications 338 inside cabins, 463 outside; 6 suites; 69 deluxe cabins with verandas. Standard dimensions, 194 square feet; 495 with twin beds (all convertible to double); 358 with upper/lower berths accommodating third/fourth berths; no singles; 4 wheelchair-accessible.

DINING *Empress of the Seas* has an elegant specialty restaurant, **Portofino** ($20 surcharge), an upgraded **Windjammer Café,** and a refurbished, bi-level **Carmen Dining Room,** the main dining room with walls of floor-to-ceiling windows spanning two decks. There are two seatings for the three meals. Menus are the same as offered on other RCI ships and include theme dinners. At the **Latte'tudes,** a combined coffee bar and ice-cream shop, passengers can enjoy specialty espresso drinks from Seattle's Best Coffee or 16 flavors from Ben & Jerry's ice cream.

Meals and snacks are served around the clock, starting with early-riser's breakfast at 6:30 a.m. and ending with the midnight buffet. All menus have health-conscious selections. Breakfast and lunch buffets are served in the upgraded, glass-domed Windjammer Café. It's also an alternative dinner restaurant, offering full table service 6:30 to 10:30 p.m., and a midnight buffet. A Sun Worshipper's lunch and afternoon tea are served poolside. The full dining room menu is available for room service at lunch and dinner.

SERVICE *Empress's* crew is eager to please. Stewards make up cabins twice a day and provide evening turndown service. The friendly dining staff quickly learns your preferences. As on all other RCI ships, they will encourage good reviews on your passenger comment cards.

FACILITIES AND ACTIVITIES Passengers on short cruises usually pack in as many activities as possible. *Empress* provides abundant choices. Topside by day are outdoor games and entertainment; elsewhere are dance classes, cards, crafts, bingo, and karaoke.

Nighttime entertainment is some of RCI's best, with good shows, music, and dancing for many tastes. Big Broadway-style productions are staged in the impressive, tiered **Strike Up the Band** lounge. Sight lines are good from almost any seat. The lounge also has a dance floor. The ship's most dazzling feature is the **Casino Royale,** offering slot machines, nine blackjack tables, roulette, craps, and wheel of fortune. Between the casino and Centrum is the newly created **Card Room.** The former High Society lounge was transformed into **Bolero's,** a Latin-themed bar offering specialty tequilas and cocktail favorites like mojitos and live entertainment. *Empress of the Seas* also now has the line's popular **Schooner Bar,** a nautical-themed lounge with sing-along piano entertainment. The **Viking Crown**

Lounge is at the stern on Sun Deck, rather than cantilevered from the stack as on other RCI ships. Nonetheless, with three walls of windows, it's a fine observation area. Late night, it's a disco.

SPORTS, FITNESS, AND BEAUTY   The large, bi-level **Fitness Center** has a glass-enclosed exercise area and an array of equipment, plus saunas, showers, and massage rooms. On deck are three whirlpools and two fountains that cascade into two pools (one for children). The beauty salon offers hair, facial, and beauty treatments (additional charge). Video golf in the **Golf Ahoy! Center** enables participants to try their skill at world-famous courses projected on the screen ($20 per hour). A computer analyzes the stroke and scores the game. Vitality activities range from aquadynamics to basketball free throws. "Dollars" earned for participation can be redeemed for T-shirts and visors.

CHILDREN'S FACILITIES   **The Adventure Ocean** area is a multipurpose, 95-square-foot playroom for children ages 3 to 12. Designed with a space-station theme, the room has an 11-foot ceiling, making room for the **Tubular Time** labyrinth of suspended tubes that are lighted and carpeted inside. Children can crawl through the tubes to a slide and clubhouse platform.

The youth program provides participants with a daily agenda, slipped under the cabin door at night. It's packed with activities, including ice-cream and pizza parties, face painting, midnight basketball, talent shows, and shore tours. Menus designed for children ages 4 to 12 offer such favorites as peanut butter sandwiches, hot dogs, and pizzas, plus salads and fruit. Babysitters (extra cost), cribs, and high chairs are available.

Brilliance of the Seas	QUALITY 8	VALUE C
Jewel of the Seas	QUALITY 8	VALUE C
Radiance of the Seas	QUALITY 8	VALUE C
Serenade of the Seas	QUALITY 8	VALUE C
REGISTRY Bahamas	LENGTH 962 feet	BEAM 106 feet
CABINS 1,050	DRAFT 26.7 feet	SPEED 25 knots
MAXIMUM PASSENGERS	PASSENGER DECKS 12	ELEVATORS 9
2,501	CREW 859	SPACE RATIO NA

THE SHIPS   With sunshine shimmering through walls of glass, Royal Caribbean's *Radiance of the Seas* lives up to her name. The ship is so bright and airy you'll want to keep your sunglasses on when you come in from an outside deck.

Launched in 2001, *Radiance* has floor-to-ceiling windows on all levels of its nine-deck atrium and in 16 public areas, plus exterior glass elevators spanning 12 decks. Passengers never have to miss a minute of the beauty of Alaska and the Caribbean or the connection with the sea.

First of the new class of ships for Royal Caribbean, *Radiance of the Seas* is a classy lady—smaller than the giant *Voyager* class and larger than the *Vision* group. She incorporates the best of her predecessors: the many entertainment and activity options of *Voyager* (including the famous climbing wall), the sleek profile of *Sovereign*, and glass galore. Her twin, *Brilliance of the Seas*, debuted in Europe in 2002. *Serenade of the Seas* followed in 2003 and *Jewel of the Seas* in 2004. The ships are Panamax class, meaning they are narrow enough—just barely—to pass through the Panama Canal.

And these ships have highlights of their own: the most balconies of any RCI ships; Internet ports in every cabin; a bookstore/coffeehouse; and gas and steam turbines said to reduce emissions, noise, and vibration. The ships reflect RCI's resortlike style, with the purser's desk called Guest Relations, its staff outfitted in resort wear (rather than nautical uniforms), and a general manager and vacation experience director intended to foster guest satisfaction.

Radiance also boasts a first at sea: self-leveling pool tables. These high-tech tables are the big attraction in the **Bombay Billiard Club,** one of four lounges clustered in the **Colony Club.** The others are the **Calcutta Card Club, Jakarta Lounge,** an intimate bar with gaming tables, and **Singapore Sling,** a piano bar with floor-to-ceiling windows offering spectacular views aft. The **Centrum,** a dramatic, airy atrium and an RCI signature, is decorated in light woods and soft tones of sand, coral, and aqua, set off with greenery, a waterfall, and colossal abstract sculpture— all part of the ship's $6 million-plus art collection.

Another memorable area is the African-themed **Solarium,** with three life-size stone elephants, a bronze of a lion cub dipping his paw in the water, a waterfall, stone relief art panels depicting gazelles and antelopes, greenery, and piped-in sounds of chirping birds. It also has a raised pool (with a countercurrent), two whirlpools, a bar, and pizzeria, all under a retractable glass roof.

On the *Jewel of the Seas,* passengers enjoy unobstructed views of the sea and landscapes afforded by the ship's nearly three acres of exterior glass in the dining rooms, lounges, ocean-facing glass elevators, and floor-to-ceiling windows in most public areas. The ship also had the highest percentage of cabins with balconies in Royal Caribbean's fleet when it was launched, and an eclectic, $5.3 million art collection with themes of landscape and light in paintings, sculptures, textiles, ceramics, and mosaics throughout the ship. The nine-story Centrum has a modern art interpretation of the Northern Lights: a stainless steel, wire, and glass sculpture with an integrated lighting system.

Other highlights include the **Coral Theater,** which introduces three productions: a tango show, *Tango Buenos Aires,* starring Argentinean dancers and musicians; and two musical reviews, *City of Dreams,* featuring the music of top artists such as Billy Joel, Elton John, and Celine Dion, and *From West End to Broadway,* a variety of music from Cole Porter to *Les Miserables.*

ITINERARIES *See* Itinerary Index.

CABINS Accommodations are spacious and attractively decorated; 70% have verandas. The most lavish, the Royal Suite, is a palatial 1,035 square feet, with 173 square feet of balcony and such amenities as a baby grand piano, wet bar, and entertainment center with 42-inch flat-screen TV, stereo, and VCR, and bath with whirlpool, bidet, and steam shower. Veranda cabins measuring 179 square feet with a 41-square-foot-balcony are situated on Decks 7, 8, 9, and 10, with the ones on Deck 10 closest to the pools and other outdoor amenities. The lowest-priced cabins are inside cabins measuring 166 square feet.

All cabins are equipped with an interactive television, telephone, computer jack, vanity table with an extendable working surface for a laptop computer, refrigerator/minibar, hair dryer, 110/220 electrical outlets, two single beds convertible to double, and reading lights by the beds. There are wheelchair-accessible cabins available in most categories.

The needs of passengers with disabilities are addressed not only in the cabins and oversize hallways, but also with special devices to aid the hearing-impaired. Listening devices are available, as well as telephone amplifiers and strobe-light door knockers and telephone ringers. For the visually impaired, cabin doors, service directories, and even elevator buttons and dining menus are written in Braille. The personalized service sometimes extends to extra assistance at the pier, early-boarding orientation, sign language interpreter, special diet accommodation, or onboard medical services.

Specifications 1,055 cabins; 238 inside, 817 outside (577 with balconies); 62 suites; 62 deluxe suites; 6 Family Suites; 65 third/fourth persons; no singles; 15 wheelchair-accessible.

DINING **Cascades,** the elegant, two-level main dining room, has a grand staircase, etched-glass mural, and a cascading waterfall. The upper level has floor-to-ceiling windows; the lower level, large windows. Two smaller dining rooms, **Breakers** and **Tides,** are ideal for private parties. Breakfast and lunch are open seating; dinner is served in two seatings. Vitality (or low-fat) selections are offered for lunch and dinner. The casual **Windjammer Café** serves buffet-style breakfast and lunch with a choice of indoor and outdoor seating. The **Seaview Café** cooks up burgers, hot dogs, and nachos. The food ranges from mediocre to delicious.

Alternative eateries include **Chops Grill,** serving steaks and other grills from an open kitchen; and **Portofino,** an upscale Euro-Italian restaurant with Tuscany-inspired decor. Fee is $20 per person at each, which covers gratuities; reservations required.

FACILITIES AND ACTIVITIES The three-level **Aurora Theatre,** the setting for Broadway-style revues, has Arctic-themed decor with sculptured balconies, sidewalls, and parterre divisions resembling glacial landscapes. The futuristic **Starquest** (with a revolving bar) and **Hollywood Odyssey** are two nightspots housed in RCI's hallmark **Viking Crown Lounge** perched high over the sea. The latter features jazz ensembles, comedians, pianists, and vocalists. The ship has a large casino, several bars, and a library reminiscent of a traditional English study, as well as **Royal Caribbean Online,** the Internet center with 12 stations.

SPORTS, FITNESS, AND BEAUTY The ocean-view **Spa,** the beauty and health center, has 12 treatment rooms, including rasul and a thermal suite ($15 to $42 for a half hour), gym with 18 treadmills and an array of equipment, and fitness activities and exercise classes. Out on deck, passengers have more challenges at the climbing wall with five separate climbing tracks, golf simulator ($20 per hour), nine-hole miniature golf course, basketball court, and jogging track.

CHILDREN'S FACILITIES The line's **Adventure Ocean** youth program offers supervised activities by age group (ages 3 to 5, 6 to 8, 9 to 11, 12 to 14, and 15 to 17) in age-appropriate activity centers. Kids earn gift coupons for participating. Facilities include a computer lab, play stations with video games, and **Adventure Beach** with splash pools and a waterslide. Teens have their own coffeehouse/disco with flat-screen televisions and soda bar. Children's menus and group babysitting are available.

Freedom of the Seas	**QUALITY 9**	**VALUE B**
Independence of the Seas	2008	
Liberty of the Seas	Preview	
REGISTRY Bahamas	**LENGTH** 1,112 feet	**BEAM** 184 feet
CABINS 1,800	**DRAFT** 28 feet	**SPEED** 21.6 knots
MAXIMUM PASSENGERS	**PASSENGER DECKS** 15	**ELEVATORS** NA
4,370	**CREW** 1,360	**SPACE RATIO** NA

THE SHIP Back in 1999 when I said *Voyager of the Seas* was cruise ship as entertainment, I could not have imagined *Freedom of the Seas.* It's a wow! and then some. Many of her features are those that are found on the *Voyager*-class ship, but many others are innovations appearing on a cruise ship for the first time.

At 160,000 tons, with a maximum capacity of 4,370 passengers, *Freedom of the Seas,* constructed in Finland, was the largest cruise ship in the world when she debuted in May 2006. The first of three in Royal Caribbean's new *Freedom* class, the giant vessel is the most innovative ship the company has built to date.

Among the most noteworthy innovations are the first boxing ring and the first surf simulator at sea and an unusual top-deck aquatic playground with three massive pool areas. They include an interactive water park, two dramatically situated whirlpools, and a dedicated sports pool—each with a different audience appeal.

The most interesting space is the **H₂0 Zone,** a colorful wonderland of large, bright sculptures doubling as interactive fountains that spray and spurt water in every direction. The oversize sculptures are in all shapes and sizes, giving passengers numerous playful opportunities—by turning wheels, setting off sensors, and dodging dumping buckets—to get soaked or to soak others.

In one corner of the water playground, a circular pool shoots a current of water in a river around a central island. Passengers can float with the flow as they are misted by one of the fountain sculptures. A shallow pool area, fed by a flamingo-shaped fountain, is a secluded space for the youngest kids. At the back of the park, a rectangular swimming pool is flanked by wading areas and fed by a waterfall cascading from an overhanging bridge. At night, the water park becomes a dramatically lit sculpture garden.

The **Solarium,** an adults-only oasis, offers another cruise-ship first. Two hot tubs, large enough for the neighborhood, are cantilevered out 12 feet from the sides of the ship and suspended 112 feet above the ocean. The panoramic views from here are definitely not for those with acrophobia. But interestingly enough, every time I passed by the pools, no one was looking out at the views—they were too busy talking to each other. The Solarium's jungle decor has tropical foliage, rain forest–inspired mosaics and murals, tall metal palm trees and hammocks, and seven-foot-tall parrot sculptures. Passengers swimming in the Solarium's pool are treated to music piped in underwater and a simulation of a coral reef.

Another first for RCI is in the main pool area at the center of the ship where there are two parallel pools. One of the pools is designated as a sports pool for activities ranging from pool volleyball to synchronized swimming competitions. The sports pool has lane markers for lap swimming. At night, the main pool area can be transformed into an open-air nightclub, with a large dance floor situated between the two pools. The ship's combined pool areas—the family pool area, adults-only Solarium, and the main pool area—are 43% larger than on the *Voyager*-class ships.

ITINERARIES *See* Itinerary Index.

CABINS Other innovations on *Freedom of the Seas* are flat-screen televisions in all cabins and six categories of family cabins designed especially for large families and groups of friends. These accommodations come in several new configurations, sizes, and price ranges.

The largest is the 14-person Presidential Suite, with a 1,215-square-foot interior and an 810-square-foot balcony equipped with a whirlpool, wet bar, eight lounge chairs, and a 14-person table for dining alfresco. The oversize suite has dual entryways, two master bedrooms with 30-inch flat-panel televisions, and bathrooms with bathtubs. Two other bedrooms will accommodate four people each, with convertible twin/queen and Pullman beds. Both rooms have a 23-inch flat-screen television. The suite's common area includes two additional bathrooms with showers, a living room with a sectional sofa that sleeps two, a card/dining table, and an entertainment center with a 42-inch plasma television.

The five other types of family accommodations are in addition to the ship's standard triples and quads. Each category includes twin beds, convertible to a queen bed and bunks. Four, eight-person Royal Family Suites (600 square feet with a 270-square-foot balcony), each with two bedrooms, include a master bedroom with a bathroom with bathtub, a second bathroom with shower, and a living area with a sectional sofa and an entertainment center with a 30-inch flat-screen television, and an alfresco dining table for eight. Each suite can be expanded to accommodate up to ten people via a connecting cabin.

Three categories with a total of 15 cabins, each for six persons, have a curtained-off sleeping alcove with bunk beds, sleeper sofa, a bathroom and shower or tub; some with walk-in closets; 1 Accessible Family (400 square feet with a 120-square-foot balcony); 8 Family Oceanview (up to 495 square feet with windows); 4 Promenade Family (335 square feet, two windows with window seats overlooking Royal Promenade); and 2 Inside Family (330 square feet).

Specifications 1,084 outside cabins, 844 with balconies; 732 inside, 558 with no window, 168 overlook Promenade; 21 Family Suites (1 for 14 persons, 4 for 8 persons, 15 for 6 persons, 1 wheelchair accessible); 32 wheelchair-accessible.

DINING *Freedom* has a very large main dining room spanning three levels. There are two seatings in this nonsmoking room. Tables are available for 4 to 12 persons. The ship has many other dining options: the casual **Windjammer Café,** serving buffet breakfast, lunch, and table-service dinner; **Jade,** an Asian-fusion specialty restaurant in the Windjammer Café; a **Johnny Rockets** diner; and several eateries along the Promenade, including the **Portofino,** an upscale Italian restaurant ($20) requiring reservations, and **Chops Grille,** a specialty restaurant for steaks and seafood. The Royal Promenade has a coffee shop serving sandwiches, pizza, and pastries; **Latte'tudes,** a coffee bar; **Sorrento's,** a pizza parlor and Italian restaurant; and **Bull and Bear Pub,** an English pub.

FACILITIES AND ACTIVITIES *Freedom of the Seas* has RCI standard features, such as the ever-popular ice-skating shows and production shows in the main theater, **Arcadia Theatre,** decorated in Art Deco style. The theater features three shows: *Marquee,* a medley of performances, the musical magic show *Now You See It!,* and *Once Upon a Time,* a narrative piece based on the Brothers Grimm's fairy tales. The disco is crowded to the wee hours, but the best action is the **Royal Promenade,** the heart of the ship, a 445-foot-long shopping, dining, and entertainment boulevard with activities throughout the day and special ones at night, including festive circus parades with bright costumes and colorful characters. Among the shops on the Promenade are **A Clean Shave** barber shop, **Book Nook** (a bookstore with French cafe seating), and **Ben & Jerry's** ice-cream parlor.

Some of the ship's 20 bars include **Olive or Twist,** which is part of RCCL's signature, glass-enclosed Viking Crown Lounge on Deck 14 that also has a private club for Crown & Anchor members. The bar has live jazz nightly shows. Cloud Nine, a quiet corner, is also part of the Viking Crown Lounge. **Bolero's** offers mojitos and Latin music; **On Air Club** is the venue for karaoke. **Wipe Out!,** on Deck 13, offers draft beer, wine, and fruit ice drinks. The **Champagne Bar,** with a wide Champagne selection, and **Vintages,** a wine bar, are on the Promenade. The always-popular **Schooner Bar,** RCCL's signature cocktail lounge and piano bar, is on Deck 4, the same deck as the lower level of the main dining room.

SPORTS, FITNESS, AND BEAUTY *Freedom's* **Fitness Center,** the largest at sea, is incredible and to my thinking, the ship's biggest wow! It should be called No Excuses. The huge gym has every type of exercise equipment and instruction imaginable, with special studios for Pilates ($10 per person), spinning, yoga (including classes on the beach in Labadee), and others, but the biggest attraction is the full-size 18-by-8-foot Everlast boxing ring. For the first time ever on a cruise ship, novices can test their chops in a variety of boxing-related activities—groups of three people in sparring sessions with freestanding Body Masters bags, supervised by a coach ($10) or Rocky wannabes three one-hour training sessions with a coach inside the ring. The workout includes a warm-up, bag work, mirror boxing, footwork, and pad work.

Some of the many novel programs are Boot Camp X-Treme circuit training for seasoned exercisers, Salsamania, a Latin-inspired exercise class incorporating dance moves and energetic music for a lively workout, and the Night Klub indoor cycling program, held in a high-tech studio outfitted with enhanced lighting features to create a nightclub-style light show throughout the class. To help familiarize passengers with all of the fitness activities available, the Center has two 65-inch interactive plasma televisions where classes and equipment are reviewed and class schedules are available.

And not to be forgotten are the climbing wall, the eight-hole minigolf course, and the much-publicized, first-on-a-cruise-ship FlowRider, a surf simulator that accommodates only two people at one time. It is surrounded by viewing stands for some to watch and even get splashed. The climbing wall (43 feet high and 44 feet wide) is 30% larger than the original on *Voyager*-class ships. The freestanding wall has a central spire, adding a new dimension to the experience. Passengers have 11 routes to choose, from easy to expert.

CHILDREN'S FACILITIES Adventure Ocean Program is RCL's program for kids ages 3 to 17. On *Freedom*, teens particularly are catered to with three areas just for them: **Fuel** nightclub, the **Living Room** hangout, and the **Back Deck** sun deck. For tiny tots ages 6 to 36 months and their parents, *Freedom* offers the line's Aqua Babies and Aqua Tots playtime programs developed by partner Fisher-Price (now available fleetwide).

Liberty of the Seas comes with similar facilities and attractions and is sailing on alternating seven-day Eastern and Western Caribbean cruises. When she debuts in May 2008, *Independence of the Seas* will begin her maiden season based in the United Kingdom and will be the largest ship ever to be home-ported in Europe.

POSTSCRIPT Royal Caribbean's reputation for delivering consistency holds up on all its ships. But remember, these are megaliners; you need patience for crowds and long lines, no matter how smoothly the ships operate. At the same time, their size and array of facilities and activities are treats in themselves, and they serve to fuel the action-packed, high-energy atmosphere aboard.

Seabourn Cruise Line

6100 Blue Lagoon Drive, Suite 400, Miami, FL 33126
☎ 305-463-3000 or 800-929-9391; fax 305-463-3010
www.seabourn.com

TYPE OF SHIPS Small, modern, ultraluxurious ocean liners.

TYPE OF CRUISES Top-shelf luxury cruises on worldwide itineraries.

CRUISE LINE'S STRENGTHS
- impeccable service
- luxurious accommodations
- exclusivity
- ship size/maneuverability
- open-seating dining
- cuisine
- worldwide itineraries

CRUISE LINE'S SHORTCOMINGS
- limited activities
- limitations on use of water sports facilities

FELLOW PASSENGERS Sophisticated, discriminating, well-heeled, experienced travelers; 80% from North America; others are from Europe and elsewhere. Age varies, depending on season and destinations. Most are age 50 and older; active business owners and professionals—doctors, lawyers, entrepreneurs—as well as honeymooners and some semiretired. They come mainly from the Northeast, Florida, California, and the Chicago area. Fifty percent or more are repeaters. The mix could include a childless couple in their 30s or multigenerational families ages 4 to 70. Passengers are likely to have sailed on other luxury vessels and stayed in five-star hotels. They know and understand quality; their expectations are high, and their judgment tough.

Recommended for Sophisticated, seasoned travelers accustomed to the best; affluent passengers whose first priority is service; those who seek exclusivity; yacht owners who want to leave the driving to others; those who shun big-ship, glitzy cruises; first-timers who seek and can afford small-ship ambience; honeymooners with rich parents; lottery winners.

Not recommended for Those unaccustomed to luxury or a sophisticated environment; anyone uncomfortable in a fancy restaurant or five-star European hotel; flashy dressers; late-night revelers; inexperienced travelers; children.

CRUISE AREAS AND SEASONS Australia/New Zealand, Caribbean, Panama Canal, South America, Southeast Asia, winter. Baltic, Black Sea, British Isles, Europe, Mediterranean, Norwegian fjords, spring/summer; Egypt, Canada, Caribbean, New England, Red Sea, autumn; transatlantic, spring, fall.

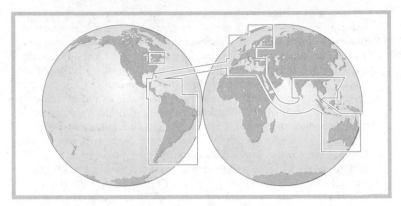

CRUISE AREAS AND SEASONS FOR SEABOURN CRUISE LINE

THE LINE Founded in 1987 by Norwegian industrialist Atle Brynestad, Seabourn Cruise Line's goal has always been to offer the world's most luxurious cruises on the most elegant ships afloat for the most discriminating travelers. Seabourn's posh ships with sleek, yachtlike profiles are small enough to be exclusive yet large enough to be spacious and offer most facilities of a large ship. The ambience is carefree elegance. Cruises follow the sun on worldwide itineraries that circle the globe in a year's time.

In 1996, with the demise of Royal Viking and Royal Cruise lines, Seabourn acquired the *Royal Viking Queen,* which was originally intended to be the third Seabourn ship. In 1999, Carnival, which had owned 50% of Seabourn Cruises, acquired 100% ownership. Seabourn remains a separate brand. With the purchase, Carnival became a major player in the luxury market. Carnival's ownership, with its deep pockets, is enabling Seabourn to increase its fleet. In 2007, it announced its intention to build two new 32,000-ton ships for Seabourn. To be built at Italy's T. Mariotti yard in Genoa, each ship will have 225 suites, and although they are more than three times the size of the vessels currently in the fleet, Seabourn says the hotel-staff-to-guest ratio will be the same as on the current fleet.

THE FLEET	BUILT/RENOVATED	TONNAGE	PASSENGERS
Seabourn Legend	1991/96/2000/03	10,000	208
Seabourn Pride	1988/97/2000/03	10,000	208
Seabourn Spirit	1989/99/2000/03	10,000	208
Seabourn Odyssey	2009	32,000	450
Unnamed	2010	32,000	450

STYLE Elegant but not stuffy, glamorous but not glitzy, Seabourn ships are like tony private clubs. Quality is key, starting with a nearly effortless embarkation and a white-gloved attendant to escort you to your suite (as luxurious as the brochure promises), where fruit and Champagne await you. Decor exudes understated elegance. Service—always attentive, never intrusive—is as polished as the silver with which you dine. You will be addressed by name by the staff after your first appearance.

Seabourn attracts both old-money travelers who disdain mainstream cruise ships and newly rich who appreciate the line's status symbolism. It also caters to stressed-out professionals and others seeking privacy. Whatever their background, they're affluent enough to be accustomed to a high level of service and style without excessive fuss.

Days at sea are for relaxing. Dress and atmosphere are informal, and time is unstructured. The usual announcements, pool games, and contests are absent. In fact, a Seabourn cruise is so low-key, you may need to read your daily agenda to know what's happening. Each cruise has one or two special events meant to be highlights. It might be a special concert in an unusual location for Seabourn passengers only; a visit to a private island, marina, or estate; or a sporting event. Evenings aboard ship are more formal; fine dining is the day's highlight. On evenings when you prefer to relax, a full-course dinner will be served en suite.

All three ships are now wired for WiFi access, enabling passengers with suitable laptop computers to receive and send e-mail and Web-surf from all suites and most public areas on board. A new satellite service has lowered costs: Internet access is $0.50 per minute, with lower bulk rates available. Phone service is $4.95 per minute. The ships offer an expanded menu of television channels, with additional sports, news, and entertainment programming. Cell phone capability for passengers to use their own phones in international waters is also available fleetwide.

Seabourn offers the ultimate in vacation flexibility by enabling passengers to choose from varied options. These include tailoring their cruise with separate and independently priced cruise fares, air-travel options, pre- and postcruise tours, hotel, and transfers. For air, the choices are Seabourn's air program with preselected carriers (economy, business, or first class); the cruise line's independent air program, booked through Seabourn; or a chartered Gulfstream to and from the ship anywhere in the world.

DISTINCTIVE FEATURES Unusual care for solo passengers. Foldout water sports marina. Personalized stationery, walk-in closets, complimentary self-service laundry. Computer learning centers. Luggage shipping. Visiting chefs. WiFi access. Personal-shopper services in many ports.

	HIGHEST	LOWEST	AVERAGE
PER DIEM	$1,422	$417	$839

Per diems are calculated from cruise line's nondiscounted *cruise-only* published fares on standard accommodations and vary by season, cabins, and cruise areas.

RATES Tips are included; government fees and taxes are additional. Prestocked minibar in cabins; wine with meals; open-bar policy throughout ships.

Special fares and discounts Advance-purchase, capacity-controlled discounts, known as EBS (Early Booking Savings), reward early birds with up to 50% savings. Combo savings of 10% are added for booking consecutive cruises totaling up to 17 days. Longer combinations of 18 days or more get 50% or more Grand Voyage savings. Future cruises booked aboard a cruise earn an extra 5% savings. For the line's other special fares, consult its brochures. Those who have sailed on Seabourn or any of the other Carnival member lines qualify for Club Signature Savings of 50% on an array of cruises throughout the world. Club Signature Value Sailings are clearly marked in Seabourn's cruise catalog and on the Web site.

- **THIRD PASSENGER:** 50% of per-person published tariff.
- **CHILDREN'S FARE:** Same as third-person rate. No infants under one year; children ages 1 to 2 sail free.
- **SINGLE SUPPLEMENT:** 125% to 200% of per-person double-occupancy basic suite, depending on cruise, and capacity controlled.

Packages
- **AIR/SEA:** Yes. First- and business-class upgrades at extra charge.
- **PRE/POST:** Yes. Many basic air/sea packages include one hotel night in the departure city; extensions available in all major gateways.
- **OTHERS:** Yes.

PAST PASSENGERS Members receive 50% savings on selected cruises and a free 14-day cruise after 140 days. There are also savings for early bookings.

THE LAST WORD To compete in the growing ultra-deluxe market, Seabourn widened its price range and began offering much more flexibility. The per diems on some sampler and promotional cruises are no more than those of mainstream cruises, and considering the all-inclusive nature of a Seabourn cruise, the mainstream lines may cost more in the end. In any year, Seabourn visits more than 300 ports in more than 100 countries. Very few cruise lines can match those numbers. If you can afford the price, you're unlikely to find any finer cruising—even on your own yacht.

Seabourn Cruise Line Standard Features

Officers Norwegian, international

Staff Dining, Cabin, Cruise: international

Dining facilities Two open-seating restaurants; one more formal, the other a casual indoor/outdoor cafe. Alfresco grill on deck some nights. En suite dining. Complementary wine.

Special diets On request, four weeks prior to sailing.

Room service 24 hours, cabin menu and full service.

Dress code By day, casual but conservative, comfortable. Dinner is a dressier affair some nights, casual (no jacket required) other nights; informal (jacket but no tie for men) or formal (black-tie optional one evening in the dining room on one-week cruise; two on two-week cruise); there are casual alternatives for dinner every night.

Seabourn Cruise Line Standard Features (continued)

Cabin amenities Flat-screen television with DVD player, CNN, ESPN, and Discovery channels; financial fax service, Bose Wave CD/stereo, direct-dial telephone, marble bathroom with twin sinks (one on *Legend*), tub and shower, deluxe toiletries, hair dryer, bathrobes, walk-in closet, minifridge, safe. Stocked bar; umbrella, atlas, personalized stationery.

Electrical outlets 110/220 AC.

Wheelchair access 4 suites.

Recreation and entertainment 3 lounges with entertainment/dance music nightly, cabaret, classical music concerts, folkloric performances in ports of call, weekly dinner dance, casino, cruise-related lectures, bridge instructor and lessons, enrichment programs.

Sports and other activities Water sports marina, outdoor pool, deck sports; parlor games.

Beauty and fitness Several saunas, outdoor whirlpools, gym, exercise classes, beauty salon, spa with massage, beauty treatments.

Other facilities Self-service laundry, laundry/dry cleaning, library, boutique, hospital, nondenominational religious services. WiFi access, medical facilities, and computer center.

Children's facilities None; children under age 18 must be accompanied by parent or adult with written permission.

Theme cruises Classical music, food and wine, others.

Smoking Dining venues and areas of lounges are designated as nonsmoking. Cigar, pipes on open decks only.

Seabourn suggested tipping No-tipping-expected policy.

Credit cards For cruise payment and onboard charges: American Express, Diners Club, Discover, MasterCard, Visa.

Seabourn Legend	**QUALITY 9**	**VALUE C**
Seabourn Pride	**QUALITY 9**	**VALUE C**
Seabourn Spirit	**QUALITY 9**	**VALUE C**
REGISTRY Bahamas	**LENGTH** 439 feet	**BEAM** 63 feet
CABINS 104	**DRAFT** 16 feet	**SPEED** 18 knots
MAXIMUM PASSENGERS	**PASSENGER DECKS** 6	**ELEVATORS** 3
208	**CREW** 165	**SPACE RATIO** 49

THE SHIPS In this age of glitzy ships, the Seabourn triplets (they are nearly identical) epitomize understatement. Clean lines, fine fabrics, and subtle styling are meant to soothe. Passengers board through a lobby that instantly reveals the ships' character. Quietly elegant, the small atrium spans five decks with a double circular stairway accented by brass railings and etched glass. A glass dome above illuminates the stairs and adjacent hallways with diffused natural light. Pastel carpeting complements blush marble and wood used throughout the vessel. The sense of space and serenity is immediate and is among the ships' most appealing features.

Public rooms occupy all of the two top levels and are aft on the two center decks. The dining room is on the lowest passenger level. In 2000, all three ships were given a stem-to-stern multimillion-dollar renovations, along with the addition of French balconies to 36 suites, a computer learning center, a cigar humidor, and an expanded gym, among other improvements. Again, in 2003, the ships were refurbished and new amenities added. More enhancements were added when the ships were renovated in late 2005 and early 2006.

The main showroom, **Magellan Lounge** (**King Olav** on *Legend;* **Amundsen Lounge** on *Spirit*), has a stage and dance floor. It is used for daytime lectures and evening entertainment. In the lobby area are the purser's and tour desk, cruise director's office, writing room, and computer center.

One flight up is a second entertainment lounge, which is cleverly glass-partitioned in three sections: a small casino, an informal bar, and a piano lounge used for activities, socializing, daytime parties, and predinner cocktails. After dinner, it's a nightclub. There's also a small book-and-video library.

The first of the two top levels contains the Sports and Spa Deck and indoor/outdoor **Veranda Café.** Another flight up is the **Observation Lounge,** a beautiful room with sloping floor-to-ceiling windows. Early-bird continental breakfast and afternoon tea are served here—both stellar times for ocean panoramas. Reference material on shore excursions, board games, and puzzles is available. A bar outside serves morning bouillon and is a popular gathering spot in fair weather. A promenade used by walkers and joggers connects the bar to a sunning deck.

ITINERARIES *See* Itinerary Index.

CABINS Accommodations—all spacious, outside suites—are among the ships' finest features. Even standard Seabourn Suites are large. Their practical design maximizes space, and appointments—wall coverings, carpets, draperies, bedcovers of fine, lightly textured fabrics—enhance harmony and elegance.

They have well-defined sitting and sleeping sections. The roomy conversation area has a sofa, two chairs, and a coffee table that can be transformed into a dining table. Two cushioned stools provide extra seating for guests. The sitting area is next to a five-foot-wide picture window placed low enough that you can lie in bed and watch the passing scenery. The window has a mechanical shade operated by a switch near the desk and a device to clean the outside automatically.

Now, 36 of each ship's 104 suites have French balconies in place of the five-foot picture window. The balconies consist of two full-length sliding glass doors opening onto a narrow Riviera-style balcony with a waist-high glass balustrade. The sliding doors can be opened to enjoy sea breezes without cutting into the interior space of the room. In the ships' tariff, these suites are designated by categories B2 and B3, and their locations are shown on deck plans. Unfortunately, the French balconies have shown not to ride well in high seas when water seeped in to such an extent that the wall-to-wall carpets and furniture had to be changed completely. Upon the first experience of this problem, all seals on balcony doors were replaced and closures changed—making for significant improvement.

A curtain separating the sitting and sleeping areas can be drawn to put sleepers in darkness. Beds can be configured as twins or a queen. The bedroom section has a long dresser/desk and a large, lighted mirror. A wall-mounted minifridge and bar is stocked with two bottles of spirits or wine that you select when you book. Replenishments cost extra. Mineral water and soft drinks are free. The bar contains Norwegian crystal glassware. On the opposite wall is a pullout writing desk, containing your personalized stationery and a small sewing kit. On a shelf opposite the bed is a flat-screen television and DVD player. CNN and other channels are available, depending on the location of the ship. The suites also have a Bose Wave stereo radio and CD player. The walk-in closet contains extra shelf space and a safe.

The marble bathroom has twin sinks (*Legend,* one sink), mirrored storage shelves, a large tub, and a shower. Thick terry robes, a hair dryer, and toiletries are supplied. Fine bed and bath linens are used throughout.

Cabin doors have a thoughtful touch: a brass clamp to hold the daily agenda, messages, and menus. A hall-side door can be used to convert adjacent standard suites into doubles.

Twenty suites on each ship can be joined, by opening a movable wall, and made into double suites, with a total of 554 square feet, two baths, one queen bed, and a separate dining area. Six larger suites are in three configurations. Classic suites have queen beds only, a larger sitting area, and a small veranda. Two Owner's Suites have a separate bedroom and living room, a master bath with shower and tub and guest bath, a table with four chairs, one walk-in and one alcove closet, two sofas, and a private veranda. Two other Owner's Suites are the largest and have large living rooms and forward-facing private verandas.

Specifications All suites: 88 are standard Seabourn Suites; 2 larger Classic Suites and 4 Owner's Suites—all with verandas, 36 with French balconies. Standard dimensions, 277 square feet; 102 suites with twins (convertible to queen); no singles; 4 wheelchair-accessible.

DINING Fine dining is central to a Seabourn cruise, and the choices are diverse. For any meal, you dine when and with whom you like in the **Restaurant** dining room or the casual **Veranda Café,** an indoor/outdoor venue for buffet breakfast and lunch. In the evening, this venue becomes a second restaurant, serving tasting menus and theme dinners by reservation. On sea days, lunch and some evenings feature alfresco dining at the **Sky Bar**

Grill. Or one can dine en suite, choosing from the 24-hour cabin menu or the dining room menu, served course by course. Morning bouillon is served in the Sky Bar, and afternoon tea with cucumber sandwiches can be enjoyed in the Observation Lounge. Weather permitting, a lavish deck barbecue dinner is offered on one evening of the cruise.

With Seabourn, the emphasis is on fresh ingredients, such as seafood, fruits, and vegetables, obtained in ports. Breads, pastries, and ice cream are prepared onboard. Menus, changed daily and repeated on a 21-day cycle, are created by celebrity chef Charlie Palmer and offer three appetizers, two soups, two salads, five entrées, three desserts, cheese, and ice cream. Generally, dishes are innovative and sophisticated. You will find a familiar fettuccine Alfredo, but you may be tempted by seared reindeer or grilled marlin with strawberry and cilantro sauce. Vegetarian and lean specialties are available daily, as are classic steak, chicken, and fish.

Menu entrées are cooked to order, and presentation is outstanding. Compatible wines are complimentary. Suggested wines are usually moderately priced; the wine list is more elaborate and offers attractive prices on rare and unusual wines bought as a package in advance. Wine is also available by the glass. Caviar available by request.

The Restaurant is a pretty room dressed in pastels where tables are set with Porsgrund china, fine crystal, silverware, and fresh flowers. Most tables seat four or six, but two, eight, and tens are available.

Breakfast and lunch appeal most to those who prefer a quiet environment and full service. Dinner is a lavish, somewhat formal affair. One evening each week calls for black tie or optional dark suit, and for all but casual nights, dress suitable for fine dining in New York or Paris is expected. Seabourn has expanded its passengers' choices by offering a more casual dining alternative in Restaurant 2 in the Veranda Café on evenings when the suggested attire for the Restaurant is black tie.

In 2006, Seabourn introduced two new dining options. The **Sky Grill** was created by turning the Sky Bar area into an alfresco dining venue, complete with candlelight and table service for grilled steak and seafood, along with a great buffet. Sky Grill can accommodate about two dozen passengers and is available one or two nights of the cruise, depending on the weather. The other innovation is **Tasting @ 2,** when the daytime casual restaurant is transformed nightly into a romantic yet casual evening spot for up to 50 passengers. The three tasting menus alternate with themed dinners such as Asian or Mediterranean cuisine, very different from those being served in the main restaurant.

Service is unfailingly superb. In fact, service in the Restaurant is the best and most professional we have encountered on any cruise ship. Unlike on other cruise ships, singles are invited to join an officer's table or one hosted by management or a social-staff member. An invitation will be clipped to your door almost daily, and the mäitre d' will seat singles with other guests, unless you indicate that you prefer to dine alone. At least once each cruise, a dinner dance is held in the Restaurant.

The informal, convivial atmosphere of the Veranda Café makes it the most popular choice for breakfast and lunch or for dinner after a long shore excursion. In the ships' most recent refurbishing, the Café got fresh new decor and new contemporary menus. The lively cafe bustles with people and conversation indoors. Outside, tables are set under protective awnings. In fair weather, the deck is one of the most delightful dining places anywhere.

The breakfast buffet offers fruit, fresh breads, and pastries, smoked fish, cheeses, and eggs, pancakes, and waffles made to order. The lunch buffet includes salads, made-to-order pasta, hot and cold seafood, chicken and meats, or grilled fish or meat on request. Hard to resist are the daily surprises: guacamole, an Asian buffet, or a cheese and dessert bar. The homemade ice cream is a passenger favorite. But these aren't your ordinary self-service buffets. An army of attentive stewards take drink orders, assist you with your plate, and bring seconds.

Seabourn is continuing its highly appreciated Chef's Circle, a guest chefs program that brings America's most creative and celebrated chefs onboard, features their signature dishes in the Restaurant, and has them give cooking demonstrations during the cruise.

SERVICE Most passengers rate service as the single best feature—and with good reason: it's impeccable. Shipwide, the thoroughly professional staff is gracious and attentive, but never intrusive. The Norwegian captain and officers, European hotel staff and stewardesses, and British and American cruise and social staff work harmoniously and are visibly proud of their ship. The ships' small size lends them to personalized service impossible on larger ships. The luxury setting offers more opportunities to provide good service, and the high crew-to-passenger ratio enables staff to deliver it.

The ship's no-tipping policy appeared to work very well, but we've recently been told that it's being modified to allow staff to accept tips for unusual service. We thought it was the result of the line's lowering its cruise prices (20% or more), but we were wrong. Gratuities are still included in the cruise price. We hope the change won't impact service. Also, to note, some guests give donations to a crew fund through the purser's office; it pays for crew parties and other activities during their free time.

FACILITIES AND ACTIVITIES The daily agenda isn't taxing but might include a cooking demonstration, afternoon lecture by a well-known person from the arts, academia, politics, or show business, port talks, bridge lessons or play, art class, galley tour, wine-and-cheese party, ice-cream social, parlor games and quizzes, or folkloric show. A movie about one of Seabourn's other cruises—and a not-too-subtle sales pitch—may be presented. Not on the schedule are bingo, horse racing, pool games, or costume parties.

The library has music and books, including some on CD. Also, cabin stewardesses will deliver DVDs to suites, upon request. The boutique beckons to shoppers. The **Computer Learning Center,** with four computers, offers classes for a fee.

Or you can do nothing at all. If the weather is fair, you'll probably be out on deck, relaxing, snoozing, soaking in the Jacuzzi, or enjoying a "massage moment" (complimentary from the spa staff). Some places offer protection in hot or cool weather.

Evening entertainment is tony, designed for sophisticated people. The ship's quartet plays easy listening and dance music in the **Club,** or a pianist/vocalist performs at the cocktail hour. Evening cabaret and variety shows staged in the **Magellan Lounge** are usually very good. They feature the cruise director and three or four social-staff members. Lounge seats are slightly tiered, providing excellent sight lines. A classical concert or program by a young artist may be offered, or the Restaurant becomes a supper club with dancing. The casino offers roulette, blackjack, slot machines, and gaming lessons.

SPORTS, FITNESS, AND BEAUTY Decks have ample space for sunning and a teak promenade for walking or jogging. Whirlpools and a small, deep swimming pool are in a peculiar spot near the Veranda Café—the pool is often shaded by the ship's superstructure, inhibiting swimmers.

The ships have a water sports platform with a 30-by-30-foot steel-meshed cage that drops into the sea, creating a protected saltwater pool. A teak border provides a launch area for paddleboats, windsurfers, kayaks, and sailboats in warm-weather ports. Two high-speed boats pull water-skiers or banana boats and also transport snorkelers and divers to choice locations. Although the ships try to use these marinas at least once a week, rough water may preclude it.

In the 2003 renovations, fitness facilities were upgraded substantially, with the gym doubled in size and more state-of-the-art equipment added, along with new cabinets and lockers. Daily stretch and exercise classes at varied workout levels, individual training, sauna, and steam rooms are available. The **Spa at Seabourn** has enhanced selections of beauty treatments and services, along with fitness classes in yoga, Pilates, and cardio Ki Bo circuit training.

Seabourn no longer has a golf program; however, the line can make arrangements for tee times on request. Seabourn's ships visit 90 ports around the world where passengers have access to more than 100 golf courses, including most of the major and famous ones.

CHILDREN'S FACILITIES Although Seabourn doesn't offer the ideal family vacation, it's a testimony to staff that three children younger than 9 years old reported having the time of their lives on a recent cruise.

SHORE EXCURSIONS Excursions are well organized and orchestrated by an experienced, knowledgeable staff. On a Norwegian fjord cruise, the briefing was the most thorough heard on any but expedition-type cruises accompanied by specialists. There's no push to sell excursions, and even off-the-shelf motor coach tours tend to be pricey. Information on excursions is available on Seabourn's newly expanded and enhanced Web site; excursions can be booked online.

Each cruise offers one event designated as an Exclusively Seabourn excursion for all passengers. These often are a cruise highlight and may be visits to private homes or local sites off the tourist track. Refreshments and entertainment are provided, and guests may be introduced to local dignitaries. For example, a Norwegian voyage offered a concert of Edvard Grieg's music at his lakeside home near Bergen, presented by Norway's foremost pianist.

In addition, the line recently added more than 75 new and unusual shore excursions created exclusively for Seabourn passengers. These excursions include special entry to sites of interest, meetings with famous personalities, and a variety of special-interest pursuits such as car racing, yacht racing, photography, and river rafting. There's a visit to Hong Kong's Cantonese Opera to watch artists apply their makeup; a ride in a horse-drawn carriage to a winery in the Medoc; and shopping in Florence markets for an Italian Cordon Bleu Cooking School class, to name a few.

POSTSCRIPT   One of Seabourn's most useful innovations has been Personal Valet Luggage Shipping, particularly considering the frequent hassle travelers encounter at airports and customs these days. By teaming up with DHL Worldwide Express, Seabourn enables passengers to ship their luggage directly from their home to their ship. The service prepares all the shipping and customs paperwork, picks up the luggage, maintains 24-hour online tracking, insurance, and delivers the shipment. The cost is based on weight. As an example, 30 pounds from the United States to Seabourn's Scandinavia/Russia cruise cost about $350.

New Ships: Scheduled to debut in June 2009, *Seabourn Odyssey,* Seabourn's new, $250 million flagship, is being designed by architects Yran & Storbraaten of Norway and built in Italy by T. Mariotti. A sister ship is expected to be launched in 2010.

The new ship mirrors the silhouette and general interior layout of the existing Seabourn ships but will add new facilities and amenities, such as more dining options, more types of suites, more verandas, more entertainment venues, and enhanced spa and recreational facilities.

Although three times the size of her smaller sisters, the new vessel will carry only twice as many guests and boast a 71.1 space ratio—among the highest in cruising. The 225 ocean-view suites (277 to 1,300 square feet) will come in 13 categories and be found on 7 of 11 passenger decks; 90% have verandas. The 22 penthouses measure 450 square feet with 100-square-foot verandas. The largest accommodations are five Owners Suites (700 square feet, including veranda) and four two-bedroom Grand Suites (1,300 square feet). All suites have granite bathrooms, separate tub and shower, twin sinks, and a stunning glass vanity.

Seabourn Odyssey will have four dining venues: The Restaurant, an open-seating gourmet dining room offering menus by celebrity chef Charlie Palmer; Veranda Café, a casual eatery with indoor-outdoor seating serving regional specialties; Restaurant 2, with innovative tasting menus; and the poolside Patio Grill for pizza and grills. It will also have a showroom, a selection of lounges and bars, and an open-bar policy.

Silversea Cruises

110 East Broward Boulevard, Fort Lauderdale, FL 33301
☎ 954-522-4477 or 800-722-9955; fax 954-522-4499
www.silversea.com

TYPE OF SHIPS Ultraluxury, all-suite small ships.

TYPE OF CRUISES Luxury cruises on worldwide itineraries.

CRUISE LINE'S STRENGTHS
- luxurious all-suite accommodations, most with verandas
- open-seating dining
- cuisine
- impeccable service
- worldwide itineraries
- congenial atmosphere
- comprehensive, all-inclusive prices

CRUISE LINE'S SHORTCOMINGS
- somewhat staid evening activities and entertainment
- shallow draft in rough seas

FELLOW PASSENGERS Diverse demographically, experienced cruisers. Many have made the rounds of the luxury ships. Well traveled and outgoing, passengers range from young professionals in their 30s to lively 80-year-olds. The majority are older than 50; couples are the rule. Passengers come from throughout the United States, but Silversea also has a sizable European following. A high number of passengers are repeaters.

Recommended for Sophisticated, knowledgeable travelers who prefer a finely crafted ship and low-key atmosphere to the glitz and games of big ships; those who appreciate exacting service in casual elegance.

Not recommended for Those for whom subtle luxury and attention to detail are unimportant; anyone uncomfortable among non-Americans. Late-night revelers or children.

CRUISE AREAS AND SEASONS Africa, Alaska, Amazon, Australia, Baltic, Canada, Caribbean, China, Far East, India, Madagascar, Mediterranean, New England, New Zealand, Northern Europe, Seychelles, South America, South Pacific, seasonally. World cruise, winter.

THE LINE Silversea Cruises was created in the early 1990s by the Lefebvre family of Rome with the Vlasov Group of Monaco, commercial and passenger shipping families that previously owned Sitmar Cruises. The name was chosen to suggest quality, luxury, and the romance of the sea.
   When the Italian-built fleet of identical twins was launched in 1994 and 1995, Silversea took the luxury market by storm with reasonable pricing, uncompromising service, outstanding accommodations, and a

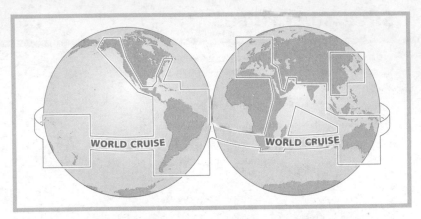

CRUISE AREAS AND SEASONS FOR SILVERSEA CRUISES

space ratio of 55.74, among the highest of any cruise ship. The ultra-deluxe six-deck ships were substantially larger than most of their direct competitors, offering big-ship facilities and all-suite accommodations in a comfortable small-ship atmosphere. Their biggest advantage was their high number of cabins with verandas. Prices cover beverage service throughout the ship (wine, liquors, and nonalcoholic drinks), stocked in-suite beverage cabinet, in-suite hors d'oeuvres and full meals, a special shoreside event on some sailings, baggage handling, and gratuities. The ratio of crew to passengers is 1 to 1.34.

Encouraged by its initial success, the line added another set of larger twins: *Silver Shadow* in 2000 and *Silver Whisper* in 2001. They are about a third bigger and carry about a third more passengers than the line's first twins. The design is similar, but with enhancements based on passengers' comments: larger bathrooms and closets, more top-grade suites, 80% of cabins with verandas, a poolside dining venue, computer center, cigar lounge, and larger spa and fitness center. The ships were built at the T. Marrotti Shipyard in Italy, where the first two ships were built.

In March 2007, Silversea Cruises announced the construction of a 36,000-ton luxury ship at the Italian shipbuilder Fincantieri, to be delivered in late 2009 with an option for a sister ship. The new ship will carry 540 passengers and represents a 40% increase in the line's capacity. Also in 2007, Silversea's ships were scheduled to call at 120 countries and visit 29 new ports, while *Silver Shadow* sails on her first world cruise.

THE FLEET	BUILT/RENOVATED	TONNAGE	PASSENGERS
Silver Cloud	1994/2001/04	16,800	296
Silver Shadow	2000	28,258	382
Silver Whisper	2001	28,258	382
Silver Wind	1995/2003	16,800	296

STYLE Sparkling clean, impeccably maintained, and luxurious in an under-stated way consistent with fine yachts, the ships offer elegance undisturbed by pretense or formality. From boarding to disembarking, passengers are attended by a crew that makes a genuine effort to know each individual and anticipate every need. This attention is direct and friendly, but never obsequious.

Suites are exceptionally comfortable and exceed their representa-tion in the line's brochure. Public areas are inviting and elegant. Structured activities are available, but they tend toward the relaxing and cerebral. Announcements, games, and contests are the exception rather than the rule.

At sea and in port, days are casual. Evenings are low-key but dressier. Most cruises include a Silversea Experience signature event—usually an excursion with dining and drinks in a beautiful setting, perhaps a private island, private club, or secluded coast.

Silversea attracts gregarious and adventuresome passengers. Although the atmosphere is social and conducive to meeting new friends, dozens of delightful nooks offer solitary time.

Through several exclusive arrangements, Silversea is introducing a se-ries of new features and amenities. With Viking Range, manufacturer of ultrapremium kitchen appliances, Silversea has introduced the first Viking Cooking School at sea. Silversea passengers can participate in cooking classes led by Relais & Châteaux–Relais Gourmands chefs hosting Sil-versea's popular culinary cruises. The new Viking culinary theaters feature a custom-designed cooking station, fully equipped with Viking profes-sional-caliber cookware, cutlery, and countertop appliances.

Another addition is the new Loro Piana boutiques fleetwide. Loro Piana, a six-generation Italian luxury textile brand, creates elegant, top-quality pieces for men and women, including accessories, gifts, and made-to-measure products—all crafted in Italy.

Through Silversea's exclusive partnership with the National Trust for Italy (*Fondo per l'Ambiente Italiano*), passengers will enjoy an enhanced program of shore excursions, cultural events, and access to some of Italy's most historic sites. FAI protects and maintains some of Italy's most beautiful architectural and cultural treasures, including ancient castles, villas, a monastery, gardens, and stretches of pristine countryside and coastline.

Silverseas ships have WiFi hot spots for computer or Blackberry con-nections, and recently the line added cell-phones-at-sea access to enable passengers to use their own cell phones in international waters. Recently, too, Silversea enhanced bedtime for its passengers with the installation of new custom-designed Sealy Posturepedic Plush Euro-top mattresses fleetwide. The top suites—Owner's, Grand, Royal, and Rossellini—got Stearns & Foster Plush ultraluxury mattresses that are 10% larger than a conventional mattress.

In 2007, Silversea tested its first cruise with no formal nights or receptions on one of *Silver Cloud's* Mediterranean cruises. Dubbed Privileged Passage, the program also included extended open hours for the fitness center and spa, requests for early embarkation and late disembarkation at no cost, a selection of complimentary tours designed to connect travelers to the places and cultures they visit, and a more casual entertainment program featuring jazz ensembles and an international DJ. Silversea says that if the program is well received, it might be added to other cruises. Stay tuned.

DISTINCTIVE FEATURES   All-suite accommodations; comprehensive air/sea travel with personalized service at intermediate travel stops; all-inclusive prices. Silversea Experience on most sailings; moderate single supplements; 365 Golf program; Internet access; Personalized Voyage program; personal e-mail.

	HIGHEST	LOWEST	AVERAGE
PER DIEM	$1,439	$488	$865

Per diems are calculated from cruise line's nondiscounted *cruise-only* published fares on standard accommodations and vary by season, cabins, and cruise areas.

RATES   Tips and onboard beverages, including select wine and spirits, in cruise-only rate; an optional air/hotel program includes round-trip airfare (with upgrades to business class available), one-night precruise deluxe hotel, transfers, and baggage handling.

Special fares and discounts   Early-booking incentive savings range from 5% to 20%; they are capacity-controlled and subject to availability. An additional advanced payment savings of 5% may be combined with the early-booking savings when payment is made in full by a specified date.

Silversea has expanded its Silver Sailing savings program, enabling passengers to save up to 50% off cruise-only fares on Vista, Veranda, and Midship Veranda suites and higher categories (Medallion to Owner's suites) up to 35% on certain cruises to the Indian Ocean, Northern Europe, and Southeast Asia, as well as Africa, Australia/New Zealand, Caribbean, Mediterranean, South America, and South Pacific cruises as in the past. The Silver Sailing offers are subject to availability; they are valid only for new cruise bookings and do not apply to land, hotel, and air programs.

- THIRD PASSENGER: Approximately 50% of the Vista or Veranda Suite per-person published rate.
- SINGLE SUPPLEMENT: 110% to 175% of per-person double-occupancy basic suite, depending on cruise.

Packages
- AIR/SEA: All cruises packaged with economy-class air; upgrades available for an additional charge, but still at special rates.
- PRE/POST: Extensive pre- and post-cruise tours. Many air/sea packages include one or more hotel nights in the departure or termination city; extensions are available.

PAST PASSENGERS   Past passengers automatically become members of the Venetian Society, named to reflect the line's Italian ownership. On their second voyage, members receive a silver pin bearing the society's winged-lion emblem, a symbol of Venice. After they have sailed for 100-, 200-, and 500-plus days, they receive sapphire, emerald, and diamond pins, respectively. Members also receive a newsletter three times yearly containing information on special discounts. Other benefits include shipboard events hosted by the captain. Members get fare reductions of 5%, 10%, and 15%, combinable with early-booking incentives, advance-payment bonus, and consecutive-cruise savings. Members may bring friends in an additional suite at some savings. They also receive $250 or $500 shipboard credits and a credit to their Society account for the days their friends cruise. Members may accrue days toward a free cruise.

THE LAST WORD Silversea got off to a great start with its first two ships, setting exceptionally high standards for itself and the industry. The second two larger ships did not draw the same level of praise initially, and the line fell into a slump. Now, after a determined effort to improve the product across the board, Silversea has made a comeback. The new food, entertainment, and enrichment programs are innovative, and the itineraries are creative, calling on some ports seldom visited by cruise ships. Officers and crew are actively involved in providing highly personalized service.

Silversea has expanded its guest lecturer program with a new series called The Spirit of Exploration. On select voyages, an internationally acclaimed adventurer will serve as the ship's Resident Explorer, hosting a series of presentations and accompanying passengers on selected shore excursions.

Silversea Cruises remains a good value for those who can afford it, and competition keeps a constant pressure on price. The cruise line's Personalized Voyages program provides prospective passengers with the utmost flexibility and convenience to customize a cruise to suit their needs.

Here's how it works: Passengers choose the length of their voyage (five nights minimum) and the embarkation and disembarkation ports from Silversea's list of more than 200 approved ports of call or on its Web site (**www.silversea.com**). To determine your cost, you select a suite category, then add up the daily rate for the days you plan to be on board. You must arrange your own air transportation, but Silversea will assist you with hotel and/or transfers in select ports, as needed, for a fee.

Silversea Cruises Standard Features

Officers Italian.

Staff Dining and Cabin: European; Cruise: British and American.

Dining facilities All meals served at one seating in restaurant; indoor/outdoor cafe for casual breakfast and lunch. Alternative dining specialty dinners on most evenings. In-suite dining.

Special diets Available on request.

Room service 24 hours, cabin menu and full-service dining room menu.

Dress code By day, casual but conservative and comfortable. Dinner is more

Silversea Cruises Standard Features (continued)

dressy. Informal (jacket, tie optional for men) or formal (two black-tie or dark-suit nights on one-week cruise; four on two-week cruise).

Cabin amenities Stocked bar, minifridge, interactive television with CNN, VCR, direct-dial telephone, marble bathroom with sink, tub, and shower, hair dryer, bathrobes, walk-in closet, safe.

Electrical outlets 110/220 AC.

Wheelchair access Limited.

Recreation and entertainment Three lounges with entertainment/dance music nightly, cabaret, classical music concerts, folkloric performances in ports of call, nightly dancing, casino, cruise-related lectures, Internet access.

Sports and other activities Outdoor pool, deck sports, bridge instructor and lessons, enrichment programs.

Beauty and fitness Two saunas, two outdoor whirlpools, small gym, exercise classes, beauty salon, spa with massage, beauty treatments.

Other facilities Self-service laundry, laundry and dry cleaning, library with books and video, hospital, cigar lounge, computer center, nondenominational religious services, Internet access.

Children's facilities None; children under age 18 must be accompanied by parent or adult with written permission.

Theme cruises Cuisine, wine, golf, music, and others.

Smoking Dining and public rooms nonsmoking except designated areas in lounges and bars.

Silversea suggested tipping No-tipping policy.

Credit cards For cruise payment and onboard charges: American Express, Diners Club, MasterCard, Visa.

Silver Cloud/Silver Wind	QUALITY 8	VALUE C
REGISTRY Bahamas	**LENGTH** 514 feet	**BEAM** 70 feet
CABINS 148	**DRAFT** 18 feet	**SPEED** 20.5 knots
MAXIMUM PASSENGERS	**PASSENGER DECKS** 6	**ELEVATORS** 4
296	**CREW** 210	**SPACE RATIO** 56.8

THE SHIPS Styled to soothe, the first Silversea twins are the antithesis of the huge floating hotels that dominate cruising. Elegance is anchored in simplicity, clean lines, earth-tone fabrics, and polished wood and brass.

The entry lobby surprises with its modest proportions. No six-story atrium here. The feeling is of boarding a yacht. The ships' layout is simple. On topmost Deck 9 are a fitness center and jogging/walking track that circles the ship. It overlooks the pool and pool bar on Deck 8, which also contains the bridge, twin whirlpools, **Panorama Lounge,** with indoor and outdoor seating, and the **Champagne Room,** an elegant wine and cigar lounge.

On Decks 4 through 7, all cabins are forward, all public areas aft. Elevators and a circular stairwell are aft of amidships. Deck 7 offers the library (on *Silver Cloud*), spa, beauty salon, and **Terrace Café** for informal dining and breakfast and lunch buffets. Deck 6 has the main lobby, travel desk, reception desk, card and conference room, and showroom, which is large enough for small production shows but small enough to be intimate. Deck 5 has a sundries shop, casino, and the **Bar,** where the showroom audience gathers. The **Library** (on *Silver Wind*) and **Restaurant** are on Deck 4. Public areas are extensive for ships of this size. Dozens of quiet places throughout the ship invite reading or watching the water.

ITINERARIES *See* Itinerary Index.

CABINS The spacious, all-outside suites are among the ships' signature features. Suites provide twin beds convertible to a queen, walk-in closet, sitting area with love seat, coffee table and side chairs, writing desk, dressing table with hair dryer, marble bathroom with full-size tub and shower, stocked refrigerator and cocktail bar, entertainment center with satellite interactive television and VCR, and direct-dial telephone. A curtain separates the sleeping and living areas.

Seventy-five percent of the suites have private teak verandas; the remainder provide picture windows. All suites are decorated in light earth tones or pastel blues with nautical trim of polished wood and brass. Other ultradeluxe extras are fine, pure-cotton bed linens and robes, down pillows, personalized stationery, fresh fruit, large umbrellas in the closets, complimentary shoe shine, and 24-hour room service.

Added in 2005 are luxury bath amenities by Acqua di Parma, the century-old Italian fragrance house, which has produced in-suite toiletries characterized by natural ingredients, delicate production processes, and meticulous attention to detail; most products are still packaged and bottled by hand. Added in all suites in 2007 were Sealy Posturepedic Plush Euro-top mattresses and in the top suites—Owner's, Grand, Royal, and Rossellini—Stearns & Foster Plush ultraluxury beds that are 10% larger than a conventional mattress.

Specifications: 102 Veranda Suites (295 square feet); 36 Vista Suites (240 square feet, no veranda); 3 Silver Suites (541 square feet); 1 Rossellini Suite (1,314 square feet with 2 bedrooms) ; 2 Royal Suites (1,031 square feet in the 2-bedroom configuration), 1 Grand Suite (1,314 square feet with 2 bedrooms), and 1 Owner's Suite (827 square feet). No singles; 2 wheelchair-accessible.

DINING The main dining room, called the **Restaurant,** is reminiscent of an exclusive club. Tables are set with Eschenbach china, Christofle silver, linen, and Schott crystal. Draped picture windows flank the elegant room, and a domed center section adds to its spaciousness. A small marble dance floor allows for occasional dinner dances. Although formal, the Restaurant is also comfortable, relaxed, and unpretentious.

Passengers aren't assigned seating times or tables; they may eat any time during published hours. Lunch and breakfast buffets in the Terrace Café provide an informal option. No late-night buffet is offered. Room service is available 24 hours and is delivered with the same attention to detail characteristic of the dining room. Service is outstanding.

Carrying fewer passengers enables Silversea ships to cook dishes to order, as in a restaurant. (However, we have received complaints from some passengers that the kitchen isn't as accommodating as the line claims or as it should be for this price, or as some competitors are.)

Silversea also provides for picky eaters, health-conscious diners, and the meat-and-potatoes set. Only the finest ingredients are used, regardless of how simple or complex the dish. Meat eaters in search of a cruise ship that can prepare a good steak, chop, or prime rib will find nirvana here. Menus offer three appetizers, a pasta, two soups, two salads, sherbet, three main courses, and usually a grilled selection. In addition are a light and healthy and a vegetarian entrée. The dessert menu is separate. Wines are included in the cruise price.

The food is excellent in quality and presentation, but for those unaccustomed to rich sauces and creams, it could be overwhelming—although you can order meals without creams or sauces. Freshness of ingredients is not a problem. One day, returning to ship aboard the tender, we were assaulted by an unexpected smell. Peering around the bulkhead, we discovered a grinning chef with a huge string of fish just purchased from local fishermen—a luxury that could never be provided on a large ship.

The casual Terrace Café high on the stern offers a commanding view of the sea. A wall of windows faces the sheltered outside dining area. Tables are always set with china, crystal, and silver. Buffet waiters take orders for drinks and hot entrées. On most evenings the cafe is transformed into **La Terrazza,** offering an à la carte experience with the finest elements of Italian cooking. Reservations may be made on board.

In 2004, the refurbished *Silver Cloud* and *Silver Wind* got a new **Champagne Room**, bringing them more in line with *Silver Shadow* and *Silver Whisper.* The Champagne Room, located on Deck 8 and adjacent to the Panorama Lounge, is a wine and cigar room offering guests a cozy venue where they can relax and settle back into sumptuous leather chairs to enjoy a select vintage or fine cigar.

Dining options also include an alternative gourmet dining venue, called **Saletta,** which means "a small room" in Italian. It's one of Silversea's new Wine Restaurants by Relais & Châteaux and features some of the world's rarest vintages, chosen by Relais & Châteaux–trained sommeliers to highlight this culinary experience. The fee is about $150 per person to dine, and advance reservations may be made on board.

SERVICE Passengers rate service in a dead heat with accommodations as these twins' best feature. Without exception, the staff is professional and attentive but never intrusive, friendly without being familiar, and thoroughly gracious in the European manner.

Working harmoniously, officers and crew form a highly effective and responsive team. A concierge is available for special services. These ships' size lends itself to more personalized service than larger ships can offer. There's no tipping. Period.

FACILITIES AND ACTIVITIES The next-day's programs, delivered nightly to your suite, are more mainstream than you might expect on an ultraluxury cruise, but they prove that even the pampered and sophisticated play bingo! A typical day might include an early power walk with the fitness instructor, a visit to the bridge, a lesson about computers or multimedia, aerobics, wine tasting by the sommelier, a bridge lecture, bingo, backgammon, shuffleboard competition, water volleyball, golf-putting competition, afternoon tea, team trivia, and line-dancing lessons.

In conjunction with Relais & Châteaux-Relais Gourmands, Silversea has a series of culinary cruises highlighted by cooking demonstrations, gala dinners, signature dishes, and regional specialties created by master chefs from around the world.

Experts lecture on the cruise area, and a folkloric show might be staged by a local group. A morning port talk will include a sales pitch for tours. Doing nothing is an option. In fair weather, you'll probably be on deck, relaxing in a lounge chair or soaking in the Jacuzzi. There are ample places in shade or sheltered from wind. In foul weather, the library stocks books, magazines, periodicals, and videos; it's open around the clock, and sports computer terminals with Internet access. Also available are daily printed news and market-wrap reports.

In the evening, there's music for dancing before and after dinner as well as evening entertainment—a variety show, comedy, and magic. The ship's small orchestra plays easy listening and dance music in the **Bar,** and a pianist or vocalist duo perform in the **Panorama Lounge.** The casino offers roulette, blackjack, slot machines, and gaming lessons. Entertainment in the **Main Lounge** spotlights individual entertainers and production shows by a six-member group. All passengers can be accommodated in the steeply tiered, two-level room. Murals of sinuous women add an Art Deco touch. Most sight lines are good. Late-night diversions consist of audience-participation games, dancing, and piano music in the Panorama Lounge.

SPORTS, FITNESS, AND BEAUTY The Pool Deck has a large swimming pool, plentiful sunbathing space, two whirlpools, and a pool bar. Blue-and-white-striped chair cushions create a nautical atmosphere. The uppermost deck has an artificial-turf-carpeted promenade for walking or jogging. The fitness center, recently expanded and moved to the top deck, now offers a panoramic ocean view in addition to ample exercise equipment and free weights. One or more daily stretch and exercise classes for various workout levels are offered; individual training is available.

The spa offers sauna, steam rooms, and beauty treatments and a comprehensive program of fitness, beauty, and spa treatments crafted for Silversea by Mandara Spa, an international spa specialist. It uses naturally blended treatments and Balinese techniques, incorporating its signature blend of exotic, traditional, and cutting-edge health and beauty programs, offering such unusual indulgences as a hot lava-rock massage and a Japanese honey steam wrap. Spa treatments can now be booked on Silversea's Web site.

CHILDREN'S FACILITIES Children are rare on Silversea cruises, and no children's facilities or programs are offered. The occasional child receives lots of attention and generally enjoys the cruise. The nice pool and all-included drinks and snacks help.

SHORE EXCURSIONS Shore excursions are administered efficiently onboard, and the line has a good batting average with them. Silversea passengers' expectations that excursion operators will provide the same level of service they receive aboard ship may be unrealistic in some regions of the world, no matter how hard the cruise lines tries. This problem is, of course, not unique to Silversea; only that the contrast from the ship to the land operation is sometimes sharper.

Excursion sales are low-key, and some cruise directors do an excellent job of matching passengers with the tours most suited to their tastes. Even off-the-shelf motor coach tours tend to be pricey. Shore excursions can now be booked online. Many cruises include one Silversea Experience, a special shore excursion showcasing an area's culture. This may be a private tour or dinner in an extraordinary location. For example, the line has hosted wine tastings at a private château and dinner at a palace in St. Petersburg, Russia.

Silver Shadow	QUALITY 8	VALUE C
Silver Whisper	QUALITY 8	VALUE C
REGISTRY Bahamas	LENGTH 610 feet	BEAM 82 feet
CABINS 194	DRAFT 19.6 feet	SPEED 21 knots
MAXIMUM PASSENGERS	PASSENGER DECKS 7	ELEVATORS 5
382	CREW 295	SPACE RATIO 73.9

THE SHIPS *Silver Shadow,* launched in 2000, was followed by her twin, *Silver Whisper,* in 2001. The noted Norwegian architectural team of Petter Yran and Bjorn Storbraaten, designers of *Silver Cloud* and *Silver Wind,* created the ships, which are slightly larger and accommodate 100 more passengers than the line's first ships. Otherwise, they are similar, more or less, to their sister ships in layout and contemporary decor. Throughout the ships, mellow wood furnishings and fine fabrics combine with marble floors and crystal chandeliers to create an elegant, stylish setting. Their passenger space ratio of 73.9 may be the highest of any cruise ship.

Silversea's hallmarks—Veranda Suites, single-seating dining, in-suite dining, Christofle silverware, fine linens, down pillows—are found aboard these ships. Among the new features were a casual poolside dining venue, a computer center, conference center, cigar lounge, and a

Champagne bar. The ships also have an observation lounge, show lounge, boutique, a larger spa, swimming pool, and whirlpools.

ITINERARIES *See* Itinerary Index.

CABINS More than 80% of the suites have teak verandas. A standard Veranda Suite measures a spacious 345 square feet, including veranda. The smallest cabins measures 287 square feet. All cabins have a walk-in closet and large Italian marble bathroom with telephone, double-basin vanity, full bath and shower, and separate toilet, and are equipped with small refrigerators and cocktail bar, entertainment center with interactive television and VCR, and fresh fruit and flowers.

The largest suites range from 701 to 1,435 square feet and include the Owner's, Grand, and Royal suites in six variations. They have enlarged balconies, separate bedrooms and living rooms, large-screen televisions, and private bars. Owner's Suites also have a guest powder room and CD stereo system. Larger suites are located amidships. Two Medallion Suites, 501 square feet each, are extremely comfortable, with enough storage space for a family of five.

All suites now have Sealy Posturepedic Plush Euro-top mattresses and the top suites—Owner's, Grand, Royal, and Rossellini—have Stearns & Foster Plush ultra-luxury mattresses that provide 10% more sleep surface than a conventional mattress.

Room service, available 24 hours a day, offers a full room-service menu. Passengers can order from the Restaurant's menu and have their meal served course by course in their staterooms. Self-service laundry facilities are available.

Specifications: 186 outside suites; 2 Owner's Suites (1,264 square feet with 2 bedrooms), 3 Grand Suites (1,286–1,435 square feet with 2 bedrooms), 13 Silver Suites (653–701 square feet), 2 Medallion Suites (521 square feet), 128 Veranda Suites (345 square feet), 35 Vista Suites (287 square feet, no veranda); 2 Royal Suites (1,312–,352 square feet), 1 Rossellini Suite (1,286–1,435 square feet with 2 bedrooms); 2 wheelchair-accessible with verandas.

DINING The **Restaurant,** the main dining room, has an elegant ambience with tables set with fine linens and Christofle silverware. It offers open seating and a variety of table configurations for two to six people. The popular bistro-style **Terrace Café,** with floor-to-ceiling windows opening onto panoramic views off the ship's aft deck, serves buffet breakfast and lunch and makes a charming setting in the evening, when it is transformed into La Terrazza, serving Italian fare with fresh and flavorful ingredients. The **Grill** is a casual poolside dining venue.

Recently, another dining alternative was added. The new gourmet restaurant, **Le Champagne,** is one of Silversea's new Wine Restaurants by Relais & Châteaux and features some of the world's rarest vintages, chosen by Relais & Châteaux–trained sommeliers to highlight the culinary experience. The fee is about $150 per person to dine, and advance reservations may be made on board.

FACILITIES AND ACTIVITIES The **Humidor,** an elegant wine and cigar bar, adjoins Le Champagne. Designed in the style of a traditional English smoking club with rich wood floors and deep galley chairs, it has a walk-in humidor stocked with Davidoff products, a Swiss-based purveyor of fine cigars and luxury merchandise, as well as a selection of Dominican, Honduran, and Cuban cigars. The lounge seats 25 and offers complimentary cognacs and cordials, along with cigars.

Of the ship's four bars, the **Casino Bar,** a small nook adjoining the casino, seems to be the most popular. Simply furnished with a semicircular cherrywood bar with ebony leather stools, it has two small leather sofas and modern-style halogen lamps and fixtures.

The ships have a shopping arcade, a library with books in various languages, videos, and seven computer terminals with Internet access. Silversea has an unusual way of charging for their use: The $0.75 per minute is charged only for as long as it takes a Web page to download and come into view. The charges then stop until another Web page is requested.

SERVICE These ships do not have as high a crew-to-passenger ratio as the smaller twins, nonetheless, they continue to receive high marks for service.

SPORTS, FITNESS, AND BEAUTY The ships have large health clubs and spas that occupy most of Deck 10. Decorated in a soothing combination of aqua and blue tiles and blonde carpets, the facility has a beauty salon and an aerobic and fitness center with weights, treadmills, stationary bikes, and other equipment. There are separate steam rooms, saunas, and changing facilities for men and women. The ships also have a heated outdoor pool and two whirlpools.

In 2007, Silversea Cruises launched a new spa concept fleetwide, starting with *Silver Shadow.* Dubbed The Spa at Silversea, it replaces Mandara spas and features new treatments and ceremonies designed to offer passengers a more personalized and holistic spa experience. The Spa has been refurbished with new artwork and contemporary furnishings. The program, part of the line's Wellness Program, offers cutting-edge body-age assessment technology that gauges body fat, cardiovascular health, strength, and flexibility to see how one's body age compares with his or her actual chronological age. Based on the results, The Spa's personal trainers design a lifestyle program for a participant and recommend a fitness regimen as well as dining options developed specifically for the Wellness Program. The program is available also for men and for couples. Elemis aromatherapy products are used, and the facility is operated by Steiner.

On many cruises, the Silver Links golf program provides the opportunity for passengers to improve their game with the help of an onboard PGA-class golf professional. The program also offers golf excursions, arranged and escorted by the ships' golf pros, to such challenging courses as Shanghai's Silport Golf Club.

POSTSCRIPT *Silver Shadow* and *Silver Whisper* are almost 70% larger than their predecessors, but not everyone agrees that bigger is necessarily better. Some passengers like the spaciousness and new facilities that the larger size provides; others prefer the more intimate experience the smaller ships offer. Still, all Silversea ships carry an impressive number of repeat passengers, and during the last two to three days of a cruise, many passengers are seen in front of the concierge desk waiting to book their next voyage.

Star Clippers, Inc.

7200 NW 19th Street, Suite #206 Miami, FL 33126
☎ **800-442-0551 or 305-442-0550; fax 305-442-1611**
www.starclippers.com

TYPE OF SHIPS Replicas of 19th-century clipper sailing ships.

TYPE OF CRUISES Casual, active, sports-oriented, sailing under canvas to out-of-the-way places.

CRUISE LINE'S STRENGTHS
- traditional sailing with some cruise-ship comforts
- camaraderie
- ship size/maneuverability
- itineraries

CRUISE LINE'S SHORTCOMINGS
- meager port information
- potential language/cultural collisions among passengers
- small cabins

FELLOW PASSENGERS International mix. About half are American, Canadian, and Latin American; the other half are European, particularly Germans, including non-English speakers. The average age is 45, but some cruises have 20- and 30-year-olds. The majority are couples, usually including about a dozen newlyweds.

As many as 50% may be repeaters, attracted by sailing on a square-rigger. Many appreciate the beauty and authenticity of the clipper ships and have no interest in the nightclubs, casinos, and glitter aboard mainstream cruise ships, which they probably have shunned.

Recommended for Independent, active travelers who seek light adventure and off-the-beaten-track itineraries, small-ship devotees, stressed-out urbanites, honeymooners and romantics captivated by the notion of sailing on a tall ship. Also, avid sailors, water sports enthusiasts, experienced cruisers weary of crowded large ships, and conservationists who appreciate environmentally friendly travel aboard ships that use their engines only when necessary. It's a great experience for children ages 7 and older who mix well with adults.

Not recommended for Those seeking gourmet cuisine, pampering, around-the-clock activity, and resort facilities of a superliner. Physically impaired travelers.

CRUISE AREAS AND SEASONS Caribbean, South Asia, winter; Mediterranean, summer; transatlantic, trans–Indian Ocean, April and October; Tahiti/Society Islands, year-round.

THE LINE Launched in 1991, Star Clippers is the dream come true of Swedish shipping entrepreneur Mikael Krafft, whose passion for sailing and building yachts and love of the clipper ship (one of America's greatest

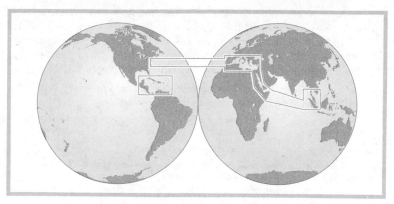

CRUISE AREAS AND SEASONS FOR STAR CLIPPERS, INC.

inventions, he says) led him to create an unusual cruise line with replicas of the sleek, mid–19th-century trading ships. Called greyhounds of the sea, they were the fastest ships afloat until the arrival of the steam age in the late 1860s.

About 100 feet longer than the original clippers and equipped with the latest marine technology, these clippers combine the romance of yesteryear's sailing with some modern amenities. They offer the excitement of manning an authentic square-rigger and cruising out-of-the-way waters of the Caribbean, Mediterranean, French Polynesia, or South Asia.

The success of Star Clippers' twins led the line to build a third ship, which is reported to be the world's largest sailing vessel. She entered service in July 2000. In 2008, Star Clipper Cruises is adding year-round Tahiti cruises on *Star Flyer,* sailing from Papeete on 7-, 10- and 11-night itineraries.

THE FLEET	BUILT/RENOVATED	TONNAGE	PASSENGERS
Royal Clipper	2000	5,000	227
Star Clipper	1991	2,298	170
Star Flyer	1992	2,298	170

STYLE Cruises have the freewheeling spirit of a private yacht and are intended to fit between budget-priced Windjammer Barefoot Cruises and pricey Windstar Cruises. They're designed for active, healthy folks who want their travel to be interesting, educational, and fun. Daytime dress is very casual (shorts and deck shoes); evenings are only a bit dressier.

CABINS are of average size and public rooms few, but the teak decks are roomy.

Cruises offer island hopping in a laid-back atmosphere with varied options at each port of call. The clippers can anchor in bays where large cruise ships cannot go. Launches take passengers to isolated beaches and places for scuba diving, snorkeling, and other water sports.

After a week's cruise, you will know many passengers on a first-name basis and most of the crew, who are both deckhands and sports instructors. You can help hoist the sails or laze about on deck watching the canvas and the sea. Itineraries ensure daylight cruising under sail. The environment is great for families with children ages 7 and up.

DISTINCTIVE FEATURES The ship and helping sail it; captain's daily briefings; PADI certification for those interested in scuba diving.

	HIGHEST	LOWEST	AVERAGE
PER DIEM	$575	$97	$272

Per diems are calculated from cruise line's nondiscounted *cruise-only* published fares on standard accommodations and vary by season, cabins, and cruise areas.

RATES Port charges are additional.

Special fares and discounts 10% discount on published rates for booking 120 days in advance on selected cruises.

- **SINGLE FARE:** Guaranteed rate, depending on season, with cabin assigned two weeks before departure.
- **SINGLE SUPPLEMENT:** 150% for categories 2 through 6 (selected seasons) of published fare. 200% for highest-category cabins, deluxe suites, and Owner's Suites.

Packages
- **AIR/SEA:** Yes.
- **PRE/POST:** Yes.
- **OTHERS:** Honeymoon.

PAST PASSENGERS Members receive special discounts and a bottle of Champagne in their cabins on boarding and are placed on the ship's VIP list.

THE LAST WORD Star Clippers provides an unusual experience on unique ships that are modern and comfortable, yet steeped in tradition. More affordable than Sea Cloud and more upscale than Windjammers, Star Clippers' ships are more authentic than those of Windstar. Yet, they definitely aren't for everyone.

The ships cannot readily accommodate disabled passengers and aren't for people who want mainstream cruising's comforts and options. English is the ships' language, but announcements are likely in other languages, depending on passenger makeup. Language can become a problem when English speakers are outnumbered by non-Anglophones, and some may feel left out of activities. Onboard charges are in euros.

Star Clippers Standard Features

Officers European.

Staff Dining, Cabin: international; Cruise: Swedish, Australian, and Hungarian.

Dining facilities One dining room for three meals with open, unassigned seating. Light breakfast, occasional buffet lunch, hors d'oeuvres on deck at 5 p.m.

Special diets Inquire in advance. Vegetarian, low-calorie standard on menus.

Room service Only for top suites on *Royal Clipper*.

Dress code Relaxed and casual. Walking shorts, bathing attire with cover-up, skirts, slacks for daytime; slacks with polo or casual shirts, no jackets required for men in evening.

Cabin amenities DVD players, radio, hair dryer, safe, cellular-satellite phone, movies, ports-of-call videos and music, bathrooms with showers, upper category with whirlpool bath and minifridge.

Electrical outlets *Star Clipper/Flyer*, 110 AC; *Royal Clipper*, 220 AC, American adapter needed.

Wheelchair access None.

Recreation and entertainment Piano bar with entertainer, outdoor deck bar for dancing and local entertainment, library/writing room, backgammon, and bridge.

Sports and other activities Two outdoor pools, water sports and equipment, sailing dinghies, windsurfers, waterskiing, underwater viewing craft, water-jet launches, and inflatables carried on board. Learn-to-sail and dive programs.

Beauty and fitness No beauty/barber service on *Star Clipper/Flyer*; spa, hair salon, gym on *Royal Clipper*. Exercise sessions.

Other facilities Dining room doubles as conference room with audiovisual equipment. Nurse on cruises; doctor and nurse on transatlantic. Ship's officers trained in emergency medicine.

Children's facilities None; younger than age 18 must be accompanied by adult.

Theme cruises None.

Smoking No smoking in cabins. At first briefing, captain emphasizes that smoking is allowed on deck or in rear of dining room.

Star Clippers suggested tipping $8 per person per day; 15% added to bar bills.

Credit cards For cruise payment and onboard charges: American Express, Master-Card, and Visa.

Star Clipper/Star Flyer	QUALITY 7	VALUE A
REGISTRY Luxembourg	LENGTH 360 feet	BEAM 50 feet
CABINS 85	DRAFT 18.5 feet	SPEED 17 knots
MAXIMUM PASSENGERS 170	PASSENGER DECKS 4	ELEVATORS None
	CREW 72	SPACE RATIO 15

THE SHIPS *Star Clipper* and *Star Flyer* are identical, with four masts and square-rigged sails on the forward mast—a barkentine configuration—with a total of 16 sails (36,000 square feet of Dacron). They are manned, not computerized, and are capable of attaining speeds up to 19 knots. A diesel engine is in reserve for calms and maneuvering in harbors.

At 226 feet, they are among the tallest ships (the cruise line says *Royal Clipper* is the tallest) and the first true sailing vessels to be classified by Lloyd's Register of Shipping since 1911. Built in Belgium, they comply with the latest safety regulations for passenger vessels on worldwide service.

The ships have four passenger decks; all but eight cabins are on the lower two. Public spaces, which were recently refurbished, are on the top two. There, amid sails and rigging, every Walter Mitty begins to salivate with anticipation. They can help hoist the sails or watch in wonder. The ships are generally under sail from late evening to the following midmorning. Under normal conditions, they use the engine only to maneuver in port. For true salts and romantics, balmy tropical air filling the white sails against a star-filled sky is the essence of bliss. Many stay up half the night savoring it.

ITINERARIES *See* Itinerary Index.

CABINS Small but comfortable, cabins are carpeted, air-conditioned, and tastefully furnished with a counter/desk and built-in seat, large mirror, wood paneling, brass lamps, and prints of sailing scenes. Two portholes admit light. Under-bed storage holds luggage or scuba gear, and closet and drawer space is adequate for informal cruising.

Most cabins are outside and have twin beds convertible to a double. They have multichannel radio, phone, DVD players, hair dryer, safe, ceiling-mounted television/video monitor (DVDs are available from the library in English and German), and 24-hour news prepared in British English, American English, Canadian English, and German. Each version includes news of interest to that group.

Bathrooms are very small. They have marble-trimmed fixtures and showers. Eight top-category cabins have a whirlpool bathtub, hair dryer, and minifridge stocked at cruise's start (occupants pay for restocks). These cabins open onto the deck; some people may feel that decreases their privacy. Cabin service is limited to cleaning. Aft cabins on lower decks are the least desirable due to engine noise.

Specifications 6 inside cabins, 78 outside; 1 suite. Standard dimensions, 120 square feet. 66 cabins with 2 lower beds (convertible to queen); 18 cabins with fixed double beds; 12 cabins accommodate third passenger; 6 inside cabins have uppers and lowers; no singles.

DINING The **Clipper Dining Room,** resplendent with shining brass and etched glass, is rather formal for such an informal ship. Seating is at tables for six among or around a forest of columns, and banquettes line the walls by portholes. All passengers and officers are accommodated at one open seating. When the ship is full, the room is crowded.

The buffet breakfast has made-to-order omelets; lunch has a different pasta daily and a self-service salad bar. A light early-morning breakfast and occasional lunch buffet are also served on deck.

Dinner selections include beef, chicken, and fish, vegetables, cheeses, and desserts. The food is plentiful but appeals mostly to those with minimal interest in epicurean delights. During a week, food can range from adequate to good, but not gourmet. The menu emphasizes fresh ingredients, fruit, salads, vegetables, and seafood. Wines are available at reasonable prices.

SERVICE Officers and deck crew are friendly, energetic, and easygoing. They mix freely and easily with passengers, helping create the ship's relaxed atmosphere. The dining and hotel staff is low-key and congenial. An easy camaraderie among officers, staff, and passengers is part of the ships' appeal.

FACILITIES AND ACTIVITIES Passengers might be found playing backgammon or bridge. The teak-paneled library/writing room resembles an English club, with large brass-framed windows, paintings of nautical scenes, and a nonworking fireplace (snuffed by the U.S. Coast Guard). Furnished with card tables and comfortable chairs, it's a reception desk at boarding and a small meeting room. A good selection of popular fiction, travel, and coffee-table books is stocked. A tiny shop sells film and souvenirs. The dining room converts to a meeting room with screen projectors and video monitors for port lectures. The captain and cruise director hold "story time," an informal briefing, on deck in late afternoon or the morning before arriving in port. Passengers congregate around the open bridge, where they can hear the captain and his mates at work and watch the sails being raised and lowered. Many lend a hand with the rigging, but few hang in for the full cruise.

A small, U-shaped piano lounge wraps the landing of the stairway between the Main Deck and dining room. It has brass-framed panoramic windows and small tables with cushioned banquettes that seat about two dozen people. The skylight overhead is actually the transparent bottom of a pool on the Sun Deck. A pianist or vocalist entertains before and after dinner. Swinging doors connect to the outdoor **Tropical Bar.** Depending on the hour, it's a social center, meeting area, stage (where the captain speaks daily), spot for light breakfast or buffet lunch, or dance floor (taped music or electronic keyboard). There's no casino.

SPORTS, FITNESS, AND BEAUTY There are two tiny outdoor pools, one filled with freshwater and one with seawater. Beginning scuba lessons are offered at the forward pool.

Exercisers can walk from the stern to the bow around the open parts of the Main and Sun decks. At 8 a.m. daily, one of the water sports teams leads a half-hour aerobics session.

In the Caribbean and South Asia, water sports are a more important element of the cruise than in the Mediterranean. The ships carry sailing dinghies, windsurfers, underwater viewing craft, boats for waterskiing and skis, snorkel gear (issued for cruise duration), scuba equipment for certified divers, volleyballs, and oversize, solid-surface kadima paddles for beach sports. The ships might anchor in a remote cove or off a deserted beach and shuttle passengers to and from shore for snorkeling, sailing, windsurfing, and swimming.

The sports and recreational staff includes multilingual instructors. Snorkeling is organized almost daily in the Caribbean. Certified divers with C cards can join trips to reefs and underwater wrecks. A charge of 65 euros covers air tank refill, personal supervision, and transport by Zodiac.

Two dive programs are available: a PADI refresher course costs 150 euros for those whose certification has lapsed within the past year, and a full PADI certification course costs 410 euros. For the latter, the line requires that divers spread the course over a two-week cruise.

SHORE EXCURSIONS Guided tours (usually $25 to $85) focus on a destination's architectural, historical, and environmental points of interest and are likely to be more interesting than those offered by mainstream ships. Fewer passengers and unusual itineraries help ensure more stimulating, personalized tours for participants.

The ships tie up in port as seldom as possible. Patented stabilizing tanks keep the ship steady at anchor. Tender service is offered every half hour until sailing time, usually around 6 p.m.

Royal Clipper	QUALITY 9	VALUE A
REGISTRY Luxembourg	**LENGTH** 439 feet	BEAM 54 feet
CABINS 114	**DRAFT** 18.5 feet	SPEED 20 knots
MAXIMUM PASSENGERS	**PASSENGER DECKS** 5	ELEVATORS None
227	**CREW** 106	SPACE RATIO NA

THE SHIP *Royal Clipper* made her debut in 2000 as the longest, largest sailing vessel ever built. Her gross tonnage of about 5,000 tons is more than twice that of *Star Clipper* or *Star Flyer*. Her appearance contrasts sharply with her running mates, which resemble large white-hull racing yachts. *Royal Clipper* is a full-rigged ship, with square sails on all five masts; the earlier four-masters are barkentine-rigged. *Royal Clipper* carries 56,000 square feet of Dacron sail, compared with 36,000 square feet on each of the small twins.

The vessel's interior, created by noted megayacht interior designer Donald Starkey of London, is more upscale than her sisters and has many new features. One of her three outdoor swimming pools—an oval center pool—has a glass bottom, which allows light into the three-deck atrium below. A circular staircase links the atrium with lounges, cabins, and public rooms. **Captain Nemo's Lounge,** on the lowest passenger deck, has 16-inch portholes looking out on marine life day and night.

On the Main Deck below the bridge is an observation lounge with wraparound windows; it is used for meetings, informal talks, and Internet connections. The Main Deck also has the purser's office, a large piano lounge, an indoor/outdoor bar, and library.

The main lounge, located amidships, is as comfortable as they come, with banquette, soft couch, and chair seating. It has a sit-up bar and a central well that looks down into the dining room two decks below.

Leaving via the aft doors, the covered **Tropical Bar** recalls the earlier *Star Clipper* pair; so, too, does the paneled Edwardian library, though aboard *Royal Clipper* both rooms are on a much larger scale.

When there is no wind, the twin Caterpillar 2,500-horsepower diesel engines can drive the ship at up to 14 knots. When maneuvering in and out of port, the captain may put up most of the sails, then use a very quiet generator to turn the ship and drive it forward to leave the harbor.

ITINERARIES *See* Itinerary Index.

CABINS Standard cabins, each with 148 square feet, are 35% larger than those on sister ships; 32 have a third fold-down bed. There are two deck cabins of 125 square feet and six inside cabins of 100 square feet. The cabins are furnished in much the same style and vary mostly by location. They have marble bathrooms with shower, television, satellite telephone, radio channels, private safe, and hair dryers.

The outstanding deluxe suites are located along a narrow central mahogany-paneled companionway with a thick sloping mast penetrating the corridor at the forward end. These luxurious cabins, measuring 215 square feet, are mahogany-paneled with rosewood framing and molding against an off-white ceiling and upper portion walls. Pale gold-framed mirrors enlarge the space, and brass-framed windows bring in light to bathe the far corner sitting alcove. Brass wall lamps and sailing ship prints round out the feel of an upward sloping ship's cabin, not a hotel-style room on a hull. One door opens to a huge marble bathroom with Jacuzzi bath—a nod to upscale cruise ship amenities. Another heavy wooden door leads to a private teak veranda with shrouds passing upward from the ship's side.

The two Owner's Suites at the stern are even larger at 355 square feet and have a private entrance and butler service. There are also two 226-square-foot deluxe cabins that open onto the aft deck.

Specifications 114 cabins, 6 inside with double bed; 90 outside—all but 4 have 2 lowers, convertible to doubles; 32 convertible to triples; 2 Owner's Suites; 14 deck suites with verandas; 2 deck suites.

DINING The handsome bi-level dining room accommodates all passengers at a single seating for all meals. The paneled room with brass wall lamps has rectangular, round, and banquette-style tables and is set low enough that in any kind of sea, the water splashes in, washing-machine fashion, over the portholes.

An omelet chef cooks to order at breakfast, and a carvery features roast beef, ham, and pork at lunch. The lunch buffets are the biggest hits on the menu for the first day at sea, providing such fare as jumbo shrimp, foie gras, artichoke hearts, herring, potato salad, lots of salad fixings, hot and cold salmon, meatballs, and sliced roast beef.

SERVICE The international crew provides friendly service, though the pace can be slow at dinner when passengers order from the menu.

SPORTS, FITNESS, AND BEAUTY At least once during the cruise, passengers with a Walter Mitty fantasy may climb (wearing safety belts) the steel mast to a crow's nest, 60 feet above the deck. They may also climb out on the netting that cascades from the bowsprit. Although passengers do not handle the sails as on Windjammers, they can enjoy being part of the navigation by helping the helmsmen on a raised platform above the bridge and chart room. They can also take lessons in sailing and rope tying.

The lower deck has an exercise room, spa, tiled Turkish bath, and beauty salon. A hydraulic platform stages the water sport activities, which include banana boats, waterskiing, diving, snorkeling, and swimming from the 16-foot inflatable raft. An interior stairway gives access to the marina. Two 60-passenger tenders, resembling military landing craft, take passengers for beach landings. Two 150-passenger fiberglass tenders ferry passengers between the anchored ship and pier.

POSTSCRIPT The ship has no special facilities for children, but when they are aboard, they are looked after well by the crew and staff, and there is much for them to observe, learn, and enjoy.

Although the overall experience and attraction of *Royal Clipper* is similar to the smaller clippers, comparisons are difficult. *Royal Clipper* is truly different. Her size, her 42 sails, the sheer amount of deck equipment, and her lavish Edwardian interiors are a sharp contrast to the smaller-scale, relatively simple sleek sisters. As one passenger saw it, "For an ocean crossing, I would want the full-rigged *Royal Clipper*; for sailing the Caribbean or Mediterranean, I would be happy with either."

Windstar Cruises

300 Elliott Avenue West, Seattle, WA 98119
☎ 206-281-3535 or 800-258-7245; fax 206-281-7110
www.windstarcruises.com

TYPE OF SHIPS   Deluxe sailing yacht/cruise ships.

TYPE OF CRUISES   Low-key, laid-back, yet luxurious, for active, affluent travelers with cosmopolitan tastes for offbeat corners in sunny climes.

CRUISE LINE'S STRENGTHS
* appealing lifestyle
* private-yacht exclusivity on small ships
* cabins
* romantic escape
* water sports

CRUISE LINE'S SHORTCOMINGS
* evening activity
* port-intensive itineraries with minimal time under canvas

FELLOW PASSENGERS   The mix is broader than generally perceived. Not all drive BMWs and Porsches: 40% have Jeeps and Fords, and 77% of those are the family version rather than sports model. Passengers range from 20 to 80 years in age, but the majority are 35 to 65 years old. Incomes differ, and they might be first-time or experienced cruisers. Despite many differences, they have one aspect in common—a lifestyle preference, even if they cannot enjoy it 365 days of the year. Passengers are likely to be well traveled, from the United States, Europe, and Latin America, and about 75% are professionals—lawyers, doctors, business executives—and probably work in high-pressure jobs. The remainder are apt to be retirees from similar pressure cookers, plus a few honeymooners. They are active and enjoy individual and low-energy sports, such as golfing, walking, and swimming.

Recommended for Active, affluent, type-A individualists, 25 to 75 years old, who really mean it when they say they want to chill out; those who abhor mainstream cruising; divers and others who enjoy water sports; experienced cruisers looking for something different; those attracted by the romance of sailing ships while wanting upscale luxury.

Not recommended for Anyone who prefers large ships, thrives on nightlife, or enjoys wearing fancy clothes; those who need to be entertained, don't relate to a sophisticated ambience; those who prefer a burger to brûlée.

CRUISE AREAS AND SEASONS   Bahamas, Caribbean, Costa Rica, Panama, winter; Greek Isles, Mediterranean, spring through fall; transatlantic, March/April and November.

THE LINE   Four masts in a row, each with enormous triangular sails and as tall as a 20-story building, tower above a deck one-and-a-half times the length of a football field and half as wide. The great sails are manned by computers designed to monitor the direction and velocity of the wind

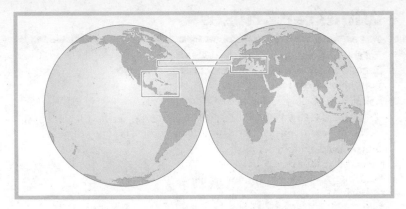

CRUISE AREAS AND SEASONS FOR WINDSTAR CRUISES

to keep the ship from heeling more than 40 degrees. The sails can be furled in less than two minutes.

These ships are wind cruisers, which on their introduction in 1985 were called the most revolutionary vessels since the introduction of the steamship. The vessels use wind power alone up to 50% of the time at sea, depending on itinerary; electrical power and backup propulsion are provided by diesel-electric engines. The ships marry the romance and tradition of sailing with the comfort and amenities of a cruise ship. Their all-outside cabins are larger, better designed, and better appointed than most standard cabins on mainstream cruise ships. The French-built vessels' shallow draft enables them to call at less-visited ports, private marinas, and secluded beaches.

Windstar Cruises was acquired by Holland America Line in 1988, and the next year both companies were purchased by Carnival Corporation. Windstar continues to operate as a separate entity. In 1998, Windstar bought the five-masted *Club Med 1,* a larger version of the Windstar ships, and after remodeling, renamed her *Wind Surf.* In early 2007, to the surprise of most cruise-watchers, Carnival sold Windstar Cruises for $100 million to Ambassadors International, Inc., which also owns the newly created Majestic America (See Part III, U.S. River Cruises).

A companion—"Degrees of Difference"—has been added to Windstar's tagline, "180 Degrees from Ordinary," to highlight the updating and upgrading of the features and amenities of all three Windstar ships. Among the new features are wireless access and cell phone capability available fleetwide.

THE FLEET	BUILT/RENOVATED	TONNAGE	PASSENGERS
Wind Spirit	1988/2003/07	5,350	148
Wind Star	1986/2003/07	5,350	148
Wind Surf	1990/98/2000/01/03/06	14,745	312

STYLE Laid-back, romantic, and informal, the cruises combine the atmosphere of a private yacht with the amenities and services of a cruise ship. From the outset, the ships have offered exclusivity because of their size, ambience, and the people they attract: upscale professionals who can afford a luxury cruise but want a less-structured environment and more unusual vacation than is available on today's typical cruises.

The ships are wonderfully quiet under sail; you can hear the ocean wash the hull and the sails snap as wind fills them. Passengers visit the open bridge to see how everything works. The captains—their hands never far from the wheel—usually give eager passengers a few minutes at the helm.

There's a casual elegance and easygoing informality about the ship and its occupants. Regardless of age, passengers seem to blend easily; by week's end, they're good friends. Pressure to keep a schedule is nonexistent. You decide how to spend your day. Even ardent type-A personalities can unwind.

Monogram Valet Luggage Service, introduced by Windstar in October 2006, enables passengers to travel luggage-free to their ship for a fee. Bags are picked up at their home and delivered to their cabin on the ship, wherever it may be. The luggage is shipped via an air valet service and requires no boxing or extra packaging. At the end of the cruise, luggage can be shipped back home. Windstar uses Universal Express, a courier company based in Boca Raton, Florida, for the luggage express service. Charges are assessed by weight, destination, and type of service. For example, it costs $257 to ship a 45-pound suitcase from Florida to Barbados. Bags are insured up to $1,000 at no extra cost with options to insure up to $10,000. The luggage service can be booked on Windstar's Web site, where details are available and a link connects to Monogram Valet Luggage Service.

DISTINCTIVE FEATURES The ship. Water sports platform; use of most sports gear is free. Wireless Internet access and cell phone capability. A passenger lucky enough to hook a fish on a deep-sea outing can have it cooked by the chef.

	HIGHEST	LOWEST	AVERAGE
PER DIEM	$659	$89	$303

Per diems are calculated from cruise line's nondiscounted *cruise-only* published fares on standard accommodations and vary by season, cabins, and cruise areas.

RATES Port charges are included; tips are extra.

Special fares and discounts Booking six months in advance saves up to 50%. Windstar frequently offers two-for-one promotions. Other discounts are on a quarterly basis.

- **SINGLE SUPPLEMENT:** 175% of the published per-person rate.

Packages

- **AIR/SEA:** Yes. Packages are available for some European cruises from select air gateways across the United States and Canada.

- **PRE/POST:** Yes.
- **OTHERS:** Yes.

PAST PASSENGERS The Foremast Club is open to all who take a Windstar cruise. They receive a quarterly newsletter, e-mails, and other literature highlighting new itineraries and special discounts, including alumni savings on select cruises.

THE LAST WORD On our first Windstar cruise, having expected passengers on the level of royalty, the ones who seemed to be enjoying themselves most were a blue-collar couple from Massachusetts on their second honeymoon—and first cruise. A Windstar cruise is a relaxing, romantic escape, but the perception more than the reality seems to put it out of reach in price and ambience for many people. Although it's definitely a way to impress your friends, deciding whether this cruise is for you shouldn't be based on price (although you get a lot for your money), but on the type of cruise it offers. Those who relate to it think it's heaven; those who don't would probably be bored.

Our only complaint is that the itineraries are so port-intensive they leave little time for passengers to enjoy the ships, particularly under sail. Windstar recently added a day at sea to some Mediterranean cruises. We think two would have been better.

Windstar's new owners took over the cruise line in April 2007, indicating that they planned to operate all the line's published itineraries (presumably through 2008), continue with the upgrading of the vessels, and maintain their staff and crew. Beyond those commitments, we expect to hear some changes in the future. Stay tuned.

Windstar Cruises Standard Features

Officers British

Staff Dining, Cabin: Indonesian and Filipino; Cruise: American, British, some European.

Dining facilities One open-seating restaurant, indoor/outdoor cafe for breakfast and lunch buffet featuring traditional and tropical specialties, occasional barbecues on the beach. Wind Surf, lunch, dinner in Degrees; espresso bar.

Special diets Sail Light menus with low-calorie, heart-smart, and vegetarian selections. Advance notice requested for others.

Room service 24 hours.

Dress code Casual and elegantly casual.

Cabin amenities Flat-screen television and DVD player, CD player, three-channel radio, international direct-dial telephone, safe, minibar and refrigerator, hair dryer, and terry robe.

Electrical outlets 110 AC (220 Wind Surf).

Wheelchair access None. Guide dogs have been permitted.

Recreation and entertainment Piano bar, casino, lounge with local musicians or ship's band, library, videocassette/CD library.

Sports and other activities Water sports platform for sailboats, windsurfers, motorized inflatables, waterskiing, scuba diving (extra charge); snorkeling equipment carried on board; saltwater pool.

Beauty and fitness Beauty salon, hot tub, sauna, masseuse, fitness room with weight-training equipment. Spa on *Wind Surf.*

Other facilities Laundry, doctor, infirmary, e-mail and Internet, WiFi access, cell phone capability.

Children's facilities None. Children's videos.

Theme cruises None currently.

Smoking Allowed in designated areas, but not in dining room.

Windstar suggested tipping A service change of $11 per person per day is added to passenger's onboard bill. A 15% service charge is added to bar bills.

Credit cards For cruise payment and onboard charges: American Express, Discover, MasterCard, Visa, traveler's checks.

Wind Spirit	QUALITY 9	VALUE C
Wind Star	QUALITY 9	VALUE C
REGISTRY Netherlands	LENGTH 440 feet	BEAM 64 feet
CABINS 74	DRAFT 13.5 feet	SPEED 8 to 12 knots
MAXIMUM PASSENGERS	PASSENGER DECKS 4	ELEVATORS None
148	CREW 94	SPACE RATIO 36

THE SHIPS The ships are identical inside and out. If not for their itineraries, they would be difficult to tell apart. Throughout, the tasteful appointments are well designed and inviting. They have the feel of a sailing ship—wood and leather, portholes, and nautical blue and white—yet they're modern, with expanses of windows creating spaciousness and space-station-white walls adorned with contemporary art.

Because the number of passengers is small, boarding is speedy. You're greeted with a glass of Champagne or chilled fruit drink and escorted to the main lounge to complete paperwork. Then you're escorted to your cabin, where your luggage should be waiting.

The cabins, gym, and sauna are on the bottom two of four passenger decks. The third deck contains a main lounge and dining salon—both handsome. Through a lounge skylight, passengers have dramatic views of the majestic sails overhead. You'll also find a bar, a tiny casino, boutique, and a new beauty salon/spa. The top deck offers a pool, bar, and veranda lounge. In 2007, under Windstar's Degrees of Difference enhancement program, both ships' public rooms and cabins were being renovated and new features added. *Wind Spirit* came out of five weeks of extensive renovations in late April while the *Wind Star* was scheduled for the same treatment in October/November, returning to service in time for her Panama Canal repositioning cruise, departing December 1, followed by a Costa Rica series for winter 2008.

ITINERARIES *See* Itinerary Index.

CABINS With the exception of the Owner's Suite, cabins are identical: large and outside. Larger than those on mainstream cruise ships, these well-designed, nicely appointed cabins make optimum use of space and are fitted with twin beds or a queen-size bed.

The marriage of tradition and technology is apparent in cabins. Each has twin portholes with brass fittings and wood cabinetwork, including a foldout vanity with makeup mirror. Amenities include flat-screen television and DVD player, international direct-dial telephone, WiFi access, CD player, safe, and minibar stocked with beer, wine, spirits, and soft drinks. Note, however, that drinks are expensive. A beer, for example, costs about $5. The newest additions to all cabins and suites are Bose Sound Dock speakers. Apple iPod Nanos preloaded with music are available for complimentary checkout, as are laptops for rent.

Bathrooms have showers, hair dryers, and terry robes. In the 2007 renovations, all cabin and suite bathrooms were being remodeled for a more contemporary look with new fixtures, open glass shelves, new cabinets, granite countertops, porcelain sinks, a magnifying mirror, and their teak floors refinished. Egyptian cotton towels and bath amenities by L'Occitane were being added.

Specifications 74 outside cabins; 1 suite with queen-size bed. Standard dimensions, 185 square feet. 73 with twin beds (convertible to queen); 11 (20 on *Wind Star*) with third berths. No singles and no wheelchair-accessible.

DINING The teak-lined dining room—nautical in design with rope-wrapped pillars—has low ceilings and subdued lighting, giving it an intimate atmosphere. Seating is open, restaurant style. Cuisine continues to be uneven, ranging from super to ordinary.

Menus by celebrity chef Joachim Splichal of Patina and Pinot Bistro in Los Angeles, whose French cooking incorporates light California style, match Windstar's casual style of cruising. Recently, Splichal created 100 new dishes. The line serves California wines to complement the cuisine; tastings are offered. Sail Light menus by Jeanne Jones, who developed the spa menus for Canyon Ranch and the Pritikin Center, are also available.

Coffee, tea, juices, and breakfast rolls are served poolside for early risers. Breakfast in the glass-enclosed veranda offers tropical fruits and freshly baked breads. Afternoon tea on the Pool Deck with pastries and finger sandwiches is popular. Room service is available 24 hours a day. In the Caribbean, a highlight is the Pool Deck barbecue, serving grilled lobster tails, shrimp, and other seafood accompanied by local music.

SERVICE The captain and European officers are affable, accessible, and visible, inviting passengers to watch the ship in operation, visiting with them, and participating in activities when possible. They welcome questions. Cabin staff and most restaurant personnel are Indonesian; deck stewards, bar personnel, and section captains are Filipino. All get very high marks.

FACILITIES AND ACTIVITIES Windstar ships don't have scheduled daily activities. You set your own schedule and make your own activities, independently or with new friends. That's what this cruise is all about. Days are passed sunbathing, reading, deep-sea fishing, swimming, and watching the ship's operation. (Readers should bring books; selections aboard are limited.) Ship's television features two current movies daily, plus satellite news around the clock.

In recent renovations, the beauty salon/spa was moved to the Main Deck and expanded to provide room for two treatment rooms and a pedicure chair. Health and exercise classes are also offered.

Nightlife is low-key and minimal. The tiny casino has blackjack tables, a Caribbean stud poker table, and slot machines. An easy-listening trio plays nightly for dancing in the lounge. You also can watch a movie in your cabin; a selection of videos available at the reception desk. A Caribbean night showcases a reggae band, and passengers young and old dance on the Pool Deck.

SPORTS, FITNESS, AND BEAUTY Water sports from the ships' foldout platform more than compensate for the absence of onboard sports. Furthermore, the ships' shallow draft enables them to stop at less-visited ports and secluded beaches and coves. On Caribbean more than Mediterranean cruises, water sports are a main attraction. Carried aboard are sailboats, windsurfing boards, snorkeling and diving equipment (including tanks), and Zodiacs to take passengers snorkeling, scuba diving, waterskiing, and deep-sea fishing. Except for scuba, gear is available free of charge.

Scuba costs $80 for one-tank dive; $150, two tanks; divers must show certification. Windstar's new Dive the Five package offers five one-tank dives for $350. A Discover Scuba Diving program, as well as a PADI Advanced Open Water Course and Adventures in Diving program are also available. The Discover Scuba resort course, divided into three sessions—classroom, pool, and dive (with instructor)—costs $140; participants can choose from any of the dive locations throughout their cruise. Dive masters and water-sports directors are well qualified, personable, and eager to help. Snorkeling and scuba trips and lessons are organized daily. Kayaking is also available. When the ships anchor off secluded islands, passengers often must wade from Zodiacs to the beach.

Each ship has a fitness room with some exercise equipment, sauna, and masseuse; Jacuzzis are on the Pool Deck. The salon offers aromatherapy.

SHORE EXCURSIONS Most excursions are half-day tours with an emphasis on tropical gardens, national parks, and other natural attractions. Prices are on the high side, costing $25 to $150. Excursions at St. Kitts in the Caribbean, for example, include a rain forest hike and horseback riding. In the Mediterranean, sightseeing is emphasized. Passengers can now book their shore excursions on the Windstar Web site in advance in conjunction with their cruise.

Wind Surf	QUALITY 7	VALUE C
REGISTRY Netherlands	LENGTH 617 feet	BEAM 66 feet
CABINS 156	DRAFT 16 feet	SPEED 12 knots
MAXIMUM PASSENGERS	PASSENGER DECKS 6	ELEVATORS 2
312	CREW 191	SPACE RATIO 48

THE SHIP *Wind Surf,* acquired by Windstar Cruises in 1997, is the former *Club Med 1,* a larger version of *Wind Star.* After extensive remodeling, the ship was rechristened *Wind Surf* and entered Windstar service in 1998. She has had several subsequent alterations, the most recent being a five-week, multimillion-dollar refit in 2006. Then, *Wind Surf* emerged with Degrees of Difference enhancements that updated her public rooms and cabins, added more luxury amenities, a spa treatment room for couples, and two new luxury suites, and improved the technical operations of the ship.

Among the new features is **The Yacht Club,** which replaced the library. Anchored by a flat-screen television and providing comfortable seating for relaxing and socializing, the new room is meant to be similar to today's coffeehouse, with an espresso bar offering gourmet coffee drinks, eight computers with Internet access, and a library of books, CDs, and DVDs for checkout. Wireless access and cell phone capability are now available on all three ships.

The ship has a meeting room that is a fully equipped conference center with new audiovisual equipment and meeting facilities for up to 50 people.

The **Wind Surf Lounge & Casino** has a nautical design, color scheme, and furniture; a beautiful teak bar; and clear sight lines to the stage from every seat. Other public rooms include a signature shop and spa and fitness center. The captain maintains an open bridge while at sea. Also available are 24-hour room service, laundry service, and a doctor's office.

ITINERARIES *See* Itinerary Index.

CABINS The deluxe outside cabins encompass 188 square feet each and offer queen-size beds (convertible to twins) and a work/desk/vanity area. They are similar in layout and decor to standard cabins on Windstar's other ships. All have flat-screen television and DVD player, CD player, safe, minibar and refrigerator, and direct-dial telephone. The bathroom has a shower, hair dryer, toiletries, and terry robe.

In the most recent renovations, all cabin and suite bathrooms were remodeled for a more contemporary look with new fixtures, open glass shelves, new cabinets, granite countertops, porcelain sinks, and a magnifying mirror. Refinished teak floors retain the popular nautical style. Egyptian cotton towels and bath amenities by L'Occitane have been added. Bose Sound Dock speakers were installed in all cabins and suites, while Apple iPod Nanos preloaded with music are available for complimentary checkout; laptops are for rent. Also in the cabins, desks now have granite surfaces, and full-length mirrors were added. Suites were given a second flat-screen television and DVD player.

The two new luxury suites on Bridge Deck are approximately 500 square feet each and include a living and dining area, separate bedroom with walk-in closet, and a marble bathroom with whirlpool tub and separate shower. Bridge Suites come with extra amenities such as chilled Champagne upon arrival, an invitation to dine with the captain, unpacking, laundry, and pressing service, evening appetizers, high-tea service upon request, complimentary bottled water in the suite, and additional L'Occitane bath amenities.

In an earlier renovation, 31 ocean-view suites were created in selected areas of top decks by combining several cabins. Each measures 376 square feet and has decor accented by teak, linen wall coverings, and original art. Each suite has a queen bed convertible to twins and a sofa bed. A curtain can be pulled across the bedroom to separate it from the living room for dining or entertaining. In addition to standard amenities, suites boast his-and-her bathrooms with shower, teak flooring, plush towels and robes, and vanity lighting.

Specifications 33 deluxe outside suites; 123 outside cabins with queen beds (convertible to twins) and sitting area. Some cabins have third berth; some side by side have adjoining private door.

DINING The ship's two dining rooms—the **Restaurant** and the smaller **Degrees**—accommodate all passengers at one open seating. Menus for both were developed by Joachim Splichal, chef and founder of the Patina group of top restaurants in Los Angeles. Passengers have the opportunity to dine in both during a cruise. Light and vegetarian menus are available. The **Verandah Café,** with covered outdoor seating where breakfast and lunch are served, has been expanded with new awnings.

Degrees (formerly the Bistro) is Wind Surf's alternative restaurant and is modeled after Splichal's Pinot Bistro. It serves a Splichal-inspired steak house menu four nights a week and offers rotating menus from Northern Italy, France, and Indonesia other nights. Reservations are required but there is still no surcharge.

All three venues have been improved with increased capacity. Degrees' decor uses French- and Italian-inspired colors, fabrics, and furniture. The glassed-in Verandah had its aft wall pushed back to enclose a portion of the deck to allow for additional indoor seating, which is preferred by guests on hot or windy days.

SPORTS, FITNESS, AND BEAUTY The 10,000-square-foot **WindSpa,** operated by Steiner, has a staff of ten and offers three kinds of treatments. Recently, a pedicure chair and a couples massage room were added and the gym got new weights and televisions. Health and exercise classes are offered for aerobics, yoga, and Pilates. Pampering includes Swedish, deep tissue, sports, and other massage, aromatherapy, hair care, manicures, pedicures, and facials, and hand, foot, and spa bath treatments. Purification treatments include herbal wraps, body masks, and mineral baths.

Treatments can be purchased in advance or on board. The Windstar brochure outlines options.

Wind Surf offers a complimentary water sports program. The ship has a water sports platform and equipment similar to that on the other Windstar vessels; two saltwater pools are located near them, as well as two hot tubs.

The ship offers an extensive dive program, including Windstar's Dive the Five package that includes five one-tank dives for $350. A Discover Scuba Diving program, as well as a PADI Advanced Open Water Course and Adventures in Diving program are also available. (See *Wind Spirit/Wind Star*, above, for details.)

POSTSCRIPT Affluent clients attracted to Windstar for casual elegance, small ships, fewer passengers, and the chance to sail with passengers of similar means and interests will find that *Wind Surf* is different. One passenger observed, "*Wind Surf* is too large to get the true feeling of a yacht. It's more of a cruise-ship experience than a sailing experience." As with so many ships sailing the Mediterranean in summer, Windstar's cruises are so port-intensive that there is little time—not enough time, in our opinion—to enjoy the ship, which as we said in the beginning, is the best thing about the cruise line. Recently, the line added some overnights in port, enabling passengers to take in some of a destination's nighttime pleasures and, perhaps, satisfying those who prefer more time in port than under sail.

EUROPEAN, ASIAN, *and* SMALLER CRUISE LINES

IN ADDITION TO THE CRUISE LINES and ships in the American mainstream of cruising already profiled in this section, another group of lines, with ships based mostly in Europe, may be of interest to readers. Space doesn't allow the same in-depth treatment, but generally they have small to midsize ships operated in the European tradition. Their interesting itineraries often visit places many Americans would need an atlas to find. Ships have English-speaking staff, although the majority of passengers may be Europeans speaking other languages. A few ships operate from U.S. or Asian ports.

The degree of luxury varies widely. Some are luxury vessels launched only in the last few years; others are renovated vintage ships that form a flotilla of new cruise lines.

Cruises appeal particularly to those who have traveled the main routes often and are looking for new destinations or a new environment in which to return to places seen previously. They also appeal to those who might never consider a typical cruise ship, preferring to explore less-traveled waters.

Also described are a few lines and ships that cater mainly to the U.S. market but weren't profiled in depth for other reasons, such as the fact that they're sold mainly through tour companies in combination with larger tour programs, they're under charter much of the year, or we had difficulty obtaining information.

Note: In parentheses after each ship name is information about the number of cabins and passengers; officers and crew; and the ship's length and tonnage (cabins/passengers; officers/crew; ship length/tonnage).

Abercrombie & Kent, Inc.
1520 Kensington Road, Suite 212, Oak Brook, IL 60523-2141; ☎ 630-954-2944 or 800-323-7308; fax 630-954-3324; www.abercrombiekent.com

Abercrombie & Kent is a prestigious international tour operator specializing in exotic journeys worldwide for affluent, sophisticated travelers with an avid interest in nature and wildlife. The cruise programs focus on Antarctica; barge and river cruises in Europe and on the Irrawady (Ayeyarwady), Nile, and Yangtze rivers; and a wide selection of other areas, such as the Galápagos, Tahiti, and Alaska. All emphasize culture and ecologically sound tourism. Most passengers are professionals, retired or semiretired, well educated, well traveled, usually ages 50 and older, in good health, and fit enough to enjoy hikes in Antarctic snows or snorkeling in the Galápagos. Singles make friends easily on these trips.

Marco Polo is a club for A&K veterans and offers a quarterly newsletter, members-only trips, a 5% discount on land arrangements on most tours, personalized luggage tags, priority on new destinations, tailored itineraries, a free lending library of A&K videotapes, and eligibility to compete in the annual Marco Polo Photo Contest. Annual membership is $95; five-year; $325; lifetime, $950; and children's memberships are available.

Explorer II **(111 CABINS, 12 BALCONY SUITES/300; BRITISH, INTERNATIONAL/146; 436 FEET/12,500 TONS)**

In early 2003, Abercrombie & Kent replaced its venerable *Explorer I,* the world's first expedition cruise ship, with the new, spacious *Explorer II,* and with one stroke changed the nature of its adventure cruises, bringing a new level of comfortable and informal refinement to Antarctic travel.

Gone are the small, spartan cabins and antiquated bathrooms of the old ship. Now passengers can enjoy modern, well-appointed, and comfortable accommodations and public rooms on a ship with more facilities and greater flexibility than might have ever been imagined in the past.

Explorer II, launched in 1996, is a stylish yet unpretentious ship that has been likened to a country-house inn, with gleaming brass, polished wood, fresh flowers, and original art decorating the walls. But beneath these amenities, there's strong steel, including an ice-strengthened hull, stabilizers, and bow thrusters that give the ship the power, stability, and agility to handle open-water cruising and the icy channels of Antarctic seas.

The Lounge on Main Deck forward is a favorite place for passengers to congregate before the day's Zodiac excursion, listen to talks by onboard naturalists and other experts, or join friends for after-dinner coffee. Two bars—the **Shackleton** and the **South Cape**—provide additional corners in which to relax. The ship's library is exceptional, with a wide range of books, as well as newspapers, games, and puzzles. The Main Deck also has the dining room aft and a beauty salon (which also offers massage) at midship. On Bridge Deck is the swimming pool, a bar and informal restaurant, lounge, card room, cinema, library, exercise room, and sauna. The ship also has a gift shop, medical center, and two elevators.

Explorer II can carry in excess of 300 passengers, but on her Antarctica voyages, A&K limits her complement to 199 passengers. The smaller number enhances the comfort level for all passengers, including the use of outside cabins and suites only, so that all passengers have their own window onto the Antarctic landscape. On the Christmas and New Year's cruise, children ages 18 and under receive a 50% discount off the adult price when sharing a cabin (except suites) with an adult.

The atmosphere on board *Explorer II* is informal and unregimented and sports an easy camaraderie among the passengers and the experts (naturalists, geologists, zoologists, historians, and ornithologists) who accompany every cruise. Each day, passengers gather for informal preexcursion briefings or posttrip wrap-ups in the ship's lounge or auditorium. Throughout the trip, they interact with the experts to exchange ideas and ask questions—at dinner, at the rail, or on a Zodiac. Staff and crew add to the experience with their informal talks and entertainment.

An accomplished pianist offers light entertainment in the Shackleton Lounge and an *Explorer II* quartet performs on selected evenings in the **Main Lounge**. Days are packed with intellectual and physical activities and the day's recap before dinner. Socializing resumes after dinner, sometimes continuing into the wee hours. A passenger may tickle the ivories or sing, but guests generally just converse. Slides, a film, or a Hollywood movie may be shown. The library is popular at any hour. Lectures are well attended. Most talks are accompanied by audiovisuals.

Explorer II offers among the most spacious and comfortable accommodations in Antarctica, many with private balconies. All cabins have vanity table/writing desk and chair, television and radio, refrigerator, direct-dial telephone, hair dryer, and binoculars. There are two Owner's Suites and ten outside suites on Bridge Deck forward, with floor-to-ceiling patio doors leading to a balcony and furnished with queen or twin beds, bathroom with tub, large double wardrobe, ample drawer space, and separate sitting area with sofa, chair, and table. The 12 outside deluxe cabins on Promenade Deck forward have twin beds or queen bed (some have a pull-out sofa for triple occupancy), bathroom with tub, separate sitting area with sofa, chair, and table, and a large picture window mirrored for privacy. Promenade Deck, midship and aft, also has 20 outside superiors with twins or queen bed, bathroom with tub, walk-in closet, armchair, and large picture window.

The standard categories (A, B, SA) are spread on two decks: 54 on A Deck, and 26 on B Deck. All are outside and have twin beds or queen, bathroom with shower, single and double wardrobes, love seat, and a picture window or porthole. Four cabins are handicapped-accessible, and four are single cabins. Laundry service is available on Deck A. For its 199 passengers, *Explorer II* carries a staff and crew of 146, who provide a high level of warm, personal service.

Explorer II has two dining rooms with open seatings and indoor and outdoor service. The menus offer international cuisine as well as selections of light fare and vegetarian dishes. Special diets can be accommodated with sufficient advance notice. "Smart casual" wear is evening attire. Smoking is not permitted in most areas of the ship, but there is a dedicated smoking room on the Bridge Deck and designated areas on the outer decks.

In addition to accommodations and meals, A&K's all-inclusive cruise prices include all bar drinks and house wines, onboard gratuities, and sightseeing. You receive a backpack, parka for Antarctica cruises, and very good precruise information.

Explorer II sails on diverse itineraries in Antarctica and neighboring islands. She claims to operate under guidelines to do all that is possible to protect the fragile Antarctic environment. Antarctic cruises are intended for serious travelers who cherish unusual opportunities and draw interesting, intellectually curious people, among whom many lasting friendships are forged. If you don't have a similar thirst for knowledge or the flexibility to deal with frequent changes caused by weather and sea, you could find yourself on the wrong ship a long way from home. Gadabouts and tourists wanting to add exotic destinations to their tally should look elsewhere.

A&K also markets some deluxe yachts, such as the famous *Sea Cloud* and the luxurious *River Cloud.* For A&K's river cruises, see Part Three. In early January 2007, Discovery World Cruises/Voyages of Discovery (see later in this chapter) took a long-term lease on *Explorer II;* however, A&K will continue to market and operate its Antarctic cruises. During the balance of the year, the ship will sail on worldwide itineraries marketed by its new leaseholder.

ITINERARIES   *See* Itinerary Index.

American Canadian Caribbean Line

(*See* Part Two, Cruise Lines and Their Ships)

American Cruise Lines
741 Boston Port Road, Suite 200, Guilford, CT 06437; ☎ 800-814-6880 or 203-453-6800; fax 860-453-0417; www.americancruiselines.com

American Eagle **(31/49; AMERICAN; 165 FEET)**

American Glory **(31/49; AMERICAN; 168 FEET)**

American Spirit **(51/100; AMERICAN; 215 FEET)**

American Star **(52/100; AMERICAN; 215 FEET)**

The small coastal ship *American Eagle,* completed in 2000 at the owner's Chesapeake shipyard in Salisbury, Maryland, takes only 49 passengers on close-to-shore trips from Maine and New England through the Chesapeake Bay to the Deep South and Florida via the Intracoastal Waterway from March to December. (For the eagle-eyed, some of the company ads and brochure photos might be familiar. American Cruise Lines first surfaced in 1974 with a previous *American Eagle,* and after operating six ships for 15 years, the company quietly went bust.)

In 2002, the *Eagle* was joined by *American Glory,* which is three feet longer and three feet wider at the beam and has 14 Veranda Suites. The larger *American Spirit,* which debuted in 2005, has 23 veranda cabins; and the latest addition, *American Star,* made her debut in June 2007.

The *American Star,* with its 6.5-foot draft, is similar in design to *American Spirit* but features more large cabins with private verandas. All cabins are fitted with flat-screen satellite television and DVD players, Internet access, hair dryer, and other amenities. The ship has an elevator to all four decks, four lounges, an Observation Deck, library, and a dining room with surrounding windows. The ship sails on 6-, 7- and 14-night cruise itineraries along the East Coast from Maine to Florida.

The ships' public spaces are roomy, considering they have only four decks. The forward-facing **Nantucket Lounge** (**Chesapeake Lounge** on *Spirit*) seats all passengers; and amidships, a ship-wide foyer offers additional comfy couch seating. A library has television, VCR, and books. The decor is a bit plain, with utilitarian-looking walls and ceilings, but the carpets and fabrics help to dress it up. The ships have an elevator with access to each floor, and equipment for the handicapped is available.

The dining room, glass-enclosed on three sides, has open seating at large, round tables. The ships do not have a liquor license; instead, there is a complimentary bar and sumptuous predinner hors d'oeuvres for the very popular cocktail hour, and there are carafes of wine on the dinner table.

Each ship has chefs from the Culinary Institute of America and Johnson & Wales University. Their expertise shows in the delicious, creative meals. The food is uniformly excellent throughout the cruise. Lunch is light fare, such as crab cakes and chicken Caesar salad. The set dinner menus, with a choice of two entrées, might be grilled artichoke hearts, hearts of palm in balsamic vinegar, Cornish game hen with wild rice, grilled catfish, broiled lobster, and desserts such as pecan peanut butter pie.

The fourth or Sports Deck, open to the sky, has deck chairs for all passengers plus tables and chairs and a putting green. Additional covered deck space faces aft, and the open deck forward of the lounge is excellent for viewing ahead.

There are five cabin categories, all with private bath and outside with windows that slide open to allow in fresh air. AA, the second grade up, measures 192 square feet and compares favorably to the line's competition. The six AAV cabins are 249 square feet, including veranda. The average size of Glory's cabins is slightly larger at 220 square feet. All ships have five single cabins priced at about a 50% premium over the AA category. Cabins are furnished with comfortable couches.

The American Cruise Lines' ships offer a low-key cruising experience with itineraries from Maine and New England to Florida that celebrate Americana, sometimes with the help of an enrichment lecturer. The passengers are mostly an amiable retired lot who like sailing in a small club setting. There may also be mothers, grandmothers, daughters, and sons. The all-American crew includes college-age men and women, some just out of high school, serving as deckhands, cleaning cabins, and waiting tables. The level of service is friendly, if sometimes haphazard. The line offers early-bird discounts to those who book six months in advance.

American Cruise Lines is building two 166-passenger luxury cruise ships that will greatly expand its horizons as they are intended for worldwide cruising. The ships, scheduled to enter service in 2008 and 2009, will be SOLAS (Safety of Life at Sea) compliant, fully stabilized, and incorporate the latest small cruise ships technology. The first ship will sail on the Canadian Maritime, the Caribbean, and Central America itineraries.

Public spaces will include a dining salon to accommodate all the passengers in one seating; four lounges, one of which also can accommodate all passengers; and on the fifth deck, a theater/lecture room with audiovisual capabilities. The ships will have a fully equipped spa and elevators to all decks.

Cabins will measure between 240 and 360 square feet, most with private balconies. They will have satellite television, Internet connections, and other modern conveniences. Throughout the ship there will be large picture windows providing unobstructed views of the scenery in the dining room, lounges, and cabins.

The cruise line says the ships will be environmentally friendly and have enhanced launch capability for travel to remote areas. The line is considering itineraries to Alaska, the Baltic, British Isles, Mediterranean, the Pacific, and South America as well Canada, the Caribbean, and Central America.

ITINERARIES *See* Itinerary Index.

American Safari Cruises
3826 18th Avenue West, Seattle, WA 98119; ☎ 206-284-0300 or 888-862-8881; fax 206-283-9322; www.amsafari.com

Safari Escape **(6/12; AMERICAN/6; 112 FEET)**

Safari Quest **(11/22; AMERICAN/9 TO 10; 120 FEET)**

Safari Spirit **(6/12; AMERICAN/6; 105 FEET)**

Formed in 1996, American Safari Cruises offers nature-oriented adventure cruises for affluent travelers on three small luxury yachts. The Alaska itineraries are off-the-beaten-track, close-up experiences of wildlife, or scenery viewing at a leisurely pace with the pampering of a luxury cruise. The line's seven- and eight-night fall cruises sail in the Pacific Northwest on the Columbia and Snake rivers, and in the San Juan Islands and British Columbia Gulf Islands. There also is a winter series of weekly cruises of Baja California and the Gulf of California, departing from Loreto.

All cabins on the vessels are outside and deluxe. Each is furnished with a king or queen bed or two twin beds (except for one cabin with one twin on *Safari Quest*), television with DVD/VCR, and private bathroom with shower or tub. Amenities include evening turndown service, terry robes, and fresh flowers.

The main gathering spot is a salon furnished with comfortable couches and chairs. A self-service bar separates the dining area and salon. The salon opens onto the sports platform, where passengers can board a launch or a two-passenger kayak. A spiral staircase links all public decks, the library and lounge, and the bridge. A promenade circles the entire yacht. The yachts have a top-deck hot tub for an under-the-stars spa experience. Upon request, fishing charters can be arranged for an additional charge.

On Alaskan itineraries, binoculars, rain jackets, and rubber boots are provided, as are wet suits, fins, and snorkel gear in the Gulf of California. A skilled and personable expedition leader accompanies each cruise and serves in lieu of a cruise director. A trained naturalist and usually university educated, the expedition leader organizes hikes and biking excursions, leads kayak explorations, and identifies wildlife en route. In the evenings and when appropriate during the day, the expedition leader lectures on the flora, fauna, geology, and the history of the areas visited. Praised by passengers as caring, enthusiastic, and knowledgeable, the expedition leaders elevate the experience from a luxury cruise to a horizon-expanding voyage of discovery.

Food aboard American Safari Cruises is as good as it gets on a cruise ship. Each day, the chef joins the passengers to discuss the menu and to describe special dishes to be prepared. An early-bird breakfast of fresh fruit, pastries, cereal, juices, and hot beverages starts at 6 a.m., with a full-service, cooked-to-order breakfast available at 8 a.m. A full-course lunch is served at 1 p.m. Hors d'oeuvres are offered nightly during the cocktail hour preceding dinner at 7 p.m. Two entrées are offered each evening—usually fresh local seafood as well as chicken, lamb, or beef. Wine with meals and all other alcoholic beverages are included in the price of the cruise. The wine selection is stellar, as are the upscale labels in the well-stocked bar. Beer drinkers will love the draft beers from a prize-winning Alaskan microbrewery.

The yachts travel in daytime for wildlife viewing and scenic exploration. In late afternoon, they anchor in a scenic, secluded cove or bay for the night, offering further discovery on foot or by Zodiacs. Sighting wildlife—whales, porpoises, harbor seals, black bears, brown bears, sea lions, bald eagles, cormorants, herons, sandhill cranes, oystercatchers, and gulls—is all but guaranteed. In the Gulf of California, sightings include the mammoth blue whale, largest creature ever to exist, other whale species, manta rays, huge pods of up to 1,000 dolphins, giant sea turtles, sea lions, and 200 species of birds, including pelicans. The yachts are small enough that the captain can change course immediately to approach something for closer inspection. Long summer days in Alaska allow kayaking, whale-watching by Zodiacs, and hiking until late evening.

All meals, excursions, and events on these cruises are strictly informal. Jeans, khakis, and shorts, along with outdoor gear appropriate to the cruise venue and time of year, are all you need. Although the expedition leader has lots of activities on tap each day, the decision to participate is yours. Soaking in the hot tub, reading, napping, and watching movies on your cabin DVD player are some of the alternatives available. Each ship also has at least one aerobic exercise machine.

The Alaska itineraries explore remote areas and small villages. They range from 7 to 14 nights. Prices cover shore excursions, including unlimited use of kayaks, guided nature walks, all private transfers, open bar, and port charges. Tips are extra. The Gulf of California seven- and nine-night series operate from December to April, while the seven-night cruises of the Pacific Northwest operate in September and October. A longer eight-night trip is available on the Columbia and Snake rivers. Golf and spa packages are available in conjunction with the Gulf of California cruises; Kids in Nature programs are featured on some Alaska and Gulf of California cruises. All three vessels are available for private full-yacht charter.

Although a luxury product, American Safari cruises represent a good value, offering a highly personalized and intimate private yacht experience for less than most upscale cruises of comparable length. Indeed, with early-booking discounts and the inclusion of wine, liquor, and all shore excursions in the price of the cruise, American Safari cruises are among the most affordable luxury cruises afloat.

American Safari passengers are typically over 40 years old, well educated, and adventurous individuals who revel in learning and discovery and who enjoy making new friends. Life aboard is, after all, an intimate experience, one that practically ensures you will become well acquainted with your fellow passengers.

ITINERARIES *See* Itinerary Index.

Bora Bora Cruises

P. O. Box 40186, Fare Tony–Vaiete, 98713 Papeete, Tahiti, French Polynesia;
☎ 689-544 505; fax 689-451 065; www.boraboracrusies.com

Tu Moana/Ti'a Moana (37/74; FRENCH; 230 FEET)

Nomade yachting by Bora Bora Cruises, launched in 2003, sails on weekly cruises of French Polynesia with its two custom-built luxury superyachts. The boutique cruise yachts are aimed at a market niche of customers who want exclusive, stylish voyages with great attention to detail, a high level of service, gourmet cuisine, and designer furnishings and amenities.

The twin vessels take their names from the native Tahitian language: *Moana* is the universal Polynesian word meaning "the sea," *Tu* and *Ti'a* carry similar meanings "to stand erect, to be upright" and "to fit, agree, answer the purpose." Thus, each ship's name literally means "comfortably upright in the sea."

Built in Australia by Austal Ships, with interiors by the well-known Swedish firm of Tillberg Design and technical oversight by V-Ships of Monaco, *Tu Moana* and *Ti'a Moana* have the sleek lines of a private luxury yacht. The vessels are identical in all areas except interior decor. Their fine finishes combine exotic hardwood interiors, original Polynesian artwork, and glass staircases with the latest technologies.

All cabins are outside ones with large windows and lovely furnishings, located on three decks. They have three different layouts with an average size of about 170 square feet. Each cabin has a queen bed with an exclusive Kenzo throw, high-quality European bed and bath linens, flat-screen television and DVD/CD player, phone, safe, minibar and refrigerator, writing desk and stationery, handblown glass bowl with fresh fruit, bedside reading lamps, bathrobes, and BBC logo beach bag. In the glass-enclosed bathroom, there are Philippe Starck–designed bath fixtures, hair dryer, adjustable showerhead, BBC bathrobe, and exclusive hypoallergenic bathroom toiletries.

The crew speaks several languages, and the French chef's creations have garnered rave reviews. Special touches include breakfast served on linen and china at tables in the warm waters of the lagoon, dinner under the moonlight on a beach, movies shown on a secluded island under the stars, and a kayak expedition for two up a tropical river. Passengers can snorkel, get a massage on the beach, or enjoy other options, including a romantic tête-à-tête dinner on a secluded *motu* or islet; a 4-by-4 island safari, horseback riding, mountain climbing, shark and manta ray feeding, aft-deck night fishing, and lagoon photo excursions.

The ships have an unusual flat-water design, which draws only 7.5 feet and allows for safe navigation in the lagoons inaccessible to larger vessels, providing passengers with a unique experience. The shallow draft enables the yachts to travel close to the shoreline and to the most beautiful coral reefs in these islands; at the same time, the ships' advanced stabilization technology provides smooth sailing in open water.

Both vessels depart Bora Bora on Monday mornings, returning to Bora Bora Sunday evenings, gliding across the calm lagoons of Huahine, Raiatea,

Taha'a, and Bora Bora on six-night, seven-day cruises. Travelers can book a 7-day cruise to the islands or a 10- or 14-day island-and-sea package combining a cruise with a stay at the Hotel Bora Bora or St. Regis in Bora Bora, and Taha'a private island resort and spa. Contact the U.S. representative, JoAnn Kurtz-Ahlers, joann@kurtzahlers.com; ☎ 949-487-0502. Most passengers are from Europe and the United States.

Bora Bora Cruises is the dream of its founder, owner, and chairman, Mehiti Degage, a young Polynesian woman whose love for the sea and lagoons of her country inspired her to provide visitors with an experience that captures the essence of these islands in a stylish, intimate manner.

ITINERARIES *See* Itinerary Index.

Croceros Australis

(*See* Part 3, Adventure and Cultural Cruises)

Cruise North Expeditions

(*See* Part 3, Adventure and Cultural Cruises)

Discovery World Cruises

1800 SE Tenth Avenue, Suite 205, Fort Lauderdale, FL 33316;
☎ **866-623-2689; fax 954-761-7768; www.discoveryworldcruises.com**

Discovery **(351/650; SCANDINAVIAN, BRITISH, DUTCH/AMERICAN, EUROPEAN, FILIPINO; 553 FEET/20,186 TONS)**

Explorer II **(111 CABINS, 12 BALCONY SUITES/300; BRITISH, INTERNATIONAL; 436 FEET/12,500 TONS)**

Founded in 2002 by well-known travel industry entrepreneur Gerry Herrod, this new cruise line offers deluxe cruises to less-traveled destinations at affordable prices, much like Orient Lines and other niche-market companies that Herrod headed in the past. The cruises focus on giving passengers in-depth exposure to their destinations, while providing the traditional comforts of its deluxe ocean liner. In 2005, All Leisure Group of the United Kingdom bought the *Discovery*, and in January 2007, All Leisure leased *Explorer* II on a long-term basis. In the United States, the cruise tours are marketed as Discovery World Cruises; in Europe, they are sold under the brand Voyages of Discovery.

Before entering service in 2003, the *Discovery*, built as the *Island Venture* in 1972 in Germany by century-old shipbuilder Rheinstahl Nordseewerke (and best known as Princess Cruises' *Island Princess*) underwent extensive, multi-million-dollar renovations that, in effect, created a new ship. She has retained her handsome, classic profile and grand ocean liner ambience, but now boasts modern safety features and amenities. At 20,000 tons—small compared with today's megaliners—*Discovery* is large enough for cruising to faraway places, yet small enough to enter remote harbors that larger vessels must bypass.

Facilities on the eight-deck ship include three restaurants, five lounges, lecture theater/cinema, a well-stocked library, bridge room, modern gym, spa and beauty center; two swimming pools, one with a retractable dome, two Jacuzzis, card room, Internet center and wireless access, boutiques, and four elevators. There is nightly entertainment, classical music concerts, and folkloric performances by local groups.

All the ship's cabins and suites are equipped with private facilities, air-conditioning, television, hair dryer, and safe. Cabins on Bridge and Promenade decks have bath and a shower; those on other decks have showers. Cabins have two lower beds or a double bed. Some cabins have one or two upper berths or a sofa bed, allowing for third or fourth person sharing. Most beds in twin cabins are arranged parallel to each other, although some are arranged in an L shape. A small number of cabins have an inter-connecting door and can be booked as adjoining cabins. Outside cabins on Bridge and Promenade decks have picture windows (the view of the Owner's Suite is obscured by lifeboats). Outside cabins on the Pacific Deck have two windows; those on Bali and Coral decks have two portholes. Outside and inside standard cabins measure 135 square feet; outside superior cabins have 194 square feet.

Most itineraries are marketed as cruise-tour vacation packages, which include extended stays and sightseeing in embarkation and/or disembarkation cities, detailed briefings on each port of call, and local cultural performances on board. A hallmark of Discovery World Cruises is its enrichment program of lectures and workshops at sea, with noted expedition leaders and area experts on each voyage. Early-bird savings up to 50% are available.

Discovery has run an unusual lecture series sponsored by the Mayo Clinic that includes a comprehensive team of distinguished medical professionals aboard select cruises. The lecture series debuted during the ship's first year, and has been repeated each year. Contact the cruise line for a schedule.

During the winter season, *Discovery* sails on cruises in the Amazon, Antarctica, Easter Island, Galápagos, Peru, and South America. Afterward the ship sails through the Panama Canal, stopping in the San Blas Islands, Costa Rica, and Belize before making a transatlantic voyage to England from Fort Lauderdale, Florida. During the remainder of the year, the ship cruises the Baltic, Black Sea, British Isles, Faroe Islands, Greenland, Iceland, the Mediterranean, North Africa, the Red Sea, Scandinavia, and the Suez Canal.

The *Explorer II* (formerly the *Minerva*) underwent refurbishing before being put into service with Voyages of Discovery/Discovery World Cruises. (See Abercrombie & Kent earlier in this chapter for a description of *Explorer II*.)

Abercrombie & Kent will continue to handle the winter Antarctica cruises and the expedition program and operations. In the summer, *Explorer II* operates under the Voyages of Discovery/Discovery World Cruises brand to the Arctic, Canada, Libya, Norwegian fjords, southern Africa, the U.S. Eastern Seaboard, and destinations similar to those of the *Discovery*.

ITINERARIES   *See* Itinerary Index.

easyCruise
easyGroup (UK), Ltd., The Rotunda, 42–43 Gloucester Crescent, London NW1 7DL; ☎ 0207-241-9000; fax 0207-482-2857; www.easycruise.com

easyCruise One **(170; GREEK/INTERNATIONAL; 4,077 TONS)**

easyCruise Two **(52/104; DUTCH)**

Upstart easyCruise, launched in May 2005, is both a new cruise line and a new concept. Billed as no-frills cruising, the new line has "unbundled" the cruise package, selling cabins on board the ship on a night-by-night basis, for a two-night minimum. Prices start at about $60 per person per night for a simply furnished basic cabin; passengers are charged for meals, housekeeping, and other onboard services.

Passengers make their own air connections to and from the ship, presumably using the abundance of low-cost European airlines, such as easyJet, which serve the Mediterranean. Initially, the line allowed passengers to hop on and off the ship, cruising for as many or as few nights as they wish, but that proved not to be practical. Now, passengers buy a specific number of days, as on other cruise ships, but still under the low-cost, no-frills concept.

The venture is the brainchild of 40-year-old Stelios Haji-Ioannou, known to one and all simply as Stelios, the founder of easyGroup, which includes easyJet.com, the successful British no-frills airline, easyHotel.com, easyCar.com, easyCinema.com, and 11 other enterprises in the same low-cost, no-frills mode.

The first ship, the 4,077-ton *easyCruise One* (previously called *Neptune*), is the former 114-passenger luxury *Renaissance II,* built in Italy in 1990. It was completely refitted with new interiors in Singapore to carry 170 passengers in a no-frills style. Cabins, pictured on easyCruise's Web site, are in the same style as easyHotel, stripped down to the basics. The line wants you to think of them as being in the currently fashionable minimalist style. Each measures about 100 to 150 square feet, has a shower unit, a lavatory and a washbasin, and one double bed or two twins. The six-deck ship has four suites with balcony (220 square feet), seven quads, 74 standard cabins, and one disabled double. Housekeeping is an optional extra.

The Mediterranean-based ship sails for no more than about six hours a day, departing in early morning, arriving at her next port by noon or early afternoon, and staying through the night to give passengers the opportunity to dine and enjoy the evening in port. Entertainment on board the vessel is limited, since presumably an evening in an interesting port would top anything the ship could offer. Food and beverages, available for purchase from the ship's restaurant and shop, have been upgraded and enhanced as a result of an early lesson the line learned—many passengers prefer to eat, especially breakfast, on the ship. Thus, the ship now has a full-fledged restaurant with menus that include local specialties as well as international ones. Also recently added was an Apivita spa where passengers can have massages and other treatments, including manicures and pedicures. There is also a new sauna and hot tub.

In August 2006, easyCruise added another vessel, *easyCruise Two,* a riverboat sailing in Holland and Belgium, and unveiled a new look that it applied to *easyCruise One,* as well. On the exterior, both vessels display the line's new logo and in place of easyCruise's dominant orange, they are painted a conservative, graphite gray with orange trim.

Inside, *easyCruise Two* has an attractive restaurant and bar, cabins showcasing a new color scheme, and windows in all rooms and cabins. The design by Netherlands premier designer, Jan Des Bouvrie, answers passenger feedback of "too much orange" and adds a more sophisticated look for the cruise line. *EasyCruise Two*'s facilities include a large canopied Sun Deck and two hot tubs, a fully equipped gym, and a resident DJ. The 90-seat **World Café** serves breakfast, lunch, and dinner. The menu offers a variety of local specialties and international dishes as well as light meals and pizzas. The boat has a new bar with a wide selection of beverages, specialty coffees, and local beers. Cabins are available as twins, doubles, bunks, or quads; all have windows and private bathrooms.

EasyCruise Two sails on a weekly itinerary round-trip from Amsterdam and visits Rotterdam, Antwerp, and Brussels. Prices start from $13 (£7) per person per night.

During the spring-to-fall season, the two ships carry mostly Europeans; in the Caribbean, the cruises are aimed at North Americans. The ages range from 20s and up, but to the surprise of the cruise lines, the average age is 40s. Tickets are sold via the Internet. Following a cruise industry practice, the best prices are available to customers who book early at **www.easyCruise.com**. In fact, the earlier they book, the less they pay. EasyCruise's calculation that its flexibility and low prices attracts a wider customer base of new travelers who have never cruised has apparently paid off.

During her maiden summer, the ship sailed the western Mediterranean from Nice, but learned that it should stay away from itineraries where travelers can easily drive, and for summer 2007 shifted to the Greek Isles. In fact, the Greece itineraries got such a good response that the cruise line extended their season from mid-May to mid-November. The offerings range from two to seven nights and can be combined to create a cruise of up to two weeks. Prices start at $39 per person for a two-night minibreak and seven-night cruise at $135 per person, based on two people sharing a standard cabin. Cabins are available in twins/doubles, quads, and suites.

In its first Caribbean winter, the ship was based in Barbados and sailed to islands in the Eastern and Southern Caribbean. That, too, has changed; now, the ship is based in St. Maarten and sails on three- and four-day itineraries that can be combined into a week's cruise. Air service was a major consideration in the change.

In late 2006, easyCruise signed a letter of intent with Neorion Holdings to build two 500-passenger cruise ships at Neorion's shipyards in Greece, with an option for two additional ships. Soon after, the line concluded another deal with Cyprus-based cruise ship operator Louis Cruises that increased the new-build agreement with Neorion Holdings to three ships, with an option for three more. The additional vessels will be owned by Louis Cruises and operated under the easyCruise brand. The deal also advances easyCruise's plan to expand the fleet via franchising. EasyCruise's owner says he has held talks with authorities to base a ship in Florida, possibly for Bahamas cruises during the winter season.

Also in 2006, Stelios Haji-Ioannou was knighted by Queen Elizabeth II for his services to entrepreneurship; and his easyHotel contracted to open a chain of 38 hotels across the Middle East, India, and North Africa.

ITINERARIES   *See* Itinerary Index.

Fred Olsen Cruise Lines

Fred Olsen House, White House Road, Ipswich IP1 5LL, United Kingdom; ☎ 01473-742434; fax 01473-292-410; www.fredolsencruises.co.uk; or c/o Borton Overseas, 5412 Lyndale Avenue South, Minneapolis, MN 55419; ☎ 612-822-4640; fax 612-822-4755; www.bortonoverseas.com

The family-operated cruise line, now in its 40th year of operation, has acquired some of the best ships that main line cruise companies sold off in favor of big ships. Over the years, it has established a reputation for well-maintained, comfortable ships and the family's dedication to their operation. The British-based line offers a classic cruise experience with small-town friendliness and reasonable prices. It caters mostly to a British clientele, but their ships—the size and ambience—have found an American and Canadian audience who shun big ships. Aimed mainly at over-age-50 travelers, the line has had a promotion, "Celebrate 60" in 2007, for the baby boomers born in 1947.

The line has a golf package available on *Black Watch, Boudicca,* and *Braemar* (and *Balmoral* from 2008) on selected cruises in the Baltic, Canary Islands, Caribbean, and Mediterranean. It consists of up to four rounds of golf ashore, the services of the resident PGA professional on board, competitions, and social activities for both players and nonplaying partners. The package must be booked in advance of one's cruise.

The Arts Club is a program of special-interest cruises operating on selected cruises. The subjects, with expert lecturers and instruction, include music, dance, antiques, gardening, wine, photography, wildlife, bridge, and more. The programs are available to all passengers and at no additional cost (except wine tasting and painting materials).

The cruise line provides a children's program with entertainment and activities on cruises over Easter, during July and August, and Christmas and New Year's on *Black Watch, Boudicca,* and *Braemar* (and *Balmoral* from 2008).

Smoking is now banned on all balconies and all restaurants on all Fred Olsen ships. It is also banned in all cabins and suites on *Boudicca,* and forward suites on Deck 9 on *Black Watch.* There are smoking areas in designated areas of lounges and bars.

Oceans is Olsen's past-passengers club and enables member to take advantage of some exclusive benefits with every booking. Members are awarded a Cruise Point for each night spent on board the line's ships since January 1, 2000; the more points one accrues, the more benefits to be enjoyed. The conditions and benefits are detailed on the line's Web site. Members are automatically enrolled upon return from their first cruise and are issued a membership number to be used when booking future cruises. The cruise line also publishes an online newsletter. British sterling is the currency of the fleet.

Note: All passengers must have traveler's insurance, which Americans must purchase in the United States, and provide their policy number to the cruise line in advance of their cruise.

Olsen is offering world cruises for two of its vessels for 2009. The *Boudicca* will sail in January from Southampton on a 97-day westbound voyage through the Caribbean, the Panama Canal, to the South Pacific, Australia (where she will visit six ports), South Africa, and the west coast of Africa to Southampton. *Black Watch* will depart Dover in February on a 104-day eastbound route through the Mediterranean, Middle East, India, Asia, Russia and the Aleutian Islands, Alaska, Vancouver, three western U.S. ports, Mexico, the Caribbean, and the Azores Islands before returning to Dover. Passengers making a deposit on one of the cruises by December 31, 2007 will receive a $950 per person onboard credit, private roundtrip car transfers between London airports and the ship, and an airfare allowance of $300 to $500 per person, depending on cabin category.

Black Prince (210/412; EUROPEAN/FILIPINO; 480 FEET/11,209 TONS)

Built in 1966 to carry both passengers and vehicles, the ship was converted to total cruise operation in 1986. The ship caters to Britons and sails on 2- to 35-night cruises from Liverpool, England, and Greenock, Scotland, to the Amazon, the Arctic, Baltic Sea, Canary Islands, Caribbean, Mediterranean, Norwegian coast, Orinoco, and South America. The ship—a good choice for gregarious travelers ages 50 and older—has an indoor **Leisure Centre** with pool, fitness area with gym, and beauty facilities, and an outdoor Leisure Centre that provides access to water sports facilities in the ocean. In addition, the ship has a casino, an outdoor pool and Jacuzzi, indoor and outdoor eating venues, and a full entertainment and activities program.

On this and other Fred Olsen Lines cruises, early-bird discounts are available for booking six months in advance; last-minute values might be reduced 50%. The *Black Prince,* as well as the line's other ships, offer theme cruises, such as music, dance, painting, bridge, wine, antiques, and more, throughout the year. Details are available on the cruise line's Web site.

Black Watch (320/807; NORWEGIAN/INTERNATIONAL; 674 FEET/28,613 TONS)

Formerly the *Royal Viking Star*, the much-loved *Black Watch* was judged too small and too old to compete in the U.S. market and was sold to Fred Olsen Lines in 1996 and given an $8 million refurbishment.

Black Watch cabins come in a bewildering number of configurations. Thirty-nine are singles. Although most are small, all are nicely appointed. Ninety percent are outside with portholes, picture window, or private veranda. Baths are well designed but very plain. All cabins have televisions and phones, and many have refrigerators.

The ship's public areas are exceptional. The library is among cruising's largest and most splendidly appointed. (Unfortunately, it's open only a couple of hours each day.) Equally impressive is the card and game room. Both rooms display artifacts from earlier ships in the Olsen fleet. The **Observa-**

tion Lounge overlooks the bow and **Lido Lounge,** the stern. Both provide live music well into the night. A third bar/lounge adjoins the main showroom; decor honors the Scottish Black Watch Regiment.

The clubby **Braemar Room,** a large lounge adjacent to the dining room, is packed with brightly colored stuffed chairs. It's a base for the British passion for tea, and occasionally hosts classical concerts. The ship also has a 170-seat auditorium.

Well-designed public areas continue outside with a promenade that encircles the ship. Also available are pools, Jacuzzis, exercise pools, golf nets, bars, cafes, casino, an Internet center, and outdoor areas (some covered) for sunning or relaxing.

Entertainment is professional, varied, and appealing to a range of ages and backgrounds. It puts to shame the offerings aboard many superliner competitors. During a recent voyage, we enjoyed Las Vegas–style production shows, an incredibly talented opera company, an illusionist, a comic, a celebrity vocalist, and classical music concerts. Lounges and the casino bustle into the wee hours. Theme cruises are varied.

For an American, the greatest pleasure aboard *Black Watch* is meeting Britons—delightful, interested, and interesting. Many hours are spent with new English, Scottish, Welsh, and Irish friends exploring the subtleties that make our cultures so similar yet so different. Some misunderstandings of idiom and accent are uproarious: Announcement of a "folkloric presentation" was heard by the Americans as a "full colonic presentation."... We couldn't wait! Because the British are gracious and friendly, being the minority was a special pleasure.

In 2005, *Black Watch* was given major surgery during a 63-day refit that saw the installation of four new engines and renovations to her passenger cabins, including the addition of 36 balconies to her Bridge Deck cabins. In January 2008, the *Black Watch* will embark on her third cruise around the world; prices for the full cruise start at £11,203 per person. Some maiden calls for the cruise line will be Papua New Guinea, Karimunjawa Island, and the South Island of New Zealand.

Boudicca (320/839; NORWEGIAN/INTERNATIONAL; 674 FEET/28,388 TONS)

The *Boudicca* began life as *Royal Viking Sky* and for a short while was the *Grand Latino* of Spanish tour operator Iberojet before being acquired by Olsen. As a sister to *Black Watch,* she would seem to be an ideal fit, further enhancing the line's style of worldwide itineraries on small, more intimate cruise ships. The purchase also gave Olsen an opportunity to expand its fleet quickly and to operate an even wider choice of itineraries for its repeat customers.

Boudicca underwent extensive, multimillion-dollar renovations prior to entering service in February 2006. In keeping with the cruise line's tradition, the refit included the creation of 44 single cabins, some with a veranda, making it an ideal choice for the solo traveler. The ship has a wide selection of cabins and suites, ranging in size from 140-square-foot inside cabins to 550-square-foot top suites with sitting room and veranda. All cabins have television, hair dryer, and luxury Molton Brown toiletries. The top suites also have a DVD/CD player, minibar, and refrigerator. All cabins are nonsmoking.

Boudicca has three dining rooms with open seating for breakfast and lunch and assigned seating for dinner. The informal **Secret Garden** is an option for breakfast, lunch, and dinner buffet and an outdoor grill for lunch, weather permitting. In the evening, musical and comedy shows are staged in the ship's show lounge. Music for dancing is available nightly. Other facilities include a fully equipped gym offering exercise classes, a spa, swimming pool, wading pool, hot tubs, and a swim-against-the-current pool; an Internet room with six computers, and two small shops. During summer and holidays, the ship has a supervised children's program.

Braemar (310/727; EUROPEAN/INTERNATIONAL; 537 FEET/19,089 TONS)

The former *Crown Dynasty* of Crown Cruise Line and *Norwegian Dynasty* of Norwegian Cruise Lines, she is one of the nicest ships in her size and price category in cruising. She is small enough to be cozy but large enough to offer modern cruise-ship amenities and facilities.

Elegant but not stuffy, *Braemar*'s decor communicates a sophistication that is apparent the moment you step on board. Expansive glass windows throughout the ship, large open decks and terraces, and a five-story atrium with walls of glass create a feeling of space and openness. Polished woods, gentle lighting, and soft hues contribute to the stylish comfort.

Built in Spain in 1993 and originally designed by Scandinavian architect Petter Yran, known for his work on many luxury ships, the pretty *Braemar* was given a face-lift by the eminent British ship-interior designer John McNeece prior to beginning her new life in August 2001.

The layout of the eight-deck ship is unusual, if not unique. The five-deck, greenery-filled atrium lobby is aft, rather than amidships. Also, it's on the starboard side rather than at the center, with windows spanning Decks 4 to 8, admitting natural light and sea views, and helping connect passengers with the sea. Four of the main public rooms are stacked vertically at the stern, allowing for large windows in virtually every area. The decks are connected by outdoor stairways and open decks.

Deck 5 is devoted to public rooms. It's anchored at both ends by lounges oriented to the port side horizontally and facing large windows (rather than the usual arrangement of lounges facing the bow or stern). The multilevel show lounge, for example, is semicircular, with the stage and dance floor on the port side. Between the lounges are shops, the photo gallery and tours desk, and the elegant **Braemar Room**—a relaxing lounge with cocktail music and a bar.

Cabins are on five decks; about two-thirds are outside. They are nicely appointed in pastels with light wood furniture and brass fixtures. All have television, phone, safe, and card-key door lock. Closet space is good, but drawer space is minimal. Many cabins are fitted with twin beds that can be converted to a queen. Bathrooms are small but have large medicine cabinets, mirrored doors, and vanities. Deluxe cabins and suites have refrigerators and sitting areas with large windows. Ten suites have private balconies. Four wheelchair-accessible cabins have large bathrooms with grab bars and wide doorways. There are four elevators.

The dining room has a skylight and panoramic windows on three sides, providing natural light and sea views for all diners. Although tables are close, noise is low. The room, decorated in muted colors with lively, contemporary art, has a variety of table configurations.

Above the dining room on Deck 5 is the **Coral Club,** a comfortable lounge with bar and a small stage for live music shows. The small dance floor comes into its own during the evening. Above on Deck 6 is the **Palms Café**—a casual indoor/outdoor cafe—more elegantly decorated than usual for a Lido cafe. Up again on Deck 7 is the **Skylark Club**—two lounges with full-service bar and which can be divided by screens or left as one large sitting and relaxing area. It's also used as the disco by night. The slot machine room is close by. The ship also has a cozy library with good sea views, a card room, an Internet center, a small casino, and a medical center.

The top deck has a swimming pool, Jacuzzis, bar, and a spa with large windows facing the bow. The spa is equipped with state-of-the-art exercise equipment, an aerobics area, and a juice bar. It also has a beauty salon with hair and body treatments, two saunas, and steam and massage rooms. Windscreens line the deck's perimeter. A wide, outside promenade circling Deck 5 provides an uninterrupted track for walking or jogging. The ship also has a golf program that is available on most Caribbean itineraries and on select Mediterranean and Canary Islands ones. It combines individual instruction on board ship and play at clubs on shore.

Despite the increasing numbers of seasoned cruisers who prefer smaller ships, their choices in the midprice range are limited. As one of the few midsize ships built in the 1990s, *Braemar* helps fill the void.

Balmoral **(400/987; NORWEGIAN/INTERNATIONAL; 614 FEET/34,242 TONS)**

Acquired from Star Cruises, the owners of Norwegian Cruise lines, the *Balmoral* was originally built in 1988 as the *Norwegian Crown* of NCL at the Meyer Werft shipyard in Germany. She sailed as the *Crown Odyssey* of Orient Lines in the 1990s and afterward returned as the *Norwegian Crown* to NCL. Over the two decades she has had several extensive renovations. When she is transferred to Olsen in autumn 2007, she will have a 90-foot section inserted at a Hamburg shipyard. It will increase her capacity by 350 berths. At the same time, she will be given an extensive refurbishment prior to joining the fleet in January 2008. When she begins sailing for Olsen, she will be the largest passenger ship in the fleet.

During the renovations, Olsen says, the public areas will be redesigned, the accommodations altered by adding balconies on many suites, converting several cabins and suites into a single accommodation, and in general, bringing the ship in line with *Black Watch* and *Boudicca*.

The *Balmoral* is expected to add a new dimension to the Olsen product, with its range of facilities and cabin sizes well suited for long-range cruising as well as shorter U.K.-based routes. The ship is due to enter service with an inaugural, 14-night Canary Islands cruise round-trip from Dover in late January 2008. She will then make a transatlantic cruise and reposition to Miami, arriving on March 1, 2008, for four Caribbean cruises—two 10-night Eastern and two 11-night Western—before returning to Europe for the summer. The following winter, the ship is scheduled to be based in Miami for the entire season.

ITINERARIES   *See* Itinerary Index.

Hapag-Lloyd Cruises
631 Commack Road, Suite 1A, Commack, NY 11725, ☎ 877-445-7447; www.hl-cruises.com; www.eurolloyd.com

Hapag-Lloyd Cruises traces its origins back to the mid-19th century and two venerable German shipping companies, Hamburg America Line of Hamburg and North German Lloyd of Bremen. Until World War II, the two companies operated some of the world's largest and fastest liners and were pioneers in the operation of pleasure cruises. With today's combined company, the cruising arm is a very small part of a giant container-shipping operation based in Hamburg. The current fleet names recall some of the two lines' most famous ships, and while greatly reduced in size, today's vessels offer the very high standards of the past.

In recent years, Americans have come aboard Hapag-Lloyd ships when chartered by special interest and university groups, and for individual bookings when the *Hanseatic* was chartered by Regent Seven Seas Cruises for Antarctica and the *Columbus* began sailing on the Great Lakes. The line claims it wants to increase the numbers of North American passengers by establishing bilingual cruises with menus, programs, entertainment, and announcements in English. Most of the crew, mainly German and Filipino, speak English. But passenger experience has found that language continues to be a barrier for those who do not understand German.

The vessels boast high space-to-passenger and crew-to-passenger ratios. They are decidedly European, yet each has her own distinct character and distinctive features. Daytime usually has everyone in an adventure mode and dress; nighttime brings out conservative fineries. Hapag-Lloyd now has a U.S. office with a toll-free booking number.

Europa (204/408; GERMAN/INTERNATIONAL/275; 652 FEET/ 28,600 TONS)

The flagship of Hapag-Lloyd Cruises, *Europa* is primarily a German ship, but to attract English-speaking travelers, Hapag-Lloyd has extended its bilingual sailings to attract more U.S. and Canadian passengers. However, the effort has not been consistent. On a recent cruise specifically marketed as a bilingual one, all officers and crew spoke English, but the entertainment was in German only, with no translation.

To take one example, on the last night of a cruise, the captain traditionally holds an auction—the money goes to charity—of the chart for that cruise. The captain is good at the task and is very animated. For those who understand German, it must be hilarious, but for non-German speakers it's difficult, as no translation is offered. Fortunately, a kind audience member translated for us, noting that one cruise netted 150,000 euros for UNICEF.

The all-suite ship, known for its attention to detail, is designed for cruisers who have refined tastes and are interested in the music, food, and art of the places the ship visits. On board, there are wine masters, three-star Michelin guest chefs, and a PGA professional to help golfers improve their game. The line provides renowned lecturers; arranges excursions for passengers to view art, architecture, and nature; and looks for cruises that provide once-in-a-lifetime experiences. *Europa's* size allows her to dock at smaller ports or anchor off remote beaches. She carries Zodiacs to reach remote areas.

Europa's spacious suites, ranging from 291 to 915 square feet, have large living and bedroom areas, a luxurious bathroom, and a minibar. All furnishings are top of the line. An infotainment system, one of the finest at sea, includes television, VCR, music center, as well as an information medium with which guests can send and receive personal e-mails free of charge. The e-mail system and the music choices are great. The exception is television, which carries Cubavision, Al Jazeera, DW, but no English-language stations, although the cruise line claims it will be adding English stations for the next season. One DW radio station does report some English-language news. Five English language films—the same five daily—are offered along with a choice of 150 German flicks (without subtitles). The cruise line has made a commitment to have more English-language choices for the next season.

Europa's Penthouse Deck has ten Deluxe Suites and two Grand Suites. Each Grand Suite has its own sauna, whirlpool, guest bathroom, and a dining table for six. Passengers on Penthouse Decks are served by personal butlers 24/7. Most of the other 192 outer suites have balconies. Two suites are specially designed for disabled persons.

The *Europa's* restaurant, which can accommodate all passengers at one seating for all meals, serves haute cuisine. Two specialty restaurants, **Oriental** and **Venezia,** offer Asian and Italian cuisine. Europa Deck has a cigar bar, piano bar, the **Clipper Lounge** for cocktails and snacks, and a boutique. On the Lido Deck, an informal indoor/outdoor cafe serves a buffet and snacks three times a day. The Lido Deck also has a club and bar, a well-stocked library (including a shelf of left-behind English-language paperbacks), and an auditorium where lectures and films (in German) are presented frequently. The ship's entertainment ranges from classical musicians to well-known popular acts.

During its 2004 refurbishing, *Europa* acquired an expanded fitness area and a new bar. The **Spa Futuresse Center** on Sports Deck is fitted with a sauna, steam bath, massage parlor, Japanese bath, and solarium. The fitness center covers three levels—all with ocean views. Top-of-the-line equipment for cardiovascular training and other exercises are available, as is a personal trainer for individual programs and fitness counseling. The golf training unit has a golf simulator, video analysis, two tee-offs, and a putting green. The swimming pool, one of the longest on any cruise ship, has a magrodome for use as an indoor as well as an outdoor pool.

The new **Sansibar** at the stem of the *Europa,* designed in cooperation with its namesake's creators on the island of Sylt, enjoys great ocean views. The sophisticated **Club Belvedere** is almost entirely glassed-in, providing another venue for sea views.

Families with children are welcome on the *Europa,* with a special children's program and staff during vacation periods. The ship has two children's areas—for younger and older children.

Europa also has a fully equipped hospital and two self-service launderettes.

For luxury and beauty, *Europa* is a wonderful cruise experience, particularly for those who understand some German, as she sails to exotic ports around the world. *Europa* is a ship for well-traveled English speakers, content to be on their own, not particularly interested in interacting with other passengers or who don't mind missing some of the action due to the language barrier. Even the mandatory fire drill is conducted in German. (The cruise line now says that in the future, all announcements and drills will also be in English when English-speaking passengers are on board. Stay tuned.)

Note: The euro is the currency of the ship. When checking prices for spa treatments, shore excursions, or a bottle of wine, it's important to remember that you are reading euros, not U.S. dollars; thus, at the current rate of exchange, prices may be considerably higher than you might think at first glance.

Bremen (82/164; GERMAN/INTERNATIONAL; 366 FEET/6,752 TONS)

Described as a world-class private club aboard a first-class exploration cruise ship, the *Bremen* (formerly *Frontier Spirit*) was constructed at the Kobe Shipyard in Japan by Mitsubishi Heavy Industries in 1990. Slightly smaller than the *Hanseatic,* the *Bremen* is a fine expedition vessel with an ice-hardened hull, which means she can sail in places such as Antarctica. Her 16-foot draft enables her to sail to remote areas of the Amazon and Orinoco rivers, and her Zodiac landing craft allows her to take passengers even farther into areas where large ships cannot go.

Public rooms include a light-filled observation lounge that is used for lectures, a roomy main lounge and bar with a small dance floor and band, and a well-stocked library. The restaurant operates on an open-seating plan for breakfast and lunch and assigned seating for dinner. Meals are prepared with high-quality ingredients. Additional amenities include a sauna, small fitness room, and a heated outdoor swimming pool, usable for polar bear types in cold-weather conditions, with a pool bar and awnings covering 60% of the deck.

All cabins, arranged in four categories, are outside and measure a standard 149 square feet. They have a sitting and bedroom area, large panoramic windows or portholes, and private bath. Eighteen cabins have private verandas. All cabins are fitted with closed-circuit television, satellite telephone, writing desk, a moderate amount of closet space for a casual cruise, and a stocked minibar; bathrooms have a hair dryer and bathrobes. In addition to the cabin amenities, suites have a large, comfortable entertaining area and separate sleeping area with twin beds convertible to queen. All cabins have a special niche for storing personal expedition gear and a warming drawer for drying wet clothing.

The *Bremen,* besides cruising for the German market, is often chartered for worldwide cruising by American special-interest and alumni groups, among whom her reputation is high.

C *Columbus* (205/420; GERMAN/INTERNATIONAL; 473 FEET/14,903 TONS)

The *C Columbus* is marketed to North Americans only for two or three Great Lakes cruises in the late summer and early fall. When built in 1997, her design included bridge wings that swivel inward to allow the ship to enter the extremely deep lock chambers in the Welland Canal linking Lakes Erie and Ontario. These bilingual cruises, but with German-speaking passengers in the majority, offer English-language printed materials, entertainment, enrichment programs, and shore excursions. Currently, the *Columbus* is the only oceangoing cruise ship plying these waters.

Cabins are of moderate size, with some inside and only two with balconies. Colorfully decorated public rooms include a forward observation lounge, adjacent to the buffet and used for breakfast, lunch, and afternoon tea seating; a sprawling, low-ceiling main lounge for lectures and cabaret shows; a cozy corner wine bar; a library with mostly German-language books; and several small gallery lounges ideal for daytime reading.

The restaurant operates with one fixed seating, and while the menu does not feature the same level of gourmet dishes as on the *Europa,* the quality of the ingredients is of the same fine standard. The menu is international with a German specialty—venison, wild boar, and wild duck are offered every night. German selections also appear at breakfast—herring, meats, and cheese—in the buffet. An Octoberfest with free beer takes place at picnic tables around the Lido pool once every cruise.

Hanseatic (92/184; GERMAN/INTERNATIONAL; 403 FEET/8,378 TONS)

A small ship offering adventure-in-luxury cruises, *Hanseatic* was launched in 1993 as one of the most luxurious, technologically advanced adventure-cruise vessels afloat, and at the time set a new level of luxury for adventure cruises. The small ship offers a high crew-to-passenger ratio and amenities typical of small luxury ships. Her rich wood, brass interiors, and fine appointments create the atmosphere of a private yacht.

Hanseatic is said to be one of the most environmentally friendly cruise ships ever built, with a nonpolluting water disposal system, a pollution-filtered incinerator, and full biological treatment plant. The sleek vessel, designated 1A Super Ice class—the highest rating for a passenger vessel—can carry passengers into the far reaches of the Arctic and Antarctica, while her shallow draft, small size, and maneuverability enable her to penetrate deep into the Amazon and other areas inaccessible to most cruise ships.

The *Hanseatic* has six passenger decks with public rooms on all of them. The reception area and all-purpose **Explorer's Lounge** is on Explorer Deck, the dining room is one flight below on Marco Polo Deck, and the **Columbus Lounge** for casual dining is one flight up on Bridge Deck. **Darwin Hall,** the lecture hall, is located on the lowest deck.

Topside, the Observation Deck is a combination sports and sun deck with a small outdoor swimming pool and a glass-enclosed indoor hot tub. The ship has a small health club with exercise equipment, sauna, massage therapy, and a beauty salon. Forward, the **Observation Lounge,** with a 180-degree span of windows, is the ship's most popular room, where passengers socialize and relax while viewing the passing scene. The lounge has a library, ocean charts, maps, and a radar monitor to follow the progress of the ship. Sometimes, alas, this lounge may be filled with smoke. It is the one place on the ship where smoke is noticeable. Passengers are allowed to smoke in all lounges and restaurants, which usually have clearly marked smoking areas.

Hanseatic's all-outside cabins come in six categories and are located on four of the ship's seven decks. All are large (standard average dimension, 236 square feet) with separate sitting areas and large windows. They are furnished with twin or queen beds, writing desk, spacious closets, a flat-screen television and VCR, radio, and a refrigerator restocked daily with soft drinks and water. The marble bathroom has a full-size bathtub, shower, and hair dryer. Some cabins accommodate third and fourth persons. Four deluxe suites have a separate sleeping area, walk-in closets, and a large entertaining area. The suites and eight deluxe cabins on Bridge Deck have butler service. The ship also has a small boutique for gifts and clothing.

The **Marco Polo Dining Room,** an attractive setting with large windows on three sides at the stern, accommodates all passengers at a single, open seating for breakfast and lunch and assigned seating for dinner. Some passengers give the food high marks; most call it uneventful. Casual breakfast and lunch buffet are served in the airy Columbus Lounge with an indoor/outdoor seating—weather permitting. At night on select evenings, the Columbus Lounge is transformed into the intimate, reservations-only (no extra charge) **Ethno Restaurant** and serves a fixed menu with a regional theme related to the area of cruising. Daily in the Explorer's Lounge, an English tea is served with piano background music. Room service offers in-cabin dining.

Life aboard is casual, unregimented, and leisurely paced, with none of the organized activity that typifies mainstream cruise ships. Every cruise has lecturers, who might include naturalists, marine biologists, geologists, zoologists, research scientists, or anthropologists. They make daily presentations with films and slides and accompany shore excursions, acting as guides; and in the late afternoon, they recap the day's visit. Four tenders and 14 Zodiac landing craft take passengers ashore, from the Far North or the Galápagos to Antarctica. Parkas and rubberized boots are issued gratis to all passengers on Arctic and Antarctic voyages; snorkel equipment is provided in the tropics.

Hanseatic cruises are designed for passengers seeking off-the-beaten-path voyages in comfort. Her passengers are small-ship devotees, affluent, 50-plus in age, adventurous, interested in natural history, and committed to preserving the environment. They are independent, active, seasoned travelers accustomed to luxury and quality. The ship globe-trots throughout the year. Although most of her cruises are light adventures, many entail considerable walking, wet landings, and climbing in and out of Zodiacs in remote areas. Anyone with physical limitations or health problems should not underestimate the difficulties they could encounter. The Antarctica itineraries involve traversing the Drake Passage, a notoriously rough stretch of water. Often, this ship is on charter to an American cruise line or group.

ITINERARIES *See* Itinerary Index.

Hebridean Island Cruises
Griffin House, Broughton Hall, Skipton, North Yorkshire, United Kingdom BD23 3AN; ☎ 011-44-1756-704-704 or 800-659-2648; fax 011-44-1756-704-794; www.hebridean.co.uk

Hebridean Princess **(30/49; ENGLISH/SCOTTISH/38; 235 FEET/ 1,420 TONS)**

Built in 1964 to carry 600 passengers, Hebridean Island Cruises redesigned the ship in 1994 to carry only 47 passengers in the style of a deluxe country inn. Accommodations vary from singles with shared facilities to suites. The ship has a lounge, restaurant, library of books and videos, and shop. She visits lochs, estuaries, and Scotland's Inner and Outer Hebrides islands on three- to eight-night cruises from March to November, usually departing from the West Highlands port of Oban. Prices start at £800 for a four-night Highland cruise.

Hebridean Spirit **(49/96; ENGLISH/SCOTTISH/70; 300 FEET/4,200 TONS)**

In 2000, Hebridean Island Cruises bought the *MegaStar Capricorn* from Star Cruises, Asia's largest cruise line, and renamed her *Hebridean Spirit.* She was given a $4.7 million renovation and redesigned to accommodate 96 guests (down from 114) in a style similar to the *Hebridean Princess.* The crew of 72 includes seven chefs! Even her superstructure has been "aged" to give the ship the style and outline of ships from the golden era of cruising.

The 49 cabins, decorated in a classical English yet contemporary style, include 18 singles (no supplementary charge). Each cabin has a sitting area and is decorated individually and named after familiar places. They have marble bathrooms with full tub and shower, a large or walk-in closet, and a tea- and coffeemaker. Eight cabins have balconies, and there are two suites.

The oceangoing vessel has enabled Hebridean Island to cruise in new waters and to offer itineraries for north European and Mediterranean destinations in summer, and from the Greek Islands through the Red Sea and the Indian Ocean to Sri Lanka in winter, on weekly cruises and normally with no repetition of ports of call. Passengers' departure points are reached by private charter to and from London. Prices for an eight-night Mediterranean cruise start at £3,915 per person for a single cabin and £3,500 per person double, and include air travel, transfers, entrance fees to attractions, house wine, shore excursions, meals, gratuities, and port or passenger taxes. Brits account for 84% of the line's passengers, with 50% repeaters.

ITINERARIES *See* Itinerary Index.

Kristina Cruises
Kirkkokatu 16, 48100 Kotka, Finland; ☎ 358-5-211-4230;
fax 358-5-211-4500; www.kristinacruises.com

Kristina Cruises, the Finland-based shipping company, has more than 50 years' experience in the cruise business. Today, the second generation of the Partanen family heads the company and operates two cruise ships.

Kristina Regina **(119/245; FINNISH/55; 327 FEET/4,295 TONS)**

The ship, which has a receptive audience among well-traveled Americans, sails on multilength itineraries that visit the Baltic region, Iceland, the Mediterranean, and West Africa. In spring of 2001, she underwent a million-dollar renovation. She has an English-speaking staff, two dining rooms and one evening restaurant, a cafe, library, health center, sauna, laundry, and Sun Decks. Dining is at one seating; menus vary. Her small size enables her to dock within walking distance of town centers.

Kristina Brahe **(57/129; FINNISH/24; 186 FEET/1,105 TONS)**

Regina's sister ship, in summer of 2003, inaugurated cruises on the route of the Russian czars between the Finnish archipelago and Lake Saimaa, taking passengers to the destinations westbound from Helsinki through the Finnish Archipelago National Park and different outer islands. The eastbound cruise leads through the Saimaa canal to Lappeenranta and on the Saimaa to Savonlinna, a town noted for its opera festival. These cruises won the Scandinavian Travel Award in 2004.

Bookings in the United States can be made through the following agencies: The Nordic Company, WI; ☎ 888-806-7226; **www.nordicco.com;** Scantours, CA; ☎ 800-223-7226; **www.scantours.com;** Five Stars of Scandinavia, WA; ☎ 800-722-4126; **www.5stars-of-scandinavia.com;** Nordic Saga Tours, WA; ☎ 800-848-6449; **www.nordicsaga.com;** Borton Overseas, MN; ☎ 800-843-0602; **www.bortonoverseas.com.** In Canada: Valhalla Travel, Ontario; ☎ 800-265-0459; **www.valhallatravel.com.**

ITINERARIES *See* Itinerary Index.

Lindblad Expeditions
(*See* Part Three, Cruising Alternatives, Adventure and Cultural Cruises)

Louis Cruise Lines
150A Franklin Roosevelt and Omonias Avenue, P.O. Box 55612;
3045 Limassol, Cyprus; ☎ 00357-25570000 (40 lines);
fax 00357-25573320; www.louiscruises.com

Louis UK, Chesterfield House, 385-387 Euston Road, London, NW1 3AU;
☎ 0800-0183883; fax + 44-2073832992; e-mail: cruise@louis-uk.co.uk

After many years of marketing its ships in North America through U.S. tour companies, the Cyprus-based Louis Cruises stepped up its U.S. presence in early 2007 by joining the Niche Cruise Marketing Alliance (NCMA), a group of 12 small U.S. and foreign cruise lines whose purpose is to help its members penetrate the U.S. market.

Louis Cruises, a well-established cruise and hotel company in the Eastern Mediterranean, began more than 30 years ago operating short cruises from Cyprus to the Eastern Mediterranean. Today with a fleet of 12 small and mid-size cruise ships, the company operates classic cruises of three to ten days out of Genoa and Marseilles to the West Mediterranean and North Africa and from Cyprus and Piraeus to Egypt and the Eastern Mediterranean.

The ships—*Coral, Orient Queen, Perla, Sapphire*—that the line sells directly sail on a wide variety of itineraries to France, Gibraltar, Italy, Portugal, and Spain; to North Africa visiting Morocco, Tunisia, Malta, and Libya; and to Greece, Turkey, and the Black Sea, plus short-term cruises from Cyprus to Israel and Egypt. Passengers on the Greek Island cruises have the option of embarking in Mykonos and disembarking in Santorini.

The seven-deck *Coral* (486 feet; 13,995 tons) has 344 air-conditioned cabins (231 outside; 113 inside), all equipped with bath with shower, phone, and radio. Most cabins have two lower beds; some have a third and/or fourth upper bed. The ship has a dining room, theater, nightclub, disco, casino, small pool, gym and sauna, jogging track, and two elevators.

The eight-deck *Orient Queen* (525 feet; 15,781 tons) has 364 air-conditioned cabins (199 outside; 165 inside), all equipped with bath with shower, phone, and plasma television. Most cabins have two lower beds or double; some have a third and/or fourth berth. All ten deluxe cabins have minibar and bathtub. The ship has a dining room, Lido buffet, disco, several bars, show lounge, casino, small pool, fitness center, beauty salon, card room, library, children's club, shops, and four elevators.

The seven-deck *Perla* (537 feet; 16,710 tons) has 395 air-conditioned cabins (261 outside; 134 inside), all equipped with bath with shower, phone, and radio. Most cabins have two lower beds; some have a third and/or fourth upper berth. The 52 suites and deluxe cabins have sofa and bathtub. The ship has two restaurants, show lounge, disco, several bars, casino, two swimming pools, spa and fitness center, ice-cream parlor, beauty salon, card room, minigolf course, children's club, shops, and four elevators.

The seven-deck *Sapphire* (489 feet; 12,263 tons) has 288 air-conditioned cabins (157 outside; 131 inside), all equipped with bath with shower, phone, and radio. Most cabins have two lower beds; some have a third and/or fourth upper berth. The ship has a dining room, disco, several bars, casino, small pool, beauty salon, card room/library, and three elevators.

Four of Louis Cruises' ships—*The Calypso, The Emerald, Thomson Destiny,* and *Thomson Spirit* are chartered to Thomson Cruises of TUI AG and a fifth one, *Arielle,* to Transocean of Germany. The line's other ships are *Ivory, Princesa Marissa,* and *Serenade.*

The NCMA Web site (**www.nichecruise.com**) has information on Louis Cruise Lines and a direct link to its Web site, as well as information on the alliance's 11 other members.

ITINERARIES *See* Itinerary Index.

Orion Expedition Cruises

A.B.N. 88 456 259 434; 26 Alfred Street, Milsons Point, Sydney N.S.W. 2061, Australia; ☎ +61-2-9033-8700 (international); 02-9033-8700 (local); fax +61-2-9033-8799 (international); fax 02-9033-8799; www.orioncruises.com.au

---

Orion **(53/106; GERMAN/EUROPEAN; 337 FEET/4,050 TONS)**

Billed as a vessel for a new age of exploration cruising, the *Orion*, which made her maiden voyage in 2003, combines the latest advances in ship design and communication technology with the style and comfort of a luxury cruise ship. From her ice-strengthened hull (rated E3, the highest rating available) to the remote viewing cameras atop its mast, no expense was spared in *Orion*'s construction.

Built at the Cassens Shipyard in Emden, Germany, *Orion* is a model of German craftsmanship and engineering, with such features as technologically advanced stabilizers, bow and stern thrusters for easy maneuverability, a surround-sound audio system in the lecture hall, and direct Internet access in every cabin.

But it's *Orion*'s luxurious accommodations that distinguish her from older, more traditional expedition ships. Each of the 22 standard cabins measures between 175 and 180 square feet, while each of the 31 suites measures from 215 to 345 square feet; eight have French balconies. All cabins are outside; many suites and the Owner's Suites have a balcony. All cabins include a sitting area or living room, flat-screen television, DVD and CD player, minifridge, private marble bathroom, ample closet space, and twin beds that can be converted to a queen. Large oval, rectangular, or sliding glass floor-to-ceiling windows offer panoramic views.

Orion's facilities include a spa, sauna, whirlpool, massage services, hairdresser, boutique, several lounges, and a library equipped with Internet access. At the center of the ship is a glass atrium that wraps around the elevator and serves *Orion*'s seven decks. The **Constellation Restaurant** accommodates all guests at a single unassigned seating; an open deck off the main lounge is available for dining alfresco. Dinner menus featuring fresh local produce are conceived by award-winning chef Serge Dansereau (of The Bathers' Pavilion, Balmoral). The ship offers 24-hour room service as well.

The spacious observation lounge on the top deck opens onto a wraparound deck for optimal viewing. The bridge also leads out to an open observation area. A mudroom on the lower deck stores parkas, boots, and other equipment used during and after a day of exploration. Ten heavy-duty Zodiac inflatable motorized boats are used for landing in shallow areas and to navigate small waterways. Several two-seater kayaks are available for individual exploration.

Onboard expedition leaders and lecturers include marine biologists, botanists, anthropologists, ornithologists, historians, and other specialists, depending on the voyage. *Orion* combines adventure through access to remote areas by Zodiac with five-star facilities on board. Each itinerary features a range of inclusive shore expeditions as well as optional excursions such as helicopter or fixed-wing flights, scuba diving, and fishing, depending on each particular voyage.

Classified with Germanischer Lloyd, *Orion* meets the latest international safety rules and regulations. The ship is served by 75 European officers and crew. Permanently based in Australian waters, *Orion* sails on a wide range of expeditions that vary by season: the Kimberley (north to west Australia) between April and September, Papua New Guinea/Melanesia in March and November, Antarctica in December and January. Most cruises are of 10 or 11 nights' duration, although there are some 7-night voyages (Hobart to Sydney), and voyages to the Antarctic are 18 nights' duration.

ITINERARIES   *See* Itinerary Index.

P&O Cruises
Richmond House, Terminus Terrace, Southampton SO143PN, England;
☎**08453-555; fax 023-8065-7409; www.pocruises.com.uk**

P&O Cruises stems from the original steamship company founded in 1837, whose principal routes served the British Empire from India to New Zealand. In 1974, P&O Cruises purchased Princess Cruises, and through it had a big impact on modern cruising, particularly on the U.S. West Coast market.

The introduction of the *Oriana* in 1995, P&O Cruises' first brand-new ship in more than two decades, signaled the start of a modern era for the cruise line, replacing her old ships and building new ships designed primarily for British passengers. *Oriana's* sister, *Aurora,* was delivered in 2000 with even more new features. In 2003, the *Oceana,* formerly the *Ocean Princess* of Princess Cruises, joined the fleet. In 2005, the line added *Arcadia* as well as *Artemis* (formerly *Royal Princess*). In 2003, P&O Cruises, along with Princess Cruises and the company's other cruise lines, were bought by Carnival Corporation after an intensive bidding war with Royal Caribbean Cruises. P&O has under construction the 115,000-ton *Ventura,* which will be Britain's largest cruise ship when she enters service in April 2008, and her near sister, a 116,000-ton ship planned for spring 2010, at an estimated cost of 535 million euros.

P&O Cruises offers moderately priced, classic cruises sailing on worldwide itineraries. P&O Cruises defines them as three different styles of cruise experience: original and authentic cruising on *Aurora* and *Oriana;* contemporary and innovative cruising on *Arcadia* and *Oceana;* and traditional and intimate cruising on *Artemis.* The line's new multimillion-dollar Elevation program of refinements to its onboard experience was introduced in early 2007 and will be rolled out fleetwide over the next two years. It encompasses dining, accommodations, entertainment, shore excursions, and the booking process.

The ships' British style cannot be overemphasized; it's what P&O passengers want. The atmosphere is very social, helped by friendly British officers who mingle with passengers and host tables at dinner, a popular feature. The ships are well organized, aboard and ashore, with excellent programs that include outstanding lecturers on port history and culture, classical pianists, afternoon teas, Sunday religious services (Anglican) with a passenger-staff choir, and varied evening entertainment. The dress code tends to be dressier than on similar ships catering to Americans. Men wear jacket and tie on most nights at sea and on formal evenings they wear tuxedos or dinner jackets, and women don cocktail and long dresses.

P&O focuses generally on three programs: cruises departing from Southampton, those based in the Caribbean in winter, and annual around-the-world voyages. Most passengers are British, of all ages and incomes. Americans, Australians, and New Zealanders are a sizable minority on around-the-world voyages. Once-in-a- lifetime shore excursions were among the 196 new shore excursions launched across the fleet in 2007. These include such adventures as an evening concert and after-hours evening visit of the Hermitage in St. Petersburg, Russia, or a Turkish bath experience in Istanbul. There are tours designed for families and other for teens, and gourmet tours such as wine tasting in Provence or a Greek gastronomy class in Corfu.

In 2008, three ships—*Aurora, Oriana,* and *Artemis*—will sail on world cruises; together, they will visit 90 ports in 48 countries on seven continents between December 2007 and April 2008. The voyages can be taken in segments ranging from 34 nights to 101 nights. Recently, P&O Cruises changed the registry on the *Arcadia, Oceana, Oriana,* and *Artemis* from British to Bermudian to allow weddings at sea with a traditional ceremony conducted by the captain. (Weddings are not recognized aboard U.K.-registered vessels.) The new *Ventura* is expected to use Bermudian colors, too.

Aurora **(939/1,874; BRITISH/INDIAN AND EUROPEAN; 886 FEET/76,000 TONS)**

Oriana **(914/2,016; BERMUDIAN/INDIAN AND EUROPEAN; 853 FEET/69,153 TONS)**

The *Oriana* is big and beautiful. New and modern, she nonetheless has the design and decor of a classic liner with traditional oil paintings, historic documents, and ship models on the walls. Interiors are as fine and refined as tea in a British parlor. No flashy neon or glitz here. The ship has an inviting calm and numerous nooks where it's easy to relax, read, write postcards, and let the world go by. It's cruising as it should be.

As part of the cruise line's new Elevation program, *Oriana* was given a multimillion-dollar refit in 2006. Among the enhancements were **Oriana Rhodes,** a 96-seat restaurant created by well-know British chef Gary Rhodes; the refurbishing of 914 cabins complete with upgraded mattresses and deluxe Egyptian cotton bed linens, towels, and robes; and a new children's club. Other cabin innovations were fitness facilities for passengers who would prefer to exercise in private; improved tea- and coffeemakers in every cabin; and a Champagne-breakfast-in-bed option.

New dining features are gourmet tasting menus in select venues, two additional gala dinners in the main restaurants, including a Chaîne des

Rôtisseurs culinary dinner, and nightly themed buffet menus in the food court offering Indian, French, Spanish, Italian, and British cuisines. A special children's tea at 5 p.m. was introduced in April 2007 on all the line's family-friendly ships, providing bibs, beakers, and children's cutlery, along with new healthy menu options.

Similar enhancements are being introduced fleetwide, and the new *Ventura* has Marco Pierre White, the youngest British chef ever to win three Michelin stars for his restaurant, as a dining consultant. He will oversee the fine-dining restaurant, **The White Room,** as well as an enhanced balcony dining, a pizzeria by the pool, and **The Beach House,** a casual restaurant catering to families.

Entertainment options tailored to the three respective styles of cruising are being added. These include more celebrity speakers, sports heroes, and television personalities; more live broadcasts of sporting events; a golf pro on *Aurora* to give lessons on the golf simulator; and a new family production show launched on *Oceana* in May.

Aurora, which debuted in 2000, came with new features and a bit more glitz as well as some firsts for a ship dedicated primarily to the British market. These include two-deck Penthouse Suites, four decks of cabins with balconies, and interconnecting family cabins. She also had P&O Cruises's first 24-hour bistro-style restaurant, coffee and chocolate bar, Champagne bar, tea- and coffee-making facilities in all cabins, a retractable dome over one swimming pool, and a virtual-reality center. Her four-deck atrium has a waterfall and Lalique glass–style sculpture and is surrounded by shops and a tour desk.

The size and spaciousness of these ships allow for a variety of public rooms and entertainment facilities, as well as some larger public rooms enabling passengers of all types to find comfortable and familiar surroundings. Vast amounts of open deck call to British sun worshippers and those who take a daily constitutional walk.

Oriana's cabins are spacious and more luxurious than on previous P&O ships and come in a wide range of configurations with ample storage space. The ship has 114 singles—an unusual feature for today's superliner. Almost all cabins, including suites, are on the three middle decks. *Aurora's* cabin choices are even wider, and include interconnecting cabins suitable for families. More than 40% of the cabins, including some standard ones, have balconies. Cabins on both ships have tea- and coffeemakers, safe, refrigerator, television, direct-dial telephone, air-conditioning, and music system; some have bathtubs, hair dryers, and minibars.

Two main restaurants offer two sittings for three meals. The cuisine is very English: lots of meat and potatoes and sauces, excellent soups but few salads. The **Conservatory** on Lido Deck, with indoor/outdoor seating, serves a buffet breakfast and lunch. The area can become very crowded at peak lunch hours.

The ships' elaborate activities programs ranges from bingo and crafts to bridge and dance classes. Port lecturers are very knowledgeable and generally have a dry, British sense of humor. They wouldn't dream of giving the shopping sales pitch heard on many Caribbean cruise ships. The comfortable library is well supplied.

Public rooms spread over two Main Decks offer a variety of atmospheres catering to class-conscious Brits. Many reflect in name and style the company's 165-year history, and range from cabaret in the **Pacific Lounge** to large production shows in **Theatre Royal.** There's **Lord's Tavern,** a cricket-themed pub, and the spacious **Crow's Nest** observation bar and lounge, with wraparound windows and a trio playing dance music before and after dinner. **Monte Carlo Casino** is small, compared with casinos on big ships sailing the Caribbean.

On *Aurora,* a West End–style theater has the latest production technology, and the new-concept main show lounge comes with a spacious bar, large dance floor, and retractable stage. Amidships is an intimate, futuristic nightclub with small dance floor and stage. One deck above, a large concert hall/cinema shows first-run films and stages concerts; there's also a business center with computers.

Activities on *Oriana's* vast open decks include deck tennis, quoits, shuffleboard, golf nets, and trapshooting. Cricket matches between passengers and officers are popular. One of two adult pools is a generous 42 feet long. Passengers take daily walks on a wide promenade sprinkled with deck chairs shaded by lifeboats. A large spa offers aerobics, a gym, whirlpools, sauna, massage, beauty and therapy rooms, and a hair salon.

On *Aurora,* a pool between Decks 11 and 12 has a waterfall and is surrounded by tiered decks. Another pool can be covered by a dome in inclement weather; still another is reserved for families at certain times of year. A netted deck area is adaptable for cricket, soccer, and tennis, and golfers can practice on the golf simulator. A well-equipped gym and aerobics studio overlook the forward pool. The spacious area is linked by stairs to health and beauty facilities.

P&O Cruises' children's program is highly praised. In peak times, four age-specific areas have separate, supervised, well-designed programs; two age groups are used at other times. Children have their own pool and Lido area, and they eat at an early sitting, with or without their parents. A staffed night nursery is available for children under age 5, and cabins have baby "listening" facilities.

Arcadia (984/1,952; BERMUDIAN/INTERNATIONAL; 952 FEET/83,000 TONS)

Arcadia, which joined the fleet in 2005, is the largest ship in the fleet. She is children-free. Among her spacious public rooms, the 11-passenger-deck ship has an array of dining options, a three-tier theater, 12 bars, nightclub, coffee and chocolate bar, spa with a thermal suite and hydrotherapy pool, an outdoor pool, five Jacuzzis, and an indoor/outdoor swimming pool with retractable dome. Other facilities include shops, a casino, a library, an observation lounge with panoramic views, Cyb@study, hair salon, art gallery, touch-screen photo gallery, and 14 passenger elevators, including two panoramic glass ones on the sides of the ship.

More than two-thirds of the cabins on the British-registered ship have balconies. **The Belvedere,** a food court so named because it commands fine views, offers informal dining around the clock with a wide choice of menus, from Asian and Italian to bistro-style dishes and a delicatessen counter. Light and airy, the decor has a soft, calm Japanese theme and is furnished with outside seating for dining alfresco. There is a two-tier main restaurant, and the ship's specialty restaurant, **Arcadian Rhodes,** is the creation of Gary Rhodes, one of Britain's best-known chefs who is noted for his innovative take on contemporary British cuisine. Rhodes has created the menu and several signature dishes for the restaurant.

Oceana (1,008/2,016; BERMUDIAN/INTERNATIONAL; 856 FEET/77,000 TONS)

Oceana (formerly *Ocean Princess*) joined the P&O fleet in fall 2003. She was part of Princess Cruises' *Sun Princess* group. (For a description of these ships, see Princess Cruises earlier in Part Two.)

Artemis (520/1,196; BERMUDIAN/INTERNATIONAL; 757 FEET/45,000 TONS)

The *Artemis* (the former *Royal Princess*), which joined P&O Cruises in spring 2005, was launched in 1984 and christened by Diana, Princess of Wales. Both made an indelible mark on the 1980s. At the time, *Artemis* was the most expensive passenger ship ever built. Her sleek lines and tapered bow looked traditional, but she had so many innovations inside that she was called revolutionary and set new standards in passenger comfort for the cruise ships that followed.

Artemis was the first cruise ship to have all outside cabins, and television with remote control, minifridge, and full bathroom with tub and shower in all cabins. She was first to have verandas in all suites, deluxe cabins, and even in some lesser categories, and large windows instead of portholes in every category. The ship, with nine passenger decks, has two acres of open teak decks, three swimming pools, and a fully equipped spa. Her decor is refined. Interiors are defined less by walls than by art, sculpture, and glass with brass railings. Live plants and abundant windows create openness throughout the ship.

Artemis's layout is unusual. Most public rooms are on the two lower levels, and virtually all cabins are on upper decks. A large foyer on the lower Plaza Deck spans two decks—the first shipboard atrium, perhaps. This greenery-filled area is dominated by a large David Norris sculpture consisting of a bronze spiral with seagulls rising over rocks. A dramatic staircase with glass balustrade curves in two wings upward to a balcony with piano lounge overlooking the foyer; it is a gathering spot where passengers enjoy prelunch or predinner drinks, entertained by a pianist-vocalist. This deck also holds the main showroom, cabaret-style lounge, casino, boutique, card room, and a theater. The ship has six elevators.

Artemis's cabins are spacious, each with picture windows, a tiled bathroom with tub and shower, retractable clothesline, mirrored medicine-cabinet door, minifridge, safe, multifunction phone, television, and four-channel music radio. High-quality interiors and attention to detail are reflected in a large dressing table with makeup lights, an easy-to-reach hair dryer, ample drawers, and large closets. In many cabins, a twin bed folds into a wall, providing extra sitting space by day. Some cabins have obstructed views, indicated on the deck plan. Standard dimensions are 168 square feet. Some cabins accommodate a third person and there are ten wheelchair-accessible cabins. Self-service launderettes offer washers, dryers, irons, and ironing boards at no charge.

Suites and cabins with verandas are very roomy. The two largest suites have separate sitting and dining rooms, Jacuzzi bathtub, separate bedroom with queen bed, and large veranda. Minisuites are similar, but without walls between bedrooms and sitting areas.

The warm, pleasant **Continental Dining Room** has a raised perimeter level delineated with brass railings. Small islands of round tables break up the space, provide privacy, and help lower the noise level and allow easy conversation. Senior dining staff is Italian and very attentive. The **Lido Café,** an indoor/outdoor cafe with tile-topped tables, serves an informal buffet breakfast, lunch, and snacks.

The show lounge has seats tiered in a semicircular fashion; sight lines are generally good, except from the back. There are several other lounges offering entertainment and playing dance music every evening, as well as a casino.

A cluster of five small pools is the centerpiece of the Lido Deck, the main outdoor recreation area. On Sun Deck, passengers sunbathe on a raised platform, play table tennis and shuffleboard, swim in one of cruising's largest lap pools, and exercise in the spa. The fitness complex has a gym with state-of-the-art equipment, sauna and massage rooms, and a large whirlpool. Joggers and walkers circle the wraparound teak promenade (four laps equal one mile).

Ventura **(1,550/3,597; BERMUDIAN; 957 FEET/115,000 TONS)**

To be launched in April 2008, the £300 million *Ventura,* designed specifically for the British market, will be 40% larger than the *Arcadia.* Three distinct elements of British culture are being brought together on the ship: fine dining, family entertainment, and modern and contemporary art.

Well-known British chef and three-star restaurateur Marco Pierre White is creating a signature restaurant, **The White Room,** and acting as a consultant to P&O Cruises. His culinary flair will also be integrated into other areas of the dining experience, such as **The Beach House,** a family dining venue, said to be a cruise-ship first as a venue designed specifically for families to dine together.

Further emphasizing *Ventura*'s family-friendly facilities, the much-loved British Toyland character Noddy will be featured in the children's area for 2 to 4 year olds. Noddy will be on board all cruises to delight youngsters at character breakfasts and during playtime.

Older children will be offered lessons in how to become a rock star and learn to play a guitar, keyboards, and drums. For the first time, P&O Cruises has designed an area specifically for parents to supervise their children under 2 years old.

Art and design are key themes for the *Ventura,* and she will be a floating showcase for the best of British contemporary art, with 7,000 pieces from 55 artists. Art experts from the famous Tate Modern museum in London will host Introduction to Modern Art cruises with seminars, presentations, and practical art classes to be held throughout the year.

The *Ventura's* design is embodied in the atrium—striking, contemporary, yet designed for purpose: the hub of the ship from which all public areas can be easily accessed. The 14-deck ship will carry a maximum of 3,600 passengers. She will have eight restaurants, six boutiques, five pools, and three show lounges, including the largest theater on a British ship; 900 cabins with private balconies and 1,200 crew members. British designer Nick Munro, renowned for his unique furniture, ceramic, and home ware designs, is creating items designed specifically for contemporary British tastes.

Ventura's cabins will be contemporary and stylish in decor with modern art on canvas, fashionable bed linens, and designer touches. Deluxe cabins will have two lower beds convertible to a king-size bed; bathroom with full-size bath and separate shower; lounge sofa, chairs and table; vanity/writing desk; flat-screen television and radio; safe, hair dryer, and refrigerator; tea- and coffee-making facilities; direct-dial telephone; and balcony furnished with teak furniture. Suites will have all these features plus butler service, a full-size Jacuzzi bath, a dressing area, DVD player and hi-fi, and trouser press and ironing board.

The ship's spa with alluring sea views, will be equipped with a thermal suite and a pool. It will offer a blend of ancient traditions and alternative therapies and a wide range of treatments, from body wraps to a makeover and a massage.

ITINERARIES *See* Itinerary Index.

Pearl Seas Cruises
741 Boston Post Road, Suite 250; Guilford, CT 06437; ☎ 203-453-4211 or 800-983-7462; fax 203-453-1877; www.pearlseascruises.com

---

Pearl Seas I **(UNNAMED) (109/210; REPUBLIC OF THE MARSHALL ISLANDS; 330 FEET)**

Pearl Seas II **(UNNAMED) (NA/210; REPUBLIC OF THE MARSHALL ISLANDS; 300 FEET)**

Pearl Seas Cruises, a new cruise line begun by the same group that operates American Cruise Line, is building two new luxury ships at Irving Shipbuilding in Halifax, Nova Scotia. The first ship is scheduled to debut in July 2008 and the second in June 2009. The cruise line's name is meant to reflect a high regard for the beauty and romance of the precious jewel from the sea. The ships have not yet been named.

The six-deck ships' interior will offer luxury accommodations with oversize suites and cabins measuring 240 to 460 square feet, and all will have private balconies. The cabins also have large picture windows that open, flat-screen satellite television and DVD, Internet access, and other amenities. The ships will have a stocked library, spa, three Observation Decks, a Sport and Exercise Deck, and an elevator to all decks. The window-lined dining room will seat all passengers at one time; leisure time can be spent in one of six lounges.

The ships will be able to travel faster, have the latest navigational technology and communication equipment, and will meet stringent regulations for fire safety and stability. They will be powered by Caterpillar diesel engines for propulsion and generators and will be stabilized by Rolls-Royce Commercial Marine active wing stabilizer units.

The first ship will spend her maiden summer and fall cruising in the Canadian Maritimes, Newfoundland, and New England, and from mid-November 2007 to April 2009, she will sail on four- to ten-night cruises in the Caribbean. The small ships have been designed for the luxury market. With a draft of only ten feet; they will be able to slip into harbors off the beaten path as well as larger, better-known ports of call.

ITINERARIES *See* Itinerary Index.

Peter Deilmann Cruises
1800 Diagonal Road, Suite 170, Alexandria, VA 22314; ☎ 703-549-1741 or 800-348-8287; fax 703-549-7924; www.deilmann-cruises.com

Peter Deilmann Cruises' *Deutschland,* launched in 1998, was built in the Art Nouveau and Art Deco style of ocean liners of the past as a traditional luxury liner in the grand European style. She has three restaurants and a Promenade Deck and accommodates 513 passengers in a variety of mostly outside staterooms. The ship is renowned in Germany (it was the venue for filming the German television version of *The Love Boat*), and the majority of the passengers are from German-speaking countries. But it also attracts different nationalities, including up to 20% from England, Canada, and the United States. Almost all sailings now offer announcements in English as well as German due to an increase in the number of English-speaking passengers.

In addition to German food, the menu includes Italian, French, American, and international selections, while reflecting the cuisine of port of call. Underscoring Deilmann's effort to appeal to Americans, hamburgers and other grilled meats, fish, and shrimp are available on the open-air Lido Deck for lunch. Each day's menu also features vegetarian dishes, both at the indoor **Lido Buffet** restaurant and the **Berlin,** the ship's main restaurant, where breakfast, lunch, and dinner are served daily. There are two seatings for dinner in the Berlin Restaurant. The waitstaff are especially friendly and the service is excellent in this plush dining venue. An alternative gourmet restaurant, the **Four Seasons,** requires advance reservations. Both intimate and quiet, the Four Seasons serves as many as six courses at a leisurely pace (dinner is routinely a two- to three-hour affair). A buffet on the Lido Deck offers breakfast, lunch, and dinner, and frequently offers dishes from the menu of the main dining salon. In the **Lili Marleen** lounge, nightly musical trios perform for both listening and dancing. The mainstay is American standards and jazz tunes.

The **Old Fritz Pub,** a cozy wood-paneled bar, opens to additional seating outdoors. Entertainment here is low-key, consisting of a pianist playing

European and American standards. The two-story **Emperor's Ballroom** serves as the ship's theater, with nightly revues and dancing. Shows include Las Vegas–style production shows, classical concerts, magicians, and stand-up comics who usually perform in German only, as does the MC. The line says an English-speaking MC is available when needed.

Cabins on the *Deutschland* feature polished burled walnut paneling and pastel yellow furnishings. Well-designed bathrooms in Italian marble are unusually spacious, but for the most part offer showers only. Amenities include a radio and color television with CNN and MSNBC and English-language films, a minifridge, two armchairs and a table, a desk, robes, slippers, a hair dryer, Molton Brown toiletries, and for outside cabins, a medium to large picture window.

The *Deutschland* provides a small but adequate fitness center and a full-service spa that was expanded recently and offers thalassotherapy, Cleopatra bath, a wide range of massages, and other beauty and health treatments. The fitness programs include daily classes in Pilates, Nordic walking, and aqua exercise. Fitness consulting sessions are also held. In 2007, Deilmann introduced new prebooked wellness packages, starting at $150 for ladies' facial, special body bath, and classic back massage. Men's grooming and relaxation packages start at $155 for a two-hour treatment. Although a notable array of outdoor activities is available, there is no place on board to run or jog. There are two swimming pools: one indoors on Deck 3 and another outdoors (saltwater).

Announcements are conducted in German. When there are enough English- speaking passengers to warrant it, announcements are repeated in English. All staff members on board speak English, some much better than others. Cabin crews are often from Eastern Europe and speak English as a second language rather than German; waitstaff come mostly from eastern Germany. Passengers get news and daily activity reports in English or German. Menus and daily wellness and spa programs are available in English. English-language shore excursions are offered in a package at up to 50% discount when prepurchased.

From time to time, Deilmann offers free air from up to 17 U.S. gateways and low air supplements from an additional 34 cities, as well as free shore excursions in connections with certain cruises. Check with the cruise line. Theme cruises have also been expanded and include golf, garden, and equestrian theme cruises as well as a music cruise.

(For Peter Deilmann River Cruises, designed for English-speaking passengers as well as European ones, see Part Three, Cruising Alternatives.)

ITINERARIES *See* Itinerary Index.

Saga Cruises
100 Cummings Center, Suite 120B, Beverly, MA 01915; ☎ 800-343-0273; www.sagacruisingusa.com

Saga Cruises is part of the Saga Group, an English firm based in Folkestone that began operating tours in 1951 for British senior citizens ages 60 and older; then, in 1995, it dropped the minimum age to 50. Companions ages 40 and up may accompany the lead passenger. Although primarily in the resort and tour business, the company recently started to market its cruises to North Americans.

While Saga may be an unfamiliar name to North Americans, its two principal ships, the *Saga Rose* and the *Saga Ruby,* were once well known in the luxury market. Graceful ships with classic ocean liner profiles, both trace their heritage to Norwegian America Line when the former ship, completed in 1965, sailed as the *Sagafjord,* while the latter came in 1973 as the *Vistafjord.* Together the Norwegian pair provided some of the most luxurious cruise experiences afloat.

After an interim period with Norwegian America Cruises, both ships were purchased by Cunard Line in 1983. Then in 1996, the *Sagafjord* was sold to the Saga Group to become the *Saga Rose.* In 2004, the *Caronia* (formerly *Vistafjord*) was given a $30 million refit before starting to cruise in early 2005 as the *Saga Ruby.*

In 2006, the company added the *Spirit of Adventure* (former *Berlin* of Deilmann), under the brand Voyages of Discovery. After a complete makeover, the 352-passenger ship began sailing on exploratory cruises offering strong enrichment programs.

Saga Rose **(322/584; EUROPEAN/FILIPINO/350; 620 FEET/24,474 TONS)**

Saga Ruby **(376/655; EUROPEAN/FILIPINO/380; 627 FEET/24,492 TONS)**

Saga Ruby and *Saga Rose,* essentially sister ships, provide one of the few traditional cruising experiences left on the high seas that is the antithesis of the mass-market megaship experience. The atmosphere is genteel and subdued inside and out on deck. You won't find art auctions, loud entertainment, inches of gold for sale, pool games, or even a casino. Think enjoying a good book in the library or a deck chair, an intense game of team trivia, serenaded afternoon tea, and a glass of port following the evening meal.

The vast majority of passengers will always be British, mostly ages 65 and older—people who have been successful financially and now have the time and money to travel. While Saga cruising is a highly social experience, some come for a quiet time and like to read and dine at a table for two. Anglophile North Americans who like a traditional but not stuffy atmosphere will enjoy the lifestyle of these two ships. Walking aboard, one enters a British-style boutique hotel with rich colors and handsome wood paneling.

The main dining rooms seem larger in scale than the rest of the ship but they are designed to take the full complement of passengers and top officers at one sitting, the later hosting tables on formal nights. The *Saga Rose*'s dining room is first seen through a glass wall between the foyer and restaurant while descending the main staircase. A two-deck-high center section, punctuated with huge chandeliers, stretches the length of the handsome space. The *Saga Ruby*'s main restaurant has a small raised section and hence is not as dramatically impressive.

Tables of two, four, six, and eight are reserved for dinner for the entire cruise, while breakfast and lunch provide open seating. Wine selections begin below $20 and bar drinks are reasonably priced, beginning at less that $3. The hotel staff is largely Filipino and many have worked with Saga Cruises since its beginning.

Because most passengers are British, the menu entrées include veal chop, chicken breast, grilled fillet of beef, and roast halibut with appetizers such as asparagus tips with Parma ham and curried carrot and parsnip soup. An international cheese board is a popular alternative dessert. Preparation and presentation are consistently good.

Saga Rose's Lido buffet, located aft of the **Ballroom,** has a superior layout to the more constricted facility on the *Saga Ruby.* Seating is available inside, and in good weather, the open deck provides additional tables under umbrellas. There are daily specials geared to the cruising regions and a delightful and sometimes quite elaborate dessert spread following the evening show.

The most attractive public space on both ships is the semicircular **Britannia Lounge,** where the windows arc 180 degrees. The room sweeps upward toward the bow, and the perimeter seating is raised above the circular center section occupied by additional chairs, a dance floor, and bandstand. Readers who like a light airy space gravitate here during the day, and at 4 p.m. a popular (and proper) afternoon tea with scones and clotted cream and those English-style crustless sandwiches takes place to the accompaniment of live music. After dinner, the room takes on a restful glow from the bands of recessed ceiling lights as passengers gather for after-dinner drinks and classical concerts.

The high-ceilinged **Ballroom** is just that, a throwback to the day when the main evening entertainment was dancing to a good band. Gentlemen hosts are on hand before and after dinner to give the ladies a twirl. Passengers today expect to be entertained, so the room hosts vocalists, instrumentalists, small acts, and local groups who come aboard in port. In the afternoon, an informal buffet-style tea extravaganza takes place and being a British ship, it is extremely well attended.

The **North Cape Bar** on the *Saga Rose* and **South Cape Bar** on the *Saga Ruby,* located portside, provide a cozy setting for drinks and a pianist. Just around the corner, a traditional theater is used for screening first-run films and hosting special interest lectures and the Sunday interdenominational worship service. The library offers a very good collection with high-back chairs for reading along the starboard side gallery. Both ships have a card room and gift shop. Facing aft over the stern, *Saga Rose's* two-tiered pair of rooms provides a computer learning center with Internet access on the upper level and the **Polaris Club,** used for trivia quizzes and a nightclub, one deck below. On the *Saga Ruby,* the upper level becomes a specialty restaurant in the evening.

Because the ships are older, the cabins vary greatly even within the same category, so have a careful look at the deck plan or ask someone who knows the ship well. One of the best features is 60 single cabins (small) on the *Saga*

Rose and 70 on the *Saga Ruby;* hence, the line attracts many passengers who are on their own or with a friend but do not wish to share a cabin.

The largest cabins and suites are located on the **Promenade Deck** and the two decks of cabins added during the Norwegian America Cruises era. Some of the two dozen balcony cabins look over, around, or between the lifeboats; they are marked in the brochures. Cabins are furnished with flat-screen television, DVD player, radio, direct-dial phone, hair dryer, 24-hour room service and fresh fruit, stocked refrigerator, and video in categories C and up. The great majority have bath with tub as well as shower. Originally designed for long-distance cruises, storage space is more than adequate.

Daytime entertainment features individual quizzes and team trivia, dance classes, bridge instruction, computer sessions, cooking demonstrations, darts, bingo, special interest, enrichment and destination talks, and navigational bridge visits. Social gatherings are hosted for passengers traveling alone. In the evening, there are stage shows with a British-humor comedian (some jokes will translate and some won't), singers, dancers, classical concerts, ballroom dancing, sing-along, and game shows.

Outdoor deck space is more than adequate for passengers who do not take the sun for long stretches. The continuous Promenade Deck has shady recesses for reading and dozing, but the small aft-facing tiered decks are the most sought-after locations for reading or conversation while gazing down on the swimmers in the outdoor pool and over the stern to the ship's wake. Games include putting practice, table tennis, deck quoits, and shuffleboard.

As the *Saga Rose* and *Saga Ruby* were originally built to cruise in cool waters, the ships have indoor pools (rare on ships today), saunas, and steam rooms deep down in the ships, two decks below the lowest passenger cabin level. The spa is relatively small but offers a generous number of treatments. Outdoor pools are located aft on Veranda Deck.

Dress alternates between formal black tie, informal jacket and tie, and casual during in-port evenings. On formal nights, about 90% of the men will be wearing dinner jackets. During the day, unlike on American-oriented ships, you will see very few men in T-shirts or jeans or women wearing shorts during the day aboard or ashore.

Spirit of Adventure (206/352; EUROPEAN/FILIPINO/168; 457 FEET/9,570 TONS)

The *Spirit of Adventure,* which operates under a separate banner, Voyages of Discovery, was launched in 2006 on exploratory cruises accompanied by archaeologists, historians, food and wine experts, and the like. The lecturers are listed in the brochure by name and expertise for each cruise. Unlike the Saga pair, this ship takes passengers ages 19 and up; hence a separate brand.

She is a small oceangoing ship by today's standards, providing an intimate atmosphere for mature adults and multigenerational British passengers. Public rooms and dining areas are located aft and along most of the promenade deck; none have views over the bow. Passengers gather in the main lounge for the lecture program and cabaret-style entertainment and retire to the **Yacht Club** for drinks and music. The large library is a major draw, with comfortable seating, a fine selection of books and DVDs, and Internet access. The ship has no casino.

Dining is open seating at tables of four to eight places, and large picture windows afford good views while enjoying mostly British-style fare with regional dishes geared to the specific cruising region. Two decks above, **The Verandah** provides breakfast, lunch, and dinner in a casual setting.

For exercise, there is the health spa with its exercise equipment, sauna, and treatment rooms. Deck space is rather limited to a small area around the small outdoor pool aft and side promenades.

The inside and outside cabins are relatively compact and none have balconies nor baths with tub. However, no fewer than 60 are set aside for single travelers, as generous a number as on the *Saga Rose* and *Saga Ruby*. Most doubles have twin beds that cannot be moved. All come equipped with a television/DVD player and refrigerator. A nice touch is a pair of binoculars.

The *Spirit of Adventure*'s itineraries, marketed separately from Saga Cruises, include Southern Europe, Mediterranean and Black seas, and via Suez into the Indian Ocean and Southeast and East Asia. Her ice-strengthened hull allows for Arctic and Antarctic cruising.

Most Saga cruises begin and end in southern England at Southampton or Dover, where the itineraries fan out to the Baltic, Greenland, Iceland, Norway, and Scotland, and south to Iberia, the Atlantic Isles, and into the Western Mediterranean and along the North African coast. A long transatlantic cruise visits the Canadian Maritimes, the St. Lawrence River Valley, and U.S. East Coast, and an annual around-the-world cruise starts out from England in early January and returns in late April. *Saga Rose*'s and *Saga Ruby*'s deep drafts of 27 feet make them good sea vessels. The reasonable fares are virtually all-inclusive, with a choice of two excursions in each port and all gratuities.

ITINERARIES *See* Itinerary Index.

SeaDream Yacht Club
601 Brickell Key Drive, Suite 1050, Miami, FL 33131; ☎ 800-707-4911; www.seadream.com

---

SeaDream I/SeaDream II **(55/110 SCANDINAVIAN/INTERNATIONAL/89; 344 FEET/4,260 TONS)**

SeaDream Yacht Club, a venture of Seabourn Cruise Line veterans, Norwegian entrepreneur Atle Brynestad (who was Seabourn's founder) and Larry Pimentel (its former president), began operating in late 2001 and early 2002, offering seven-day summer Mediterranean and winter Caribbean cruises on the luxury twin ships *SeaDream I* and *II* (formerly *Sea Goddess I* and *II*). The twin megayachts, as the line calls them, were redesigned and refitted at Lloyd Werft's shipyard in Bremerhaven, Germany, prior to their entering service.

The handsome twins are meant to provide a totally different experience from today's typical cruise, one that more closely resembles yachting. Like yachts, the ships offer an open and unstructured ambience and provide passengers the ability to move at their own pace and to make personal choices. "No clocks, no crowds, no lines, no stress" could be the company's motto.

These are the SeaDream differences the owners cite:

- **Flexible Schedules and Itineraries** SeaDreams yachts depart their first port and arrive at their last port as scheduled, but frequently, the port calls in between are not run by a strict timetable. Captains have the authority to adjust for local opportunities. If they want to visit a small island fish market so the chef can pick up the catch of the day, that's fine. If the weather and the snorkeling are perfect in a small secluded bay and passengers want to remain longer, that's okay, too.

- **Overnight in Key Ports** Most cruise ships arrive at ports of call at about 8 a.m. and sail at 5 or 6 p.m. of the same day. SeaDream yachts overnight at such ports as Monte Carlo and St. Tropez, where the action doesn't even get started until late in the evening.

- **Officers and Staff as Guides** Passengers might visit a small-town pastry shop with the chef, go snorkeling with the captain, or go hiking, biking, or golfing with the officers. What better guides to have, SeaDream says, than those who know their sailing regions like the backs of their hands?

- **No Tuxedos or Gala Gowns** SeaDream has no dress code; rather it stresses the casual nature of yachting.

The outdoor features of *SeaDream I* and *II* include alcoves for sunning on double Balinese sun beds, a private massage tent on deck, a large-screen golf simulator, movies on deck by the outdoor swimming pool, and a water sports marina at the stern where there is equipment for kayaking, waterskiing, windsurfing, wave running, snorkeling, and Sunfish sailing. Tai chi, yoga, and aerobics classes are also offered. The Balinese beds are elevated so that you can see over the railing. We are told the beds are so dreamy, some passengers even spend the night outside under the stars on them.

Indoors, passengers have an Asian-style spa and fitness center with elliptical treadmills mounted with flat-screen televisions, as well as free weights and recumbent bikes. A personal trainer is available. Spa treatment can now be booked online at **www.seadreamspa.com**. The spa, open from 8 a.m. to 8 p.m. daily, offers an extensive range of Asian treatments such as traditional Thai massage, shiatsu massage, and Javanese body scrub. All spa offerings are for men as well as women. The spa also operates a salon for manicures, pedicures, and other beauty treatments.

The ships also have a **Main Lounge** with a 61-inch flat-screen television, a piano bar, casino, and a library with books, CDs, DVDs, and computer outlets. Laptop computers are available. Passengers are given their own onboard e-mail address.

Each ship accommodates from 47 to 55 couples, depending on the configuration. Of the 55 cabins, all but one are Yacht Club category with 195 square feet. Sixteen of these are convertible to Commodore Club cabins of 390 square feet with his and her bathroom facilities and a dining area accommodating four. The 450-square-foot Owner's Suite has a bedroom, a bathroom with a tub and separate shower with a view of the sea, a living room and dining area, and a guest bathroom.

All cabins are Internet-ready and have an entertainment center with a flat-screen television, CD and DVD systems with an extensive selection of movies, and other offerings. A personal jukebox with more than 100 digital music programs is also available. All bathrooms have multiple-jet massage showers and lighted magnifying mirrors.

The cuisine is guaranteed to be top rate, with such luxuries as having all the bread baked aboard and including specialty breads such as multigrain, sourdough, pumpernickel, and focaccia.

Staff and crew number 89; most have been sailing on their respective ships for several years. The yachts, suitable for small meetings and incentive groups, are very popular for charter.

In 2006, SeaDream made an irresistible offer to its passengers sailing on voyages out of Rome—an opportunity to drive a Ferrari. The adventure got such heavy response that there weren't enough Ferraris available. But not to worry. SeaDream is continuing to offer the program.

SeaDream makes a specialty of calling at new ports and ports where large ships cannot go. In 2007, the line added such new European ports as the Greek island of Paxoi, Molyvos on Lesvos, Phytagorion on Samos, Naousa on Paros, and Kotor, a UNESCO World Heritage site, in Montenegro. In 2008, the cruise line plans to add more stops in Croatia on cruises from Venice. In the Caribbean, SeaDream has added Anegada, BVI; Barbuda, sister island of Antigua; Montserrat; St. Bart; and the Puerto Rican islands of Vieques and Culebrita, a wildlife refuge.

ITINERARIES *See* Itinerary Index.

Star Cruises
Star Cruises Terminal, P.O. Box No. 288, Pulau Indah, Pelabuhan Barat, 42009 Port Klang, Malaysia; ☎ 60-3-3101-1313; fax 60-3-3101-1406; www.starcruises.com

Malaysian-based Star Cruises, owned by Genting Group, a publicly traded investment group, is a phenomenon in Far Eastern cruising. Launched in 1993 with two ships, today it's the third-largest cruise operator in the world, with 22 ships in service (and four more new builds in the pipeline) under the Star Cruises, Norwegian Cruise Line/NCL America, Orient Lines, and Cruise Ferries brands. Five of the Star-brand ships operate in Asia year-round, while the sixth, the *SuperStar Libra,* splits its time between India and the Mediterranean. Star's strengths are its food, variety of entertainment, family-friendly features, and friendly (and patient) crew, which knows how to cater to a diverse mix of passengers.

Star Pisces (780/1,020; SCANDINAVIAN/INTERNATIONAL; 581 FEET/40,053 TONS)

The ship is a former Baltic ferry designed for the regional Asian market. The ship sails on one-night cruises from Hong Kong to the South China Sea, catering largely to families and first-time cruisers. The ship is exceedingly well maintained and has no fewer than ten food and beverages options.

Child-care facilities are extensive. Activities and entertainment are geared to the whole family, with karaoke, table tennis and other sports, a library, spa, boutiques, and big-name performances. The ship earns high marks for its food and incredibly friendly crew.

SuperStar Gemini **(400/800; INTERNATIONAL/470; 538 FEET/19,093 TONS)**

Built in 1992 in Spain for more than $100 million, *SuperStar Gemini* (the former *Crown Jewel*) was the first of the SuperStar group launched in 1995 and offers mostly seven-night cruises from Singapore to Southeast Asian ports. She has a continental restaurant plus an international inside/outside buffet, several bars and entertainment venues, swimming pool, gym and sauna, shops, Internet room, and children's center.

SuperStar Virgo **(980/1,960; INTERNATIONAL/1,100; 879 FEET/76,800 TONS)**

SuperStar Virgo arrived in 1999. A classic megaliner on par with NCL's newest ships, she has multiple Vegas-style entertainment lounges, nine restaurants (four serving exclusively Asian fare), and excellent facilities for children. *SuperStar Virgo* does a good job catering to both Asian and non-Asian clientele. Singaporean Chinese and Malays are in the majority on most cruises, followed by a sizable contingent of Indians from the Subcontinent and Australians, and a handful of Europeans, North Americans, and other Asians.

A public observation area near the bridge offers interesting information and videos about the navigation and engine operations. The ship offers a casino, spa, and fitness center, shops, library and Internet center, and an impressive indoor/outdoor children's space that includes an outdoor play area with themed pool. Cabins are on the small side, but are comfortable and stylish, and offer extras like tea- and coffeemakers.

The ship's cruising speed is a zippy 25.5 knots, enabling her to include more ports of call on her itineraries. She sails on one- to five-night cruises to Malaysia and Thailand, round-trip from Singapore.

MegaStar Aries/MegaStar Taurus **(36/72; INTERNATIONAL; 270 FEET/3,264 TONS)**

The *MegaStars* are the most deluxe of Star's brands. Formerly *Aurora I* and *II*, the ships were among the most luxurious small ships built in the 1990s. The ships each carry only 72 passengers and 80 crew members and operate short cruises year-round from Malaysia, Singapore, and Kuala Lumpur. They are most often chartered to corporations, groups, or wedding parties.

ITINERARIES *See* Itinerary Index.

Travel Dynamics International

132 East 70th Street, New York, NY 10021; ☎ 212-517-7555 or 800-257-5767; fax 212-774-1545; www.traveldynamicsinternational.com

Travel Dynamics International specializes in educational and cultural cruises, aboard small deluxe ships. The customized programs are designed for well-traveled, destination-oriented individuals who want a learning experience but don't want to forgo their comfort. Itineraries span the globe and include exotic as well as familiar destinations. Lecturers and academics knowledgeable about the destination accompany the cruises. The company currently operates two small ships described below.

Callisto (17/34; GREEK/EUROPEAN/18; 164 FEET/435 TONS)

This small luxury yacht, built in Germany, underwent comprehensive renovation and refurbishment prior to her debut in 2000. The ship has 17 outside cabins, 11 with large panoramic windows, and 6 on Daphne Deck with three large portholes each. Public areas include a spacious lounge, a library, and a dining room accommodating all passengers at one open seating. There are two broad decks for sunbathing and dining alfresco and a swimming platform at the vessel's stern.

All cabins are air-conditioned with generous storage space and have full- or queen-size beds, marble bathroom with shower radio, telephone, refrigerator, and television with VCR/DVD. The four-deck ship has a draft of eight feet and a speed of 14 knots. It is equipped with Zodiac landing craft. The bridge is outfitted with state-of-the-art navigational and communications equipment.

Callisto flies the Greek flag and is equipped with the latest navigational instruments, including satellite communication systems. The ship offers e-mail service. She sails to the Adriatic, Greek Islands, the Mediterranean, Turkey, and West Africa.

Corinthian II (57/114; EUROPEAN/75; 297 FEET/4,200 TONS)

The deluxe, all-suite *Corinthian II* offers a classic yachtlike atmosphere and fine accommodations. Originally built in 1992, the ship was redecorated and refurbished in 2005. *Corinthian II* accommodates all guests in 57 outside suites, each affording sea views. Suites have a sitting area, television/DVD, minifridge, safe, and other amenities, as well as a marble-appointed bathroom. Several suites include private balconies accessed via sliding glass doors. Fresh flowers and fruit provide a bright touch in every suite.

The *Corinthian II*'s spacious and finely decorated public areas include a library stocked with books related to the itinerary and other volumes. Four computer terminals with Internet access are accessible for e-mail. The ship has an elegant lounge as well as **The Club,** a space with picture windows for panoramic views and a relaxing place to enjoy musical arrangements by the ship's pianist. The restaurant serves fine cuisine prepared by European chefs and can accommodate all guests at a single unassigned seating or alfresco on the wide Sun Deck, which is specially equipped for outdoor dining. Other facilities onboard include a gym, beauty salon, Sun Deck with whirlpool, and elevator serving all passenger decks. *Corinthian II* has an ice-strengthened hull for voyages into Antarctic waters and is equipped with a fleet of Zodiac inflatable craft for excursions ashore.

ITINERARIES *See* Itinerary Index.

The World/ResidenSea, Ltd.
**5200 Blue Lagoon Drive, Suite 790, Miami, FL 33126; ☎ 800-970-6601
(North America rentals); 305-259-5151; fax 305-269-1058;
www.residensea.com**

The World **(165 RESIDENCES: 106 APARTMENTS;
19 STUDIO APARTMENTS; 40 VERANDA STUDIOS;
NORWEGIAN/320; 644 FEET/43,000 TONS)**

The World, the first residential cruise ship ever built, was launched from Oslo in March 2002 to begin her cruising odyssey and confounded the skeptics (us included), who said it would never happen. Five weeks later, she sailed to America on her maiden voyage.

Billed as the world's first residential resort community at sea continuously circumnavigating the globe, *The World* has 165 residences, most available for rent. A staff of about 250 attends them.

Here's what she offers on her 12 decks: two- and three-bedroom private apartments ranging from 1,106 to 3,242 square feet, with decor by five top designers and fully furnished down to the Christofle flatware and Wedgewood china; four theme restaurants featuring French, Mediterranean, and Asian cuisine, plus a delicatessen; enrichment activities such as lectures and seminars; full-size tennis court; a retractable marina for water activities; two pools; a top-deck, open-air, full-shot driving range, 40-course golf simulators, real grass putting greens, two artificial greens, a sand bunker, and a PGA-certified golf director; a fitness center; the Swiss spa **Clinique La Prairie;** and an art gallery, casino, Internet cafe, library, two conference rooms, nightclub, meditation chapel, and several boutiques. Oh, yes, and three emergency wards, full-time doctor and nurse, as well as a telemedicine hookup with Mount Sinai-Cedars Hospital in Miami Beach. Activities on board are deliberately kept to a minimum, but there are some typical cruise pastimes such as bridge and other games, trivia, lectures, movies, afternoon tea, and enrichment programs.

Passengers enjoy all this while traveling the world: 140 ports in more than 40 countries with planned itineraries of 6 to 17 days, and attending such special events as America's Cup in Valencia, Spain, and a New Year's Eve gala in Funchal, Portugal. And the price (ah, yes, if you have to ask): apartments range from $825,000 to $7.3 million, with an average price of $2.8 million. And then there's the annual maintenance fee, which includes housekeeping, and varies based upon square footage. As of June 2006, all of the apartments in the ship's original inventory have been sold.

Who, you ask, bought these apartments? According to its management company, they are home owners who have two or three residences, are age 55, and are first-generation entrepreneurs who have built their worth as computer-chip makers, real-estate developers, and the like. They are very active, have an affinity for the sea, maybe own a yacht or have cruised a lot, and they guard their privacy.

North Americans constitute the largest number of buyers, followed by Norwegians, Brits, Germans, Australians, and Swiss. Some owners stay aboard for three months a year, just as they would, say, at their condo in Aspen or their villa in the south of France.

The World's management says the ship is for people who hate having to pack a suitcase to travel, who really miss sleeping in their own beds when they're away, and who long to see the world without ever having to leave the comforts of home. It seems such a simple idea that it's surprising no one ever floated it before.

The apartment owners bought out the original developers in 2006, and now they own the ship. ResidenSea, Ltd., remains the managing company of *The World*. Rentals can be booked through travel agents or ResidenSea. Rentals are for a minimum six nights; rates begin at approximately $1,300 per person double and include onboard dining, beverages, port charges, gratuities, and taxes.

ITINERARIES   *See* Itinerary Index.

PART THREE

CRUISING
ALTERNATIVES

RIVER *and* BARGE CRUISES

A RIVER CRUISE IS NOT ONLY a different way to see a country, it's a different country you will see. Whether you sail down the Danube or the Yangtze, up the Hudson or the Nile, or float on European channels or the Erie Canal, the cruise will be a new travel experience, even if you have visited the same area by land.

The river cruise most familiar to U.S. travelers is probably steamboating on the Mississippi, but there are many kinds of river cruises, their character shaped by the location and nature of the waterway. An adventure cruise on the Amazon, for example, is quite different from barging in Burgundy. Nonetheless, river cruises share certain characteristics, and all are light-years from an ocean cruise.

To begin with, boats (a vessel is a ship on the ocean, but a boat on a river) offering river cruises are small. Most boats carry 100 to 200 passengers, although some of the new riverboats accommodate 250 or more, and Majestic America's *American Queen* takes 436 passengers. Barges that glide along small canals and waterways are much smaller, taking as few as 6 and never more than 24 passengers.

The small size of vessels and the nature of the waterways provide an intimate look at the cruise locale, heightening the sense of place and history in a way ocean liners never can. The destination, not the boat, is the main attraction on a river cruise.

Cabins are small but comfortable. The ambience is informal, the dress casual. Except on some large riverboats, nightly entertainment is absent. Passengers are left to their own devices, and many rediscover the pleasure of conversation and friendship.

RIVER AND BARGE CRUISES IN EUROPE

RIVER CRUISES ARE AVAILABLE ON MAJOR RIVERS worldwide, but the largest selection—an estimated 400 passenger riverboats—is in

Europe on the Danube, Rhine, Rhone, Seine, and Volga, where rivers have been thoroughfares of commerce and culture for centuries. The growth in recent years has been phenomenal.

European cruises—most between April and November—take you to the Continent's great cities through beautiful scenery laced with ancient forts, mighty cathedrals, and storybook castles. They dock in the heart of a different town each day. Some river cruise lines include sightseeing tours in their cruise fare. If not, passengers may book optional tours for a fee or they can easily sightsee on their own.

River cruises reveal Europe the way it was meant to be seen. Almost all historic buildings were built facing the river, so when the boat docks in front of Pillnitz Palace on the Elbe, for example, passengers enter the way guests of Augustus the Strong did centuries ago.

Some itineraries overnight in port, allowing passengers to attend local shows or dine ashore. Others sail at night so passengers wake refreshed for the next day of sightseeing.

More than a dozen companies offer such cruises; the largest, Viking River Cruises, is typical in its itineraries. Its fleet of 25 ships sails the length of the Rhine, as well as the Elbe, Moselle, Rhone, Saône, and Seine. The Danube and Rhine-Main-Danube Canal were added in 1994, when the North and Black seas were linked for the first time.

Riverboats and barges have completely different styles. Canals and smaller rivers deep in the countryside are traversed by barges, which glide gently through some of the most beautiful and historic areas of England and Europe. The pace is so leisurely (three or four knots per hour) that passengers can get off to walk in the woods or bike in the village and not be left behind. The tortoiselike pace, the utter peace and relaxation, are for some the best vacation they ever had. For others, it's like watching grass grow.

By day, passengers lounge on deck, play cards, read, and watch the boat navigate the locks. They can walk or bike, discovering interesting places and friendly people, and reboard at the next lock. The price usually includes a choice of guided tours by minibus or bicycle to nearby castles, wineries, and medieval towns.

Hotel barges, as they are known, are like floating country inns. They vary in size, carrying from 6 to 51 passengers on cruises of 3, 6, or 13 days. Cabins are small and bathrooms are tiny, but the barges, such as those of French Country Waterways, are luxurious. Many serve outstanding gourmet cuisine prepared by Le Cordon Bleu chefs. Regional wines, normally included in the cruise price, flow generously. The atmosphere is very informal—and very romantic.

The following is a sampling of the offerings from companies with U.S. offices or representatives. Note that several companies offer the same boats; agreements may not be exclusive.

Note: In parentheses after each boat name is information (where available) about the number of cabins and passengers; officers and crew; and the boat's length (cabins/passengers; officers/crew; boat length).

Abercrombie & Kent, Inc.
1520 Kensington Road, Suite 212, Oak Brook, IL 60523-2156; ☎ 630-954-2944 or 800-323-7308; fax 630-954-3324; www.abercrombiekent.com

(*Also see* Abercrombie & Kent under Yangtze River Cruises and Nile River Cruises, all later in this chapter.)

Absoluut 2 (4/8; FRENCH/BRITISH/4; 128 FEET)
Six nights Burgundy-Champagne or Holland.

Actief (6/11; BRITISH/5; 100 FEET)
Six nights on the River Thames.

Alouette (3/6; FRENCH/BRITISH/4; 98 FEET)
Six nights on the Canal du Midi.

Amaryllis (4/8; FRENCH/BRITISH/6; 129 FEET)
Six nights in Burgundy and Beaujolais.

Anacoluthe (24/50; FRENCH/13; 210 FEET)
 Six nights in Normandy and Ile-de-France.

Anjodi (4/8; FRENCH/BRITISH/4; 100 FEET)
Six nights on the Canal du Midi and in Provence.

Charlemagne (16/32; FRENCH/12; 217 FEET)
Six nights in Holland and on the Moselle, Neckar, and Rhine rivers in Germany.

Fleur de Lys (3/6; FRENCH/BRITISH/6; 129 FEET)
Six nights in Burgundy and Beaujolais.

Hirondelle (4/8; FRENCH/BRITISH/4; 128 FEET)
Six nights in Burgundy and the Franche-Comté.

L'Art de Vivre (4/8; FRENCH/BRITISH/4; 100 FEET)
Six nights in Burgundy.

La Belle Epoque (6/12; FRENCH/BRITISH/5; 128 FEET)
 Six nights in Burgundy and Chablis.

La Bonne Amie (4/8; FRENCH/5; 126 FEET)
Six nights in the Upper Loire.

La Bonne Humeur (4/8; FRENCH/5; 126 FEET)
Six nights in Ile-de-France and the Upper Loire.

La Nouvelle Etoile (4/8; FRENCH/DUTCH/5; 129 FEET)
Six nights in Holland or France (Northern Burgundy, Champagne, Alsace-Lorraine) or Moselle region in Germany.

Le Bon Vivant (4/8; FRENCH/4; 126 FEET)
Six nights in the Upper Loire.

L'Impressionniste **(6/12; FRENCH/BRITISH/5; 126 FEET)**

Six nights in Provence, the Camargue, and Languedoc.

Libellule **(10/20; FRENCH/7; 128 FEET)**

Six nights in Southern Burgundy and Beaujolais.

Litote **(10/20; FRENCH/7; 128 FEET)**

Six nights in central Burgundy.

Lorraine **(11/22; FRENCH/7; 128 FEET)**

Six nights in Alsace-Lorraine.

Magna Carta **(4/8; BRITISH/4; 117 FEET)**

Six nights on the River Thames.

Marjorie II **(6/12; FLEMISH/5 TO 6; 128 FEET)**

Six nights Holland-Belgium, Northern Burgundy.

Napoleon **(6/12; FRENCH/BRITISH/6 TO 7; 129 FEET)**

Six nights in the Vallee du Rhone and Provence.

Prosperite **(4/8; FRENCH/5; 128 FEET)**

Six nights in central Burgundy.

River Cloud **AND** *River Cloud II (see descriptions later in this section)*

Roi Soleil **(3/6; FRENCH/4; 98 FEET)**

Six nights in Provence, the Camargue, Languedoc, and Canal du Midi.

Savoir Faire **(6/12; BRITISH/FRENCH/DUTCH/7; 132 FEET)**

Six nights in Holland, Upper Loire and Burgundy, or Champagne.

Scottish Highlander **(4/8; BRITISH/4; 117 FEET)**

Six nights on the Caledonian Canal in the Scottish Highlands.

Serenite **(6/12; GERMAN/6; 126 FEET)**

Six nights in Germany (Berlin and Mecklenburg lakes) or France (Burgundy, Loire Valley, or Provence and the Camargue).

Shannon Princess II **(5/10; IRISH/5; 105 FEET)**

Six nights on the River Shannon and Lough Derg in Ireland.

Avalon Waterways
5301 South Federal Circle, Littleton, CO 80123; ☎ 877-380-1540 or 877-797-8791; www.avalonwaterways.com

Avalon Artistry/Avalon Poetry **(87/84, 2/4 SUITES; 178/176 PASSENGERS; CREW OF 43; 426 FEET)**

Avalon Imagery/Avalon Tranquility **(81, 4 JUNIOR SUITES; 170 PASSENGERS; CREW OF 43; 443 FEET)**

Avalon Tapestry **(80, 2 JUNIOR SUITES; 164 PASSENGERS; CREW OF 43; 443 FEET)**

Avalon Waterways, a division of Globus Tours, offers a new generation of river cruise boats built specifically for the North American market, with nonsmoking interiors and English-speaking crews. The boats feature some of the largest cabins and suites available on river cruises, with comfortable beds and large windows to view the passing scenery. European cuisine tailored to North American tastes is served at an open single seating in a spacious restaurant; wine is included with all onboard dinners; coffee and tea are available throughout the day. The company says its enrichment program is "geared for the way North Americans like to travel, with lively itineraries, time for individual discovery, and onboard entertainment."

The well-appointed boats have a two-story lobby, lit by a central glass skylight, and both the dining room and lounge have floor-to-ceiling windows with panoramic views. The boats are equipped with state-of-the-art technology and have a **Sky Bar, Club Lounge,** exercise room with fitness equipment, walking track, whirlpool, hair salon, massage service, and gift shop. The Sky Deck is fitted with newly developed shade systems, which are lowered when passing under a bridge then promptly raised again.

All cabins are outside ones. Some have picture windows, while 70% have floor-to-ceiling sliding glass doors to enjoy the passing scenery. The *Poetry* has four junior suites (two on the *Artistry*), each 258 square feet, and standard cabins of 172 square feet. On the *Artistry,* for example, all cabins have a granite bathroom, ample closet, radio, telephone, satellite television, minibar, safe, and hair dryer. Beds may be configured as twins or one queen; connecting cabins are available.

The cruise-tour itineraries range from 9 days in Holland and Belgium, to 12 days on the Lower Danube/Black Sea cruising from Budapest to Bucharest (with two nights in Budapest), to a cruise from Nuremberg to Budapest with a three-night stay in Prague. Other cruise-and-land combinations from 9 to 20 days are available with time spent in places such as Paris or Berlin. Discounts for AARP members are available.

The company also offers Nile and Yangtze river and Galápagos cruises.

The Barge Lady
101 West Grand Avenue, Suite 200, Chicago, IL 60610; ☎ 312-245-0900 or 800-880-0071; fax 312-245-0952; www.bargelady.com

A variety of barges on the canals of Belgium, France, Germany, Great Britain, Holland, Ireland, and Scotland; multigenerational, small-group, and wine-tasting cruises featured. More recently, the company has added European rivers (*River Cloud* on the Danube, Rhine, and others), and Alaska, Pacific Northwest, and Mexico (American Safari Cruises).

Crown Blue Line
980 Awald Road, Suite 302, Annapolis, MD 21403; ☎ 888-355-9491; fax 410-280-2406; www.crownblueline.com

Specializes in self-drive boats with a large fleet of small boats operating in England, Ireland, Scotland; extensively in France; and others in Belgium,

Italy, Germany, and Holland. The fleet consists of about three dozen types of boats and more than 600 vessels. The company is affiliated with Le Boat, Inc. (see listing later in this section).

Peter Deilmann Cruises
1800 Diagonal Road, Suite 170, Alexandria, VA 22314; ☎ 703-549-1741 or 800-348-8287; fax 703-549-7924; www.deilmann-cruises.com

This European line markets nine riverboats and the luxury ocean liner *Deutschland*. In addition to traditional cruises, the line has special-interest ones for music, golf, gardens, and cycling as well as hiking and wellness theme cruises on its weekly cruises on the Elbe, Danube, Neckar, Rhine, Moselle, Oder, Rhône, Saône, Seine, Vltava, and other rivers from late March through early November.

Starting in March 2008, Peter Deilmann Cruises will expand its no-smoking restrictions on its nine riverboats from all cabins, corridors, and restaurants to include all areas inside the vessels without exception. Smoking will be permitted on open decks only.

Casanova **(48/96; GERMAN/EUROPEAN; 338 FEET)**

Built in 2001, this deluxe boat offers spacious outside cabins with French doors on the upper deck and picture windows on the lower. All cabins have a private bathroom, telephone, radio, desk, and chair. Facilities include a single-seating dining room, lounge, bar, library, dance floor, boutique, and beauty salon. The boat sails seven-night cruises on the Danube, Moselle, Rhine, Dutch and Belgian canals, and Rhine-Main Canal.

Cezanne **(50/100; EUROPEAN; 356 FEET)**

Built in 1993, this boat was purchased by the line and completely renovated in 2000 with elegant furnishings and a panoramic dining room and lounge. Twin cabins are 162 square feet; queen cabins, 178 square feet. In 2005, the boat introduced weekly cruises on the Seine River, sailing from Paris and Rouen on two different itineraries.

Danube Princess **(94/198; EUROPEAN/GERMAN; 364 FEET)**

Facilities include an outdoor swimming pool, single-seating dining room, two bars, conference room, library, gift shop, and beauty salon. Cabins have a private bathroom, telephone, radio, and television. Between March and early November, the ship sails on seven-day Danube cruises from Munich to Austria, Hungary, Serbia, and Romania to the Black Sea.

Dresden **(53/106; EUROPEAN/GERMAN; 320 FEET)**

Facilities include a single-seating dining room, bar, gift shop, beauty salon, fitness equipment, sauna, library, infirmary, and laundry room. All cabins have a private shower and toilet, telephone, radio, television, and hair dryer. *Dresden* sails seven-night Elbe cruises from Hamburg and Dresden, visiting Meissen, Magdeburg, and Wittenberg.

Frederic Chopin **(41/79; EUROPEAN/GERMAN; 272 FEET)**

The *Frederic Chopin*, a luxury vessel that debuted in 2002, sails on seven-night cruises on the Elbe between Prague and Potsdam (Berlin) and five cruises on the Oder River in Germany and Poland between Potsdam and Stralsund. All cabins on the upper deck have French doors.

Heidelberg **(56/110; EUROPEAN; 360 FEET)**

Introduced in 2004, the ship has a fitness center and spa with sauna, steam room, and massage facilities. All cabins on two upper decks have French doors, and four cabins on the lower cabin deck have large portholes. Cabins are a spacious 190 square feet. She sails on the Rhine and Moselle rivers, Rhine-Main Canal, and Dutch and Belgium canals in Belgium, France, Germany, Holland, and Switzerland from April through October.

Katharina von Bora **(41/79; EUROPEAN/GERMAN; 272 FEET)**

Double- and twin-bedded cabins have French doors on upper decks, picture windows on the lower deck. The vessel operates various itineraries on the Elbe River between Potsdam (Berlin) and Prague. She also sails five cruises on the Oder River in Germany and Poland between Potsdam and Stralsund.

Mozart **(100/200; EUROPEAN/GERMAN; 396 FEET)**

This deluxe boat, refurbished in 2006, has large, all-outside cabins with spacious private bathrooms, television, minibar, hair dryer, and telephone. Facilities include a new indoor swimming pool, whirlpool, sauna, and fitness center. From March to October, the boat sails seven-night Danube cruises departing from Passau and calling at Bratislava, Budapest, Duernstein, Esztergom, Melk, and Vienna. Classical music cruises are also scheduled in April and October.

Princesse de Provence **(70/140; GERMAN/EUROPEAN; 363 FEET)**

Refurbished in 2005, all cabins have a private bathroom, telephone, and radio, and upper deck cabins have French doors. Hair dryer and terry robes available on request. Facilities include single-seating dining room, lounge, two bars, library, infirmary, gift shop. Between March and November, the boat sails seven-night cruises round-trip from Lyon or between Arles and Lyon calling at Chalon-sur-Saône, Macon, Viviers, Trevoux, and Avignon.

Elegant Cruises & Tours
24 Vanderventer Avenue, Port Washington, NY 11050; ☎ 516-767-9302 or 800-683-6767; fax 516-767-9303; www.elegantcruises.com or www.seacloud.com

River Cloud **(45/90; EUROPEAN; 360 FEET)**

Launched in 1996, the splendidly appointed *River Cloud* is one of the finest boats on European waterways. Interiors convey 1930s luxury reminiscent of the Orient Express. She offers the impeccable service and fine cuisine for which her famous sister ship, *Sea Cloud,* is known.

The elegant dining room serves meals in a single, open seating in a relaxed, friendly atmosphere. Breakfast and lunch are buffet style; dinner is served at tables. Menus feature continental specialties and complimentary fine wines, beer, and soft drinks. The centerpiece of the handsome lounge—encircled by windows at the bow,—is a seven-foot Steinway grand piano. It's much in use during afternoon tea and music cruises, when renowned pianists and opera stars are aboard. Amenities include a library, boutique, hair salon, exercise room, sauna, putting green, and large-scale chessboard. All cabins have telephone, radio, television, air-conditioning, safe, and marble bathroom with shower and hair dryer. The Dutch-built *River Cloud* sails on the Danube, Main, Moselle, and Rhine, April through October.

River Cloud II (44/88; EUROPEAN; 338 FEET)

Launched in late spring 2001, this boat sails the Danube River Valley. Her public rooms include a lounge and library, restaurant, boutique, and hair salon. The air-conditioned ship has 13 junior suites with windows, 20 double-bed cabins with portholes, and 10 twin-bedded cabins. All have direct-dial telephone, television with DVD player, radio and music channels, minibar, emergency button, and bath with shower, hair dryer, bathrobes, and toiletries. A fruit basket, half bottle of Champagne, bottled water, and soft drinks are replenished daily.

River Cloud II operates on the Upper Danube and Lower Danube to the Danube Delta from April through October.

The cruises are also sold through Dailey-Thorp Travel of New York, ☎ 212-307-1555; Abercrombie & Kent, ☎ 800-323-7308; and other U.S. companies.

In addition to the European river boats described above, Elegant Cruises owns and operates the *Andrea* and the *Monet* and also markets *Galapagos Explorer II* in the Galápagos, as well as the *Sea Cloud,* which spends winter in the Caribbean and summer in the Mediterranean, Adriatic, and Aegean (see chapter on Sailing Ships).

The handsome 106-passenger *Andrea* began her career as the popular *Harald Jarl* of Norwegian Coastal Voyages, where she developed a following over the years. Purchased and extensively renovated in 2003 by Elegant Cruises, the re-christened *Andrea* provides an intimacy and classic cruising often lacking in larger vessels. The ship's cabins are tastefully decorated with lower beds (either separated or connected) and private facilities. The ship also has ample deck space, ideal for viewing beautiful scenery, comfortable public areas and lounges, a restaurant, and outdoor cafe. She operates expedition cruises in Antarctica from November through March, with the balance of the year spent in the Adriatic, Baltic, British Isles, and Mediterranean.

The deluxe *Monet,* with 31 outside cabins, is the ideal size for calling at small island ports and coastal towns of the Adriatic. In 2007, the ship marks her seventh year of cruising along the Dalmatian coast. Weekly departures from Venice are offered from April through October; early spring and late fall value cruises are leisurely 14-night programs that include all shore excursions.

Les Etoiles
**c/o Karen Bull Associates, 3355 Lenox Road, Suite 750, Atlanta, GA 30326;
☎ 800-280-1492 or 404-237-1841**

La Nouvelle Etoiles (4 SUITES/8; FRENCH; 128 FEET)

Seven- and 13-day trips to Belgium, France, Germany and Holland, April through September.

European Waterways/Go Barging

c/o 35 Wharf Road, Wraysbury, Staines, Middlesex, TW19 5JQ, England;
☎ 44-0-1784-482-439 or 800-394-8630; fax 44-0-1784 483-072;
www.gobarging.com

*Actief/Alouette/Anjodi/Athos/Hirondelle/L'Arte de Vivre, La Belle Epoque/
La Dolce Vita/La Reine Pedauque/L'Impressionniste/Magna Carta/Nymphea/
Savoir Faire/Scottish Highlander/Serenite/Shannon Princess/St. Louis* **(3 TO
6/6 TO 12; FRENCH/FRENCH AND ENGLISH; 80 TO 128 FEET)**

The company offers six-night cruises on the rivers and canals of Belgium,
the Czech Republic, England, France, Germany, Holland, Ireland, Italy, and
Scotland. European Waterways also owns a medley of barges and riverboats
for 6 to 12 passengers in Scotland and France. All cruises can be geared to
special interests, such as golf, sportfishing, horseback riding, fine dining,
cycling, wildlife, poetry, and more.

The company has an extensive Web site with pictures and descriptions
of its boats, itineraries, and virtual tours, as well as links to its theme cruises
and newsletter.

French Country Waterways

P.O. Box 2195, Duxbury, MA 02331; ☎ 781-934-2454 or 800-222-1236;
fax 781-934-9048; www.fcwl.com

As its name implies, French Country Waterways' five boats, or hotel barges,
as they are known, concentrate on the small rivers and canals that crisscross
France, through a navigational system that began in the early 17th century.
Unlike many barge and riverboat operators, French Country Waterways
owns and operates all its fleet. Lunches and dinners are accompanied by
Grand Cru and Premier Cru wines and all cruises include a dinner ashore in
a Michelin-starred restaurant. The line's handsome brochure details each of
the barges and its itineraries with descriptions and photographs that convey an accurate and inviting look at its cruises.

Adrienne **(6 SUITES/12; FRENCH/ENGLISH; 128 FEET)** Upper Loire Valley.

Esprit **(9/18; FRENCH/ENGLISH/7; 128 FEET)**
Cote d'Or wine region (Burgundy Canal, Saône River, Canal du Centre from
Dijon to St. Leger-sur-Dheune).

Horizon II **(4/8; FRENCH/ENGLISH/6; 128 FEET)**
Two Upper Burgundy itineraries (Burgundy Canal between Tanley and
Pouillenay; and Tanley and Auxerre).

Nenuphar **(6/12; FRENCH/ENGLISH/6; 128 FEET)**
Champagne region. The boat was relaunched in 2007 after being renovated.

Princess **(4/8; FRENCH/ENGLISH/6; 128 FEET)**
Alsace-Lorraine region.

Gota Canal

c/o Norwegian Coastal Voyage, Ltd.; 405 Park Avenue, New York, NY
10022; ☎ 212-319-1300 or 800-323-7436; fax 212-319-1390;
www.norwegiancoastalvoyage.us

Three vintage ships—M/S *Juno*, M/S *Wilhelm Tham*, and M/S *Diana*—were
built in 1874, 1912, and 1931, respectively, and are lovingly maintained to
preserve their classic interiors. They ply the historic Gota Canal between
Stockholm and Göteborg, Sweden's largest port, from May to September.
The 118-mile canal, an engineering landmark, hand-excavated from 1809 to
1832, provides a journey back in time—through lush countryside to
medieval castles, ancient towns, and a Viking city. The unusual route links
the Baltic and North seas via three canals, eight lakes, and a river.

Designed to fit the narrowest canal locks, the recently renovated vessels
sail across Sweden at a leisurely five to ten knots on tree-lined canals bordered by fields and forests, the 11-lock Berg staircase, huge lakes Vanern
and Vattern, and by many islands. Sightseeing, which varies according to
cruise length and direction, may include Lacko and Stegeborg castles, the
Birka Viking city on Bjorko Island, the medieval towns of Vadstena and
Soderkoping, the seaside resort of Trosa, and the Royal Hunting, Trollhat-
ten Canal, and Motala Motor museums.

The ships retain their stylish Art Nouveau decor, reminiscent of the heyday of upper-class sailings, with mahogany paneling, brass fittings, and
paisley fabrics. Each has a lounge with a bar and small library, a dining room
featuring French cuisine with a Swedish twist and a large wine selection.
There are 25 to 29 cozy cabins with bunk beds, washbasin and shared toilets, and showers with privacy locks.

Seven- and nine-day air-inclusive cruise tours are scheduled from mid-
May to mid-September; a 15% discount applies to cabin rates at certain
times during the season. Packages including round-trip flights from New
York are available. Rates are lowest in May and September.

Le Boat, Inc.

980 Awald Road, Suite 302, Annapolis, MD 21403; ☎ 800-992-0291;
fax 410-280-2406; www.leboat.com; www.connoisseurafloat.com

Le Boat, now affiliated with the self-drive specialist Crown Blue Line, offers
a wide range of cruises in Europe and specializes in barge charters, often
representing owner-operated barges, and self-drive canal boats on canals in
Belgium, Britain, France, Germany, Holland, Ireland, Italy, and Scotland. At
most of the European destinations, one-way cruises that start and finish in
different places are available. Discounts for early bookings, family, and
groups are also offered. The company also features special-interest cruises—
food and wine, fishing, golf, and others. Connoisseur Holidays Afloat is the
British counterpart of Le Boat and is based in Portsmouth, England.

Viking River Cruises
5700 Canoga Avenue, Suite 200, Woodland Hills, CA 91367;
☎ **818-227-1234 or 877-66VIKING (877-668-4546); fax 818-227-1237;**
www.vikingrivercruises.com

Viking River Cruises, a global company with U.S. headquarters in Los Angeles, California, offers Europe, Russia, Ukraine, and China cruises. In Europe, the line has a variety of itineraries ranging from 7 to 14 days on the Danube, Dnieper, Elbe, Main, Rhine, Rhone, Saône, Seine, and Volga rivers. Those sold in North America cover inclusive programs created specifically for English-speaking passengers. (See the China cruises section later in this chapter for the line's Yangtze River program.) The following is a sampling of the fleet in Europe that caters to North Americans.

Viking Burgundy/Viking Seine **(76/154; FRENCH/INTERNATIONAL; 365 FEET)**

Built in 2000, the sister ships cruise the best of France. Two seven-night cruises trace the Rhone and Saône rivers through Burgundy, Provence, and the scenery of the Ardeche region as well as Paris. A 14-night cruise, France's Finest, combines Paris and the heart of Normandy with Burgundy and Provence.

Viking Kirov/Viking Pakhomov/Viking Surkov **(110/212; 430 FEET)**
Viking Lomonosov **(112/202; 423 FEET)**

Built between 1979 and 1990 and refurbished in 2003, the boats sail the Volga and Svir rivers in Russia. From May to October, these boats sail on 10- and 11-day Waterways of the Czars cruises between St. Petersburg and Moscow.

Viking Lavrinenkov **(110/212; 423 FEET)**

Built 1990; refurbished 2003, the boat cruises the Dnieper River in Ukraine on a 14-night cruise round-trip from Kiev.

Viking Europe/Viking Neptune/Viking Pride/Viking Spirit
(75/150; 40; 365 FEET)

These sister ships sail a variety of European destinations including Austria, Eastern Europe, Germany, and Hungary. Some examples are 14 nights, Amsterdam to Budapest (or reverse); seven nights, Danube between Budapest and Nuremberg (or reverse); and nine nights round-trip from Amsterdam.

Viking Schumann **(60/124; 311 FEET)**

Built in 1991 and refurbished 2001, the boat has all outside cabins. She sails on 11-night cruises with seven days on the Elbe from Magdeburg to Melnik plus two overnights in both Berlin and Prague.

Viking Sky **(75/150; 360 FEET)**

Built in 1999, the deluxe ship has all outside cabins. She embarks on nine-night round-trip cruises from Amsterdam to tour Holland and Belgium's waterways. Another option: 12 nights between Vienna and Amsterdam or reverse.

Viking Sun **(99/198; 44; 433 FEET)**

Built in 2004, this is Viking River Cruises newest ship and features French

windows in the cabins. She sails on 12-night Rhine cruises from Basel to
Antwerp or reverse.

YANGTZE RIVER CRUISES IN CHINA

THE CHINESE APTLY CALL THE YANGTZE "Changjiang" (long
river). Rising from the Tibetan plateau, it plunges through mountain
passes into Sichuan to form a border between Hubei and Hunan
before reaching the fertile plains of Jiangsu and Shanghai, a journey
of almost 4,000 miles.

The Yangtze (a local name) is more than a scenic wonder. It was
the site of epic battles in the second century BC, and archaeological
excavations suggest that the area was a cradle of Chinese civilization.

The river remains the great highway of central China, carrying
passenger ferries, patrol boats, and barges piled with coal, limestone,
timber, and cement. Small freighters deliver supplies to towns built
into the cliffs and collect the fruit grown in terraced orchards. The
river is always busy, especially as it narrows into gorges. There, traffic control is essential, and cruise ship captains are in telephone
contact with shore pilot stations as they steer the shallow-draft vessels between gravel shoals.

The Three Gorges: Qutang, Wu, Xiling

Qutang Gorge, also known as Wind Box Gorge, is five miles long, but
never wider than 490 feet. Limestone cliffs erupt on each side in sheer
walls up to 4,000 feet tall. The cliff face is pitted with caves, and there
remains visible an old towpath—the only way through the gorge
before the biggest boulders were cleared from the river.

Less than an hour after leaving the Qutang Gorge, cruise-ship passengers enter 25-mile-long **Wu Gorge.** Its cliffs are so high and steep
that the sun rarely touches the water. Twelve peaks dominate the skyline. According to myth, they're a goddess and her handmaidens who
chose to be turned to stone to stand sentinel over the river.

Midway through the gorge is the border between Sichuan and
Hubei provinces. The exit from the gorge is only 164 feet across, the
narrowest part of the river.

It takes another day for cruise ships to reach **Xiling Gorge,** the
longest canyon, which winds 47 miles through small gorges amid
fierce rapids. On each side are examples of the mountains beyond
mountains of classic Chinese scenery.

Three Gorges Dam

The Three Gorges Dam, located in Sandouping, at the eastern mouth of
the gorges, is nearly completed. It's massive. The dam wall is almost two
miles long and 607 feet tall. Behind it, a lake is filling that will eventually
stretch 373 miles and cover 418 square miles, raising the water level of
Xiling Gorge and a portion of the Wu Gorge. A million or more people
are being evacuated in anticipation of the dam's completion in 2009.

Supporters say the multibillion-dollar dam will control flooding and generate 84.7 billion kilowatt hours of electricity a year for Shanghai and the Lower Yangtze Basin. Opponents say it will destroy the environment and build a reservoir of toxic silt in an earthquake-prone region. Either way, it adds poignancy to a Yangtze cruise.

With the bulk of the construction now completed, the reservoir continues to fill. The lake behind the dam will raise water levels in the Xiling and Wu gorges. Cruise boats journey through a new, five-stage lock to go around the dam wall.

The first Westerners to sail up the Yangtze River were British colonial administrators who established the inland port of Hankow (now part of Wuhan) in the 1840s. The most adventurous continued into the sparsely populated wilderness upstream and found the Three Gorges.

Transport was by sailing ships, which were hauled by teams of trackers through raging rapids and over great boulders, until English trader Archibald Little pioneered steamship service from Wuhan, finally reaching Chongqing (formerly Chungking) in 1898. The voyage remained extremely hazardous until the 1950s, when the Chinese blasted away the largest boulders.

Regular cruises through the gorges were introduced in the early 1980s and became an established part of many all-China itineraries. The gorges are on the 120-mile (192-kilometer) stretch of river between Baidicheng and Yichang. Some itineraries between Chongqing and Yichang reduce the trip by a day and night. However, it has often proven difficult to arrange air or land passage to or from Yichang. Most cruises thus cover the full 850-mile (1,370-kilometer) section between Chongqing and Wuhan.

Shore Excursions (Upstream or Downstream)

SHENNONG STREAM/DANING RIVER GORGES All cruises offer a side trip up one of the Yangtze's tributaries for a closer look at its natural grandeur. Excursions feature fast-flowing, crystal-clear streams with shifting, pebbled shoals and sheer cliffs pocked with caves, clad in waterfalls, and encrusted with ferns. With the rising waters of the river, some of the lesser gorges are also now fully accessible by larger boats, and tributaries previously difficult to navigate are now readily available to visitors.

Shennong Stream is a better option than Daning River, partly because the journey is taken in wooden longboats, which are steered, pushed, and sometimes hauled by husky young men of the Tujia minority. Shennong Stream is also a good option because it is one of the shallower tributaries. The half-day excursion includes a visit to a Tujia-style house, where local dance is performed and worthwhile souvenirs are sold.

ZIGUI This historic town, poised on the cliffs at the entrance to Xiling Gorge, exudes an air of ancient certainty, but it will be swallowed by the dam's reservoir. Only one building will be preserved:

The temple dedicated to Chu Yuan, the scholar and statesman who drowned himself in 278 BC in protest of his government's policy, will be moved downstream with the population. Travelers will lose a town whose main street is packed with sidewalk kitchens, vegetable stalls, alfresco hairdressers, one-room tailors, and an alley of pool tables.

SHASHI/JINGZHOU Upstream from Wuhan, this bustling port contains the remains of a royal capitol from the seventh century B.C. Some original walls are maintained, and the museum contains a 2,000-year-old mummy.

YUEYANG TOWER This gold-tiled pavilion on the Hunan banks of the river, upstream from Wuhan, was built in AD 716 as a military lookout. It was later expanded to provide a belvedere over scenic Dongting Lake.

FENGDU Near the western entrance of Qutang Gorge, this ancient cliff town is reputed to be where people's spirits go after death. To placate unhappy and potentially dangerous phantoms, a temple sells "passports to hell" and other souvenirs.

SHIBAOZHAI This cliffside temple complex, between Chongqing and the first gorge, has a 12-story red pagoda and hilltop temple. Built right into the cliff and called the Pearl of the Yangtze, the temple is an architectural treasure from the Ming Dynasty, dating to the mid-16th century. Some excursions visit it.

Cruise Lines and Ships

Dozens of ships offer cruises through the Yangtze gorges. Many are Chinese-owned and marketed internationally by Changjiang Cruise Overseas Travel Company (**www.ccotc.com**), with offices throughout Asia.

A new generation of vessels caters to travelers whose interest has been fueled by reports that the gorges' days are numbered. These ships operate on regular itineraries designed to allow passage through the gorges during daylight. The timing concerns produce shore excursions that are conveniently located, interesting, varied, and appropriate to the area's history. The season lasts from late February to early December. Summer is extremely hot; in winter, the water level is low and temperatures are colder, often below freezing. There are almost weekly departures of the four-day, three-night downstream cruise from Chongqing and the five-day, four-night upstream trip from Wuhan.

However, those reports that the gorges' days are numbered are a bit exaggerated. Overall, the river will rise some 575 feet in total, but the gorges themselves are so deep that they will be less affected than some have claimed. While the landscape will change, the reality is that the water will not submerge the gorges. In fact, since Stage Two of the dam is already complete, the river will rise only about another 131 feet at the dam's completion. In addition, the deeper water will open even newer vistas to cruisers, since the lesser gorges, which previously held little water, will be fully navigable, and visitors will have the opportunity to explore previously inaccessible areas of the river.

Note: In parentheses after each boat name is information (where available) about the number of cabins and passengers; officers and crew; and the boat's length (cabins/passengers; officers/crew; boat length).

Abercrombie & Kent, Inc.
1520 Kensington Road, Suite 212, Oak Brook, IL 60523; ☎ 630-954-2944 or 800-323-7308; fax 630-954-3324; www.abercrombiekent.com

East King/East Queen **(78 TO 86/186 TO 190; CHINESE; 300 FEET)**

The twin boats *East King* and *East Queen* (operating March through November) are fast and modern. All cabins are spacious—about 183 square feet—and have picture windows, minibars, satellite television, international direct-dial telephones, safes, terry robes, hair dryers, and well-designed bathrooms. There are two Royal Suites, which can be combined with a tea lounge for seminars, groups, or small meetings. The main dining room serves Western and Chinese meals. Public facilities include a nightclub, karaoke room, an enclosed Observation Deck with cafe, a business center, and a 100-seat function room. Recreational facilities include a swimming pool, card rooms, gym, and sauna.

Victoria Cruises
57-08 39th Avenue, Woodside, NY 11377; ☎ 212-818-1680 or 800-348-8084; fax 212-818-9889; www.victoriacruises.com

Victoria Anna **(133 CABINS, 20 SUITES/308; CHINESE; 348 FEET/6,200 TONS)**

Victoria Empress **(91 CABINS, 8 SUITES/198; CHINESE; 3,868 TONS)**

Victoria Katarina **(119 CABINS, 14 SUITES/266; CHINESE; 324 FEET/ 5,780 TONS)**

Victoria Prince/Victoria Queen/Victoria Star **(93 CABINS, 10 SUITES/206; CHINESE; 4,587 TONS)**

Victoria Rose **(63 CABINS, 2 SUITES; 130; CHINESE; 2,428 TONS)**

Victoria Cruises, a New York–based Sino-American joint venture, with American management, operates vessels with the wedding-cake look and character of Mississippi riverboats. Each boat has four decks (*Victoria Anna,* five decks) and an observation area and offers single-seating dining with Chinese and Western cuisine.

Ships come in two categories: premier and classic. Premier ships include all of the vessels listed above, with the exception of the *Victoria Rose,* a classic ship and smaller than the others; it was rebuilt in 2001 and maintains the same high-quality standards on board. The premier ships are new or newly rebuilt vessels, and have a higher level of comfort and decor as well as private balconies for every cabin. Introduced in 2004, *Victoria Katarina* has floor-to-ceiling windows and a mix of modern and traditional architecture.

All cruises have professional, multilingual Western cruise directors and trained local staff. Meals on all boats are served in a single-seating **Dynasty** dining room. Western and Chinese buffets are offered at breakfast and lunch; dinners are served banquet style. Passengers can enjoy cultural immersion both ashore and on board; tai chi is offered mornings on the boats, as are lectures in Chinese culture and history and live traditional performing arts. An onboard boutique sells Chinese gifts and souvenirs. The boats have cocktail lounges, game rooms, business centers, health, and other facilities.

Victoria Anna, another premier vessel, made her scheduled debut in 2006. She is the largest ship in the company's fleet, with 133 standard cabins, 16 junior suites, 2 deluxe suites, and 2 Shangri-La suites. The cabins have bathrooms with a shower and bathtub, television with HBO and BBC broadcasts, and private balconies. There is a single-seating main restaurant and an à la carte restaurant on the top deck. The boat has a three-story atrium lobby, two lounges, three bars, a fitness room, lecture room, reading room, beauty salon, mini-spa, gift shop, Observation Deck, Internet access, and two elevators.

Four- to nine-day itineraries are operated round-trip from Chonqqing, between Chonqqing and Yichang, and between Chonqqing and Shanghai. Victoria Cruises provides cruises on the Yangtze exclusively for such tour operator partners as Pacific Delight Tours, Uniworld, Ritz Tours, and a host of others that are listed on Victoria Cruises' Web site.

Viking River Cruises, Inc.

5700 Canoga Avenue, Suite 200, Woodland Hills, CA 91367;
☎ **877-66-VIKING (877-668-4546) or 818-227-1234; fax 818-227-1237;**
www.vikingrivercruises.com

Viking Century Sky **(153/306; EUROPEAN/CHINESE 168; 415 FEET)**
Viking Century Sun **(153/306; EUROPEAN/CHINESE 168; 415 FEET)**

Europe's largest river-cruising company launched its first boat in China on the Yangtze River in March 2004. With local branch offices in Beijing and Chongqing, Viking River Cruises is headquartered in Los Angeles, California, and oversees all its cruise-tour components, from ship operations and shore excursions to land programs, tours, hotel selections, meals, and cultural performances. Each program has English-speaking escorts and guides.

Viking's Swiss hotel-management staff oversees all food and beverage service and a crew of 168. A variety of food, from the traditional family-style Chinese cuisine to Western selections and even an on-deck barbecue, is available. English is the primary language on board as well as during shore excursions and tours.

Included as part of all Yangtze cruises is an excursion on a local ferry along the scenic Lesser Three Gorges, a tributary of the Yangtze formerly difficult to navigate. One itinerary includes a three-night stay in Lhasa, Tibet. Pre- and postcruise land extensions are available for Hong Kong and Guilin. All cruise tours include Yangtze River cruises of varying duration in addition to land stays in Beijing, Xian (home of the terra-cotta warriors), and Shanghai.

Itineraries range from 9 to 15 nights and include all shore excursions and tours, meals, five-star and deluxe hotels, intra-Asia flights, and English-speaking escorts. With its policy of contributing to the regions in which it sails, Viking River Cruises has helped rebuild three elementary schools in the Hubei province. Passengers on the Cultural Delights itineraries have the opportunity to visit one of the schools and meet the local children.

In April 2005, Viking introduced another ship, almost twice as large as the *Viking Century Star,* the first ship. The purpose-built *Century Sky* is one of the most luxurious of the Yangtze cruise vessels, with all-outside cabins with balconies, baths with shower, telephone, television, safe, hair dryer, and air-conditioning. The five-deck boat has a restaurant, observation lounge and bar, gym, sauna, massage room, Sun Deck, business center, beauty salon, doctor, and laundry service.

In 2006, Viking River Cruises launched the *Viking Century Sun* on the Yangtze. A twin of *Viking Center Sky,* the five-deck vessel has an observation lounge, restaurant, sauna, Sun Deck, bar, massage room, beauty salon, Internet bar, and two elevators. All cabins are air-conditioned and have private bathroom with shower and a balcony.

Other Yangtze River Cruises

Many other U.S.-based companies offer Yangtze cruises. All include the cruises as part of longer China itineraries ranging from 12 to 24 days and often use the boats of Victoria Cruises or Viking River Cruises. The following is a small sample:

China Vacation	☎ 888-285-8933	www.china-vacation.com
General Tours	☎ 800-221-2216	www.generaltours.com
Maupintour	☎ 800-255-4266	www.maupintour.com
Orient Flexi-pax Tours	☎ 800-223-7460	www.orientflexipax.com
Pacific Bestours	☎ 800-688-3288	www.bestour.com
Pacific Delight Tours	☎ 800-221-7179	www.pacificdelighttours.com
SITA World Travel	☎ 800-421-5643	www.sitatours.com
Travcoa	☎ 800-992-2003	www.travcoa.com
Uniworld	☎ 800-360-9550	www.uniworld.com
Vacations To Go	☎ 800-338-4962	www.vacationstogo.com
Visits Plus	☎ 800-321-3235	www.visitsplus.com

OTHER ASIAN RIVER CRUISES

Orient Express Hotels, Trains, and Cruises
1114 Avenue of the Americas, 38th Floor, New York, NY 10036;
☎ **800-524-2420; fax 401-351-7220; www.orient-express.com**

Road to Mandalay **(66/118; EUROPEAN/BURMESE; 305 FEET)**

Unusual cruises in Myanmar (formerly Burma) are offered by Orient Express Hotels, Trains, and Cruises, the company that operates the famous Orient Express. The boat sails from February to April and July to December on three- to seven-night itineraries on the Irrawaddy (Ayeyarwady) River between Mandalay and Bagan and round-trip from Mandalay. Generally, the cruises are part of a package departing from Bangkok, Thailand, with round-trip flights to Yangon.

The German-built *Road to Mandalay,* a deluxe cruiser, previously sailed the Rhine and Elbe. Before starting these cruises in 1996, the boat was renovated. Facilities include a pool, large Sun Deck, observation lounge, and several bars. The dining room accommodates all passengers in a single seating and serves international and Asian cuisine. The three cabin types include some singles. All have a private bath and air-conditioning. Doubles have twin beds; larger cabins have a sitting area. Two even more exotic journeys: One seven-night cruise sails round-trip from Bagan , while an 11-night adventure visits a little-known region north of Mandalay to beyond Bhamo, stopping just short of the China border. Unlike the tranquil flood plains surrounding the lower Irrawaddy, the northern landscape changes as the ship enters the Three Narrows region, marked with lush forests and towering cliffs.

NILE RIVER CRUISES

NO TRIP TO EGYPT IS COMPLETE without a cruise on the Nile. It is the perfect way to enjoy the Egyptian countryside as well as to see ancient temples and monuments, because the most famous sites are clustered along the great river. Your first view of the Nile snaking through the desert will illustrate dramatically why the river has been so important throughout Egypt's history. Quite literally, Egyptian civilization would not exist without the Nile. Beyond the green ribbon—the land irrigated by the Nile—the desert stretches endlessly into the horizon. The Nile flows so gently that ships glide as though unmoving. Riverbanks, always near, give passengers an intimate view of rural life in Upper Egypt. Along the riverbanks and in the fields of the green valley, Egyptians live today much as they have for thousands of years. Life and land have a continuity bridging the centuries, as visitors will see in the ancient drawings on temple and tomb walls and the present scenes of the countryside. The sense of tranquillity is an overwhelming sensation throughout a Nile cruise and is a total contrast from the roar and clamor of Cairo—the juxtaposition makes the pastoral setting of the Nile Valley all the more remote.

Nile Itineraries

Those beginning their cruise in Upper Egypt may travel from Cairo to Luxor or Aswan by plane or train. They can begin their trip in Aswan and cruise to Luxor or do the reverse. We recommend the former, as the trip then saves the best for last: climaxing with sightseeing at **Karnak** and the **Valley of the Kings** at Luxor.

Aswan was the capital of Nubia in ancient times and an important trading place. Today, it's primarily a winter resort and the administrative center for the **High Dam** and surrounding region. Aswan is dotted with antiquities. The most important is the **Temple of Philae**— one of many temples saved from the High Dam's reservoir—on an island in the river. The botanical gardens, also on an island, and a view of the Aga Khan's mausoleum (not open to the public) are standard stops on the popular excursion made by local felucca, the graceful sailboats of the Nile.

From Aswan, Nile steamers sail downstream (north) to Luxor, stopping at **Kom Ombo, Edfu,** and **Esna**—sites of temples dating from the Ptolemaic, or Greek, period. One temple has a wall carving bearing the only known likeness of Queen Cleopatra. Luxor is the modern town next to the ancient city of Thebes, capital of Egypt for most of its illustrious early history. Most boats dock on the east bank near the Luxor Museum or the **Sofitel Winter Palace Luxor** hotel, which are walking distance from **Luxor Temple** and a short carriage ride from the colossal **Karnak Temple.** A full-day excursion visits the west bank's **Valley of the Kings,** where tombs of Tutankhamen and other pharaohs were found; the **Valley of the Queens;** and the **Tombs of the Nobles,** which contain important art.

Longer cruises of six nights sail north from Luxor to Qena to visit the **Temples of Dendera** and **Abydos,** considered the most important temple in Egypt for its artwork. Visits beyond Abydos to **Tel al Amarna,** capital of revolutionary pharaoh Akhenaton and his wife, Nefertiti; Minya, central Egypt's largest town; and **Beni Hassan,** site of tombs containing drawings showing ancient Egyptians at play, must be made by road or rail from Cairo.

Lake Nasser and Abu Simbel

Construction of the Aswan High Dam created Lake Nasser, which stretches more than 300 miles south from Aswan to the Sudanese border. As waters rose, the famous temple of **Abu Simbel** would have been inundated had it not been moved to higher ground in a colossal 1950s international project. For decades while the waters rose, visitors flew or drove to the site of Abu Simbel. Now, they can go by Nile steamer, departing from the south side of the dam. (See Misr Travel below.)

Nile River Journeys

Nile river boats range from cozy, friendly, and clubby to very luxurious. Some accommodate as few as 20 passengers; the largest carry 150 or more passengers. Cabins, smaller than those on standard cruise ships, are well-appointed and comfortable; on many new ships, suites are available. Most have twin lower beds (some have pull-down bunks for a third person), a dressing table or nightstand, closet, and private bathroom with shower. Boats holding 80 or more passengers have lounges for reading and relaxing, a bar, Sun Deck, dining room with table service, and evening entertainment. Laundry service is available. Some offer table tennis or a tiny swimming pool.

The boat's small size limits its recreational and entertainment facilities, but these aren't important on a Nile cruise, where antiquities and scenery are the attractions. Roaming room is surprisingly ample. Deck chairs invite lounging and watching history float by.

Newer four- and five-star vessels offer four- and six-night cruises between Luxor and Aswan. Some add **Dendera** and feature cruises of six or seven nights.

Nile cruises are divided into three seasons (prices include all meals, service, taxes, and guided sightseeing).

HIGH SEASON (October to April) Five-star boats range from $200 to $450 per person per night; four-star, approximately $150 to $210.

SHOULDER SEASON (May and September) 10% to 15% off high-season rates.

LOW SEASON (June to August) 15% to 50% off high-season rates. Generally, U.S. tour companies do not visit Upper Egypt during this period.

Although prices are lower in summer and many of the boats are air-conditioned, the heat in sightseeing areas can be intense. Large groups walking generate dust in which it's difficult to breathe; a dust mask or handkerchief over the mouth is helpful. Boat food usually is quite good. Be very careful to eat only fruits and vegetables that can be peeled.

More than 200 boats sail on Nile cruises. Unless you have the opportunity to inspect a vessel yourself, book only with established companies. Five-star boats operated by Mena House Oberoi, Movenpick, Sheraton, and Sonesta are among those used by major U.S. tour companies.

If you arrive in Egypt without reservations and decide to cruise, make inquiries and reservations through the managing company's office in Cairo, where cabin space is controlled. If you wait until you arrive in Luxor or Aswan to find space, you might have to walk among ships and ask the boat manager if a cabin is available.

If you have ample time, however, the latter method lets you see the ship, its cabins, and cleanliness (important, especially on boats of less than five stars) before booking. And if you're good at bargaining, you may negotiate a price better than you would have received in Cairo.

A selected list of companies and Nile river boats marketed in the United States follows. *Note:* In parentheses after each boat name is information (where available) about the number of cabins and passengers; officers and crew; and the boat's length (cabins/passengers; officers/crew; boat length).

Abercrombie & Kent, Inc.

1520 Kensington Road, Suite 212, Oak Brook, IL 60523; ☎ 800-323-7308; fax 630-954-3324; www.abercrombiekent.com

Sun Boat III (18 CABINS AND SUITES)

The four-deck boat has a restaurant, upper Sun Deck with heated swimming pool, lower Sun Deck with lounge and bar. Cabins have direct-dial phone, safe, mini-bar, CD player. Renovated in 2005.

Sun Boat IV **(40 CABINS AND SUITES; 220 FEET)**

The five-deck boat has a restaurant, upper Sun Deck with small pool, gift shop, lounge and bar, library and lower Sun Deck. Cabins have direct-dial phone, safe, mini-bar, CD player. Renovated in 2006, the Art Deco interiors by Egyptian designer Mohammed Noaman used bold colors and Egyptian motifs. Floor-to-ceiling windows were added in the cabins on the Main Deck, the Bridge Deck, and the Promenade Deck, and teak flooring laid in all the outdoor areas and teak and Egyptian marble on the Sun deck.

Cruises of four to eight days between Luxor and Aswan (or reverse) are normally included in the tour company's various small group and independent itineraries in Egypt. There are year-round twice-monthly and monthly departures. The *Sun Boat IV* has eight or more departures monthly, sailing every Saturday for three-night cruises and Tuesday on four-night ones.

Esplanade Tours
160 Commonwealth Avenue, Suite L3, Boston, MA 02116; ☎ 617-266-7465 or 800-426-5492; fax 617-262-9829; www.esplanadetours.com

Regency/Regina/Royale **(30 TO 70/50 TO 102; EGYPTIAN; 238 FEET)**

This luxury group's boats, owned and operated by Travcotels of Egypt, are fully air-conditioned. Each has lounges, bars, panoramic windows, single-seating dining, two Sun Decks, a swimming pool, gift shop, beauty salon, and laundry facilities. Cabins measure 230 square feet; suites have 380 square feet. All have a television, DVD player, minifridge, and bathroom with shower, toilet, bidet, and hair dryer. The boats offer three-, four-, and seven-night cruises between Luxor and Aswan or a Lake Nasser cruise between Aswan and Abu Simbel. They are included in Esplanade's 14-day Egypt package and in customized trips that are the company's specialty.

Mena House Oberoi Hotels
Pyramids Road, Giza, Cairo, Egypt 12556; ☎ 20-2-383-3222; fax 20-2-383-7777; www.oberoihotels.com

Oberoi Philae **(50 DOUBLE CABINS, 4 SINGLES, 4 SUITES)**

The boat is operated by Oberoi Hotels, an international chain with hotels in Cairo. The *Oberoi Philae* resembles a paddle wheeler. Each cabin has floor-to-ceiling sliding glass doors leading to a private balcony. Jacket and tie are preferred for men at dinner. The ships sail on three- to seven-night cruises between Luxor and Aswan. Oberoi also operates the twin boats, *Shehrayar/Shehrazah* (59 cabins and suites).

Misr Travel
630 Fifth Avenue, Suite 1460, New York, NY 10111; ☎ 212-332-2600 or 800-223-4978; fax 212-332-2609; www.misrtravel.org

Misr Travel has been taking tourists to Egypt for more than 70 years, and its network of 29 local offices at all major Egyptian tourist sites and in many of

Egypt's leading hotels can be comforting to travelers. Misr offers a myriad of packages in Egypt and neighboring countries, with different cruise options. Packages can be customized with add-ons as well.

Misr offers several cruise tours that included a Nile cruise. For example, a nine-day Classic Egyptian Tour with year-round departures includes four nights at a Hilton, Marriott, or Sheraton Hotel in Cairo with full breakfast buffet and a four-night cruise on a Sonesta-, Movenpick- or Oberoi-managed Nile cruise boat. Also included are air transportation between Cairo and the ship, transfers, and sightseeing. During the cruise portion of the journey, passengers visit the Valley of the Kings and Queens, the Colossi of Memnon, the Temples of Karnak, Luxor, Edfu, Kom Ombo, and Philae and Aswan.

For those short on time and low on funds, Misr also offers a lower-cost option on their Extraordinary Egypt package and Budget Cruncher packages. Passengers spend several nights in Cairo and three nights onboard a Movenpick- or Oberoi-managed Nile cruiser, and also get local flights, transfers, a full-day guided tour of Cairo, and round-trip air from New York. An optional excursion to Abu Simbel by air from Aswan is available for an additional cost.

Misr Travel offers programs using the boats— *Eugenie* (50 cabins/100 passengers), *Nubian Sea* (60/120), *Kasr Ibrim* (60/120), and *Prince Abbas* (60/120)—that make three- and four-night cruises on Lake Nasser between Aswan and Abu Simbel. All the boats have outside cabins with private baths. The four-night program sails south from Aswan on Monday and ends at Abu Simbel on Friday; three-night cruises sail north on Friday from Abu Simbel to Aswan. The highlight is a daylight visit to Abu Simbel, and a special feature is a candlelight dinner on deck in front of the floodlit temple of Ramses II and a performance of the son et lumiere. The price is about $220 per person per night, double occupancy in winter; it is lower in off-season. All meals and shore excursions are included.

Nabila Nile Cruises
605 Market Street, Suite 507, San Francisco, CA 94105; ☎ 415-979-0160 or 800-443-6453; www.nabilatours.com

King of Thebes (**65 CABINS**)

El Nabitan

Queen Nabila of Abu Simbel (**60 CABINS, 2 SUITES**)

Queen of the Nile (**70 CABINS**)

Queen of Sheeba (**78 CABINS**)

Ramses King of the Nile (**71 CABINS**)

These ships sail on four-, five-, and eight-day cruises between Luxor and Aswan. Also offered are three- and four-night cruises on Lake Nasser between Aswan and Abu Simbel. All cabins have air- conditioning, minifridge, hair dryer, television, and telephone.

Sonesta Hotels, Resorts & Nile Cruises
116 Huntington Avenue, Ninth Floor, Boston, MA 02116; ☎ 800-SONESTA (766-3782); www.sonesta.com; Sonesta Nile Cruises, 4 El Tayaran Street, Nasser City, Cairo, Egypt; ☎ 20-2-2628111; fax 20-2-2628765; www.sonesta.com

Sonesta Moon Goddess (48 CABINS/2 SUITES; EGYPTIAN)

Sonesta Nile Goddess (63 CABINS/2 SUITES/136; EGYPTIAN)

Sonesta Star Goddess (33 SUITES/66; EGYPTIAN)

Sonesta Sun Goddess (58 CABINS/4 SUITES; EGYPTIAN)

Three four- to seven-night cruises between Luxor and Aswan are offered. The all-suite, five-star *Sonesta Star Goddess* is the company's newest, most luxurious boat. Designed and built in Cairo, the ship has four decks and measures 237 feet in length and 46 feet in width. The ship has 33 suites, each with a private terrace and elegant, sophisticated modern decor. There are three sizes, each category named for a famous composer: 27 deluxe Beethoven Suites, four slightly smaller Mozart Suites, and two larger, superior Chopin Suites.

UNITED STATES AND CANADIAN RIVER CRUISES

THE MISSISSIPPI HAS NORTH AMERICA'S best-known river cruises, but there are others. Spectacular scenery is the main attraction. In the Northeast, the favorite season is autumn, with its brilliant foliage.

Note: In parentheses after each boat name is information about the number of cabins and passengers; officers and crew; and the boat's length (cabins/passengers; officers/crew; boat length).

American Canadian Caribbean Line (*See* Part Two.)

American Cruise Lines
(*See* Part Two, under European and Smaller Cruise Lines.)

American West Steamboat Company
(*See* Majestic America Line below.)

Cruise West (*See* Part Two.)

Delta Queen Steamboat Company
(*See* Majestic America Line below.)

Majestic America Line
2101 Fourth Avenue, Suite 1150, Seattle, WA 98121; ☎ 206-292-9606; 800-434-1232; 800-543-1949; www. majesticamericaline.com

Majestic America Line (MAL), a subsidiary of Newport Beach, California–based Ambassadors International, Inc. (a cruise, marine, and travel and event company) is a new cruise line formed in 2006 through the combination of American West Steamboat Company and Delta Queen Steamboat Company. The line sails classic boats and cruise ships on rivers and coastal waters through America's heartland, the Pacific Northwest, and Alaska.

Although MAL is a new company, it has inherited a proud history. At the time of the MAL acquisition, Delta Queen Steamboat Company was the country's oldest line of American-flagged cruise vessels, whose forerunner was founded in 1890. After World War II, the *Delta Queen* was purchased by Tom Greene, who remodeled and inaugurated her on Mississippi River cruises in 1948. The company was acquired by new owners in 1973, renamed the Delta Queen Steamboat Company, and the larger *Mississippi Queen* was added. The *American Queen,* the largest steamboat ever built, arrived in 1995. After the tragedy of 9/11, Delta Queen Steamboat Company's ownership changed twice until its three ships were acquired by MAL last year. American West Steamboat Company was a much younger company, dating from 1995, but when it did start it brought back to the Pacific Northwest a tradition more than a century old.

The ships and their cruises appeal to anyone interested in American history, culture, and literature and those who enjoy the relaxed pace and shoreline visibility that river cruises offer. They also appeal to anyone uneasy about ocean voyages or straying far from home.

Passengers are likely to be a mix of ages, nationalities, families, couples, singles, and grandparents traveling with grandchildren. They are often repeaters who have sailed on the steamboats many times; a surprising number of passengers live near the river. For most passengers, the real destination of these cruises is the steamboats. People seem to love their homespun, star-spangled slice of Americana.

While you're floating down the Mississippi on one of these "wedding cakes" at a lazy nine knots per hour, visions of Huck Finn and Tom Sawyer are sure to arise. Nostalgia is thick when a morning mist hangs over the shoreline, and the only sounds are the low hum of engines and the red paddle wheel churning the river's muddy water. Mark Twain wrote that the Mississippi at morning has a "haunting sense of loneliness, isolation, remoteness from the worry and bustle of the world. The dawn creeps in stealthily, the tranquillity is profound and infinitely satisfying."

After breakfast, the cruise Riverlorian relates colorful bits of river history. Later, your boat, festooned in red, white, and blue flags, arrives in a port with its calliope (an organlike instrument with whistles sounded by steam or compressed air) in full song. Most likely, you'll be met by townsfolk who personally offer passengers directions. It's an experience not likely found on standard cruises.

Majestic America recently launched its comprehensive Web site. Segments for each ship include 360-degree video of public rooms and cabins, with simultaneous indication of their location on accompanying deck plans. There are descriptions of the cruises and their destinations along with a calendar of cruises for the full year.

The new owners have also undertaken an upgrade of all cabins and suites with premium pillow-top mattresses, pillow options, 300-thread-count bed linens, and deluxe duvet covers. Flat-screen televisions with DVD players have been added to accommodations on the *American Queen, Mississippi Queen,* and *Contessa. Columbia Queen, Empress of the North,* and

Queen of the West already had television with DVD. American-crafted ice buckets and glasses have been added in all cabins. Bathrooms fleetwide now have a revitalizing massage showerhead, makeup mirror, good-quality soap, shampoo, and lotion, and premium robes and towels, custom-milled in America. Suites have additional amenities, including bath slippers, safe, coffee/tea maker, refrigerator, and a new digital entertainment system.

Majestic America Line is working with American culinary experts to develop menus that celebrate the country's regional flavors. Northwest celebrity chef, author, and consultant Kathy Casey of Kathy Casey Food Studios is creating a lineup of signature American dishes using local, fresh, seasonal ingredients. Food Network chef and author Sara Moulton has fashioned the American Cocktail Party for Majestic America. This party, available to passengers prior to dinner, features hors d'oeuvres paired with signature drinks. Excellent American wines from some of the country's finest wineries are also available. Rounding out the dining experience are new table settings using fine American artisinal china and fresh seasonal floral arrangements inspired by regional landscapes.

American Queen (222/436; AMERICAN; 418 FEET/3,707 TONS)

The *American Queen* was named the flagship vessel for Majestic America Line in spring 2007. Constructed in Amelia, Louisiana, she was the largest passenger vessel built in a U.S. shipyard in more than four decades when she made her debut in 1995. No expense was spared in re-creating the luxurious setting of yesteryear. The vessel merges Victoriana and the grand style of 19th-century steamboats with modern shipbuilding technology and amenities. Her white exteriors are laden with gingerbread filigree, and a 45-ton red paddle wheel turns at the stern. Inside are a bathing pool, gym, conference center, and two elevators.

The *American Queen* rises 97 feet from the waterline to the top of its fluted stacks, making quite a show. The stacks and pilothouse can be lowered to enable the vessel to pass under low bridges. The six-passenger-deck vessel is powered by two 1930s Nordberg steam engines salvaged from the *Kennedy,* a dredge belonging to the U.S. Army Corps of Engineers.

A Victorian theme employs period wallpaper, floral carpets and fabrics, brass fixtures, etched glass, and antiques or good reproductions. Even modern plumbing and electrical fixtures are disguised as antiques. Each cabin is named after a river town, waterway, historic figure, or steamboat. The several cabin categories are distributed on all but the lowest passenger deck. Some cabins have bay windows; 27 have verandas. Three-fourths are outside; most have French doors. Midrange standard cabins are considerably larger than on her sister boats. Standard dimensions are 141 and 190 square feet. Cabins are more senior friendly, with larger bathrooms, emergency call buttons by each bed, and levers (rather than handles) on doors.

Interior designers borrowed liberally from historic steamboats, particularly the 1878 *J. M. White,* called the most graceful and spacious steamboat of her time. Her dining saloon—which Mark Twain described as "dainty as a drawing room; when I looked down her long, gilded saloon, it was like gazing through a splendid tunnel"—was copied and named the **J. M. White Dining Room.** Located on Main Deck, the lowest passenger deck, the dining room spans two decks. Tall windows have ornate fretwork arches. A drop ceiling divides the room and each side has a vaulted space with huge mirrors in spectacular gilt frames dating from the 1880s. A custom-built mahogany Victorian piano bar accents the vessel's Victorian decor.

The **Mark Twain Gallery** around the upper level of the dining room honors the author whose *Life on the Mississippi* captured the essence of steamboating. Books and curio cases contain exhibits on regional wildlife and steamboat history and river memorabilia. Furnishings include Tiffany-style lamps and writing tables. Window areas provide cozy nooks for reading, writing, or watching the scenery.

Forward from the gallery to starboard is the **Gentlemen's Card Room,** a masculine room meant to resemble Teddy Roosevelt's library. Cases are filled with books typical of late-19th-century homes, with many first-person accounts of exploration and vintage how-to books.

From the gallery to midship is the purser's lobby and grand, gilded staircase under a spectacular filigreed ceiling, also harking to the *J. M. White.* Beyond are the **Grand Saloon's** upper level and the lively **Engine Room Bar** overlooking the paddle wheel.

Forward on Texas Deck is the cruise line's signature Front Porch of America, complete with swings and rockers. Above, Promenade Deck has a full-circuit walkway and the **Calliope Bar.** Stairs behind the bar lead to the topmost Sun Deck, small exercise room, and bathing pool (essentially a large hot tub). The Observation Deck also has a full-circuit promenade (seven laps equal a mile).

A lounge and bar at the dining room entrance links the lobby and Grand Saloon below, used for nightly entertainment and dancing. Designed as an idealized 1880 opera house, the theater has a proscenium stage and is ringed with private boxes on the second-story balcony.

Columbia Queen (75/150; AMERICAN/57; 218 FEET)

The *Columbia Queen* was built in 2000 for a reported $43 million in early 20th-century riverboat style to start a new operation in the Pacific Northwest. But the two companies that tried fell on hard times and the finely appointed vessel sat idle for three years until it was acquired by Majestic America Line in 2006.

The boat features a blend of Victorian and Pacific Northwest decor, using warm mahogany paneling, plush leather furniture, Tiffany stained-glass chandeliers and lamps, brass accents, and Northwest artwork. The cabins offer modern amenities similar to those found on oceangoing cruise ships. All cabins and the four suites are equipped with twin beds convertible to kings, satellite television and DVD player, boat-to-shore telephone, and bath with a glass-enclosed shower, hair dryer, and iron and ironing board. Most cabins have private verandas, French doors with balconies, or doors that open directly onto the deck. There is one wheelchair-accessible cabin and two elevators.

The **Astoria Room,** a handsome two-tiered space on the Main Deck, serves a dual purpose. Dressed in richly upholstered banquettes and chairs and crystal chandeliers, the room is large enough to seat all passengers at one time. Later in the evening, the room is transformed into the main show lounge and theater for passengers to enjoy entertainment or dance under authentic Tiffany stained-glass chandeliers.

Other facilities include the rustic **Explorer Bar,** a piano bar with large windows revealing panoramic views, and the **Lewis & Clark Lounge,** an intimate space for cocktails and hors d'oeuvres, reached by a large stairwell with a mahogany banister and ornate iron grillwork. The Lounge is furnished with overstuffed library chairs and a mahogany bar with an eight-foot mirrored bar back. The **Back Porch,** at the rear of the observation deck, provides a venue for passengers to enjoy breakfast, a light lunch, or cocktails, or to relax in the ladder-back rocking chairs and read or watch the world go by.

Contessa (24/48; AMERICAN; 104 FEET/98 TONS)

Although odd-looking with its catamaran hulls and three-deck-tall, wedge-shaped superstructure, the *Contessa* (formerly *Executive Explorer* of now-defunct Glacier Bay Cruise Line) is ideal to sail less traveled waters. Streamlined and powerful, she's able to zip between ports faster than most small passenger ships on the Alaska scene.

Public areas are pleasantly furnished and decorated with Native Alaskan art. The **Vista View Lounge** and Vista cabins above it have a wall of windows overlooking the bow. An open top deck and covered area on the middle deck are best for wildlife viewing. An open area at the stern is another option.

The ship was completely renovated in 2005. All the well-appointed cabins have large windows, refrigerator, flat-screen television and DVD players, and considerable closet space. The bathrooms are small, arranged in the space-saving head style (toilet is in the shower stall); sinks and vanities are in the main cabin area. Most cabins have twin beds that convert to queen size. One small cabin has upper and lower berths and accommodates two people but is suggested as a single. Two Vista Deluxe cabins have a sitting area, queen-size beds, larger closets, and a wall of windows providing a wraparound view. Standard cabins measure approximately 135 square feet. There is no elevator.

Meals are served at one open seating in one dining room. Service, more like that found at a friendly bed-and-breakfast than at a resort, is cordial and warm, capable and professional. Members of the hotel staff, most of them young and mostly from Alaska and the Pacific Northwest, do double and triple duty, cleaning cabins, serving meals, and helping carry luggage on and off the ship.

The ship has only two public rooms—one lounge with the vessel's only bar, library, board games, and videotapes; and one dining room. There are no exercise or entertainment facilities. Shipboard activities are focused mainly on observing nature and wildlife. In the evenings, the naturalists give talks on wildlife, native culture, and history. Entertainment is provided by Alaska itself and by passenger interaction. Guests often gather on the open top deck for incredible views of the coastline.

Delta Queen (87/174; AMERICAN; 285 FEET/3,360 TONS)

The *Delta Queen,* which celebrated 80 years on America's rivers in 2007, is the only remaining authentic example of the thousands of overnight paddle-wheel steamers that once plied the nation's rivers. She has the warmth of a bed-and-breakfast, and her small-town friendliness mirrors the heartland ports she visits.

From the outside, this waterborne piece of history looks rather ordinary, except for her paddle wheel. Inside, however, she enchants with Tiffany-style stained glass, brass fittings, and rich, polished woods from another era. Simply knowing the *Delta Queen* is the real thing makes you appreciate every ceiling molding and creak in the floor. There's no other cruise vessel like her, and there never will be, because passenger vessels can no longer be built of wood. Indeed, *Delta Queen's* elaborate superstructure, which adds so much to her character, was almost her undoing.

In the 1920s, the boat was one of two steamers commissioned by the California Transportation Company for luxury overnight travel on the Sacramento River between Sacramento and San Francisco. Their steel hulls were fabricated in Scotland, and reassembled in California. The wheel shafts and cranks were forged in Germany. Her American-built superstructure was crafted from pine, oak, teak, mahogany, and Oregon cedar. The *Delta Queen* and her twin, *Delta King,* were launched in 1927 and became famous for their deluxe appointments. The *Delta Queen* might have died as other steamboats did, but during World War II, the U.S. Navy commandeered her, painted her battleship gray, and used her to ferry troops across San Francisco Bay.

At war's end, the U.S. Maritime Commission auctioned the boat. Tom Greene, president of Cincinnati-based Greene Line Steamers, forerunner of the Delta Queen Company, bought her for only $46,250. Greene had the vessel towed 5,378 miles in a 37-day trip to New Orleans via the Panama Canal. From there, she steamed on her own up the Mississippi and Ohio rivers to Pittsburgh, where she was refitted to her original state. She made her Mississippi River debut in June 1948.

By 1962, the ship's demise seemed imminent, but publicist Betty Blake revived the tradition of steamboat races to draw attention to the venerable steamer. It worked. But in 1969, the *Delta Queen* returned to death's door when federal safety standards banned wooden vessels as fire hazards. Blake organized a letter and petition campaign that won a congressional exemption the boat still enjoys. The riverboat was made fire-resistant, but in November 1970 she again faced demise. Another act of Congress saved her, placing her on the National Register of Historic Places. More than a million dollars was spent to enhance fire resistance. In 1989, she was designated a National Historic Landmark.

To ocean veterans, a cruise on the *Delta Queen* requires reorientation. Large cruise ships take at least a day to figure out; *Delta Queen* requires less than an hour. The intimate boat is like a small inn. At the speed of eight knots per hour, the ship averages 100 miles a day (an automobile covers that distance in 90 minutes or less), but after a day, distance and speed become irrelevant. Life aboard is a tonic for stress; seasickness is no issue. Passengers settle in to watch the passing scenery and a lively parade of barges and towboats heaped with grain, coal, scrap iron, and fuel. (Binoculars are helpful.) Approaching ports becomes a major event. The ship's throaty whistle and cheerful tunes from her century-old calliope announce her arrival and draw people to the river.

Cabins fall into several categories, all outside with private showers. Hair dryers are allowed. Four of six suites have picture windows framed by stained glass, a conversation area, queen-size bed, bathtub, and shower; the other two have smaller sitting areas and shower only. Suites are furnished with antiques, while the homey furnishings in standard cabins range from good reproductions to collectibles. A few standard cabins have double beds; the remainder has twins. All are small but comfortable and clean, ranging from 44 square feet for the smallest quarters to 156 square feet for top accommodations. There are no elevators.

Cabins on two of the three decks face wide promenades dubbed the front porch of America. Rooms on Cabin Deck open inside onto the quiet **Betty Blake Lounge,** but they have outside-facing windows. Bathrooms are small but functional; many have sinks outside the bathroom door.

All meals are served in the **Orleans Dining Room** at two seatings for dinner. Wide windows on two sides frame a river panorama. Continental breakfast is served in the **Forward Cabin Lounge** and coffee and iced tea are available all day. The dining room is the boat's largest room and doubles as the entertainment lounge after the second-seating dinner. Service is provided by cheerful, fresh-faced young Midwesterners whose attitude is infectious and genuinely appreciated by passengers.

The laid-back *Delta Queen* offers simple pleasures. Despite images of riverboat gamblers, there's no casino; passengers settle for bingo or horse racing or they can also head for a casino ashore in some destinations. The softly lighted **Betty Blake Lounge,** furnished with armchairs, sofas, desks, and bookcases, is fine for reading or board games.

The *Delta Queen*'s centerpiece is the **Grand Staircase,** which links the Forward Cabin Lounge to the **Texas Lounge** upstairs. An ornate bronze filigree railing, scrolled latticework, and hardwood paneling accent this impressive stairway, which is crowned by a Tiffany chandelier. At the Texas Lounge entrance is a plaque recognizing the *Delta Queen*'s landmark status. The wood-paneled lounge's piano bar is a magnet for the sing-along crowd. Wide windows provide the ideal setting for watching the river and sunsets.

Mississippi Queen **(206/412; AMERICAN; 382 FEET/3,364 TONS)**

If the *Delta Queen* is a floating country inn, her larger sister, *Mississippi Queen*, is a stately Victorian showboat. Proud and pretty, she rolls down the river like the grandest float in a parade. On board, it's the Fourth of July—a red, white, and blue celebration of Americana amid Victoriana. Polished brass railings, beveled mirrors, crystal chandeliers, and Victorian-style chairs evoke the turn of the century, yet the *Mississippi Queen* offers seven decks of comfort and many modern cruise-ship amenities, including bathing pool, six lounges and bars, a small gym, library, gift shop, two elevators, cabin telephones and flat-screen televisions, some private verandas, and a beauty salon.

Modern comforts aside, this ship is a true steamboat, powered by an authentic steam engine. Her huge paddle wheel is not just for show. In the **Paddle Wheel Lounge** on Texas Deck, you can watch through floor-to-ceiling windows as the bucket planks churn to drive the vessel.

The *Mississippi Queen*'s modern side is best appreciated in her cabins. All accommodations have air-conditioning, wall-to-wall carpeting, telephones, flat-screen televisions, and private bathrooms. Standard cabins (123 square feet) are compact and have tiny bathrooms with showers. Suites and outside deluxe cabins have private verandas, but only suites have bathrooms with tubs and showers. Each cabin displays historical art pertaining to its name. Cabin staff attends rooms twice daily to replenish towels and ice. There is one wheelchair-accessible cabin.

Two seatings are offered at dinner; open seating for breakfast and lunch. A band plays nightly for dancing in the **Grand Saloon.**

Empress of the North (112/223; AMERICAN/84; 360 FEET)

Empress of the North, the first stern-wheeler to cruise Alaska's Inside Passage in more than 100 years, was launched by American West Steamboat Line in 2003. And she came with an important feature—105 out of her 112 cabins have balconies.

The comfortable cabins and suites are large and richly decorated and have picture windows or verandas and private baths. They also have a telephone, minibar, desk, television, and DVD player, among other amenities. The vessel has a show lounge and several bars. Onboard entertainment includes lectures and showboat-style revues.

The elegant main dining room offers open seating for all meals. A casual top-deck bar and grill serves sandwiches and other snacks.

The ship's cruises have a strong focus on history, culture, and wildlife, with both a fun and educational approach. A historian or naturalist accompanies every cruise. Passengers enjoy the small-ship cruise experience with an American staff that will be addressing them by name soon after they have come aboard. The onboard atmosphere is casual but with a touch of elegance.

Passengers will find an art and artifacts brochure in their cabins, enabling them to take a self-guided tour of the ship's impressive art collection, ranging from cowboy art to gold-rush-era photos. There is also a rare collection of Russian nesting dolls, Fabergé eggs, and native Alaskan masks and carvings.

Queen of the West (71/142; AMERICAN/47; 230 FEET)

The deluxe paddle wheeler *Queen of the West*, launched in 1995 by American West Steamboat Company, was the first overnight passenger stern-wheeler to be built and operated in the West in 80 years. The boat is propelled solely by her three-story-high churning paddle wheel. But unlike earlier craft, the *Queen* doesn't rely on a steam engine. Instead, she is powered by a revolutionary hydraulic propulsion system that uses environmentally safe biodegradable hydraulic oil. Her 45-foot-long bow ramp allows passengers to go ashore anywhere along the river, much as the 19th-century vessels did.

The all-outside cabins and suites are large, comfortable, and richly decorated and have picture windows or verandas and private baths. All cabins have a telephone, minibar, television, and DVD player, among other amenities.

The ship's elegant main dining room offers open seating for all meals, with one dinner seating time. The **Calliope Bar & Grill,** located on the Vista View Deck, is a 24-hour self-service snack bar with a large canopy-covered area that can be enclosed for all-weather comfort. The **Columbia Showroom,** forward on the Explorer Deck has a bar, dance floor, stage, and big-screen television. By day, the elegant window-walled lounge is a popular place to relax and watch the passing scenery; it is also used for special presentations. In the evening, it's the venue for cocktails with live music and for showboat entertainment and dancing after dinner. The lounge's decor, with rich upholstery and dark mahogany accents, reflects the sophistication of 19th-century paddle wheelers.

With more than 100 framed pieces lining the walls on four decks, the collection gives travelers an historical view of the Columbia and Snake rivers. Among the artists represented are famed cowboy artist Charles M. Russell, John Clymer, Cameron Blagg, and Jody Bergsma. Their works depict Native Americans, everyday scenes from the Old West, and the difficult existence along the Oregon Trail.

RiverBarge Excursion Lines, Inc.
201 Opelousas Avenue, New Orleans, LA 70114; ☎ 504-365-0022 or 888-462-2743; fax 504-365-0000; www.riverbarge.com

River Explorer (98/198; AMERICAN; 295 FEET)

Similar in concept to European barges, *River Explorer* was the first boat of its kind when it was inaugurated in 1998. She's a modern, American-built, American-flagged and American-crewed hotel barge; the vessel consists of two connected custom-built barges propelled by a 3,000-horsepower towboat. The forward barge contains public rooms, including a dining room accommodating all passengers at a single, open seating for all meals, a two-deck showroom, exercise and games area, library, gift shop, and **Pilot House Lounge,** a re-creation of a river pilothouse complete with equipment and windows overlooking the bow. Art depicting river exploration decorates public areas. Among the amenities are a never-empty cookie jar, a "raid the fridge" policy for sandwiches and snacks, and 24-hour coffee service.

The aft barge contains all 98 cabins, each measuring 200 square feet. All are outside and have picture windows. Upper-deck cabins have balconies. All have twin or super-queen-size beds, satellite television, VCR, telephone with computer port, minifridge, coffeemaker, iron, and bathroom with tub.

River Explorer sails from New Orleans on four- to ten-day excursions encompassing six geographic regions. Itineraries feature the Cumberland, Illinois, Kanawha, Mississippi, Ohio, and Tennessee rivers, Atchafalaya basin, and Gulf of Mexico Intracoastal Waterway. From time to time, the line offers special theme cruises.

Prices begin at $995 per person, double, for a four-day excursion. Taxes, port charges, most shore activities, and tipping are included. Alcoholic beverages cost extra.

St. Lawrence Cruise Lines/Canadian River Cruise Vacations

253 Ontario Street, Kingston, Ontario, Canada K7L 2Z4; ☎ 613-549-8091 or 800-267-7868; fax 613-549-8410; www.stlawrencecruiselines.com

Canadian Empress (32/66; CANADIAN; 108 FEET)

The *Canadian Empress* is a replica of a steamboat but with modern conveniences and amenities. Built in 1981, she was designed to reflect the classic style of North American turn-of-the-century riverboats with brass handrails and ornate metal ceilings, recapturing the grace of a turn-of-the-century lifestyle. Her size and shallow draft allow her to navigate the islands and through locks, some of which are inaccessible to larger vessels and provide an up-close experience. A congenial Canadian crew provides good service in a comfortable atmosphere.

The boat sails on three-, five-, and six-night cruises between May and October on the St. Lawrence and Ottawa rivers. Boarding ports include Kingston, Ottawa, and Quebec City. Cruise fares include most sightseeing tours and attractions.

AMAZON RIVER CRUISES

MANY MAINSTREAM SHIPS WITH SOUTH AMERICAN itineraries include an Amazon River cruise. They enter on the Atlantic delta and sail upriver to Manaus. The river is very wide; any intimate view must be obtained aboard small crafts on tributaries. More exotic regions of the Upper Amazon are reached mainly from Iquitos, Peru, or via Ecuador.

Note: In parentheses after each boat name is information (where available) about the number of cabins and passengers; officers and crew; and the boat's length (cabins/passengers; officers/crew; boat length). Many companies offering tours from the United States use the same boats on the Amazon; these include the following:

Amazon Clipper (8/16; PERUVIAN; 65 FEET)

Three-night cruises explore the tributaries to bird-watch, fish for piranha, and visit Amazon Ecopark, a nature reserve and wildlife rehabilitation sanctuary. *Clipper's* cabins have private bathrooms, bunk berths, as well as nighttime air-conditioning. Facilities include a covered salon, bar, dining area, library, and fully equipped kitchen with freezer. Local cuisine is served—mainly fresh fish. Mineral water is provided.

Amazon Explorer (8/16; PERUVIAN; 85 FEET)

Three- or six-night round-trip cruises upriver from Iquitos. The steel-constructed boat has a small air-conditioned lounge, dining room/bar, and Sun Deck. The cabins are outside doubles with bunk beds; all are air-conditioned and have private bath/shower.

Arca (13/31; PERUVIAN; 98 FEET)

Three- to six-night trips on the Upper Amazon. The air-conditioned, steel-hull riverboat operates between Iquitos and the twin cities of Tabatinga, Brazil, and Leticia, Colombia. She offers ten twin-bedded cabins with upper/lower berths and three triples with lower beds. All cabins have private bathroom and shower. The boat has a lounge/bar and covered and uncovered deck areas.

Rio Amazonas (21/44; PERUVIAN; 146 FEET)

Three- to six-night explorations of the Upper Amazon, sailing downriver on Sunday from Iquitos to the twin cities of Tabatinga, Brazil, and Leticia, Colombia; upriver on Wednesday from Leticia. Itineraries can be combined. The ship has an air-conditioned dining room and library, covered and uncovered deck areas, and hot tub. Upper-deck cabins have picture windows and private bathrooms with shower. Sun Deck cabins are larger, offering three twin beds, a closet, and a chair.

Most of the following companies also offer Galápagos cruises as well as Amazon ones. See listings in the next section, Adventure and Cultural Cruises.

Ecotour Expeditions

P.O. Box 128, Jamestown, RI 02835-0128; ☎ 800-688-1822 or 401-423-3377; fax 401-423-9630; www.naturetours.com

Tucano (9/18; PERUVIAN/7; 80 FEET)

The *Tucano,* built in 1997 and extensively renovated and refurbished in 2004, is designed in the tradition of the steamboats that navigated the Amazon in the late 19th century, giving her a shallow draft and a large volume of interior space. She is very wide at the base and has a flat bottom, drawing only five feet, enabling her to explore remote Amazon rivers where V hulls cannot navigate. Routinely, the *Tucano* crosses the sandbars that cover the entrances of many rivers in Amazonia, and continues deep into the wilderness, exploring small rivers where wildlife is abundant but which are closed to most other passenger vessels.

Due to the typical calm Amazon waters, *Tucano* is able to have three decks, resulting in her large interior space and the all-important large windows—70—all of which are three feet high and can be opened. Every cabin has at least four of these windows, making the cabins bright and airy. All cabins have private bathrooms with shower, toilet, and sink. The boat is air-conditioned and has wood-paneled walls, a large Observation Deck, a living room, a wide balcony around the front of the vessel and a collection of science and nature reference books.

Seven-night cruises depart year-round. Air transportation can be arranged from Miami. The trips on the Amazon and tributaries are accompanied by naturalists. The company also offers Galápagos cruises.

Iberostar Grand Amazon Cruises
**2566 Le Jeune Road, Coral Gables, FL 33134; ☎ 888-923-2722 or
305-774-9225; fax 305-774-4810; www.iberostar.com**

Iberostar Grand Amazon (72/148; BRAZILIAN; 270 FEET)

In 2005, the Spanish hotel company, Iberostar, launched its first cruise ship
on the Amazon River in Brazil. Built in Manaus at a cost of $12 million and
styled like Nile River boats after the owner and architects made several
trips to Egypt for that purpose, the *Iberostar Grand Amazon* is the most
deluxe riverboat on the Amazon.

The four-deck vessel has 72 spacious cabins and two suites, all with air-
conditioning, small private balcony, private bathroom with a countertop of Brazilian marble, a large glass-enclosed shower (only suites have tubs), hair dryer, and
an ingenious light sensor that turns the lights on/off when you step inside.

The cabins, each measuring 240 square feet—unusually large for
riverboats—are identical in size and layout and are very comfortable. They
are furnished with a queen or twin beds, a dressing table that can double as
a desk, leather easy chair, night tables, mini-bar, television monitor for
movies, safe, phone, and generous closet space and drawers. There is good
lighting with bedside switches for all lights. The two suites have almost 500
square feet with a separate bedroom and sitting/dining room and a
veranda that extends around both rooms.

Two dining venues serve local and international cuisine, offer fresh fruit
and vegetables, and feature local fish from the Amazon, along with excellent lamb, pork, and beef from Brazil. The main dining room on the lower
deck, accommodating all passengers at one time, has open seating for three
meals with flexible times. It serves a buffet for breakfast and lunch, but at
dinner passengers have a choice of the buffet or a menu with two selections for four courses, or they can take from both. All tables seat 8 people,
except the Captain's table which seats 12. A second dining venue for light
breakfast and lunch and a bar are in the covered area of the top open-air
deck. Another section of the deck has a swimming pool surrounded by
comfortable wooden deck lounges and a hot tub (with lukewarm water).

The riverboat's other facilities include a large lounge with a bar that
does duty as the lecture room, show lounge, and disco; a small gym with
exercise equipment; one elevator; a boutique; a clinic with nurse available
24/7; and laundry service. Internet access is planned.

Decor throughout the vessel is low-key and pleasant and features generous use of Brazilian hardwoods and crafts. In the cabins, for example, several
walls are faced with golden blond Brazilian hardwoods and artwork reflecting
Amazonian traditions; several public rooms have lovely parquet floors.

The boat has an expedition staff of five to eight men, depending on the
number of passengers. All come from the Manaus region and are knowledgeable about the flora and fauna of the Amazon. Daily excursions of two
to three hours are scheduled for 8 a.m. and 4 p.m.; special outings for birding are offered at 6 a.m. at least twice during the week. The boat carries

four launches, each holding up to 22 people; more launches are added as needed. Normally, passengers are divided by language—Portugese, Spanish, English, French, German, Italian—as necessary. At least two guides accompany every expedition.

Departing from Manaus, the *Iberostar Grand Amazon* sails on two itineraries: A four-night cruise (Sunday–Thursday) along the Rio Negro, the main tributary of the thousand tributaries that spill into the Amazon River; and a three-night one (Thursday–Sunday) along the Solimoes River, the name given to the Amazon prior to its arrival at Manaus. A third option combines the two itineraries into a seven-day cruise. The boat stops at several points along the Amazon jungle, offering excursions on small boats to explore certain areas up close.

Back on the ship after an excursion, passengers can attend lectures on Amazon history, flowers, fish, birds, and more with audio-visual accompaniment. During the week, two evening shows are performed by a lively folklore group from Manaus. And we particularly appreciate that there are none of the endless announcements heard on many cruise ships.

In addition to the standard inclusion of all meals and entertainment on the boat, all beverages and excursions are also included in the price. Dress throughout the cruise is casual.

For many people, a cruise on the Amazon is reason enough to take this trip, but when they can combine it with stylish accommodations, good food, and outstanding service, it's truly a winner.

International Expeditions
1 Environs Park, Helena, AL 35080; ☎ 205-428-1700 or 800-633-4734; fax 205-428-1714; www.ietravel.com

La Amatista **(15/30; 125 FEET)**

La Turmalina **(14/28; 115 FEET)**

La Turquesa **(23/46)**

This 25-year-old company uses exploratory vessels sailing from Iquitos, past the start of the Amazon, exploring its tributaries. These include the Ucayali, Maranon, and Tapiche rivers and the Pacaya-Samiria National Reserve, all viewed from excursion craft and on foot along jungle trails. Naturalists/ guides accompany the outings. All cabins have private facilities and air-conditioning. Nine-day cruises make weekly departures throughout the year. The company also offers Galápagos cruises and others in Central and South America as well as Patagonia on the *Via Australis,* and Antarctica, British Isles, Greenland, and Spitsbergen on the 96-passenger *Polar Star.*

Ladatco Tours
2200 South Dixie Highway, Suite 704, Coconut Grove, FL 33133; ☎ 305-854-8422 or 800-327-6162; fax 305-285-0504; www.ladatco.com

Ladatco is a tour company that promotes and sells cruises on the following boats:

Amazon Clipper Premium **(8/16; PERUVIAN; 66 FEET)**

La Amastista/La Esmeralda/La Turmalina **(11 TO 15/22 TO 30; PERUVIAN; 91 TO 115 FEET)**

Tucano **(9/16; 80 FEET)**

Amazon Clipper Premium, a two-deck riverboat refurbished for overnight touring, has cabins with bunk beds, private baths, and air-conditioning. Three- to four-day cruises depart on Wednesday from Manaus on the Amazon and Negro rivers; a six-day cruise combines the two. A multilingual local guide accompanies all cruises.

La Amastista, La Esmeralda, and *La Turmalina* offer six-day cruises, round-trip, departing Sunday from Iquitos. Three-night cruises are also available. The itinerary includes bird-watching, jungle walks, and fishing in the Ataquari River.

Tucano sails year-round from Manuas on seven-night Heart of the Amazonia cruises. (See Ecotour Expeditions earlier in this section.)

Marco Polo Expeditions/PTS, Inc./Galápagos Cruises
1467 Industrial Avenue, Escondido, CA 92029; ☎ 866-672-4533 or 858-672-4533, fax 858-672-4505; www.ptsincorporated.com

Three-night *Desafio* cruises depart year-round from Manaus to the Amazon and tributaries accompanied by a multilingual naturalist. Continental and Brazilian cuisine is served buffet style. The three-day *Tucano* program includes a jungle walk to explore flora. The *Uncano* also sails on a nine-day Amazon adventure. The company also uses the *Amazon Clipper, Arca, Rio Amazonas,* and others, as well as offering three- to seven-night cruises in the Galápagos on a variety of vessels, including the *Galapagos Legend, Galapagos Explorer II, Coral I,* and *Coral II* on year-round departures.

Tara Tours
6595 Northwest 36th Street, Suite 306, Miami, FL 33166; ☎ 305-871-1246 or 800-327-0080; fax 305-871-0417; www.taratours.com

The tour company utilizes a variety of vessels and offers Amazon cruises from both Iquitos and Manaus. Among its vessels are *Rio Amazonas* (21/44; Peruvian; 146 feet), *La Amastista, La Esmeralda, La Turmalina* (11 to 15/22 to 30; Peruvian; 90 to 125 feet), and *La Aquamarina* (16/29).

Eight-night Amazon packages offered year-round from Miami to Iquitos include boat trips and one night at a hotel in Lima, Peru, plus jungle walks, visits to native villages, and English-speaking naturalists. The company also offers cruises of the Galápagos.

ADVENTURE *and* CULTURAL CRUISES

THE DIFFERENCE BETWEEN AN ADVENTURE or expedition cruise and an educational or cultural cruise is often a matter of semantics or marketing. And although there are differences, there are also similarities, particularly in the type of person to whom they appeal—namely, experienced travelers who prefer an intellectually stimulating or educational environment when they travel and do not need (or want) the activities and entertainment typical of mainstream cruises. They prefer the hands-on learning that adventure and educational cruises provide as well as the companionship of like-minded travelers.

Ships offering adventures or expeditions generally are informal and small, accommodating fewer than 150 passengers. Their small size enables them to visit places large ships cannot go. Vessels providing educational or cultural cruises might be larger and more formal. In all cases, the itineraries (which tend to be two weeks or longer) and the opportunity to learn from experts are the main attractions.

In the last two or three years, more deluxe ships have been added in the adventure and cultural cruises category, bringing with them a new level of comfort and expanded facilities. But the majority are still comfortable workhorses that safely ply icy waters or jungle rivers. They have cozy, functional cabins, friendly service, and good food, served at one open seating, often family style. Dress is casual. Most ships maintain an open bridge.

Cruises are almost always seasonal to take advantage of optimum weather and wildlife conditions. On board, passengers attend lectures by specialists and have time to enjoy fellow shipmates. Ports are likely to be remote and passengers travel by Zodiac boats to the most inaccessible areas, often making wet landings where no docks are available.

On shore, participants view wildlife and scenery, hike into coastal forests, or encounter remote cultures. Not all cruises require heavy exertion—many are light adventure, nothing more than a short walk. In the evening, staff naturalists and guest lecturers recap the day's excursion in well-attended sessions. On educational or cultural cruises, lecturers are likely to be historians, anthropologists, museum authorities, and area specialists. Many such trips are sponsored by universities and museum groups, often as an alumni fund-raiser.

Destinations might be world-renowned sites visited by general tours, but participants on cultural cruises get in-depth information and excursions led by experts rather than the commercial guides that regular cruise lines use. Participants also are likely to attend cultural and folklore events. It isn't unusual for adventure and cultural cruises to overlap in their activities, particularly those offering light adventure (or soft adventure, the unappealing term the travel trade uses).

Not only do these cruises appeal to the same type of people—they may appeal to the same exact people.

If you've never tried an adventure/expedition cruise, there are a few things you need to consider. Adventure cruises are not exactly laid-back affairs. You might be rousted out of bed at 5:30 a.m. to see a whale, a penguin, or nearly anything else within the purview of the cruise's educational program. Even if you're not rolled out at 5:30 a.m., you'll probably have to rise by 6:30 or 7 a.m. to dress and have breakfast before the day's activities commence. If you try sleep in, you can often count on some announcements over the public address speaker that can be heard in your cabin. Such cruises tend to pack a lot into a day. On some ships, you scarcely have time for a shower and a change of clothes before dinner is served, except on days at sea.

Before you book an adventure/expedition cruise, carefully scrutinize the itinerary and make some inquiries about the likelihood of rough seas. An Antarctic cruise, for example, must traverse the Drake Passage for two days southbound and two days northbound from South America. The Drake Passage can be one of the roughest seas on the planet—perhaps not the place to be if you've never cruised before or if your experience is limited to the calm waters of the Caribbean. But if you're lucky, as Kay was on her Antarctic expedition, the passage can be as smooth as a lake.

Because many adventure/expedition cruises are at the ends of the earth or halfway around the world, you need to pay attention to all aspects of your travel plans. We recommend an intermediate layover both coming and going, as well as an extra day in the port of embarkation. If you're going to the Far East or Australia, try to arrange a night in Hawaii or California before continuing to your final destination. If you're headed to Antarctica, you might want to spend a night in Santiago or Buenos Aires on the return. Once when coming home from Antarctica, Bob ignored his own advice. After two days bouncing across the Drake Passage, he disembarked the ship at 8:30 a.m., then had to wait until 1 p.m. for a four-hour flight to Santiago. He had another four-hour layover in Santiago before boarding a nine-hour flight to Houston and connecting on to his final destination. By the time he got home, he'd been traveling for 32 hours (not counting the Drake Passage).

If your cruise package includes a stopover (and many do), it pays to check out the city where you'll be stopping. A Galápagos Islands adventure cruise included an overnight in Quito, Ecuador. Those folks who didn't check out Quito before leaving home were astonished to learn upon arrival that it sits in the Andes at an elevation of 9,350 feet. Not only did most not have warm clothing they were heading for the equator and sea level, after all—but they discovered it was quite impossible to acclimate to that altitude in one day. An equally compelling reason for an overnight stopover and an extra night in the port city is the opportunity to deal with lost luggage. Believe us, the worst time to have your luggage disappear is when you're about to embark on an adventure/expedition cruise. Chances are you've spent weeks rounding up the specialized clothing and gear required for the cruise, but if you have a day or more prior to boarding for your luggage to catch up with you, you'll be fine 90% of the time. In a worst-case scenario, when your lost luggage stays lost, you'll still have time to re-equip in local stores before sailing.

Another precaution we take is to avoid luggage transfers between airlines. On an itinerary from Fort Lauderdale to Iceland for an expedition cruise out of Reykjavik, for example, we took an early Delta flight to New York's JFK International Airport, where we claimed our bags and then personally rechecked them with Icelandair. We were perfectly happy to suffer an extra hour or two at JFK for the peace of mind of knowing that our bags were safely checked with Icelandair to Reykjavik.

Adventure/expedition cruises don't require physical training, but participants should be in good condition and able to endure some exertion. More importantly, they need to be flexible in temperament as well as body. They should be good sports, keep a sense of humor, and be ready to forgo comforts occasionally. Adventure or expedition cruises take participants off the beaten path worldwide. They tend to be more expensive than mainstream cruises because fewer people share the cost and because it costs more to operate a ship in remote areas. Also, shore excursions are usually included, and lecturers must be accommodated in cabins that otherwise draw revenue.

Participants tend to be strong environmentalists who expect fellow travelers to share their views. They like to be outdoors, are active, well traveled, well educated, intellectually curious, affluent, and perhaps semiretired professionals age 50 or older. They often belong to a museum or natural history group. They probably read *Audubon*, *National Geographic,* or *Smithsonian* magazines, watch public television, and support the local zoo.

Following is a representative list of companies offering adventure/expedition or educational/cultural cruises. They provide brochures, usually with deck plans of vessels they use, and descriptions of itineraries. Being specialists, they usually can answer questions with more firsthand authority than a travel agent—unless it's an adventure travel specialist—or a mainstream cruise line can.

Regarding Galápagos cruises, in an effort to prevent overcrowding at certain visitor sites, the Galápagos National Park Service has revised the itineraries of many tour boats. Check with the tour company for the latest information.

Note: In parentheses after each boat name is information (where available) about the number of cabins and passengers; officers and crew; and the boat's length (cabins/passengers; officers/crew; boat length/tonnage).

Abercrombie & Kent, Inc. (*See* Part Two.)

Small boats are chartered for Galápagos cruises, including *Eclipse* (27/48; Ecuadoran; 210 feet), among others. In Antarctica, the company uses *Explorer II*.

African Safari Club Ltd.
Northside House, Tweedy Road, Bromley, Kent BR1 3WA, UK;
☎ **+44-208-466-0014; fax +44-208-466-0020; www.africansafariclub.com**

Royal Star **(111/255; GREEK/130; 472 FEET/5,600 TONS)**

Royal Star (formerly *Ocean Islander*) was built in 1956 and extensively renovated in 1994. The cabins are small but nicely decorated; bathrooms are tiny with shower only. Most cabins (96) are outside and have air-conditioning, safe, and phone. Some triples and quads are available. Suites have a minibar and television/VCR. Room service menu is limited. A nice, small vessel with attractive decor and a friendly ambience, it offers excellent itineraries. The ship has a casino, library, one elevator, small pool, massage room and sauna, shuffleboard, darts, and bingo. The **Belvedere Restaurant** has two seatings and offers international cuisine and afternoon tea with good service. There's also a poolside buffet at lunch. Entertainment is limited and low-key in the two lounges and piano bar.

Royal Star passengers tend to be couples ages 40-plus and European. Although children are welcome, the ship has no facilities or special arrangements for them. The ship sails on 14- to 21-day cruises, many of which are combined with safari packages in Kenya. She sails from Mombassa to Zanzibar and Mahe in the Seychelles. The club has its own charter aircraft taking passengers from London to the ship's location. *Royal Star* is represented in the United States by Global Quest Journeys, 185 Willis Avenue, Mineola, NY 11501; ☎ 516-739-3690 or 800-221-3254; fax 516-739-8022; **www.globalquesttravel.com.**

American Safari Cruises
(*See* Part Two under European and Smaller Cruise Lines.)

Canodros, S.A.
Canodros 2735, P.O. Box 59-9000, Miami, FL 33159-9000;
☎ **800-613-6026; www.canodros.com**

Galápagos Explorer II **(50/100; ECUADORAN; 295 FEET)**

The luxury, all-suite ship, built in 1990 as the *Renaissance III*, sails on three-, four-, and seven-night cruises weekly in the Galápagos Islands. Cruises can be combined with three or more nights at Kapawi Ecological Reserve, an unusual native Indian-owned and -operated base camp in the Amazon.

Ecuadoran-owned and -operated, the ship has classic lines and interiors throughout. Cabins, all with sitting rooms, are air-conditioned and have queen or two twin beds, telephone, television for VCR use, refrigerator-bar, full-length wardrobe, marble bath, and 110-volt electrical outlets. Also onboard are an outdoor pool and whirlpool, boutique, library, observation deck, karaoke bar, and massage suite. The vessel has satellite communications and carries a doctor onboard.

The elegant, nonsmoking restaurant offers one informal open seating. International and Ecuadoran cuisine is served; special diets can be accommodated. A lunch buffet is served on deck. Staff will prepare additional dishes on request. All bar drinks—including bottled water—are complimentary; only name wines, Champagne, and minibar contents cost extra. Cruise price also includes twice-daily tours escorted by naturalists.

The ship always anchors offshore, and passengers are tendered on dinghies for dry or wet landings. In keeping with the company's environmental commitment, all soaps, detergents, and shampoo used on board are biodegradable. The ship produces its own fresh water and is equipped with a sewage treatment system to minimize environmental impact. Chlorine isn't used on board. Paper and nontoxic solids are incinerated, metal cans are compacted for recycling, and nonbiodegradable trash is returned to port.

The ship is used extensively by tour companies offering Galápagos/South America tour programs.

Compagnie Polynesienne de Transport Maritime
2028 El Camino Real South, Suite B, San Mateo, CA 94403;
☎ **650-574-2575 or 800-972-7268; www.aranui.com**

Arnaui III (85/200; MARQUESAN)

The world has shrunk to the point that most places on earth can be reached by air, but there are a few exceptions, such as the French Polynesian Marquesas and Tuamotu (or Tuomotu) Islands in the South Pacific. These islands have been accessible by passenger freighters named *Aranui* (meaning "great highway" in the Maori language) since 1959. In 2003, a brand-new one arrived, the 200-passenger *Aranui III*, to take over the 16-day round-trips from Papeete, Tahiti. She carries all manner of cargo and 20-foot containers to the remote archipelago and is crewed mostly by Marquesans.

The passengers' quarters are of a high standard and include a main lounge, library, video room, gym, small shop, laundry, and outdoor swimming pool with a bar. The dining room can accommodate all passengers at one seating. The food is both international and Polynesian, with ingredients such as pork, poultry, fish, fruits and vegetables, and imported beef. French wines are included with lunch and dinner, which are served family style while breakfast is a buffet. Many passengers are French (French Polynesia is still part of France), and others are European, Australian, and American.

The ship has a total of 85 cabins and suites. They include 63 standard, moderate-size twins with portholes, shower, and toilet that are plainly appointed with light wood furnishings; 12 larger deluxe cabins with windows, more colorful decor, darker wood furnishings, a refrigerator, and bathtub; and 10 suites, 8 with private balconies. Some cabins will accommodate a third person.

The ship sails year-round from Papeete, about every other week, on a 14-day voyage, calling at two Tuamotu and six Marquesas islands, all with spectacular scenery and some with beautiful volcanic peaks. Most days are spent at anchor off an island, while the ship loads and unloads cargo; two days are spent at sea. Time in port varies from a few hours to a full day. The *Aranui's* arrival is a major event for each of these islands.

Activities include watching locals harvest black pearls, swimming from fine sandy beaches, snorkeling over coral reefs, exploring archaeological ruins by jeep and on foot, buying handicrafts, and enjoying barbecues. Shore excursions are included in the fare. Scuba diving, horseback riding, and helicopter tours are extra. A 14-day voyage on *Aranui III* starts at about $3,600 per person, double occupancy.

Although assistance is provided, passengers need to be able to negotiate ladders into whale boats and disembark through the surf. March to August is the dry season, but with an occasional shower. September to February is the rainy season. Daytime temperatures hover in the 80s and fall into the 60s and 70s after dark.

Cruise North Expeditions, Inc.

1920 Avenue Road, Toronto, Ontario, Canada M5M 4A1; ☎ 866-263-3220 or 416-789-3752; fax 416-789-1974; www.cruisenorthexpeditions.com

Lyubov Orlova (59 CABINS, 2 SUITES/110; RUSSIAN, CANADIAN, INUIT/64; 328 FEET/4,251 TONS)

Cruise North Expeditions, the Inuit-owned cruise line launched in July 2005, has revolutionized travel to the remote Canadian Arctic, a virtually undiscovered part of the world, by making it affordable, accessible, and authentic. The Inuit are the indigenous people of the Canadian Arctic, popularly known as the Eskimo.

The *Lyubov Orlova*, a Russian vessel with an ice-strengthened hull, a Russian captain and crew, was built in Yugoslavia in 1976, refurbished in 1999, and further upgraded in 2002. She is the only passenger ship docked in the Canadian Arctic with cruises starting in Kuujjuaq, at the northern limit of the great Boreal Forest. That's a clear advantage over other cruise ships that must sail into the region from distant locations, such as Greenland, requiring extra travel days at sea. Cruise North Expeditions chartered the ship in 2006 for five summer seasons from Quark Expeditions (see entry later in this chapter), which takes the ship on Antarctic voyages during the winter months.

The Cruise North package includes a short two-hour flight from Montreal to Kuujjuaq on its sister company, First Air, a Canadian airline that has served the northern region for more than 50 years. Kuujjuaq (population 2,500) is the main town and commercial center of Nunavik, the northernmost district of Quebec Province. It sits on the Koksoak River at the tree line, 914 miles north of Montreal and a few hundred miles below the North Pole. Arriving passengers will be surprised to see soft green hills and wide valleys covered with evergreen forests interspersed with lakes where the winter snows have melted. There were no buildings, no houses, and no roads in the landscape until a few minutes before the plane begins its landing. Any idea that the Arctic is similar to Antarctica will be quickly dispelled.

Cruise North is making a determined effort to have the local Inuit inhabitants actively involved in the cruise operation. At the same time, this venture is helping the Inuit preserve their culture by sharing their traditions and customs with passengers. By being in direct contact with Cruise North passengers and welcoming them to their homeland, Inuit hosts help passengers appreciate the indigenous people's deep reverence for the natural world, its scenic wonders, and wildlife.

Cruise North operates a series of 7- to 12-night Arctic cruises from June through September. Normally during that time, the average daily temperature is about 50 degrees and can even reach 70 degrees. The Arctic wildlife and scenery are certain to delight passengers when they see magnificent polar bears, walrus, Beluga whales, bearded seals, musk oxen, and up to 22 species of birds, including huge colonies of the indigenous thick-billed murre against the awesome backdrop of icebergs, towering cliffs, mountains, and fjords.

The cruises feature an experienced expedition team and daily lectures by naturalists, ornithologists, and historians who review the region's history, particularly the impact of European traders and the explorers who searched for the Northwest Passage. The Inuit members talk about their culture with insights into their society—a society in transition, adjusting from the traditional life of Eskimos to life in modern Canada. On several nights, passengers can watch some excellent films, including *Nanook of the North*, the classic, award-winning feature that vividly portrays the difficult life and extreme hardship that Inuits faced early in the last century, and *Climate On The Edge*, a documentary on the effects of climate change in the Arctic by the National Film Board of Canada.

In small settlements like Kimmirut (population 400) on the coast of Baffin Island, passengers are met by townspeople who act as their guides and a bevy of children, often shyly selling their soapstone carvings, an art for which the Inuit are famous. Kimmirut, once an important trading post, has a new promise of wealth—rubies and sapphires being mined only two miles from town. Sample gems are on display, along with a fine collection of soapstone carvings at the Sopher Gallery in town. Next to the Kimmirut Information Centre with exhibits on the region's history and culture, a tent invites passengers inside to watch women making traditional bannock (a staple similar to doughnuts) and removing the blubber from a seal skin using an *uluk*, the traditional Inuit working knife.

The daily pattern of the voyage is typical of expedition cruises: awakened at 6:30 a.m. with a weather report, breakfast at 7 a.m. and board the Zodiacs to depart for the day's outing by 8 a.m. Passengers are advised to dress in layers, always prepared for a wet landing with waterproof boots, rain pants, and windbreaker, and on some days, a parka. Cruise North Expeditions sends useful information, including maps, to passengers in advance of their cruise.

Cruise North's six itineraries—Arctic Explorer, Baffin Adventure, High Arctic, Hudson's Wake, Labrador North, and Newfoundland and Labrador—include visits to ancient Inuit archaeological sites and entertainment by the Inuit community of traditional Inuit drum dancing and throat singing. Prices start at U.S. $2,995 per person, double occupancy for a seven-night package. Generally, air transportation and taxes are extra. Pre- and postcruise options in the Arctic for small groups are offered and include kayaking, hiking, and a stay at a wilderness lodge.

Most cabins on the *Lyubov Orlova* have two lower berths and a porthole, a small private bath with shower, and are furnished with a chest of drawers and ample closet space. Cabins on the upper deck open onto the deck. The ice-strengthened ship has four decks. Public rooms, situated on one deck, include a forward lounge, small bar, and library stocked with Arctic-related literature, a window-lined dining room that accommodates all passengers at one seating, an aft Observation Deck, and wide promenades, excellent for viewing wildlife and passing scenery.

Cruise North Expeditions is owned by the Makivik Corporation of Quebec, a successful investment corporation born of the first modern-day Aboriginal land claim settlement agreement in Canada (the JBNQA of 1975). Makivik also owns First Air and Air Inuit. The cruise line is headed by Adamie Alaku, the Inuk chairman, and Dugald Wells, a professional engineer and expedition cruise veteran who began his career in the Arctic 20 years ago as a research scientist onboard Canadian icebreakers. The deck staff and engine crew are Russian. The expedition leader, guides, lecturers, chef, and bartender are mostly Canadian, including some Inuit. Reservations can be made through travel agents or The Travel Network in Toronto at ☎ 866-263-3220 or 416-789-3752.

Cruceros Australis/USA
4014 Chase Avenue, Suite 215, Miami Beach, FL 33140; ☎ 305-695-9618 or 877-678-3772; fax 305-534-9276; www.australis.com

Mare Australis **(63/129; CHILEAN; 236 FEET)**

Via Australis **(64/136; CHILEAN; 236 FEET)**

From October to April, the two virtually identical expedition ships of Cruceros Australis sail the Magellan Strait and Beagle Channel, exploring Chilean-Argentinean Patagonia and Tierra del Fuego, one of the most beautiful and unexplored regions of the world at the tip of continental South America. While the departure ports are sizable and interesting, once the cruises are under way the accent is on nature on a grand scale, with ships cruising deep into fjords for close-up experiences of crackling ice fields and wildlife encounters or scenery viewing at a leisurely pace.

The company launched operations on this routing in 1990 with the *Terra Australis*, which was replaced by the more luxurious *Mare Australis* in 2002, with the *Via Australis* added in 2005. Both ships were custom-built in the Valdivia shipyard in Chile and carry Chilean officers and crew.

Cruises ply the waters between Punta Arenas, Chile, and Ushuaia, Argentina, on two different three- and four-night itineraries. With two ships crossing back and forth, the cruise line can offer passengers the option of weekly sailings on three-night or four-night cruises from either port; however, about half of those cruising opt for the seven-night journey, cruising round-trip from either Punta Arenas or Ushuaia.

All cruises have daily Zodiac excursions that differ with the itinerary. Passengers taking the full cruise will sail along magnificent Glacier Alley, observe colonies of elephant seals and sea lions, walk among colonies of Magellanic penguins, visit Cape Horn National Park, hike along the glacier of Pia Fjord, and poke around Puerto Williams, the most southerly town in the world. Weather can affect some shore excursions. Many passengers opt to explore more of Patagonia with land tours, combining Torres del Paine National Park in Chile with El Calafate and its impressive Glacier Perito Moreno in Argentina, with their three- or four-night sailings. These land/sea circuits are offered and operated by *Cruceros Australis* and should be requested at the time of the cruise booking.

Activities schedules are issued daily and briefings are held prior to all disembarkations for Zodiac excursions. In this rather unknown corner of the world, lectures by knowledgeable naturalists are an important part of the cruise experience. They are held daily, introducing passengers to the flora and fauna of the Magellanic forest; marine mammals and birds of Patagonia; history and navigation in the Beagle Channel, Strait of Magellan, or Cape Horn; and history and customs of the native peoples.

The ships have four enclosed decks, with spacious, inviting public areas; the top Observation Deck is totally open, affording grand vistas of the passing scene. The views are almost as panoramic in the **Sky Lounge** on Deck Four, which has an open bar; here, most night activities take place, and in addition to the **Game Room,** it's the only place on board where smoking is permitted. The **Yamana Lounge** on Deck Three has a bar, small library, video and audio equipment, as well as wide-window views. Both lounges are used for lectures and light evening entertainment from a folklore show to bingo, special films, or a tango performance. The bridge is open to passengers, and on board also is a shop and first aid service from the resident doctor.

The **Patagonia dining room** is on Deck One, and the food on board the *Cruceros Australis* ships is very good—a mix of regional and international cuisine. For early risers, coffee and sweet rolls are available. Both breakfast and lunch are buffet service; breakfast has a full range of choices, from juice and fruits to cereal, cheeses, and cold cuts to hot dishes prepared to order; lunch includes cold and hot choice dishes, salads, and a table of various desserts. Each evening, canapés (including Latin specialties such as empanadas) and trays of pisco sours are served in the lounge before dinner. For dinner, along with the first course, soup course, and dessert choice, two or three entrées are offered, including excellent beef and lamb, fish, and seafood. All beverages, including beer, Chilean and Argentine wines, and liquors are included in the ships' tariff.

There is a shipwide equality in all cabins, measuring 161 square feet with outside positions and windows. These are nicely decorated and well-appointed cabins with two low twin beds (that can be moved together for queen-size sleeping), bathroom with shower, reasonable storage and closet space, independently controlled heater, safety box, closet, and 110-/220-volt power outlets. The *Mare Australis* has three triples with pull-down beds, the *Via Australis* has seven.

Passengers are mostly mature, well-seasoned travelers, a mix of North and South Americans, as well as Europeans; lectures and excursions cater to various language groups aboard, although most passengers seem to speak some English. This is an informal ship, requiring that passengers bring warm and waterproof clothing rather than dressy outfits. The atmosphere is friendly and passengers are generally committed to enjoying the adventure of cruising in the wakes of Darwin, Fitz Roy, and Magellan.

Ecotour Expeditions
P.O. Box 128, Jamestown, RI 02835-0128; ☎ 800-688-1822 or 401-423-3377; fax 401-423-9630; www.naturetours.com

This operator uses three small sister ships, *Eric, Flamingo,* and *Letty* (10/20; 83 feet) as well as the *Beluga* (8/16; 110 feet) All cabins and dining rooms are air-conditioned and all cabins have private bathrooms with showers. The vessels are comfortable, but not luxurious. On the upper Dolphin Deck, cabins have two twin lower beds and picture windows, except one cabin that has one double bed. Booby Deck cabins have one double bed and picture windows; while the lower Iguana Deck cabins have two twin lower beds and portholes. Two Iguana cabins have an upper berth and can be used as triples. The *Beluga* has a large dining room, salon, and a full Sun Deck. Of its eight cabins, two have queen-size beds, three bunk beds, and three have two twin beds. The cruises depart on Fridays; on each island passengers visit two to three different sites.

Ecoventura S.A. (*See* entry for Galápagos Network.)

Esplanade Tours (*See* Nile River Cruises earlier in Part Three.)

Galápagos Cruises
c/o Adventure Associates, 13150 Coit Road, Suite 110, Dallas, TX 75240; ☎ 972-907-0414 or 800-527-2500; fax 972-783-1286; www.metropolitantouring.com or www.adventure-associates.com

Adventure Associates is the U.S. representative of Quito-based Metropolitan Touring, Ecuador's leading tour company, and the oldest company offering Galápagos cruises. Ships are well run and have excellent guides.

Isabela II **(21/40; ECUADORAN; 166 FEET)**

Completely renovated in February 2000, this ship's new look includes an enlarged reception area, a redesigned library, and a new multimedia system for briefings and lectures. The mahogany-paneled dining room and library were totally refurbished along with the lounge and cabins. The redesigned Sun Deck now has a bar, observation area for whale- and dolphin-watching, and a solarium. The air-conditioned ship offers satellite telephone, e-mail, and fax service. She sails from Baltra on Fridays on seven-night cruises of the Galápagos Islands; shorter cruises are offered on Tuesday departures. Children under age 12 who share a cabin with adults get a 25% discount off the regular price. Prices do not include Ecuador/Baltra flights or national park entrance fee.

Santa Cruz (46/90; ECUADORAN; 237 FEET)

Offering three-, four-, and seven-night Galápagos cruises, this ship, renovated in 1998, is one of the largest and most comfortable sailing in
Galápagos waters. Food and service are good, and the ship is well run. All
cabins were refitted, and passengers can choose singles, doubles, or suites.
The air-conditioned ship is mostly carpeted and has a large dining room,
cocktail lounge, bar, library, Jacuzzi, and spacious decks. Three-night cruises
visit the southern islands; four-night tours visit the central and northern
groups. The two can be combined. Naturalist guides, trained and licensed
by Galápagos National Park, give nightly briefings on the next day's visit
and accompany passengers on excursions. Passengers are divided into
groups of 20 people or fewer. In 2005, the company introduced enhancements to its established routes with visits to Sante Fe Island, home to
endemic land iguanas, a large sea lion colony, and the Galápagos' oldest
rocks; Dragon Hill on Santa Cruz, where marine iguanas bask on black lava
and a lagoon attracts flamingos; La Galapaguera, the giant-tortoise breed-
ing station; and Stephen's Bay on San Cristobal, with indigenous Chatham
mockingbirds, lava lizards, and a white coral beach.

Adventure Associates offers other ships in the Galápagos and also has
Upper Amazon cruises on the 26-passenger *Manatee Amazon Explorer.*

Galapagos Network

**5805 Blue Lagoon Drive, Suite 160, Miami, FL 33126; ☎ 305-262-6264 or
800-633-7972; fax 305-262-9609; www.ecoventura.com**

This tour company offers year-round, five- to ten-night cruises in the Galápagos Islands on its fleet of small vessels. Cruises are designed for the well
educated, well traveled, and those eager to learn about nature, ecology, and
environmental issues. The boats' size allows them to visit remote islands.
Naturalist guides lecture and lead walks. Passengers are ferried to the
islands by launches.

Life aboard a Galapagos Network cruise, especially on the *Letty, Eric,* and
Flamingo I, is, well, familial. The small number of passengers and Ecuadoran
crew connect almost immediately in a friendship that only ripens over the
duration of the cruise. The whole crew—from the captain to the cook—is
invested in sharing the rugged beauty and abundant wildlife of the Galápagos, and their enthusiasm is impossible to resist.

Dining features Ecuadoran specialties, which in spice, aroma, and taste
are always a surprise. Some dishes exhibit characteristics of provincial Mexican cuisine; others, remarkably, would be at home in an Indian (as in
Mumbai) restaurant. But it's all good, even if it keeps you guessing.

One of the Galapagos Network's greatest strengths is its land support.
From the time you step off your international flight, there is someone to
watch over you. Most itineraries include an overnight in either Quito or
Guayaquil in quirky but totally wonderful (and totally Ecuadoran) local
hotels. Following an overnight, passengers continue on by plane the next
day to the Galápagos.

Sky Dancer **(8/16; ECUADORAN; 100 FEET)**

Built in the United States, this live-aboard dive vessel has a spacious dining area that serves both Ecuadoran and international cuisine, fully stocked bar, main salon with entertainment center, allocated personal dive storage, and Sun Deck. Cabins are air-conditioned and have private bathrooms. *Sky Dancer* attracts hard-core divers who can take as many as four dives per day on a preplanned, seven- or ten-night itinerary. Dive in the Northern Islands of Wolf and Darwin, famous for hammerhead sharks, giant manta rays, and whale sharks.

Eric/Flamingo I/Letty **(10/20; ECUADORAN; 83 FEET)**

Built in 1993, *Letty* is the newest of three luxury yachts. All are air-conditioned. Cabins have private bathrooms, VCRs, and stereo equipment. *Letty* departs on Monday; the others depart on Sunday. Approximately four hours per day are spent on each island. The boats are well suited for families or groups. Five- to seven-night itineraries include the western islands of Fernandina and Isabela, as well as Española, Tower, Santa Cruz, Bartolome, South Plaza, Santiago, and San Cristobal. In addition, passengers may lunch at a ranch on Santa Cruz. The ships depart from San Cristobal every Sunday for the week's cruise.

Galapagos Yacht Cruises

c/o Galapagos, Inc., 7800 Red Road, Suite 112, South Miami, FL 33143; ☎ 305-665-0841 or 800-327-9854; fax 305-661-1457; www.galapagoscruises.net

Three-, four-, and seven-night cruises of the Galápagos on a dozen ships as different as the deluxe 100-passenger *Galapagos Explorer II* and the 16-passenger catamaran M/V *Millenium*, which has air-conditioned cabins, each with private balcony, some with Jacuzzis, Sun Deck, and large social area.

Skorpios III **(49/125)**

This is one of several companies that use the ship for their Chile program. *Skorpios III* was constructed in 1994 and 1995 to international standards for SOLAS and A-1 Ice, among others. She is equipped with fire, navigational, security, and lifesaving equipment and satellite phone service. The ship sails every Sunday from Puerto Natales, about 153 miles north of Punta Arenas, on a five-day cruise through the channels and fjords that border the Southern Ice Field in the Chilean Patagonia, considered the third largest reserve of freshwater on the planet and home to the most spectacular glaciers in the Southern Hemisphere.

International Expeditions

One Environs Park, Helena, AL 35080; ☎ 205-428-1700 or 800-633-4734; fax 205-428-1714; www.ietravel.com

Evolution **(18/32)**

The four-deck expedition ship is fully air-conditioned and has 14 cabins and 4 suites that measure about 200 square feet each, including a generous-size bath with shower and hair dryer. There is an Observation Deck, a Sun Deck with a small pool, a canopied bar on the roof deck, a library/video room, and an infirmary with a doctor aboard every voyage. Meals are served in the dining room in one seating or outdoors, weather permitting. Satellite phone and e-mail access is available from the bridge when necessary. The ship carries regular kayaks and special acrylic sea kayaks for underwater viewing; scuba and snorkeling equipment; and wet suits. All cruises are accompanied by naturalist guides. Ten-day Galápagos itineraries are offered monthly year-round.

Kleintours

Avenue Eloy. Alfaro N 34–151 and Catalina Aldaz, Quito, Ecuador; ☎ 888-50-KLEIN or 593-2-2267-000; fax 593-2-2442-389; www.kleintours.com

Coral I/Coral II (20/36)

These two vessels offer three-, four-, and seven-night cruises. Three-night cruises depart on Sunday; four-night cruises, Wednesday.

Galapagos Legend (50/100 ;ECUADORAN/68; 300 FEET)

Built in Germany in 2002, this ship has 50 outside cabins, of which four are large suites and 24 are junior suites, and 3 inside cabins. All cabins have a private bathroom, hair dryer, and television. This boat offers three-, four-, and seven-day cruises. Three-day cruises depart on Monday; four-day cruises depart on Thursday. Seven-night cruises depart on Monday, Wednesday, or Thursday. The ship has a dining room, where continental cuisine and Ecuadoran specialties are served, and a bar, pool, and conference room for up to 70 persons. The ship is air-conditioned and has a lounge, library, 24-hour coffee bar, observatory, jogging track, boutique, and clinic. The ship sails year-round from Baltra to the Galápagos Islands, accompanied by naturalist guides. Longer itineraries can include stay-overs in Quito, Ecuador.

Lindblad Expeditions

96 Morton Street, Ninth Floor, New York, NY 10014; ☎ 212-765-7740 or 800-397-3348; fax 212-265-3770; www.expeditions.com

Lindblad Expeditions describes its mission as "providing travelers with a more thoughtful way to see the world, avoiding crowded destinations, and seeking out natural ones." The company offers a wide selection of expedition cruises using six small ships in various offbeat destinations around the world. The globe-roaming company was founded in 1979 by Sven-Olof Lindblad, son of the late Lars-Eric Lindblad, who pioneered modern expedition cruising. Each cruise is designed to take travelers to remote areas in comfort and safety.

Lindblad Expeditions chartered four other ships in 2007 and operates cruises for universities or groups.

In 2004, Lindblad took two major steps: the company added a second ship, the *Islander,* to its weekly Galápagos series and joined forces with the National Geographic Society to combine their travel and expedition strengths in three broad areas:

1. Creating an education program to enhance passengers' expedition experience and bring the findings to an audience far beyond expedition participants.

2. Adding technological innovations across the Lindblad fleet, with particular focus on the *Endeavor,* renamed *National Geographic Endeavour,* where state-of-the-art equipment will allow for more extensive underwater exploration.

3. Establishing an expert advisory panel of researchers, scientists, and explorers, including oceanographer and National Geographic Society explorer-in-residence Sylvia Earle and National Geographic Society contributing photographer-in-residence Emory Kristof, to help shape the alliance's conservation, research, and education initiatives. The best part for Lindblad passengers is the opportunity to interact with the National Geographic Society team as well as Lindblad's expedition leaders and naturalists.

National Geographic Endeavour **(61/110; SCANDINAVIAN/ INTERNATIONAL; 295 FEET)**

The *Endeavour,* after being renamed, sailed on its inaugural voyage in April 2005. Throughout the year, the ship operates from Antarctica to Scandinavia on 12- and 25-night itineraries. She has been outfitted to allow for more extensive exploration, including Zodiac landing craft, sea kayaks, snorkel gear, and high-tech underwater equipment such as a remotely operated video camera (ROV) that transmits live underwater pictures back to the ship.

The five-deck ship has a lounge with a bar and facilities for films and lectures, a library, small swimming pool, fitness center, sauna, hair salon, gift shop, and Observation Deck. Meals are served in one seating with unassigned tables in an informal setting. All cabins are outside above the waterline and have windows or portholes and private baths; there are a few singles. The ship provides a passenger e-mail station, and laundry services. A doctor and massage therapist are on board. From time to time, the company offers cruises geared to families and others designed for travel photography buffs.

Islander **(24/48; ECUADORAN; 164 FEET)**

This new, fully air-conditioned ship has a lounge with bar and facilities for films and lectures, a library, small gift shop, doctor's office, and deck space for lounging in the sun or shade. All meals are served in one seating and offer an international menu with Ecuadoran specialties. All cabins on the three-deck ship are outside and have windows and private baths. The ship carries Zodiac landing craft, snorkeling gear, and wet suits. The ship sails in the Galápagos year-round, departing Saturdays, and underscores Lindblad's 40 years of exploration in the region.

Lord of the Glens **(29/54; SCOTTISH; 150 FEET)**

A classic luxury yacht with rich mahogany finishes and teak decks, the vessel has two lounges, a small library and bar, and two open-air viewing areas. The cabins are outside with large windows (some have portholes), bathrooms with shower, bathrobes, hair dryer, phone, television, and safe. Meals that stress local fare and fresh products are served in a single seating in the room-with-a-view dining room. From May to September, the vessel offers ten-night or longer cruises in the heart of the Scottish Highlands, visiting historic places and extraordinary scenery. For a 14-day trip, the Heart of the Highlands cruise is combined with a Royal Scotsman train ride through countryside between Edinburgh and Inverness.

Polaris (41/80; SWEDISH/FILIPINO AND SWEDISH; 238 FEET)

Polaris offers Galápagos cruises year-round. Ten-day land and sea itineraries are accompanied by outstanding naturalists, including Dr. Lynn Fowler, who has conducted wildlife research in the area for more than 20 years. The fully air-conditioned ship has a lounge with bar and facilities for films and lectures, a library, gift shop, doctor's office, and covered deck with tables and chairs. All meals are served in one seating and offer an international menu with Ecuadoran specialties. All cabins on the four-deck ship are outside and most have windows (except a few on the lower deck that have portholes) and private bath. The ship carries Zodiac landing craft, a glass-bottom boat, snorkeling gear, and wet suits. Polaris sails on ten-day programs with a nine-night voyage visiting six islands in the Galápagos.

Sea Bird/Sea Lion (37/70; AMERICAN; 152 FEET)

The twin ships have a lounge with bar and facilities for films and lectures, a library, and outside deck with chairs. All meals, prepared by American chefs, are served in one seating. All cabins on the four-deck ship are outside and have windows (except four on the lower deck that have portlights) and private bath. The ship carries Zodiac landing craft, kayaks, snorkeling gear, and wet suits, and has an e-mail station. From May to September, the ships sail on 7- and 11-night Alaska cruises; in autumn and spring they move to the Columbia and Snake rivers to Hells Canyon and Lewis and Clark sites, as well as Idaho and Montana. In winter, they offer a series of cruises to Baja California and the Gulf of California timed for optimum whale-watching.

Sea Voyager (32/62; COSTA RICAN; 175 FEET)

Acquired in summer 2001 from Temptress Cruises, this ship has all-outside cabins with private bathrooms and air-conditioning. She was completely refurbished in 2001 and sails most of the year on Baja California, Costa Rica, and Panama cruises.

MTS (Melanesian Tourist Services)

P.O. Box 707, Coastwatchers Avenue, Madang, Papua New Guinea; or USA Sales Office, MTS, P.O. Box 65515, Tucson, AZ 85728; ☎ 310-809-6700; fax 310-785-0314; www.mtspng.com; e-mail: mtsusa@cox.net

MTS Discoverer (21/42; NEW GUINEAN; 117 FEET)

The MTS Discoverer was built exclusively for expeditional cruising up the mighty Sepik River and around the Bismarck and Trobriand islands. She can cruise for 30 days without the need to take on fuel and water. She is fast, comfortable, and equipped with five tenders and a helicopter (subject to conditions). The vessel is air-conditioned; her facilities include a restaurant, library, in-house television system, bar, lounge, covered deck space, dive shop, laundry, and gift shop. All cabins have private bathroom, satellite phones, and public address system.

The ship meets international safety requirements and is the only vessel of its kind in Papua New Guinea. She sails on four- and five-night cruises on the Sepik River, and seven-night cruises of the Trobriands and the remote islands of Bismarck and North Solomon. The cruises remain flexible to take advantage of the opportunity to witness an authentic local ceremony that may occur along the way or ensure maximum shore time in the villages.

MTS, a Papua New Guinea–owned and –operated company, was founded in 1975 to develop the country's tourism in a sustainable manner. MTS operates full inbound services and is based in Madang with offices in Port Moresby, Japan, and North America.

Metropolitan Touring

(*See* entry for Galápagos Cruises.)

National Geographic Expeditions

1145 17th Street NW, Washington, D.C. 20036; ☎ 888-966-8687; www.nationalgeographicexpeditions.com

National Geographic Expeditions offers a wide selection of worldwide programs, including more than 20 cruises or journeys in which a cruise is part of the itinerary. The programs use a total of 16 ships as different as the 227-passenger *Royal Clipper* along the Dalmatian coast and the 64-passenger riverboat *Mekong Pandaw* in Vietnam and Cambodia; five of the ships are operated by Lindblad Expeditions. In 2004, the National Geographic Society and Lindblad Expeditions joined to offer excursions that combine the expertise of both. (See Lindblad Expeditions, above, for details.) Lindblad's 110-passenger *Endeavor* was renamed *National Geographic Endeavour* and was outfitted with new equipment such as sea kayaks and high-tech underwater equipment to enhance the expeditions.

Orient Lines (*See* Part Two.)

Orion Expeditions Cruises

(*See* Part Two, European, Asian, and Smaller Cruise Lines.)

Quark Expeditions

1019 Boston Post Road, Darien, CT 06820; ☎ 203-656-0499 or 800-356-5699; fax 203-655-6623; www.quarkexpeditions.com

This expedition operator, a pioneer in Arctic and Antarctic expedition cruises, handles a large fleet of Russian- and Yugoslavian-built ships for polar travel, all with Russian officers and crew. The fleet includes icebreakers, adventure ships, and expedition ships. All ships are equipped with Zodiacs. Some icebreakers have helicopters. Each voyage is accompanied by an expedition leader, assistant expedition leader, lecturers, and Zodiac pilots who may be from the United States, Europe, Australia, or South America, depending on destinations and their expertise. Antarctica departures are varied and include the Antarctic Peninsula, Weddell Sea, South Georgia, Falkland Islands, Ross Sea, New Zealand, and Australian sub-Antarctic islands. Most cruises depart from Ushuaia, Argentina, but some depart from Auckland, New Zealand, or Hobart, Tasmania. The icebreakers sail on various itineraries in the High Arctic and to the North Pole.

In May 2007, Quark Expeditions was acquired by UK-based First Choice Holidays PLC, and has joined First Choice's Activity Holidays sector, a growing international collection of adventure travel companies.

Akademik Shokalskiy (**30/50; RUSSIAN; 213 FEET**)

Professor Multanovskiy (**30/50; RUSSIAN; 226 FEET**)

The *Professor Multanovskiy,* built in Finland in 1982 for polar and oceanographic research, has been refurbished since her conversion to a passenger ship. She has two dining rooms, a lounge, bar, library, lecture room, sauna, and infirmary. There are twin and triple cabins; some with private baths and others with shared baths. From November to March, the ice-strengthened adventure ship sails to the Antarctic Peninsula, South Shetlands, South Georgia, and the Falklands round-trip to Ushuaia. *Akademik Shokalskiy* is a sister ship of *Professor Multanovskiy* and was upgraded in 2006.

Orlova (**59/110; RUSSIAN/70; 295 FEET**)

Built in 1976, refurbished in 1999, and upgraded in 2002 and 2006, this expedition ship is fully equipped with a lounge for lectures and entertainment, library, bar, and a dining room. Accommodations include twin and triple cabins and suites, all with a lower berth, private bathroom, porthole or window, and ample storage. Meals, prepared by international chefs, are served at a single seating in a window-lined dining room. *Orlova* operates cruises to the Antarctic Peninsula and South Georgia during the winter season and is chartered in summer by Cruise North Expeditions for cruises in the Canadian Arctic. (See Cruise North Expeditions earlier in this chapter.)

Sarpik Ittuk (**45/96; RUSSIA/38; 239 FEET**)

Owned by Arctic Umiaq Line, a Greenland-based shipping company, the expedition ship was built in Denmark in 1992, renovated in 1999, and underwent a multimillion-dollar refurbishment in 2006 before joining the Quark fleet in November of that year. Her sister ship is expected to debut for the 2007 to 2008 season. Accommodations include twin, triple, and dedicated single cabins, all with private facilities. Berths can be lower or a combination of upper and lower. The ship has a panoramic observation lounge. Meals, prepared by international chefs, are served in the dining room at a single seating. *Sarpik Ittuk* sails on ten-day voyages of Antarctica, Falkland Islands, and South Georgia during the winter season.

Kapitan Khlebnikov (**54/108; RUSSIAN/70; 369 FEET**)

This Antarctic icebreaker, built in 1980 and refurbished in 1992 and 2006, became the first ship to circumnavigate Antarctica with passengers in 1997. All cabins and suites are outside ones and have two lower berths, private bath, desk, and large closet. There are two dining rooms, a lounge and bar, conference room, indoor swimming pool, gym and sauna, library of polar books and videos, shop, and small clinic with doctor. The ship's satellite communication system provides phone, fax, and e-mail facilities when conditions permit.

The icebreaker sails a variety of itineraries in both polar regions. In the Arctic, the ship sails either west to east from Russia to Greenland or east to west from Scandinavia to Greenland. In the Antarctic, the ship sails to the Weddell Sea to visit an emperor penguin rookery and from the Antarctic peninsula to the Ross Sea or from the Weddell Sea to Prydz Bay. The icebreaker is equipped with a helicopter and Zodiacs.

Ocean Nova **(42/82; RUSSIA/38; 239 FEET)**

Owned by Arctic Umiaq Line, a Greenland-based shipping company, the expedition ship was built in Denmark in 1992, renovated in 1999, and underwent a multimillion dollar refurbishment in 2006 before joining the Quark fleet in November of that year. The latest renovation enhanced the ship's expedition facilities, added a glass-enclosed observation lounge, and refitted all passenger cabins with new beds, furniture, and fixtures. Her sister ship is expected to debut for the 2008 season. Accommodations include twin, triple, and dedicated single cabins, all with private facilities. Berths can be lower, or a combination of upper and lower. Meals, prepared by international chefs, are served in the dining room at a single seating. The ship also has a lounge/library. *Ocean Nova* sails on ten-day voyages of Antarctica, Falkland Islands, and South Georgia during the winter season.

Yamal **(50/100; RUSSIAN/140; 465 FEET)**

One of the world's most powerful icebreakers, the *Yamal* has a lounge, bar, library, gift shop, clinic, dining room, lecture room, gym, sauna, pool, and two helicopters. She departs on 16-day expeditions round-trip from Murmansk to the geographic North Pole.

St. Helena Line
Andrew Weir Shipping, Ltd., Dexter House, 2 Royal Mint Court, London EC3N 4XX, England; ☎ 44-020-7575-6480; fax 44-020-7575-6200; www.aws.co.uk

St. Helena **(49/128; BRITISH/ST. HELENIAN)**

The island of St. Helena, a British South Atlantic territory located 1,200 miles off the coast of Africa, may be the world's most significant place with no airport. For the mountainous island's 4,000 inhabitants, the 6,767-ton Royal Mail Ship (RMS) *St. Helena* provides the sole link to the outside world (at least until the island's new airport opens in 2010). For visitors, the voyage is one of the last true ocean liner experiences, plus, it gives passengers the bonus of a full week on the island. The trips begin either at Cape Town, South Africa, and sail via Namibian ports to St. Helena and Ascension islands and return south (about three weeks) or, less frequently, sail from England and call at Las Palmas, Ascension, St. Helena, and onto Cape Town (about four weeks).

The passenger, mail, and cargo service began in 1978 and operates under a contract with the British government. The present ship was purpose-built in a Scottish shipyard in 1989 to serve the islands, offering the comfortable facilities of a small liner for 128 passengers and a British and St. Helenian crew of 65. One-way fares between Cape Town and St. Helena range from £288 to £1,107.

The homey public rooms include a two-section forward observation lounge with a bar, and a video lounge for screening films and reading. The **Sun Lounge** looks onto the outdoor pool. Here, a light breakfast and lunch are served daily. The dining room, on a lower deck, operates with two reserved sittings at dinner. The food is good British fare, such as tasty soups, curries, roasts, and well-prepared fish.

All plainly furnished cabins are outside, with windows or portholes, twin beds, and upper and lower berths. Most have a private shower and toilet. Budget accommodations, reserved for the Saints, as the St. Helenians are called, are sometimes available for non-island passengers.

The local passengers are Saints—a people of mixed British, South Asian, East Indian, and Malagasy origin—and visitors from Britain, France, Germany, South Africa, and the United States. Cargo includes mail and parcels, refrigerated and frozen food, medical equipment and drugs, construction materials, textbooks, and vehicles. In short, everything the islanders require.

During the daily cycle, passengers establish a routine of reading, socializing on deck, visiting the bridge or engine room, and taking a swim or playing deck tennis with the officers. In the evening, the purser hosts games, quizzes, and pantomime, all old-fashioned shipboard fun. There's also a captain's cocktail party.

St. Helena, the principal destination, spreads across the horizon beneath a low cloud clinging to the mountain peaks. The ship anchors off Jamestown, a pastel-colored 19th-century Georgian town sandwiched into a deep valley. Through and round-trip passengers get the bonus of a week on the island while the cargo is discharged and the ship makes a passenger run to Ascension and back. Most visitors stay at two small hotels in Jamestown, while others choose self-catering cottages up in the hills. Jamestown offers a small museum, a pretty Anglican church, a few shops, and a couple of restaurants, but the principal attraction is Main Street, the island's social center where everyone gathers to talk.

Napoleon spent six years here, from 1815 until his death in 1821; Longwood, his permanent residence and gardens, is open to visitors. Nearby, Deadwood Plain is home to the island's indigenous wire bird. The governor's house, a handsome 1791 Georgian mansion, is home to a giant Seychellois tortoise named Jonathan, reputed to about 175 years old. There are miles of walking trails around the coast and down to secluded bays. After a week, the ship returns to the island and embarks passengers for a continuation of the voyage. Once a year, the *St. Helena* also makes a three-week round-trip voyage to the even more remote island of Tristan da Cunha, located about halfway between South Africa and South America. This one sells out well in advance.

Wilderness Travel
1102 Ninth Street, Berkeley, CA 94710; ☎ 510-558-2488 or 800-368-2794; fax 510-558-2489; www.wildernesstravel.com

This adventure tour company offers Galápagos programs almost year-round, some with up to three departures monthly. The company combines cruises on small yachts with hiking in areas not usually covered by conventional excursions. As an example, the *Sagitta* (10/16; 120 feet), a sailing yacht, boasts three full masts, two decks, and cabins with private bathrooms, hot showers, and air-conditioning; a library, dining room, salon, and conference room with video. The crew is made up of the captain, first mate, engineer, two sailors, a cook and assistant, cabin attendant, and naturalist guide.

The *Diamante* (6/12; 112 feet), a brigantine schooner motor sailer, is a modern, scaled-down version of the great naval training ships. She has an airy deckhouse that includes the main salon/dining room. The beamed salon is decorated with beautiful mahogany and teak and offers 360-degree visibility onto the passing scenery. It is also possible to dine outside, around a teak table aft of the pilothouse. The six cabins have upper and lower berths, private facilities with fresh hot- and cold-water showers.

The company also has a combination cruise of the Galápagos and the haciendas of Ecuador, with an optional extension to the Kapawi rain forest; and a full program of expedition cruises to Antarctica and the South Pacific.

NORWEGIAN COASTAL CRUISES *and* CRUISE FERRIES

THE CRAGGY COAST OF NORWAY, deeply indented like the fingers on your hand, was carved eons ago by massive glaciers. Crevasses, which we call fjords, can be ten miles long. From their dark, mirror-like waters rise almost vertical cliffs, and awesome mountains climb to several thousand feet on each side.

Often at the head of fjords are snow-capped peaks. In some places, glaciers inch toward the North Sea. Along the shores are tiny fishing villages and isolated farmhouses. Farther up the mountains are lodges where hikers bed down in summer and Olympic hopefuls fine-tune their skiing in winter.

The setting is beautiful; late May through early autumn is ideal for cruising, although the other months are popular with some for the unusual experience those times offer. Most major lines with ships in Europe offer Norwegian fjord cruises, mostly in May and June. Itineraries differ slightly, but the program is essentially the same: departing from Bergen, Copenhagen, Dover, Harwich, or Oslo and going as far north as Trondheim, Norway's original capital and third-largest city, or Tromso, the largest town north of the Arctic Circle. Others continue to the North Cape, the northernmost point in Europe, and to Spitsbergen, a group of islands studded with massive glaciers. Another way to cruise the coast—the way Norwegians do— is on the Norwegian Coastal Express.

On the Coastal Express

Billed as the world's most beautiful voyage, especially when the weather cooperates, the Coastal Express offers relaxed and informal adventure. Aboard the *Kong Harald,* the feeling is that of a small, modern floating hotel. On the first morning at sea, a sheer mountain wall plunges into the narrow channel, and, to port, Norwegian Sea breakers pile up against low-lying islands. At a briefing, the courier reminds everyone that this is a working ship and that local passengers will be boarding and leaving at each port. The diesel engine throbs rhythmically in the background. At Bodo, a city at the northern end of Norway's main rail line, about 100 passengers typically board for the six-hour crossing to the Lofoten Islands. Automobiles come aboard, and forklifts maneuver whole fish, bundles of evergreen saplings, and building materials.

During brief port calls, you can walk briskly to the main shopping street to buy souvenirs and newspapers. On one excursion, during the stop at Harstad, passengers attend a short worship service in a fortress church. There are visits to the North Cape promontory; an excursion from Kirkenes, the voyage's turnaround port, to the Russian border; and a cruise into the **Trollfjord,** a one-mile passage between sheer rock cliffs bubbling with falling water. The moon reflects in the turning basin as the captain revolves his ship in a tight half circle. During the warmer months, the ship sails well inland to take in the spectacular **Geirangerfjord.** By voyage's end, round-trip passengers have shared a 2,500-mile feast of dramatic scenery, shore visits, fresh—if somewhat repetitious—food, and constantly changing weather.

Norwegian Coastal Voyage, Ltd. (NCV)

405 Park Avenue, New York, NY 10022; ☎ 212-319-1300 or 800-323-7436; fax 212-319-1390; www.norwegiancoastalvoyage.us

Eleven working passenger-cargo ships, known as Hurtigruten ("fast route" in Norwegian), operate a daily passenger and cargo service from Bergen to 35 ports on Norway's coast, well beyond the North Cape to Kirkenes, near the Russian border. A Norwegian institution since 1893, the ships operate year-round through all weather and are a lifeline for the people in small, often isolated communities along the way. The vessels, while increasingly cruise-oriented, provide transportation for locals and haul cargo ranging from automobiles and farm equipment to frozen fish.

The ships also carry tourists who may board and disembark at any port. Many visitors, however, take the 2,500-mile round-trip voyage as a 12-day cruise. Others sail one-way and return by road or air. (Some open-water passages can be rough; passengers should come prepared.)

Time in port varies from as little as 15 minutes to several hours. There are shore excursions (about $20 to $40) at a few ports, and more-costly trips leave the ship at one port, travel inland, and rejoin it at another.

The best time to make the trip is mid-May to July, the period with 24 hours of daylight. Some travelers prefer the quieter months of early spring and fall. Summer sailings fill quickly, although space is often available at short notice. During the off-season, cabins usually are plentiful.

In the height of summer, some stretches are crowded with deck passengers, especially between the mainland and islands. Generally, about half of the passengers are local commuters or those attending an onboard conference; the balance is an international mix. There are usually quite a few English-speaking people, and always many Germans. Announcements are made in the languages required by passenger makeup. Meals are served at two seatings when traffic warrants. Breakfast and lunch are buffet-style. Dinner is from a set menu; tables are reserved. Dietary requests should be made when booking. Continental and Norwegian dishes are served. Lunch offers the widest selection of hot and cold foods. Because of hefty taxes, alcoholic beverages are expensive—$6 or more for a beer is common. Entertainment is limited to the gorgeous scenery, enlivened by commentary, good conversation, cargo handling, and the festive occasion of crossing the Arctic Circle. The line provides an excellent guidebook. In summer, the newest ships might have a band for dancing.

Norwegian Coastal Voyage, Inc., markets the service in North America. The service has 11 ships in four classifications: Millennium, Contemporary,

Midgeneration, and Traditional. In addition, NCV launched a newly built exploration ship, MS *Fram,* in April 2007.

Millennium Ships

The *Finnmarken* and *Trollfjord,* completed in spring 2002, and the *Midnatsol,* completed in 2003, are 15,000 tons and take 643, 674, and 674 passengers, respectively. Of the three new ships, the *Finnmarken* appears to be the more innovative, with features such a Jugend-style (Art Nouveau) interiors, an indoor/outdoor cafe, wine bar, two panoramic lounges, an indoor pool, a racquet court and gym, four conference rooms, and 14 suites with private balconies. The *Trollfjord* has 21 suites (8 with balconies), glass elevators, a sauna and fitness room, and eight conference rooms. The cargo is handled via ramps through the side doors. The standard amenities are the same as the new ships. The *Midnatsol,* meaning "the midnight sun," has its interiors dedicated to the Norwegian summer, and natural light pours in through the big glass windows. Like the *Trollfjord,* the ship has some suites with balconies as well as amenities like a sauna, gym, and library. All three Millennium vessels have an Internet cafe.

Contemporary Ships

The *Kong Harald, Nordkapp, Nordlys, Nordnorge, Polarlys,* and *Richard With,* all completed since 1993, add to the Hurtigruten the concept of the cruise ferry, with its greater comfort (well established and popular in Baltic waters). Large and boxy (390 feet long and 63 feet wide), the ships take as many as 490 passengers in relatively roomy accommodations. Cargo is handled via ramps.

The modern cabins are mostly outside. They have foldaway beds and two lower berths, audio channels, automated wake-up calls, tiled baths with showers, and hair dryers.

Public rooms have the fashionable look of modern cruise ships, with rich fabrics, thick carpets, and ample use of brass, glass, and veneers. Norwegian sculptures and painted seascapes are attractive features. A top-deck wraparound observation lounge is for viewing. A middle deck offers a cocktail lounge, library/card room, conference rooms, a souvenir shop, playroom, video arcade, 24-hour cafeteria, 240-seat restaurant, and private dining room. Also aboard are a sauna, small gym, and passenger laundry.

Midgeneration Ships

The *Lyngen* and the *Vesteraalen,* built in 1982 and 1983, respectively, then rebuilt and enlarged later in the same decade and refurbished in 1995, carry up to 320 passengers. Cabins are smaller and decidedly plainer, but most are outside and all have private bathrooms with showers. The ships have forward-facing observation lounges and glass-enclosed top-deck lounges. Freight and vehicles are handled via roll-on ramps.

Traditional Ships

The 114-passenger *Nordstjernen,* built in 1956, is one of two remaining Traditional ships. She has very small outside and inside cabins, some without private facilities. The best cabins sell out fast. The ship possesses rich character, teak decks, and a battered hull from thousands of dockings. There are two lounges (the forward facing one is nonsmoking), a restaurant, and a cafeteria, the latter used by short-run passengers. Cargo and vehicles are loaded by crane. This ship is no longer in year-round service.

The *Nordstjernen* summer cruises around Spitsbergen feature naturalist guides and Zodiac landings. The packages combine round-trip flights from New York to Oslo and Longyearbyen, the Svalbard capital and ship's departure point for the four-day cruise. Hotel and breakfast in each capital, selected cabin category, all meals on the cruise, shore excursions, transfers, port charges, air taxes, and gratuities are included in the package.

Norwegian Coastal Voyage also sells the 100-passenger *Polar Star,* an expedition ship rebuilt from a Swedish icebreaker, on eight-day Spitsbergen circumnavigation packages from Longyearbyen. *Polar Star* sails along Spitsbergen's northwest coast to the Russian mining town of Barentsburg, Prins Karl Forland Island, the Ny-Alesund research center, old whaling sites, spectacular fjords, and, weather and ice permitting, cross the 80° N.L. line. The more comprehensive *Polar Star* voyages continue along the coast to fjords in the archipelago's isolated northern and eastern regions. The ship's route and landing sites depend on weather and ice conditions, adding Hinlopen Strait and glacier-covered Nordaustlandet Island. The ship also offers cruises to Greenland, Iceland, Labrador, and Newfoundland.

The *Lofoten,* the second of the classic ships, was completed in 1964 and given a major refit in 2003. Like the *Nordstjernen,* she substitutes for the *Nordnorge* and *Nordkapp* when these ships leave the rotation in October for cruises to Antarctica and the Chilean fjords, returning in April. The *Lofoten*'s maritime character and paneled interiors are a well-maintained delight. With berths for 171 passengers, her cabins are small, with the majority having upper and lower berths; about half have private facilities. There are two forward observation lounges from which to watch the cargo handling, a dining room spanning the width of the ship, a cafeteria, and a bar aft. In the summer, the *Lofoten* is used on a fjords cruise program, including the 11-day Lofoten Islands and Western Fjords and 10-day Fjords to the North cruises.

New Expedition Ship

Recently, Norwegian Coastal Voyage has become even more active in expedition cruises to Greenland and Antarctica, with the addition of its new deluxe expedition ship, the 12,700-ton MS *Fram* (160 cabins/

318 berths). Launched in April 2007, the ship was built especially for cruising the iceberg-laden waters around Greenland.

The eight-deck *Fram*, built by Italian shipyard Fincantieri, was named after the polar ship built and used by Norwegian explorer Fridtjof Nansen on a three-year expedition around Greenland in the late 1800s. Greenland's culture inspired the ship's interior design while at the same time incorporating a Scandinavian feel with the extensive use of wool, leather, and oak.

Continuing NCV's tradition of having original artwork as a theme on all its ships, Ane Birthe Hove, from Nuuk, Greenland, was chosen as the ship's main artist and several other artists from Greenland and Norway were given commissions. The ship's architect, Arne Johansen, made use of concept terms from the Inuit language in describing the design philosophy: *Imaq*, or "sea", describes the ship's main dining room, situated aft and close to the sea; *Nunami* means "ashore," and refers to the forward areas where the main reception and lobby are situated; and *Qilak*, or "sky," is the term for the ship's glass-enclosed observation salon offering panoramic views of the outside scenery—from the sea to the sky. Additional highlights include meeting facilities, a wellness center with saunas, workout room and two glass-screened heated outdoor whirlpools, a bistro, a passenger bridge viewing selected data from the ship's bridge and her library.

The MS *Fram*'s season began in May with a 15-day expedition package from Reykjavik, Iceland, to the eastern and southern Greenland coasts (reversed in September at the end of the season). During the summer months, she sails on two itineraries: a 12-day program focusing on Greenland's Disko Bay region, and a 19-day, more extensive voyage that explores the island's west coast as far as Storapaluk, about 800 miles from the North Pole. The 20 or so villages and towns visited by the *Fram* run the gamut—from Uummannaq, where passengers can hike to Santa's summer cabin and the massive Eqip Sermia glacier, to Uunartoq, home to the country's best hot springs, and Nuuk, the largest, oldest town and the island's capital. Two to three nights are spent in Reykjavik with a range of optional excursions.

In September 2007, the MS *Fram* was scheduled to sail on what is believed to be the first Artic-to-Antarctica World Cruise. The 66-day expedition will visit 44 ports in 17 countries on four continents, taking a longitudinal route from pole to pole. The voyage begins in Reykjavik, Iceland, and proceeds through the Arctic to Canada, the eastern United States, Western Caribbean, the Panama Canal transit, the west coast of South America, Chilean fjords, and Antarctica, ending in Ushuaia, Argentina, on November 22.

From the fall foliage of the U.S. East Coast to the Chilean fjords and Antarctica, the variety of seasons and scenery in one cruise is breathtaking. (A reverse itinerary up the east coast of South America, the west coast of Africa, the Mediterranean and along the coast of Western Europe is planned for the spring of 2008.) From December to March, MS *Fram* joins the *Nordnorge* in Antarctica on three itineraries: a 13-day expedition round-trip from Buenos Aires; a 19-day Antarctica, Argentina, and the Chilean fjords voyage, and a 21-day voyage to the Falklands, South Georgia, and Antarctica.

EUROPEAN CRUISE FERRIES

"CRUISE FERRY" IS AN INADEQUATE TERM for a sophisticated breed of ship that takes passengers on overnight sea voyages but provides most of the comforts and amenities of a deluxe liner. Still, that's the name. And cars, recreational vehicles, and large trucks are indeed below deck.

Operating throughout Northern Europe, the ferries crisscross the Baltic and North seas, linking cities such as Copenhagen and Oslo, Stockholm and Helsinki, Newcastle and Bergen. Creative train-ferry itineraries often include the Eurail Pass network. Most passengers are Scandinavians (Danish, Finnish, Norwegian, Swedish), traveling to visit Scandinavian friends and relatives or simply cruising. Germans are second-most numerous among passengers. North Sea sailings also attract Britons.

Larger, newer ships offer varied restaurants. Options include quality à la carte dining, a 60-item smorgasbord, and simpler, cheaper cafeteria meals. The *Silja Europa* even has a McDonald's. After-dinner entertainment includes cabarets, dancing, gambling, and films. There are playrooms, video arcades, saunas, and on some ships, duty-free shopping (purchases can be rolled to checkout in supermarket carts). English is widely spoken.

Cabins vary from well-appointed rooms with windows and cruise-ship amenities to large family cabins with private showers. Most accommodations are away from the activity and noise of public rooms. Young Scandinavians come aboard to party on weekend sailings, so be prepared for some public drunkenness.

The following lines are represented in North America. They offer the most extensive routes and some of the newest and most sophisticated ships. However, they're only a sampling of a wider network spanning all European seas, including the Mediterranean. Most major intercity services operate year-round. Ships occasionally may change routes or be sold.

Color Line

THE FLEET	BUILT/RENOVATED	TONNAGE	PASSENGERS
Bohus	1971	8,772	1,422
Christian IV	1982	21,699	1,860
Color Fantasy	2004	76,600	2,770

THE FLEET	BUILT/RENOVATED	TONNAGE	PASSENGERS
Color Festival	1985/86	34,314	2,000
Color Viking	1985	19,763	1,720
Kronprins Harald	1987	31,914	1,432
Peter Wessel	1981/88	29,704	2,100
Prinsesse Ragnhild	1981/92	35,438	1,875
Silvia Ana (FAST DAY FERRY)	1996	7,895	1,043

NORWEGIAN-BASED COLOR LINE OPERATES six international cruise ferry lines between ten ports in Norway, Germany, Demark, and Sweden. For example, it sails between Oslo, Norway, and Kiel, Germany; between Bergen, Stavanger, and Hirtshals in northern Denmark; and between Oslo or Kristians, Norway, and Hirtshals, Denmark. The largest and most impressive of its ships is the *Color Fantasy,* which is more than twice the size of the *Kronprins Harald;* both of those vessels operate the Oslo-to-Kiel route, and leave daily from either port for the 20-hour overnight run. The ships enter and leave Oslo via the scenic Oslofjord, a two-hour stretch. Most passengers are German or Norwegian.

The departures from Newcastle that connect two to three times weekly in Bergen with Norwegian Coastal Express evening northbound departures are operated by the Fjord Line's 20,581-ton *Jupiter,* formerly the *Color Viking.* The Fjord Line also operates the *Fjord Norway* between Norway and Denmark. Ship details, timetables, and prices are available on the Web site, **www.colorline.com.**

DFDS Seaways

THE FLEET	BUILT/RENOVATED	TONNAGE	PASSENGERS
Crown of Scandinavia	1994	35,498	2,026
Dana Sirena	2002	22,400	600
Fjord Norway	1986/2006	31,360	1,600
King of Scandinavia	1987	31,395	2053
Pearl of Scandinavia	1989/2001	40,039	2,166
Queen of Scandinavia	1981/98	34,093	1,756

DANISH-OWNED DFDS SEAWAYS OPERATES cruise ferries between England and Denmark, England and Norway, England and the Netherlands, and Denmark and Norway.

The largest ships operate between Copenhagen and Oslo, with scenic departures from both cities at 5 p.m. and arrival about 9 a.m. the next day. The northbound route from Copenhagen passes Hamlet's Castle at Helsingor, and enters the Oslofjord at dawn. Two-night round-trip cruises are popular from Oslo and Copenhagen. They give passengers time ashore between the morning arrival and late-afternoon departure. The Copenhagen pier is adjacent to the central business district, and the Oslo pier is a short bus ride from the city's center.

DFDS departs year-round from Harwich, England, which can be reached by boat or train from London. It has year-round, overnight services three to four times a week to Esbjerg on the Danish west coast. Additional sailings operate from Newcastle to Stavanger, Bergen, and Amsterdam.

Silja Line

THE FLEET	BUILT/RENOVATED	TONNAGE	PASSENGERS
Silja Europa	1993	59,914	3,013
Silja Festival	1986/92	34,414	1,916
Silja Serenade	1990	58,376	2,852
Silja Symphony	1991	58,377	2,852

OPERATING SOME OF THE LARGEST CRUISE FERRIES, Silja Line is the best-known Scandinavian ferry company. The ships are cities at sea; some carry as many as 3,000 passengers. In early 2007, Silja Line was acquired by Tallink Line (See section that follows).

Although busy, the ships are designed to avert crowding and long queues. Cruise-ship-style atriums are the centerpiece; nearby are eateries, lounges, and bars for all incomes. The prestige route is Stockholm to Helsinki. A ship leaves each port at 5 every night year-round (the sun shines until 10 p.m. or later in summer, this being the Land of the Midnight Sun) and arrives the next day at 9:30 a.m. The extended passage time includes a middle-of-the-night call in the Aland Islands that permits the continuation of duty-free shopping, a major attraction for high-taxed Scandinavians. The two-hour passage through the Stockholm archipelago is a highlight; to enjoy the entire transit, be up before 7 a.m. The ship docks conveniently next to central Helsinki; passengers on the two-night round-trip have the day ashore. Extended stopovers are easily arranged. Arrival in Stockholm is slightly less convenient, with a subway connection to the city center.

The overnight Stockholm to Turku, Finland, route is offered daily. A companion daylight service takes about 11 hours.

Tallink Silja Line

THE FLEET	BUILT/RENOVATED	TONNAGE	PASSENGERS
AutoExpress 2, 3, 4	2007	NA	NA
Kapella	1974	NA	50
Regal Star	1999	NA	79

THE FLEET	BUILT/RENOVATED	TONNAGE	PASSENGERS
SuperFast VII, VIII, IX	2001	NA	676/728
Tallink Galaxy	2006	NA	2,800
Tallink Meloodia	1978/98	NA	1,500
Tallink Regina Baltica	1980/2002	NA	1,500
Tallink Romantika	2002	NA	2,500
Tallink Victoria I	2004	NA	2,500
Vana Tallinn	1974/2000	NA	800

TALLINK SILJA OY IS ONE OF THE LEADING passenger and cargo shipping companies in the Baltic. The Tallink brand began in 1989, as a Finnish-Soviet joint venture with one chartered vessel, the Tallink ferry, primarily to transport tourists on the 48-mile route between Helsinki and Tallinn. Over the next decade, the company grew, always with chartered vessels, until 1997, when a new management team acquired three vessels. The following year, the company hit a milestone of 2 million passengers. Between 2002 and 2004, Tallink acquired two high-class cruise ferries, Romantika and her sister vessel, Victoria I, and the following year, placed orders for two new high-speed ships to be delivered in 2007 and 2008. The same year, Tallink was listed on Tallinn Stock Exchange.

In 2006, Tallink introduced its new cruise vessel *Galaxy*, to operate between Helsinki and Tallinn, acquired three Superfast ferries, started operating between Finland and Germany, and in 2007, finalized the acquisition of Silja Line, one of the largest, best-known Scandinavian ferry companies. It also launched a new service, the Tallink Shuttle, providing scheduled service year-round in all weather conditions between Helsinki and Tallinn. The Shuttle has four restaurants, two bars and more than 1,500 square meters of shopping area, and a business class where one can relax in a quiet setting, enjoy a meal, and use the fax and Internet.

Viking Line

THE FLEET	BUILT/RENOVATED	TONNAGE	PASSENGERS
Alandsfarjan	1972	NA	963
Amorella	1988	34,384	2,450
Cinderella	1989	46,398	2,500
Gabriella	1992	35,492	2,420
Isabella	1989	35,154	2,450
Mariella	1985	37,860	2,500
Rosella	1980	16,850	1,700
Viking ADCC	2009	15,600	1,500
Viking XPRS	2008	34,000	2,500

THE RED-HULLED SHIPS OF VIKING LINE, Silja Line's main competitor, cruise similar routes. The Stockholm-to-Turku daylight voyage calls at Mariehamn in the beautiful Aland Islands, about halfway between Sweden and Finland. The Stockholm-to-Helsinki route may be taken as a two-night round-trip cruise that includes two dinners and two breakfasts. The berth in Stockholm is closer to the city center than Silja's, while the Helsinki location is similar. The Web site, **www.vikingline.fi,** has ship details, timetables, and prices.

Viking Line has two new ships under construction. The first one, the 2,500- passenger *Viking XPRS,* a fast ferry, is expected to debut in January 2008 on the Helsinki-to-Tallinn route. The second ship, 1,500-passenger *Viking ADCC,* slated for 2009, will sail on the Mariehamn-to-Kapellskär route.

INFORMATION AND RESERVATIONS

Borton Overseas (for Viking Line)
5412 Lyndale Avenue South
Minneapolis, MN 55419
☎ 612-822-4640 or 800-843-0602
fax 612-822-4755
www.bortonoverseas.com; www.vikingline.fi

DFDS Seaways (USA) Inc. and Silja Line
6801 Lake Worth Road, Suite 107
Lake Worth, FL 33567
☎ 800-533-3755 ext. 114
fax 561-432-2550
**www.seaeurope.com; www.europeonsale.com;
www.silja.us; www.tallinkusa.com**

Nordic Saga Tours (for Color Line)
303 Fifth Avenue South, Suite 109
Edmonds, WA 98020
☎ 800-848-6449 or 425-673-4800
fax 425-673-2600
www.nordicsaga.com; www.colorline.com
The tour operator also represents Scandinavian Seaways, Fjord Line, and other European cruise ferries.

Traghettionline S.r.l.
Via Brigata Liguria 4
16121 Genoa, Italy
www.traghettionline.net
Traghettionline, an Italian company with years of experience in sea transportation, provides information on some 90 ferry companies in Europe, North America, Australia, and Asia on its Web site. The Internet service enables users to book a ferry, receive the ticket directly at home, and pay with a credit card or bank transfer.

SAILING SHIPS

PEOPLE CHOOSE TO CRUISE for reasons as diverse as the amazingly wide range of ships, itineraries, and services available. For many, however, there is a longing that transcends midnight buffets, luxurious cabins, and myriad ports of call. These are individuals who are transfixed and enchanted by the lure of the sea itself. The feeling of being under way, the buffeting wind, the salt sea spray over the bow, and the twinkling phosphorescent wake are to them the stuff of dreams. There is no bingo, afternoon tea, or stylish air-conditioned lounge for these folks. Rather, you'll find them on deck leaning on the starboard rail, taking in every white-capped wave.

Almost all are landlubbers—individuals whose imagination draws them to the sea—and many of them first experience the sea aboard a large, modern cruise ship. It doesn't take long for them to realize, however, that no matter how grand a particular floating resort might be, they desire a much more intimate relationship with the sea. Opting for a smaller cruise ship does the trick for some, but for others it's not enough. Sooner or later, these folks discover the wonderful world of cruising under sail.

Cruising under sail is cruising in concert with the sea. By definition, sailing uses currents, tides, and winds to the advantage of the sailor, always working with natural forces and never against them. Pursuing this harmony precipitates any number of outcomes (the elements are not always cooperative, you know), but it's always an adventure. Bringing home the reality of weather and sea conditions, sailing is for many a life-changing experience—an epiphany.

If you want to try sailing on for size, you have a wide selection of alternatives. Choices range from medium-size cruise ships with computer-controlled sails and powerful, supplemental engines to tiny schooners with no motor at all, where every passenger must help work the boat. Accommodations range from conventional cruise-ship staterooms to tiny cabins accessible only by descending a ladder through a hatch. Some voyages are veritable courses in sailing and seamanship; others demand nothing beyond normal cruise ship passenger passivity.

If you've not sailed before, if you enjoy the amenities of a larger cruise ship, or you're uncertain how much of an adventure you want, consider sailing with either **Star Clippers** or **Windstar Cruises** (both described in detail in Part Two, Cruise Lines and Their Ships). Star Clippers operates four- and five-masted, square-rigged ships with small (by cruise ship standards), air-conditioned cabins with private baths. You'll find a small pool, a library, and even a piano lounge. Star Clippers vessels carry a maximum of 170 or 227 passengers, depending on the vessel.

Windstar, which operates three four-masted ships with triangular sails, costs about $350 to $550 per day before any applicable discounts, compared with an average non-discounted per diem of about $268 on Star Clippers. Two Windstar ships carry about 150 passengers, and one ship, *Wind Surf*, accommodates 308. Cabins on these ships approximate the size of those on mainstream cruise ships, and there's even a casino and a disco. Whereas a crew sets the sails in the traditional way aboard Star Clippers ships (you can pitch in if you want), sails on Windstar are computer-controlled. Ships of both lines have powerful diesel-electric engines. Windstar uses its engines for propulsion up to 50% of the time, whereas Star Clippers employs its engines primarily to get into and out of port.

Similar to Windstar's *Wind Surf* is **Club Med's** five-masted, computer-controlled sailing ship *Club Med 2*. The length of two football fields, *Club Med 2* carries almost 400 passengers with a per diem ranging from $130 to more than $350, depending on season and itinerary. Smaller, luxury ships with large cabins and many mainline cruise ship amenities are **Sea Cloud's Cruises'** *Sea Cloud* (64 passengers) and *Sea Cloud II* (94 passengers). The sailing cruise lines mentioned in this section offer itineraries that can take you all over the world.

Less expensive, but offering a more authentic, hands-on experience are the **Maine Windjammer Association** cruises and **Windjammer Barefoot Cruises.** The Maine Windjammer Association is the marketing arm for 12 individually owned and operated traditional tall ships, all schooners, ranging in size from 46 to 132 feet. The fleet operates exclusively along the midcoast region of Maine, with the majority of itineraries in the verdant, island-studded waters of Penobscot Bay. Most of the schooners were built between 1871 and 1945 as working boats for hauling cargo or fishing and were converted to passenger-carrying ships within the last 20 years or so. Nine of the 12 schooners are designated National Historic Landmarks.

Cruises depart Camden, Rockland, or Rockport from May through October for three- to six-day itineraries that include short ports of call at small islands and at historic Maine coastal villages. Days, for the most part, are spent sailing. The schooners anchor in protected coves or tie up at small, picturesque maritime communities at night. Meals are served family style, sometimes in the galley and sometime on deck, and feature local produce and seafood among other selections. A lobster bake on a forested island is a highlight of many cruises. While most of the schooners accommodate 12 to 29 guests, the 46-foot *Mistress* carries only 6, and the *Victory Chimes,* the largest sailing vessel flying American colors, carries 40.

About 1,000 miles south, the Caribbean is home water to Windjammer Barefoot Cruises. Although the names are similar ("windjammer" is nautical slang for a seaman on a sailing ship), Windjammer Barefoot Cruises is related to the Maine Windjammers in concept only. Windjammer Barefoot Cruises operates four sailing vessels and one motorized vessel year-round, on a variety of 6- to 13-day Caribbean and Bahamas itineraries, particularly the Eastern Caribbean, including the Grenadines, and farther south to Aruba, Bonaire, Curaçao, and occasionally Panama and Costa Rica.

All of its sailing craft are larger than those of the Maine fleet, with the largest carrying 122 passengers and the smallest 64. Facilities are not as extensive as those of the *Sea Clouds, Club Med 2,* or Clipper and Windstar ships described earlier, but are more luxurious than those of the relatively spartan Maine fleet. Most Windjammer Barefoot cabins are air-conditioned and offer a private bath. Air-conditioning isn't generally needed in Maine, and schooner passengers usually share toilet and bathing facilities. Dining is of comparable quality in both fleets, with meals distinguished by fresh, locally available meat, seafood, vegetables, and fruit. On both Maine Windjammer and Windjammer Barefoot vessels, you can help the crew sail the ship. On the Barefoot cruises, however, such activity is take-it-or-leave-it, while Maine schooner captains frequently count on passengers to help out. On ships of either fleet, you can avail yourself of a fairly extensive sailing education during your time aboard.

For all the similarities, however, there are likewise some striking differences. The Maine experience is all about sailing, while the Barefoot ships spend most of the day in port or anchored in a secluded cove, where diving, water sports, or sunning are the main attractions. In fact, on a Barefoot cruise, most of the sailing is done between the hours of dinner and breakfast—the exact opposite of a Maine schooner.

If you think this type of cruising will appeal to you, take a moment to check out the respective Windjammer Web sites (**www.sailmainecoast.com** and **www.windjammer.com**). Potentially critical differences will become immediately apparent. The Caribbean cruise line's site screams fun, sun, and warm-weather delights. The Maine Windjammers' site, in contrast, emphasizes the peace and serenity of sailing, rugged Maine coastline scenery, and maritime skills and history. On Barefoot cruises, morning Bloody Marys, afternoon rum swizzles, and wine with dinner are provided in the price of the cruise. On a Maine schooner, no alcohol at all is served or sold, except at lobster bake events, though passengers are invited to bring their own private stock. Days start early in Maine, while in the Caribbean, sleeping in is definitely an option.

Climate additionally differentiates the two sail cruise options. The Caribbean is a perfect destination during the cold-weather months of the year, while Maine offers a great escape from the heat during the summer and early fall.

Finally, regardless which cruise line you choose, you should know that seasickness is rare on sailing ships. This is because the wind stabilizes the ship in the water and prevents almost all of the side-to-side rolling motion that is the primary cause of seasickness.

Note: In parentheses after each boat name is information about the number of cabins and passengers; officers and crew; and the boat's length (cabins/passengers; officers/crew; boat length).

Classic Cruises of Newport
Christie's Landing, Newport, RI 02840; ☎ 800-395-1343 or 401-849-3033; dock office ☎ 401-847-0298; fax 401-849-3023; www.cruisenewport.com; www.cruisearabella.com

Arabella (20/40; AMERICAN; 160 FEET)

Favored by sailing enthusiasts, romance seekers, and travelers who enjoy soft adventure, *Arabella,* a luxury schooner, offers cruises from late December through early May throughout the British and U.S. Virgin Islands, as well as St. Maarten, which the ship uses as a home port for part of the winter when she visits Anguilla and St. Bart's.

The Caribbean excursions, combining sailing, swimming, kayaking, and snorkeling with day trips and island dining, depart from St. Thomas on six-night sails. One sample itinerary might include St. John, U.S.V.I., and Norman Island; Jost Van Dyke, Tortola, Virgin Gorda, and Peter Island, B.V.I.; and Culebra and Vieques, Puerto Rico.

Arabella has 20 air-conditioned cabins, each with satellite television, viewing portholes, private bath, and communications capabilities that allow guests to conduct business while at sea. She also houses an on-deck hot water spa, a lounge and bar, and water sports equipment for passenger use.

Rates for Caribbean cruises range from $1,295 to $2,195 per person, based on double occupancy, and include all daytime meals, four dinners ashore, and optional excursions. The cruise departs Sunday afternoon and returns to St. Thomas on Saturday at or before noon. At the end of her Caribbean season, *Arabella* sails north in the spring (and south in the fall) and spends June through September along the New England coast. Summer and fall cruises of four and five nights from Newport stop in Nantucket, Martha's Vineyard, Cuttyhunk, and Provincetown. Those cruises start at $995 per person, double occupancy. In September, the ship sails on a wine-tasting cruise that visits vineyards from Rhode Island to Martha's Vineyard.

Arabella is part of the Newport-based Atlantic Stars Hospitality Group which has hotels in New York City, Newport, Miami Beach, and Martha's Vineyard, a restaurant in South Beach, Miami, and cruise vessels on day trips around Newport Harbor and Narragansett Bay.

Club Med
75 Valencia Avenue, Coral Gables, FL 33134; ☎ 800-CLUB MED or 800-258-2633; fax 305-443-0562; www.clubmed2.com/FR/clubdescroisires

Club Med 2 (190/392; FRENCH; 614 FEET)

One of the world's largest cruise ships with sails offers casual, sports-oriented, all-inclusive vacations with an easy lifestyle for active, upscale vacationers. The ship sails on seven-day Caribbean cruises in winter, Mediterranean cruises in summer, and transatlantic voyages in spring and fall.

After two decades of spreading the gospel of all-inclusive resort vacations, Club Med applied its resort formula to a cruise ship, *Club Med 2*. Built in 1992, the 14,000-ton vessel marries today's technology to yesteryear's seafaring. She is as long as two football fields and rigged with five 164-foot masts and seven computer-monitored sails; there's no listing or heeling and no officers on deck—they are on the bridge monitoring computers.

Club Med 2 has an open, nautical feeling and is glitz-free, but loses much of the intimacy that makes the Windstar line's smaller version so appealing. She is spacious and has multiple Burmese teak decks. Interiors by the well-known European designer Albert Pinto evoke understated luxury through meticulous craftsmanship and the use of fine mahogany, quality fabrics, and leather reminiscent of classic sailing ships. Walls of windows afford sea and shore views.

The cabins are large, comfortable, and handsomely decorated with hand-rubbed mahogany cabinetwork. All cabins are outside and have twin portholes. They're fitted with twin or queen-size beds, a mahogany desk, large mirrors, ample closets, a television, radio, safe, refrigerator, minibar, and satellite telephone, which is also used to order room service. The teak-floored baths have showers, hair dryers, and fluffy bathrobes. Electrical outlets are 110/220 AC. In all, there are 190 outside cabins; 6 suites. Standard dimensions are 188 square feet. There are no single cabins but you can book a cabin as a single by paying a supplement of 40% on the Deck C price.

The cruises are basically a French—Club Med says "international"—product with the same informal, carefree ambience of Club Med villages, but in deluxe surroundings with cruise ship amenities. Integral to both operations are GOs—*gentils organisateurs*—the social hosts and hostesses who keep the action and smiles going day and night. Most GOs are Mauritian, French, and other Europeans, or Americans who speak very good French. Their first task when you board is to familiarize you with the ship and answer questions. They organize shipboard activities and can usually give valuable tips on the best bars and restaurants in ports of call.

The ship has two ocean-view dining rooms, each with a different menu featuring French cuisine. **Le Grand Bleu,** an open-air veranda cafe on the top deck, serves a casual breakfast, luncheon buffets, and theme dinners featuring cuisine from around the world. **Le Deauville** is a more intimate formal dining room. The à la carte menu offers several choices for each course.

Dinner is a serious affair lasting up to two hours or longer. Complimentary wine from Club Med's private label, beer, and bottled water accompany lunch and dinner. Smokers are in the majority on board and have the run of the ship. Restaurants have nonsmoking sections, but smoking is allowed in all public areas. Unlike at Club Med villages, breakfast can be enjoyed in your cabin. There is 24-hour room service, and laundry service is available for an extra charge.

Both restaurants have waiters and unreserved, unassigned seating at tables for two or more, with continuous service during dining hours. Officers and staff dine with passengers. Most seven-night Caribbean itineraries offer a lobster beach picnic.

The ship has several lounges, a nightclub, piano bar, and disco. The **St. Tropez Piano Bar,** one of several bars, is the most popular for afternoon tea with French pastries and music and for after-dinner drinks (at prices higher than average). A lounge that doubles as a theater has a bar, stage, bandstand, and dance floor. A different show or program is presented here each evening by GOs—some more entertaining than others and all amateur. Some passengers find this fun, while others say the luxury prices they pay merit more professional entertainers.

There's a small library, card tables and chairs in a lounge, and a boutique. Party seekers make their way to the disco with its lighted dance floor. One night in the Caribbean is Carnival.

Sports facilities include a teak sports platform at the stern that unfolds into the sea to become a marina when the ship is at anchor. The vessel carries sailboards, sailboats, snorkels, fins, and masks and provides free lessons in waterskiing, windsurfing, sailing, and snorkeling. Two ski boats with scuba equipment take certified divers on diving trips. The scuba program is a good value.

The less ambitious can retire to a chaise lounge around the two outdoor, saltwater swimming pools. Even when the ship is full, space to lounge is ample. The supervised fitness center has exercise equipment that passengers use while enjoying a panoramic view from the top deck. Aerobics and water exercise in the pool are offered daily. Several decks below are a sauna and massage room. *Club Med 2* also has a beauty salon and spa with massage therapists and treatments—all at additional cost.

The Club Med imprint is obvious. Officers and crew are Mauritian; the staff, dressed in impeccable white shirts, shorts, and socks, handle dining and hotel duties and earn praise for their friendly, professional service. The energetic, attractive GOs are managed by the chef du village, the cruise director. These cheery camp counselors do it all: helm the reception desk, run activities, teach sports, and entertain. In the Caribbean, the ship visits a port each day and sails at night. Unfortunately for those who love sailing, passengers get very little opportunity to experience the pleasure of sailing under canvas.

The ship attracts a range of passengers that changes with the cruise, season, and location. Typically, passengers are 30 to 60 years old. The majority are couples. Children younger than age 8 are not accepted. Most passengers like the informality and sociability of the GO concept. On the other hand, the constant interaction between the young, bouncy GOs and passengers creates a summer camp atmosphere that is not for everyone.

The GO team is bilingual in English and French, but French is the ship's primary language. That could be a problem for English speakers who aren't up to the language challenge, or who might feel there's unequal treatment. Club Med's attitude is: this is a French-European or international product. The cruise is, after all, an experience in which Americans might lunch with people from Normandy, snorkel with Italians, and have cocktails with Austrians. That's part of the attraction.

Per diems start around $350 per person but may vary by season, cabin, and cruise areas. Tips, wine and beer at lunch and dinner, and most water sports are included in the fare; port charges are additional. Club Med offers specially priced cruises occasionally, but it does not discount prices.

Coastal Cruises

P.O. Box 798, Camden, ME 04843; ☎ 207-785-5670 or 800-992-2218; www.schoonermaryday.com

Mary Day (15/30; American; 90 feet)

This two-masted schooner sails on three- to six-day cruises along the Maine coast. Some cruises are themed ones, such as Lighthouses or Audubon Naturalist, while others focus on special events like the Great Schooner Race or a folk festival.

Maine Windjammer Association

P.O. Box 1144P, Blue Hill, ME 04614; ☎ 800-807-WIND; www.sailmainecoast.com

Formed in 1977, the Maine Windjammer Association is made up of 12 privately owned and operated traditional tall ships that once belonged to commercial fleets. They delivered everything from fish and granite to coal and Christmas trees along U.S. coasts. The two- and three-masted schooners range from 46 to 132 feet long. Seven are National Historic Landmarks, some older than 100 years.

The windjammers offer three- to six-day cruises from mid-May to October, departing Rockland and Camden on scenic Penobscot Bay, Maine. With more than 3,000 islands, the Maine coast is one of the best and most beautiful sailing areas anywhere. Ships sail by day, about 10 a.m. to 4 p.m., and anchor each night at a deserted inlet or quiet port or village where passengers can go ashore. Passengers may participate in all aspects of sailing, from hoisting sails and taking the wheel to helping in the galley.

Meals are served family style and include fresh seafood, roasts, garden salads, chowder, and homemade breads and desserts. A lobster bake on an island is featured on every six-day trip and most three-day cruises. Accommodations are simple: single, double, or triple cabins with comfortable mattresses, fresh linens, and plenty of blankets. Shipboard life is relaxed and informal.

Each windjammer carries 6 to 40 passengers and a crew of two to ten. Cruises are ideal family vacations, appropriate for most ages. (Check with individual captains regarding children. Teens ages 12 years and up are accepted on most boats. However, because of an increasing demand for family cruises, two of the vessels are now offering cruises with a minimum age of 5 and 6, respectively. Some windjammers have theme cruises ranging from photography and lighthouse cruises to wine tasting and whale-watching. The tall ships gather annually for an all-day race in which passengers can participate.

Three- to six-day cruises range from $400 to $950 per person. Charter rates are available. All vessels undergo rigorous U.S. Coast Guard inspections and carry ship-to-shore radios and electronic navigational devices.

Air transportation is available to departure ports via Portland International Jetport, with limousine service to the Rockland/Camden area.

Commuter air service is available from Boston, and buses run from Boston and Portland. All vessels offer free parking.

Member vessels are *American Eagle, Angelique, Grace Bailey, Heritage, Isaac H. Evans, Lewis R. French, Mary Day, Mercantile, Mistress, Nathaniel Bowditch, Stephen Taber,* and *Victory Chimes.* The association provides descriptive brochures as well as a short DVD.

Although all are windjammers, each boat is different and special in its own way. The *Angelique,* for example, has a deck house salon—a passenger lounge above deck. This gives passengers a warm, cozy alternative to the galley on rainy days. The *Grace Bailey* offers a combination lounge/galley below deck large enough to accommodate an upright piano. Most toilet and bath facilities are shared. Some schooners, like the *American Eagle,* with hallways running fore and aft below decks, offer toilets and hot showers situated adjacent to passenger cabins. On other ships, the communal heads are accessed from the Main Deck. A few vessels, including *Victory Chimes,* may have some cabins with private toilets in the cabin.

Cabins for the most part are very small—a place to sleep or change clothes, but not a place to hang out. Most cabins include a reading light and private sink, sometimes with hot and cold fresh running water, sometimes just with cold water. Storage space in the cabins is minimal, sometimes problematic when two or more share a cabin. A few ships offer 110-volt electrical outlets for hair dryers and such, but this is more the exception than the rule.

During fair weather, almost everyone hangs out on deck, where lunch and sometimes other meals are served. Some ships have built-in benches on deck, while others provide collapsible chairs. On rainy days, a galley with a wood stove affords refuge from the elements during and between meals. While anchored, both in dry and wet weather, a canvas tarp is deployed over much of the deck.

Passengers should be reasonably agile. Access to lower decks is almost always by ladder, with the exception of the *Victory Chimes* and the *Heritage,* which substitute rather steep stairs.

Music, in the form of informal jam sessions or sing-alongs, is a favorite evening's entertainment on many schooners, including the *Stephen Taber, Grace Bailey, Victory Chimes, Angelique,* and *Mary Day.* The *Grace Bailey* and *Angelique* carry upright pianos, and the *Mary Day* carries an organ. Passengers are strongly encouraged to bring any sort of acoustic (that is, nonelectrical) instrument. On ships without captain or crew of a musical bent, storytelling is a preferred pastime. Regardless of the activity, it's a rare night when festivities go beyond 11 p.m.

In a rather marked departure from the rest of the cruise industry, no alcoholic beverages are sold or served on Maine Windjammer schooners (with the exception of educational wine tasting events or on some vessels, a lobster bake). Although guests are invited to bring their own stash, most precruise instructional material makes it clear that excessive imbibing will not be tolerated.

Itineraries are quite flexible, with no particular urgency to be at a certain place at a particular time. Many captains ad-lib their itineraries en route, responding to the weather and the stated preferences of the passengers. And speaking of captains, they are as diverse as the ships. There are several husband-and-wife teams, some partnering gentlemen captains, and on the *Isaac H. Evans,* the fleet's only solo female captain. Some of the couple-captains bring their children along (amazingly socially acclimated and well behaved).

Summer weather in Maine is all over the map, although you can usually count on good wind. May and June are very unpredictable both in terms of temperature and rainfall. July is almost always warm, but with more rain than the predictably dry and warm August and September. Regardless of the time of year, good rain gear is essential.

Sea Cloud Cruises
32–40 North Dean Street, Englewood, NJ 07631; ☎ 201-227-9404 or 888-732-2568; fax 201-227-9424; www.seacloud.com

Sea Cloud (32/64; INTERNATIONAL; 360 FEET)

One of the world's most luxurious sailing ships, the *Sea Cloud* was built in 1931 as a wedding present from financier E. F. Hutton for his bride, Marjorie Merriweather Post. The ship has 32 air-conditioned cabins with phone, safe, hair dryer, and bathrobes. The elegant dining room accommodates all passengers at one seating; complimentary wines are served at lunch and dinner. A library and boutique are available.

The four-masted bark sails on different itineraries year-round. She plies the Eastern Caribbean in winter and the Mediterranean during the remainder of the year, and she is marketed by several U.S. companies. Sea Cloud Cruises also owns the luxurious *River Cloud* sisters, which sail European rivers (see River and Barge Cruises in Europe, earlier in Part Three).

Sea Cloud II (47/94; INTERNATIONAL; 384 FEET)

The legendary *Sea Cloud* got a sibling in 2001. The 384-foot, $40 million vessel is square-rigged with three masts (rather than *Sea Cloud*'s four), and her 29,687 square feet of sail are manually operated, with the crew climbing the masts and clambering along the spars to set the square-rigged sails. Modern with the highest safety standards, the vessel is traditional in appearance and offers opulent 1930s decor. Forty-seven luxurious cabins range from 129 to 236 square feet, those on the Promenade Deck with ornate marble bathtubs and marble mantels; two Owner's Suites each contain 290 square feet, with separate shower stalls and four-poster beds. Large deck areas and a swimming platform provide plentiful outside space for jogging, walking, lounging, sunning, and dining. The ship has an alfresco bar, an attractive restaurant, an elegant lounge with large arched windows, an inviting sauna and gymnasium, and a sunny, well-stocked library with windows overlooking the foredeck. The European/Asian crew is attentive and efficient—you could almost be on a private yacht—and the cuisine, predominantly French and German, is outstanding. Many of the cruises are chartered to museum and alumni groups (but there are normally cabins available for nonmembers). Nightlife tends to consist of lectures, wine tastings, and recitals by soloists or chamber groups.

Sea Cloud II's all-weather cruising ability sets her apart from Sea Cloud, which is generally restricted to sunny climes. The new ship cruises through the North Sea and Baltic in summer, the Mediterranean in autumn, and the Caribbean in winter.

The office also handles the River Cloud I and River Cloud II, which are described earlier in the chapter under European River Cruises/Elegant Cruises.

Star Clippers, Inc. (See Part Two.)

Windjammer Barefoot Cruises, Ltd.
P.O. Box 190120, Miami Beach, FL 33119-0120; 1759 Bay Road, Miami Beach, FL 33139; ☎ 305-672-6453 or 800-327-2600; fax 305-674-1219; 305-7505; www.windjammer.com

For sailors young or just young at heart with good sea legs and a Captain Mitty spirit, Windjammer Barefoot Cruises offers a chance to stand watch at the wheel or climb the mast and live out your fantasies. The line has a fleet of famous tall ships, including those once owned by Aristotle Onassis, the Duke of Westminster, and financier E. F. Hutton. Most cabins have bunk beds, private facilities, and steward service. Itineraries are super, including the Grenadines (often called the world's most beautiful sailing waters) and less-visited destinations in the Eastern and Southern Caribbean. Most cruises are seven days; some have different southbound and northbound legs that can be combined.

A sample seven-night St. Vincent and the Grenadines cruise starts at $1,100 per person double. Be sure to visit the cruise line's Web site. Special promotions are featured almost every week. Each ship's itineraries are accompanied with a map and information on the port and hotels. On summer sailings between June and August, Windjammer's Junior Jammer Kids Club, a program of chaperoned activities for children ages 6 and older, allows kids to sail for free when accompanied by two full-fare adults or for half fare when accompanied by one adult. The kids learn to sail and have full days of activities.

Legacy (61/122; AMERICAN/WEST INDIAN; 294 FEET)

Built in 1959, this ship was a meteorological research and exploration vessel for the French government. She was acquired by Windjammer in 1989, stripped to her hull, and converted into a four-masted barkentine, debuting in 1998.

The well-designed vessel has her original portholes, wide stairways, hand-carved South American wood, and custom interiors. All cabins are air-conditioned and have private bathrooms with showers. They are simply decorated and have wooden wardrobes, full-length mirrors, and either bunk, double, or twin beds (some have sofa beds). The most luxurious cabin, Burke's Berth, has a platform double bed, entertainment center, bar, and picture windows.

The top deck, with its large bar, entertainment by local bands, and hermit crab races, is action central. The captain gives a morning briefing there on the day's activities. Meals are served family style in the dining room, which is air-conditioned. A small lounge contains the only television and VCR, along with books and games. *Legacy* offers Junior Jammers Kids Club, a summer program of chaperoned activities for children ages 6 to 12.

Legacy is based year-round on the Pacific coast of Costa Rica and sails on seven-day itineraries departing on Sundays. She offers scuba diving courses for beginners as well as for certified divers. There is also birding, hiking, and a kids' program in summer. Her home port is Herradura.

Mandalay (72 PASSENGERS; BRITISH/WEST INDIAN; 236 FEET)

Mandalay is queen of the fleet. Formerly the yacht of financier E. F. Hutton and an oceanographic research vessel of Columbia University, she has three masts and 22,000 square feet of sail. Under Hutton's ownership, she was considered the world's most luxurious private yacht. When she retired in 1981 from Columbia, nearly half the existing knowledge of the ocean floor had been gathered by the ship.

From October to May, *Mandalay* alternates on 14-day cruises between Antigua and St. Maarten, exploring the French and Dutch West Indies. From May to September, she sails on Panama cruises, departing on Sundays from Colon.

Polynesia (54/112; BRITISH/WEST INDIAN; 248 FEET)

This legendary fishing schooner has been featured in articles in *National Geographic* magazine and various television productions. She joined the Windjammer fleet in 1975 after extensive remodeling added 8 Admiral Suites, 2 Commodore Suites, and 40 regular cabins, all double occupancy. All have private bathrooms and showers, wood paneling, and tile floors. Three Ensign cabins were built, each accommodating six. New plumbing, air-conditioning, and a teak deck were installed. The curved stern contains a specially designed dining salon with large tables, each depicting an island on *Polynesia*'s itinerary.

Probably the most popular Windjammer ship, *Polynesia* sails from November to May on seven-day Caribbean itineraries from St. Maarten to Anguilla and the British Virgin Islands, depending on wind. In summer through early fall, she is based in Aruba and offers the Junior Jammers Kids Club summer program. Occasionally, she offers singles' cruises as well as theme cruises.

Yankee Clipper (64 PASSENGERS; BRITISH/WEST INDIAN; 197 FEET)

In 1927, German industrialist Alfred Krupp built this ship as the *Cressida*, probably the world's only armor-plated private yacht. Adolf Hitler was aboard during World War II to award the Iron Cross to a U-boat captain. She was confiscated as a war prize and commandeered by the U.S. Coast Guard. After the war, she was acquired by the wealthy Vanderbilt family, renamed *Pioneer*, and sailed off the West Coast. Joining Windjammer's fleet in 1965, she was rechristened *Yankee Clipper*. Extensive remodeling gave her a third mast, continuous upper deck, and cabins with private bathrooms and showers. She's one of the fastest tall ships.

Yankee Clipper offers seven-day Caribbean cruises year-round, leaving Grenada for St. Vincent, Bequia, Mayreau, Union Island, Carriacou, and the Tobago Cays, departing on Sundays.

Windstar Cruises (*See* Part Two.)

Zeus Tours and Yacht Cruises

c/o Tourlite International, 120 Sylvan Avenue, Englewood Cliffs, NJ 07632; ☎ 201-242-1770; 800-272-7600; fax 201-242-8085; www.zeustours.com

The Zeus Group, which has been in operation for almost a half-century, offers Greek Isles, eastern Mediterranean, and Central and South American cruises in its own and chartered vessels. The cruises are sold in the United States through Tourlite International.

Among their wide range of offerings are several set itineraries with frequent sailing dates on the following vessels:

Diogenis V **(24/49; GREEK; 165 FEET)**

From April to October, this vessel operates seven-night Aegean Mosaic cruises round-trip from Heraklion, Crete, visiting such destinations as Aghios Astypalea, Karpathos, Nicolaos, Rhodes, Santorini, and Simi. The vessel offers air-conditioned cabins with private facilities, a dining room, lounge bar with stereo music/TV, and a Sun Deck equipped with sun chairs.

Viking Star **(24/42; GREEK; 106 FEET)**

The vessel operates seven-night Ionian Odyssey cruises round-trip from Corfu, with port calls at Albania and such Greek Isles as Scorpios and Parga. The vessel was constructed in the mid-1990s and has 24 outside cabins, 19 on the main deck, and 5 on the lower deck; one dining room and adjacent bar/lounge; and a Sun Deck with sun beds and chairs.

FREIGHTERS

FREIGHTER TRAVEL MAY BE THE LEAST-UNDERSTOOD segment of the cruise industry. You don't read or hear much about it, and cargo lines that offer passenger service rarely advertise in the mainstream media. Most travel agents, too, lack experience and expertise in booking freighter cruises.

Freighters roam the globe, visiting ports famous and exotic but usually industrial and removed from city centers and tourism attractions. They offer a carefree, informal environment conducive to total relaxation, and they may cost less than conventional cruise ships on a per diem basis.

Before the post–World War II boom in air travel and cruises, freighters were a significant mode of international travel. Expanding air routes, lower fares, and the growth of the cruise industry gradually relegated freighter travel to a minor niche in the cruise market.

Cargo lines have since recognized a revival of interest and the economics inherent in carrying passengers. Ten passengers at roughly $100 a day each adds up to good found money over the course of a year, and at the small cost of perhaps providing one extra steward and additional food. A few companies operate combined container and passenger vessels that can accommodate large numbers of passengers. But more typical are the 100 or more traditional freighters currently in service—mostly container ships—that accommodate from 2 to 12 passengers. Many enjoy brisk bookings and operate at capacity during peak seasons. However, extra regulations since 9/11 have caused several freight lines to reconsider the practicality of passenger service. Always call to confirm all information before making travel plans or reservations, and then deal with a freighter travel specialist who can keep you apprised of departure, embarkation time, and arrangements.

FREIGHTERS: DEFINING THE BREED

WHAT EXACTLY IS A FREIGHTER? First, let's say what it is not. A modern freighter isn't a rusty tramp steamer sailing on a mission of intrigue or romance as popularized in movies and novels. The vast majority of cargo vessels today are less than 30 years old. Imposing and boxy, they're loaded with sophisticated navigation and communication equipment. Most are containerized, that is, their freight is carried in large metal containers resembling railway box cars systematically stacked below and above decks. Some carry bulk items in holds such as iron ore or grain.

The International Conventions and Conferences on Marine Safety define the passenger-carrying freighter as a vessel principally engaged in transporting goods that is licensed to carry a maximum of 12 passengers. Those licensed to carry more than 12 are defined as combination passenger-cargo ships. The latter must meet stricter safety standards and carry more staff, including a doctor. They also have the advantage of gaining preferred docking privileges over ordinary freighters.

Nowadays, most cargo ships run on fixed schedules along established routes, except for those in so-called tramp service. Tramps don't sail regular routes or schedules and can be hired to haul almost anything, anywhere, anytime. A few take passengers. However, many of today's freighters are often chartered for specific periods of time, so their fixed schedules and routes may change.

Why People Choose Freighters

Traveling by freighter offers a rare opportunity to truly get away from it all. There are no crowds, no planned activities, no lines, no dress code, and no hoopla. The atmosphere aboard a freighter is relaxed and unstructured. Passengers can be as active or as lazy as they choose.

Freighters are for travelers who want to see the world on their own terms and are flexible about schedule changes and port substitutions. Most are veteran travelers who have become bored or disillusioned with conventional tours, cruises, and popular vacation destinations. Their sense of adventure and yearning for discovery demand something different.

A glance at freighter itineraries often reveals ports that would be impractical or prohibitively expensive to visit any other way. While some ships will dock in ports close to places you will want to visit, others may be berthed at a sprawling container terminal miles from the city. Often the ship and/or its port agents will help with hiring taxis or provide some basic touring information. But veteran freighter travelers know to come prepared with some knowledge of what they want to see, then perhaps ask local residents to suggest how to get there and back by their vessel's posted all-aboard notice. Time ashore is often limited, as modern ships can load or unload hundreds of containers in only a few hours; a long stay rarely exceeds 24 hours.

Freighter travelers recognize good value, and, on a per diem basis, there are few better travel values than freighters. With careful research and planning, you can roam the world for months aboard a freighter for roughly $90 to $250 per day. And unlike cruise ships with their large assortment of pay-as-you-go activities and amenities, there are few opportunities to spend more money on board a freighter beyond the fare.

Some people are attracted by the camaraderie they enjoy with fellow passengers. Sailing with usually no more than a dozen like-minded, well-informed veteran travelers in a low-key, relaxing atmosphere is their ideal travel environment and often leads to lasting friendships. On the other hand, if you have a list of books that you have been eager to read, here's your chance. Be aware, some passengers are avid bridge players, and others can't wait to bend an elbow when the sun is over the yardarm.

Is Freighter Travel for You?

Judging from the high rate of repeat bookings, once a freighter traveler, always a freighter traveler. If you haven't tried it but you've read this far, you may be a good candidate.

You must usually have plenty of time, as most trips are long, although voyages of one to two weeks also exist. Most folks just can't get away for a 30-, 60-, or 90-day trip. For that reason alone, the majority of freighter travelers are retirees, teachers and professors, self-employed professionals, and the occasional artist or writer. Common characteristics include an extensive travel background, love of the sea, preference for independent travel, and a general dislike of formality.

Wherever on this planet your imagination might roam, chances are you can go there on a freighter. Some of the more exotic and popular routes (round-trip from the United States) include South Africa from New York (46 days), the East or West Coast to New Zealand and Australia (38 to 66 days), around the world from New York (90 days or longer), Marquesas Islands from Tahiti (16 days), Mediterranean from the East or West Coast (42 to 60 days), and South America from the East or Gulf Coast (42 to 70 days). Shorter one-way transatlantic trips, such as Montreal to England, France, or Belgium, are an average of 8 to 11 days, and trips from the U.S. East Coast to the Mediterranean, some ranging from 10 to 20 days, are available.

Accommodations and Facilities

The majority of cargo liners have spacious, comfortable accommodations equal to, and often better than, those found on cruise ships. Normally they are located in a multistory superstructure at the stern. The cabins and public spaces may be on two to four different decks, so vertical movement is often the norm. Cabins have showers and sometimes bathtubs. In most cases they're air-conditioned and have a tastefully furnished lounge area. Often, they have taped music, service phones, VCRs or DVD players, minifridges, and picture windows rather than portholes.

Comfy, smartly decorated public lounges invite card games, conversation, and evening cocktails. Most vessels have large-screen televisions and an extensive library of videos and DVDs. The lounge may be shared with the officers, or there may be a separate one for passengers. Smoking policies will vary, too. Many cargo liners have small pools, exercise rooms, and saunas for officer and passenger use, and plenty of deck space for walks.

Some lines offer single cabins; others charge a single supplement, usually less than 50%. You should ask if your assigned cabin window is likely to be blocked by a container during any part of the voyage. Because freighters are working vessels, most lines won't accept preteen children for passage. Those that do usually charge the adult fare for children. Pets aren't permitted.

An open-bridge policy prevailed among freighters in the past; some freighters may still have one, others may not. Policies on bridge access are more strict since 9/11. Some lines and governments in port destinations may prohibit noncrew passengers from gaining bridge access. When the vessel does have an open bridge, you're welcome to watch officers and crew in action, except during critical maneuvers such as docking. On some freighters, passengers are free to go almost anywhere, while on others there are sensible security and safety rules. Obviously during rough weather, the container decks are off-limits. Pampering is not part of the program, although the crew may be very attentive. Basic services are handled by stewards who usually double as cabin attendants and waiters. A washer and dryer are generally available for passenger use. Phone and fax services are always available in emergencies, but policies on casual use vary.

Ships carrying more than 12 passengers have a doctor on board and generally have a small hospital or treatment center. But medical services aboard freighters carrying 12 or fewer passengers are limited. All, however, carry basic medical supplies and someone aboard will be trained in first aid. In case of serious illness, the captain will contact the nearest ship or shore station with a doctor available for advice. In a grave emergency, the victim will be transferred to a ship with appropriate medical facilities or be put ashore at the nearest port. Costs incurred in medical evacuation and treatment are the passenger's responsibility. All freighters taking fewer than 12 passengers have age limits; many will not take passengers over age 79, and some have a cutoff as low as 70 years of age.

In view of this, you're advised to take out travel health insurance with medical evacuation coverage and to carry more than enough of any medications you require. (See Part One of this book for insurance information.)

Dining and Food

Every freighter has a comfortable dining room shared by officers and passengers. On some ships, the officers share their tables with passengers; on others, they eat at separate tables. Dining is the day's special event and an opportunity to socialize. Most officers are congenial, eager to please, and happy to share their knowledge of the ship, the sea, and the world. Most freighter food is of good restaurant quality, well-prepared, and plentiful. Menus often feature the national cuisine of the ship's and/or officers' origin, which are as wide-ranging as British, German, Ukrainian, or Indian. The deck crew's nationality may be entirely different.

Breakfast and lunch are usually presented buffet-style, while dinners are served at tables, often in four or five courses. Coffee and tea are available anytime, and between-meal snacks are provided. While beer, wine, and liquor are available on most ships, it may be necessary for you to BYOB.

PLANNING YOUR FREIGHTER VOYAGE

THE MAJORITY OF FREIGHTERS book up early, especially for peak summer months and on voyages to tropical climes during northern winters. Start early yourself—six months or more—to get your choice of ship and routing, and a year ahead is not unusual on popular voyages. Planning, booking, and confirming your voyage can take much longer than you imagined. Depending on itinerary, you may have to obtain travel documents, such as visas, make arrangements concerning your home or business, get a physical check-up and inoculations, and decide on trip and travel health insurance options. Fewer than 40 nations require U.S. citizens to carry visas, but those that do will require some planning to avoid a potentially nasty situation. These are all reasons to engage a freighter travel specialists, especially when it is your first trip on a freighter.

Ford's Freighter Travel Guide
19448 Londelius Street
Northridge, CA 91324
☎ 818-701-7414

You might start by consulting a current issue of **Ford's Freighter Travel Guide,** a comprehensive twice-a-year guide listing almost all passenger-carrying freighter itineraries. Your local university library may have a copy. A subscription costs $24 (plus $1.98 sales tax for California residents). Single copies are $15.95.

TravLtips Cruise and
Freighter Association
P.O. Box 580188
Flushing, NY 11358-0188
☎ 718-224-0435 or
800-872-8584
fax 718-224-3247
www.travltips.com

A smart move would be to join **TravLtips Cruise and Freighter Association;** membership costs $20 per year per couple or $35 for two years). You'll connect with this loose-knit group of thousands of freighter and offbeat cruising buffs and receive bimonthly issues of *TravLtips,* the association magazine, periodic issues of *Roam the World by Freighter,* which includes members' reports of voyages, access to the association's travel planning and reservation services, and member-only invitations on special and unusual cruises.

Another very useful resource is California-based **Freighter World Cruises.** Printed twice monthly, The *Freighter Space Advisory* reports cabin availability, descriptions, departure dates from the U.S. and foreign ports, en route ports of call, and fares. You can subscribe online at **www.freighterworld.com;** a one-year subscription costs $29. Both of these resources can help you select a vessel or voyage and book it, plus handle air and other travel arrangements.

Freighter World Cruises
180 South Lake Avenue
Suite 335
Pasadena, CA 91101-2655
☎ 626-449-3106 or
800-531-7774
fax 626-449-9573
www.freighterworld.com

Canada-based **The Cruise People** has been in business since 1972, and employs a full-time freighter travel specialist. By accessing the Web site, **www.thecruisepeople.ca,** you can get on the e-mail list for promotions on freighter voyages and cruises.

All three companies' Web sites list the ever-changing freighter voyage opportunities, and access is free.

Many cargo lines are represented by the above or similar specialized agents. These services can be a real blessing, particularly to first-timers, because booking passage on a freighter is neither quick nor easy.

You need lead time. Because freighter schedules are prone to change, some lines require wait-listing (no charge) until firm schedules are released. Only then will waiting passengers be given an option on a cabin. A deposit—usually 10 to 20%—is required only after a cabin option is accepted. Final payment is usually due 45 to 60 days before sailing.

The Cruise People
1252 Lawrence Avenue East
Suite 210
Don Mills, Ontario
Canada M3A 1C3
☎ 416-444-2410 or
800-268-6523
fax 416-447-2628
www.thecruisepeople.ca

During the months before sailing, the departure date may shift a few days and the routing may change. (For example, you may be going to Wellington rather than Auckland.) This proves the value of having an experienced agent to keep you informed of changes and to help deal with them, as well as your need for flexibility in schedule and attitude.

Every freighter company has its own policies affecting passengers. Most have literature outlining these policies and describing their ships and itineraries. Obtain such materials through your travel agent or freighter travel specialist or directly from the line, and read everything thoroughly—including the fine print. Pay particular attention to the company's cancellation policy, and take it into account when you consider trip cancellation insurance. Also, it may be wise to take out deviation insurance in case a voyage suddenly becomes longer by a week or more, because some lines will charge you for the extra days.

Your Health and Safety

Cargo lines require passengers ages 65 or older to present a certificate of good health from their doctor before booking can be completed. Review your itinerary with your physician regarding potential risk of disease or infection and any immunizations or protective medicines needed. Up-to-the-minute immunization recommendations are available from the **U.S. Centers for Disease Control's** 24-hour hotline in Atlanta: ☎ 877-394-8747. You'll need a touch-tone phone and fax machine to receive faxed messages. You may also check for information on the CDC Web site at **www.cdc.gov**. You may also want to stay informed about potential unrest in the countries you are visiting. The U.S. State Department publishes travel advisories at **travel.state.gov/travel/warnings.html**. If something happens en route, the shipping line may change the itinerary. Or, if it is safe to call for handling cargo, you may be advised or even required to stay aboard.

Clothing and Essentials

Packing for a 90-day freighter voyage should be no different from selecting your gear and garments for a 10-day trip. Nor should it weigh more; cargo lines, unlike cruise lines, aren't obligated to provide baggage service. Don't bring more than you can handle, although crewmembers are likely to help you carry your luggage up a steep gangway.

Casual attire is the rule. It's possible there might be a special occasion calling for slightly dressier clothes, or that restaurants ashore may require them. For everyday wear, bring low-heeled, nonskid, rubber-soled shoes. They are essential for safe maneuvering aboard ship in rough seas and during normal rolling conditions. Be prepared for just about any kind of climate. Light wraps (even in the tropics) and rain gear are essential.

Foul weather is almost a certainty during any long voyage, and many freighter veterans pack a lightweight, two-piece rain suit (parka and pants) and rubber boots. They also are handy for wading through the dust and residue that cakes bulk-loading docks. Bring binoculars, some reading material (don't overdo; most ships have extensive libraries), washcloths, and facial tissue.

Electrical current on most foreign-flagged freighters is 220/250 AC. You'll need a voltage converter and plug adapter to use your appliances. Funds for shipboard expenses should be in U.S. currency. Traveler's checks are generally accepted, but very few lines take credit cards or personal checks.

Some lines say they have no policy on tipping. A few say that their stewards who serve passengers get extra pay and suggest that tipping be reserved for exceptional or special service. The norm seems to be $1.50 per passenger per day to the room steward and an equal amount to the dining steward.

Smoking is allowed on nearly all freighters because many officers and crew members smoke. A few lines bar smoking in dining rooms. The majority of officers and crew who smoke are courteous around nonsmoking guests, and most passengers say smoking is not a big problem.

FREIGHTER TRAVEL COMPANIES

BELOW IS A SMALL SAMPLE of freighter companies offering cruises; all can be booked through The Cruise People, Freighter World Cruises, and TravLtips. These agents are able to supply detailed information on these and other freighter companies and ships with the facilities to carry passengers.

BANK LINE/ANDREW WEIR SHIPPING, LTD. General cargo ships take 12 passengers sailing from Dunkirk and Le Havre, France, on a round-the-world service via the Panama and Suez canals. The route includes South Pacific islands, Papua New Guinea, Singapore, Malaysia, then Algeciras, Spain, ending at Hamburg, Germany. 100 to 105 days.

CANADA MARITIME Container ships accommodating from three to eight passengers operate regular transatlantic services on three routes from Montreal to two or three European ports—Liverpool and Thamesport, England; Le Havre, France; Antwerp, Belgium; and Hamburg, Germany. 18 to 20 days round-trip; one-way passage is also available. **www.canmar.com.**

CMA CGM, THE FRENCH LINE Four container ships take six passengers, sailing from New York; Norfolk, Virginia; and Savannah, Georgia, then via the Panama Canal to the South Pacific, Australia, Singapore, Saudi Arabia, and Egypt; through the Suez Canal to Mediterranean and Northern European ports; and then west to New York. All in about 84 days.

GRIMALDI FREIGHTER CRUISES Roll-on/roll-off ships take nine to ten passengers from Southampton, England, to ports in Italy, Greece, Turkey, Cyprus, Israel, and Egypt, and return via several Northern European ports back to Southampton. Complete voyage takes about 35 days. **www.Grimaldi-Freightercruises.com.**

LYKES LINES LTD. Four container ships accommodate five passengers, sailing from Houston to New Orleans, San Juan, then transatlantic to Italian and Spanish ports, returning via Mexican ports to Houston. About 42 days. **www.lykesline.com.**

PZM POLISH STEAMSHIP COMPANY Bulk carriers take six passengers, sailing from Amsterdam (Ijmuiden) to the Great Lakes ports of Cleveland, Ohio; Burns Harbor, Indiana; Duluth, Minnesota; and Thunder Bay, Ontario. The one-way westbound trip lasts about 12 to 21 days. The return is a tramp service with eastbound ports not known in advance. They could be in Northern Europe, the Mediterranean, and North Africa. Complete voyage takes about 60 days.

REEDEREI F. LAEISZ Four container ships take four passengers, leaving from Long Beach, California, for Pusan, South Korea, and Shanghai, China, and return to Long Beach in about 28 days. The company also operates nine ships that accommodate eight passengers and sail from Long Beach to East Asian ports, Sri Lanka, then via the Suez Canal to Northern European ports, returning via Suez to East Asian ports and back to Long Beach in about 84 days. **www.laeiszline.de.**

ITINERARY INDEX

Abercrombie & Kent, Inc.

Explorer II **HOME PORT** Ushuaia
November–March, 13–19 nights, Antarctica. Includes 1-night hotel in Santiago and flights between Santiago and Ushuaia–round-trip from Ushuaia.

African Safari Club Ltd.

Royal Star **HOME PORT** Mombassa
January–February, 14 nights, South Africa, from Mombassa to Cape Town.

February, 18 nights, Indian Ocean, round-trip from Mombassa to Mahé.

April–October, December, 4 and 11 nights, Indian Ocean Islands, various itineraries round-trip from Mombassa.

November, 13 nights, Seychelles, round-trip from Mombassa to Mahé.

American Canadian Caribbean Line

Grande Caribe **HOME PORTS** Philadelphia, Warren (RI), and others
May 9, 12 nights, intracoastal between Philadelphia and Jacksonville.

May 23 and November 10, 14 nights, Atlantic coastal waterways between Warren and Jacksonville; and reverse.

June, August, 5 nights, New England, round-trip from Warren to Newport, Province-town, Plymouth, Martha's Vineyard, Nantucket; or Portland via Cape Cod Canal, Salem, Gloucester, Newburyport, Portsmouth, Portland; 7 nights, coast of Maine, round-trip from Portland to Bath, Rockland, Bar Harbor, Castine, Belfast, Port Clyde.

June, July, September 3, 12 nights, Erie Canal/Saguenay between Warren and Quebec City and return voyage; Fall Foliage between Warren and Quebec City; return October.

Grande Mariner **HOME PORTS** Providenciales, St. Thomas, Warren, and others
November 2007, April 2008, 14 nights, Warren to Jacksonville and reverse.

December 2007, 11 nights, Nassau to Mayaguana Island, Long Island, Acklins Island, Exuma Cays, Staniel Cay, Norman's Cay.

January, February, 11 nights, St. Thomas to St. John, Tortola, Salt Island. Or St. Maarten to Antigua via Marigot, Saba, St. Kitts, Nevis. Return February.

March 14, 11 nights, round-trip from Nassau to Spanish Wells, Eleuthera, Harbour Island, Governor's Harbour, Exuma Cays, Staniel Cay, Warderick Wells Cay; 7 nights, from Charleston to Jacksonville via Beaufort, Savannah, Brunswick, Jekyll Island, St. Marys, Fernandina Beach. Return April.

May, July, 15 nights, Chicago to West Point via Manistee, Mackinac Island, Wyandotte, Cleveland, Erie, (eastbound only), Buffalo, Rochester, Oswego, Troy, Kingston; return June, August.

June, July, August, 6 nights, round-trip from Chicago to Holland, Manistee, Mackinac Island, Sturgeon Bay (WI), Milwaukee.

September, 12 nights, Erie Canal/Saguenay, from Warren to Quebec City; return September.

October, 12 nights, Northeastern Fall Foliage, from Warren to Quebec City; return October.

American Cruise Lines

American Star **HOME PORTS** Baltimore, Bangor, Charleston, Jacksonville, Providence

November, May, 7 nights, Mid-Atlantic Inland Passage, between Baltimore and Charleston. Or 14 nights, between Baltimore and Jacksonville.

April–May, November–December, Saturday, 7 nights, Antebellum South, from Charleston to Jacksonville.

May, June, 7 nights, New England Islands, round-trip from Providence to New Bedford, Nantucket Island, Martha's Vineyard, Bristol/Fall River, Newport, Block Island.

May, October, 7 nights, Chesapeake Bay, round-trip from Baltimore to Williamsburg/Yorktown, Tangier/Solomons Island, Cambridge, Oxford, St. Michaels, Annapolis.

June–September, Saturday, 7 nights, Maine Coast, round-trip from Bangor; some cruises depart from/return to Portland.

October, 7 nights, Hudson River Fall Foliage, round-trip from New York to West Point, Catskill, Albany, Kingston, Sleepy Hollow, cruise Hudson River.

November–December, 7 nights, Great Rivers of Florida, round-trip from Jacksonville.

American Spirit **HOME PORTS** Baltimore, Charleston, New York, Providence
March–May, November–December, Saturday, 7 nights, Antebellum South between Charleston (SC) and Jacksonville.

June–September, 7 nights, New England Islands, round-trip from Providence.

November 2007, May–June, October–November 2008, 7 nights, Chesapeake Bay, round-trip from Baltimore.

October, 7 nights, Hudson River Fall Foliage, round-trip from New York.

November–December, 7 nights, Great Rivers of Florida, round-trip from Jacksonville.

November, May, 7 nights, between Baltimore and Charleston. Or 14 nights, between Baltimore and Jacksonville.

American Glory **HOME PORTS** Baltimore, Charleston, Jacksonville, New York
November–December, April–May, Saturday, 7 nights, Antebellum South between Charleston and Jacksonville.

June–September, 7 nights, New England Islands, round-trip from Providence; July 26 and August 6, 10 nights, Grand New England Cruise, from Providence to Bar Harbor, Martha's Vineyard, Rockland, Nantucket, Camden, and other ports.

May–June, November, 7 nights, Chesapeake Bay, round-trip from Baltimore.

September–October 2008, Saturday, 7 nights, Hudson River Fall Foliage, round-trip from New York.

November–December 2007, February–March, December 2008, 7 nights, Great Rivers of Florida, round-trip from Jacksonville.

November, May, 7 nights, between Baltimore and Charleston. Or 14 nights, between Baltimore and Jacksonville.

American Eagle **HOME PORTS** Baltimore, Charleston
November 2007, 7 nights, Antebellum South between Charleston and Jacksonville. Or Great Rivers of Florida, round-trip from Jacksonville.

June–November, Saturday, 7 nights, Chesapeake Bay, round-trip from Baltimore to Williamsburg/Yorktown, Tangier Island/Solomons Island, Cambridge, Oxford, St. Michaels, Annapolis. Or Baltimore to Charleston via Chesapeake Bay, Norfolk, Oriental, Morehead City, Wilmington, Myrtle Beach, Charleston. Or 14 nights, between Baltimore and Jacksonville.

American Safari Cruises

Safari Escape **HOME PORTS** Friday Harbor, Juneau
May–September, 8 nights, Alaska, between Juneau and Prince Rupert (BC); mid-May to late August, calling at Tracy Arm, Sawyer Glaciers, Stephens Passage, Frederick Sound, Petersburg, Canoe Pass, Meyers Chuck, Misty Fjords, Ketchikan.

May and September, 14 nights, Inside Passage repositioning cruises, between Seattle and Juneau.

September–October, 7 nights, San Juan Islands and fjords of Canada, round-trip from Friday Harbor (WA) to Sidney, Victoria, Princess Louisa Inlet, and Vancouver; Roche Harbor, Jones Island.

Safari Quest **HOME PORTS** Astoria, Juneau, La Paz, Lewiston, San Francisco
October–November, 3 and 4 nights, round-trip from San Francisco to Petaluma and Carneros regions and Napa Valley.

January–March 23, November–December, 7 nights, Loreto, round-trip from Loreto to Gulf of California, Baja Peninsula, La Paz, includes hiking, whale-watching, kayaking. Or November–December, March–April, 9 nights, round-trip from Loreto to Baja Peninsula. Or December 2007, November 2008, 7 nights, Scuba Diving, Gulf of California. Or January, 7 nights, Stargazing, Baja California, telescopes on board for viewing.

May–September, 7 nights, Alaska, between Juneau and Sitka, via Glacier Bay National Park, Icy Strait, Inside Passage, and reverse.

September, 14 nights, Alaska, between Seattle and Juneau via San Juan Islands, Friday Harbor, Canadian Inside Passage, Prince Rupert, Ketchikan, Canoe Pass, Petersburg, Glacier Bay National Park. Includes kayaking in fjords, hiking to hot springs, tour of Saxman Totem Village.

September–October, 11 nights, Columbia and Snake rivers, from Lewiston (ID) to Astoria (OR) or reverse.

Safari Spirit **HOME PORTS** Friday Harbor, Juneau
November–December 2007, March–April 2008, 5 or 6 nights, Wine Charters on Columbia River between Wenatchee and Portland via North Columbia Valley, Walla Walla Appellation, Red Mountain and Yakima Valley Appellation, Maryhill Museum/Columbia Gorge Appellation, Columbia River Gorge/Bonneville Dam.

May–September, 8 nights, Alaska between Juneau and Petersburg via Tenakee Springs, Alaska's Inside Passage, Glacier Country. The adventure cruise includes whale-, wildlife-, and bird-watching and kayaking.

May, September, 14 nights, Alaska between Seattle and Juneau.

September–November 2008, 8 nights, Columbia and Snake rivers, between Lewiston (ID) and Astoria (OR).

Bora Bora Cruises

Tu Moana/Ti'a Moana **HOME PORT** Bora-Bora
Year-round, Monday, 6 nights, Society Islands lagoon cruising, round-trip from Bora-Bora to Taha'a, Raiatea (2 days), Huanine, overnight in Bora-Bora.

Carnival Cruise Lines

Carnival Celebration **HOME PORT** Jacksonville
Year-round, 4 to 5 nights, Bahamas round-trip from Jacksonville. 4 nights, alternate Thursdays to Freeport and Nassau; or 5 nights, alternate Mondays and Saturdays to Key West and Nassau; 2 days at sea.

Carnival Conquest **HOME PORT** Galveston
Year-round, Sunday, 7 nights, Western Caribbean, round-trip from Galveston to Montego Bay, Grand Cayman, Cozumel, 3 days at sea.

Carnival Destiny **HOME PORT** San Juan
Through 2007, Sunday, 7 nights, Southern Caribbean, round-trip from San Juan.

January 2008–April 2009, Sunday, Southern Caribbean, round-trip from San Juan to St. Thomas, Dominica, Barbados, St. Kitts, La Romana (overnight).

Carnival Ecstasy **HOME PORT** Galveston
Year-round, 4 to 5 nights, Western Caribbean from Galveston. 4 nights, alternate Thursdays to Cozumel; 5 nights, alternate Mondays and Saturdays to Progresso (Yucatan) and Cozumel; all with 2 days at sea

Carnival Elation **HOME PORTS** Port Canaveral, San Diego
Year-round, 4 to 5 nights, Baja Mexico, round-trip from San Diego. 4 nights, alternate Thursdays to Cabo San Lucas; 5 nights, alternate Mondays and Saturdays to Cabo San Lucas and Ensenada; all with 2 days at sea.

Carnival Fantasy **HOME PORT** New Orleans
Year-round, 4 to 5 nights, Western Caribbean, round-trip from New Orleans. 4 nights, alternate Thursdays to Cozumel; 5 nights, alternate Mondays and Saturdays to Costa Maya and Cozumel; all with 2 days at sea.

Carnival Fascination **HOME PORT** Miami
Year-round, 3 to 4 nights, Bahamas and Western Caribbean, round-trip from Miami. 3 nights, Fridays to Nassau; 4 nights, Monday to Key West, Calica/Playa del Carmen, or Cozumel.

Carnival Freedom **HOME PORTS** Fort Lauderdale, Miami
November 2007–April 2008, Saturdays, 7 nights, alternating Eastern/Western Caribbean, round-trip from Miami to San Juan, St. Thomas, and St. Maarten; or Cozumel, Grand Cayman, Ocho Rios, 3 days at sea. April, 7 nights, to Half Moon Cay, St. Thomas, San Juan, Grand Turk, 2 days at sea.

April 26, 14 nights, transatlantic from Miami to Civitavecchia (Rome); November, 16 nights, transatlantic from Civitavecchia to Fort Lauderdale.

May–October, 12 nights, Mediterranean and Greek Isles, round-trip from Civitavecchia to Naples, Venice, Dubrovnik, Messina, Sicily, cruising by Stromboli volcano, Barcelona, Cannes, Livorno; or Naples, Rhodes, Izmir; Istanbul, Dardanelles, Athens, Katakolon, Livorno.

Carnival Glory **HOME PORT** Port Canaveral
Year-round, Saturday, 7 nights, alternating Eastern and Western Caribbean, round-trip from Port Canaveral to Nassau, St. Thomas/St. John, and St. Maarten; or Cozumel, Belize City, Costa Maya, Nassau.

Carnival Holiday **HOME PORT** Mobile
Year-round, 4 to 5 nights, Western Caribbean, round-trip from Mobile. 4 nights, alternate Thursdays to Cozumel; 5 nights, alternate Mondays to Cozumel, Calica/ Playa del Carmen; 5 nights, alternate Saturdays to Cozumel and Costa Maya.

Carnival Imagination **HOME PORT** Miami
Year-round, 4 to 5 nights, Western Caribbean, round-trip from Miami. 4 nights, alternate Thursdays to Key West and Calica/Playa del Carmen with 1 day at sea; 5 nights, alternate Mondays and Saturdays to Grand Cayman and Ocho Rios, with 2 days at sea.

Carnival Inspiration **HOME PORT** Tampa
Year-round, 4 to 5 nights, Western Caribbean, round-trip from Tampa. 4 nights, alternate Thursdays to Cozumel; 5 nights, alternate Mondays to Grand Cayman and Cozumel; 5 nights, alternate Saturdays to Grand Cayman and Calica; all with 2 days at sea.

Carnival Legend **HOME PORT** Tampa
Year-round, Sunday, 7 nights, Western Caribbean, round-trip from Tampa to Grand Cayman, Cozumel, Belize; Costa Maya with 2 days at sea.

Carnival Liberty **HOME PORTS** Fort Lauderdale, Miami
Through May 2008, 6 and 8 nights, alternating Western/Eastern Caribbean, round-trip from Fort Lauderdale. 8 nights, Saturday, to either Costa Maya, Puerto Limon (Costa Rica), Colon (Panama), or San Juan, St. Thomas/St. John, Antigua, Tortola/Virgin Gorda, and Nassau. 6 nights, alternate Sundays to Freeport, Grand Cayman, and Cozumel. 6 nights, alternate Sundays to Freeport, Key West or Nassau, Grand Cayman and Costa Maya or Ocho Rios.
June 2008–May 2009, Saturdays, 7 nights, alternating Eastern and Western Caribbean, round-trip from Miami to San Juan, St. Thomas, and St. Maarten; or Cozumel, Grand Cayman, Ocho Rios.

Carnival Miracle **HOME PORTS** Fort Lauderdale, New York
October 2007–February 2009, 8 nights, alternating Southern/Western Caribbean, round-trip from Fort Lauderdale to St. Maarten, St. Lucia, St. Kitts or Colon, Limon, Belize.
April, 6 nights, Bermuda, round-trip from New York to King's Wharf (overnight) and Newport with 2 days at sea.
June, August–October 2008, 8 nights, Eastern Caribbean, round-trip from New York to San Juan, St. Thomas, Tortola with 4 days at sea.
October, 2 nights, Cruise to Nowhere, round-trip from New York.

Carnival Paradise **HOME PORT** Long Beach
Year-round, 3 to 4 nights, Mexico, round-trip from Long Beach. 3 nights, Friday to Ensenada; 4 nights, Monday to Ensenada and Catalina Island; both with 1 day at sea.

Carnival Pride **HOME PORT** Long Beach
Year-round, 7 nights, Mexican Riviera, Sundays, round-trip from Long Beach to Puerto Vallarta, Mazatlan, Cabo San Lucas with 3 days at sea.

Carnival Sensation **HOME PORT** Port Canaveral
Year-round, 3 to 4 nights, Bahamas, round-trip from Port Canaveral. 3 nights, Thursdays to Nassau; 5 nights, Sundays to Freeport and Nassau; both with 1 day at sea.

Carnival Spirit **HOME PORTS** San Diego, Vancouver, Whittier
October–April, 8 nights, Mexican Riviera, round-trip from San Diego to Acapulco, Zihuatanejo/Ixtapa, and Manzanillo.
May, October, 12 nights, Hawaii, between Honolulu (overnight) and Vancouver, calling at Kona and Hilo; Maui (Lahaina), cruise the Na Pali Coast. September 24 reverse.
October, 12 nights, Hawaii between Honolulu and Ensenada, calling at Kauai

(Nawiliwili), Kona, Hilo, Lahaina, Kahului (Maui).

May–September, Wednesday, 7 nights, Alaska between Vancouver and Whittier, calling at Prince William Sound, College Fjord, Lynn Canal, Sitka, Juneau, Skagway, Ketchikan, and the Inside Passage; or reverse; or Glacier Bay round-trip from Vancouver via Inside Passage to Juneau, Glacier Bay, Skagway, Ketchikan.

Carnival Splendor (debuts 2008) **HOME PORT** London (Dover), Rome (Civitavecchia), Fort Lauderdale

July 13, Inaugural 12 nights, Northern Europe from London (Dover) to Copenhagen, Warnemunde (Berlin), Helsinki, St. Petersburg, Russia (2-day call), Tallin, Estonia, and Amsterdam. Other departures July 25 and August 6, 18, 30.

September 11–23, 12 nights, Western Mediterranean from London (Dover) to Rome (Civitavecchia) via Le Havre, Vigo, Spain, Lisbon, Malaga and Barcelona, Cannes, Livorno.

September 23, 12 nights, Mediterranean from Rome to Naples, Venice (2-day call), Dubrovnik, Croatia, Messina, Sicily, Barcelona, Cannes, Livorno.

October 5 and 17, 12 nights, Mediterranean, Turkey and Greece from Rome to Naples, Marmaris, Izmir (Ephesus), Istanbul, Athens (Piraeus), Katakolon, Livorno; with overnight at Rome (Civitavecchia).

October 29, 16 nights, transatlantic from Rome to Fort Lauderdale via Barcelona, Palma de Mallorca, Malaga, Funchal (Madeira), Portugal, St. Maarten.

November 22–February 2009, 7 nights, Caribbean from Fort Lauderdale to Casa de Campo/La Romana, Dominican Republic; St. Thomas/St. John, San Juan, and Nassau.

Carnival Triumph **HOME PORT** Miami

Through April 2008, Saturday, 7 nights, alternating Eastern and Western Caribbean, round-trip from Miami to San Juan, St. Thomas, St. Maarten, or Grand Turk; or Cozumel, Grand Cayman, Ocho Rios; or Half Moon Cay, St. Thomas, San Juan, Nassau, or Grand Turk.

Carnival Valor **HOME PORT** Miami

Year-round, Sunday, 7 nights, alternating Eastern and Western Caribbean, round-trip from Miami to Nassau, St. Thomas, and St. Maarten with 3 days at sea; or Grand Cayman, Belize City; Isla Roatan (Honduras); Grand Cayman and Costa Maya with 2 days at sea.

Carnival Victory **HOME PORTS** Charleston, Miami, New York, Norfolk

Winter, Sunday, 7 nights, alternating Eastern and Western Caribbean, round-trip from Miami to San Juan, St. Maarten, and St. Thomas; or Costa Maya, Grand Cayman, Ocho Rios.

May–June, and October, 5 nights, Bahamas, round-trip from Charleston to Nassau and Freeport.

June, October, 6 nights, Bahamas, round-trip Norfolk to Nassau.

June, October, 2 nights, Cruise to Nowhere.

June–September, alternate Mondays and Saturdays, 4 to 5 nights, Canada, round-trip from New York to Halifax (4 nights); or Saint John, Bay of Fundy, 2 days at sea and Halifax (5 nights).

September, 7 nights, Fall Foliage, round-trip from New York to Boston, Portland, St. John, New Brunswick, Bay of Fundy, Halifax with 2 days at sea.

November, 24 nights, Athens to Singapore

Celebrity Cruises

Azamara Journey **HOME PORTS** Buenos Aires, Cape Liberty, Valparaiso

January 28, 2008, 12 nights, Carnaval, round-trip from Buenos Aires to Punta del Este, Sao Paulo, Rio de Janeiro, Montevideo.

January–March, 10–18 nights, Antarctica from Valparaiso to Buenos Aires; round-trip. April–November, Europe.

Azamara Quest **HOME PORTS** Acapulco, Athens, Miami, Rome, Singapore
January, 14 nights, Caribbean, round-trip from Miami to Mayaguez, Ponce, St. John, Antigua, Dominica, Guadeloupe, Virgin Gorda, Samana, Grand Turk.

January, March, 14 nights, from Miami to Acapulco via Port Antonio, Cartagena, Puerto Limon, Panama Canal, Fuerte Amador, Puerto Caldera, San Juan del Sur, Huatulco. Return March from Acapulco to Huatulco, San Juan del Sur, Cristobal, Puerto Caldera, San Andres Island, St. Tomas de Castilla, Playa del Carmen.

February–March, 14 nights, round-trip from Miami to Virgin Gorda, Cabrits, Dominica, St. Vincent, Tobago, St. Bart's, St. John, Ponce, Samana, Grand Turk.

April 12, 14 nights, transatlantic from Miami to Rome (Civitavecchia) via Ponta Delgada, Azores, Malaga, Alicante, Menorca, Gijon, Bonifacio, Corsica.

April, September, 14 nights, Italy, round-trip from Rome to Bari, Split, Venice, Ravenna, Taormina, Sorrento, Porto Cervo, Sardinia, Florence.

May–September, 14 nights, Western Mediterranean, round-trip from Rome via Sorrento, Valletta, Tunis, Barcelona, Sete, Provence, Monte Carlo, Portofino, Florence/Pisa.

June–July, October–November, 14 nights, Greece and Turkey from Rome to Athens via Sorrento, Chios, Istanbul, Canakkale, Bodrum, Gethiye, Antalya, Limassol, Alexandria.

July–August, 14 nights, Black Sea from Rome to Athens via Kusadasi, Istanbul, Sinop, Yalta, Sevastopol, Odessa, Varna.

June–August , 14 nights, Athens to Kusadasi, Sorrento, Livorno (Florence/Pisa), Greece's lesser-known islands.

November, 24 nights, Athens to Singapore.

Celebrity Century **HOME PORTS** Amsterdam, Barcelona, Miami
January 19, 2 nights, Bahamas, round-trip from Miami to Nassau.

January–April, 4 or 5 nights, Western Caribbean, round-trip from Miami to Key West, Cozumel or Key West, George Town, Grand Cayman.

April 28, 14 nights, transatlantic from Miami to Amsterdam via Nassau, Bermuda (overnight), Ponta Delgada, Cornwall, La Coruna, Paris, Dover.

May, 5 nights, Scandinavia, round-trip from Amsterdam to Copenhagen, Oslo. Or 12 nights, to Edinburgh, Inverness/Loch Ness, Kirkwall, Belfast, Dublin, St. Peter Port, Channel Islands, Paris.

June–August, 12 nights, Scandinavia and Russia, round-trip from Amsterdam to Copenhagen, Stockholm, Helsinki, St. Petersburg, Tallinn, Klaipeda. Or to Ny-Alesund, Arctic Circle, Alta, Honningsvag, Tromso, Molde, Olden, Bergen. Or 10 nights, to Cork, Belfast, Ny-Alesund, Flam, Bergen. Or 8 nights, to Barcelona via Zeebrugge, Cherbourg, Vigo, Lisbon, Tangier.

September–October, 10 or 11 nights, Western Mediterranean, round-trip from Barcelona to Provence, Nice, Florence, Rome, Naples/Capri, Valletta, Tunis or Provence, Nice, Florence, Rome, Ajaccio, Gibraltar, Casablanca, Tangier.

December 1, 14 nights, westbound transatlantic from Barcelona to Miami via Cartagena, Gibraltar, Marrakech, Agadir, Canary Islands.

December 1, 2008, 14 nights, transatlantic from Barcelona to Miami.

Celebrity Constellation **HOME PORTS** Cape Liberty, Fort Lauderdale, Harwich
September 2007–March 2008, 10 or 11 nights, Caribbean, round-trip from Fort Lauderdale to St. Thomas, St. Kitts, Barbados, St. Lucia, St. Maarten; or Grand Cayman, Aruba, Cartagena, Cristobal Pier, Cozumel.

April 11, 13 nights, transatlantic from Fort Lauderdale with an overnight stay in King's Wharf, Bermuda, to Harwich via Cork, Brest, Normandy, Cherbourg.

April 24, 9 nights, Scotland and Ireland, round-trip from Harwich to Edinburgh, Inverness/Loch Ness, Belfast, Dublin, St. Peter Port, Channel Islands.

May–August, 14 nights, Scandinavia and Russia, round-trip from Harwich to Amsterdam, Berlin, Stockholm, Helsinki, St. Petersburg, Tallinn, Copenhagen.

September 9, 14 nights, transatlantic from Barcelona to Cape Liberty via Malaga, Morocco, Cadiz, Lisbon (overnight), the Azores, St. John's.

September–October, 13 nights, Canada/New England, round-trip from Cape Liberty to Newport, Bar Harbor, Quebec City, Saguenay River, Halifax, Portland, Boston.

October 30, 11 nights, Bermuda/Caribbean reposition from Cape Liberty to Fort Lauderdale via Bermuda (overnight), St. Maarten, Aruba, Labadee.

Celebrity Galaxy   **HOME PORTS**   Miami, Rome, San Juan

December 22, 2007, 13 nights, Caribbean, round-trip from San Juan to St. Thomas, Aruba, Bonaire, Curaçao, Grenada, Barbados, St. Kitts, Tortola.

January–April, 10 nights, Southern Caribbean, round-trip from San Juan to Tortola, St. Maarten, St. Lucia, Barbados, Grenada, Curaçao, Aruba; 11 nights, add Dominica.

April, 14 nights, transatlantic from San Juan to Rome.

May–December, 10 nights or October, 11 nights, Eastern Mediterranean, round-trip from Rome to Sicily, Athens, Mykonos, Kusadasi (Ephesus, Turkey), Rhodes, Santorini, Naples/Capri; or Mykonos, Rhodes, Santorini, Istanbul, Kusadasi, Piraeus (Athens), Naples/Capri.

December 5, 14 nights, transatlantic from Rome (Civitavecchia) to San Juan via Marrakech, Agadir, Lanzarote, Tenerife, Santa Cruz, Tortola.

Celebrity Infinity   **HOME PORTS**   Buenos Aires, San Diego, Valparaiso, Vancouver; others vary with itinerary

November 2007–March 2008, 14 and 15 nights, Buenos Aires to Valparaiso and reverse via Montevideo, Puerto Madryn, Port Stanley, Falkland Islands, Cape Horn, Ushuaia, Punta Arenas, Strait of Magellan, Chilean Fjords, Puerto Montt.

March, 14 nights, from Valparaiso to Fort Lauderdale via La Serena, Arica, Lima, Manta, Panama Canal, Cartagena, Ocho Rios.

April 13, 15 nights, Panama Canal from Fort Lauderdale to San Francisco via Montego Bay, Cartagena, Panama Canal, Punta Arenas, Costa Rica, Huatulco, Acapulco, Cabo San Lucas.

May–September, Sunday, 7 nights, Alaska, round-trip from Vancouver to Ketchikan, Juneau, Sitka, and cruising the Inside Passage and Hubbard Glacier.

Celebrity Mercury   **HOME PORTS**   San Diego, Seattle

December 2007–March 2008, 14 or 15 nights, New Zealand/Australia, Auckland to Sydney via Tauranga, Napier, Wellington, Christchurch, Dunedin, Dusky Sound, Doubtful Sound, Milford Sound, Melbourne, Newcastle.

March, 15 nights, Australia/New Zealand, round-trip from Auckland to Tauranga, Raro-tonga, Cook Islands, Moorea, Bora-Bora, Fanning Island, Kiribati, Hilo, Honolulu, Oahu.

May–September, 7 nights, round-trip from Seattle to Juneau, Skagway, Hubbard, Ketchikan, Prince Rupert.

Celebrity Millennium   **HOME PORTS**   Barcelona, Fort Lauderdale

December 2, 2007, April, 14 nights, transatlantic/Canary Islands, from Barcelona to Malaga, Seville, Lanzarote, La Palma, Labadee.

December 2007–April 2008, 7 nights, Caribbean, round-trip from Fort Lauderdale to San Juan, Tortola, Catalina Island (Casa de Campo), Dominican Republic, Labadee.

May–November, 7–14 nights, Alaska; Australia/New Zealand.

Celebrity Solstice (debuts 2008) **HOME PORT** TBA
December 14, 2008, inaugural cruise, 7 nights, round-trip Eastern Caribbean calling at San Juan, St. Kitts, St. Maarten; itinerary will alternate with San Juan, St. Maarten, Tortola, and Labadee through April 12, 2009.

Celebrity Summit **HOME PORTS** Fort Lauderdale, Los Angeles, San Juan, Southampton
January, April, 14 nights, Panama Canal from Los Angeles to San Juan via Cabo San Lucas, Acapulco, Huatulco, Punta Arenas, Panama Canal, Cristobal Pier, Aruba, Curacao.

January–April, 7 nights, Southern Caribbean, round-trip from San Juan to St. Maarten, Dominica, Grenada, Bonaire, Aruba.

March 29, 12 nights, eastbound transatlantic from San Juan to Southampton via Ponta Delgada, Vigo, Gijon, La Rochelle, Cherbourg.

April, 12 nights, Southampton to Barcelona via Paris, La Rochelle, Bilbao, Gijon, Vigo, Lisbon, Casablanca, Seville.

May–November, 12 nights, Mediterranean from Barcelona to Venice via Nice, Florence, Rome, Naples/Capri, Athens, Santorini, Dubrovnik, and reverse.

November 29, 14 nights, westbound transatlantic from Barcelona to San Juan via Malaga, Madeira, Lanzarote, Tenerife, La Palma, St. Maarten.

Celebrity Xpedition **HOME PORT** Baltra (Galápagos Islands)
Year-round, 7 nights, Galápagos Islands, round-trip from Baltra to North Seymour, San Cristobal, Punta Suarez, Cormorant Point, Baroness, Outlook, Las Bachas, Bartolome, Elizabeth Bay, Punta Espinoza, Puerto Egas, Dragon Hill, Puerto Ayora.

Classic Cruises of Newport

Arabella **HOME PORTS** Newport, St. Maarten, St. Thomas, and others
All itineraries are sample ones as all stops are subject to the captain's discretion and may vary due to weather or unforeseen circumstances.

December 2007, February–March 2008, 6 nights, St. Bart's, round-trip from St. Maarten to Anguilla, St. Bart's; 6 nights, round-trip from St. Thomas to Culebra, Vieques, Jost van Dyke, Tortola, St. John.

January–April, 6 nights, U.S. Virgin Islands and British Virgin Islands, round-trip from St. Thomas.

June–September, 5 nights, New England, round-trip from Newport.

July–August, 5 nights, Maine, round-trip from Camden.

Costa Cruises

Costa Allegra **HOME PORTS** Hong Kong, Shanghai, Singapore
October–December, January, March–June, 14 nights, round-trip from Hong Kong to Manila, Kota Kinabalu, Bandar Seri Bagawan (Brunei), Singapore, Ho Chi Minh City, Da Nang, Sanya.

January, 7 to 16 nights, Far East, from Singapore and Hong Kong to Ho Chi Minh City, Da Nang, Sanya. Manila, Kota Kinabalu, Bandar Seri Bagawan.

February, Vietnam, round-trip from Hong Kong.

February–October, 3 to 5 nights, Far East; 3 to 4 nights, round-trip from Shanghai to Hong Kong; 5 nights, round-trip from Shanghai to Cheju, Nagasaki, Kagoshima.

Costa Atlantica **HOME PORTS** Amsterdam, Guadeloupe, Savona
December 2007, 13 nights, transatlantic from Savona to Guadeloupe
December 2007–March 2008, 7 nights, Southeastern Caribbean, from Guadeloupe.
April 4, 3 nights, round-trip from Savona to Barcelona, Ajaccio.
April 29, September 11, 5 nights, Tunisia/Malta, round-trip from Savona to Ajaccio, Tunis, Valletta, Naples.
May 7, 9 nights, from Savona to Amsterdam via Barcelona, Palma de Mallorca, Malaga, Cadiz, Lisbon, Vigo, Dover. Reverse September 2.
May–September, 11 nights, Baltic and Russia or Norwegian fjords/North Cape, round-trip from Amsterdam to Copenhagen to either Stockholm, Helsinki, St. Petersburg (overnight), Tallinn, Ronne; or Hellesylt, Honningsvag, Tromso, Gravdal, Trondheim, Andalsnes, Bergen.
June, 13 nights, fjords/Iceland, to Hellesylt, Geiranger, Trondheim, Gravdal, Honningsvag, Akureyri, Honningsvag, Reykjavik, Thorshavn (Faroe Islands).
July 6, 14 nights, Spitsbergen, round-trip from Amsterdam to Bergen, Hellesylt, Geiranger, Honningsvag, Bear Island, Magdalenefjord, Ny-Alesund, Longyearbyen, Tromso, Olden.
August, 10 or 12 nights, Baltic to Copenhagen, Stockholm, Helsinki, St. Petersburg, Tallinn, Ronne (Bornholm); 11 nights, add Oslo, overnight St. Petersburg.
September–November, 10 nights, Egypt/Turkey/Greece, round-trip from Savona to Naples, Messina, Alexandria, Limassol, Turkey, Santorini, Katakolon.

Costa Classica **HOME PORTS** Savona, Trieste
November 2007, March–April and October–November 2008, 11 nights, Canary Islands, round-trip from Savona to Barcelona, Casablanca, Agadir, Arrecife, Tenerife, Funchal, Malaga.
December 2007, 17 nights, transatlantic from Savona to Santos.
January, 11 nights, round-trip from Santos to Rio de Janeiro, Cabo Frio, Salvador Bahia, Buzios; 11 nights, add Recife, Maceio, Ilheus.
February, 19 nights, transatlantic from Santos to Savona via Rio de Janeiro, Ilheus, Salvador Bahia, Maceio, Recife, St. Vincent, Tenerife, Funchal, Casablanca, Gibraltar, Barcelona.
May, 8 nights, round-trip from Savona to Barcelona, Alicante, Gibraltar, Lisbon, Cadiz, Malaga.
June, 6 nights, from Savona to Trieste via Naples, Valletta, Corfu, Dubrovnik, Venice.
June–September, 7 nights, Greek Isles/Croatia, round-trip from Trieste to Ancona, Santorini, Mykonos, Piraeus, Corfu, Dubrovnik.
September, 5 nights, from Trieste to Savona via Bari, Corfu, Valletta, Naples.

Costa Concordia **HOME PORT** Rome
December, 9 nights, round-trip from Civitavecchia to Savona, Barcelona, Alicante, Cadiz, Lisbon, Gibraltar, Malaga.
December 2007–April 2008, 10 or 11 nights, Eastern Mediterranean, round-trip from Civitavecchia to Savona, Katakolon, Piraeus, Rhodes, Limassol, Alexandria; 11 nights, add Izmir.
April–November, 7 nights, round-trip from Civitavecchia to Savona, Barcelona, Palma de Mallorca, Tunis, Valletta, Palermo.

Costa Europa **HOME PORTS** Dubai, Savona
December 5, 2007, 18 nights, Savona/Dubai, from Savona to Dubai via Naples,

Alexandria, Port Said, Suez Canal transit, Sharm el Sheikh, Aqaba, Safaga, Hodeidah, Al-Mukalla, Salalah, Muscat.

December 2007–February 2008, 7 nights, Dubai/Oman/Bahrain, round-trip from Dubai to Muscat, Fujairah, Abu Dhabi, Manama (Bahrain).

February 24, 16 nights, from Dubai to Savona via Muscat, Salalah, Al-Mukalla, Safaga, Sharm el Sheikh, Suez Canal transit, Alexandria, Naples.

March–August, 8 or 10 nights, round-trip from Savona to Malaga, Cadiz, Lisbon, Gibraltar, Alicante, Barcelona, or reverse from Barcelona.

April, 3 nights, round-trip from Savona to Barcelona, Ajaccio.

April, June, 11 nights, Black Sea, round-trip from Savona to Naples, Dardanelles, Istanbul, Yalta, Odessa, Bosporus, Santorini, Katakolon.

April and October–November, 11 nights, Egypt/Libya, round-trip from Savona to Naples, Alexandria, Limassol, Rhodes, Valletta, Tripoli. Or 10 nights, Egypt/Cyprus/ Greece, round-trip from Savona to Naples, Alexandria, Cyprus, Rhodes, Piraeus, Katakolon.

May–September, 11 nights, Canary Islands, round-trip from Savona to Barcelona, Casablanca, Agadir, Arrecife, Tenerife, Funchal, Malaga.

Costa Fortuna HOME PORTS Fort Lauderdale, Savona
November, 15 nights, transatlantic from Savona to Fort Lauderdale via Barcelona, Tenerife, Guadeloupe, St. Maarten, Catalina Island, Nassau.

November 2007–March 2008, 7 nights, alternating Western/Eastern Caribbean, round-trip from Fort Lauderdale to Cozumel, Grand Cayman, Ocho Rios (or Montego Bay), Grand Turk. Or 7 nights, to San Juan, St. Maarten, Tortola, Nassau or San Juan, St. Thomas, Catalina Island/La Romana, Nassau.

April, 7 nights, Bermuda, round-trip from Fort Lauderdale to Nassau, King's Wharf (2 overnights).

April, 17 nights, transatlantic from Fort Lauderdale to Savona via Nassau, Catalina Island, St. Maarten, Guadeloupe, Barbados, Tenerife, Funchal, Barcelona.

April, 5 nights, from Savona to Venice via Naples, Valletta, Corfu, Dubrovnik.

May–November, 7 nights, Greek Isles, round-trip from Venice to Bari, Katakolon, Santorini, Mykonos, Rhodes, Dubrovnik.

Costa Magica HOME PORTS Santos, Savona
December 2007–February 2008, South America, 6 nights, round-trip from Santos to Rio de Janeiro, Salvador Bay, Ilhbela; 7 nights, add Ilheus (Brazil).

March, 15 nights, transatlantic from Santos to Savona via Rio de Janeiro, Salvador Bahia, Tenerife, Casablanca.

March–November, 7 nights, Mediterranean, round-trip from Savona to Naples, Palermo, Tunis, Palma de Mallorca (overnight), Barcelona, Marseille.

Costa Mediterranea HOME PORTS Copenhagen, Fort Lauderdale, Savona, Venice
November 2007, 15 nights, transatlantic from Savona to Fort Lauderdale via Barcelona, Casablanca, Tenerife, Barbados, St. John's, St. Maarten, Nassau.

December 2007, 7 nights, Bermuda, round-trip from Fort Lauderdale to Cozumel, Grand Cayman, Ocho Rios (or Montego Bay), Grand Turk.

December 2007–April 2008, 7 nights, alternating Eastern/Western Caribbean, round-trip from Fort Lauderdale to San Juan, St. Thomas, La Romana, Grand Turk, or Key West, Grand Cayman, Roatan, Cozumel.

April, 16 nights, transatlantic from Fort Lauderdale to Savona via Key West, San Juan, St. Thomas, St. Maarten, Antigua, Funchal, Malaga.

April, May, 5 nights, Tunisia/Malta, round-trip from Savona to Ajaccio, Tunis, Valletta, Naples.

May, 10 nights, from Savona to Copenhagen via Malaga, Cadiz, Lisbon, Vigo, Dover, Amsterdam.

May–September, 7 nights, Baltic and Russia or fjords, round-trip from Copenhagen to Tallinn, St. Petersburg, Helsinki, Stockholm or Flam, Hellesylt, Geiranger, Bergen, Stavanger, Oslo.

September, 10 nights, from Copenhagen to Savona via Dover, Le Havre, Vigo, Lisbon, Cadiz, Malaga.

September–November, 8 nights, round-trip from Savona to Malaga, Cadiz, Lisbon, Gibraltar, Alicante, Barcelona.

Costa Romantica **HOME PORTS** Dubai, Savona

November 30, 2007, 22 nights, from Savona to Dubai via Civitavecchia, Katakolon, Alexandria, Port Said, Suez Canal transit, Sharm el Sheik, Aqaba, Safaga, Hodeidah, Al-Mukalla, Salalah, Muscat, Fuhjairah, Abu Dhabi, Manama.

December 2007–March 2008, 7 nights, Dubai/Oman/Bahrain, round-trip from Dubai to Muscat, Fujairah, Abu Dhabi, Manama.

March, 16 nights, from Dubai to Savona via Muscat, Salalah, Al-Mukalla, Safaga, Sharm el Sheikh, Suez Canal transit, Alexandria, Naples.

April, 5 nights, round-trip from Savona to Ajaccio, Tunis, Valletta, Naples.

May 1, 4 nights, to Civitavecchia via Barcelona, Palma de Mallorca, Ajaccio

May–November, 7 nights, alternating Greece/Turkey and Tunisia/Libya/France, round-trip from Civitavecchia to Catania, Patmos, Mykonos, Izmir, Santorini or Catania, Valletta, Gabes, Tripoli, Tunis, Eolie Islands.

Costa Serena **HOME PORTS** Savona, Venice

December 2007, January–April, 10 or 11 nights, round-trip from Savona to Barcelona, Casablanca, Tenerife, Funchal, Malaga; 11 nights, add Arrecife.

April, 5 nights, from Savona to Venice via Naples, Valletta, Corfu, Dubrovnik; return November, Bari replaces Dubrovnik.

April–November, Greece/Turkey/Croatia, round-trip from Venice to Bari, Katakolon, Izmir, Istanbul, Dubrovnik.

Costa Victoria **HOME PORTS** Kiel, Santos, Savona

December 2007–February 2008, 9 or 22 nights, Brazil/Argentina/Uruguay, Tierra del Fuego, 9 nights, round-trip from Santos to Rio de Janeiro, Buenos Aires, Punta del Este, Porto Belo; 22 nights, add Montevideo, Puerto Madryn, Punta Arenas, Garibaldi Bay, Ushuaia, Port Stanley.

March, 3 nights, round-trip from Santos to Rio de Janeiro, Ilha Bela, Portobelo.

March, 18 nights, transatlantic from Santos to Savona via Rio de Janeiro, Ilheus, Salvador Bahia, Recife, Dakar, Tenerife, Funchal, Lisbon, Cadiz, Malaga.

April, 8 nights, round-trip from Savona to Malaga, Cadiz, Lisbon, Gibraltar, Alicante, Barcelona.

May 6, 10 nights, from Savona to Hamburg via Malaga, Cadiz, Lisbon, Vigo, La Coruña, Le Havre, Dover, Amsterdam.

May–August, 6, 7, or 11 nights, Fjords or Baltic and Russia, round-trip from Kiel to Hellesylt, Geiranger, Bergen, Stavanger, Aarhus; 7 nights, add Flam, or Stockholm, Helsinki, St. Petersburg, Tallinn; 11 nights, add Riga, Klaipeda, Gdynia, Ronne.

June, July, 14 nights, Spitsbergen, round-trip from Kiel to Hellesylt, Geiranger, Tromso,

Magdalenefjord, Ny-Alesund, Longyearbyen, Honningsvag, Hammerfest, Molde, Andalsnes, Bergen.

June, 14 nights, Iceland/North Cape, round-trip from Kiel to Hellesylt, Geiranger, Trondheim, Gravdal, Honningsvag, Akureyri, Reykjavik, Kirkwall, Lerwick (Shetland Islands).

September, 10 nights, Kiel/Savona, between Kiel and Savona via Dover, Cherbourg, Leixos, Lisbon, Cadiz, Malaga.

September, 13 nights, Black Sea, round-trip from Savona to Naples, Santorini, Mykonos, Izmir, Dardanelles, Istanbul, Bosporus, Costanta (Romania), Odessa, Yalta, Bosporus, Piraeus, Katakolon.

September–November, 11 nights, Canary Islands, round-trip from Savona to Barcelona, Casablanca, Agadir, Arrecife, Tenerife, Funchal, Malaga.

Cruise North Expeditions, Inc.

Lyubov Orlova **HOME PORT** Kuujjuaq
Weather, drifting ice, sea, tides, and other conditions dictate itinerary and excursions; routes and landing sites will vary from one expedition to the next.

June, 7 nights, Newfoundland and Labrador, round-trip from St. John's to Terra Nova National Park, St. Anthony, L'Anse aux Meadows, Red Bay, Battle Harbour, Gannet Islands, The Wonderstrands, Rigolet, Happy Valley-Goose Bay; 8 nights, Labrador North, round-trip from Happy Valley-Goose Bay, Makkovik, Hopedale, Nain, Hebron, Nachvak Fjord/Eclipse Harbour, Killiniq, Kuujjuaq.

July–August, 7 nights, Baffin Adventure, from Kuujjuaq to Iqaliut and reverse to Akpatok Island, Quaqtaq and Diana Island, Killiniq and the Button Islands, Cape Dorset and Mallikjuak Territorial Park, Kimmirut for Katannilik Territorial Park (Soper Heritage River), Kekerten Territorial Historic Park and Auyuittuq National Park, Pangnirtung.

July–August, 8 nights, Artic Explorer/Hudson's Wake, round-trip from Kuujjuaq, or from Kuujjuaq to Churchill via Akpatok Island, Kangiqsujuaq, Digges Island and Mansel Island, Walrus Island, Cape Dorset and Mallikjuak Territorial Park, Kimmirut for Katannilik Territorial Park (Soper Heritage River), Inukjuaq, Churchill.

August–September, 8 nights, High Arctic from Kuujjuaq to Akpatok Island, Qikiqtarjuaq, Auyuittuq National Park, Baffin Island, Pond Inlet, Bylot Island, Milne Inlet, Lancaster Sound, Resolute Bay.

Cruise West

Pacific Explorer **HOME PORTS** Colon, Los Sueños, Panama City
December 2007, January–April, 9 nights, Costa Rica and Panama, cruise tours including San Blas Islands, Portobelo, Panama Canal, Darién Jungle, Isla de Coiba, Golfo Dulce, Corcovado National Park, Manuel Antonio National Park.

November–December, June–July, 7 nights, between Panama and Costa Rica.

Spirit of Alaska **HOME PORT** Juneau
May–August, 3 to 4 nights, Alaska Glacier Bay, round-trip from Juneau to Skagway, Haines, Sitka, Glacier Bay. Positions between Juneau and Seattle, 10 nights, May and August–September.

Spirit of Columbia **HOME PORTS** Whittier, Juneau
May–August, 3 to 4 nights, Prince William Sound, round-trip from Anchorage/Whittier to Blackstone Bay, College Fjord, Knight Island, Chenega Glacier, Cordova, Turnagain Arm. Positioning cruises between Juneau and Seattle, 10 nights, May and September.

May and August–September, Gold Rush Alaska Inside Passage.

Spirit of Discovery **HOME PORTS** Juneau, Ketchikan, Portland

April 2008, 7 nights, Taste of the Pacific Northwest, food and wine cruise, Columbia and
Snake rivers, round-trip from Portland to Columbia River Gorge, Snake River, Hells
Canyon, Walla Walla, The Dalles, Maryhill Museum, Astoria, Fort Clatsop, eight sets
of locks.

May and September, 10 nights, Gold Rush Inside Passage between Juneau and Seattle.

June–August, 8 nights, Alaska Wilderness Inside Passage, round-trip from Juneau to
Endicott Arm, Tracy Arm, Frederick Sound, Sitka, Icy Strait, Elfin Cove, Glacier Bay
National Park.

Spirit of Endeavour **HOME PORTS** Juneau, Ketchikan, Seattle

September, 7 nights, Gulf Islands/British Columbia, Pacific Northwest Coastal Escape,
round-trip from Seattle to Vancouver, Granville Island, Princess Louisa Inlet, Nanaimo,
Gulf Islands, Sidney, Victoria, Friday Harbor, San Juan Islands, Port Townsend.

May and September, 10 nights, Alaska Gold Rush Inside Passage between Juneau and
Seattle.

June–August, 8 nights, Wilderness Alaska Inside Passage, round-trip from Juneau to
Gastineau Channel, Tracy Arm, Frederick Sound, Icy Strait, Elfin Cove, Sitka, Glacier
Bay National Park, Skagway, and Haines.

Spirit of Nantucket **HOME PORT** Juneau, Ketchikan

May and September, 10 nights, Gold Rush Inside Passage between Juneau and Seattle.

June–August, 8 nights, Alaska Wilderness Inside Passage, round-trip from Juneau to
Gastineau Channel, Tracy Arm, Frederick Sound, Sitka, Icy Strait, Elfin Cove, Glacier
Bay National Park.

Spirit of '98 **HOME PORTS** Juneau, Ketchikan, Portland

April–September, October, April, 7 nights, Columbia and Snake rivers, round-trip from
Portland to Columbia River Gorge, Snake River, Hells Canyon, Walla Walla, The Dalles,
Maryhill Museum, Astoria, Fort Clatsop, eight sets of locks.

May–August, 8 nights, Inside Passage between Ketchikan and Juneau via Misty Fjords,
Metlakatla, Petersburg, Frederick Sound, Tracy Arm, Sitka, Glacier Bay, Skagway, Haines.
Repositions between Juneau and Seattle, 10 nights, May and August–September.

Spirit of Oceanus **HOME PORTS** Anchorage, Vancouver; and others

January–March, Three itineraries in the South Pacific: Island Sanctuaries, Pearls of
Polynesia, and Legends of the Pacific.

April and October, Japan, Treasures of the Orient; November, Japan, South Korea,
China, and Vietnam.

May–August, Alaska, three itineraries: Coastal Odyssey, Voyage of the Bering Sea, and
In Harriman's Wake.

September, Ring of Fire itinerary in the Kuril Islands.

Spirit of Yorktown **HOME PORT** Varies with itinerary

January–March, and December, Baja Mexico's Sea of Cortès Whales and Wildlife,
round-trip from La Paz to Isla Partida, Los Islotes, Isla Espiritu Santo, Cabo San Lucas,
Bahia Magdalena, Boca De Soledad, La Entrada (for Magdalena Bay), San Carlos.

May and August–September, Alaska Gold Rush Inside Passage, round-trip from Juneau
to Skagway, Haines, Elfin Cove, Idaho Inlet, Glacier Bay National Park, Sitka, Tracy Arm.

September–October, California Wine Country, round-trip from Redwood City to
Sausalito, Sacramento, Vallejo, and San Francisco.

Crystal Cruises

Crystal Serenity **HOME PORT** Varies with itinerary

November 9, 10 nights, transatlantic from Lisbon to Miami via Azores/Ponta Delgada, Bermuda/Hamilton.

November, 11 nights, from Miami to Costa Rica via Grand Turk, St. Bart's, St. Maarten, Aruba, Panama Canal or from Costa Rica, Panama Canal, St. Lucia, Antigua, St. Maarten, Grand Turk.

December 2007, 10 or 14 nights, Caribbean, round-trip from Miami to Grand Turk, St. Bart's, Antigua, St. Kitts, Tortola; 14 nights, round-trip from Miami to Tortola, Barbados, St. Lucia, St. Bart's, Curaçao, Aruba, Key West.

January, 15 nights, from Miami to Los Angeles via Grand Cayman, Cartagena, Panama Canal, Costa Rica, Puerto Chiapas, Acapulco, Cabo San Lucas.

January–April, World Cruise, from Los Angeles.

January, 13 nights, from Los Angeles to Papeete via Honolulu, Maui/Lahaina, Raiatea, Moorea.

February, 11 nights, from Papeete to Auckland via Huahine, Bora-Bora, Apia, Lautoka.

February, 14 nights, from Auckland to Sydney via Christchurch, Wellington, Dunedin, cruising Dusky Sound, Doubtful Sound, Milford Sound, Hobart, Melbourne.

February, 17 nights, World Cruise from Sydney to Hong Kong via Brisbane, Cairns, Darwin, Brunei/Bandar Seri Bagawan.

March, 12 nights, from Hong Kong to Singapore via Da Nang/Chan May, Ho Chi Minh City, Bangkok/Laem Chabang, Ko Samui, Singapore.

March, 14 nights, from Singapore to Mumbai via Kuala Lumpur/Port Kelang, Phuket, Yangon (two overnights), Cochin.

April, 16 nights, World Cruise from Mumbai to Civitavecchia via Salalah, Luxor and Karnak/Safaga, Suez Canal, Alexandria/Cairo, Crete/Aghios Nikolaos, Sicily/Catania, Naples.

April 26, 11 nights, from Civitavecchia to London/Southampton via Monte Carlo, Valencia, Gibraltar, Lisbon, La Coruña.

May, 12 nights, from London/Southampton to Civitavecchia via Bordeaux, Le Verdon, Bilbao, Lisbon, Gibraltar, Barcelona, Villefranche.

May, 11 nights, from Civitavecchia to Venice via Sorrento, Sicily, Corfu, Dubrovnik, Trieste.

May, 7 nights, from Venice to Athens via Katakolon, Santorini, Kusadasi, Mykonos. Return June, 7 nights, via Kusadasi, Santorini, Sarande, Split.

June, 12 nights, from Venice to Barcelona via Dubrovnik, Sorrento, Civitavecchia, Florence/Livorno, Monte Carlo, Marseille. Return via Porto Venere, Civitavecchia, Sorrento, Katakolon, Corfu, Dubrovnik, Trieste.

July, 12 nights, from Venice to Athens/Piraeus via Katakolon, Santorini, Samos, Kusadasi, Istanbul.

July, 12 nights, from Athens/Piraeus to Monte Carlo via Kusadasi, Mykonos, Sarande, Civitavecchia, Florence/Livorno, Portofino, St. Tropez.

July, 12 nights, from Monte Carlo to Venice via Marseille, Barcelona, Florence/Livorno, Civitavecchia, Sorrento, Corfu, Dubrovnik.

August, 12 nights, from Venice to Athens/Piraeus via Katakolon, Mykonos, Yalta, Odessa, Constanta, Black Sea, Istanbul. Athens/Piraeus to Civitavecchia via Kusadasi, Santorini, Rhodes, Crete, Corfu, Sicily, Sorrento.

September, 7 nights, from Civitavecchia to Venice via Katakolon, Corfu, Dubrovnik, Trieste.

September, 12 nights, from Venice to Monte Carlo via Dubrovnik, Sicily, Sorrento, Civitavecchia, Florence/Livorno, Elba.

September, 12 nights, from Monte Carlo to Athens/Piraeus, Civitavecchia, Sorrento, Mykonos, Kusadasi, Istanbul.

October, 12 nights, from Athens/Piraeus to Civitavecchia via Volos, Kusadasi, Rhodes, Alexandria/Cairo, Sardinia, Naples.

October, 12 nights, from Civitavecchia to Barcelona via Naples, Sicily, Gibraltar, Malaga, Cartagena, Valencia, Mallorca.

October, 12 nights, Canary Islands, from Barcelona to Lisbon via Valencia, Malaga, Cadiz/Seville, Casablanca, Tenerife, Las Palmas, Madeira/Funchal.

November, 10 nights, transatlantic from Lisbon to Miami via Azores/Ponta Delgada, Grand Turk.

December, 11 nights, from Miami to Costa Rica via Grand Turk, Tortola, St. Bart's, Aruba, Panama Canal; reverse, 14 nights, round-trip from Miami to Tortola, St. Maarten, St. Bart's, Antigua, St. Lucia, Barbados, Curaçao, Aruba.

Crystal Symphony   **HOME PORT**   Varies with itinerary

November, 10 nights, from Miami to Costa Rica via Tortola, St. Bart's, Curaçao, Panama Canal; reverse.

November, December, 7 nights, round-trip from Miami to Cozumel, Belize City, Puerto Costa Maya, Key West.

December, 14 nights, Mexican Riviera, round-trip from Los Angeles to San Diego, Cabo San Lucas, Acapulco, Zihuatanejo/Ixtapa, Puerto Vallarta, Mazatlan, La Paz, San Diego.

December 2007–January 2008, 11 nights, from Miami to Costa Rica via St. Thomas, St. Maarten, Antigua, Aruba, Panama Canal; reverse; 13 nights from Miami to Los Angeles via Cozumel, Panama Canal, Acapulco, Cabo San Lucas; 16 nights from Los Angeles to Miami via Cabo San Lucas, Costa Rica, Panama Canal, Aruba, St. Kitts, San Juan.

February, 14 nights, from Miami to Los Angeles via Cozumel, Grand Cayman, Cartagena, Panama Canal, Costa Rica, Acapulco, Cabo San Lucas.

February, 7 nights, Mexican Riviera, round-trip from Los Angeles to Cabo San Lucas, Mazatlan, Puerto Vallarta.

March, 17 nights, transpacific from Los Angeles to Hong Kong via Oahu/Honolulu. March, 15 nights, from Hong Kong to Beijing via Kobe, Hiroshima, Shanghai, Dalian; return; 15 nights, from Beijing to Hong Kong via Dalian, Shanghai, Osaka. Both include 3-nights precruise land program in Beijing.

April, 11 nights, Southeast Asia from Hong Kong to Singapore via Da Nang/ Chan May, Ho Chi Minh City, Bangkok; 16 nights, from Singapore to Dubai via Phuket, Cochin, Marmagao, Mumbai, Muscat, Doha.

May, 14 nights, from Dubai to Athens/Piraeus via Salalah, Luxor and Karnak/Safaga, Aqaba, Suez Canal, Alexandria/Cairo; 13 nights, from Athens to London via Sicily/Taormina, Malaga, Cadiz/Seville, Lisbon, Oporto, Bordeaux.

June, 11 nights, Baltic Sea and Russia from London to Stockholm via Oslo, Copenhagen, Ronne, St. Petersburg (2 overnights), Helsinki.

June, 11 nights, from Stockholm to Copenhagen via St. Petersburg (2 overnights), Helsinki, Berlin.

June, 14 nights, North Cape and Arctic Circle from Copenhagen to London/Dover via Geiranger/Hellesylt, Trondheim, cruising Svartisen Glacier, Arctic Circle, Honningsvag, North Cape, Bear Island, Sorkapp, Arctic Circle, Longyearbyen, Ny Alesund, Olden, Bergen.

July, 11 nights, round-trip from London/Dover to Edinburgh/Rosyth, Dublin, Liverpool, Belfast, Guernsey/St. Peter Port.

July, 11 nights, Baltic Sea and Russia from London to Stockholm via Oslo, Copenhagen, Helsinki, St. Petersburg, Tallinn.

August, 7 nights, to Copenhagen via Tallinn, St. Petersburg, Helsinki; return; 11 nights, via Berlin, Gdansk, Helsinki, St. Petersburg, Tallinn.

August, 11 nights, to London/Dover via Helsinki, St. Petersburg (2 overnights), Copenhagen, Oslo.

September,14 nights, transatlantic from London/Dover to New York via Invergordon, Tórshavn, Reykjavík, Nuuk, Atlantic Ocean crossing, Halifax.

September–October, 11 nights, New England and Canada from Montreal to New York via Quebec City, Corner Brook or St. John, Halifax, Bar Harbor, Boston, Newport.

October,12 nights, from New York to Miami via Bermuda/Hamilton, St. Maarten, Antigua, Aruba, Grand Cayman/George Town.

November, 13 nights, from Miami to Los Angeles via Grand Cayman, Cartagena, Panama Canal, Acapulco, Cabo San Lucas; 7 nights, Mexican Riviera, round-trip from Los Angeles to Cabo San Lucas, Mazatlan, Puerto Vallarta.

December, 15 nights, from Los Angeles to Valparaiso via Cabo San Lucas, Costa Rica, Guayaquil, Lima; 18 nights, South America, Cape Horn and Antarctica, from Valparaiso to Buenos Aires via Puerto Montt, Punta Arenas, Cape Horn, Ushuaia, Antarctica, Elephant Island, Falkland Islands/Antarctica, Port Stanley, Puerto Madryn, Montevideo.

Cunard Line

Queen Elizabeth 2 **HOME PORT** Southampton; others vary with itinerary
November 2007, 14 or 16 nights, Mediterranean, round-trip from Southampton to Lisbon, Cagliari, Athens, Zakynthos, Palermo, Naples, Gibraltar or Malaga, Palermo, Alexandria, Kusadasi, Athens, Rome.

November 2007, June 2008, 10 or 11 nights, Atlantic Isles, round-trip from Southampton to La Coruna, Funchal, Lanzarote, Tenerife, Las Palmas, Lisbon, or Bilbao, Funchal, Tenerife, Las Palmas, Lisbon.

December 2007, 8 nights, Christmas Markets, round-trip from Southampton to Oslo, Hamburg, Rotterdam, Zeebrugge; 21 nights, round-trip from Southampton to Ponta Delgada, Antigua, St. Kitts, Curaçao, Bonaire, Barbados, Funchal.

January 6, westbound transatlantic from Southampton to New York.

January–April, 90 nights, World Cruise, round-trip from New York via Barbados, Brazil, Uruguay, Port Stanley, Chile, Easter Island, Tahiti, Tonga, New Zealand, Australia, New Zealand and Australia, Singapore, Vietnam, Hong Kong, Shanghai, Japan, Honolulu, Acapulco, Panama Canal, Costa Rica, Jamaica, Fort Lauderdale. Six segments from 34 to 77 nights available.

April 12, eastbound transatlantic from New York to Southampton.

May–September, 4 to 20 nights, Europe, round-trip from Southampton to Baltic, Norwegian Fjords, Channel Islands, England/Ireland/France, Iberia, Canary Islands, Western and Eastern Mediterranean, or Egypt/Turkey; 16 nights, Mediterranean, round-trip from Southampton to Lisbon, Gibraltar, Valletta, Cephalonia, Dubrovnik, Trieste, Split, Corfu, and Cadiz.

May, August, October, 10 or 12 nights, Mediterranean, round-trip from Southampton to Lisbon, Sardinia, Cannes, Barcelona, and Gibraltar or Naples/Capri, Rome, Florence/Pisa, Cannes, Barcelona, and Gibraltar. Or 15 nights, round-trip from Southampton to Lisbon, Sardinia, Corfu, Dubrovnik, Trieste, Valletta, Gibraltar; Naples/Capri, Messina, Dubrovnik, Zakinthos, Athens, Gibraltar, Vigo; or Athens, Zakinthos, Palermo, Naples/Capri, Valencia.

June–July, 7 or 13 nights, Norway, round-trip from Southampton to Bergen, Hellesylt, Geiranger, Flam, and Stavanger or Bergen, Trondheim, Gravdal, Longyearbyen, Tromso, Hellestylt, Geiranger, Stavanger. Or 12 nights, Iceland and Norway, round-trip from Southampton to Reykjavik, Grundarfjordur, Akureyri, Hellesylt, Geiranger, Flam, Stavanger, Oslo.

July, 11 nights, round-trip from Southampton to Lisbon, Corsica, Rome, Monte Carlo, Barcelona, and Gibraltar.

July, August, October, 3 or 5 nights, round-trip from Southampton to Rotterdam, Zeebrugge, or Bilbao, La Rochelle, St. Peter Port.

Late September, 6 Farewell Voyages: September 30, 10 days, British Isles Voyage round-trip from Southampton around British Isles; October 10, final transatlantic crossing to New York; October 16, final transatlantic back to Southampton, both in tandem with QM2; October 22, 5 days, round-trip from Southampton to France and Spain; October 27, 15 days, Mediterranean round-trip from Southampton; November 11–27, final voyage from Southampton to Mediterranean, Suez Canal to Dubai.

Queen Mary 2 **HOME PORTS** Cherbourg, Fort Lauderdale, Hamburg, New York, Southampton

October 2007–April 2008, 10 nights, Caribbean, round-trip from New York to St. Kitts, Barbados, St. Lucia, St. Thomas.

December–January, 14 nights, Caribbean, round-trip from New York to St. Maarten, Curaçao, Grenada, Barbados, Dominica, St. Kitts, St. Thomas.

February, March, Panama and Caribbean, round-trip from New York to Limon, Cristobal, Curaçao, Bonaire, St. Lucia, St. Thomas; 4 days, from New York to Eleuthera.

April–October, November, 6 nights, transatlantic eastbound between Southampton and New York, interspersed with occasional cruises in Europe, New England/Canada and to nowhere. Transatlantic westbound from Southampton to New York and to/from Hamburg and Cherbourg via Southampton.

May 22, 5 nights, Memorial Day, round-trip from New York to Halifax, Nova Scotia, and Boston.

June, September, 11 or 12 nights, Mediterranean, round-trip from Southampton to Vigo, Barcelona, Monte Carlo, Rome, Gibraltar, and Lisbon; 12 nights, add Naples/Capri.

July 2, 6 nights, Independence Day, round-trip from New York to Boston, Bar Harbor, Halifax.

September, 7 nights, Splendor of Autumn, round-trip from New York to Halifax, St. John, Portland, Boston, Newport.

October, 4 nights, Halloween Getaway, round-trip from New York to Eleuthera.

November–December 2008 and 2009, 8 nights, Caribbean between New York and Fort Lauderdale via St. Kitts, Grenada, Bonaire; 10 nights, round-trip from Fort Lauderdale to Curaçao, Grenada, Barbados, St. Lucia, St. Kitts, St. Thomas; 14 nights, to Panama, Bonaire, Grenada, Barbados, St. Lucia, Dominica, St. Kitts, Tortola.

Queen Victoria (debuts December 2007) **HOME PORTS** Barcelona, New York, Rome, Southampton, Venice

December 11, 2007, 10 nights, Maiden Voyage, round-trip from Southampton to Rotterdam, Copenhagen, Oslo, Hamburg, Bruges.

December, 16 nights, Canary Islands, round-trip from Southampton to Vigo, Lisbon, Malaga, Funchal, Las Palmas, Lanzarote, Tenerife, Casablanca, Gibraltar.

January–April, 99 or 105 nights, World Cruise, round-trip from New York (return from Southampton on QM2) via Panama Canal, Mexico, Los Angeles, Hawaii, Pago Pago, Fiji, New Zealand, Australia, Malaysia, Hong Kong, Vietnam, Thailand, Singapore, India,

Sri Lanka, Dubai, Oman, Egypt, Suez Canal, Greece, Italy, Spain, Portugal. Eight segments from 35 to 68 days available.

April 22, 10 nights, Canary Islands, round-trip from Southampton to Madeira, Tenerife, Gran Canaria, Lisbon, and Vigo.

May, 4 nights, round-trip from Southampton to Paris, Rotterdam, and Zeebrugge.

May 6, 14 nights, Mediterranean, round-trip from Southampton to Seville, Corsica, Rome, Naples/Capri, Valletta, La Goulette, and Gibraltar. Or August, 12 nights, between Southampton and Venice (overnight) via Gibraltar, Cannes, Florence/Pisa, Rome, Sicily, Corfu, and Dubrovnik.

May, 7 nights, Norwegian fjords, round-trip from Southampton to Bergen, Hellesylt, Geiranger, Ny-Alesund, and Stavanger.

May–July, 14 nights, Russian Rendezvous, round-trip from Southampton to Zeebrugge, Oslo, Copenhagen, Stockholm, Helsinki, St. Petersburg (overnight), Tallinn, and Gdansk. Or 12 nights, to Bergen, Tromso, Honningsvag (North Cape), Trondheim, Hellesylt, Geiranger, Olden, and Stavanger.

August, October, 12 nights, Mediterranean, departing Venice (overnight) via Dubrovnik, Katakolon, Mykonos, Istanbul, Kusadasi, Sicily, Rome, Florence/Pisa, Marseille, and Barcelona. Or between Barcelona and Rome via Monte Carlo, Florence/Pisa, Naples/Capri, Valletta, Crete, Izmir, Athens, and Sicily.

September, 12 nights, Greek Isles, departing Rome via Naples/Capri, Santorini, Izmir, Istanbul (overnight), Samos, Athens, Zakinthos, Dubrovnik, and Venice. Or 12 nights, Crimean Coast, between Venice and Rome via Kusadasi, Istanbul (overnight), Odessa, Yalta, Athens, Sicily, and Rome. Or November, from Rome and Athens, via Naples/Capri, Sicily, Valletta, Alexandria (for Cairo/Giza), Port Said, Kusadasi, Istanbul, Kepez, Volos, and Athens. Or between Rome and Southampton via Naples/Capri, Sicily, Katakolon, Dubrovnik, Valletta, La Goulette, and Malaga.

December, 22 nights, Caribbean, round-trip from Southampton to Ponta Delgada, Antigua, St. Kitts, St. Lucia, Grenada, Barbados, Madeira, and Vigo.

Discovery World Cruises

Discovery **HOME PORTS** Barbados, Buenos Aires, Montego Bay, and others
December 2007–January 2008, 15 nights, Antarctica, round-trip from Buenos Aires to Ushuaia, cruise the Drake Passage, Point Wild, Antarctic Sound, Hope Bay, Deception Island, King George Island, Arctowski Station, Point Wild, Gerlache Strait, Waterboat Point, Lemaire Channel, Half Moon Island, Cape Horn. Or 19 nights, Antarctic Peninsula and South Georgia, round-trip from Buenos Aires to Ushuaia, Port Stanley, Grytviken, Elsehul, Gold Harbour (South Georgia), cruise Scotia Sea, Coronation Island, Point Wild, Antarctic Sound, Hope Bay, Gerlache Strait, Half Moon Island, cruise Cape Horn, and Ushuaia.

February, 20 to 48 nights, Antarctica and Chilean fjords from Buenos Aires to Santiago, San Cristobal or San Jose via Ushuaia, Drake Passage, Deception Island and King George Island, Antarctic Sound, Hope Bay, Gerlache Strait, Waterboat Point, Lemaire Channel, Half Moon Island, cruise Cape Horn, Beagle Channel, Punta Arenas (Chile), Strait of Magellan and Chilean fjords, Puerto Montt, Valparaiso (20 nights); add Robinson Crusoe Island, Easter Island (Rapa Nui), Arica (Machu Picchu option), Lima, Manta (Ecuador), Galápagos Islands, (40 nights); add Fort Amacor, Panama Canal, San Blas Islands, Puerto Limon (48 nights).

February, 12 to 26 nights, Galápagos/Easter Island/Panama Canal, between Santiago and Lima or Quito to Robinson Crusoe Island, Easter Island, Arica, Lima (23 nights), Manta, Galápagos, Quito (26 nights).

March, 12 nights, between Quito and San Jose, Costa Rica via San Cristobal, Fort Amador, Panama Canal, San Blas Islands, Puerto Limon.

April, 11 or 23 nights, Amazon between Montego Bay and Manaus or Barbados or Manaus and Barbados via Curaçao, Tobago, Amazon River, Santarem, Boca de Valeria, Manaus, Parintins, Alter do Chao, Devil's Island, Trinidad, Grenada, St. Vincent.

April, 11 to 39 nights, Amazon/Caribbean/Atlantic Isles from Montego Bay to London; 16 nights, Caribbean and Atlantic, between Barbados and London via St. Lucia, Antigua, Horta, Angra do Heroismo, Ponta Delgada.

Disney Cruise Line

Disney Magic **HOME PORTS** Los Angeles, Port Canaveral

January–May, 7 nights, alternating Eastern and Western Caribbean, round-trip from Port Canaveral to St. Thomas, Castaway Cay or Key West, Grand Cayman, Cozumel, Castaway Cay.

May 10, 15 nights, repositioning from Port Canaveral via Castaway Cay, Aruba, Panama Canal, Acapulco, Puerto Vallarta, Cabo San Lucas, Los Angeles with 8 days at sea.

May–August, 7 nights, Mexican Riviera from Los Angeles to Cabo San Lucas, Mazatlan, Puerto Vallarta with 3 days at sea.

August 17, 15 nights, repositioning from Los Angeles via Cabo San Lucas, Puerto Vallarta, Acapulco, Panama Canal, Cartagena, Aruba, Castaway Cay, Port Canaveral with 7 days at sea.

September, 5 nights, Bahamas, round-trip from Port Canaveral to Nassau with 2 days at Castaway Cay.

September–December, 7 nights, round-trip from Port Canaveral to Costa Maya with 2 days at Castaway Cay.

Disney Wonder **HOME PORT** Port Canaveral

Year-round, 3 to 4 nights, round-trip from Port Canaveral on Thursday to Nassau and Castaway Cay (3 nights); or on Sundays to Nassau, Castaway Cay, plus a full day at sea (4 nights). Cruise can be combined with Disney World packages for a 7-night vacation.

May–August, 4 nights, Bahamas, from Port Canaveral to Nassau with 2 different days at Castaway Cay.

easyCruise

easyCruise One **HOME PORT** Varies with itinerary

December–April, Caribbean, Friday, round-trip from St. Maarten, calling at St. Bart's, Anguilla, return to St. Maarten (Monday), St. Kitts, Antigua, Nevis. Travelers can begin their cruise in St. Maarten on Friday or Monday, or in Antigua on Wednesday.

June–October, 3 to 7 nights, Greek Isles, round-trip from Piraeus; 3 nights to Poros, Spetes; 4 nights to Mykonos, Paros, Sifinos; 7 nights to Milos, Ios, Amorgos, Naxos, Folegandros, Serifos.

easyCruise Two **HOME PORTS** Amsterdam, Brussels.

3 to 7 nights, Holland, 3 nights, from Amsterdam to Brussels via Rotterdam, Antwerp; 4 nights, from Brussels to Amsterdam via Antwerp and Rotterdam; 7 nights, round-trip from Amsterdam to Rotterdam, Antwerp, Brussels, and return.

Fred Olsen Cruise Lines

Balmoral **HOME PORTS** Dover, Miami, New York , Rome

January, round-trip from Dover to Lisbon, Cadiz, Las Palmas, Tenerife, Funchal, Vigo.

February–March, segments up to 30 nights, transatlantic and Caribbean from Dover to Miami, and round-trip from Miami.

April, 17 nights, Miami to Rome via Nassau, Bermuda, Funchal, Malaga, Ajaccio.

May–June, 9 to 21 nights, Mediterranean, round-trip from Rome and Rome to Dover via Tunis, Valletta, Corfu, Brindisi, Dubrovnik, Venice, Palermo, Cagliari, Gibraltar, Lisbon.

July–October, 7 to 13 nights, Norway, round-trip from Dover to Bergen, Olden, Flam, Gudvangen, Eidfjord, Hardangerfjord.

July–August, Iberia and Morocco, 3 to 11 nights, round-trip from Dover to Lisbon, Cadiz, Malaga, Tangier, Gijon, La Rochelle.

September, 14 nights, Western Mediterranean, round-trip from Dover to Lisbon, Gibraltar, Barcelona, Sete, Ajaccio, Mahon, La Coruna.

November, Bermuda and Bahamas, New York to Miami via Bermuda, Port Canaveral, Nassau.

Black Prince **HOME PORTS** Greenock, Liverpool

January–March, 13 to 35 nights, Portugal/Caribbean, round-trip from Liverpool to Lisbon, Arrecife, La Palmas, Tenerife, Funchal, Oporto, and round-trip to Tenerife, Barbados, Trinidad, Puerto Ordaz, Cano Araguaito, Grenada, St. Lucia, Dominica, St. Kitts, Antigua, St. Maarten, Funchal.

March, 16 nights, Eastern Mediterranean, round-trip from Liverpool

April–June, 7 to 21 nights, Canary Islands, Eastern Mediterranean or Iberia, round-trip from Greenock.

June–July, 8 to 11 nights, Norway, round-trip from Greenock.

July–August, 7 to 13 nights, Iberia, Western Mediterranean or France/Ireland, round-trip from Liverpool.

September, 21 nights, Adriatic, round-trip from Liverpool.

October, 12 nights, Canary Islands, round-trip from Liverpool; 14 nights, Western Mediterranean, round-trip from Greenock.

Black Watch **HOME PORTS** Dover, Southampton

January–April, 107 nights, World Cruise from Dover, calling at Portugal, Canary Islands, Caribbean, Panama Canal, Lima, Easter Island, Pitcairn, Tahiti, Raratonga, New Zealand (North and South islands), Australia (Sydney, Brisbane, and Cairns), Papua New Guinea, Karimunjawa Island, Singapore, India, Sri Lanka, Egypt, Jordan, Suez Canal transit, Malta, Spain.

April, 11 nights, France and Spain, round-trip from Dover.

May, 22 nights, Mediterranean, round-trip from Dover.

June–September, 7 to 28 nights, Baltic or North Cape, 14 nights, round-trip from Dover or from Southampton to Dover.

August, 8 to 13 nights, Western Mediterranean or Iberia, round-trip from Southampton.

October, 8 nights, Iberia, round-trip from Dover.

Boudicca **HOME PORTS** Newcastle, Southampton

January 2008, 12 nights, Portugal, round-trip from Southampton to Funchal, San Sebastian la Gomera, Tenerife, Las Palmas, Lisbon.

January–March, 72 nights, Cape Horn/Panama Canal, Southampton to Lima via Lisbon, Funchal, Tenerife, St. Vincent, Salvador, Rio de Janeiro, Itajai, Montevideo, Buenos Aires, Puerto Madryn, Port Stanley, Cape Horn, Beagle Channel, Punta Arenas, Chilean fjords, Puerto Montt, Valparaiso, Coquimbo, Arica, Calla, Manta, Panama Canal, Puerto Limon, Roatan, Jamaica, Grand Turk, Bermuda, Azores.

April, 21 nights, Greece, round-trip from Southampton.

May, 13 or 21 nights, Canary Islands or Adriatic, round-trip from Southampton.

May–August, 8 to 14 nights, Norway or Baltic, round-trip from Southampton, round-trip from Leith, round-trip from Newcastle.

July, 13 nights, France and Spain, round-trip from Newcastle.

Braemar **HOME PORTS** Barbados, Dover, Malaga, Montego Bay, Rome, Southampton
January–April 2008, 14 or 15 nights, Caribbean, round-trip from Barbados.

April, 16 nights, return to Southampton from Montego Bay via Santiago, Santo Domingo, Tortola, St. Maarten, Funchal.

May–June, 8 nights, Norway and Denmark, round-trip from Dover.

July–October 2008, 11 to 14 nights, Eastern and Western Mediterranean from Dover to Rome, round-trip from Rome.

September–October, 14 nights, Black Sea, round-trip from Rome.

October 2008, 15 nights, transatlantic, Malaga to Barbados.

Hapag-Lloyd Cruises

Bremen **HOME PORT** Varies with itinerary
November 2007, 12 nights, Africa, South America from Dakar to Buenos Aires; 19 nights, Patagonia, Buenos Aires to Ushuaia via Magellan Strait, Punta Arenas, Drake Passage, South Shetland Islands, Antarctic Peninsula, Cape Horn.

November 30–February 26, 15 to 21 nights, Antarctica, various itineraries, round-trip from Ushuaia via Falkland Islands, South Georgia, South Orkney Islands, Antarctic Peninsula, Melchior Islands, Drake Passage, Cape Horn.

C Columbus **HOME PORT** Varies with itinerary
December 8, 2007, 12 nights, Caribbean and Mexico, round-trip from Miami to Ocho Rios, Grand Cayman, Progresso, New Orleans, Key West.

December 2007–April 2008, 138 nights, Around the World, 10 segments, from Miami to Nice via Barbados, Rio de Janeiro, Walvis Bay, Durban, Mahé, Port Kelang, Singapore, Dubai, Nice.

Europa **HOME PORT** Varies with itinerary
November 2007–April 2008, 157 nights, World Cruise from Barcelona to Dubai in 11 stages from 10 to 22 nights via Santa Cruz, Rio de Janeiro, Manaus, La Guaira, Acapulco, Honolulu, Cairns, Manila, Laem Chabang, Singapore. Also available in 6 stages from Acapulco to Dubai for 91 days.

April, 16 nights, Dubai to Limassol via Abu Dhabi, Khasav, Muscat, Salalah, Aden, Hodeidah, Sharm el Sheikh, Aqaba, Safaga, Suez Canal transit, Port Said.

May, 1 to 13 nights, Aegean, Limassol to Naples, Naples to Nice, round-trip from Nice, Nice to Bilbao.

June, 12 nights, Bay of Biscay from Bilbao to Hamburg; 14 nights, British Isles, round-trip from Hamburg.

July, 14 nights, Far North, Hamburg to Kiel via Copenhagen, St. Petersburg, Helsinki, Stockholm, Gdynia. 4 nights, Sansibar, Kiel to Hamburg, via Baltic Canal, Borkum; 19 nights, Fjords, round-trip from Hamburg to Kirkwall, Reykjavik, Akureyri, Spitsbergen, Skarsvag, Tromso, Hellesylt, Geiranger, Bergen.

August, 4 nights, Baltic Sea, from Hamburg to Kiel via Heligendamm, Gudhjem, Copenhagen; 9 to12 nights, Norway fjords or Baltic Sea, round-trip from Kiel.

September, 14 nights, Adriatic, Barcelona to Piraeus.

November–December, 13 to19 nights, Indian Ocean, Africa, Cape Town, South America, from Dubai to Port Louis, Port Louis to Cape Town, Cape Town to Buenos Aires, Buenos Aires to Valparaiso.

Hanseatic **HOME PORT** Varies with itinerary
November 2007, 14 or 28 nights, South Seas, Noumea to Tahiti via Fiji, Tonga, Niue, Cook Islands, Bora-Bora, Tahiti to Easter Island via Moorea, Matavia, Takapoto, Marquesas, Napuka, Mangareva, Pitcairn.

December 2007 8 nights, Patagonia, from Easter Island to Punta Arenas; 20 nights, Antarctica, Punta Arenas to Ushuaia via Falkland Islands, South Georgia, South Sandwich Islands, South Orkney Islands, South Shetland Islands, Antarctic Peninsula, Cape Horn.

February, 17 to 18 nights, Antarctica, round-trip from Ushuaia.

Hebridean Island Cruises

Hebridean Princess **HOME PORT** Oban
April–November, 4 to 8 nights, Scotland, various itineraries, round-trip from Oban including the Inner and Outer Hebrides, mainland Scotland, Northern Island, Firth of Clyde Islands.

July, November, 7 to 8 nights, U.K. and Norway from Scrabster to Bergen, round-trip from Bergen, Bergen to Scrabster, Portland to Tilbury.

Hebridean Spirit **HOME PORT** Varies with itinerary
April, 10 nights, Canary Islands from Santa Cruz to Funchal via Tenerife, San Sabastian, La Estaca, Santa Cruz, Porto Santo, Funchal, Madeira.

April, 12 nights, Morocco from Funchal to Gibraltar via Santa Cruz, La Estaca, Las Palmas, Arrecife, Essaouira, Ceuta.

May–October, 7 to 13 nights, Mediterranean, Adriatic, Greek Isles, Turkey, various itineraries, from Seville to Barcelona, Barcelona to Nice, Nice to Cagliari, Cagliari to Catania, Catania to Brindisi, Brindisi to Pula, Pula to Bari, Bari to Volos, Volos to Thessaloniki, Thessaloniki to Istanbul, Istanbul to Constanta, Constanta to Kusadasi, Kusadasi to Corfu, Corfu to Palermo, Palermo to Valeta, Valletta to Cagliari, Cagliari to Marseille, Marseille to Barcelona, Barcelona to Tenerife.

August, 7 nights, Spain from Gibraltar to Seville via Cadiz, Portimao, Huelva.

August, 7 to 13 nights, Black Sea from Istanbul to Costanta and Constanta to Kusadasi.

October–November, 9 to 12 nights, Atlantic from Tenerife to Funchal, Funchal to Cape Verde, Santiago Islands to Funchal.

Holland America Line

Amsterdam **HOME PORTS** Fort Lauderdale, Los Angeles, Seattle; others vary with itinerary
January 4, 114 nights, World Voyage, round-trip from Fort Lauderdale to Caribbean, Panama Canal, French Polynesia, New Zealand, Australia, Indonesia, Brunei, Philippines, Hong Kong, Vietnam, Singapore, India, Oman, Egypt, Suez Canal transit, Egypt, Turkey, Russia, Ukraine, Greece, Italy, Croatia, Libya, Gibraltar, Lisbon, Madeira, Bermuda, New York. Seven segments from 17 to 55 nights available.

April, November, 14 to 18 nights, Fort Lauderdale to Seattle, Vancouver or Los Angeles via Panama Canal, Golfo Dulce, Punta Arenas, Puerto Chiapas, Santa Cruz, Huatulco, Acapulco, Cabo San Lucas, Los Angeles, Victoria, Vancouver, Seattle. From San Diego to Fort Lauderdale via Cabo San Lucas, Puerto Vallarta, Huatulco, Puerto Quetzal, Puerto Caldera, Panama Canal, Cartagena, Half Moon Cay.

May, 4/5 nights, Los Angeles to Vancouver and Vancouver to Seattle.

May–September, Alaska via Glacier Bay, round-trip from Seattle to Stephens Passage, Juneau, Tracy Arm and Sawyer Glaciers or Glacier Bay National Park, Sitka, Ketchikan, Victoria.

September 29, 65 nights, between Seattle and San Diego, calling at Aleutian Islands, Russia, Japan, China, Hong Kong, Vietnam, Thailand, Singapore, Indonesia, Australia, New Caledonia, Fiji, Samoa, Hawaii. Seattle to San Diego (65 nights), Seattle to Singapore (33 nights), Singapore to San Diego (32 nights).

Eurodam **HOME PORTS** Copenhagen, Fort Lauderdale, New York

July–August, Norwegian fjords and Scotland, 10 nights, round-trip from Copenhagen to Oslo, Ny-Alesund, Vik, Aurlandsfjord, Flam, Sognefjord, Stavanger, Newcastle upon Tyne, South Queensferry, Invergordon. Or Baltic, round-trip from Copenhagen to Tallinn, St. Petersburg, Helsinki, Stockholm, Warnemunde, Arthus. Or 15 nights, from Copenhagen to New York via Oslo, Stavanger, Bergen, Torshavn, Reykjavik, Prince Christian Sound, St. John, St.-Pierre, Sydney, Halifax.

September–October, 10/14 nights, New York to Quebec City, Quebec City to Fort Lauderdale via Newport, Boston, Bar Harbor, Halifax, Sydney, Prince Edward Island, Gulf of St Lawrence, Saguenay Fjord, Quebec City. Reverse via New York to Quebec City.

October–December, 5/7 nights, Caribbean, round-trip from Fort Lauderdale to Nassau, Half Moon Cay; or Grand Turk, Tortola; or Puerto Rico, St. Thomas, Half Moon Cay. Or to Half Moon Cay, Aruba, Curaçao.

Maasdam **HOME PORTS** Boston, Fort Lauderdale, Montreal; others vary with itinerary

January–April, October–December, 10 nights, Eastern/Southern Caribbean, round-trip from Fort Lauderdale to St. Maarten, St. Lucia, Barbados, Martinique, Tortola or Half Moon Cay, St. Thomas, Dominica, Curaçao, Aruba.

January, 15 nights, Fort Lauderdale to San Diego via Half Moon Cay, Cartagena, Panama Canal, Golfo Dulce, Punta Arenas, Puerto Chiapas, Huatulco, Acapulco, Cabo San Lucas.

February, reverse via Cabo San Lucas, Mazatlan, Puerto Vallarta, Puerto Quetzal, San Juan del Sur, Panama Canal, Cartagena, Nassau.

May–June, August–October, 7 to 10 nights, Canada/New England, between Montreal and Boston or Fort Lauderdale; or Fort Lauderdale to Montreal via the Saguenay Fjord, Prince Edward Island; Sydney and Halifax, Nova Scotia and Bar Harbor. Fort Lauderdale to Montreal includes Charleston, New London, Newport, Quebec.

July, 35 nights, transatlantic/Voyage of the Vikings, round-trip from Boston to Sydney, Corner Brook, St. Anthony, Qaqortoq (Julianehab), Prince Christian Fjord; Isafjordur, Seydisfjordur, Lerwick, Stavanger, Oslo, Nieuw Waterweg, Cherbourg, Milford Haven, St. Georges Channel, Dublin, Liverpool, Belfast, Little Minch Stornoway, Torshavn, Faroe Islands, Skopunar Fjord; Reykjavik, Nanortalik, St. John, St Pierre, Bar Harbor; 17 nights, Boston to Rotterdam; 18 nights, Rotterdam to Boston.

Noordam **HOME PORTS** New York, Rome

January–April, October–December, 10 to 11 nights, Eastern/Southern Caribbean, round-trip from New York to Grand Turk, Tortola, St. Maarten, St. Thomas, San Juan.

April and October, 15 nights, transatlantic, New York to Rome via Ireland Island (Bermuda), Funchal, Lisbon, Cadiz, Casablanca, Barcelona, Monte Carlo, Livorno, Civitavecchia, Toulon, La Goulette, Valletta, Messina, Naples; or reverse, 14 nights, add Cartagena.

April–September, 10 nights, Eastern/Western Mediterranean, round-trip from Rome to Dubrovnik, Corfu, Katakalon, Santorini, Kusadasi, Malta, Messina (Eastern) or to Livorno, Monte Carlo, Barcelona, Palma de Mallorca, La Goulette, Palermo, and Naples.

October, 14 nights, transatlantic from Rome to New York via Livorno, Monte Carlo, Barcelona, Cartagena, Cadiz, Bermuda.

Oosterdam **HOME PORTS** San Diego, Seattle
January–April, October–December, 7 nights, Mexican Riviera, round-trip from San Diego to Cabo San Lucas, Puerto Vallarta, Mazatlan.

May–September, 7 nights, Alaska, round-trip from Seattle to Stephens Passage, Juneau, Hubbard Glacier, Sitka, Ketchikan, Victoria.

Prinsendam **HOME PORT** Varies with itinerary
January 3, 68 nights, South America and Antarctica, round-trip from Fort Lauderdale to Grand Cayman, Puerto Limon, Panama Canal, Fuerte Amador, Quito, Guayaquil, Salaverry, Callao, Lima, Arica, Coquimbo, Valparaiso, Puerto Montt, Chilean fjords, Puerto Chancabuco, Darwin Channel; Seno Eyre Fjord and Pius X Glacier, Isla Angel and Isla San Marez, Magellan Straits, Punta Arenas, Cockburn and Beagle channels; Cape Horn and Drake Passage, Anvers Island, Cuverville Island, Petermann Island, Deception Island, Livingston Island, Half Moon Island, Hope Bay, Paulet and Elephant Islands; Cumberland Bay, South Georgia, Stanley, Buenos Aires, Montevideo, Rio de Janeiro, Salvador da Bahia, Recife, Fortaleza, Belem, Amazon River; Santarem, Boca da Valeria, Manaus, Parintins, Devil's Island, Barbados, Mayaguez, Half Moon Cay; 12-, 27-, 29-night segments available. Can be combined with Africa Voyage.

March 11, 73 nights, Grand Africa, Fort Lauderdale to Lisbon via Grand Turk, San Juan, St. Maarten, Funchal, Casablanca, Agadir, Dakar, Banjul, Tema (Accra), Lome, Cotonou, Wavis Bay, Cape Town, Durban, Richards Bay, Reunion, Port Louis, Seychelles; Mombassa, Salalah, Safag, Suez Canal; Alexandria, Tripoli, Malaga, Cadiz, Lisbon. Fort Lauderdale to Cape Town, 33 nights; Cape Town to Lisbon, 40 nights available.

May 23, 11 nights, Bordeaux from Lisbon to Amsterdam via Gijon, Bilbao, La Rochelle, Bordeaux, Brest, St. Peter Port, Dover, Zeebrugge.

June and August, 14/16 nights, round-trip from Amsterdam to Kiel Canal transit, Warnemunde, Helsinki, St. Petersburg, Tallinn, Stockholm, Klaipeda, Ystad, Copenhagen, Oslo. Scandinavia routes also include Lulea, Hudiksvall, Mariehamn, Visby Karlskrona, Lim Fjord.

July, 14 nights, Amsterdam to London via Newcastle upon Tyne, Rosyth, Invergordon, Belfast, Barrow in Furness, Liverpool, Dublin, Dunmore East, Milford Haven, St. Peter Port (Guernsey); 21 nights, from London to Amsterdam via Oslo, Kristiansand, Bergen, Ny-Alesund, Akureyri, Jokullfjordur Fjord, Cape Farewell, Qaqortoq, Nuuk, Prince William Sound, Reykjavik, Lerwick, Rosyth.

August, round-trip from Amsterdam to Kiel Canal, Warnemunde, Helsinki, St. Petersburg, Tallinn, Stockholm, Gdansk, Ronne, Copenhagen, Oslo.

September, 14 nights, Amsterdam to Rome via Antwerp, Cover, Santander, Coruna, Leixos, Lisbon, Portimao, Gibraltar, Marseille, Monte Carlo, Livorno.

September, October, 14 nights, Black Sea from Rome to Athens via Strait of Messina, Dubrovnik, Sarande, Argostoli, Istanbul, Trabzon, Sochi, Sevastopol, Nesebur, Dardanelles, Kusadasi. Athens to Rome via Alexandria, Ashdod, Haifa, Antalya, Rhodes, Kusadasi, Santorini, Gabes, Valletta, Messina.

October 20, 24 nights, transatlantic, Athens to Fort Lauderdale via Kusadasi, Santorini, Katakolon, Civitavecchia, Livorno, Monte Carlo, Barcelona, Cartagena, Gibraltar, Casablanca, Arrecife, Tenerife, Funchal.

November, 26 nights, Amazon, round-trip from Fort Lauderdale to Grand Turk, Aruba, Bonaire, Grenada, Devil's Island, Amazon River, Santarem, Boca de Valeria, Manaus, Parintins, Alter do Chao, Barbados, Dominica, St. Thomas, Half Moon Cay.

Rotterdam **HOME PORTS** Athens, Lisbon, Rio de Janeiro, Valparaiso; others vary with itinerary

April, 18 nights, Japan, Eastern Russia, Alaska, Osaka to Vancouver via Yokohama, Hako-
date, Kuril Islands, Petropavlovsk, Kodiak, Homer, Glacier Bay, Sitka, Inside Passage.

May–September, 7 nights, Alaska between Vancouver and Inside Passage, Tracy Arm,
Sawyer Glaciers, Skagway, Glacier Bay National Park, Ketchikan.

September, 30 to 35 nights, Vancouver to San Diego, San Francisco to San Diego or
round-trip from San Diego to Hilo, Kona, Honolulu, Nawiliwili, Raiatea, Bora-Bora,
Papeete, Nuku Hiva.

October, 16 nights, San Diego to Fort Lauderdale via Cabo San Lucas, Acapulco, Santa
Cruz Huatulco, Puerto Chiapas, Puerto Quetzal, Puerto Caldera, Panama Canal,
Cartagena, Half Moon Cay.

November, 13 to 26 nights, round-trip from Fort Lauderdale to Callao or return via Half
Moon Cay, Grand Turk, Santa Marta, San Blas Islands, Panama Canal, Manta,
Salaverry, Callao, Guayaquil, Manta, Panama Canal, Puerto Limon, San Andres Island,
George Town, Key West.

December, 14 nights, Southern Caribbean, round-trip from Fort Lauderdale to Half
Moon Cay, St. Thomas, St. John's. St. Lucia, Barbados, Trinidad, El Guamache,
Curaçao, Aruba, Grand Turk. Or round-trip from Tampa to Key West, Belize City,
Santo Tomas de Castilla, Costa Maya.

Veendam **HOME PORTS** San Diego, Tampa, Vancouver; others vary with itinerary
January, March–April, 7 nights, November–December, Western Caribbean, round-trip
from Tampa to Key West, Belize City, Santo Tomas de Castilla, Costa Maya.

January–March, November, 14 nights, round-trip from Tampa to Half Moon Cay,
St. Thomas, Dominica, Barbados, Grenada, El Guamache, Bonaire, Aruba. Or 7 nights,
round-trip from Tampa to Costa Maya, Montego Bay, Grand Cayman.

April, 15 to 19 nights, Panama Canal, Tampa to San Diego, or Vancouver via Grand
Cayman, Cartagena, Panama Canal, Golfo Dulce, San Juan del Sur, Puerto Chiapas,
Santa Cruz Huatulco, Acapulco, Cabo San Lucas.

May–September, 7 nights, Alaska to Inside Passage, round-trip from Vancouver to
Juneau, Skagway, Glacier Bay, Ketchikan. Or from Anchorage to Vancouver to
Hubbard Glacier, Icy Strait Point, Skagway, Juneau, Ketchikan, Inside Passage. Or
Vancouver to Anchorage to Ketchikan, Icy Strait, Juneau, Kitka, Hubbard Glacier.

September, October, 32 to 36 nights, Panama Canal/Amazon, Vancouver or San Diego to
Tampa via Victoria, San Diego, Cabo San Lucas, Acapulco, Santa Cruz Huatulco, Puerto
Chiapas, Puerto Caldera (Costa Rica), Panama Canal, Aruba, Grenada, Santarem, Boca
de Valeria, Manaus, Parintins, Amazon River, Barbados, Grand Turk, Half Moon Cay.

Volendam **HOME PORTS** Fort Lauderdale, Vancouver
January–February, November–December, 14 nights, Australia and New Zealand,
Sydney to Auckland via Melbourne, Burnie, Milford Sound, Dunedin, Christchurch,
Picton, Queen Charlotte Sound, Wellington, Napier, Tauranga, White Island, Mayor
Island, Alderman Islands, Mercury Islands.

January–April, 10 nights, round-trip from Fort Lauderdale to Half Moon Cay, Aruba,
Curaçao, Panama Canal, Limon Bay, Manzanillo Bay, Puerto Limon. Or reverse.

April, 15 or 19 nights, Fort Lauderdale to San Diego to Vancouver via Cartagena,
Panama Canal, Golfo Dulce, Punta Arenas, Manzanillo, Puerto Vallarta, Mazatlan,
Topolobambo, Cabo San Lucas.

May–September, 7 nights, Vancouver and Anchorage to Ketchikan, Juneau, Skagway,
Glacier Bay National Park, College Fjord, or reverse, add Haines, Inside Passage.

September, 29 to 33 nights, South Pacific and New Zealand from Vancouver, Seattle, or
Los Angeles to Auckland via Hilo, Lahaina, Honolulu, cross the equator, Pago Pago,
Apia Fiji, Port-Vila, Ile des Pins, Noumea, Bay of Islands, Tauranga, Napier, Wellington.

October–December, 14 nights, Auckland to Sydney via Mercury Islands, Tauranga, Napier, Wellington, Christchurch, Dunedin, Fjordland National Park, Burnie, Melbourne; 17 nights, add Queen Charlotte Sound, Melbourne.

Westerdam **HOME PORTS** Fort Lauderdale, Seattle; others vary with itinerary
March–December, 7 nights, Eastern Caribbean, round-trip from Fort Lauderdale to Grand Turk, Puerto Rico, St. Thomas, Half Moon Cay. Or alternating Eastern/Western Caribbean, round-trip from Fort Lauderdale to Half Moon Cay, Grand Turk, Grand Cayman, Costa Maya or Grand Turk, St. Maarten, Tortola, Half Moon Cay.

April, October, 3 days, Eastern Caribbean.

April, 19 nights, Panama Canal, Fort Lauderdale to San Diego or Seattle, via Half Moon Cay, Cartagena, Panama Canal, Golfo Dulce, Punta Arenas, Santa Cruz Huatulco, Acapulco, Cabo San Lucas.

May–September, 7 nights, Alaska, round-trip from Seattle to Glacier Bay National Park, Juneau, Sitka, Ketchikan, Victoria.

Zaandam **HOME PORTS** Fort Lauderdale, San Diego, Seattle
January, March, November, 15 nights, Hawaii, round-trip from San Diego to Hilo, Honolulu, Lahaina, Kona, Ensenada.

January–February, April, September–December, 15 to 19 nights, San Diego to Vancouver, round-trip from San Diego, round-trip from Vancouver or Seattle to Vancouver via Hilo, Honolulu, Nawiliwili, Na Pali Coast, Lahaina, Kona, Ensenada or Astoria, Victoria.

April, 18/19 nights, round-trip from Vancouver or Seattle to Vancouver via Hilo, Honolulu, Nawiliwili, Na Pali Coast, Lahaina, Kona, Astoria, Victoria.

May–August, 7 nights, Alaska, round-trip from Vancouver between Anchorage to Skagway, Glacier Bay National Park, College Fjord.

Zuiderdam **HOME PORTS** Fort Lauderdale, Seattle, Venice
January–March, 7 nights, Eastern Caribbean, round-trip from Fort Lauderdale to Grand Turk, Tortola, Half Moon Cay, or Puerto Rico, St. Thomas, Half Moon Cay.

March, 18 nights, transatlantic from Fort Lauderdale to Rome via Half Moon Cay, Funchal, Lisbon, Cadiz, Casablanca, Barcelona, Monte Carlo, Livorno.

April, June–September, 14 nights, round-trip from Venice to Split, Piraeus, Dardanelles, Istanbul, Mykonos, Kusadasi, Santorini, Katakolon.

May–October, 12 nights, between Venice and Barcelona to Dubrovnik, Kerkira, Argostoli, Santorini, Catania, Naples, Civitavecchia, Livorno, and reverse.

October, 17 nights, transatlantic, Venice to Fort Lauderdale via Dubrovnik, Kerkira, Messina, Civitavecchia, Cartagena, Cadiz, Funchal, Half Moon Cay.

November–December 2008, 10 nights, round-trip from Fort Lauderdale to Half Moon Cay, Aruba, Curaçao, Panama Canal, Limon Bay, Manzanillo Bay, Puerto Limon.

Kristina Cruises

Kristina Brahe **HOME PORTS** Helsinki, Kotka; others vary with itinerary
April–August, 1 to 7 nights, Finland, Finnish Archipelago, Lake Saimaa on lunch cruises and minicruises round-trip from Kotka, round-trip from Helsinki; round-trip from Lappeenranta; between Kotka and Helsinki, Lappeenranta and Puumala; Lappeenranta and Savonlinna. Special bird-migration sailings in May and midsummer sailings in June.

Kristina Regina **HOME PORTS** Dakar, Helsinki, Las Palmas, and others
November–December and February–March, 7 nights, Canary Islands, fly-cruise including air from Helsinki, round-trip from Las Palmas to Arrecife, Puerto del Rosario, Tenerife, San Sebastian de la Gomera, Santa Cruz de la Palma, Puerta la Estaca, El Hierro.

December–January, 10 to 11 nights, West Africa/Cape Verde Islands, fly-cruise including air from Helsinki, round-trip from Banjul to Dakar and the Cape Verde Islands.

March–June, 7 nights, Mediterranean, Adriatic, and Western Europe as ship repositions from Las Palmas to Helsinki for summer cruises.

July–August, 3 to 7 nights, round-trip from Helsinki, visa-free cruises to St. Petersburg, round-trip from Helsinki (3 nights); Norwegian Fjords; Baltic Sea; Iceland, Faroe Islands, and Shetland Islands.

Lindblad Expeditions

Islander **HOME PORT** Guayaquil
March–May, September, December, 9 to 15 nights, Galápagos Islands, round-trip from Guayaquil to Galápagos, Santa Cruz, Bartolome, Santiago, Santa Cruz, Isabela, Fernandina, Floreana, Espanola.

Lord of the Glens **HOME PORTS** Bergen, Edinburgh; others vary with itinerary
May–September, 12 to 14 nights, Highlands and Edinburgh, round-trip from Edinburgh/Inverness to Culloden, Loch Ness, Fort Augustus, Caledonian Canal, Laggan Locks, Banavie, Neptune's Staircase, Tobermory, Isles of Mull and Iona, Isle of Skye, Armadale, Loch Carron, Gariloch. Optional land excursions available.

August, 14 nights, Vikings and Celts from Bergen to Portsmouth via Shetland Islands, Moussa and Fair Isles, Orkney Islands, Inverewe Gardens and Callanish, St. Kilda Outer Hebrides, Iona and Staffa Inner Hebrides, Donegal, Aran Islands, Skellig Islands, Dingle Peninsula, Isles of Scillly, Dartmouth.

National Geographic Endeavour **HOME PORTS** Santiago, Ushuaia
November 2007–February 2008, 12 to 22 nights, Antarctica, South Georgia and the Falklands, round-trip from Santiago/Ushuaia to Antarctica (6 days exploring the Peninsula, walk, cruise in Zodiacs, kayak) (12 nights); add Elephant Island, South Orkney Islands, South Georgia Island, Port Stanley, Falkland Islands (22 nights).

Polaris **HOME PORT** Guayaquil
March–May, September, December, 9 nights, Galápagos Islands, round-trip from Guayaquil to Galápagos, Santa Cruz, Bartolome, Santiago, Santa Cruz, Isabela, Fernandina, Floreana, Espanola.

Sea Bird/Sea Lion **HOME PORTS** La Paz
January–March, 7 nights, Baja, round-trip from La Paz/San Carlos to Bahia Magdalena, Gorda Banks, Los Cabos, Islas Los Islotes, Espiritu Santo, cruise Gulf of California.

May–August, 7 nights, Alaska from Juneau to Sitka via Tracy Arm, Petersburg, Frederick Sound, Glacier Bay National Park, Point Adolphus.

Sea Voyager **HOME PORT** Panama City
January–March, Panama Canal and Costa Rica, Panama City to Herradura via Gatun Lake, Panama Canal transit, Gulf of Panama Islets, Gulfe Dulce, Osa Peninsula, and reverse.

Louis Cruise Lines

Coral **HOME PORTS** Genoa, Marseilles
April–December, 7 nights, Western Mediterranean, round-trip from Genoa to Marseilles and round-trip from Marseilles to Palma, Almeria, Malaga, Gibraltar, Tangier, Ibiza, Barcelona.

Sapphire **HOME PORTS** Genoa, Naples, Piraeus
May–October, 10 nights, Eastern Mediterranean, round-trip from Piraeus via Kusadasi, Patmos, Mykonos, Santorini, Katakolon, Messina, Marseilles, Genoa, Naples and round-trip from Genoa to Naples, Piraeus, Kusadasi, Patmos, Mykonos, Santorini, Katakolon, Messina, Marseilles.

November, 8 nights, Libya from Nice to Marseilles and round-trip from Marseilles, via Genoa, Civitavecchia, Tunis, Tripoli, Malta, Cagliari.

Serenade **HOME PORT** Limassol

April–July, 2 nights, Egypt, round-trip from Limassol to Port Said.

May–August, 2 nights, Holy Land, round-trip from Limassol to Haifa.

May–July, 3 nights, Rhodes, round-trip from Limassol to Rhodes, and round-trip from Limassol to Rhodes and Kos.

June, 5 to 6 nights, Greek Islands, 6 nights, round-trip from Limassol to Rhodes, Mytilmi, Ayion, Thessaloniki, Kos; 5 nights, round-trip to Rhodes, Mytini, Piraeus, Tinos, Kos.

Majestic America Lines

American Queen **HOME PORTS** New Orleans; others vary with itinerary

April–December, 3 to 7 nights, Explore the Mississippi, various itineraries from New Orleans, Memphis, St. Louis, Cincinnati, Pittsburgh, Minneapolis, Louisville, Chattanooga.

Columbia Queen **HOME PORT** Varies with itinerary

April–October, 7 nights, Northwest Rivers from Klickitat Dock to Astoria to Pendleton, Clarkston, Longview.

Contessa **HOME PORT** Ketchikan

May–September, 7 nights, Alaska Adventure from Ketchikan to Sitka, calling at Wrangell, Thomas Bay, Dawes Glacier, Juneau, Glacier Bay National Park.

Delta Queen **HOME PORTS** New Orleans; others vary with itinerary

April–November, 6 to 11 nights, Explore the Mississippi, various itineraries from New Orleans, Memphis, Cincinnati, Nashville, Chattanooga, St. Louis, Little Rock, Birmingham, Mobile.

Empress of the North **HOME PORTS** Juneau, Portland, Seattle

April–September, 7 to 12 nights, Alaska Adventure, round-trip from Portland to Klickitat Dock, Pendleton, Clarkston, Port of Rainier, Astoria (7 nights). From Seattle to Juneau via Victoria, Vancouver, Ketchikan, Wrangell, Petersburg, Sitka, Glacier Bay National Park, Skagway, Dawes Glacier (12 nights). Round-trip from Juneau to Skagway, Glacier Bay National Park, Sitka, Petersburg, Wrangell, Dawes Glacier (7 nights).

October–December, 7 nights, Northwest Rivers, round-trip from Portland to Klickitat Dock, Pendleton, Clarkston, Port of Rainier, Astoria.

Mississippi Queen **HOME PORTS** New Orleans; others vary with itinerary

April–November, 3 to 11 nights, Explore the Mississippi, various itineraries from New Orleans, Memphis, Cincinnati, Nashville, St. Louis, Pittsburgh.

Queen of the West **HOME PORT** Portland

April–December, 7 nights, Northwest Rivers, round-trip from Portland to Klickitat Dock, Pendleton, Clarkston, Longview, Astoria.

MSC Cruises

MSC Armonia **HOME PORTS** Rio de Janeiro, Venice, and others

December 2007, 18 nights, from Venice to Dubrovnik, Tunis, Malaga, Casablanca, Tenerife, Recife, Salvador, Buzios, Rio de Janeiro.

December 2007–March 2008, 4 nights, Brazil, round-trip from Rio de Janeiro to Portobelo, Ilhabela; 7 nights, to Recife, Maceio, Salvador; 8 nights, Rio de Janeiro to Buenos Aires, Punta del Este, Ilhabela; 6 nights to Salvador, Maceio, Ilheus; Portobelo, Buenos Aires; Punta del Este, Ilhabela; 3 nights, to Ilha Grande, Ilhabela; 9 nights, to Santos, Punta del Este, Buenos Aires, Ilhabela, Santos; 3 nights, to Ilha Grande, Santos.

April, transatlantic to Mediterranean.

Summer, 11 nights, Cape North; 10 nights, Baltic/Norwegian fjords

Fall, 11 nights, Eastern Mediterranean from Genoa to Egypt or the Black Sea.

MSC Fantasia (debuts late 2008) **HOME PORTS** TBA
Ship will sail alternating Canary Island and Egypt itineraries.

MSC Lirica **HOME PORTS** Fort Lauderdale, Genoa, Hamburg, Kiel

November 2007 and May 2008, 17 nights, transatlantic, Genoa to Fort Lauderdale and reverse.

December 2007, 7 nights, Eastern/Southern Caribbean, round-trip from Fort Lauderdale to Key West, Montego Bay, Grand Cayman, Cozumel; or to San Juan, St. Thomas, Cayo Levantado, Nassau; 7 nights, round-trip from Fort Lauderdale to Key West, Grand Cayman, Cozumel, Nassau.

December 2007–March 2008, 10 nights, Caribbean, round-trip from Fort Lauderdale to San Juan, St. Maarten, St. Lucia, Antigua, Tortola, Cayo Levantado or to Cozumel, Puerto Limon, Cristobal, Cartagena, Cayo Levantado.

April 29, 17 nights, transatlantic eastbound from Fort Lauderdale to San Juan, St. Thomas, Funchal, Vigo, Le Havre, Dover, Amsterdam, Hamburg.

May–September, 3 nights, Germany, Denmark, round-trip from Hamburg to Kalundborg, Kiel; 7 nights, Kiel to Copenhagen, Visby, Riga, Helsinki, St. Petersburg; or Kiel to Copenhagen, Oslo, Kristiansand, Bergen, Eidfjord; or Kiel to Copenhagen, Visby, Tallinn, St. Petersburg, Helsinki; round-trip from Kiel to Copenhagen, St. Petersburg, Helsinki, Riga, Visby; or, Kiel to Copenhagen, Harwich, La Coruna, Lisbon, Gibraltar, Malaga, Olbia, Genoa.

September–November, 3 nights, from Genoa to Civitavecchia/Rome, Olbia; or 7 nights, Mediterranean, round-trip from Genoa and Rome to Marseille, Valencia, Tangier, Malaga, Civitavecchia/Rome.

Winter 2008–2009, 10 nights, Deep Caribbean and Panama.

MSC Melody **HOME PORTS** Durban, Genoa, Barcelona

November 2007, 21 nights, from Genoa to Naples, Port Said, Suez Canal, Aqaba, Safaga, Seychelles, Mauritius, Reunion, Durban.

Summer, 7 nights, round-trip from Barcelona, calling at Ibiza, Tunis, Messina, Livorno, Monte Carlo.

MSC Musica **HOME PORT** Genoa, Venice

November 2007–February 2008, 11 nights, from Genoa to Ajaccio, Malta, Rhodes, Alexandria, Tripoli, Messina, Naples. Or to Barcelona, Gibraltar, Tenerife, Funchal, Arrecife, Malaga, Civitavecchia/Rome.

March 16–October, 7 nights, Eastern Mediterranean, round-trip from Venice visiting Greek islands of Katakolon, Santorini, Mykonos, Piraeus, and Corfu and Bari and Dubrovnik.

MSC Opera **HOME PORTS** Santos, Trieste, Kiel

November 5, 18 nights, from Trieste to Ancona, Tunis, Malaga, Tenerife, Fortaleza, Salvador, Rio de Janeiro, Santos.

November 2007–March 2008, 3 nights, Brazil, round-trip from Santos to Ilha Grande, Rio de Janeiro; 4 nights, add Buzios; or to Portobelo, Rio de Janeiro; 5 nights, to Portobelo, Ilha Grande, Rio de Janeiro; or 7 nights, to Buenos Aires, Punta del Este, Portobelo; or to Buzios, Salvador, Ilheus, Ilha Grande; or to Buzios, Copacabana, Salvador, Ilha Grande.

Summer, 7 nights, alternating Norwegian Fjords and Baltic Capitals.

Fall, 7 nights, Mediterranean from Trieste to the Greek islands and Dubrovnik.

MSC Orchestra **HOME PORTS** Genoa, Venice

November 3, 2007, 11 nights, Mediterranean between Venice and Genoa to Split, Athens, Rhodes, Heraklion, Tunis, Palma de Mallorca, Barcelona, Marseille.

November 2007–March 2008, 11 nights, round-trip from Genoa to Barcelona, Casablanca, Tenerife, Funchal, Malaga, Rome. Or to Katakalon, Athens, Rhodes, Alexandria, Limassol, Marmaris, Heraklion, Naples.

March–October, 7 nights, from Barcelona or Genoa to Naples, Palermo, Tunis, Palma, Marseille.

November–December 2008, 11 nights from Genoa or Rome to Barcelona, Casablanca, Tenerife, Funchal, Malaga

December 16, 2008, 17 nights, Christmas–New Year's transatlantic cruise from Genoa arriving in Fort Lauderdale January 3, 2009.

January–March 2009, 7 nights, alternating Eastern and Western Caribbean round-trip from Fort Lauderdale.

MSC Poesia (debuts 2008) **HOME PORT** Venice

April–November, 7 nights, inaugural Eastern Mediterranean round-trip itineraries from Venice, calling at Bari, Katakalon, Izmir, Istanbul, Dubrovnik.

MSC Rhapsody **HOME PORTS** Genoa, Venice

November 2007–March 2008, 11 nights, round-trip from Genoa to Barcelona, Casablanca, Tenerife, Funchal, Malaga, Rome. Or 11 nights, Mediterranean, round-trip from Genoa to Katakalon, Athens, Rhodes, Alexandria, Limassol, Marmaris, Heraklion, Naples.

March–October, 7 nights, Western Mediterranean, round-trip from Genoa calling at Livorno, Salerno, Taormini, Sardinia, Malta, Tunisia.

MSC Sinfonia **HOME PORT** Genoa, Buenos Aires

November 19, 2007, 20 nights, transatlantic between Genoa and Buenos Aires.

December 2007–February 2008, 3 to 9 nights, South America, round-trip from Buenos Aires.

February 27, 21 nights, transatlantic between Buenos Aires and Venice.

March–October, 7 nights, Western Mediterranean, round-trip from Genoa or Rome to Monte Carlo, Valencia, Malta, Tunis, Rome.

Norwegian Coastal Voyage

Kong Harald, Nordlys, Nordstjernen, Midnatsol, Vesteraalen, Lofoten, Nordkapp, Finnmarken, Polarlys, Narvik, Lyngen, Richard With, Trollfjord **HOME PORT** Bergen

Year-round, 12 nights, Norwegian Coastal Voyage, round-trip from Bergen northbound to Kirkenes stopping at 34 ports and returning southbound visiting the same ports, but those visited in the day northbound will be visiting during the night southbound and vice versa. One-way, 7-night segments, northbound (Bergen to Kirkenes) and 6-night segments, southbound (Kirkenes to Bergen) available. Or 12 to 18 nights, Norway and Scandinavia, various itineraries with unescorted land tours and including the Norwegian Coastal Voyage.

April–October, 14 nights, Scandinavian Sampler from Reykjavik to Oslo, Bergen, Norwegian Coastal Voyage, Kirkenes; 18 nights, Norway Splendor from Oslo to Bergen via Ulvik, Gudvangen, Bergen, Kirkensbergen.

May–September, 15 nights, Norway from Bergen to Oslo via land tour of Lofthus, Balestrand, Bergen, embark for Norwegian Coastal Voyage, Vadso, Karasjok, Alta. Or 13 nights, Norway from Oslo to Bergen via Alta, Karasjok, Kirkenes, Bergen, Ulvik, Flam.

Fram **HOME PORTS** Reykjavik, Santiago, Ushuaia

May–June, September (reverse), 15 nights, Reykjavik to Kangerlussuaq, round-trip from Reykjavik to Tasiilaq, Skjoldungen, Uunartoq, Qassiarsuk, Qaqortoq, Ivittuut, Nuuk, Kangerlussuaq.

June–August, 12 nights, Disko Bay, round-trip from Reykjavik to Sismiut, Qeqertarsuaq, Uummannaq, Ukkusissat, Eqip Sermia, Illulissat, Evighedsfjorden, Kangerlussuaq. Featuring PolarCirkel boat landings, excursions, and lectures by expert guides.

August–September, 19 nights, Disko Bay and Thule, round-trip from Reykjavik to Kangerlussuaq, Sismiut, Qeqertarsuaq, Uummannaq, Ukkusissat, Kullorsuaq, Dundas, Siorapaluk, Qaanaaq, Upernavik, Eqip Sermia, Illulissat, Evighedsfjorden, Kangerlussuaq.

November–February, 13 nights, Chile and Antarctica, round-trip from Santiago to Ushuaia, Drake Passage, Antarctic Peninsula (Half Moon island, Whaler's Bay, Ukrainian Vernadsky Base, Almirante Brown, Port Lockroy, Neko Harbor, Polish Arctowski Base, Petermann Island).

Nordnorge **HOME PORTS** Buenos Aires, Santiago

November–February, 19 nights, Antarctica, Argentina and Chilean fjords from Santiago to Buenos Aires via Punta Arenas, Strait of Magellan, Puerto Natales, Beagle Channel, Cape Horn, Drake Passage, Antarctica, and reverse.

October–November, 21 nights, The Falklands, South Georgia, Antarctica, round-trip from Buenos Airs to Stanley, Sounders Island, South Georgia, Antarctica, Ushuaia.

Nordstjernen **HOME PORT** Oslo

June–August, 9 days, Spitsbergen Arctic Adventure, round-trip from Oslo to Longyearbyen, Magdalenefjord, Woodfjord, Smeerenburgfjord, Ny Alesund, Prins Karls Forland, Longyearbyen. Featuring expedition guides and PolarCirkel boat landings.

Polar Star **HOME PORT** Oslo

June–August, 12 nights, Grand Arctic Expedition, round-trip from Oslo to Longyearbyen, Ny Alesund, Magdalenefjord, Smeerenburgfjord, Woodfjord, Hinlopen Strait-Austfonna Glacier, Longyearbyen. Featuring expedition guides and Zodiac landings.

Norwegian Cruise Line

Norwegian Dawn **HOME PORT** Miami

November 2007–April 2008, 7 nights, Eastern Caribbean, round-trip from Miami, to Samana (Dominican Republic), Tortola, St. Thomas, Great Stirrup Cay.

April–September, Bermuda, round-trip from New York.

Norwegian Dream **HOME PORTS** Dover, Houston, Valparaiso

November 2007, 14 nights, Chilean fjords/Tierra del Fuego, round-trip from Valparaiso to Concepcion (Talchuano), Puerto Chacabuco, Punta Arenas, Ushuaia Argentina (overnight), Puerto Montt, and Valdivia. Or 18 nights, Chilean fjords/Strait of Magellan, from Valparaiso to Buenos Aires via Coquimbo, Concepcion, Valdivia (Corral), Puerto Montt, Puerto Chacabuco, Punta Arenas, Ushuaia, cruise Cape Horn, Stanley (Falkland Islands), Puerto Madryn, Montevideo.

December 2007–March 2008, 14 nights, Chilean fjords/Tierra del Fuego from Buenos Aires to Valparaiso via Montevideo, Puerto Madryn, Stanley, cruise Cape Horn, cruise Beagle Channel, Punta Arenas, cruise Strait of Magellan, Puerto Chacabuco cruise Darwin Canal, and Puerto Montt, and reverse.

April, 18 nights, Americas from Valparaiso to Los Angeles via Coquimbo, Iquique, Arica (optional tour to Machu Picchu), Lima, Trujillo, cross the equator, Punta Arenas, Acapulco, Puerto Vallarta.

May–September, 7 days, Boston to Bermuda.

Norwegian Gem HOME PORTS Barcelona, London, New York
December 3, 2007, 9 nights, transatlantic from Barcelona to Boston via Madeira.

January–February, 10 to 11 nights, Southern Caribbean, round-trip from New York via St. Thomas, Antigua, Barbados, St. Maarten; 11 nights, add Grenada, Dominica, Tortola instead of St. Maarten.

February–April, 7 nights, Bahamas, round-trip from New York via Orlando (Port Canaveral), Great Stirrup Cay, and Key West.

April 19, 2008, 15 days, transatlantic return from New York.

Early May–November 9, 7 nights, Western Mediterranean, round-trip from Barcelona to Malta, Naples, Rome (Civitavecchia), Florence/Pisa (Livorno), Nice (Villefranche).

Norwegian Jewel HOME PORTS Barcelona, Miami
November 2007–April 2008, 9 and 14 nights, Southern Caribbean, round-trip from Miami, to Samana, Tortola, Antigua, Barbados, and St. Lucia; 14 nights, add Cozumel and Grand Cayman; 5 nights, Western Caribbean, round-trip from Miami to Cozumel and Grand Cayman.

February, 2 nights, Weekend Cruise, round-trip from Miami.

May 5–September 17, 12 nights, Baltic Capitals, round-trip from London (Dover) to Copenhagen, Berlin (Warnemunde), Tallinn, Estonia, St. Petersburg (2 days), Helsinki, Stockholm. August 9, 2-day sampler cruise from London (Dover); September 4, 13 days, adds Oslo.

Norwegian Majesty HOME PORTS Boston, Charleston
October–November 2007, 5 to 7 nights, Bermuda, round-trip from Boston or Charleston with overnights in Bermuda.

January–April, 7 nights, Western Caribbean, round-trip from Charleston to Grand Cayman, Cozumel, and Key West.

Norwegian Pearl HOME PORTS Miami, New York, Vancouver
October 2007–April 2008, 9 nights, alternating Southern/Western Caribbean, round-trip from Miami via Samana, Tortola, Antigua, Barbados, and St. Lucia; 5 nights, via Cozumel and Grand Cayman; 14 nights, round-trip from Miami via Cozumel, Grand Cayman, Samana, Tortola, Antigua, Barbados, St. Lucia.

May 4–September 14, 7 nights, Alaska, round-trip from Seattle to Juneau, Skagway, Ketchikan, Victoria, Glacier Bay.

Norwegian Spirit HOME PORT New York
November 2007, 15 nights, Southern Caribbean from New York to New Orleans via St. Thomas, St. Lucia, Barbados, Aruba, Costa Maya, Santo Tomas de Castilla (Guatemala), Belize, and Cozumel.

November 2007–March 2008, 7 nights, Western Caribbean, round-trip from New Orleans to Costa Maya, Santo Tomas de Castilla, Belize, and Cozumel.

Norwegian Star HOME PORTS Los Angeles, Seattle
December 2007, January–April 2008, 8 nights, Mexican Riviera, round-trip from Los Angeles to Acapulco (overnight), Zihuatanejo/Ixtapa, Cabo San Lucas.

May 3–September 13, 7 nights, Alaska, round-trip from Seattle to Ketchikan, Juneau, Skagway, Prince Rupert, Sawyer Glacier.

Norwegian Sun HOME PORTS Miami, New Orleans, Seattle
January–April, 7 nights, Western Caribbean, round-trip from Miami to Roatan, Belize City, Costa Maya, Great Stirrup Cay.

April 20, 19 days, Panama Canal.

May 11–August 31, 7 nights, Alaska, round-trip from Vancouver to Inside Passage, Ketchikan, Juneau, Sawyer Glacier, Skagway.

NCL America

Pride of Aloha **HOME PORT** Honolulu

Year-round, 7 nights, round-trip from Honolulu (Sunday) or Kahului (Saturdays) to Nawiliwili (overnight), Hilo; cruise by Mount Kilauea; Kona, Kahului (overnight); Honolulu.

September–December 2007, February–March 2008, 11 nights, Hawaii, round-trip from Honolulu to Hilo, nighttime viewing of Kilauea volcano, Lahaina, cruising south coast of Molokai, Kona, Kahului (2 days), cruise north coast of Oahu and Napali Coast, and Nawiliwili (2 days).

January–April, 11 nights, Fanning Island, round-trip from Honolulu to Hilo, Fanning Island, Kahului, Kona, Nawiliwili (2 days), and late-afternoon cruise of Napali Coast.

Pride of America **HOME PORT** Honolulu

Year-round, 7 nights, Saturday, round-trip from Honolulu to Hilo, Kahului (2 days), Kona, Nawiliwili (2 days), Kona. The ship is in port every day and offers scenic cruising on Sunday evening (Mount Kilauea) and Thursday morning.

Pride of Hawaii/Norwegian Jade **HOME PORTS** Barcelona, Honolulu, Istanbul, Southampton

To February 2008, 7 nights, Monday, round-trip from Honolulu to Hilo, Kahului (2 days), Kona, and Nawiliwili (2 days).

Late March–November, 12 to 14 nights, Eastern and Western Mediterranean, from Barcelona, Istanbul, and Athens (Piraeus) to Rome (Civitavecchia), Naples, and Venice; or, Dubrovnik and Ephesus; or, Mykonos, Santorini, Iraklion, Crete, Corfu, Katakolon, Alexandria.

Late March–November, North Cape, Western Europe, and British Isles, round-trip from London (Southampton); two 2-night samplers and four 14-night Western Mediterranean with calls in Malaga (Cordoba), Barcelona (overnight), Nice (Ville-franche), Florence/Pisa (Livorno), Rome (Civitavecchia), Gibraltar, Lisbon, Vigo.

Late March–November, 12 nights, North Cape, round-trip from Southampton to Norway, cross the Arctic Circle and cruise by Svartisen Glacier.

Late March–November, 13 nights, British Isles and Northern Europe, round-trip from Southampton to France, England, Ireland, Scotland, Germany, the Netherlands, and Belgium.

Late March–November, 13 nights, Western Europe, from Southampton to Barcelona or return via Villefranche, Livorno, Civitavecchia, Naples, Cagliari, Sardinia, Granada (Malaga), Gibraltar, Seville (Cadiz), Lisbon, Vigo.

Oceania Cruises

Insignia **HOME PORT** Varies with itinerary

December 2007–February 2008, 12 nights, Rio de Janeiro and Buenos Aires via Ilha Grande, Parati, Santos, Itjai, Rio Grande, Montevideo. Or 16 and 20 nights, Antarctica/Patagonia, Buenos Aires to Valparaiso, Valparaiso to Buenos Aires.

March, 15 nights, transatlantic from Rio de Janeiro to Barcelona via Salvador, Recife, Porto Grande, Agadir.

April–July, 10 to 12 nights, Mediterranean/Greek Isles to Barcelona, Venice to Rome, Athens, Barcelona, or Venice to Barcelona, Rome to Venice.

July–October, 12 to 14 nights, Rome to Venice, Venice to Barcelona, Barcelona to Istanbul, Istanbul to Athens, Athens to Rome, Athens to Istanbul, Rome to Venice, Barcelona to Lisbon.

November, 14 nights, transatlantic, Lisbon to Rio de Janeiro via Funchal, Porto Grande, Recife, Salvador.

Nautica **HOME PORT** Varies with itinerary

November 2007–February 2008, April, 15 to 27 nights, Asia/Australia from Rome to Singapore, Singapore to Sydney, Sydney to Auckland.

February–May, Asia, 15 to 25 nights, Sydney to Bangkok, Bangkok to Beijing, Beijing to Hong Kong, Hong Kong to Athens.

June–July, November, 10 to 14 nights, Mediterranean/Greece, Athens to Rome, Rome to Barcelona, Barcelona to Istanbul, Barcelona to Athens, Rome to Istanbul, Istanbul to Athens.

August–October, 12 nights, Mediterranean and Greek Isles, Rome to Athens, Athens to Istanbul, Istanbul to Athens, Istanbul to Venice, Venice to Athens, Istanbul to Rome.

Regatta **HOME PORT** Miami; others vary with itinerary

November 2007, 12 nights, transatlantic from Barcelona to Miami via Ponta Delgado (Azores), Bermuda.

November–December 2007, 26 nights, Caribbean and Amazon, round-trip from Miami to Tortola, St. Bart's, St. Lucia, Tobago, Santarem, Boca de Valeria, Manaus, Parintins, Devil's Island, Barbados, Dominica, Antigua, Virgin Gorda, Samana, Grand Turk.

December 2007–March 2008, 10 and 12 nights, Eastern Caribbean, round-trip from Miami to Virgin Gorda, St. Bart's, Dominica, St. Lucia, Antigua, Tortola, Samana, Grand Turk, and reverse.

January, 16 nights, from Miami to Los Angeles via Playa del Carmen, Cozumel, San Andres, Panama Canal, Punta Arenas, Puerto Quetzal, Acapulco, Cabo San Lucas.

February–March, 14 nights, Mexico/Central America, round-trip from Miami to Playa del Carmen, Cozumel, Belize, Santo Tomas, Roatan, Puerto Limon, Colon, Cartagena, Grand Cayman.

March, 12 nights, transatlantic from Miami to Barcelona.

April–May and September–November, 10 to 16 nights, Mediterranean/ Northern Europe from Barcelona to Rome, Venice, Barcelona; Rome to Stockholm; 14 nights, London to Barcelona, Barcelona to Venice, Venice to Rome, Athens to Barcelona.

June, 14 nights, Northern Europe, Stockholm to London via Tallinn, St. Petersburg, Helsinki, Gdansk, Copenhagen, Berlin, transit Kiel Canal, Amsterdam, Bruges.

July–August, 14 nights, Northern Europe, London to Stockholm, Stockholm to London.

November, 14 nights, transatlantic, Barcelona to Miami via Tangier, Ponta Delgada, Bermuda.

Orient Lines

Marco Polo **HOME PORT** Varies with itinerary

December 2007–January 2008, 11 to 42 nights, Antarctica, round-trip from Ushuaia; Ushuaia to Valparaiso, Buenos Aires or Rio de Janeiro via Drake Passage, Lemaire, Paradise Harbor, Half Moon Island, Cape Horn, Punta Arenas, Straits of Magellan, Chilean fjords, Puerto Chabuco, Puerto Montt, Santiago, Chilean fjords, Punta Arenas, Stanley, West Point, Punta del Este, Itajai.

January–February, 9 to 52 nights, South America/Mediterranean, Valparaiso to Buenos Aires, Rio de Janeiro or Lisbon, Buenos Aires to Rio de Janeiro, Buenos Aires to Rome via Chilean fjords, Straits of Magellan, Ushuaia, Stanley, Argentina, Uruguay, Brazil, Cape Verde, Canary Islands, Morocco, Gibraltar, Spain, Morocco, Tunisia, Malta.

March, 15 to 27 nights, from Lisbon to Rome via Tangier, Ceuta, Malaga, Alicante, Tunis, Valetta; Rome to Athens, add Tripoli, Benghazi, Alexandria, Iraklion; Rome to Venice, add Ephesus, Istanbul, Mykonos, Korcula; round-trip from Rome, add Zadar, Dubrovnik, Corfu, Taormina, Capri/Pompeii.

April, 10 to 26 nights, from Athens to Venice, Rome or Barcelona, Venice to Rome, Barcelona or London; 12 to 34 nights, Mediterranean/Norwegian fjords, from Rome to Barcelona, London or Copenhagen via Sardinia, Sicily, Malta, Tunisia, Spain, Morocco, Portugal, Guernsey, Belgium, Zeebrugge, Scotland, Shetland Islands, Norway, Sweden, Denmark.

May, 10 to 34 nights, from Barcelona to London, Copenhagen; London to Copenhagen, Stockholm, round-trip Copenhagen, Copenhagen to Stockholm.

June–July, 10 to 41 nights, from Stockholm to Copenhagen, Reykjavik, Copenhagen round-trip, Copenhagen to Reykjavik, Reykjavik to Copenhagen, Stockholm; Copenhagen to Stockholm, London.

August, 10 to 38 nights, Northern Europe, Western Europe, Morocco from Stockholm to Copenhagen, London, Barcelona, Athens; London to Barcelona, Athens, Venice.

September–November, 10 to 26 nights, Mediterranean and Black Sea from Barcelona to Athens, Rome; Athens to Venice, Barcelona; Venice to Rome, Barcelona, Athens; Rome to Barcelona, Athens, Istanbul; Barcelona to Athens, Istanbul, Venice; Athens to Istanbul, Venice, Rome; Istanbul to Venice, Rome, Barcelona.

Orion Expedition Cruises

Orion **HOME PORTS** Cairns, Sidney; others vary with itinerary

November 2007, March 2008, 10 nights, Melanesian Island Cultures from Cairns, to Rabaul (overnight onboard; optional charter flight to Cairns) via Milne Bay, Deboyne Lagoon, Trobriand Islands, Gizo Island, Kennedy Island, Marovo Lagoon.

November 2007, March, April 2008, 11 nights, Papua New Guinea Highland Cultures from Rabaul (optional charter flight from Cairns; overnight onboard) to Cairns via Sepik River, Madang, Tami Islands, Tufi, D'Entrecasteaux Islands, Samarai and Kwato Islands, Milne Bay.

November, 4 nights, Coastal repositioning from Cairns to Sydney.

December 2007, 5 nights, Tasmania East Coast from Sydney to Hobart via Eden, Flinders Island, cruising Wineglass Bay, Coles Bay, Port Davey; 18 nights, Antarctica, from Hobart to Bluff (Invercargill) via Macquarie Island, exploring Commonwealth Bay region, Auckland Islands, Snares Island (cruising), and reverse.

February, 16 nights, Melanesia and Solomon Islands from Auckland to Rabaul (overnight onboard) via Noumea, Tanna Island, Pentecost Island, Utupua Island, Santa Ana Island, Rennell Island, Marovo Lagoon, Gizo Island, Kennedy Island.

April 15, 4 nights, Coastal repositioning from Cairns to Darwin.

April–September, 10 to 11 nights, Kimberley Coastline, round-trip from Darwin (10 nights) to Vansittart Bay, Hunter River (for Mitchell Falls), Horizontal Waterfalls/ Talbot Bay, Broome (overnight), Montgomery Reef/Raft Point, Bigge Island, King George Falls, or Broom to Darwin or reverse (11 nights) to Cape Leveque, Montgomery Reef/Raft Point, Hunter River (for Mitchell Falls), Bigge Island, King George Falls, Wyndham (for East Kimberley), Roti, Kupang.

P&O Cruises

In 2008, three ships, Aurora, Oriana, and Artemis, will sail on world cruises; together, they will visit 90 ports in 48 countries on seven continents between December 2007 and April 2008. The voyages can be taken in segments.

South Africa and Australia (Cairns, the Whitsundays, Brisbane, Sydney, Burnie, Melbourne, Adelaide, Albany and Perth).

April–December, round-trip cruises from Southampton: April and July, 12 nights to Canaries, Atlantic; April, 22 nights, Spain, Caribbean; May, 13 nights, Mediterranean; May, 9 nights, Canaries, Atlantic; June, 14 nights, Norwegian fjords; 17 nights, Mediterranean; July, 14 nights, Mediterranean; 16 nights, Mediterranean; August, 13 nights, Mediterranean; September, 7 nights, Europe; September, 18 nights, Mediterranean, Black Sea; 21 nights, Caribbean, Atlantic; October, 3 nights, Europe; 2 nights, Belgium; 14 nights, Mediterranean, Tunisia; November, 10 nights, Canaries, Atlantic; 18 nights, Sou–Sou to Mediterranean, Tunisia, Egypt; December, 12 nights, Canaries, Atlantic; 22 nights, Caribbean, Atlantic.

Ventura **HOME PORTS** Barbados, Barcelona, Southampton, and others
April 18, 14 nights, Western Mediterranean, maiden cruise, round-trip from Southampton to Barcelona, Villefranche, Florence/Pisa, Santa Margherita, Rome, Alicante, Gibraltar; reverse September.

May, 7 nights, Western Mediterranean, round-trip from Southampton to Vigo, Lisbon, Bilbao, Brest.

May, July, August, 14 nights, Canary Islands, round-trip from Southampton to Corunna, Madeira, La Palms, Tenerife, Gran Canaria, Lanzarote, Cadiz, Lisbon, Vigo; 7 nights, Iberia, round-trip from Southampton to Corunna, Bilbao, La Rochelle, Brest, St. Peter Port.

May, August, 14 nights, Western Mediterranean, round-trip from Southampton to Vigo, Lisbon, Palma, Barcelona, Cannes, Rome, Ajaccio, Gibraltar.

June, 7 nights, The Fjords, round-trip from Southampton to Bergen, Flam, Sognefjord, Olden, Nordfjord, Stavenger.

June, 14 nights, Baltic, round-trip from Southampton to Oslo, Copenhagen, Stockholm, Helsinki, Tallinn, Warnemunde, Bruges.

July, 14 nights, Western Mediterranean, round-trip from Southampton to Barcelona, Cannes, Florence/Pisa, Santa Margherita, Rome, Alicante, Gibraltar.

August, 16 nights, Eastern Mediterranean, round-trip from Southampton to Malaga, Cephalonia, Dubrovnik, Venice, Korcula, Corfu, Gibraltar.

September, 2 nights, round-trip from Southampton to Bruges. Canary Islands, round-trip from Southampton to Madeira, Gran Canaria, Tenerife, Lanzarote, Lisbon, Vigo.

October, 14 nights, Western Mediterranean, round-trip from Southampton to Barcelona, Monte Carlo, Florence/Pisa, Elba, Rome, Alicante, Gibraltar; 15 nights, repositioning from Southampton to Barbados via Tenerife, St. Lucia, Antigua, St. Maarten, Dominica.

November, December 2008, January, February, 2009, 15 nights, Caribbean, round-trip from Barbados to St. Vincent, Bonaire, Aruba, Catalina Island, Tortola, St. Maarten, St. Lucia, Martinique, Grenada; 15 nights, round-trip from Barbados to Antigua, Grand Turk, Cayo Levantado, St. Kitts, St. Lucia, St. Maarten, Tortola, Dominica, St. Vincent.

March 14, 2009, 13 nights, repositioning from Barbados to Southampton via St. Vincent, Grenada, St. Lucia, Tenerife.

Peter Deilmann Cruises

Deutschland **HOME PORTS** Dubai, Lisbon, Monte Carlo; others vary with itinerary
September–October 2007, 9 nights, Mediterranean from Lisbon to Monte Carlo via Portimao, Ibiza, Mahon, Barcelona, Sete; 7 nights, round-trip from Monte Carlo to Livorno Civitavecchia, Naples, Palermo, Cagliari, Ajaccio.

November–March, 12 nights, Middle East, Monte Carlo to Aqaba via Heraklion, Tartous, Beirut, Port Said, Suez, Sharm-el-Sheikh; 13 nights, Aqaba to Dubai via Aqaba, Safaga, Hodeidah, Aden, Salaiah, Muscat, Fujairah.

December, 14 nights, India/Thailand, Dubai to Phuket via Khor Fakkan, Mumbai, Cochin, Colombo; 19 nights, Singapore/Indonesia, Phuket to Hong Kong via Singapore, Benoa, Ujung Pandang, Pare Pare, Sandakan, Puerto Princesa.

January–February, 16 nights, Southeast Asia, Hong Kong to Singapore via Haiphong, Halongbay, Da Nang, Ho Chi Minh City, Sihanoukville, Tioman Island; 18 nights, Singapore to Hong Kong via Sihanoukville, Da Nang, Hong Kong, Naha, Shanghai, Xiamen; 13 nights, Hong Kong to Yangon to Da Nang, Singapore, Phuket; 13 nights, Sri Lanka/Maldives, Yangon to Mumbai via Colombo, Male (Maldive Islands), Cochin, New Magalore and Marmagoa.

March, 10 nights, Middle East, Mumbai to Dubai via Fujairah, Khasab, Manama, Doha, and Abu Dhabi; 19 nights, from Dubai to Istanbul via Abu Dhabi, Khasab, Muscat, Salalah, Aden, Safaga , Suez, Port Said, Kusadasi , and Canakkale.

April, 9 nights, Black Sea, round-trip from Istanbul (with flights to and from Frankfurt) to Nessebar, Constanta, Odessa, Yalta, Sotschi, Sinop, and Mudanya.

Princess Cruises

Caribbean Princess **HOME PORTS** Fort Lauderdale, New York
To May 2008, Sunday, 7 nights, Eastern Caribbean, round-trip from Fort Lauderdale to St. Maarten, St. Thomas, Princess Cays.

May–August, 9 nights, Eastern Caribbean, round-trip from New York to Grand Turk, San Juan, St. Thomas, Bermuda (West End), and reverse.

August–October, Sunday, 7 nights, Canada and New England, round-trip from New York to Halifax, St. John (New Brunswick), Bar Harbor, Boston, Newport; and reverse.

October, 7 nights, Bermuda/Eastern Caribbean, between New York and San Juan to St. Kitts, Antigua, St. Thomas.

Coral Princess **HOME PORTS** Fort Lauderdale, Vancouver
October–April, 10 nights, Panama Canal, round-trip from Fort Lauderdale to Aruba, Cartagena, Panama Canal to Gatun Lake, Cristobal, Costa Rica, Ocho Rios (or Montego Bay).

April 2007 and September 2008, 15 to 17 nights, Panama Canal, repositions between Fort Lauderdale and Vancouver; available in segments.

May–September, 11 nights, Alaska between Vancouver and Whittier via Inside Passage, Ketchikan, Juneau, Skagway, Glacier Bay, College Fjord; 7 nights, to Anchorage; 7 nights, reverse from Fairbanks to Vancouver.

Crown Princess **HOME PORTS** Copenhagen, Fort Lauderdale, New York, San Juan
November 2007–April 2008, alternating Sundays, 7 nights, Southern Caribbean, round-trip from San Juan to Barbados, St. Lucia, Antigua, Tortola, St. Thomas. Or April 26, 7 nights, from San Juan to St. Thomas to St. Kitts, Grenada, Bonaire, Aruba; or, San Juan, Tortola, St. Thomas, Antigua, St. Lucia, Barbados.

May, 15 or 25 nights, transatlantic between Fort Lauderdale and Copenhagen; 15 nights, to Azores, Lisbon, Vigo, Southampton, Paris/Normandy, Oslo; or 25 nights, add Copenhagen, Stockholm, Helsinki, St. Petersburg (overnight), Tallinn, Gdansk, Oslo.

May, 10 nights, Scandinavia and Russia, round-trip from Copenhagen to Stockholm, Helsinki, St. Petersburg (overnight), Tallinn, Gdansk, Oslo; or June, July, August, Berlin, Helsinger (Denmark) instead of Oslo.

September, 28 nights, transatlantic between Copenhagen and Fort Lauderdale to Stockholm, Helsinki, St. Petersburg (overnight), Gdansk, Oslo, Copenhagen, London

(Dover), Dublin, Belfast, Reykjavik, Qaqortoq, St. Johns, New York. Or September, 18 nights, Iceland to Greenland.

Dawn Princess **HOME PORTS** San Francisco, Seattle, Sydney
September 2007–April 2008, Sunday, 7 nights, Mexican Riviera, round-trip from San Diego to Cabo San Lucas, Mazatlan, Puerto Vallarta.

Diamond Princess **HOME PORTS** Los Angeles, Vancouver
September 19, 2007–April 16, 2008, 15 nights, Hawaii, round-trip from Los Angeles to Hilo, Kilauea volcano, Kona, Honolulu, Kauai, Maui, and Ensenada.

May, 3 to 7 nights, Pacific Coast between Los Angeles and Vancouver.

May–September, 12 to 14 nights, Alaska between Vancouver and Whittier, Juneau, Skagway, Ketchikan, plus cruising College Fjord, the Inside Passage and Glacier Bay National Park.

Emerald Princess **HOME PORTS** Barcelona, Fort Lauderdale, Rome, Venice
November 2007, 17 nights, Venice to Fort Lauderdalecombined with 12 nights, Grand Mediterranean Cruise between Venice and Barcelona to Athens, Kusadasi (Turkey), Istanbul, Mykonos, Naples/Capri, Rome (Civitavecchia), Florence/Pisa, Marseille; and reverse.

November 2007–March 2008, 10 nights, Eastern Caribbean, round-trip from Fort Lauderdale to Princess Cays, St. Thomas, St. Kitts, Barbados, St. Lucia, Antigua, or reverse.

December 2007–April 2008, 10 nights, alternating Southern Caribbean, round-trip from Fort Lauderdale to Aruba, Bonaire, Grenada, Dominica, St. Thomas, Princess Cays.

April, 16 or 28 nights, transatlantic between Fort Lauderdale and Barcelona or Venice to Madeira, Seville, Gibraltar, Sardinia, Rome, Florence/Pisa, Marseille, Barcelona; 28 nights, add Marseille, Florence/Pisa, Rome, Naples/Capri, Mykonos, Istanbul, Kusadasi, Athens.

June, July, 12 nights, Greek Isles between Venice and Rome to Dubrovnik, Corfu, Katakolon, Athens, Mykonos, Kusadasi, Rhodes, Santorini, Naples/Capri.

June, August, 12 nights, between Rome (Civitavecchia) and Venice to Monte Carlo, Florence/Pisa, Naples, Santorini, Kusadasi, Mykonos, Athens, Katakolon, Corfu.

September 21, 30 nights, transatlantic between Barcelona and Fort Lauderdale to Marseille, Florence/Pisa, Rome, Naples/Capri, Mykonos, Istanbul, Kusadasi, Athens, Venice, Naples/Capri, Rome, Florence/Pisa, Cannes, Barcelona, Seville, Lisbon, Azores Islands. Or October, 17/18 nights, transatlantic from Venice to Fort Lauderdale between Naples/Capri, Civitavecchia (Rome), Cannes, Barcelona, Seville, Lisbon, Azores Islands; 18 nights, add Florence/Pisa.

Golden Princess **HOME PORTS** Los Angeles, San Francisco, Seattle
May 2008, 1 to 6 nights, Pacific Coast between Seattle and Vancouver, Vancouver to Los Angeles.

September 2007–April 2008, 7 nights, Mexican Riviera, round-trip from Los Angeles to Puerto Vallarta, Mazatlan, Cabo San Lucas.

May–September, Saturday, 7 nights, Inside Passage, round-trip from Seattle to Juneau, Skagway, cruise Tracy Arm Fjord, Ketchikan, Victoria.

Grand Princess **HOME PORTS** Fort Lauderdale, London, New York, Rome, Venice
November 2007–April 2008, Saturday, 7 nights, Western Caribbean, round-trip from Fort Lauderdale to Ocho Rios, Grand Cayman, Cozumel, and Princess Cays.

May–October, 12 nights, Greek Isles and Mediterranean between Rome (Civitavecchia) and Venice calling at Monte Carlo, Florence/Pisa, Naples, Santorini, Kusadasi, Mykonos, Athens, Katakolon, Corfu. Or between Venice and Rome to Dubrovnik, Corfu, Katakolon, Athens, Mykonos, Kusadasi, Rhodes, Santorini, Naples/Capri.

June–August, 12 nights, North Cape and Norwegian Fjords, round-trip from London to Stavanger, Hellesylt/cruise Geiranger Fjord, Trondheim, Honningsvag, Tromso, Flam, Bergen. Or, 12 nights, British Isles, round-trip from Southampton to Guernsey, Cork, Dublin, Belfast, Glasgow, Inverness/Loch Ness, Edinburgh (South Queensferry), Paris/Normandy. Or 12 nights, round-trip from London to Bergen, Olden/Nordfjord, Hellesylt/cruising Geiranger Fjord, Ny Alesund, Akureyri, Reykjavik, Belfast. Or August, 12 nights, between London and Rome to Paris/Normandy, Vigo, Lisbon, Seville, Casablanca, Gibraltar, Barcelona, Cannes, Florence/Pisa.

October, 12 nights, Egypt and Aegean, round-trip from Rome to Naples/Capri, Athens, Kusadasi, Istanbul, Mykonos, Port Said (Cairo/Giza), Alexandria.

November, 21 and 33 nights, transatlantic between Rome and Fort Lauderdale to Naples/Capri, Athens, Kusadasi, Istanbul, Mykonos, Port Said, Alexandria, Rome, Florence/Pisa, Cannes, Barcelona, Gibraltar, Casablanca, Dakar, Fortaleza, Devil's Island, Dominica.

Island Princess **HOME PORTS** Acapulco, Fort Lauderdale, Los Angeles, Vancouver

November 2007 and January 2008, 10 to 11 nights, Panama Canal; 10 nights, between Acapulco and San Juan to Huatulco, Puerto Quetzal, Puerto Corinto, Costa Rica, Panama Canal, Cartagena, Aruba; reverse December 26, 11 nights, between San Juan and Acapulco to add Curaçao, San Juan del Sur.

February, March, April 6, 15 nights, Panama Canal between Fort Lauderdale and Los Angeles, calling at Ocho Rios, Cartagena, Panama Canal, Punta Arenas, San Juan del Sur, Puerto Quetzal, Aruba, Huatulco. Or 19 nights, Pacific Panama Canal, round-trip from Los Angeles to Cabo San Lucas, Acapulco, Huatulco, Costa Rica, Panama Canal (overnights), Puerto Corinto, Puerto Quetzal, Ixtapa/Zihuatanejo, Puerto Vallarta.

May 16, 3 nights, Pacific Coast from Los Angeles to Vancouver.

May–September 2007, Alaska, Vancouver to Anchorage.

Pacific Princess **HOME PORTS** Fort Lauderdale, Honolulu, Rome, Vancouver

December, 26 nights, South Pacific/South and Central America between Papeete and Fort Lauderdale to Bora-Bora, Moorea, Pitcairn Island, Easter Island, Pisco (San Martin, Peru), Lima (Callao, overnights for Machu Picchu), Quito, Panama Canal, Cristobal, San Blas, and Limon.

January 10, 102 days, World Cruise between Fort Lauderdale and London (Southampton) via Grand Cayman, San Blas Islands, Panama Canal, Quito, Lima (overnights). To Easter Island, Tahiti, Rarotonga, Auckland, Sydney, Cairns/Great Barrier Reef, Papua/New Guinea, Micronesia, Guam, Japan, Shanghai, Hong Kong, Vietnam, Cambodia (for Angkor Wat), Bangkok, Singapore, Phuket, Sri Lanka, India, Dubai, Safaga (for Luxor), Suez Canal, Athens, Sorrento/Capri, Rome, Cannes, Barcelona, Gibraltar, Lisbon, Ireland, France, Southampton.

April 22, 16 nights, Mediterranean between Southampton and Venice to Paris/Normandy, Lisbon, Gibraltar, Barcelona, St. Tropez, Florence/Pisa, Rome, Sorrento, Dubrovnik.

May, September, October, 12 nights, Holy Land between Venice and Athens to Split, Alexandria, Port Said, Jerusalem (Ashdod), Haifa, Kusadasi, Patmos, Santorini. Or between Athens and Rome, add Sorrento/Capri. Reverse June, November.

June, July, August, September, 12 nights, Mediterranean between Rome and Venice to Portofino, Monte Carlo, Corsica, Sorrento/Capri, Messina, Valletta, Corfu, Kotor,

Split, Ravenna. Reverse June, July. Or between Athens and Civitavecchia to Istanbul, Yalta, Odessa, Varna, Volos, Santorini, Capri. Or Rome to Sardinia (Cagliari), Malaga, Gibraltar, Casablanca (Marrakech), Tunis, Valletta, Messina, Sorrento/Capri.

November, 12/21/33 nights, Holy Land, Passage to the Amazon, and transatlantic between Athens and Venice (12 nights) or Manaus (21 nights) to Santorini, Patmos, Kusadasi, Jerusalem, Haifa, Port Said, Alexandria, Split Venice, Split, Naples/Capri, Rome, Casablanca, Santarem, Boca de Valeria.

Royal Princess **HOME PORTS** Barcelona, Fort Lauderdale, Rome
November 28, 24 nights, transatlantic between Rome to Fort Lauderdale to Portofino, Monte Carlo, Barcelona, Gibraltar, Casablanca, Dakar, Fortaleza, Devil's Island, Dominica, St. Bart's.

December, 16 nights, Southern Caribbean, round-trip from Fort Lauderdale to St. Bart's, St. Lucia, Bequia, Tobago, Devil's Island, Barbados, Dominica, Virgin Gorda, Samana.

January–April, 14 nights, Amazon River between Fort Lauderdale and Manaus, to St. Bart's, St. Lucia, Tobago, Devil's Island, Amazon River ports of Santarem, Boca da Valeria, Parintins, and Manaus. Reverse on alternate cruises.

April, 23/39 nights, Scandinavia/Russia, transatlantic between Fort Lauderdale and Stockholm or Rome to Azores, Lisbon, Cork, Dartmouth, Paris/Normandy, Amsterdam, Helsinki, St. Petersburg, Tallinn. Transatlantic return, add Cannes, Florence/Pisa.

May, June, July, 16 nights, Europe between Stockholm and Rome to Tallinn, St. Petersburg, Helsinki, Amsterdam, London (Dover), Paris/Normandy, Lisbon, Cannes, Florence/Pisa. Return June, August.

August 9, 21/37 nights, North Atlantic/transatlantic between Rome or Stockholm and Montreal to Florence/Pisa, Cannes, Lisbon, Paris/Normandy, London (Dover), Helsinki, St. Petersburg, Tallinn; 21 nights from Stockholm, Helsinki, St. Petersburg, Bornholm, Copenhagen, Oslo, Scrabster, Faroe Islands, Reykjavik, Qaqortoq, Corner Brook, Quebec City.

Sapphire Princess **HOME PORTS** Anchorage, Beijing, Sydney, Vancouver; others vary with itinerary
November, December 2007, 16 nights, Southeast Asia and China between Beijing and Bangkok to Nagasaki, Shanghai, Okinawa, Taipei, Hong Kong, Nha Trang, Ho Chi Minh City, Singapore. Reverse October 27, November 18.

December, 20 nights, Australia and Asia between Bangkok and Sydney to Ko Samui, Singapore, Ho Chi Minh City, Kota Kinabalu, Darwin, Cairns, Great Barrier Reef, and Brisbane.

January, February, March, 12 nights, Australia and New Zealand between Sydney and Auckland to Melbourne, Hobart cruise Fiordland National Park, Dunedin, Christchurch, Tauranga.

April, 31 nights, Hawaii, Tahiti and South Pacific between Sydney and Los Angeles to Melbourne, Tasmania, Fiordland National Park, Dunedin, Auckland, Fiji, Pago Pago, Rarotonga, Bora-Bora, Tahiti, Honolulu, and Hilo.

May 14, 3 nights, Pacific Coast, Los Angeles to Vancouver.

Sea Princess **HOME PORTS** Barbados, Montego Bay, Southampton
November, December, 14 nights, Grand Caribbean Islander, round-trip from Barbados to Dominica, Antigua, Tortola, St. Thomas, Grand Turk, Montego Bay, Curaçao, Bonaire, Isla Margarita, Grenada, and Trinidad.

November 2007–March 2008, 14 nights, alternating Eastern Caribbean, round-trip from Barbados to St. Lucia, Antigua, St. Maarten, St. Thomas, Grand Turk, Montego Bay, Grand Cayman, Aruba, Bonaire, Caracas and Grenada.

April 12, 2008, 14-28 nights, transatlantic between Barbados and Southampton via Grand Cayman, St. Vincent, St. Lucia, St. Maarten, St. Thomas, Antigua, Azores (28 nights); Southampton, Vigo, Lisbon, Barcelona, Cannes, Rome, Naples/Capri, Corsica, Gibraltar.

April–August, 14 nights, Mediterranean round-trip from London to Vigo, Lisbon, Barcelona, Cannes, Rome, Naples/Capri, Corsica, Gibraltar.

May, 7 nights, Iberian round-trip from London to Vigo (Spain), Lisbon, La Rochelle, Brest.

August 16, 28 nights, transatlantic between Southampton and New York via Iceland and Greenland, Seville (Cadiz), Barcelona, Monte Carlo, Florence/Pisa, Rome, Sardinia, Mallorca, Gibraltar, London, Bergen, (14 nights), Shetland Islands, Faroe Islands, Akureyri, Reykjavik, Greenland, Newfoundland (28 nights)

Star Princess **HOME PORTS** Buenos Aires, Copenhagen, Fort Lauderdale, Rio de Janeiro, Rome, Venice

November, 12 nights, Egypt and Aegean, round-trip from Rome to Naples/Capri, Athens, Kusadasi, Istanbul, Mykonos, Port Said, Alexandria.

December, 17 nights, Mediterranean/transatlantic from Rome to Fort Lauderdale to Naples/Capri, Florence/Pisa, Genoa, Cannes, Barcelona, Cartagena, Gibraltar, Casablanca, Madeira. Combine with Egypt and Aegean for 29 nights.

December, 21 nights, Brazilian Adventure between Fort Lauderdale and Buenos Aires to Dominica, Barbados, Grenada, Trinidad, Devil's Island, Fortaleza, Recife, Salvador, Rio de Janeiro, Montevideo.

January, February, 16 nights, Antarctica and South America, round-trip from Buenos Aires to Falkland, Antarctic Peninsula (Elephant Island, Antarctic Sound, Deception Island, Gerlache Strait, Neumayer Channel, Schollaert Channel, Sigma Island, Boyd Strait), Cape Horn, Ushuaia, Punta Arenas, and Montevideo.

January–March, 18 or 22 nights, Rio de Janeiro to Iguazú Falls, Buenos Aires, followed by 12 nights, Buenos Aires to Santiago cruise or a 16-night round-trip Buenos Aires cruise. Or 17 nights, Lima to Cuzco, Machu Picchu, Santiago combined with 12-day Buenos Aires to Santiago cruise before or after; 12 nights, Cape Horn and Strait of Magellan between Buenos Aires and Santiago to Montevideo, Falklands, Cape Horn, Ushuaia, Punta Arena, and Puerto Montt.

April, 15 and 23 nights, Santiago to Acapulco or Seattle, calling at La Serena, San Martin, Lima, Quito, Fuerte Amador, Punta Arenas, Huatulco, Acapulco; 23 nights, add Ixtapa, Puerto Vallarta, Cabo San Lucas, San Francisco; 8 nights, Mexico between Acapulco and Seattle to Ixtapa, Puerto Vallarta, Cabo San Lucas, San Francisco.

Summer 2008, Seattle to Alaska.

Sun Princess **HOME PORTS** Seattle, Sydney

November 2007 and March 2008, 28 nights, Around Australia, round-trip from Sydney.

December 2007–February 2008, 14 nights, New Zealand, round-trip from Sydney to Fiordland National Park, Dunedin, Christchurch, Wellington, Taranga, Auckland, Bay of Islands; 9 nights, Australia and South Pacific, round-trip from Sydney to Noumea, Lifou, Isle of Pines; 12 nights, round-trip from Sydney to Noumea, Champagne Bay, Wala, Vila, Mystery Island, Isle of Pines; 10 nights, round-trip from Sydney to Noumea, Ouvea, Vila, Wala.

February, 8 nights, Australia and South Pacific, round-trip from Sydney to Port Arthur, Hobart, Coles Bay, Tasmania, Melbourne; 42 nights, to Milford Sound, Dunedin, Christchurch, Wellington, Napier, Tauranga, Auckland, Bay of Islands, Sydney, Brisbane, Whitsunday, Darwin, Broome, Exmouth, Fremantle, Bunbury, Albany, Adelaide, Melbourne, Tasmania (Burnie), Hobart.

Tahitian Princess **HOME PORT** Papeete

January–May, 10 nights, round-trip from Papeete to Huahine, Rarotonga, Cook Islands cruise Raiatea, Bora-Bora (overnights), Moorea.

Summer 2008, 14 nights, Alaska, round-trip from Vancouver to Skagway, Juneau, Ketchikan, Glacier Bay, Sitka, Victoria, Kodiak Island Valdez.

Quark Expeditions

All visits to research stations are subject to permission and can only be confirmed locally. Itineraries are flexible and up to two or three Zodiac landings are attempted in a day based on sea and weather conditions.

Akademik Shokalskiy **HOME PORT** Ushuaia

November 2007–February 2008, 12 nights, Antarctic Peninsula, same itinerary as *Professor Multnovaskiy,* below.

November 2007–February 2008, 20 nights, Antarctic Quest, round-trip from Ushuaia to Beagle Channel, the Falkland Islands, Stanley, South Georgia, South Shetland Islands, Antarctic Peninsula, Drake Passage.

Kapitan Khlebnikov **HOME PORT** Ushuaia

October–November 2007, 14 nights, Snow Hill Island Safari, round-trip from Ushuaia or between Ushuaia and Stanley to Drake Passage, Weddell Sea, Snow Hill Island, Iceberg Alley, Antarctic Peninsula. Presentations by ornithologists, helicopter flights to Emperor Penguin Show Hill Rookery.

December, 38 nights, Semicircumnavigation from Stanley to Fremantle via Falkland Islands, to Shag Rocks, South Sandwich Islands, Weddell Sea, Georg von Neumayer Station, Emperor Penguin rookeries, Riiser-Larsen Ice Shelf, Enderby Land coast, Mawson Station, Zongshan Station.

Ocean Nova **HOME PORT** Ushuaia

November 2007–March 2008, 11 to 12 nights, Discovering the Peninsula, round-trip from Ushuaia to Beagle Channel, Drake Passage, Antarctic Peninsula, Neko Harbor, Paradise Bay, Lemaire Channel. Up to three Zodiac landings attempted in a day. On 12-day itineraries, an extra day is spent on the Peninsula.

December 2007–February 2008, 20 nights, Explorers' Route, round-trip from Ushuaia to Beagle Channel, Falkland Islands, Stanley, South Georgia, South Shetland Islands, Antarctic Peninsula, Drake Passage.

Orlova **HOME PORT** Ushuaia

November 2007–March 2008, 11 to 12 nights, Discovering the Peninsula, same itinerary as *Ocean Nova,* above.

January–February, 20 nights, Explorers' Route, same itinerary as *Ocean Nova,* above.

Professor Multanovskiy **HOME PORT** Ushuaia

December 2007, 12 nights, Antarctic Peninsula, round-trip from Ushuaia to the Beagle Channel, Drake Passage, Antarctic Peninsula, Neko Harbor, Paradise Bay, Lemaire Channel, Drake Passage.

December 2007–January 2008, 15 nights, Southern Expedition, round-trip from Ushuaia to the Drake Passage, Antarctic Peninsula, Loubert Coast, Drake Passage.

December 2007–March 2008, 20 nights, Antarctic Quest, round-trip from Ushuaia to Beagle Channel, the Falkland Islands, Stanley, South Georgia, South Shetland Islands, Antarctic Peninsula, Drake Passage.

Regent Seven Seas Cruises

Explorer II **HOME PORT** Ushuaia

January 21, February 1, 11 to 14 nights, Antarctica, round-trip from Ushuaia to the Falkland Islands, Drake Passage, and Antarctic Peninsula; 14-night itinerary also includes South Georgia Island.

Paul Gaugin **HOME PORT** Papeete

Year-round, Saturday, 7 to 14 nights, French Polynesia from Papeete, Tahiti, to Raiatea, Tahaa (Motu Mahana), Bora-Bora, and Moorea; 11 to 14 nights includes Society Island/Tuamotus/ Marquesas itineraries. Summer voyages include Ambassadors of the Environment program with Jean-Michel Cousteau's Ocean Futures Society, promoting ocean responsibility and engaging youngsters with fun learning activities.

Seven Seas Mariner **HOME PORTS** Fort Lauderdale, Seward, Vancouver; others vary with itinerary

January–April, 60 nights, Circle South America, round-trip from Fort Lauderdale to 30 ports in 15 countries including Colombia, Panama, Ecuador, Peru, Chile, Argentina, Falkland Islands, Uruguay, Brazil, French Guyana, and several Caribbean islands. Available in four segments.

April, 16 nights, Panama Canal, cruise from Fort Lauderdale (combinable with Voyager's 115-night World Cruise) to San Francisco via Cartagena, Panama Canal, Punta Arenas, Huatulco, Acapulco, Cabo San Lucas, San Diego

May, 7 to 12 nights, Caribbean, round-trip from Fort Lauderdale.

April, 26 nights, Hawaii/Tahiti, round-trip from San Francisco.

May–September, 7 nights, Alaska from Vancouver to Seward and Seward to Vancouver.

October–December, Grand Asia, from Seward to Osaka, Hong Kong, Bangkok, Singapore, Sydney.

Seven Seas Navigator **HOME PORTS** Fort Lauderdale; others vary with itinerary

October 2007–April 2008, 7 to 14 nights, Caribbean/Mexico, round-trip from Fort Lauderdale.

April and October, 8 nights, transatlantic, Fort Lauderdale to Madeira or reverse.

The Discovery Collection, 82 nights, five-continents; six segments:

September 27, 11 nights, Grand Mediterranean, from Monte Carlo to Athens.

October 8, 15 nights, Egypt, the Red Sea, and Arabia, from Athens via the Suez Canal and ending in Dubai.

October 23, 9 nights, Dubai to Mumbai via Bahrain, Qatar, United Arab Emirates; 2 days cruising Arabian Sea.

November 1, 20 nights, Indian Ocean from Mumbai to the Maldives, Seychelles, Madagascar, Mombasa, Cape Town.

13 nights, Diamonds and Gems, around the Cape of Good Hope to Walvis Bay (Namibia), Jamestown (St. Helena), followed by 4 days cruising the South Atlantic to Rio de Janeiro.

December 4, Rio to Fort Lauderdale via several calls along Brazil coast to Barbados, Dominica, Puerto Rico, and Turks and Caicos

December 2008–January 2009, 11 nights, Caribbean, round-trip from Fort Lauderdale.

Seven Seas Voyager **HOME PORTS** Copenhagen, Fort Lauderdale, Horta, Stockholm; others vary with itinerary

January–April, 115 nights, World Cruise from San Francisco to Fort Lauderdale with calls to 51 ports in 26 countries throughout the South Pacific, Orient, and Arabia, as well as the Mediterranean and Bermuda.

15 nights, Norway cruise to the North Cape and Spitzbergen.

April, 8 nights, transatlantic from Fort Lauderdale to Horta.

May–June, 7 to 10 nights, Mediterranean from Horta to Barcelona, Monte Carlo to Athens, Athens to Venice, Venice to Monte Carlo.

June–August, 7 to 15 nights, Baltic/Northern Europe from Dover to Copenhagen; round-trip from Stockholm, Stockholm to Copenhagen, Copenhagen to Stockholm, and Copenhagen to Southampton.

September–November, 7 to 11 nights, Mediterranean from Southampton to Monte Carlo, Venice, Istanbul, Athens to Istanbul, Monte Carlo, Rome, Funchal.

November, 9 nights, transatlantic from Funchal to Fort Lauderdale.

December 2008–January 2009, Caribbean/Mexico, 7 to 11 nights, round-trip from Fort Lauderdale to Aruba, Curaçao, St. Kitts, and St. Lucia.

RiverBarge Excursion Lines, Inc.

River Explorer **HOME PORTS** Memphis, Nashville, New Orleans, St. Louis; others vary with itinerary

October–November 2007, July–August 2008, 4 to 11 nights, Expanding Frontiers, various itineraries from Nashville to St. Louis, St. Louis to Nashville, round-trip to Nashville, Nashville to Cincinnati.

November 2007, March, April 2008, 8 nights, CaJunes and Creoles, round-trip from New Orleans to Morgan City, Atchafalaya River Basin, Baton Rouge, Creole Plantation.

December 2007, March–May 2008, 6 to 8 nights, Delta South, various itineraries round-trip from New Orleans, New Orleans to Memphis, Memphis to New Orleans.

January–February, 7 to 8 nights, Route of Jean Lafitte, various itineraries from New Orleans to Galveston, Galveston to Port Isabel, Port Isabel to Galveston, Galveston to New Orleans.

May, 7 nights, round-trip from Memphis to St. Louis to Cape Girardeau, Chester, Ste. Genevieve, Grafton.

June, 8 nights, round-trip from St. Louis; St. Louis to Cincinnati or round-trip from Cincinnati.

Royal Caribbean International

Adventure of the Seas **HOME PORT** San Juan

Year-round, Sunday, 7 nights, Southern Caribbean, round-trip from San Juan to Aruba, Curaçao, St. Maarten, St. Thomas. April to October, alternate Sundays, cruises to St. Maarten, Antigua, St. Lucia, Barbados, and reverse.

Brilliance of the Seas **HOME PORTS** Barcelona, Miami, Southampton

October–November 2007 and April–November, 2008, 12 nights, Mediterranean, round-trip from Barcelona to either Villefranche (Nice/Monte Carlo, France), Livorno (Florence/Pisa), Naples, Rome, Mykonos, Kusadasi (Ephesus), Piraeus, Santorini, and Venice (Italy), Dubrovnik , and Corfu; or Villefranche (Nice/Monte Carlo), Livorno (Florence/Pisa), Naples, and Rome, Athens, Santorini, and Mykonos, and Kusadasi.

November, December, and April, 15 nights, transatlantic westbound, Barcelona to Miami via Alicante, Spain; Gibraltar, United Kingdom; Lisbon, Portugal; Tenerife, Canary Islands; Madeira (Funchal), Portugal; St. John's, Antigua or reverse.

December 2007, 4 nights, Bahamas, round-trip from Miami to Key West, Coco Cay. 12 nights, Caribbean/Panama Canal, round-trip from Miami to Key West, Grand Cayman; Panama Canal, Cristobal (Panama), Cartagena, Aruba, Curaçao.

January, 9 nights, Western Caribbean, round-trip from Miami to Curaçao, Aruba, Ocho Rios, Labadee.

January–April, , 10 and 11 nights, Southern Caribbean/Panama Canal, round-trip from Miami to Aruba, Panama Canal, Cristobal, and Puerto Limon, Grand Cayman. (10 nights); or Labadee, Aruba, Curaçao, Panama Canal, Cristobal, Puerto Limon (11 nights); or April 4, add Grand Cayman.

May 19, 10 nights, from Southampton to Barcelona via Le Havre/Paris, Vigo, Lisbon, Tangier, Corsica, Villefranche/Nice.

May–December, 12–15 nights, Mediterranean, round-trip from Barcelona to Cannes, Livorno, Civitavecchia, Naples/Capri, Venice, Split, Croatia, Tunisia. Or Mediter-ranean/Greek Isles, round-trip from Barcelona to Villefranche, Livorno, Civitavecchia, Mykonos, Kusadasi, Piraeus, Santorini, Naples/Capri; 14 nights, Canaries and Portugal.

Empress of the Seas **HOME PORTS** Fort Lauderdale, Norfolk, San Juan
November 2007–March 2008, 3, 5, 9, and 11 nights, Southern Caribbean, round-trip from San Juan, alternating itineraries to St. Maarten, St. Bart's, St. Kitts, Antigua, St. Lucia, Barbados, Isla Margarita, Curaçao, Aruba (11 nights); to St. Maarten, St. Lucia, Barbados, Isla Margarita, Curaçao, Aruba (9 nights); St. Kitts, St. Maarten, Tortola (5 nights); or St. Thomas, St. Maarten (3 nights); or St. Kitts, St. Maarten (3 nights). Ship will be transferred to Pullmantour in March 2008.

Enchantment of the Seas **HOME PORT** Fort Lauderdale
Year-round, 4 and 5 nights, Western Caribbean, round-trip from Fort Lauderdale; 4 nights, alternating Thursdays to Key West, Cozumel; 5 nights, alternating Mondays to Belize City, Cozumel, Key West; 5 nights, alternate Saturdays to Grand Cayman, Costa Maya. Or alternate Thursdays, 4 nights, to Coco Cay, Key West.

Explorer of the Seas **HOME PORTS** Cape Liberty (New Jersey)
November 4, 2007, 7 nights, Bermuda, round-trip from Cape Liberty to Kings Wharf, Bermuda (overnights); Boston.

November 2007–March 2008, Southern Caribbean, round-trip from Cape Liberty to St. Maarten, Antigua, Dominica, Barbados, St. Kitts, St. Thomas, San Juan.

December 23, 12 nights, to San Juan, St. Thomas, Dominica, Barbados, St. Kitts, Antigua.

April, 5 nights, Bermuda, round-trip from Cape Liberty to Kings Wharf, Bermuda. Or 9 nights, Eastern Caribbean, to Labadee, Casa De Campo, St. Thomas, San Juan. Or 9 nights, Bermuda/Caribbean, round-trip from Cape Liberty to Kings Wharf, St. Maarten, St. Thomas, San Juan.

Freedom of the Seas **HOME PORT** Miami
Year-round , Saturday, 7 nights, Western Caribbean, round-trip from Miami to Labadee, the line's private resort in Haiti. Ocho Rios, Grand Cayman, Cozumel. Alternate Sundays, 7 nights, Eastern Caribbean to San Juan, St. Thomas, St. Maarten.

Grandeur of the Seas **HOME PORTS** Baltimore, Tampa, san Juan
November 25, 2007, 13 nights, Caribbean repositioning, round-trip from Baltimore to Tampa via Bermuda (overnights), St. Maarten, Curaçao, Aruba, Grand Cayman, Cozumel.

December 2007–April 2008, 4 and 5 nights, Western Caribbean, round-trip from Tampa to Grand Cayman, Costa Maya, Belize, Cozumel, Progresso, Key West.

Various iteneraries include: April–October, Bermuda, Caribbean, and Canada/New England from Norfolk, Virginia and Baltimore.

Independence of the Seas **HOME PORTS** Southampton, Fort Lauderdale
May, August, 4 nights, round-trip from Southampton to Cork, Ireland, St. Peter Port, Channel Islands.

May, 10 nights, and October, 11 nights, Canary Islands, round-trip from Southampton to Madeira, Canary Islands, Vigo.

May–September, 14 nights, Mediterranean, round-trip from Southampton to Gibraltar, Barcelona, Villefranche, Livorno, Cagliari, Sardinia, Malaga, Lisbon, Vigo. Or to Gibraltar, Cannes, Livorno, Civitavecchia (Rome), Sardinia, Cadiz/Seville, Lisbon, Vigo. Or 10 nights, round-trip from Southampton to Gibraltar, Barcelona, Lisbon, Vigo.

Winter 2008–2009, Eastern and Western Caribbean, round-trip from Fort Lauderdale.

Jewel of the Seas **HOME PORTS** Fort Lauderdale, Harwich, Boston
November–April, 6 and 8 nights, alternating Eastern and Western Caribbean, round-trip from Fort Lauderdale to either San Juan, St. Thomas, St. Maarten, Tortola, Nassau; or Key West, Cozumel, Costa Maya, Belize, Grand Cayman.

March 30, 11 nights, transatlantic from Fort Lauderdale to Southampton via Bermuda (overnights); Le Havre (Paris).

May–August, 12 nights, Baltic or Norwegian fjords, round-trip from Harwich to either Oslo, Copenhagen, Stockholm, Helsinki, St. Petersburg (2 days), Tallinn; or Paris, Plymouth, Cork, Belfast, Glasgow, Bergen, Ny-Alesund, Flam, Amsterdam.

June 27, 13 nights, round-trip from Harwich to Klaipeda, Lithuania; Tallinn, St. Petersburg, Helsinki, Stockholm, Copenhagen, Oslo, Norway.

September–November, transatlantic/New England/Canada/Caribbean

Legend of the Seas **HOME PORTS** Barcelona, Rome, Santo Domingo
December 1, 2007, 15 nights, transatlantic from Barcelona to Santo Domingo via Tenerife, Santa Cruz, Canary Islands; Barbados, St. Vincent, Dominica, St. Kitts, Tortola.

December 2007–March 2008, alternate Sundays, 7 nights, Southern Caribbean, round-trip from Santo Domingo to St. Kitts, Guadeloupe, Martinique, Barbados, St. Lucia. Or St. Maarten, Grenada, Margarita Island, Aruba. Or December 30, to St. Kitts, Martinique, Barbados, St. Lucia. Or St. Maarten, Dominica, Grenada, Margarita, Aruba.

April–November, 12 nights, Eastern Mediterranean, round-trip from Civitavecchia (Rome), to Mykonos, Kusadasi, Rhodes, Alexandria; Piraeus, Naples/Capri. Or 13 nights, to Portofino, Livorno (Florence/Pisa), Messina, Split; Venice, Dubrovnik, Naples/Capri.

November–December, Rome/Dubai/Singapore/Shanghai and return.

Liberty of the Seas **HOME PORT** Miami
December 2007–April 2008, 7 nights, alternate Saturdays, Western Caribbean, round-trip from Miami to Labadee, Montego Bay, Grand Cayman, Cozumel. Or Eastern Caribbean, round-trip from Miami to San Juan, St. Maarten, Labadee.

Majesty of the Seas **HOME PORT** Miami
Year-round, Bahamas from Miami, 3 nights on Fridays to Nassau, and Coco Cay (RCI private island); 4 nights, on Mondays add Key West.

Mariner of the Seas **HOME PORT** Port Canaveral
Year-round, Sunday, 7 nights, Eastern/Western Caribbean, round-trip from Port Canaveral to either to Coco Cay, St. Thomas, St. Maarten; or to San Juan, St. Maarten, St. Thomas; or Labadee, Ocho Rios, Grand Cayman, Cozumel.

Monarch of the Seas **HOME PORT** Los Angeles
Year-round, 3 and 4 nights, Mexican Riviera, round-trip from Los Angeles; 3 nights, Fridays, to Ensenada; 4 nights, Mondays, to Ensenada, San Diego, Catalina Island.

Navigator of the Seas **HOME PORT** Barcelona, Fort Lauderdale, Rome
November 5, 2007, 13 nights, transatlantic westbound from Southampton to Fort Lauderdale via La Coruna, Spain; Lisbon, Madeira, Canary Islands.

November 2007–March 2008, 6 nights, Western Caribbean, round-trip from Fort Lauderdale to Cozumel, Belize, Costa Maya; or 5 nights, to Ocho Rios, Key West; or to Cozumel, Belize. Or 5 nights, to Ocho Rios, Grand Cayman; 4 nights to Key West, Cozumel; or to Key West, Cozumel, Belize.

April–June, 4 nights, round-trip from Barcelona to Palma de Mallorca, Ibiza. Or 5 nights, to Marseilles, Sardinia, Palermo. Or 5 nights, to Cannes, Livorno, Civitavecchia (Rome).

July–August, 7 nights, Eastern Mediterranean, round-trip from Civitavecchia to Messina, Piraeus, Kusadasi, Crete.

September–October, 10 nights, round-trip from Civitavecchia to Messina, Thessaloniki, Istanbul, Malta; 11 nights, from Barcelona to Palma de Mallorca, Sardinia, Piraeus, Istanbul, Malta; 12 nights, from Civitavecchia to Barcelona via Palermo; Piraeus, Kusadasi, Istanbul, Thessaloniki, Malta, Sardinia.

Radiance of the Seas **HOME PORT** Fort Lauderdale

November 4, 2007, 15 nights, Panama Canal from Los Angeles to Fort Lauderdale via Cabo San Lucas, Acapulco, Huatulco, Punta Arenas, Costa Rica; Panama Canal, Cristobal; Cartagena. April reverse.

November 2007–March 2008, Sundays, 8 nights, Eastern Caribbean, round-trip from Fort Lauderdale to San Juan, St. Thomas, Antigua, St. Maarten, Nassau.

May–September, Alaska.

September–December, Hawaii, Panama Canal, South America.

Rhapsody of the Seas **HOME PORTS** Shanghai, Singapore, Sydney, Seattle

November 24, 16 nights, from Sydney to Singapore via Brisbane; Cid Harbour, Cairns (Yorkey's Knob), Komodo, Lombok, Bali; Singapore (overnights).

December, 2 nights, Malaysia, round-trip from Singapore to Kuala Lumpur (Port Kelang); 5 nights, to Kuala Lumpur (Port Kelang), Penang, Phuket; 4 nights, to Phuket, Langkawi; 3 nights, to Kuala Lumpur (Port Kelang), Penang.

January, 12 nights, from Singapore to Hong Kong via Sihanoukville, Cambodia; Bangkok, Thailand (overnights); Ho Chi Minh City, Nha Trang, Hue, Hanoi (Haiphong), Vietnam (overnights); reverse.

January–May, 5 nights, round-trip from Hong Kong to Okinawa, Taipei (Keelung), Kaoshiung; 3 nights, Sanya and Hainan Island to Kaoshiung; 5 nights, to Hanoi (overnights), Hue; Sanya; 5 nights, Korea and Japan, round-trip from Shanghai to Fukuoka; Pusan, Seoul (Pyeongtaek), Cheju Island; Nagasaki; 7 nights, Korea and Japan to Seoul, Cheju Island, Pusan, Kagoshima; 5 nights, Asian Legacies, to Fukuoka, Pusan, Cheju Island; 7 nights, Pearls of the Orient, to Seoul, Cheju Island, Pusan, Kagoshima.

May–September, Alaska, Hawaii; October–December, South Pacific, Australia, New Zealand.

Serenade of the Seas **HOME PORTS** San Juan, Vancouver

October, Sunday, 7 nights, Alaska Inside Passage, round-trip from Vancouver to Juneau, Skagway, Hubbard Glacier, Ketchikan; 11 nights, Hawaii, Vancouver to Honolulu and Honolulu to Ensenada via Hilo, Kailua, Kona, Lahaina, Nawiliwili; 12 nights, Panama Canal, San Diego to San Juan.

October–April, Saturday, 7 nights, round-trip from San Juan to St. Thomas, St. Maarten, Antigua, St. Lucia, Barbados.

May–September, Sunday, 7 nights, Alaska Inside Passage, round-trip from Vancouver to Juneau, Skagway, Hubbard Glacier, Ketchikan, Misty Fjords.

Sovereign of the Seas **HOME PORT** Port Canaveral
Year-round, Friday and Monday, 3 and 4 nights, Bahamas from Port Canaveral to Nassau and Coco Cay; 4 nights, to Coco Cay, Nassau (overnights).

Splendour of the Seas **HOME PORTS** Lisbon, Sao Paulo (Santos), Venice
November 2007, 10 nights, Mediterranean from Venice to Lisbon via Dubrovnik, Croatia, Santorini, Tunis, Malaga, Casablanca (Marrakech).

December 4, 14 nights, transatlantic from Lisbon to Sao Paulo via Madeira; Santa Cruz, Canary Islands, Mindelo, Cape Verde, Recife, Salvador de Bahia, Rio de Janeiro; 2 nights, round-trip from Sao Paulo at sea.

December 2007–February 2008, 8 nights, from Sao Paulo to Buenos Aires, Punta del Este, Portobelo, Ilhabela, Brazil. Or Buzios, Rio de Janeiro, Portobelo, Florianopolis, Ilhabela; to Rio de Janeiro, Buenos Aires, Punta del Este, Portobelo; 6 nights, to Buzios, Cabo Frio, Angra Dos Reis, Ilhabela.

February 2, 8 nights, Carnaval, round-trip from Sao Paulo to Rio de Janeiro (overnights), Salvador de Bahia (overnights), Ilheus, Buzios.

February, 15 nights, to Valparaiso via Rio de Janeiro, Buenos Aires, Puerto Madryn, Cape Horn, Ushuaia, Punta Arenas, Straits of Magellan, Chilean fjords, Puerto Montt; 13 nights, from Valparaiso to Buenos Aires via La Serena (Coquimbo), Chile; Puerto Montt, Chilean fjords, Straits of Magellan, Punta Arenas, Ushuaia, Cape Horn, Puerto Madryn, Montevideo.

March, 13 nights, from Buenos Aires to Valparaiso via Punta del Este, Puerto Madryn, Cape Horn, Ushuaia, Punta Arenas, Straits of Magellan, Chilean fjords, Puerto Montt, La Serena, Chile; 15 nights, from Valparaiso to Sao Paulo via Puerto Montt, Chilean fjords, Straits of Magellan, Punta Arenas, Ushuaia, Cape Horn, Puerto Madryn, Argentina, Buenos Aires, Rio de Janeiro.

April, 14 nights, transatlantic eastbound from Sao Paulo to Lisbon via Rio de Janeiro, Salvador de Bahia, Recife, Brazil, Agadir, Casablanca, Tangier; 3 nights, round-trip from Venice to Dubrovnik; 4 nights, round-trip from Venice to Dubrovnik, Corfu; 6 nights, from Lisbon to Venice via Gibraltar, Sardinia, Dubrovnik.

May–November, 7 nights, Greek Isles, round-trip from Venice to Piraeus, Mykonos, Katakolon, Corfu, Split, Croatia; 7 nights, to Dubrovnik, Kusadasi, Santorini, Corfu; or to Piraeus, Mykonos, Katakolon, Corfu, Split, Croatia; 6 nights, to Piraeus, Mykonos, Split, Croatia.

Vision of the Seas **HOME PORTS** Los Angeles, Seattle, Vancouver.
January–December, Sunday, 7 nights, Mexican Riviera, round-trip from Los Angeles to Cabo San Lucas, Mazatlan, and Puerto Vallarta.

Voyager of the Seas **HOME PORTS** Barcelona, Galveston
September–November 2007, Saturdays, 7 nights, Mediterranean, round-trip from Barcelona to Villefranche (Nice), Livorno (Florence/Pisa), Civitavecchia (Rome), Naples, Palermo. Or 10 nights, Canary Islands and Morocco, to Lanzarote, Tenerife, Santa Cruz, Canary Islands, Lisbon, Malaga. Or 11 nights, add Madeira.

December 8, 2007, 15 nights, transatlantic from Barcelona to Galveston via Cartagena, Madeira, Canary Islands, San Juan, Labadee, Cozumel.

December 2007–April 2008, 7 nights, Western Caribbean, alternate Sundays, round-trip from Galveston to Montego Bay, Grand Cayman, Cozumel; or to Roatan, Costa Maya, Cozumel; or to Cozumel, Roatan, Costa Maya, Progreso.

May–November, Saturday, 7 nights, Mediterranean, round-trip from Barcelona to Villefranche (Nice), Livorno (Florence/Pisa), Rome, Naples/Capri, Palermo.

Saga Cruises

Saga Rose **HOME PORTS** Southampton
January–March, 100 nights, World Cruise, round-trip from Southampton to Funchal,
    Antigua, Curaçao, Ecuador, Peru, Easter Island, Pitcairn Island, Tahiti, New Zealand,
    Australia, Whitsunday Islands, Papua New Guinea, Indonesia, Hong Kong, Vietnam,
    Singapore, Malaysia, Sri Lanka, India, Oman, Jordan, Egypt, Greece, Malta, Spain,
    Portugal. Available in 11 segments from 21 to 63 nights.

Saga Ruby **HOME PORTS** Marseilles, Southampton
November 2007, 16 nights, Mediterranean, various itineraries round-trip from
    Marseilles to Rome, Katakolon, Heraklion, Rhodes, Limassol, Haifa, Alexandria,
    Piraeus, Valletta; 13 nights, Morocco, from Marseilles to Southampton.

December, 18 nights, Canary Islands, round-trip from Southampton to Ferrol,
    Casablanca, Funchal, Santa Cruz, San Sebastian, Tenerife, Las Palmas, Arrecife, Lisbon.

January–March, 83 nights, Grand South American Adventure, round-trip from
    Southampton via Funchal, Dakar, Porto Grande, Puerto Ordaz, Devil's Island, Brazil,
    Argentina, Uruguay, Port Stanley, Antarctica, Ushuaia, Chile, Peru, Ecuador, Costa Rica,
    Panama, Colombia, Curaçao, Venezuela, Barbados, Azores. Available in five segments.

Seabourn Cruise Line

Seabourn Legend **HOME PORTS** Barcelona, Fort Lauderdale, Nice, Rome,
    St. Thomas; others vary with itinerary
January–February, 14 to 28 nights, Panama, Belize and Costa Rica, Fort Lauderdale to
    Caldera Yucatan Channel, Belize, Roatan, Costa Rica, Panama Canal transit, Puerto
    Quepos, San Juan del Sur.

February–March, 7 to 25 nights, Panama Canal and Caribbean from Fort Lauderdale to
    St. Thomas via Panama Canal, Puerto Moin, Roatan, Belize, San Juan, St. John,
    Guadeloupe, Antigua, St. Maarten, Virgin Gorda.

April, transatlantic Caribbean/Portugal from St. Thomas to Lisbon via San Juan, Fort
    Lauderdale, Funchal.

May–October, Mediterranean/French and Italian Rivera from Rome, Nice, Barcelona;
    available in segments.

October–November, 7 to 34 nights, transatlantic from Rome to Fort Lauderdale via
    Italy, Monte Carlo, Malta, Alicante, Seville, Gibraltar, Malaga, Tenerife.

December, 7 to 14 nights, Caribbean, round-trip from Fort Lauderdale or Barbados to
    Fort Lauderdale via St. Thomas, St. Bart's, Bequia, St. Maarten, Virgin Gorda, San Juan.

January–February 2009, 14 nights, Panama, Belize, Costa Rica from Fort Lauderdale to
    Caldera and reverse.

February–March, 6 to 14 nights, from Fort Lauderdale to St. Thomas and reverse.

March, Caribbean and transatlantic, from St. Thomas to Lisbon via St. Bart's, Virgin
    Gorda, San Juan, Fort Lauderdale, Funchal.

Seabourn Pride **HOME PORTS** Fort Lauderdale, London; others vary with itinerary
January–March, 12 to 72 nights, South America, round-trip from Fort Lauderdale to
    Panama Canal, Valparaiso, Buenos Aires, Rio de Janeiro, Manaus.

March–May, 14 to 49 days, transatlantic with sailings to Mediterranean/Europe, from
    Fort Lauderdale to Lisbon, Venice, London, Copenhagen; available in segments.

June–August, 9 to 26 nights, Scandinavia and Russia from Copenhagen to St.
    Petersburg, Helsinki, Stockholm, Warnemunde, Ronne, Flam, Ny-Alesund, Svolvaer,
    Tromso, Bergen, Ulvik, Eidfjord, Stavanger, and round-trip from Copenhagen.

September–October, 14 to 42 days, Europe from London to Lisbon via Dublin, Paris, Bor-
    deaux, Funchal, Canary Islands, Casablanca, Gibraltar, Malaga, Cadiz, Seville, Portimao.

October–November, 7 to 23 nights, transatlantic from Lisbon to Barbados with Caribbean sailings round-trip from Barbados and from Barbados to Fort Lauderdale.

December 2008–February 2009, 7 to 74 nights, South America from Fort Lauderdale to Buenos Aires via Panama Canal, Guayaquil, Arica, Puerto Montt, Castro, Chilean fjords, Punta Arenas, Cape Horn, Ushuaia.

Seabourn Spirit **HOME PORTS** Hong Kong, Singapore; others vary with itinerary
January–March, 14 to 28 nights, Asia, Vietnam, Thailand and Malaysia from Singapore to Hong Kong, round-trip Singapore, Hong Kong to Singapore.

March, 8 to 30 nights, China/Asia, Singapore to Shanghai, round-trip from Hong Kong, Shanghai to Hong Kong, Shanghai to Singapore, or Hong Kong to Singapore; 14 to 63 nights, Asia/Africa/India/Arabia/Egypt, from Hong Kong to Dubai, Alexandria, Piraeus, or Istanbul.

April, 11 to 18 nights, India/Arabia/Asia/Africa from Singapore to Dubai, Alexandria, Piraeus, or Istanbul. Dubai to Istanbul; or Alexandria to Piraeus or Istanbul.

May–July, 7 to 21 nights, Mediterranean, Alexandria to Athens or Cairo; Athens to Istanbul; Venice to Civitavecchia, Athens, or Istanbul.

August–October, 7 to 35 nights, Aegean, from Civitavecchia, Athens, Istanbul.

October–December, 7 to 56 nights, repositions from Civitavecchia to Singapore via Athens, Istanbul, Alexandria, Cairo, Dubai, and followed by Asia cruises round-trip from Singapore or Hong Kong or reverse; Shanghai to Hong Kong, Singapore.

SeaDream Yacht Club

SeaDream I **HOME PORTS** St. Thomas, San Juan; others vary with itinerary
December 2007–April 2008, 7 nights, Eastern Caribbean, round-trip from San Juan to Culebrita, Esperanza, St. John, St. Maarten, St. Bart's, Virgin Gorda, Jost van Dyke. Round-trip from St. Thomas; and St. Thomas to San Juan via St. John, St. Bart's, Guadeloupe, Nevis, Jost van Dyke.

April–May, 12 nights, transatlantic, San Juan to Seville; November; 11 nights, Lisbon to San Juan.

May–October, 5 to 9 nights, Mediterranean, Adriatic, Greek Isles from Seville, Monte Carlo, Civitavecchia, Istanbul, Piraeus, Venice

SeaDream II **HOME PORTS** Miami, Tenerife; others vary with itinerary
November 2007, 11 nights, transatlantic, Tenerife to Miami.

November, 11 nights, Miami to St. Thomas via Port Lucaya, Nassau, Egg Island, Turks and Caicos, Jost van Dyke, St. Maarten, St. Bart's, Virgin Gorda.

November 2007–April 2008, 4 to 14 nights, Southern/Eastern Caribbean, round-trip from Barbados, St. Thomas, San Juan, Antigua, or from St. Thomas to San Juan; San Juan to St. Thomas; St. Thomas to Barbados; Barbados to Antigua.

April, 12 nights, transatlantic, Barbados to Malaga.

May–October, 4 to 7 nights, Mediterranean from Nice, Monte Carlo, Rome, Piraeus, Dubrovnik, Venice.

Silversea Cruises

Silver Cloud **HOME PORT** Varies with itinerary
November 2007–March 2008, 7 to 15 nights, Africa, Seychelles, Arabian Peninsula, with inaugural calls at Farquhar Islands (Seychelles) and Jeddah (Saudi Arabia) from Port Said, Mahé, Port Louis, Mombassa, Dubai.

April–June and September–October, 7 to 14 nights, Mediterranean from Athens, Istanbul, Monte Carlo, Barcelona, Rome (spring), and London, Monte Carlo, Venice, Athens, Istanbul (fall).

June–August, 10 to 15 nights, Baltic from London to Copenhagen or reverse; Copenhagen to Stockholm or reverse; round-trip from Copenhagen.

November, 16 nights, transatlantic from Barcelona to Barbados; 7 nights, round-trip from Barbados to Dominica, St. Bart's, Antigua, St. Lucia.

November–December, 7 to 16 nights, South America from Barbados to Rio de Janeiro; Rio de Janeiro to Buenos Aires; Buenos Aires to Santiago.

Silver Shadow **HOME PORTS** Fort Lauderdale, San Francisco; others vary with itinerary

November–December 2007, 15 nights, Panama Canal, Fort Lauderdale to San Diego, San Diego to Fort Lauderdale.

December, 10 to 14 nights, Southern Caribbean, round-trip Fort Lauderdale.

January–May, 110 nights, World Cruise, round-trip from Fort Lauderdale; 26 countries and 52 ports of call, including the Panama Canal, the Mexican Riviera, Hawaii, Northern Mariana Islands, the Marshall Islands, Pohnpei, Guam, Okinawa, Iwo Jima, Far East, Egypt, Italy, Spain, Caribbean. Highlights include overnight calls in Hong Kong, Ho Chi Minh City, Bangkok, Mumbai, Barcelona. Eight segments from 9 to 21 days available.

May, 15 nights, Panama Canal, Fort Lauderdale to Los Angeles.

June–September, 9 to 12 nights, Alaska, round-trip from San Francisco; round-trip from Vancouver; Los Angeles to Vancouver; San Francisco to Vancouver; Seward to Vancouver; Vancouver to Los Angeles.

September–October, 9 to 16 nights, Hawaii and French Polynesia from Los Angeles to Puerto Caldera; Puerto Caldera to Santiago; Santiago to Papeete; Papeete to Los Angeles, including Silversea's maiden visit to Rangiroa and Nuku Hiva (Marquesas Islands). Voyage can be combined for a 53-day South Pacific cruise, round-trip from Los Angeles.

November, 15 nights, Panama Canal, Los Angeles to Fort Lauderdale.

Silver Whisper **HOME PORT** Varies with itinerary

January–March, 9 to 18 nights, Australia, New Zealand, Far East, South Pacific from Sydney, Auckland, Hong Kong, Singapore; including inaugural calls at Wewak, Papua New Guinea, Jayapura, Cebu Island, and Keelung and Kaohsiung, Taiwan.

April–May, 7 to 15 nights, Africa and Indian Ocean from Singapore to Dubai, round-trip from Dubai, Dubai to Athens.

June–September, 6 to 7 nights, Mediterranean from Athens, Nice, Barcelona, Rome, Monte Carlo, Athens, Venice, Istanbul. New destinations include Collioure, Palamos, Annaba, Tinos, Porec, and Trogir. Segments can be combined for longer cruises.

October–December, 9 to 15 nights, Arabian Peninsula, Australia, New Zealand, and Far East from Dubai, Singapore, Hong Kong, Sydney, including new destination, Krabi.

Silver Wind **HOME PORT** Varies with itinerary

November 2007–February 2008, 8 to 16 nights, South America, Rio de Janeiro to Buenos Aires, Buenos Aires to Santiago, Buenos Aires to Rio de Janeiro.

February, 15 nights, repositioning, Rio de Janeiro to Barbados.

March, 7 to 8 nights, Southern Caribbean, Barbados to San Juan, round-trip from San Juan.

April–May, 9 to 15 nights, Canary Islands from San Juan to Las Palmas via St. Bart's, St. Lucia, Barbados, Porto Grande, Porto Praia, Dakar, Tenerife, and from Las Palmas to Lisbon via St. Cruz de la Palma, Funchal, La Horta, Ponta Delgada, Oporto.

May–November, 7 to 15 nights, Mediterranean/Northern Europe from London, Stockholm, Copenhagen, maiden call to Kokkola (Gulf of Bothnia).

November, 11 to 18 nights, repositioning, Lisbon to Las Palmas; Las Palmas to Cape Town with maiden visit to Banjul.

December, 14 nights, Africa from Cape Town to Port Louis; Port Louis to Cape Town, with inaugural call in Maputo.

Star Clippers, Inc.

Note: All ports may not be included on every Star Clipper cruise, as itineraries are subject to weather conditions and alterations by the captain, in search of calm sailing and best anchorage.

Royal Clipper   **HOME PORTS**   Barbados, Rome, Venice

November 2007–April 2008, Saturday, 7 nights, Southern Caribbean, round-trip from Barbados alternating to either St. Lucia, Dominica, Antigua, St. Kitts, Iles des Saintes, Martinique; or Grenadines, Grenada, Tobago Cays, St. Vincent; Martinique, St. Lucia.

December 29, 2007, 11 nights, Caribbean and Panama Canal from Barbados.

April and November, 16 to 22 nights, transatlantic between Barbados and Rome; available in segments.

May–June, 7 nights, Western Mediterranean, alternating cruises round-trip from Rome to either Capri, Amalfi, Taormina, Lipari; or Ponza, Sorrento, Capri (evening call), Amalfi, and Taormina.

June–October, 10 and 11 nights, Mediterranean, alternating cruises between Rome and Venice calling at Ponza, Capri, Taormina, Corfu, Kotor, Dubrovnik, Korcula, Hvar, Rovinj, and reverse without Rovinj.

October, 12 nights, Mediterranean from Rome to Lisbon via Bonifacio, Mahon, Ibiza, Motril, Safi, Casablanca, Tangier, Cadiz, Portimao.

Star Clipper   **HOME PORTS**   Lisbon, Phuket, Singapore; others vary with itinerary

November–March, Saturday, 7 nights, Far East, alternating southern and northern routes, round-trip from Phuket or Phuket and Singapore: round-trip from Phuket to Batong Group, Penang, Ko Lipe, Ko Khai Nok, Phang Nga/Ko Hong, Similan Islands; or Suring Islands, Similan Islands, Ko Rock Nok, Langkawi, Phi Phi Islands, Phang Nga/Ko Khai Nok. Phuket and Singapore via islands, Phang Nga/Ko Dan Hok, Ko Adang, Penang, and Malacca; or Malacca, Langkawi, Ko Lipe, Ko Khai Nok.

March, October, 37 nights, Indian Ocean from Athens to Phuket via Mykonos, Rhodes, Alexandria, Port Said, Suez Canal, Sharm el Sheik, Safaga, Salalah, Goa, Cochin, Colombo, Simian Islands.

April, September, 12 nights, Mediterranean from Lisbon to Barcelona or Cannes to Athens.

May–September, 7 nights, alternating Ligurian and Tyrrhenian, round-trip from Cannes to Calvi, Bonifacio, Costa Smeralda, Portoferraio (Elba), Portofino, St. Tropez; or Ile Rousse/St. Florent, Bastia, Portovenere, Portofino, Monte Carlo, Porquerolles.

Star Flyer   **HOME PORTS**   Athens, Barbados, Papeete; others vary with itinerary

December 2007–June 2008, 7 to 11 nights, Tahiti, alternating Society Islands and Society Islands and Marquesas. Round-trip from Papeete via Huahine, Raiatea, Tahaa, Bora-Bora, Cook Bay, Opunoh; or Fakarava, Tiputa, Rangiroa Lagoon, Tiputa, Bora-Bora, Raiatea, Huahine, Moorea.

July–September, 5 to 11 nights, Eastern Mediterranean, alternating cruises from Athens to Venice via Mykonos, Santorini, Yithion, Corfu, Kotor, Dubrovnik, Korcula, Hvar, Mali Losinj, and reverse. Or round-trip from Athens to Rhodes, Bodrum, Dalyan River, Santorini, Hydra or Kusadasi, Pythagoria, Patmos Delos/Mykonos, Sifnos.

September, 14 nights, Mediterranean from Athens to Malaga via Mykonos, Santorini, Yithian, Katakolon, Taormina, Palermo, Palma, Ibiza, Motril.

October, 22 nights, repositioning from Malaga to Barbados.

November, 11 nights, Caribbean and Panama Canal between Barbados and Panama City.

Star Cruises

Star Pisces HOME PORT Hong Kong
Year-round, 1 night to nowhere from Hong Kong catering to gamblers and first-time cruisers. Subject to change.

SuperStar Aquarius HOME PORT Hong Kong
June-October, 1 night to nowhere from Hong Kong catering to gamblers and first-time cruisers. Subject to change.

SuperStar Gemini HOME PORT Singapore
April, 7 nights, Malaysia/Thailand, round-trip from Singapore to Kuala Lumpur, Langkawi Island, Krabi, Phuket Island, Penang.

Year-round, 7 nights, Straits of Malacca, round-trip from Singapore to Kuala Lumpur, Krabi, Phuket, Langkawi, Kuala Lumpur (revisit).

April–September, 7 nights, South China Sea, round-trip from Singapore to Ko Samui, Ho Chi Minh City, Tioman Island.

May, July, September, 11 nights, Asia from Hong Kong to Singapore via Halong Bay, Nha Trang, Kota Kinabalu, Kuching.

May, July August, 10 to 21 nights, Asia, round-trip from Singapore to Ko Samui, Bangkok, Ho Chi Minh City, Da Nang (10 nights), Hong Kong, Halong Bay, Nha Trang, Kota Kinabalu, Kuching (21 nights).

SuperStar Libra HOME PORT Mumbai
October–May, 2 to 5 nights, India, round-trip from Mumbai to Kadmat (Lakshadweep) and Goa (5 nights), or Kadmat (3 nights); to Goa (2 and 3 nights)

SuperStar Virgo HOME PORT Singapore
October–March, Southeast Asia, round-trip from Singapore to Penang, Phuket (3 nights); or to Malacca, Kuala Lumpur (2 nights); combine for 5-night cruise.

April–September, 2 to 5 nights, Southeast Asia, round-trip from Singapore to Phuket, Langkawi (3 nights); or to Singapore, Redang Island (2 nights); combine for 5- night cruise.

Travel Dynamics International

Callisto HOME PORTS Athens, Dakar, Dubrovnik
October–December, 9 to 13 nights, Greece, Greek Isles, Turkey, Crete, in-depth educational fly-cruise tours from the United States, sailing round-trip from Athens plus precruise tours of Greece (Athens or Thessaloniki).

December–March, 16 nights, Rivers of West Africa, fly-cruise tours from the United States, sailing from Dakar, Senegal, to the Casamance River, the Gambia, and Saloun River plus precruise tour of Mali and Timbuktu.

April–August, 11 to 12 nights, Adriatic, Greece, Greek Isles, in-depth educational fly-cruise tours from the United States, sailing round-trip from Athens, between Dubrovnik and Athens, or between Dubrovnik and Rab, plus pre- and postcruise tours.

Corinthian II HOME PORTS Athens, Ushuaia; others vary with itinerary
September–November, 11 to 13 nights, Eastern Mediterranean, fly-cruise from the United States, sailing from Barcelona to Venice; Venice to Istanbul; round-trip from Athens to Black Sea; Athens to Naples, or reverse; Athens to Tunis.

December–February, 13 nights, Antarctica, fly-cruise tours from the United States, sailing round-trip from Ushuaia to the Antarctic Peninsula plus a precruise stay in Buenos Aires.

April–June, 10 to 14 nights, Mediterranean, in-depth educational fly-cruise tours from the United States, sailing from Malaga to Nice; Seville to Venice; round-trip from Palermo; Palermo to Athens, round-trip from Athens; Athens to Anzio.

Windjammer Barefoot Cruises

Legacy **HOME PORT** Herradura

October 2007–May 2008, 7 nights, Costa Rica (Pacific coast), round-trip from Herradura to Coiba, Drakes Bay, Golfito, Granito Del Oro, Isla Secas, Quepas.

Mandalay **HOME PORTS** Antigua, Colon, St. Maarten

November–April, 12 nights, between Antigua and Grenada, calling at Antigua, Bequia, Tobago Cays, Carriacou, Dominica, Grenada, and to Iles des Saints, Martinique, Mayreau, Nevis, St. Lucia, St. Vincent.

November 2007, 7 nights, Panama and San Blas Islands, round-trip from Colon to Achu Tupu, Coco Banderos, Nalunega, Portobello, Tuborgana.

November 2007–May 2008, 7 nights, West Indies between Antigua and St. Maarten, calling at Nevis, St. Bart's, St. Eustatius, St. Kitts, St. Lucia.

Polynesia **HOME PORTS** Aruba, St. Maarten, Tortola

September–October, 5 nights, ABC Islands, round-trip from Aruba.

November 11, 2007, 6 nights, Singles Cruise, repositioning from St. Lucia to St. Maarten, calling at Dominica, Guadalupe, Antigua, Nevis, St. Bart's, St. Maarten.

November 2007–May 2008, 7 nights, British Virgin Islands and French West Indies between Tortola and St. Maarten calling at Anguilla, Jost Van Dyke, Norman Island, Virgin Gorda.

December, 5 nights, round-trip from St. Maarten to a selection of the following islands: St. Maarten, St. Bart's, Anguilla, Tintamarre, Saba, St. Eustatius (Statia), Nevis, St. Kitts.

Yankee Clipper **HOME PORT** Grenada

Year-round, Monday, 7 nights, Grenadines, round-trip from Grenada to Carriacou, Bequia, St. Vincent, Mayreau, Union Island, Tobago Cays.

Windstar Cruises

Wind Spirit **HOME PORTS** Athens, Istanbul, Rome, St. Thomas; others vary with itinerary

December 2007–April 2008, 7 nights, round-trip from St. Thomas to St. Maarten, St. Bart's, Tortola, Jost Van Dyke, and overnight on board in St. John and Virgin Gorda.

April and November, 14 nights, transatlantic, St. Thomas to Lisbon and reverse.

April and October, 7 nights, Western Mediterranean from Lisbon to Barcelona; Barcelona to Rome; Rome to Nice, Nice to Barcelona, Barcelona to Lisbon.

May–October, Saturday, 7 nights, Eastern Mediterranean/Greek Isles from Rome to Athens and reverse; Athens to Istanbul or reverse.

December, Caribbean cruises from St. Thomas resume.

Wind Star **HOME PORTS** Athens, Istanbul, Puerto Caldera; others vary with itinerary

November, December 2007, 14 nights, Panama Canal from Puerto Caldera to Barbados.

December 2007–March 2008, Saturday, 7 nights, Costa Rica, round-trip from Puerto Caldera to San Juan del Sur; Playas del Coco, Quepos, Bahia Paraiso, Curu, and Tortuga Island (Costa Rica).

April and October, 7 nights, Western Mediterranean from Lisbon to Barcelona; Barcelona to Rome and reverse; Rome to Barcelona; Barcelona to Lisbon.

May–July, October, Saturday, 7 nights, Eastern Mediterranean from Rome to Athens, Athens to Istanbul or reverse, Athens to Rome.

December 2008, March 2009, Costa Rica cruises from Puerto Caldera resume.

Wind Surf **HOME PORTS** Barbados; others vary with itinerary
November 2007, April 2008, 13 to 14 nights, transatlantic, Lisbon to St. Thomas, Barbados to Lisbon or reverse.

December 2007–April 2008, 7 nights, Caribbean, round-trip from Barbados to either Tobago, Bequia, Dominica, St. Lucia, Mayreau, Grenada, Tobago; or Nevis, St. Maarten, St. Bart's, Isles des Saintes, St. Lucia.

April–November, October, 7 nights, Western Mediterranean from either Lisbon, Barcelona, Marseille, Rome, Venice, or Monte Carlo.

December, April, 7-night cruises from Barbados resume.

The World/ResidenSea

The World **HOME PORT** Varies with itinerary as it continually sails around the world.
January–December, from Canary Islands to Senegal, Sao Tome/Principe, Namibia, South Africa, Mauritius, Madagascar, Seychelles, Oman, United Arab Emirates, India, Sri Lanka, Maldives, Oman, Jordan, Egypt, Suez Canal transit, Turkey, Greece, Russia, Ukraine, Bulgaria, Montenegro, Croatia, Italy, Slovenia, Malta, Monaco, Corsica, France.

CRUISE SHIP INDEX

KEY A = Adventure | E = European Cruise Ferry | F = Freighter
G = Galápagos | GR = Greek Islands | M = Mainstream | NC = Norwegian Coastal
O = Others | R = River | SS = Sailing Ship

KEY A = Adventure | E = European Cruise Ferry | F = Freighter
G = Galápagos | GR = Greek Islands | M = Mainstream | NC = Norwegian Coastal
O = Others | R = River | SS = Sailing Ship

SHIP	CRUISE LINE	TYPE	PAGE
Eugenie	Misr Travel	R	537
Eurodam	Holland America Line	M	282, 303–304
Europa	Hapag-Lloyd Cruises	M	488–490
Evolution	International Expeditions	A	563–564
Explorer II	Abercrombie & Kent/ Discovery World Cruises	M/A/R	472–474, 479–480
Explorer of the Seas	Royal Caribbean International	M	404, 412–415
Finnmarken	Norway Coastal Voyage	NC	574
Fjord Norway	DFDS Seaways	NC	578–579
Flamingo	Ecotour Expeditions/Galapagos Network	A/G	561–563
Fleur de Lys	Abercrombie & Kent	R	518
Fram	Norwegian Coastal Voyage	NC	575–577
Frederic Chopin	Peter Deilmann Cruises	R	521–522
Freedom of the Seas	Royal Caribbean International	M	404, 424–427
Gabriella	Viking Line	EC	580–581
Galapagos Explorer II	Canodros, S.A.	G	555–556
Galapagos Legend	Galapagos Yacht Cruises/Kleintours/ Marco Polo Expeditions	A/G	564
Golden Princess	Princess Cruises	M	366, 375–382
Grace Bailey	Maine Windjammer Association	SS	589
Grand Princess	Princess Cruises	M	366, 376–382
Grande Caribe	American Canadian Caribbean Line	M	146, 149–151
Grande Mariner	American Canadian Caribbean Line	M	146, 149–151
Grandeur of the Seas	Royal Caribbean International	M	404, 407–412
Hanseatic	Hapag-Lloyd Cruises	A	491–493
Hebridean Princess	Hebridean Island Cruises	E	493
Hebridean Spirit	Hebridean Island Cruises	M	493
Heidelberg	Peter Deilmann Cruises	R	522
Heritage	Maine Windjammer Association	SS	589
Hirondelle	Abercrombie & Kent/European Waterways	R	518
Horizon II	French Country Waterways	R	524
Iberostar Grand Amazon	Iberostar Grand Amazon Cruises	R	549–550
Independence of the Seas	Royal Caribbean International	M	404, 424–427
Insignia	Oceania Cruises	M	346, 348–353

KEY A = Adventure | E = European Cruise Ferry | F = Freighter
G = Galápagos | GR = Greek Islands | M = Mainstream | NC = Norwegian Coastal
O = Others | R = River | SS = Sailing Ship

KEY   A = Adventure | E = European Cruise Ferry | F = Freighter
G = Galápagos | GR = Greek Islands | M = Mainstream | NC = Norwegian Coastal
O = Others | R = River | SS = Sailing Ship

Peter Wessel	Color Line	EC	578
Polar Star	Norwegian Coastal Voyage	A	575
Polaris	Lindblad Expeditions	A/G	566
Polarys	Norwegian Coastal Voyage	NC	574
Polynesia	Windjammer Barefoot Cruises	SS	592
Pride of Aloha	NCL America	M	317,338–343
Pride of America	NCL America	M	317, 338–343
Pride of Hawaii	NCL America	M	317, 338–343
Prince Abbas	Misr Travel	R	537
Princesa Marissa	Louis Cruise Lines	M	495
Princess	French Country Waterways	R	524
Princesse de Provence	Peter Deilmann Cruises	R	522
Princesse Ragnhild	Color Line	EC	578
Prinsendam	Holland America Line	M	282, 297–300
Professor Multanovsky	Quark Expeditions	A	568
Project Genesis	Royal Caribbean International	M	404
Prosperite	Abercrombie & Kent	R	519
Queen Elizabeth 2	Cunard Line	M	254, 261–264
Queen Mary 2	Cunard Line	M	254, 257–261
Queen Nabila of Abu Simbel	Nabila Nile Cruises	R	537
Queen of Scandinavia	DFDS Seaways	EC	578–579
Queen of Sheeba	Nabila Nile Cruises	R	537
Queen of the Nile	Nabila Nile Cruises	R	537
Queen of the West	Majestic America Line	R	545–546
Queen Victoria	Cunard Line	M	254, 264–267
Radiance of the Seas	Royal Caribbean International	M	404, 421–424
Ramses King of Thebes	Nabila Nile Cruises	R	537
Regal Star	Tallink Silja Line	NC	579–580
Regatta	Oceania Cruises	M	346, 348–353
Regency	Esplanade Tours	R	536
Regina	Esplanade Tours	R	536
Rhapsody of the Seas	Royal Caribbean International	M	404, 407–412
Richard With	Norwegian Coastal Voyage	NC	574
Rio Amazonas	Marco Polo Expeditions	R	548, 551
River Cloud	Abercrombie & Kent/The Barge Lady/ Elegant Cruises & Tours	R	519, 520
River Cloud II	Abercrombie & Kent/Elegant Cruises	R	519
River Explorer	RiverBarge Excursion Lines, Inc.	R	546–547

KEY A = Adventure | E = European Cruise Ferry | F = Freighter
G = Galápagos | GR = Greek Islands | M = Mainstream | NC = Norwegian Coastal
O = Others | R = River | SS = Sailing Ship

KEY A = Adventure | E = European Cruise Ferry | F = Freighter
G = Galápagos | GR = Greek Islands | M = Mainstream | NC = Norwegian Coastal
O = Others | R = River | SS = Sailing Ship

KEY A = Adventure | E = European Cruise Ferry | F = Freighter
G = Galápagos | GR = Greek Islands | M = Mainstream | NC = Norwegian Coastal
O = Others | R = River | SS = Sailing Ship

DESTINATION INDEX

Note: This index is organized according to continents, oceans, and seas.

SUBJECT INDEX

Unofficial Guide to Cruises Reader Survey 2007–2008

If you would like to express an opinion about your cruise or this guide-book, complete the following survey and return to:

Unofficial Guide Reader Survey
P.O. Box 43673
Birmingham, AL 35243

Name of ship: _____

Today's date: _____

Date, duration, and destination of cruise: _____

Was this your ☐ 1st ☐ 2nd ☐ 3rd ☐ 4th ☐ 5th or more cruise?

Would you take another cruise on this ship? ☐ Yes ☐ No

Recommend it to a friend? ☐ Yes ☐ No

Do you plan to cruise ☐ within a year ☐ within next 3 years?

Your age: ☐ teens ☐ 20s ☐ 30s ☐ 40s ☐ 50s ☐ 60s ☐ 70s

☐ over 80

You are: employed ☐ self-employed ☐ retired

Your line of work: _____

Please score items below from 1 to 10 with 10 being the highest or best. Feel free to add your comments.

Value for money: _____

Total cruise experience: _____

Your overall impression of the ship (*appearance, appeal, furnishings and decor, cleanliness, sports and recreation facilities, consistency, comfort, boarding/disembarking procedures*): _____

Cruise director (*available, helpful, friendly*): _____

Cruise staff: _____

Dining room food (*choices, quality, taste, presentation*): _____

Breakfast and lunch buffet: _____

Dining room service: _____

Bar service: _____

Cabin (*size, layout, soundproofing, cleanliness, appearance, condition*): _____

Bathroom: _____

Cabin attendant (service, attitude): _____

Enrichment programs, lectures, games *(variety and quality)*: _____

Entertainment in the main lounge: _____

Entertainment in other lounges: _____

Children's programs: _____

Youth counselors: _____

Shore excursions (guides, variety, advanced information, value): _____

MORE QUESTIONS:

Was the food quality better, worse, or about what you expected? _____

Were wine and bar prices low, moderate, or high? _____

Was the music level tolerable or too loud, especially by the pool? _____

Were you bothered by announcements over the public address system? _____

Was the promotion of shipboard shops low key, moderate, or hard sell? _____

Was the lifeboat drill well executed? _____

Did you choose your cruise for its itinerary? _____

Which ports of call did you like best? _____

Were port talks poor or helpful? _____

Did the speakers plug specific shops? _____

*Was passenger information available prior to the cruise? in your cabin?
during the cruise?* _____

YOUR HOMETOWN:

How did you learn about your cruise? _____

How did you learn about this book? _____

Where did you buy your cruise? _____

When and where did you buy this book? _____

If you are available for a telephone interview, please give us your name,
address, telephone number, and a convenient time to call.

_____

_____

_____

THANK YOU!